LIFE OF BRANT.

Jos Brant
Thayendanegea

LIFE OF

JOSEPH BRANT—THAYENDANEGEA,

INCLUDING THE

INDIAN WARS

OF THE

AMERICAN REVOLUTION.

BY William L. Stone.

NEW-YORK:

Published by Alexander V. Blake.

1838

LIFE

OF

JOSEPH BRANT—THAYENDANEGEA:

INCLUDING

THE BORDER WARS

OF THE

AMERICAN REVOLUTION,

AND

SKETCHES OF THE INDIAN CAMPAIGNS OF GENERALS
HARMAR, ST. CLAIR, AND WAYNE,

AND OTHER MATTERS

CONNECTED WITH THE INDIAN RELATIONS OF THE UNITED STATES
AND GREAT BRITAIN, FROM THE PEACE OF 1783 TO
THE INDIAN PEACE OF 1795.

BY WILLIAM L. STONE.

IN TWO VOLUMES.

VOL. II.

NEW-YORK:
ALEXANDER V. BLAKE, 38 GOLD STREET.

1838.

Republished, 1970
Scholarly Press, 22929 Industrial Drive East, St. Clair Shores, Michigan 48080

Standard Book Number 403-00226-5
Library of Congress Catalog Card Number: 75-108544

Entered according to the Act of Congress of the United States of America, in the
year 1838, by GEORGE DEARBORN & Co., in the Clerk's Office of the District Court
for the Southern District of New-York.

This edition is printed on a high-quality,
acid-free paper that meets specification
requirements for fine book paper referred
to as "300-year" paper

CONTENTS.

CHAPTER IV.

CHAPTER V.

CHAPTER VI.

CHAPTER VII.

CHAPTER VIII.

CHAPTER IX.

CHAPTER XII.

CHAPTER XIII.

CHAPTER XIV.

LIFE

OF

JOSEPH BRANT—THAYENDANEGEA, &c.

CHAPTER I.

THE policy of waging a more decisive war against the Indians, and the loyalists associated with them in their barbarous irruptions upon the frontier settlements, has been adverted to more than once already. General Washington had long entertained the opinion that the mere establishment of a chain of military posts along the Western and North-western frontiers would not answer the purpose; and that the only method of affording efficient protection to the inhabitants of those borders, would be to carry the war into the heart of the enemy's country. By a resolution of the 25th of February, Congress had directed the Commander-in-chief to take the most effectual means for pro-

tecting the inhabitants, and chastising the Indians for their continued depredations ; and it was now his determination to put
the resolve in execution, by carrying the war directly into the
most populous country of the Six Nations ; to cut off their settlements, destroy their crops, and inflict upon them every other
mischief which time and circumstances would permit.*

Those who have been accustomed to contemplate the whole
race of North American aboriginals as essentially alike, viewing
them all as the same roving, restless, houseless race of hunters
and fishermen, without a local habitation, and with scarce a
name, have widely misunderstood the Indian character, and
must know but little of its varieties. They have, indeed, many
traits and characteristics in common ; but in other respects the
moody Englishman is not more unlike his mercurial neighbor
on the other side of the channel, than is the Mohawk unlike the
Sioux. It is the remark of a popular writer of the day,† that
" those who are familiar with the reserved and haughty bearing
" of the forest tribes, cannot fail, when an opportunity of compa-
" rison is afforded, to be struck with the social air and excitable
" disposition which mark their prairie brethren, and so decidedly
" distinguish the " gens du large" from "les gens des feuilles,"
" as the voyageurs term the different races. The Pawnees, fol-
" lowing the buffalo in his migrations, and having always plenty
" of animal food to subsist upon, are a much better fed and larger
" race than those who find a precarious subsistence in the forest
" chase. While the woodland tribes, who, though not so plump
" in form, are of a more wiry and perhaps muscular make, have
" again a decided advantage in figure and gait over the " gens du
" lac," or fishing and trapping tribes of the North-west, that pass
" most of their time in canoes. This difference in character and
" physical appearance between the different Indian races, or rather
" between those tribes who have such different methods of gain-
" ing a livelihood, has never been sufficiently attended to by
" modern authors, though it did not escape the early French
" writers on this country. And yet, if habit have any effect in
" forming the temper and character of a rude people, it must of
" course follow, that the savage who lives in eternal sunshine upon

* Letter of Washington of March 4, to Governor Clinton, and also from the same
to General Gates of March 6, 1779.
† Charles F. Hoffman, Esq.

" flowery plains, and hunts on horseback with a troop of tribesmen
" around him, must be a different being from the solitary deer-
" stalker, who wanders through the dim forest, depending upon his
" single arm for a subsistence for his wife and children." But
the higher state of social organization among the Six Nations
greatly increased the difference. They had many towns and
villages giving evidence of permanence. They were organized
into communities, whose social and political institutions, simple
as they were, were still as distinct and well-defined as those of
the American confederacy. They had now acquired some of the
arts, and were enjoying many of the comforts, of civilized life.
Not content with small patches of cleared lands for the raising
of a few vegetables, they possessed cultivated fields, and orchards
of great productiveness, at the West. Especially was this the
fact with regard to the Cayugas and Senecas. The Mohawks
having been driven from their own rich lands, the extensive
domains of the two westernmost tribes of the confederacy
formed the granary of the whole. And in consequence of the
superior social and political organization just referred to, and
the Spartan-like character incident to the forest life, the Six Nations, though not the most numerous, were beyond a doubt the
most formidable, of the tribes then in arms in behalf of the
Crown.* It was justly considered, therefore, that the only way
to strike them effectively, would be to destroy their homes and
the growing products of their farms; and thus, by cutting off
their means of supply, drive them from their own country deeper
into the interior, and perhaps throw them altogether upon their
British allies for subsistence. It was likewise the design to extend the operations of the expedition as far as Niagara, if possible—that post, of all others in the occupation of the enemy, enabling his officers to maintain an extensive influence over his
savage allies.†

---

* "The Six Nations were a peculiar and extraordinary people, contra-distinguish-
ed from the mass of Indian nations by great attainments in polity, in negotiation, in
eloquence, and in war."—*Discourse of De Witt Clinton before the New-York Hist.
Society*—1811.

† Since these sheets were in the hands of the printer, the author has discovered an
official manuscript account of a grand Indian council held at Niagara, in September,
1776, by Colonel John Butler, and Lieutenants Matthews, Burnit, and Kinnesley,
and Ensign Butler, with the Hurons, Chippewas, Ottawas, Pottawatamies, Mississagas, Senecas, Cayugas, Onondagas, Oneidas, Tuscaroras, Mohawks, Dela-

The plan of this campaign was well devised and matured. It was to be commenced by a combined movement of two divisions—the one from Pennsylvania, ascending the valley of the Susquehanna to the intersection of the Tioga river, under General Sullivan, who was invested with the command in chief; and the other from the North, under General James Clinton, which was to descend the Susquehanna from its principal source, and after forming a junction with Sullivan, the whole to proceed, by the course of the Chemung river, into the fertile country of the Senecas and Cayugas. This expedition was intended as the principal campaign of that year; since the relative military strength and situation of the two contending powers rendered it impossible that any other offensive operations could be carried on by the Americans at the same time.*

wares, Nanticokes, Squaghkies, and Connoys—in presence of Lieut. Colonel John Caldwell, then in command at Niagara. It appears that only one Oneida sachem was present, and one Tuscarora. They adopted an address, which was unanimously signed by the chiefs attending the Congress, declaring their intention to embark in the war, and abide the result of the contest of the King with his people. They also made a strong appeal to the Oneidas and Tuscaroras, " to quit the Bostonians, and be strong and determined to fulfil their engagements to the King." They also exhorted the Mohawks to be strong, and assured them " that they, and all their western brethren, would fly to their assistance at the first call," &c.—*Manuscripts of Gen. Gansevoort.*

   * It was the original purpose of General Washington to invest General Gates with the command of this expedition, and the appointment was tendered to that officer by letter, on the 6th of March. Gates declined it, in a manner not very agreeable to the Commander-in-chief. The latter, in writing subsequently to the President of Congress upon the subject, in the course of sundry explanations, not unmingled with strictures upon the conduct of Gates, wrote as follows :—" The plan of operations for the campaign being determined, a commanding officer was to be appointed for the Indian expedition. This command, according to all present appearances, will probably be of the second, if not of the first, importance for the campaign. The officer conducting it has a flattering prospect of acquiring more credit than can be expected by any other this year ; and he has the best reason to hope for success. General Lee, from his situation, was out of the question ; General Schuyler, (who, by the way, would have been most agreeable to me,) was so uncertain of continuing in the army, that I could not appoint him ; General Putnam I need not mention. I therefore made the offer of it, for the appointment could no longer be delayed, to General Gates, who was next in seniority, though, perhaps, I might have avoided it, if I had been so disposed, from his being in a command by the special appointment of Congress. My letter to him on the occasion I believe you will think was conceived in very candid and polite terms, and that it merited a different answer from the one given to it."—*Letter of Washington to the President of Congress, April* 14, 1779. The answer of Gates referred to by the Commander-in-chief, was in the following words :—" Last night I had the honor of your Excellency's letter. The man who

On the 2d of June, General Clinton received his instructions from Sullivan, to proceed forthwith in the measures of co-operation according to the plan of the campaign already indicated, viz : the descent of the Susquehanna by the northern forces, to unite with the main division at Tioga. Preparations for the enterprise, however, were already in a state of great forwardness, since General Washington had been in free communication with Governor Clinton upon the subject ; and the latter, with the General his brother, had been actively engaged in anticipation of the order.* Accordingly, batteaux had already been provided at Schenectady, which, after ascending the Mohawk to Canajoharie, were thence to be transported over land to the head of Otsego Lake at Springfield, while at the same time a large quantity of provisions had been thrown into Fort Schuyler in case of emergency. After making all his arrangements, and ordering the different corps which were to compose his command, to concentrate at Canajoharie, General Clinton arrived at that post on the 16th of June, where he found himself at the head of fifteen hundred troops.

The portage from the Mohawk river at Canajoharie to the head of Otsego Lake is about twenty miles. On the 17th, General Clinton commenced the transportation of his boats and stores across the country—the region being hilly, and the roads excessively bad. Two hundred boats were found to be necessary, and four horses were required for the draught of each boat. The troops were disposed by regiments along the route, both for

---

undertakes the Indian service, should enjoy youth and strength ; requisites I do not possess. It therefore grieves me that your Excellency should offer me the only command to which I am entirely unequal. In obedience to your command, I have forwarded your letter to General Sullivan," &c.—*Sparks's Life and Correspondence of Washington.*

* General James Clinton was at that time in command of the Northern department. The troops assigned for this campaign were, the brigades of Generals Clinton, Maxwell, Poor, and Hand, to which last brigade were assigned, in addition, all the detached corps of Continental troops on the Susquehanna. The independent companies of the State of Pennsylvania were likewise ordered upon the expedition, together with Colonel Van Courtlandt's regiment, Butler's, Alden's, and the rifle corps. Colonel Gansevoort's regiment formed a part of Clinton's brigade. This brigade had already been ordered by the Commander-in-chief himself to rendezvous at Canajoharie, subject to the orders of Sullivan, either to form a junction with the main body by the way of Otsego, or to proceed up the Mohawk and co-operate as circumstances might best permit.—*Letter of instructions from the Commander-in-chief to General Sullivan.*

safety, and to assist at difficult points of ascent. But, notwithstanding these obstacles, and the magnitude of the enterprise,
General Clinton was enabled to announce to his immediate superior, by letter on the 26th, that one hundred and seventy-three
of the boats had already reached the head of the lake; that
thirty more were on their way; and that the residue, making
up the complement of two hundred and twenty, would be forwarded thither immediately on their arrival from Schenectady.
The provisions and stores for a three months' campaign had
likewise been already transported across the carrying-place; so
that the expedition was nearly in readiness to commence its
final movement.* In a letter to General Schuyler announcing
the same intelligence, the General spoke particularly of the
alacrity and spirit with which the inhabitants of the country
had rallied to his assistance. He likewise bestowed high praise
upon Colonel Willett, acting as a volunteer, for his timely and
energetic assistance in forwarding the arrangements. In performing this labor, no other interruption took place than what arose
from the arrest of two spies, formerly inhabitants of the county,
one of whom was named Hare, a lieutenant in the British service, and the other a Tory sergeant named Newberry,—the
same wretch whose name has already occurred as a brutal murderer at Cherry Valley. They had left the Seneca country
with sixty warriors of that tribe, to be divided into three parties,
one of which was to fall upon Cherry Valley again, the other
upon Schoharie, and the third to be employed in lurking about
Fort Schuyler. They were tried by a court-martial, convicted,
and " hanged pursuant to the sentence of the court, and to the
" entire satisfaction of all the inhabitants of the county."†

* General Washington was greatly displeased at the amount of stores and baggage by which Clinton was encumbered, apprehending "the worst consequences"
from the obstacles his stores would interpose to the rapidity of his march, and also
from the publicity which would as a consequence be given to his movements. Although he had left it optional with Sullivan to direct Clinton to join him by the route
of the Susquehanna, yet the Commander-in-chief evidently preferred that the more
northern route should be taken. He wrote to Sullivan upon the subject with more
sharpness than he was wont to do.—[See Letter of Washington to Sullivan, July 1,
1779.] The event, however, aided by the sagacity of Clinton in the adoption of a
measure presently to be noted, proved that he took the right direction.

† Letter from General Clinton to General Schuyler. In General Schuyler's answer to this letter, he says, speaking of the execution of Hare—" In executing Hare,
you have rid the State of the greatest villain in it. I hope his abettors in the country will meet with a similar exultation."—Gen. Clinton's Manuscripts.

It was the desire of General Sullivan that Clinton should employ in his division as large a number of the Oneida warriors as could be induced to engage in the service. The latter officer was opposed to this arrangement; but at the importunities of Sullivan, the Rev. Mr. Kirkland, their missionary, who was now a chaplain in the army, had been summoned to Albany for consultation. From thence Mr. Kirkland was despatched to Pennsylvania directly to join Sullivan's division, while to Mr. Deane, the interpreter connected with the Indian commission at Fort Schuyler, was confided the charge of negotiating with the Oneida chiefs upon the subject. At first all went smoothly with the Indians. The Oneidas volunteered for the expedition, almost to a man; while those of the Onondagas who adhered to the cause of the Americans, were equally desirous of proving their fidelity by their deeds. Under these circumstances Clinton wrote to Sullivan on the 26th, that on the following Saturday, Mr. Deane, with the Indian warriors, would join him at the head of the lake. A sudden revolution, however, was wrought in their determination by an address to the Oneidas from General Haldimand, received at Fort Schuyler on the 22d. This document was transmitted to them in their own language; and its tenor was so alarming, as to induce them suddenly to change their purpose—judging, very correctly, from the threats of Haldimand, that their presence was necessary at home for the defence of their own castles. Still, Mr. Deane wrote that an arrangement was on foot, by which he hoped yet to obtain the co-operation of a considerable number of the Oneida warriors. The basis of this arrangement was, that in the event of an invasion of their country by the Indians, whom the Canadian commander had threatened to let loose upon them, the garrison at Fort Schuyler should not only assist them, but receive their women and children into the fort for protection.

General Haldimand's address was written in the Iroquois language, of which the following translation was made by Mr. Deane, and enclosed to General Clinton :—

*" A translation of his Excellency Gen. Haldimand's speech
to the Oneida Indians in the Rebel Interest. as delivered
to them in the Iroquois language.*

" BROTHERS : Be very attentive to what I, Ashanegown, the
Great King of England's representative in Canada, am going to
say. By this string of wampum I shake you by the hand to
rouse you that you may seriously reflect upon my words.

A string of wampum.

"BROTHERS : It is now about four years ago since the Bostonians began to rise, and rebel against their Father, the King
of England, since which time you have taken a different part
from the rest of the Five Nations, your confederates, and have
likewise deserted the King's cause, through the deceitful machinations and snares of the rebels, who intimidated you with their
numerous armies, by which means you became bewildered, and
forgot all of your engagements with, and former care, and
favor from the Great King of England, your Father. You
also soon forgot the frequent bad usage, and continual encroachments of the Americans upon the Indian lands throughout the
Continent. I say, therefore, that at the breaking out of these
troubles you firmly declared to observe a strict neutrality in
the dispute, and made your declaration known to Sir Guy
Carleton, my predecessor, who much approved of it, provided
you were in earnest. I have hitherto strictly observed and examined your conduct, and find that you did not adhere to your
assertion, although I could trace no reason on the side of government as well as the Indians, why you should act so treacherous and double a part ; by which means, we, not mistrusting
your fidelity, have had many losses among the King's subjects,
and the Five Nations your friends and connexions ; and finding you besides, proud and haughty on the occasion, as if you
gloried in your perfidy, doubtless in sure confidence as if your
friends, the rebels, were getting the better at last ; and captivated
with that pleasing opinion of yours, you have presumed twice,
during the course of last winter, to send impertinent and daring
messages to the Five Nations, as if you meant to pick a quarrel
with them. In consequence of this your daring and insolent
behavior, I must insist upon, by this belt of wampum, that you
declare yourselves immediately on the receipt of this my speech

* Copied by the author from the M . among the papers f General Clinton.

and message, whether you mean to persist in this your daring
and insulting course, and still intend to act as you have hitherto
done, treacherously under the cloak of neutrality, or whether
you will accept of this my last offer of re-uniting, and reconciling
yourselves with your own tribes, the Five Nations. Do not
imagine that the King has hitherto treated the rebels and their
adherents with so much mildness and indulgence, out of any
apprehensions of their strength, or getting the better! No, by
no means. For you will find that in case you slight or disre-
gard this my last offer of peace, I shall soon convince you that
I have such a number of Indian allies to let loose upon you, as
will instantly convince you of your folly when too late, as I
have hardly been able to restrain them from falling upon you
for some time past. I must therefore once more repeat to you
that this is my last and final message to you; and that you
do not hesitate, or put off giving me your direct and decisive
declaration of peace or war, that in case of the latter, (knowing
that there are still some of your nation who are friends to the
King and the Five Nations,) I may give them timely warning
to separate themselves from you.

"BROTHERS: Let me lastly convince you of the deceit and
dissimulation of your rebel brethren, General Schuyler, Parson
Kirkland, and others; have they not told you, in the beginning
of the rebellion, that they wanted not your assistance, and to
have your blood spilt; and you likewise declared that you would
not join them, but remain neuter? Have either of you stuck to
your word? No! you basely broke it, and seemed from the
beginning to be of mutual hostile sentiments against the King
and his allies, and soon after manifested it by your actions.
What confirms me in this opinion, and proves your deceitful
and treacherous dispositions, is your behavior during the course
of the last war, when you likewise acted a double part in clandestinely joining and carrying intelligence to the French in
this country; which I myself am a witness to, and also was told
of it by your friend, the late Sir William Johnson, who, notwithstanding your base behavior, upon promising that you would be
true and faithful for the future, forgave you, and received you
into favor again, advising you to be more prudent and honest in
time to come; and frequently after that loaded you with the
King's bounty and favor. But he was no sooner dead than you

ungratefully forgot his good advice and benedictions ; and in opposition to his family and Indian friends, and every thing that
is sacred, adopted the cause of rebels, and enemies to your
King, your late patron Sir William Johnson, and your own
confederacy and connexions. These are facts, Brothers, that,
unless you are lost to every sense of feeling, cannot but recall in
you a most hearty repentance and deep remorse for your past
vile actions.   *The belt.*

" FRED. HALDIMAND."

On the 30th of June, Clinton wrote to Sullivan that his arrangements were complete—that all his stores and munitions of
every description were at the lake, with two hundred and ten
batteaux—and every thing in readiness for embarkation the
moment his orders to that effect should be received. On the
1st of July he proceeded to the lake himself, and the expedition
moved from its head to the Southern extremity—there to await the
orders of his superior. While lying at this place, a letter was received from General Schuyler, announcing the return from Canada
of a spy, who had been despatched thither for information. He
brought word, that on the 18th of June four hundred and fifty
regular troops, one hundred Tories, and thirty Indians, had been
sent forward from Montreal to reinforce the Indians against
whom this expedition was preparing ; and that they were to be
joined by half of Sir John Johnson's regiment, together with a
portion of the garrison at Niagara. From this intelligence it
was evident that the Indian country was not to be taken without a struggle.

On the 5th Mr. Deane arrived, at the head of thirty-five
Oneida warriors. The object of their visit was in person to
apologize for the absence of their brethren from the expedition,
and to make those explanations, in regard to their own altered
situation, already communicated by Mr. Deane by letter, together with the address of General Haldimand, which had
caused their alarm. A conference took place with General
Clinton on the same day, at which the Oneidas delivered their
message in the following speech :—

" BROTHER : We suppose you imagine we have come here
in order to attend you upon your expedition, but we are sorry
to inform you that our situation is such as will not admit of it.

" BROTHER : From intelligence which we may depend upon, we have reason to believe that the Six Nations mean to embrace the opportunity of our absence in order to destroy our castles ; these accounts we have by spies from among them, and we know that a considerable body of them are now collected at Cayuga for that purpose, waiting in expectation of our warriors leaving the castle to join you.

" BROTHER : It was our intention to have joined you upon your intended route, and hope you will not think hard of it that we do not ; but such is our present danger, that in case we leave our castle it must be cut off, as a large party of the enemy are waiting for that purpose.

" BROTHER : This is a time of danger with us. Our brethren, the Americans, have always promised us assistance for our protection whenever we stand in need of it ; we therefore request that, agreeable to these promises, we may have some troops sent to our assistance in this time of great danger. Should you send a body of troops to our assistance and protection, and the enemy attack us, and we should have the fortune to beat them, we will with those troops pursue them, and join you down in their country ; or if they should not make an attack upon our castle in a short time, we will march through their castles until we join you."   *A belt.*

To which General Clinton made the following reply :—

" BRETHREN : Our present expedition is intended to chastise those nations who have broken their faith with us, and joined our enemies. The force we have is quite sufficient for that purpose. Our route is planned in the great council of this country. It is not my desire that the whole of your warriors should leave their castles. I have given a general invita' on to our Brethren the Oneidas, the Tuscaroras, and such Onoi Jagas as may have entered into friendship with us. In order to give all our Indian friends an equal chance of evidencing their spirit and determination to partake of our fortune, I am entirely satisfied that such only should join me as think proper. It is not for want of warriors that I have given you this invitation, but that every warrior who is a friend to these United States may have an equal opportunity of punishing the enemies of our country.

" As your situation is such as causes you to suppose your castle in danger of being destroyed by your enemies in case of your absence, I by no means desire that more of your warriors should leave your castles than your council think proper to permit.

" As yet I am fully persuaded that all our enemies of the Six Nations will find too much to do at home, to suffer any of their warriors to go abroad to do mischief. If you should be satisfied after a little while that your castles are out of danger, and the whole or any part of your warriors think proper to come to us, I shall be glad to see you ; and in the meantime perhaps you may be as serviceable where you are, as if you were with us.

" I shall immediately give orders to the officers commanding at Fort Schuyler to send some troops to your castle, and write to Colonel Van Schaick, who commands in my absence, to afford you every assistance in his power, as I am not authorized to order any of the troops now with me on any other command, being directed by our Great Chief and Warrior to proceed with the whole of these troops on the present route."

In the course of the interview, the sachems informed General Clinton that a party of about three hundred Indians, with a few Tories, had marched from Cayuga ten days before, for the purpose of hanging upon his outskirts and harassing his march to Tioga. Still it was supposed not to be their intention to do any serious fighting, until the invading forces should have advanced a considerable distance up the Tioga or Chemung river. Indeed, it was evidently the purpose of the enemy to make no stand, until the forces of Sullivan and Clinton should arrive in the neighborhood of the works of defence which the Indians and Tories had been constructing, even before the battle of Wyoming, on the banks of the Chemung.

In consequence of the requisition of the warriors, in their speech, General Clinton issued an order to the commanding officer at Fort Schuyler to detach a command of thirty or forty men to the Oneida fort, to be recalled as circumstances might require. With this understanding, and the assurances in the General's answer to their speech, the ten principal warriors, specially charged with the explanations, took their departure the same evening for their own castle—leaving the remaining twenty-five to accompany the expedition.* General Clinton was

---

* All but two of these, however, and those of the meaner sort, deserted the expedition before they arrived at Tioga.

impatient of delay, as appears by a letter addressed to his brother
on the next day, from which the following is an extract :—

GENERAL TO GOVERNOR CLINTON.

" *Camp on the south end of* }
" *Otsego Lake, July* 6th, 1779. }

" DEAR BROTHER,

"I have the pleasure to inform you that I am now at this
place, with two hundred and eight boats, with all the stores,
provisions, and baggage of the army; and I am well convinced
that such a quantity of each hath never before been transported
over so bad a road in so short a time and with less accidents, so
that I am now in the most readiness to move down the Susquehanna, whenever I receive General Sullivan's orders for that
purpose.   I have thrown a dam across the outlet, which I conceive will be of infinite importance, as it has raised the lake at
least two feet, by which the boats may be taken down with less
danger than otherwise, although, from the intricate winding of
the channel, I expect to meet some difficulties on the way.   It
is uncertain when I shall leave this place.

" I received a letter from General Sullivan yesterday, dated at
Wyoming July 1st, in which he informs me that he was anxiously waiting the arrival of his stores from Sunbury—that he
expected them daily—that it was determined in council that that
army should proceed almost as far as Tioga previous to my
leaving the lake, as by that means he might make a diversion in
my favor, and facilitate my movements down the river.   This
I imagine to be in consequence of a letter which he probably has
received from General Washington, and one I received from
him dated the first instant, in which his Excellency expresses
his surprise at my taking so much stores with me, when it was
determined that all the supplies of the army should come up
with General Sullivan, and that nothing more should be brought
with me than was absolutely necessary for the troops until the
junction was formed at Tioga.   However, as it was General
Sullivan's orders to bring what provision I could, and as his
Excellency added in his letter to me that it was not his intention to contravene any orders I may receive from General Sullivan, I ordered the whole to be forwarded to this place; which
I have happily effected, and of which I do not repent, as I be-

lieve I shall fall short of many articles.   *   *   *   *
*   *   *   The troops are in good health and high spirits,
and every thing seems to promise a most favorable and successful campaign." *   *   *   *   *   *   *   *

No attempts were made by the enemy to molest General
Clinton while thus detained at Otsego Lake. Still, his proceedings were not left entirely without observation, and there
were two individual affrays happening in his vicinity, which
deserve special mention. The name of David Elerson, one of
the bold spirits associated with Murphy in Morgan's rifle corps,
has already occurred in a former chapter. The detachment to
which he belonged had been ordered from Schoharie to join
this expedition. While lying at the head of the lake, Elerson
rambled off to an old clearing, at the distance of a mile or more
from camp, to gather pulse for dinner. Having filled his knapsack, while adjusting it in order to return to camp, he was
startled at the rustling of the tall and coarse herbage around
him, and in the same instant beheld some ten or a dozen Indians, who had crept upon him so cautiously as to be just on
the point of springing to grasp him. Their object was clearly
rather to make him a prisoner than to kill him, since he might
easily have been shot down unperceived. Perhaps they wanted
him for an *auto-da-fé*, perhaps to obtain information. Seizing
his rifle, which was standing by his side, Elerson sprang forward to escape. A shower of tomahawks hurtled through the
air after him ; but as he had plunged into a thicket of tall weeds
and bushes, he was only struck on one of his hands, his middle finger being nearly severed. A brisk chase was immediately
commenced. Scaling an old brush-wood fence, Elerson darted
into the woods, and the Indians after him. He was as fleet as
a stag, and perceiving that they were not likely soon to overtake, the pursuers discharged their rifles after him, but luckily
without effect. The chase was thus continued from eleven till
three o'clock—Elerson using every device and stratagem to
elude or deceive the Indians, but they holding him close. At
length, having gained a moment to breathe, an Indian started
up in his front. Drawing up his rifle to clear the passage in
that direction, the whizz of a bullet fleshing his side, and the
crack of a rifle, from another point, taught him that delays were
particularly dangerous at that spot. The Indian in front, how-

ever, had disappeared on his presenting his rifle, and Elerson
again darted forward. His wounded side bled a little, though
not enough to weaken him. Having crossed a ridge, he paused
a moment in the valley beyond, to slake his thirst—his mouth
being parched, and himself almost fainting. On rising from
the brook, the head of one of his pursuers peeped over the crest
of the hill. He raised his rifle, but such was his exhaustion
that he could not hold it steady. A minute more, and he would
have been in the power of the savage. Raising his rifle again,
and steadying it by the side of a tree, he brought the savage
tumbling headlong down the hill. In the next moment his
trusty rifle was re-loaded and primed, and in the next the whole
group of his pursuers came rushing over the ridge. He again
supposed his minutes were numbered ; but being partly sheltered by the trunk of a huge hemlock, they saw not him, but
only the body of their fallen comrade yet quivering in the agonies of death. Drawing in a circle about the body of their companion, they raised the death wail ; and as they paused, Elerson made another effort to fly. Before they resumed the pursuit, he had succeeded in burying himself in a dark thicket of
hemlocks, where he found the hollow trunk of a tree, into which
he crept. Here he lay ensconced two full days, without food
or dressings for his wound. On the third day he backed out of
" the loop-hole of his retreat," but knew not which way to proceed—not discerning the points of compass. In the course of
two or three miles, however, he came to a clearing, and found
himself at Cobleskill—having, during his recent chase, run over
hill and dale, bog, brook, and fen, upward of twenty-five miles.

At about the same time, and probably by the same party of Indians, the premises of a Mr. Shankland, lying in their track, situated in the outskirts of Cherry Valley, were assaulted. Residing
at the distance of two or three miles from the village, his house
had escaped the common destruction the preceding Autumn.
But he had nevertheless removed his family to the valley of the
Mohawk for safety, and had returned to his domicil accompanied only by his son.* They were awakened just before dawn
by the assailants, who were endeavoring to cut away the door
with their hatchets. Taking down his two guns, Mr. Shankland directed his son to load them, while he successively fired

---

* The late Thomas Shankland, Esq. of Cooperstown.

to the best advantage. But not being able to see the enemy, he determined upon a sortie. Having a spear, or espontoon, in the house, he armed himself therewith, and carefully unbarring the door, rushed forth upon the besiegers, who fled back at his sudden apparition. One of the Indians whom he was specially pursuing, tumbled over a log, and as Mr. Shankland struck at him, his spear entered the wood, and parted from the shaft. Wrenching the blade from the log, he darted back into the house, barred the door, and again commenced firing upon the assailants. They had been so much surprised by his rushing out upon them, that they neither fired a shot, nor hurled a tomahawk, until he had returned to his castle, and barred the sally-port. During that part of the affray, his son, becoming somewhat frightened, escaped from the house, and ran for the woods. He was pursued, overtaken, and made captive. The father, however, continued the fight—the Indians firing through the casements at random, and he returning the shots as well as he could. At one time he thought of sallying forth again, and selling his life to the best advantage; but by thus doing, he very rightly judged that he should at once involve the life of his son. The Indians, growing wearied of fighting at such disadvantage, at last attempted to make sure of their victim by applying the torch, and the house was speedily in flames. But it so happened that between the rear of the house and the forest, a field of hemp interposed—into which Mr. Shankland contrived to throw himself from the house, unperceived by the Indians. Concealed from observation by the hemp, he succeeded in reaching the woods, and making good his retreat to the Mohawk. Meantime the Indians remained by the house until it was consumed, together, as they supposed, with the garrison. They then raised a shout of victory, and departed*—several of their number having been wounded by the courageous proprietor.

Greatly to his vexation, as appears from his letters, General Clinton was detained at Otsego, by the tardy movements of his commander below, during the whole month of July and the first week in August—until, indeed, his troops became impatient to a degree.† But the General was not idle in respect to every

---

* Campbell's Annals.

† By a letter from the Commander-in-chief to General Sullivan, it appears that in the organization of the expedition the latter had been compelled to encounter greater

arrangement that might add to their security or contribute to their success. In the letter to his brother, last quoted, he dis closed one capital stroke of generalship, which not only contributed largely to his successful descent of the river, but was of great service in other respects. The damming of the lake, and the accumulation, by this means, of a vast reservoir of water, by rendering more certain and expeditious the navigation of the river, was an exceedingly happy thought. And when at length orders were received for his embarkation on the 9th of August, his flotilla was not only borne triumphantly along upon the pile of the impatient waters accumulated for the occasion, but the swelling of the torrent beyond its banks caused wide and unexpected destruction to the growing crops of the Indians on their plantations at Oghkwaga and its vicinity. They were, moreover, greatly affrighted at the sudden and unexpected rise of the waters in the dryest season of the year, especially as there had been no rains—attributing the event to the interposition of the " Great Spirit," who thus showed that he was angry with them. The whole expedition was indeed calculated to impress them with terror—as it might have done a more enlightened and less superstitious people. The country was wild and totally uninhabited, excepting by scattered familes of the Indians, and here and there by some few of the more adventurous white settlers, in the neighborhood of Unadilla. The sudden swelling of the river, therefore, bearing upon its surge a flotilla of more than two hundred vessels, through a region of primitive forests, and upon a stream that had never before wafted upon its bosom any craft of greater burthen than a bark canoe, was a

difficulties than had been anticipated. He was disappointed in regard to the Pennsylvania independent companies—to supply which deficiency, Lieutenant-Colonel Albert Pauling was directed to march across from Warwasing, and join Clinton at Oghkwaga. Governor Clinton himself had intended to lead this regiment, but General Washington, believing that the influence of his presence was needed elsewhere, induced him to relinquish that design. The delays of Sullivar. therefore, may not have arisen from any fault of his own. Still, the inactivity of General Clinton at Otsego Lake, and of Sullivan at Wyoming, was no more irksome to the former than to Brant himself. This active warrior had probably led in person the three hundred Indians spoken of by the Oneidas as having gone forth to hang upon the flanks of General Clinton, and annoy his troops by skirmishes during the march. Becoming weary, however, of waiting for a foe whose movements were apparently so tardy, Brant determined on making the irruption into Minisink, of which a history has been given in the last preceding chapter

spectacle which might well appal the untutored inhabitants of the regions thus invaded.

During these energetic proceedings of Clinton, it has been seen that Sullivan was very dilatory in his movements, and his conduct in the early part of the campaign gave particular dissatisfaction to Congress. His requisitions for supplies were enormous, and several of his specifications of articles, such as eggs, tongues, and other luxuries, were considered so unsoldierlike as to create disgust. However, having completed his arrangements, he left Wyoming on the 31st of July, and ascended the Susquehanna to Tioga, with an expedition far more formidable as to numbers, and not less imposing in other respects, than was the descending division under General Clinton—though he had not the advantage of riding upon so majestic a flood. Sullivan reached Tioga on the 11th of August, and on the following day pushed out a detachment twelve miles toward Chemung, which was attacked by a body of Indians—losing, during the brush, seven men killed and wounded. The detachment returned to Tioga on the 13th, after having burnt one of the Indian towns.

General Clinton with his division, having been joined at Oghkwaga by a detachment of Colonel Pauling's levies from Warwasing, arrived at Tioga and formed a junction with Sullivan on the 22d of August. The entire command amounted now to five thousand, consisting of the brigades of Generals Clinton, Hand, Maxwell, and Poor, together with Proctor's artillery and a corps of riflemen. So long had the expedition been in progress, that it was well understood the Indians and Tories were not unprepared to receive them; and in moving up the Tioga and the Chemung rivers, the utmost degree of caution was observed to guard against surprise. A strong advanced guard of light infantry preceded the main body, which was well protected by large flanking parties. In this way they slowly proceeded in the direction of the works of the enemy, upon the Chemung at Newtown. On the 28th, an Indian settlement was destroyed, together with fields of corn, and other Indian products yet unharvested.[*]

---

[*] The instructions of the Commander-in-chief were peremptory, that Sullivan was not even to listen to propositions of peace until after he should have "very thoroughly completed the destruction of their settlements."

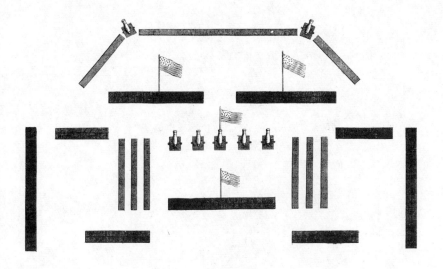

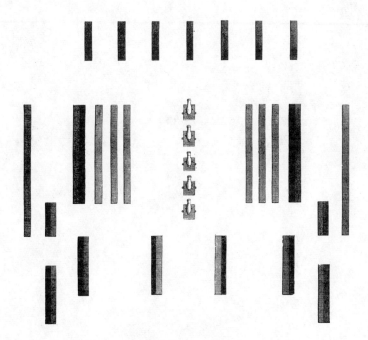

The Indians, determined to risk a general action in defence of their country, had selected their ground with judgment, about a mile in advance of Newtown.* Their force was estimated by General Sullivan at fifteen hundred, including five companies of British troops and rangers, estimated at two hundred men. The enemy, however, only allowed their force to consist of five hundred and fifty Indians, and two hundred and fifty whites—in all, eight hundred.† Brant commanded the Indians, and the regular troops and rangers were led by Colonel John Butler, associated with whom were Colonels Sir John and Guy Johnson, Major Walter N. Butler, and Captain M'Donald.‡ The enemy had constructed a breast-work of half a mile in length, so covered by a bend of the river as to expose only the front and one of the flanks to attack ; and even that flank was rendered difficult of approach by resting upon a steep ridge, " nearly parallel to the general course of the river, terminating " somewhat below the breast-work. Farther yet to the left was " still another ridge, running in the same direction, and leading " to the rear of the American army. The ground was covered " with pine, interspersed with low shrub oaks, many of which, " for the purpose of concealing their works, had been cut and " brought from a distance, and stuck down in their front, ex- " hibiting the appearance of untransplanted shrubbery. The " road, after crossing a deep brook at the foot of the hill, turned " to the right, and ran nearly parallel to the breast-work, so as " to expose the whole flank of the army to their fire should it " advance without discovering their position." § Detachments of the enemy, communicating with each other, were stationed on both hills, for the purpose of falling upon Sullivan's right and rear the moment the action should commence.

The enemy's position was discovered by Major Parr, commanding the advance guard, at about 11 o'clock in the morning of the 29th of August. General Hand immediately formed the light infantry in a wood, at the distance of about four hundred yards from the breast-work, and waited until the main body of

---

* The site of the present town of Elmira.   † Gordon.

‡ It is not quite certain whether both the Johnsons were engaged in this action. Sir John was there, and the author has somewhere seen the name of Guy Johnson as having likewise been in the battle of the Chemung.

§ Marshall.

the army arrived on the ground. A skirmishing was, however, kept up by both sides—the Indians sallying out of their works by small parties, firing, and suddenly retreating—making the woods at the same time to resound with their war-whoops, piercing the air from point to point as though the tangled forest were alive with their grim-visaged warriors. Correctly judging that the hill upon his right was occupied by the savages, General Sullivan ordered Poor's brigade to wheel off, and endeavor to gain their left flank, and, if possible, to surround them, while the artillery and main body of the Americans attacked them in front.* The order was promptly executed ; but as Poor climbed the ascent, the battle became animated, and the possession of the hill was bravely contested. In front the enemy stood a hot cannonade for more than two hours.† Both Tories and Indians were entitled to the credit of fighting manfully. Every rock, and tree, and bush, shielded its man, from behind which the winged messengers of death were thickly sent, but with so little effect as to excite astonishment. The Indians yielded ground only inch by inch ; and in their retreat darted from tree to tree with the agility of the panther, often contesting each new position to the point of the bayonet—a thing very unusual even with militiamen, and still more rare among the undisciplined warriors of the woods. Thayendanegea was the animating spirit of the savages. Always in the thickest of the fight, he used every effort to stimulate his warriors, in the hope of lead ing them to victory. Until the artillery began to play, the whoops and yells of the savages, mingled with the rattling of musketry, had well-nigh obtained the mastery of sound. But their whoops were measurably drowned by the thunder of the cannon. This cannonade " was elegant," to adopt the phraseology of Sullivan himself, in writing to a friend, and gave the Indians a great panic. Still, the battle was contested in front for a length of time with undiminished spirit. But the severity of fighting was on the flank just described. As Poor gallantly approached the point which completely uncovered the enemy's rear, Brant, who had been the first to penetrate the design of the American commander, attempted once more to rally his forces, and with the assistance of a battalion of the rangers, make a

* Letter from General Sullivan to a gentleman in Boston.
† Idem. Vide Remembrancer, vol. vii.

stand. But it was in vain, although he exerted himself to the utmost for that purpose—flying from point to point, seeming to be everywhere present, and using every means in his power to re-animate the flagging spirits, and re-invigorate the arms of his followers. Having ascended the steep, and gained his object without faltering, the enemy's flank was turned by Poor, and the fortunes of the day decided. Perceiving such to be the fact, and that there was danger of being surrounded, the retreat-halloo was raised, and the enemy, savages and white men, pre-cipitately abandoned their works, crossed the river, and fled with the utmost precipitation—the Indians leaving their packs and a number of their tomahawks and scalping-knives behind them. The battle was long, and on the side of the enemy bloody.* Eleven of their dead were found upon the field—an unusual circumstance with the Indians, who invariably exert themselves to the utmost to prevent the bodies of their slain from falling into the hands of their foes. But being pushed at the point of the bayonet, they had not time to bear them away. They were pursued two miles, their trail affording indubitable proof that a portion of their dead and wounded had been carried off. Two canoes were found covered with blood, and the bodies of fourteen Indian warriors were discovered partially buried among the leaves. Eight scalps were taken by the Americans during the chase.† Considering the duration of the battle, and

---

* Mr. John Salmon, late of Livingston County, (N. Y.) who was a member of a detachment of the rifle corps in this expedition, in a letter written for Mary Jemi-son's Narrative, speaks of a second stand made by the Indians at a place above Newtown called the Narrows—" Where," he says, " they were attacked by our men, who killed them in great numbers, so that the sides of the rocks next the river ap-peared as though blood had been poured on them by pailfuls. The Indians threw their dead into the river, and escaped the best way they could." No other account makes mention of any such incident, unless, indeed, Mr. Salmon refers to the killing of the eight warriors whose scalps were taken during the flight, according to one of Sullivan's letters to a gentleman in Boston, which may be found in Almon's Re-membrancer, and which is the authority for this statement in the text. The MS. journal of Capt. Fowler, in the author's possession, commences only the day after the battle.

† " On the next morning [after Sullivan's arrival at Catharine's town,] an old woman of the Cayuga nation was found in the woods, who informed us that on the night after the battle of Newtown, the enemy having fled the whole time, arrived there in great confusion early the next day; that she heard the warriors tell their women that they were conquered, and must fly; that they had a great many killed, and vast numbers wounded. She likewise heard the lamentations of many at the loss of their connexions. In addition, she assured us that some other warriors had

the obstinacy with which it was maintained, the loss of the Americans was small almost to a miracle. Only five or six men were killed, and between forty and fifty wounded. Among the American officers wounded were Major Titcomb, Captain Clayes, and Lieutenant Collis—the latter mortally. All the houses of the contiguous Indian town were burnt, and the corn-fields destroyed.*

The Americans encamped that night on the field of battle; and on the following day, the wounded, together with the heavy artillery, and wagons, and all such portions of the baggage as would not be required, and could not well be transported in the farther prosecution of the flying campaign now to be performed, were sent back to Tioga. Only four brass three-pounders and a small howitzer were retained; and the whole army was at once placed upon short allowance,—the soldiers submitting cheerfully to the requisition, the moment the necessity of the measure was explained to them in a speech by their commander. These and other dispositions having been made, the army moved forward on the 31st, in the direction of Catharine's town, situated

met Butler at that place, and desired him to return and fight again. But to this request they could obtain no satisfactory answer; for, as they observed, 'Butler's mouth was closed.' The warriors, who had been in the action, were equally averse to the proposal."—*Sullivan's Official Account.*

* The strength of the enemy's force at Newtown was never ascertained with any degree of certainty; although, as heretofore stated in the text, it was the opinion of Sullivan, and also of his general officers, that it must have exceeded fifteen hundred. Still, the two prisoners taken estimated them only at eight hundred. They admitted, however, that, in addition to the five companies of rangers engaged in the action, all the warriors of the Senecas, and six other nations of Indians, were engaged. In order to determine the amount of their force with as much accuracy as could be attained, General Sullivan examined their breast-work, the extent of which was more than half a mile. The lines were flanked in every part by bastions in front, and a dwelling-house also, in front of the works, had been converted into a block-house and manned. The breast-work appeared to have been fully manned, though, as Sullivan supposed, by only a single rank, Some part of the works being low, the enemy were compelled to dig holes in the ground to cover themselves in part. A very thin scattering line, designed, as was supposed, for communicating signals, was continued from those works to that part of the mountain ascended by General Poor, where a large body had been stationed, as heretofore stated, for the purpose of falling upon the flank of the Americans. The distance from the breast-work to that point was at least one mile and a half. From thence to the hill on the American right was another scattering line of about one mile, and on the hill a breast-work, with a strong party, destined, as it was supposed, to fall upon the American rear. But this design was frustrated by the movements of Clinton, as already mentioned.— *Vide Sullivan's Official Report.*

near the head of Seneca Lake, and the residence of the celebrated Catharine Montour. On their way thither, Sullivan destroyed a small settlement of eight houses, and a town called Knawaholee, of about twenty houses, situated on a peninsula at the conflux of the Tioga and Cayuga branches. Several corn-fields were destroyed at this place, and a number of others, also very large, about six miles up the Tioga, by Colonel Dayton and the rifle corps, who were detached thither upon that service.

The Indians and Tories acted unwisely in retreating so far as they did from the battle of Newtown, since the march of Sullivan thence to Catharine's town was of the most difficult and fatiguing description. They were compelled to traverse several narrow and dangerous defiles with steep hills upon either side, the passage of which might have been rendered exceedingly annoying to their invaders by a vigilant enemy. The route lay along the streams ; and such was the sinuous course of one of them, almost swelling to the size of a river, that they were obliged to ford it several times—the men up to their middles in water. Worse than all, they were compelled to thread their way through a deep-tangled hemlock swamp. The night came on exceedingly dark, and the sufferings of the troops were great. General Sullivan was advised not to enter the swamp until the next day, but he rejected the counsel, and obstinately pushed forward. So fatigued, however, was the army, that General Clinton, whose division brought up the rear, was obliged to pass the night in the swamp without pack or baggage. Neither Brant nor the Butlers displayed their wonted sagacity on this occasion, or the Americans might have been made to suffer severely for their rashness in penetrating such a thicket at such an hour. The excuse of the Indians, who were roasting corn not many miles distant, was, that the way was so bad, and the night so dark, they did not dream of Sullivan's advancing under such circumstances.

Disappointed by the Oneidas, upon whose assistance General Sullivan had counted as guides and runners through the Indian country, but only four of whom had continued with the expedition, the General despatched one of these from Catharine's town to the castle of that nation, with an address, calling upon all who were friendly to the Americans, to prove the sincerity of their professions by joining his forces immediately.

The messenger, Oneigat, was also instructed to give his nation an account of the battle at Newtown. He did not, however, rejoin the expedition until near its close. He then reported that on his arrival at the Oneida castle, a council was convened, and that his people were delighted with the news of which he was the bearer. Obedient, moreover, to the summons which he had borne thither, seventy of their warriors had set out with him to join the army, and thirty more were to follow the next day. But on that day, near the Onondaga village, they met their brother, Conowaga, from the army, who informed them that the General had already advanced as far as Kanasadagea, and had men enough—only wanting a few good guides. In consequence of this information, the Oneida warriors had turned back—transmitting, however, by him, an address to the General, interceding in behalf of a clan of the Cayugas, who, they declared, had always been friendly to the United States. As an evidence of this fact, they referred to the cases of several prisoners, who, as it was alleged, had been surrendered by them to General Schuyler. The Oneidas, therefore, besought General Sullivan not to destroy the fields of these friendly Cayugas, who, if deprived of their corn, would fall upon them for support, and they already had a heavy burden upon their hands in the persons of the destitute Onondagas. General Sullivan immediately sent a speech in reply, commending the Oneidas for their fidelity to the United States, but expressing his surprise at their interposing a word in behalf of any portion of the Cayugas, whose whole course had been marked, not only by duplicity, but by positive hostility. He therefore distinctly informed the Oneidas that the Cayugas should be chastised. Nor did he fail to execute his purpose, as will in due time appear.[*]

The brigade of General Clinton rejoined the main army on the 2d of September, and the whole encamped at Catharine's town, which was entirely destroyed on the following day, together with the corn-fields and orchards. The houses, thirty in number, were burnt. The work of destruction, marking that extraordinary campaign, was now begun in earnest. It was considered necessary by the Commander-in-chief, or his orders

* See Sullivan's address, and the message of the Oneidas in reply, Almon's Remembrancer, for 1780, Part I.

would not have been so peremptory upon the subject, nor his satisfaction so great after its accomplishment.* Still, at this distance of time, when the mind glances back not only to the number of towns destroyed, and fields laid waste, but to the war of extermination waged against the very orchards, it is difficult to suppress feelings of regret—much less to bestow a word of commendation. It has been asserted that some of the officers, among whom were General Hand and Colonel Durbin, objected to this wanton destruction of the fruit-trees, as discreditable to American soldiers; but the Indians had been long and cruelly provoking the Americans by the ferocity of their attacks upon the border settlements, and it had been judged expedient to let the arm of vengeance fall heavily upon them. "The Indians," said Sullivan, "shall see that there is malice enough in our " hearts to destroy every thing that contributes to their support;" † and well did he fulfil the threat.

The comparative state of civilization to which the Six Nations had arrived, has been glanced at in the opening of the present chapter. Still it is apprehended that but few of the present generation are thoroughly aware of the advances which the Indians, in the wide and beautiful country of the Cayugas and Senecas, had made in the march of civilization. They had several towns, and many large villages, laid out with a considerable degree of regularity. They had framed houses, some of them well finished, having chimneys, and painted. They had broad and productive fields; and in addition to an abundance of apples, were in the enjoyment of the pear, and the still more delicious peach. But after the battle of Newtown, terror led the van of the invader, whose approach was heralded by watchmen stationed upon every height, and desolation followed weeping in his train. The Indians everywhere fled as Sullivan advanced, and the whole country was swept as with the besom of destruction. On the 4th, as the army advanced, they destroyed a small scattering settlement of eight houses; and two days afterward reached the more considerable town of Kendaia, containing about twenty houses neatly built, and well finished. These

---

* See letter of Washington to Colonel John Laurens, Sept. 28, 1779; to the President of Congress, Oct. 9; and to the Marquis de Lafayette, October 20, of the same year—*Sparks, Vol.* vi.

† Gordon.

were reduced to ashes, and the army spent nearly a day in destroying the fields of corn and the fruit-trees. Of these there were great abundance, and many of them appeared to be very ancient. While thus engaged, the army was joined by one of the inhabitants of Wyoming, a captive who had escaped from the Indians. He informed them that all had been terror among the Indians since the battle of Newtown, and that Kendaia had been deserted two days before in the greatest confusion. He likewise stated various reasons for believing that the enemy had suffered greatly in that battle—that he had heard some of the Indian women lamenting the loss of their connexions, and that Brant had taken most of the wounded up the Tioga river in water craft, which had been previously made ready in case of defeat. It was farther believed that the King of Kanadaseagea had been killed at Newtown. He had been seen on his way thither, and had not returned. From the description given of his dress and person, moreover, it was believed by General Sullivan that he had seen his body among the slain.

On the 7th of September, Sullivan crossed the outlet of the Seneca Lake, and moved in three divisions upon the town of Kanadaseagea—the Seneca capital—containing about sixty houses, with gardens, and numerous orchards of apple and peach trees. It was Sullivan's object to surround the town, and take it by surprise. But, although Butler had endeavored to induce the Indians to make a stand at that place, his importunities were of no avail. They said it was of no use to contend with such an army ; and their capital was consequently abandoned, as the other towns had been, before the Americans could reach it. A detachment of four hundred men was sent down on the west side of the lake, to destroy Gotheseunquean,* and the plantations in the neighborhood ; while at the same time a number of volunteers, under Colonel Harper, made a forced march in the direction of the Cayuga Lake, and destroyed Schoyere. Meantime the residue of the army was employed, on the 8th, in the destruction of the town, together with the fruit-trees, and fields of corn and beans.† Here, as elsewhere, the work of destruction was thorough and complete.

---

* Thus spelled by General Sullivan, whose official account is in part the basis of this narrative. Captain Theodosius Fowler, in his diary, writes it Karhauguash.

† Journal of Capt. Fowler.

In leaving their town, the Indians had fled with such precipitancy that a young white male child, about seven or eight years old, was left behind, asleep. It was taken in charge by an officer, who, from ill health, was not on duty. In retiring from the campaign, for the same cause, he took the child with him, and nothing more of its history is known. This flight of the Indians was universal ; and of all commanders, Sullivan seems to have been least successful in finding the enemy of whom he was in search, save only when the enemy wished to be found. Upon this feature of the present campaign it has been remarked, that although the bravery of this officer was unimpeachable, yet he was altogether unacquainted with the science of Indian warfare, and was sure to use the best means to keep the savages at such a distance, that they could not be brought unwillingly to an engagement. For instance, he persisted in the practice of having cannon fired from his camp, mornings and evenings, forgetting what every one else perceived, that the Indians were thus notified of his position and the rapidity of his marches—thus being enabled daily to retreat from his approach exactly in time.*

From this point a detachment of sixty men, with the lame and sick, was sent back to Tioga. The main army then moved forward upon Kanandaigua, at which place it arrived in two days. Here they " found twenty-three very elegant houses, " mostly framed, and in general large,"† together with very extensive fields of corn—all of which were destroyed. From Kanandaigua they proceeded to the small town of Honeoye, consisting of ten houses, which were immediately burnt to the ground. A post was established at Honeoye, to maintain which a strong garrison was left, with the heavy stores and one field-piece. With this precautionary measure the army prepared to advance upon the yet more considerable town of Genesee—the great capital of the western tribes of the confederacy—containing their stores, and their broadest cultivated fields.

Hearing of Sullivan's continued advance, and of his purpose to strike their towns upon the Genesee, the Indians once more began to think of giving battle. A council of their towns was convened, the result of which was a determination to intercept

* Letter of John Salmon, in the Appendix of Mary Jemison's Life.
† General Sullivan's official account.

the invaders, and strike another blow in defence of their homes. They felt that if unopposed, the destruction of their towns would be inevitable, and their fate could be no worse should they meet and fight the conqueror—whatever might be the result. Their first precaution was to place their women and children in a place of security, in the woods at a distance from their town ; so that, in the event of being themselves defeated, the non-combatants would have an opportunity to escape. Having made their preparations, the warriors took the field again—selecting for their battle-ground a position between Honeoye Creek and the head of Connissius Lake.* Placing themselves in ambush, they awaited the approach of Sullivan's forces. They rose, however, upon the advance-guard of the Americans, and after a brisk skirmish, the latter fell back upon the main body—of which the Indians did not await the arrival. The only fruit of this attack, on behalf of the Indians, was the capture of two Indian prisoners of the Oneida tribe. Of itself, this incident was insignificant ; but a transaction grew out of it of thrilling interest, and strongly illustrative of Indian character. One of the Indians thus taken, was General Sullivan's guide, and had, moreover, been very active in the contest, rendering the Americans frequent and important services. On that account he was a prisoner of consequence. But there was another feature in the case not altogether unworthy of note. This faithful Indian had an elder brother engaged with the enemy, who, at the beginning of the war, had exerted all his power to persuade the younger into the British service also, but without success. At the close of this skirmish the brothers met for the first time since their separation, when they had respectively chosen to travel different war-paths ; the younger a prisoner to the elder. The latter had no sooner recognized his brother after the *melée*, than his eyes kindled with that fierce and peculiar lustre which lights up the burning eyes of a savage when meditating vengeance. Approaching him haughtily, he spoke as follows :—

"BROTHER ! You have merited death ! The hatchet or the war-club shall finish your career ! When I begged of you to follow me in the fortunes of war, you were deaf to my cries : you spurned my entreaties !

---

* At or near a place now called Henderson's Flats. Vide Life of Mary Jemison and letter of John Salmon.

"Brother ! You have merited death, and shall have your deserts ! When the rebels raised their hatchets to fight their good master, you sharpened your knife, you brightened your rifle, and led on our foes to the fields of our fathers !

"Brother ! You have merited death, and shall die by our hands ! When those rebels had driven us from the fields of our fathers to seek out new houses, it was you who could dare to step forth as their pilot, and conduct them even to the doors of our wigwams, to butcher our children and put us to death ! No crime can be greater ! But though you have merited death, and shall die on this spot, my hands shall not be stained with the blood of a brother !— *Who will strike ?*"

A pause of but a moment ensued. The bright hatchet of Little Beard, the sachem of the village, flashed in the air like the lightning, and the young Oneida chief was dead at his feet.* The other captive, who was also an Oneida sachem, was then informed by Little Beard that he was warring only against the whites, and that his life should be spared ; adding, farther, that at a suitable time he should be restored to liberty. Distrusting the good faith of the chief, however, the captive watched an opportunity for escape, and very shortly afterward accomplished his purpose—but in a manner which produced another tragic catastrophe, as will presently appear.

From Honeoye, General Sullivan advanced in two days upon a town containing twenty-five houses, called Kanaghsaws. There were large corn-fields to be destroyed here also, and a bridge to be constructed over an unfordable creek intervening between Kanaghsaws and Little Beardstown, lying next in the route to Genesee—so called from the name of a celebrated chief then residing there. While delayed by these obstacles, Lieutenant Boyd, of the rifle corps, was detached with twenty-six men to reconnoitre that chieftain's town, where also was a castle. Having performed that duty, and in doing so killed and scalped two Indians† in the otherwise deserted village, he had commenced his return to the main division. It so happened that

---

* This was truly a shocking transaction, but not *so* shocking as that of the horrible fratricide before recorded at Wyoming, nor so shocking as the attempt of the brother of Colonel Frey at Oriskany. The Indian had far the most humanity, and far the highest sense of honor and duty.

† Captain Fowler's Journal. One of these Indians was shot and scalped by Murphy, whose name has already occurred in connexion with the Schoharie wars.

Boyd was passing at no great distance from the party of Indians having the Oneida prisoner in charge. The latter was guarded by two Indians, between whom he was walking arm in arm, when, at a favorable moment, he suddenly broke from their grasp, and fled at the top of his speed in the direction of Sullivan's army. The Indians, in goodly numbers, turned out in pursuit, and while running, fell in with the party of Lieutenant Boyd.* By this time the Indians in pursuit after the fugitive numbered several hundred, under the immediate command of Joseph Brant, who seems suddenly to have made his appearance for the occasion.† Indeed, according to one authority, Brant was not concerned with the pursuit, but had previously secreted himself in a deep ravine, with a large party of his Indians and Butler's rangers, for the express purpose of cutting off Boyd's retreat.‡ Discovering his situation, and in fact surrounded by fearful odds, Boyd saw, of course, that his only chance of escape was to strike at some given point, and cut his way through the ranks of the enemy. It was a bold measure; but there was no alternative, and he made three successive attempts to accomplish his purpose. In the first, several of the enemy fell, without the loss of a single man on his own part. But he was repulsed. The Indians stood their ground nobly; and in the second and third attempts upon their line by Boyd, his whole party fell except himself and eight others. In the next moment several of these were killed, while a few succeeded in flight—among whom was the bold Virginian, Murphy. Boyd was himself taken prisoner, and one other man named Parker. The Lieutenant immediately solicited an interview with Thayendanegea, and making himself known as a freemason, was assured by the chief of protection.§ One of the party under Lieutenant Boyd was a brave Oneida warrior, named Honyerry, who served him as a guide. This faithful Indian had served long with the Americans, and, as the reader has already seen, was particularly distinguished in the battle of Oriskany, where so many of the Mohawk and Seneca warriors fell. On the present occasion, moreover, he acquitted himself with signal courage. Being an

* Life of Mary Jemison.

† Captain Fowler and John Salmon both state the number of Indians engaged in this affair at upward of five hundred.

‡ John Salmon's letter.   § Idem.

excellent marksman, his rifle did great execution. The Indians knew him, and as they closed in upon the little band, poor Honyerry was literally hacked to pieces.* It was a dear victory, however, to the enemy. The firing was so close before the brave party was destroyed, that the powder of the enemy's muskets was driven into their flesh. The enemy had no covert, while Boyd's party was, for a portion of the time at least, possessed of a very advantageous one. The enemy were, moreover, so long employed in removing their dead, that the approach of General Hand's brigade obliged them to leave one of the number among the dead riflemen ; together with a wagon load of packs, blankets, hats, and provisions, which they had thrown off to enable them to act with more agility in the field.†

From the battle-field Brant conducted Lieutenant Boyd and his fellow captive to Little Beard's town, where they found Colonel Butler with a detachment of the rangers. While under the supervision of Brant, the Lieutenant was well treated and safe from danger. But the chief being called away in the discharge of his multifarious duties, Boyd was left with Butler, who soon afterward began to examine him by questions as to the situation, numbers, and intentions of General Sullivan and his troops. He, of course, declined answering all improper questions ; whereat Butler threatened that if he did not give him full and explicit information, he would deliver him up to the tender mercies of the Indians. Relying confidently upon the assurances of the generous Mohawk chieftain, Boyd still refused, and Butler fulfilled his bloody threat—delivering him over to Little Beard and his clan, the most ferocious of the Seneca tribe.‡ The gallant fellow was immediately put to death by torture ; and in the execution there was a refinement of cruelty, of which it is not known that a parallel instance occurred during the whole war. Having been denuded, Boyd was tied to a sapling, where the Indians first practised upon the steadiness of his nerves by hurling their tomahawks apparently at his head, but so as to strike the trunk of the sapling as near to his head as possible without hitting it—groups of Indians, in the meantime, brandishing their knives, and dancing around him

---

* Captain Fowler's Journal. † Sullivan's Official Account.

‡ Letter of Salmon. There is some reason to doubt which of the Butlers was the actor in this instance—the father, Colonel John, or the more severe Captain, his son.

with the most frantic demonstrations of joy. His nails were pulled out, his nose cut off, and one of his eyes plucked out. His tongue was also cut out, and he was stabbed in various places.* After amusing themselves sufficiently in this way, a small incision was made in his abdomen, and the end of one of his intestines taken out and fastened to the tree. The victim was then unbound, and driven round the tree by brute force, until his intestines had all been literally drawn from his body and wound round its trunk. His sufferings were then terminated by striking his head from his body. It was then raised upon a pole in triumph. Parker, the other captive, was likewise beheaded, but not otherwise tortured. After the conclusion of this tragedy, the Indians held a brief council to determine whether to offer any farther resistance to General Sullivan, or to yield their country to his ravages without opposition. They finally came to the decision that they were not sufficiently powerful to oppose the invaders with success, and thereupon decided to leave their possessions, for the preservation of their lives and those of their families. The women and children were thereupon sent away in the direction of Niagara, while the warriors remained in the forests about Little Beard's town, to watch the motions of the Americans.†

As soon as the main division had heard of the situation of Boyd, they moved forward—arriving, however, only in season to bury the bodies of the slain.‡ This tragic occurrence took place on the 13th of September. On the same day Sullivan moved forward to a place called Gathtsegwarohare, where the enemy, both Indians and rangers, were apparently disposed to make a stand. The troops were immediately brought into order of battle, and General Clinton's brigade commenced a movement with a view of outflanking and gaining the enemy's rear. But

---

* Sullivan's Official Account.

† Life of Mary Jemison. According to Colonel Butler's statement, after his examination Boyd was sent forward with a guard to Niagara ; but, while passing through Genesee village, an old Indian rushed out and tomahawked him. But Salmon says he was put to death by the most cruel tortures, and so says the official report of General Sullivan. Mary Jemison, who was with the Indians, gives the details from which the present account is drawn. It is to be hoped, however, that Colonel Butler was not accessary to the cruelty ; and in justice to his memory, it must be admitted that it was not a transaction characteristic of him.

‡ They were buried at a place now called Groveland, where the grave was very recently to be seen.

discovering the movement, the enemy retreated with precipitation. Sullivan encamped on the ground—the men sleeping on
their arms, in the expectation of an attack. But the enemy did
not disturb their repose; and on the 14th the army continued
its advance, and crossed the Genesee river. Arriving at Little
Beard's town,* they found the mutilated bodies of Boyd and
Parker, which were buried on the bank of Beard's Creek, under
a clump of wild plum trees.†

The valley of the Genesee, for its beauty and fertility, was
beheld by the army of Sullivan with astonishment and delight.
Though an Indian country, and peopled only by the wild men
of the woods, its rich intervales presented the appearance of
long cultivation, and were then smiling with their harvests of
ripening corn. Indeed, the Indians themselves professed not
to know when or by whom the lands upon that stream were
first brought into cultivation. Nearly half a century before,
Mary Jemison had observed a quantity of human bones washed
down from one of the banks of the river, which the Indians held
were not the remains of their own people, but of a different race
of men who had once possessed that country. The Indians,
they contended, had never buried their dead in such a situation. Be all this, however, as it may, instead of a howling
wilderness, Sullivan and his troops found the Genesee flatts, and
many other districts of the country, resembling much more the
orchards, and farms, and gardens of civilized life. But all was
now doomed to speedy devastation. The Genesee castle was
destroyed. The troops scoured the whole region round about,
and burnt and destroyed every thing that came in their way.
Little Beard himself had officiated as master of ceremonies at
the torturing of Boyd; and his town was now burnt to the
ground, and large quantities of corn, which his people had laid
up in store, were destroyed by being burnt or thrown into the
river. " The town of Genesee contained one hundred and
" twenty-eight houses, mostly large and very elegant. It was
" beautifully situated, almost encircled with a clear flatt, ex-
" tending a number of miles; over which extensive fields of corn
" were waving, together with every kind of vegetable that could
" be conceived."‡ But the entire army was immediately en-

---

* The place is now called Leicester.
† On the road now running from Moscow to Geneseo.   ‡ Sullivan's Account.

gaged in destroying it, and the axe and the torch soon transform-
ed the whole of that beautiful region from the character of a garden to a scene of drear and sickening desolation.   Forty Indian
towns, the largest containing one hundred and twenty-eight
houses, were destroyed.*   Corn, gathered and ungathered, to
the amount of one hundred and sixty thousand bushels, shared
the same fate ; their fruit-trees were cut down ; and the Indians
were hunted like wild beasts, till neither house, nor fruit-tree, nor
field of corn, nor inhabitant, remained in the whole country.   The
gardens were enriched with great quantities of useful vegetables,
of different kinds.   The size of the corn-fields, as well as the
high degree of cultivation in which they were kept, excited
wonder ; and the ears of corn were so remarkably large, that
many of them measured twenty-two inches in length.   So numerous were the fruit-trees, that in one orchard they cut down
fifteen hundred.†

It is in connexion with this campaign that the name of the
celebrated Seneca orator, *Sagayewatha*, or *Red Jacket*, first
occurs in history, or rather, will now for the first time thus occur, since it has never yet been mentioned at so early a date by
any previous writer.   It is well known by all who are ac-

* It has already been seen that this wide-spread destruction was the result of the
express instructions of General Washington.   It was in reference to this fact, that,
when addressing President Washington at an Indian council held in Philadelphia,
in 1792, Cornplanter commenced his speech in the following strain :—" FATHER :
" The voice of the Seneca nation speaks to you, the Great Counsellor, in whose
" heart the wise men of all the Thirteen Fires have placed their wisdom.   It may
" be very small in your ears, and we therefore entreat you to hearken with attention :
" for we are about to speak to you of things which to us are very great.   When your
" army entered the country of the Six Nations, we called you the TOWN DESTROYER ;
" and to this day, when that name is heard, our women look behind them and turn
" pale, and our children cling close to the necks of their mothers.   Our counsellors
" and warriors are men, and cannot be afraid ; but their hearts are grieved with the
" fears of our women and children, and desire that it may be buried so deep as to be
" heard no more."

† Ramsay. See, also, History of the British Empire, 2 volumes—anonymous.
While Sullivan was at Genesee, a female captive from Wyoming was re-taken.
She gave a deplorable account of the terror and confusion of the Indians.   The women, she said, were constantly begging the warriors to sue for peace ; and one of the
Indians, she stated, had attempted to shoot Colonel Johnson for the falsehoods by
which he had deceived and ruined them.   She overheard Butler tell Johnson that
after the battle of Newtown it was impossible to keep the Indians together, and
that he thought they would soon be in a miserable situation, as all their crops would
be destroyed, and they could not be supplied at Niagara.

quainted with Indian history, that Brant and Red Jacket were irreconcileable enemies. The origin of this enmity has never yet been known to the public, and it has by some been imputed to the jealousy entertained by Brant of the growing reputation of his younger and more eloquent rival. But such is not the fact. Brant ever acknowledged the great intellectual powers of Red Jacket, but always maintained that he was not only destitute of principle, but an arrant coward. In support of these opinions, he asserted that Red Jacket had given him much trouble and embarrassment during this campaign of General Sullivan, and was in fact the principal cause of the disgrace and disasters of the Indians. In relating a history of the expedition to a distinguished American gentleman,* Brant stated that after the battle of Newtown, Red Jacket was in the habit of holding private councils with the young warriors, and some of the more timid sachems, the object of which was to persuade them to sue for peace, upon any—even ignominious terms ; and that at one time he had so far succeeded as to induce them to send privately, and without the knowledge of the principal war chiefs, a runner into General Sullivan's camp, to make known to him the spirit of dissatisfaction and division that prevailed among the Indians, and to invite him to send a flag of truce with certain propositions calculated to increase their divisions and produce a dishonorable peace. Brant, who was privately informed of all these proceedings, but feared the consequences of disclosing and attempting to suppress them by forcible means, despatched, secretly also, two confidential warriors to way-lay the flag when on its route from the American to the Indian camp, and to put the bearer of it to death, and then return secretly with his despatches. This was accomplished as he directed, and all attempts at farther negotiations thereby prevented. It was certainly a bold measure ; and how far Brant's conduct therein is susceptible of justification, or even palliation, will depend on a variety of minute circumstances which it is now too late to ascertain.

Having completed the objects contemplated by the expedition to the point at which he had arrived, General Sullivan re-crossed the Genesee with his army on the 16th of September, and

---

* The late Secretary of War, General Peter B. Porter.

set out on his return. Why he did not follow up his success, and strike at the enemy's citadel at Niagara, which at that time was in no situation for formidable resistance, is a question difficult of solution. Unquestionably, in the organization of the expedition, the conquest of Niagara, the head-quarters of the foe of all descriptions, and the seat of British influence and power among the Indians, was one of the principal objects in view. But perhaps the forces of the American General had become too much weakened by sickness and fatigue, (they had not lost a hundred men in battle,) to allow of a farther advance. Certain it is, that the most important feature of the enterprise was not undertaken; and it will be seen in the sequel, that but small ultimate advantage resulted from the campaign. Stimulated by a yet keener thirst for revenge, clouds of savages were afterward again and again seen to sweep through the valley of the Mohawk with the scalping knife and the torch. The excuse offered by Sullivan himself was, the want of provisions; but this deficiency might have been most abundantly supplied from the ample stores of the Indians, which were either burnt or thrown into the river.

The return of the army was along the same track by which it had advanced. On the 20th, having re-crossed the outlet of Seneca Lake, Colonel Zebulon Butler was detached with the rifle corps and five hundred men, to pass round the foot of Cayuga Lake, and lay waste the Indian towns on its eastern shore; while on the next day, Lieutenant Colonel Dearborn, with two hundred men, was detached to perform the same service along the south-western shore. The main army pursued the most direct route to the Chemung and Tioga. On the 26th Colonel Dearborn's detachment returned, and on the 28th they were rejoined by Colonel Butler, who had burnt three towns of the Cayugas, including their capital.* Dearborn had burnt six towns in his route, destroying at the same time large quantities

---

* The Oneidas, it will be recollected, had been interceding in behalf of the Cayugas, or at least a portion of them. Upon this point General Sullivan wrote in his official report as follows:—"I trust the steps I have taken in respect to the Cayu- "gas will prove satisfactory. And here I beg leave to mention, that on searching "the houses of these pretended neutral Cayugas, a number of scalps were found, "which appeared to have been lately taken, which Colonel Butler showed to the "Oneidas, who said that they were then convinced of the justice of the steps I had "taken."

of corn. On the same day Colonels Van Courtlandt and Dayton were detached upon a similar service, for the destruction of
large fields of corn growing upon the banks of the Tioga and
its tributaries.

On the 30th of September the army reached its original point
of concentration at Tioga, where, it will be recollected, a fort
had been thrown up, and left in charge of a small garrison.
This work was destroyed on the 3d of October. The army
then resumed its return march, and passing through Wyoming,
arrived at Easton on the 15th. The distance thence to the Genesee castle was two hundred and eighty miles. With the exception of the action at Newtown, the achievements of the army
in battle were not great. But it had scoured a broad extent of
country, and laid more towns in ashes than had ever been destroyed on the continent before. The red men were driven
from their beautiful country—their habitations left in ruins, their
fields laid waste, their orchards uprooted, and their altars and
the tombs of their fathers overthrown.

There was, however, an episode to this campaign, if such a
phrase may be allowed in military history, which, unexplained
as it has been, appears like a very strange movement on the
part of General Sullivan. It has been seen in the earlier portion of the present work, that when the great body of the Mohawks retired to Canada with the Johnsons, preparatory to taking up the hatchet against the Americans, the clan at the lower
castle declined accompanying them. Thus far, moreover, during the whole progress of the war, they had preserved a strict
neutrality. They had neither molested their white neighbors,
nor been molested themselves ; but were living quietly, cultivating their grounds in the midst of the best settled portion ot
Tryon County, or following the chase at their pleasure—and
on terms of perfect amity and good-will with their white neighbors. By some means or other, however, General Sullivan had
imbibed a distrust of these people, and on the 20th of September,
while at the foot of Seneca Lake, he detached Colonel Gansevoort, with a corps of one hundred men, to Fort Schuyler.
From thence his orders were peremptory that he should proceed forthwith down the Mohawk to the said lower Indian castle, make all the Indians captives if possible, destroy their castle, and then proceed immediately with the said prisoners to

head-quarters—the order explicitly forbidding that any of the prisoners so taken should be left at Albany ; and the Colonel was at the same time enjoined, amidst all these measures of hostility, to show the Indians, so to be dispossessed and carried away by violence, " such necessary marks of civility and atten-" tion as might engage a continuance of their friendship, and " give evidence of our pacific disposition toward them !" This was truly a surprising order, and, as the event proved, as uncalled for and unjust as it was incomprehensible. As Colonel Gansevoort's official report of his proceedings under this order will present the best view of the whole transaction, it is inserted entire :—

COLONEL GANSEVOORT TO GENERAL SULLIVAN.

" Albany, October 8, 1779.

" Sir,

" Agreeably to my orders, I proceeded by the shortest route to the lower Mohawk castle, passing through the Tuscarora and Oneida castles (towns), where every mark of hospitality and friendship was shown the party. I had the pleasure to find that not the least damage nor insult was offered any of the inhabitants. On the 25th I arrived at Fort Schuyler, where, refreshing my party, I proceeded down the river, and on the 29th effectually surprised the lower Mohawk castle, making prisoners of every Indian inhabitant. They then occupied but four houses. I was preparing, agreeable to my orders, to destroy them, but was interrupted by the inhabitants of the frontiers, who have been lately driven from their settlements by the savages, praying that they might have liberty to enter into the Mohawks' houses, until they could procure other habitations ; and well knowing those persons to have lately lost their all, humanity tempted me in this particular to act in some degree contrary to orders, although I could not but be confident of your approbation ; especially when you are informed that this castle is in the heart of our settlements, and abounding with every necessary ; so that it is remarked that these Indians live much better than most of the Mohawk river farmers. Their houses were very well furnished with all necessary household utensils, great plenty of grain, several horses, cows, and wagons ; of all which I have an inventory, leaving them in the care of Major

Newkirk, of that place, who distributed the refugees in the several houses. Such being the situation, I did not allow the party to plunder at all.

" The prisoners arrived at Albany on the 2d instant, and were closely secured in the fort. Yesterday, the 7th, I received a letter from General Schuyler, (of which I enclose a copy,) respecting the prisoners, desiring that the sending the prisoners down might be postponed until an express shall arrive from General Washington. Agreeably to this request, a sergeant and twelve men are detained to keep charge of the prisoners until his pleasure is known.

" It is with the greatest regret I mention my indisposition being so great as to hinder my taking charge of the party to head-quarters. I have been several days confined, and my surgeon informs me that my complaint is bilious fever. Captain Sytez takes command of the detachment, and will proceed with all expedition to head-quarters with the baggage of the several regiments, where I hope shortly to join the army. I remain, &c. &c."

It seems that General Schuyler, then at the head of the Northern Commission of the Indian Department, having heard of the harsh measure adopted in regard to the lower castle Mohawks, had interposed in their behalf. The following is the letter referred to by Colonel Gansevoort, a copy of which was enclosed to General Sullivan :—

GENERAL SCHUYLER TO COLONEL GANSEVOORT.

" *Albany October* 7, 1779.

" DEAR SIR,

"Having perused Gen. Sullivan's orders to you respecting the Indians of the lower Mohawk castle and their property, I conceive they are founded on misinformation given to that gentlemen ; these Indians have peaceably remained there under the sanction of the public faith repeatedly given them by the commissioners of Indian affairs, on condition of peaceable demeanor ; this contract they have not violated to our knowledge. It is therefore incumbent on us, as servants of the public, to keep the public faith inviolate ; and we therefore entreat you to postpone the sending the Indians from hence until the pleasure of his Excellency, Gen. Washington, can be obtained, and a letter is already despatched to him on the occasion, and in which we have mentioned this application to you. I am, dear Sir, your most obedient, humble servant,

" Ph. Schuyler,

" *President of the Board of Commissioners*
" *of Indian affairs, N. Department.*"

Copies of these letters were at the same time enclosed to the Commander-in-chief by Colonel Gansevoort, and the result was a speedy release of the poor Indians, with directions from General Washington that the Commissioners should "lay them " under such obligations for their future good behavior as they " should think necessary."*

Thus ended the memorable campaign of General Sullivan against the country of the Six Nations ; and, however harshly that officer may have been spoken of by others, it is certain, from the letters of the Commander-in-chief, that his conduct was viewed in that quarter with the most decided approbation. The officers of the several corps engaged in the expedition held separate meetings, and testified the warmest regard in his behalf, and their approbation of the manner in which he had conducted the campaign. On the 14th of October Congress passed a resolution of thanks to General Washington for directing this expedition, and to " General Sullivan and the brave officers and " soldiers under his command for its effectual execution." But at the very time of the adoption of the resolution, it was evident that it was carried by a reluctant voice. Sullivan had made such high demands for military stores, and had so freely complained of the government for inattention to those demands, as to give much offence to some members of Congress and to the Board of War.† He, in consequence, resigned his commission on

---

* MS. letter of Washington to Colonel Gansevoort. In justice to General Sullivan respecting this crusade against the little neighborhood of friendly Mohawks, it should be stated that he acted under misinformation. In his official report, written from Tioga, September 30, he said :—" I directed Colonel Gansevoort to destroy the " lower Mohawk castle in his route, and capture the inhabitants, consisting of only " six or seven families, who were constantly employed in giving intelligence to the " enemy, and in supporting their scouting parties when making incursions on our " frontiers. When the Mohawks joined the enemy, those few families were un- " doubtedly left to answer those purposes, and keep possession of their lands."

† Allen's Biographical Dictionary.

the 9th of November, under the convenient pretext of ill health. The resignation was accepted by Congress on the 30th of that month—accompanied, however, by a vote of thanks for past services.

But there was yet another expedition against the Indians, devised and executed in conjunction, or rather simultaneously, with that of General Sullivan. This movement took place under the direction of Colonel Daniel Brodhead, then commanding at Fort Pitt, and was originally designed by the Commander-in-chief, after accomplishing the destruction of the Mingo, Munsey, and a portion of the Seneca Indians settled on the Alleghany river, for co-operation with that of Sullivan, by a junction at Niagara—a point, as it happened, unattained by either. Preparatory to this campaign, Washington had written to Colonel Brodhead, on the 22d of March, directing him to throw forward detachments of troops, the first to take post at Kittaning, and the second at Venango, and to build stockade forts at both places—observing the greatest possible secresy in regard to ulterior operations.* From various unforeseen difficulties, the project of a direct co-operation with Sullivan was abandoned on the 21st of April, and Colonel Brodhead was directed to make the necessary reconnoissances for a movement against Detroit, should such an expedition be deemed advisable.† The result, however, was an independent campaign against the tribes or clans of Indians last above mentioned, inhabiting the head waters of the Alleghany river, French Creek, and other tributaries of the Ohio. Colonel Brodhead left Pittsburgh on the 11th of August, at the head of six hundred rank and file, including volunteers and militia, with provisions for one month. The first Indian town designed to be attacked was Cannowago. On their way thither, four days after their departure from Fort Pitt, Colonel Brodhead's advanced guard met a party of between thirty and forty Indian warriors descending the Alleghany in canoes. The Indians landed to give battle; but were defeated after a sharp brush, and put to flight, leaving five warriors dead, and evident marks that others had been carried off wounded. On arriving at Cannowago, the troops were mortified

---

* Letter from Washington to Colonel Brodhead, March 22, 1779—Vide Sparks's Life and Correspondence, vol. vi.

† Letter from the same to the same, April 21, 1779.

to find that the town had been deserted for eighteen months.
Proceeding onward, however, they successively entered severai
towns, which were abandoned by the Indians on their approach.
They were all destroyed, together with the adjacent corn-fields.
At the upper Seneca town, called Yoghroonwago, they found a
painted image, or war-post, clothed in dog-skin. There were
several towns in the vicinity of this place, containing, in all, one
hundred and thirty houses, some of which were large enough to
accommodate three or four families each. These were all destroyed, together with their fields of corn, so extensive that the
troops were occupied three days in accomplishing the object. The
old towns of Buckloons and Maghinquechahocking, consisting
of thirty-five large houses, were likewise burnt. The Indians
had fled so precipitately as to leave some packages of skins and
other booty, to the value of three thousand dollars—all of
which was taken. Fields of corn were destroyed at least to the
extent of five hundred acres. From the number of new houses
building, and the extent of lands preparing for cultivation, it
was conjectured that it was the intention of the whole Seneca
and Munsey nation to plant themselves down in those settlements.* The distance traversed by Colonel Brodhead, going
and returning, was four hundred miles, and not a man was lost
during the expedition.

The thanks of Congress were likewise voted to General
Washington for devising, and to Colonel Brodhead for executing, this expedition. It has already been remarked, that as
but few of the enemy were slain in these expeditions, the only
immediate effect, beyond the destruction of provisions and
property, was to exasperate the Indians. A more remote effect
was to throw the whole body of the hostiles of the Six Nations
back upon their British employers, for their entire support the
following winter. Another consequence was, that from the
want and distress of the Indians during that winter, a mortal
disease was superinduced among them, which swept great
numbers into eternity.

---

* Official account of Colonel Brodhead. Upon this expedition, in connexion
with that of Sullivan, the historian, Ramsay, remarks—" In this manner the savage
" part of the war was carried on. Waste, and sometimes cruelty, were inflicted and
" retorted, with infinite variety of scenes of horror and disgust. The selfish passions
" of human nature, unrestrained by social ties, broke over all bounds of decency or
" humanity."

Still another effect of these sweeping invasions of the Indian country, was, at least for the time being, to terrify some of the tribes yet more remote. On Colonel Brodhead's return to Fort Pitt, September 14th, he found the chiefs of the Delawares, the principal chiefs of the Wyandots or Hurons, and the King of the Maquichee branch of the Shawanese, awaiting his arrival. Three days afterward the Colonel held a council with these forest dignitaries, on which occasion *Doonyontat,* the Wyandot chief, delivered the following speech :—

" BROTHER MAGHINGIVE KEESHUCH,* listen to me !

" BROTHER : It grieves me to see you with the tears in your eyes. I know it is the fault of the English.

" BROTHER : I wipe away all those tears, and smooth down your hair, which the English, and the folly of my young men, have ruffled.

" Now, my Brother, I have wiped away all the stains from your clothes, and smoothed them where my young men had ruffled them, so that you may now put on your hat, and sit with that ease and composure which you would desire.

Four strings of white wampum.

" BROTHER : Listen to the Huron chiefs.

" BROTHER : I see you all bloody by the English and my young men. I now wipe away all those stains, and make you clean.

" BROTHER : I see your heart twisted, and neck and throat turned to the one side, with the grief and vexation which my young men have caused ; all which disagreeable sensations I now remove, and restore you to your former tranquility, so that now you may breathe with ease, and enjoy the benefit of your food and nourishment.

" BROTHER : Your ears appear to be stopped, so that you cannot listen to your Brothers when they talk of friendship. That deafness I now remove, and all stoppage from your ears, that you may listen to the friendly speeches of your Brothers, and that they may sink deep into your heart.

Seven strings of white wampum.

" BROTHER : Listen to me. When I look around me, I see the bones of our nephews lie scattered and unburied.

---

* The Indian name conferred upon Colonel Brodhead.

"BROTHER: I gather up the bones of all our young men on both sides, who have fallen in this dispute, without any distinction of party.

"BROTHER: I have now gathered up the bones of our relations on both sides, and will bury them in a large deep grave. and smooth it over so that there shall not be the least sign of bones, or any thing to raise any grief or anger in any of our minds hereafter.

"BROTHER: I have now buried the bones of all our relations very deep. You very well know that there are some of your flesh and blood in our hands prisoners: I assure you that you shall see them all safe and well.

Eight strings of white wampum.

"BROTHER: I now look up to where our Maker is, and think there is some darkness still over our heads, so that God can hardly see us, on account of the evil doings of the King over the great waters. All these thick clouds, which have arisen on account of that bad King, I now entirely remove, that God may look and see us in our treaty of friendship, and be a witness to the truth and sincerity of our intentions.

Four strings of white wampum.

"BROTHER: As God puts all our hearts right, I now give thanks to God Almighty, to the chief men of the Americans, to my old father the King of France, and to you, Brother, that we can now talk together on friendly terms, and speak our sentiments without interruption.

Four strings of black and white wampum.

"BROTHER: You knew me before you saw me, and that I had not drawn away my hand from yours, as I sent you word last year by Captain White Eyes.

"BROTHER: I look up to Heaven, and call God Almighty to witness to the truth of what I say, and that it really comes from my heart.

"BROTHER: I now tell you that I have for ever thrown off my father the English, and will never give him any assistance; and there are some amongst all the nations that think the same things that I do, and I wish that they would all think so.

"BROTHER: I cannot answer for all the nations, as I don't know all their thoughts, and will speak only what I am sure of.

"BROTHER: Listen to me. I love all the nations, and hate

none, and when I return home they shall all hear what you say and what is done between us.

" BROTHER : I have just now told you that I loved all the nations, and I see you raising up the hatchet against my younger Brother, the Shawanese.* I beg of you to stop a little while, as he has never yet heard me ; and when he has heard me, if he does not choose to think as we do, I will tell you of it immediately.

" BROTHER : I intend to speak roughly to my younger brother, and tell him not to listen to the English, but throw them off, and listen to me, and then he may live as I do.

" BROTHER : I thank you for leaving the fortress at Tuscarawas, and am convinced by that that you have taken pity on us, and want to make us your friends.

" BROTHER : I now take a firmer hold of your hand than before, and beg that you will take pity upon the other nations who are my friends ; and if any of them should incline to take hold of your hand, I request that you would comply, and receive them into friendship.   *A black belt of eleven rows.*

" BROTHER : Listen. I tell you to be cautious, as I think you intend to strike the man near to where I sit, not to go the nighest way to where he is, lest you frighten the owners of the lands who are living through the country between this and that place.†

" BROTHER : You now listen to me, and one favor I beg of you is, that when you drive away your enemies, you will allow me to continue in possession of my property, which, if you grant, will rejoice me.

" BROTHER : I would advise you, when you strike the man near where I sit, to go by water, as it will be the easiest and best way.

" BROTHER : If you intend to strike, one way is to go up the Alleghany, and by Presq' Isle ; another way is to go down this river and up the Wabash.

" BROTHER : The reason why I mentioned the road up the

---

* Colonel Clarke, the captor of Hamilton, was at that time preparing to invade the principal Shawanese towns—a purpose which he executed some time afterward. —*Author.*

† Referring to the projected movement of Colonel Brodhead against Detroit—a purpose never executed.

river is, that there will be no danger of your being discovered until you are close upon them, but on the road down the river you will be spied.

"BROTHER : Now I have told you the way by Presq' Isle, and that it is the boundary between us and your enemies ; if you go by the Wabash, your friends will not be surprised.

"BROTHER : You must not think that what I have said is only my own thoughts, but the opinion of all the Huron chiefs, and I speak in behalf of them all. If you grant what favors I have asked of you, all our friends and relations will be thankful and glad as far as they can hear all round.

"BROTHER : The reason why I have pointed out these two roads is, that when we hear you are in one of them, we will know your intentions without farther notice ; and the Huron chiefs desired me particularly to mention it, that they may meet you in your walk, and tell you what they have done, who are your enemies, and who are your friends, and I, in their name, request a pair of colors to show that we have joined in friendship.

Fourteen strings of black wampum.

"BROTHER : The chiefs desired me to tell you that they sent Montour before to tell you their intention, and they leave him to go with you, that when you meet your Brothers, you may consult together, and understand one another by his means."

On the 19th Colonel Brodhead addressed the Huron chief in reply, after the Indian form. He told him, distinctly, that fair words were no longer to be taken, unless their sincerity was attested by their deeds. In regard to the roads to Detroit, he said he should select whichever he pleased. As for the Shawanese, the Colonel told the chief that he had sent them a fair speech, which they had thrown into the fire, and he should not now recall Colonel Clarke. And in regard to the people of the chief himself, the Colonel demanded, as the basis of peace, that they should stipulate to restore all American prisoners in their hands ; to kill, scalp, and take, as many of the English and their allies as they had killed and taken of the Americans ; and on every occasion to join the Americans against their enemies. The Wyandots assented to the terms, and hostages were required for the faithful performance of their agreement.

The Delawares were at that time at peace with the United States, and a small body of their warriors had accompanied Colonel Brodhead on the expedition from which he had just returned. The business having been closed with the Huron chief, the Delawares interposed in behalf of the Maquichee clan of the Shawanese. These Indians were now apparently very humble ; but, apprehensive that they might not perhaps manage their own case very well, the Delawares had kept them back from the council, and undertaken their cause themselves. *Kelleleman*, a Delaware chief, informed Colonel Brodhead that on arriving there, their grand-children* had addressed them thus :—

"GRANDFATHERS : We are humble, and are now come unto you. Now I am come to you, I take my hands and wipe your eyes, that you may clearly see the light, and that these are your grand-children who now appear before you, and likewise remove every obstruction from your eyes, that you may hear and understand me. I also compose your heart, that you may be disposed to pity your poor grand-children, as your ancient chiefs used to pity their grand-children, the Maquichees, when they were poor or humble before them. Now, my grandfathers, I tell you to pity your grand-children, the Maquichees, and whatever you direct them to do, will be done. Now you have heard your grand-children speak, and you will judge what to say to your brother, Maghingive Keeshuch.

Two strings of white wampum.

" Now, grandfathers, here is a little tobacco to fill your pipes, that you may consider and pity your grand-children the Maquichees."

Kelleleman farther reported to Colonel Brodhead, that after the foregoing speech, *Keeshmattsee*, a Maquichee chief, rose and said to the Delawares :—

"GRANDFATHERS : I now take my chief and counsellor, Nimwha, and set him down on the ground before you, that he may assist you in considering the distressed situation of your grand-children."

Another Delaware chief, named *Killbush*, then addressed Colonel Brodhead thus :—

"BROTHER MAGHINGIVE KEESHUCH : Listen to me. You always told me that when any nations came to treat of peace, I

---

* In Indian parlance the Delawares were styled the "Grandfathers" of the Shawanese ; and hence the use, in these proceedings, of the terms reciprocally of "Grand-children" and "Grandfathers."

should first speak to them, and tell you my sentiments of them; which I am now come to do in regard to my grand-children, the Maquichees.

"I told them I was much obliged to them for clearing my eyes, my ears, and composing my heart, and that it was time, for many bad things enter into my ears."

Then turning to the Maquichees, Killbush continued his speech:—

"I remember you told me to pity you, and it is true I have pitied you, my grand-children, the Shawanese.

"Now I tell you, my grand-children, it is very well you put me in mind of my wise ancestors, who, out of pity, took you up and placed you before them.

"MY GRAND-CHILDREN: The Maquichees, it is true, you have done no harm, but I see some stains of blood upon you. which the mischief and folly of some of your young men have occasioned. Now, my grand-children, I will advise you how to be cleansed from your bloody stains; deliver to our brother Maghingive Keeshuch all his flesh and blood which are prisoners in your hands, and the horses you have stolen from the Americans. My grand-children, when you have done this, you will then be clean; your flesh and heart will be the same as mine, and I can again take you up and set you down before me. as our wise chiefs formerly did.

"Now, my grand-children, I tell you that for several years past you have been fraught with lies, which I am tired of hearing, and in future you must tell me nothing but the truth.

"Now listen to me, my grand-children; you see how dreadful the day looks, and how thick the clouds appear; don't imagine this day to be like that on which you first came to your grandfathers. I tell you that I have finished the chain of friendship. The thirteen United States and I are one. I have already assisted my brother in taking the flesh of the English and the Mingoes. You told me just now, that whatever I told you, you would do; now I offer you the flesh of the English and Mingoes to eat, and that is the only method I know of by which your lives may be preserved, and you allowed to live in peace," (delivering them a string of wampum and two scalps.) They received the string and scalps, and said they were glad to know this; and, as they had before said, whatever their grandfathers told them, they would do, so they told them again on receiving the scalps. They said, "now, grandfathers, I am very glad to hear what you have said; I have got in my hand what you say will save my life," and immediately sang his war-song. The speaker, having danced, delivered the scalps to the king, who likewise rose and sang the war-song, and said; "Now, my grandfathers, although you have often sent good speeches to the other tribes of the Shawanese nation, yet they would not receive them, but still took up the tomahawk to strike your brothers. I will now go and deliver them what I now have in my hands, which I suppose they will receive."

These proceedings were closed by the following speech from one of the Delawares to Colonel Brodhead :—

"BROTHER : We now let you know the result of our council respecting the Maquichees.

"BROTHER : Listen. This is the way I have considered the matter, and if I am mistaken I am very sorry for it. Brother, let us both consider of it. I thought when I looked in his eyes that he was sincere.

"BROTHER : I think the Maquichees are honest. In former times they were the best of the Shawanese nation. I think we may take them by the hand ; and you know you told me that any nation I took by the hand, you would also receive."

The conference appears to have been satisfactory to Colonel Brodhead. But if the Maquichee clan of the Shawanese preserved their fidelity, the main body of the nation became none the less unfriendly by their means. And although Colonel Brodhead had admonished them that he would not countermand the orders to Colonel Clarke to strike them, it so happened that the first and severest blow was struck by the Shawanese themselves. It was but a short time after the closing of the council at Fort Pitt, that a detachment of seventy men from the Kentucky district of Virginia, under the command of Major Rodgers, was surprised while ascending the Ohio, and nearly exterminated. The Kentuckians were drawn ashore by a stratagem. At first a few Indians only appeared, standing upon a sand-bar near the mouth of the Licking river, while a canoe, with three other Indians, was paddling toward them as though to receive them on board. Rodgers immediately put in to the Kentucky shore, and having made fast his boats, went in pursuit. Only five or six Indians had been seen, and Rodgers, presuming that the whole party would not probably exceed fifteen or twenty at farthest, felt perfectly sure of an easy victory—having seventy men, well armed and provided. Proceeding cautiously toward the point where he supposed he should surround the enemy, and having adjusted his movements with that design, at the very moment when he was preparing to rush forward and secure them, he found himself with his whole force in the midst of an ambuscade ! The Indians rose in a cloud of hundreds on all sides of him, and pouring in a close and deadly fire upon the Americans, rushed upon the survivors tomahawk in hand. Major Rodgers, and forty-five of his men were killed almost instantly. The residue ran for the boats, but the guard of only five men who had been left in charge, had sought security by putting off in one of them, while the Indians had already anticipated the fugitives by taking possession of the others. The possibility of retreat being thus cut off, the brave fellows now turned furiously upon the enemy ; and as night was approaching, after a sharp fight for some time, a small number, aided by the darkness, succeeded in effecting their escape to Harrodsburgh.

Among the wounded in this sharp and bloody encounter, who escaped both death and captivity, were Captain Robert Benham, and another man, whose cases, together, form a novel and romantic adventure. Benham was shot through both hips, and the bones being shattered, he instantly fell. Still, aided by the darkness, he succeeded in crawling among the thick branches of a fallen tree, where he lay without molestation through the night and during the following day, while the Indians, who had returned for that purpose, were stripping the slain. He continued to lie close in the place of his retreat until the second day, when, becoming hungry, and observing a raccoon descending a tree, he managed to shoot it—hoping to be able to strike a fire, and cook the animal. The crack of the rifle was followed by a human cry, which at first startled the Captain ; but the cry being repeated, several times, the voice of a Kentuckian was at length recognized ; the call was returned ; and the parties were soon together. The man proved to be one of his comrades, who had lost both of his arms in the battle. Never before did misery find more welcome company. One of the parties could use his feet, and the other his hands. Benham, by tearing up his own and his companion's shirts, dressed the wounds of both. He could load his rifle and fire with readiness, and was thus enabled to kill such game as approached, while his companion could roll the game along upon the ground with his feet, and in the same manner collect wood enough together to cook their meals. When thirsty, Benham could place his hat in the teeth of his companion, who went to the Licking, and wading in until he could stoop down and fill it, returned with a hat-full of water. When the stock of squirrels, and other small game in their immediate neighborhood, was exhausted, the man on his legs would roam away, and drive up a flock of wild turkies, then abundant in those parts, until they came within the range of Benham's rifle. Thus they lived, helps, meet for each other, during the period of six weeks, when they discovered a boat upon the Ohio, which took them off. Both recovered thoroughly from their wounds.*

No other events of moment occurred in the region professedly embraced in the present history, during the residue of the year 1779; and the progress of the war in other parts of the Union had been marked with but few signal actions. The active operations of this year between the British forces proper and the Americans, had commenced in the south, to the command of which section of the country General Lincoln had been assigned at the close of 1778. The first occurrence was the surprise and defeat, on the 3d of March, of General Ash, commanding a body of fifteen hundred North Carolina militia, stationed at the confluence of Briar Creek, on the Savannah river, by the British General Provost. There were about sixty regular troops under General Ash, who fought well. But the militia, as usual, threw away their arms and fled, with the exception of about three hundred, who were either killed or taken. In May, General Provost invested Charleston, but raised the siege on the approach of Lincoln upon his rear. He at first retired to the island, but soon withdrew to Savannah, where he was in turn besieged by Lincoln in October. on the land side, and by the French fleet under the Count D'Estaing by water.

---

* Captain Benham afterward served with bravery in the Indian wars of 1789–94, sharing the disaster of St. Clair and the victory of Wayne. At the close of the Revolution, he purchased the land whereon he was wounded at the time of Rodgers's defeat, built a house there, and there lived and died.

Repulsed in an injudicious assault, after much brave fighting by both Americans and French, the fleet of the latter left the continent, and the siege was raised—the militia flying to their homes, and General Lincoln retiring to Charleston.   In this assault, among other proud spirits, fell the brave Polish Count Pulaski—who had signalized himself in his own country by carrying off King Stanislaus from his capital, assisted by only a party of associate Catholic conspirators.   The only relief to this disastrous affair, was the capture, by Colonel John White of Georgia, and Captain Elholm, with four other men, of a British detachment of one hundred men, forty sailors, and five armed vessels, at Ogechee, by a very ingenious and efficacious stratagem.   Kindling a large number of fires, after the manner of an encampment, they summoned the British commander, Captain French, to surrender, or they would cut his flotilla to pieces. Supposing, by the lines of fires, that there was a greatly superior force against them, the enemy surrendered at discretion.

In the middle and northern sections of the Union, the contest during the Summer had assumed the character rather of a predatory warfare than of regular campaigns.   Sir George Collier and General Matthews made a plundering expedition on the coast of Virginia, and after sacking Norfolk and parts adjacent, returned to New-York with their booty.   In July a combined expedition by land and water was directed, under Sir George and Governor Tryon, against Connecticut.   New-Haven was taken and sacked.   Several houses in East Haven were burnt.   Fairfield, Green's Farms, and Norwalk, were likewise taken, plundered, and laid in ashes.   The Americans, consisting chiefly of militia, under General Lovell, made an attempt upon a British post at Penobscot, which was commenced gallantly.   But the arrival of Sir George Collier's fleet, with reinforcements, obliged the General to abandon the enterprise.   These untoward events, however, were relieved by Major Lee's surprise and capture of the British fort at Paulus Hook, and by the still more brilliant affair of the capture of Stony Point by General Wayne.

THE succeeding year opened inauspiciously to the American
arms. No sooner had Sir Henry Clinton heard of the departure
of Count D'Estaing from the Southern coast with the French
fleet, than he prepared for a formidable descent upon South
Carolina. Charleston was the first and most prominent object
of attack. The expedition destined upon this service left New-
York about the close of January, and in due season the troops
effected their landing about thirty miles from Charleston. The
object of the enemy could not be mistaken, and General Lincoln
made every exertion for the defence of the important post entrusted to his command, by increasing his forces and strengthening his works. Before the middle of April the town was
invested by sea and land, and Lincoln was summoned to surrender—which summons with modest firmness he declined to
obey. Clinton having succeeded in all his preliminary operations
—Tarleton having cut up Colonel White's cavalry on the Santee, and Fort Moultrie having surrendered to the Royal Navy—
the garrison, finding itself without reasonable hope of relief, proposed terms of capitulation, which were rejected by the British
commander. Hostilities were meantime prosecuted with great
energy, and after a tremendous cannonade and bombardment,
lasting from the 6th to the 11th of May, General Lincoln was
forced into a capitulation. His garrison consisted, all told, of
about five thousand men—of whom no more than two thousand

were continental troops. The loss was heavy—including upward of four hundred pieces of cannon.

Having accomplished this object, Sir Henry divided his forces into three columns, dispatching them in as many directions, with a view of overrunning the whole Southern states. Clinton, himself, returned to New-York; and then commenced that remarkable course of partizan warfare in the South, which called forth so much of high and chivalrous daring in Marion, Sumpter, and their associates in arms, and which was attended with so many brilliant exploits. There are no more vivid and thrilling pages in American history than the records of those partizan operations, the incidents of which amounted to little in themselves, separately considered; but in the general results they were of infinite importance to the cause of the republic—since the invaders were, in fact, weakened by every victory, while defeat did not discourage the Americans, who were gaining both moral and physical strength by the protraction of the struggle. But these distant glances are incidental—the North being the main field of research.

The devastation of their country by General Sullivan—the destruction of their houses, as well as their means of subsistence—had driven the Indians back upon Niagara for the winter of 1779-80—the usual winter-quarters of Brant, Guy Johnson, and the Butlers—father and son. As had been anticipated by the American Commander-in-chief, the Indians suffered greatly by destitution and consequent sickness during that winter, which was one of unexampled rigor in North America.* But neither the inclemency of the weather, nor the wants of the Indians at Niagara, prevented them from fulfilling the threat of Sir Frederick Haldimand against the Oneidas. Their villages and castle were invaded by the hostile Indians, aided by a detachment of British troops, or more probably by a corps of Butler's rangers, and entirely destroyed—their castle, their church, and their dwellings being alike laid in ashes; while the Oneidas themselves were driven down upon the white settlements for protection and support. They were subsequently planted in the neighborhood of Schenectady, where they were

---

* The harbor of New-York was not merely choked with ice for a time during the Winter of 1779-80, but so thoroughly frozen that cannon were wheeled over to the city on the ice from Staten Island.

supported by the government of the United States until the close of the war.*

Aside from the destruction of the Oneida country, it is believed that no important object was undertaken by Thayendanegea until the opening of Spring. It may be noted, however, incidentally, as an illustration of the character of the Mohawk chief, that during this winter he was married to his third wife, at the fort of Niagara, under circumstances somewhat peculiar. Among the prisoners taken to that post from Cherry Valley, was a Miss Moore, who, being detained in captivity with Mrs. Campbell and others, was courted and married by an officer of the garrison. Thayendanegea was present at the wedding; and although he had for some time previous been living with his wife, bound only by the ties of an Indian marriage, he nevertheless embraced the opportunity of having the English marriage ceremony performed, which was accordingly done by Colonel Butler, acting as one of the King's commission of the peace for Tryon County.

But the chief was seldom inactive. The month of April found him on the war-path, at the head of a small party of Indians and Tories, whom he led against the settlement of Harpersfield, which was taken by surprise and destroyed. In consequence of their exposed situation, most of the inhabitants had left the settlement, so that there were but few persons killed, and only nineteen taken prisoners. Proceeding from Harpersfield, it was Brant's design to make an attack upon the upper fort of Schoharie, should he deem it prudent to encounter the risk, after duly reconnoitering the situation of the fort and ascertaining its means of defence. The execution of this part of his project was prevented by an unexpected occurrence. Harpersfield was probably destroyed on the 5th or 6th of April. It

---

* There is difficulty in ascertaining the exact time of Brant's invasion of the Oneida towns. Although an important event in the border wars, the author has not been able to obtain dates or particulars. The fact is well known : and President Kirkland, (son of the Oneida Missionary,) has spoken of the incident several times in his communications to the Massachusetts Historical Society—published in their valuable collections. In one of those communications, Dr. Kirkland remarks that this dispersion of the Oneidas, and the devastation of their country, were greatly detrimental to their nation. When the war came on, they had attained to some degree of regularity, industry, and prosperity. But, driven from their homes, reduced to want, dependence, and abject poverty, their habits became more intemperate and idle than ever, and they never recovered from their depression.

happened that nearly at the same time, Colonel Vrooman, who was yet in command of Old Schoharie, had sent out a scout of fourteen militia-minute-men, with directions to pass over to the head waters of the Charlotte river, and keep an eye upon the movements of certain suspected persons living in the valley of that stream. It being the proper season for making maple sugar, the minute-men were likewise directed to remain in the woods and manufacture a quantity of that article, of which the garrison were greatly in want. On the 2d of April, this party, the commander of which was Captain Alexander Harper, commenced their labors in the "sugar-bush," at the distance of about thirty miles from Schoharie. They were occupied in the discharge of this part of their duty, very cheerfully and with good success, for several days, entirely unapprehensive of danger ; more especially as a new fall of snow, to the depth of three feet, would prevent, they supposed, the moving of any considerable body of the enemy, while in fact they were not aware of the existence of an armed foe short of Niagara. But their operations were most unexpectedly interrupted. It seems that Brant, in wending his way from Harpersfield toward Schoharie, fell suddenly upon Harper and his party on the 7th of April, at about two o'clock in the afternoon, and immediately surrounded them—his force consisting of forty-three Indian warriors and seven Tories. So silent and cautious had been the approach of the enemy, that the first admonition Harper received of their presence, was the death of three of his little band,* who were struck down while engaged in their work. The leader was instantly discovered in the person of the Mohawk chief, who rushed up to Captain Harper, tomahawk in hand, and observed—" Harper, I am sorry to find you here !" " Why are you sorry, Captain Brant?" replied the other. " Because," rejoined the chief, " I *must* kill you, although we were school-mates in our youth,"—at the same time raising his hatchet, and suiting the action to the word. Suddenly his arm fell, and with a piercing scrutiny, looking Harper full in the face, he inquired—" Are there any regular troops at the forts in Schoharie ?" Harper

---

* The late General Freegift Patchin, of Schoharie, was one of Harper's party, as also were his brother, Isaac Patchin, Ezra Thorp, Lt. Henry Thorp, and Major Henry. It is from Priest's Narrative of the captivity of General Patchin, that the author obtained the facts of this transaction.

caught the idea in an instant.   To answer truly, and admit that
there were none, as was the fact, would but hasten Brant and
his warriors forward to fall upon the settlements at once, and
their destruction would have been swift and sure.   He therefore
informed him that a reinforcement of three hundred Continental troops had arrived to garrison the forts only two or three
days before.   This information appeared very much to disconcert
the chieftain.   He prevented the farther shedding of blood, and
held a consultation with his subordinate chiefs.   Night coming
on, Harper and his ten surviving companions were shut up in
a pen of logs, and guarded by the Tories, under the charge of
their leader, a cruel fellow named Becraft, and of bloody noto-
riety in that war.   Controversy ran high among the Indians
during the night—the question being, whether the prisoners
should be put to death or carried to Niagara.   They were
bound hand and foot, but were so near the Indian council as to
hear much of what was said, and Harper knew enough of the
Indian tongue to comprehend the general import of their debates.   The Indians were for putting them to death ; and Becraft frequently tantalized the prisoners, by telling them, with
abusive tones and epithets, that " they would be in hell before
morning."   Brant's authority, however, was exerted effectually
to prevent the massacre.

On the following morning Harper was brought before the
Indians for examination.   The Chief commenced by saying
that they were suspicious he had not told them the truth.   Harper, however, had great coolness and presence of mind ; and
although Brant was eyeing him like a basilisk, he repeated his
former statements without the improper movement of a muscle,
or betraying the least distrustful sign or symptom.   Being satisfied, therefore, of the truth of his story, Brant determined to retrace his steps to Niagara.   This he did with great reluctance—
admitting to Captain Harper that the real object of his expedition was to fall upon Schoharie, which place, as they had been
informed, was almost entirely undefended.   He had promised
to lead his warriors to spoils and victory, and they were angry
at being thus cut short of their expectations.   Under these cir
cumstances of chagrin and disappointment, it had only been
with great difficulty that he could restrain his followers from putting them to death.   Brant then said to Captain Harper, that he

and his companions should be spared, on condition of accompanying him as prisoners of war to Niagara.

Their march was forthwith commenced, and was full of pain, peril, and adventure. The prisoners were heavily laden with the booty taken from Harpersfield, and well guarded. Their direction was first down the Delaware, where they stopped at a mill to obtain provisions. The miller was a Tory, and both himself and daughters counselled Brant to put his prisoners to death. On the following day they met another loyalist, who was well acquainted with Brant, and with Captain Harper and his party. He assured the former that Harper had deceived him, and that there were no troops at Schoharie. The Captain was, therefore, brought to another scrutiny; but he succeeded so well in maintaining the appearance of sincerity and truth, as again to avert the upraised and glittering tomahawk. On the same day an aged man, named Brown, was accidentally fallen in with and taken prisoner, with two youthful grandsons; the day following, being unable to travel with sufficient speed, and sinking under the weight of the burden imposed upon him, the old man was put out of the way with the hatchet. The victim was dragging behind, and when he saw preparations making for his doom, he took an affectionate farewell of his little grandsons, and the Indians moved on, leaving one of their number, with his face painted black—the mark of an executioner—behind with him. In a few moments afterward, the Indian came up, with the old man's scalp dangling from between the ramrod and muzzle of his gun.

Having descended the Delaware a sufficient distance, they crossed over to Oghkwaga, where they constructed floats, and sailed down the Susquehanna to the confluence of the Chemung, at which place their land-travelling again commenced. Being heavily encumbered with luggage, and withal tightly pinioned, the prisoners must have sunk by the way, at the rate the Indians travelled, and would probably have been tomahawked but for the indisposition of Brant, who, providentially for the prisoners, was attacked with fever and ague—so that every alternate day he was unable to travel. These interruptions gave them time to rest and recruit. Brant wrought his own cure by a truly Indian remedy. Watching upon the southern side of a hill, where serpents usually crawl forth in the Spring to bask in the sunbeams, he caught a rattlesnake, which was immediately made into soup, of which he ate. A speedy cure was the consequence.

But a new trial awaited the prisoners soon after they reached the Chemung. During his march from Niagara on this expedition, Brant had detached eleven of his warriors to fall once more upon the Minisink settlement for prisoners. This detachment, as it subsequently appeared, had succeeded in taking captive five athletic men, whom they secured and brought with them as far as Tioga Point. The Indians sleep very soundly, and the five prisoners had resolved at the first opportunity to make their escape. While encamped at this place during the night, one of the Minisink men succeeded in extricating his hands from the binding cords, and with the utmost caution unloosed his four companions. The Indians were locked in the arms of deep sleep around them. Silently, without causing a leaf to rustle, they each snatched a tomahawk from the girdles of their unconscious enemies, and in a moment nine of them were quivering in the agonies of death. The two others were awakened, and springing upon their feet, attempted to escape. One of them was struck with a hatchet between the shoulders, but the other fled. The prisoners immediately made good their own retreat, and the only Indian who escaped unhurt, returned to take care of his wounded companion. As Brant and his warriors approached this point of their journey, some of his Indians having raised a whoop, it was instantly returned by a single voice with the *death yell!* Startled at this unexpected signal, Brant's warriors rushed forward to ascertain the cause. But they were not long in doubt. The lone warrior met them, and soon related to his brethren the melancholy fate of his companions. The effect upon the warriors, who gathered in a group to hear the recital, was inexpressibly fearful. Rage, and a desire of revenge, seemed to kindle every bosom, and light every eye as with burning coals. They gathered round the prisoners in a circle, and began to make unequivocal preparations for hacking them to pieces. Harper and his men of course gave themselves up for lost, not doubting that their doom was fixed and irreversible. But at this moment deliverance came from an unexpected quarter. While their knives were unsheathing, and their hatchets glittering, as they were flourished in the sunbeams, the only

survivor of the murdered party rushed into the circle and interposed in their favor. With a wave of the hand as of a warrior entitled to be heard—for he was himself a chief—silence
was restored, and the prisoners were surprised by the utterance of
an earnest appeal in their behalf. It has already been observed
that Captain Harper knew enough of the Indian language to understand its purport, though unfortunately not enough to preserve
its eloquence. In substance, however, the Chief appealed to his
brother warriors in favor of the prisoners, upon the ground that
it was not they who had murdered their brothers; and to take
the lives of the innocent would not be right in the eyes of the
Great Spirit. His appeal was effective. The passions of the
incensed warriors were hushed, their eyes no longer shot forth
the burning glances of revenge, and their gesticulations ceased
to menace immediate and bloody vengeance.

True, it so happened that the Chief who had thus thrown
himself spontaneously between them and death, knew all the
prisoners—he having resided in the Schoharie canton of the
Mohawks before the war. He doubtless felt a deeper interest in
their behalf on that account. Still, it was a noble action, worthy of the proudest era of chivalry, and in the palmy days of
Greece and Rome, would have ensured him almost " an apothe-
osis and rites divine." The interposition of Pocahontas, in favor of Captain Smith, before the rude court of Powhattan,
was perhaps more romantic; but when the motive which
prompted the generous action of the princess is considered, the
transaction now under review exhibits the most of genuine
benevolence. Pocahontas was moved by the tender passion—
the Mohawk sachem by the feelings of magnanimity, and the
eternal principles of justice. It is matter of regret that the name
of this high-souled warrior is lost, as, alas! have been too many
that might have served to relieve the dark and vengeful portrai-
tures of Indian character, which it has so well pleased the white
man to draw! The prisoners themselves were so impressed
with the manner of their signal deliverance, that they justly attributed it to a direct interposition of the providence of God.

The march was now resumed toward Niagara, along the
route travelled by Sullivan's expedition the preceding year.
Their sufferings were great for want of provisions—neither
warriors nor prisoners having any thing more than a handful

of corn each for dinner. A luxury, however, awaited them, in
the remains of a horse which had been left by Sullivan's expedition to perish from the severity of the winter. The wolves
had eaten all the flesh from the poor animal's bones, excepting
upon the under side. When the carcass was turned over, a
quantity of the flesh yet remained, which was equally distributed
among the whole party, and devoured. On reaching the Genessee river, they met a party of Indians preparing to plant corn.
These laborers had a fine horse, which Brant directed to be instantly killed, dressed, and divided among his famishing company.
They had neither bread nor salt; but Brant instructed the prisoners to use the white ashes of the wood they were burning as
a substitute for the latter ingredient, and it was found to answer
an excellent purpose. The meal was partaken of, and relished
as the rarest delicacy they had ever eaten. In regard to provisions, it must be mentioned to the credit of Captain Brant,
that he was careful to enforce an equal distribution of all they
had among his own warriors and the prisoners. All fared exactly alike.

On his arrival at the Genessee river, and in anticipation of
his own departure with his prisoners for Niagara, Brant sent
forward a messenger to that post, bearing information of his approach, with the measure of his success and the number of his
prisoners. But it was not merely for the purpose of conveying
this intelligence that he dispatched his *avant courier*. He
had another object in view, as will appear in the sequel, the
conception and execution of which add a link to the chain of
testimony establishing the humanity and benevolence of his
disposition. Four days more of travel brought the party to
within a few miles of the fort; and the Tories now took special
delight in impressing upon the prisoners the perils and the sufferings they must endure, in the fearful ordeal they would have
to pass, on approaching the two Indian encampments in front of
the fort. This ordeal was nothing less than running the gauntlet, as it is called in Indian warfare—a doom supposed to be
inevitable to every prisoner; and one which, by direct means, even
Thayendanegea himself had not sufficient power to prevent.

The running of the gauntlet, or rather compelling their prisoners to run it, on the return of a war-party to their camp or
village, is a general custom among the American aboriginals—

a preliminary that must precede their ultimate fate, either of
death or mercy. It is not always severe, however, nor even
generally so, unless in respect to prisoners who have excited the
particular animosity of the Indians ; and it is often rather a scene
of amusement than punishment. Much depends on the courage
and presence of mind of the prisoner undergoing the ordeal.
On entering the village or camp, he is shown a painted post at
the distance of some thirty or forty yards, and directed to run
to, and catch hold of it as quickly as possible. His path to the
post lies between two parallel lines of people—men, women,
and children,—armed with hatchets, knives, sticks, and other
offensive weapons ; and as he passes along, each is at liberty to
strike him as severely and as frequently as he can. Should he
be so unfortunate as to stumble, or fall in the way, he may
stand a chance to lose his life—especially if any one in the
ranks happens to have a personal wrong to avenge. But the
moment he reaches the goal he is safe, until final judgment has
been pronounced upon his case. When a prisoner displays
great firmness and courage, starting upon the race with force
and agility, he will probably escape without much injury ; and
sometimes, when his bearing excites the admiration of the
savages, entirely unharmed. But woe to the coward whose
cheeks blanch, and whose nerves are untrue ! The slightest
manifestation of fear will deprive him of mercy, and probably
of his life.[*]

* Heckewelder. " In the month of April, 1782, when I was myself a prisoner, at
Lower Sandusky, waiting for an opportunity to proceed to Detroit, I witnessed a
scene of this description which fully exemplified what I have above stated. Three
American prisoners were one day brought in by fourteen warriors from the garrison
of Fort McIntosh. As soon as they had crossed the Sandusky river, to which the
village lay adjacent, they were told by the Captain of the party to run as hard as they
could to a painted post which was shown to them. The youngest of them, without a
moment's hesitation, immediately started for it, and reached it fortunately without
receiving a single blow ; the second hesitated for a moment, but recollecting himself, he also ran as fast as he could, and likewise reached the post unhurt. But the
third, frightened at seeing so many men, women, and children, with weapons in their
hands ready to strike him, kept begging the Captain to spare his life, saying he was
a mason, and would build him a large stone house, or do any work for him that he
should please. 'Run for your life,' cried the Chief to him, 'and don't talk now of
building houses !' But the poor fellow still insisted, begging and praying to the
Captain ; who, at last, finding his exhortations vain, and fearing the consequences,
turned his back upon him, and would not hear him any longer. Our mason now
began to run, but received many a hard blow, one of which nearly brought him to

Such was the scene which Harper and his fellow-prisoners now had in near prospect. They of course well knew the usages of Indian warfare, and must expect to submit. Nor was the chance of escape from injury very cheering, enfeebled and worn down as they were by their journey and its privations. Miserable comforters, therefore, were their Tory guards, who were tantalising them in anticipation, by describing this approaching preliminary cruelty. But on emerging from the woods, and approaching the first Indian encampment, what was the surprise of the prisoners, and the chagrin of their conductors, at finding the Indian warriors absent from the encampment, and their place supplied by a regiment of British soldiers! There were only a few Indian boys and some old women in the camp; and these offered no violence to the prisoners, excepting one of the squaws, who struck young Patchin over the head with an instrument which caused the blood to flow freely. But the second encampment, lying nearest the fort, and usually occupied by the fiercest and most savage of the Indian warriors, was yet to be passed. On arriving at this, also, the Indians were gone, and another regiment of troops were on parade, formed in two parallel lines, to protect the prisoners. Thus the Mohawk chief led his prisoners directly through the dreaded encampments, and brought them safely into the fort. Patchin, however, received another severe blow in this camp, and a young Indian menaced him with his tomahawk. But as he raised his arm, a soldier snatched the weapon from his hand, and threw it into the river.

The solution of this unexpected deliverance from the gauntlet-race was this:—Miss Jane Moore, the Cherry Valley prisoner whose marriage to an officer of the Niagara garrison has already been mentioned, was the niece of Captain Harper—a fact well known to Brant. Harper, however, knew nothing of her marriage, or in fact of her being at Niagara, and the chief had kept the secret to himself. On his arrival at the Genessee river, his anxious desire was to save his prisoners from the cruel ordeal-trial, and he despatched the runner, as before mentioned, with a message to Jane Moore's husband, whose name was

the ground, which, if he had fallen, would at once have decided his fate. He, however, reached the goal, not without being badly bruised, and he was, besides, bitterly reproached and scoffed at all round as a vile coward; while the others were hailed as brave men, and received tokens of universal approbation."—*Idem*

Powell, advising him of the fact, and proposing an artifice, by
which to save his wife's uncle, and his associates, from the accustomed ceremony.   For this purpose, by concert with Brant,
Powell had managed to have the Indian warriors enticed away
to the Nine Mile Landing, for a frolic, the means of holding
which were supplied from the public stores.   Meantime, for the
protection of the approaching prisoners from the violence of the
straggling Indians who remained behind, Powell caused the two
encampments to be occupied in the manner just described.   It
was a generous act on the part of Brant, well conceived and
handsomely carried through.   The prisoners all had cause of
gratitude ; and in the meeting with his niece in the garrison,
Captain Harper found a source of pleasure altogether unexpected.

The prisoners, nevertheless, were doomed to a long captivity.
From Niagara they were transferred to Montreal, thence to a
prison in Chamblee, and thence to Quebec.   They were afterward sent down to Halifax, and only restored to their country
and homes after the peace of 1783.   Their sufferings, during
the three intervening years, were exceedingly severe, particularly in the prison at Chamblee, which is represented as having
been foul and loathsome to a degree.*

* In the early part of this narrative of Harper's and Patchin's captivity, the name
of Becraft, a Tory, occurs as one of their captors.   His conduct toward the prisoners was particularly brutal throughout.   On one occasion, when he and his Tory
associates were enumerating their exploits, Becraft boasted of having assisted in
massacring the family of a Mr. Vrooman, in Schoharie.   The family, he said, were
all soon despatched, except a boy of fourteen years old, who ran from the house.
Becraft pursued and overtook him at a fence which he was attempting to climb.
He there deliberately cut his throat, took his scalp, and hung his body across the
fence !   After the peace, he had the hardihood to return to Schoharie.   But no sooner
was it known, than a party of several indignant citizens, among whom were the
prisoners who heard him make the confession here given, assembled and seized
him.   They stripped him naked, bound him to a tree, and ten of them, with hickory
whips, gave him a tremendous castigation.   They plied the whips with full vigor,
and at intervals paused, and informed him for what particular misdeeds they were to
inflict the next ten scorpion lashes, and so on.   Having punished him thus, they dismissed him with a charge never to show himself in that county again.   He never did.
Another of these Tories, who were guarding Harper and his party during the
same night of their journey, made a yet more horrible confession than that of Becraft.   His name was Barney Cane.   He boasted of having killed, upon Diamond
Island, (Lake George,) one Major Hopkins.   A party of pleasure, as he stated, had
been visiting the island on a little sailing excursion, and having lingered longer upon

The Indians were likewise early busy in other directions. Some scattering settlements, situated between Wyoming and the older establishments, were fallen upon by them, and a number of persons killed, several houses burned, and eight prisoners carried away.

But the Dutch border settlements along the base of the Kaatsbergs, or Catskill mountains, from Albany down to Orange county, were again severe sufferers during this period of the revolutionary war. Many of the inhabitants were friendly to the royal cause, and numbers of them had joined the royal standard. Some of these served as leaders and guides to the Indians, in parties for prisoners, scalps, and plunder. This petty mode of warfare was reduced to such a system, that those engaged in it were supplied with small magazines of provisions, concealed in the earth and among clefts of rocks at suitable distances from the western sides of the Kaatsbergs, over to the Delaware, and thence down to the point whence they were wont to cross with their prisoners and booty to the Susquehanna, and thence again by the usual track, along the Chemung and Genesee rivers to Niagara. The sacking of Minisink, and the incursions into Warwasing, in the preceding year, have already been chronicled. But there were several irruptions into the Dutch settlements farther north, along the western borders of Ulster County, in the Spring of 1780, some of which were marked by peculiar features of atrocity, or of wild adventure. Among these was an attack, by a small party of Indians and Tories, upon the families of Thomas and Johannes Jansen, wealthy freeholders in a

---

that beautiful spot than they were conscious of, as night drew on, concluded to encamp for the night—it being already too late to return to the fort. "From the shore "where we lay hid," said Cane, "it was easy to watch their motions; and perceiv- "ing their defenceless situation, as soon as it was dark we set off for the island, "where we found them asleep by their fire, and discharged our guns among them. "Several were killed, among whom was one woman, who had a sucking child, "which was not hurt. This we put to the breast of its dead mother, and so we left "it. But Major Hopkins was only wounded, his thigh bone being broken; he "started from his sleep to a rising posture, when I struck him," said Barney Cane, "with the butt of my gun, on the side of his head; he fell over, but caught on one "hand; I then knocked him the other way, when he caught with the other hand; "a third blow, and I laid him dead. These were all scalped except the infant. In "the morning, a party from the fort went and brought away the dead, together with "one they found alive, although he was scalped, and the babe, which was hanging "and sobbing at the bosom of its lifeless mother."—*Gen. Patchin's Narrative*

beautiful but secluded portion of the town of Shawangunk. One of these gentlemen was a colonel of militia. Both had erected substantial stone-houses, and were living in affluence. Their mansions were plundered by Indians and Tories, who were known to them; several of their neighbors and their negroes were made prisoners; and among those who were slain, under circumstances of painful interest, were a Miss Mack and her father, residing somewhat remote in one of the mountain gorges; and also a young lady on a visit at Shawangunk, from the city of New-York. From considerations of acquaintance-ship with the Jansens, however, the females of their families were not injured, although their houses were plundered and their barns laid in ashes.*

The same savage party, or rather a party composed in part of the same band of Tories and Indians who had committed the outrages just related, fell upon a settlement in the town of Sauger-ties, in May of the same year—making prisoners of Captain Je-remiah Snyder and Isaac Snyder his son. After plundering his house of provisions and money, they marched the Captain and his son over the mountains to the Delaware, and thence to Niagara, by the same route traversed by Thayendanegea and his warriors in conducting Harper and his fellow captives to that post. The adventures of these prisoners during their rough and wearisome journey were but the counterpart of those en-dured a month before by Captain Harper and his company, ex-cepting that their captors, being acquaintances, rendered their sufferings less severe. Their supplies of food, though coarse, were sufficient. They were pinioned at night, and the Indians lay upon the cords by which they were fastened to saplings, or other fixtures of security. They met several parties of Indians and Tories after crossing the Susquehanna, and on one occa-sion fell in with a beautiful white woman, married to an Indian. By all these they were treated kindly. While traversing the valley of the Genessee, their principal Indian conductor, named Runnip, pointed them to a couple of mounds by the way-side. " There lie your brothers," said he to Captain Snyder, in Dutch. " These mounds are the graves of a scout of thirty-six men,

---

* An elab rated narrative of this tragic visitation was published fifteen or twenty years ago by Charles G. De Witt, Esq.

" belonging to Sullivan's army, which had been intercepted and
" killed by the Indians."*

On their arrival at Niagara, the prisoners were less fortunate
than Harper and his companions had been, since they were compelled to run the gauntlet between long lines of the savages—a
ceremony which they looked upon with great dread, particularly
on account of their debilitated condition and the soreness of
their feet.   But in this operation they were favored by their
captors, who interposed to prevent injury.   In his narrative,
Captain Snyder described fort Niagara at that time as a structure of considerable magnitude and great strength, enclosing an
area of from six to eight acres.   Within the enclosure was a
handsome dwelling-house, for the residence of the Superintend
ent of the Indians.   It was then occupied by Colonel Guy John
son, before whom the Captain and his son were brought for ex
amination.   Colonel Butler, with his rangers, lay upon the opposite, or northern side of the river.   At a given signal, the Colonel, with two of his subalterns, crossed over to attend the examination.   Indeed, the principal object for the capture of Captain
Snyder seems to have been to obtain information.   Their examination was stern and searching, but the examiners were unable to elicit enough of news to compensate for the trouble of
their taking.

Captain Snyder described Guy Johnson as being a short, pursy
man, about forty years of age, of stern countenance and haughty
demeanor—dressed in a British uniform, powdered locks, and a
cocked hat.   His voice was harsh, and his tongue bore evidence
of his Irish extraction.   While in the guard-house, the prisoners were visited by Brant, of whom Captain Snyder says—" He
" was a likely fellow, of a fierce aspect—tall and rather spare—
" well spoken, and apparently about thirty (forty) years of age.
" He wore moccasins, elegantly trimmed with beads—leggings
" and breech-cloth of superfine blue—short green coat, with two
" silver epaulets—and a small, laced, round hat.   By his side
" hung an elegant silver-mounted cutlass, and his blanket of
" blue cloth, purposely dropped in the chair on which he sat, to
" display his epaulets, was gorgeously decorated with a border
" of red."   He asked many questions, and among others, from

* The Indian referred to the company of Lieut. Boyd.

whence they came.   On being answered Æsopus, he replied—
" That is my fighting ground."   In the course of the conversation, Brant said to the younger Snyder—" You are young, and
you I pity ; but for that old villain there," pointing at the father,
" I have no pity."   Captain Snyder was of course not very favorably impressed toward the Mohawk chief, and has recorded
his dislike.

The Snyders found many acquaintances at the head-quarters
of the Indians and loyalists, some of whom were prisoners like
themselves, and others in the ranks of the enemy.   From Niaga
ra, the two prisoners were transported by water, first to Carleton
Island in the St. Lawrence, and thence, at a subsequent period,
to Montreal.   At the latter place they were employed at labor,
and regularly paid their wages, which enabled them to purchase
various little comforts to meliorate their condition.   Indeed, they
were so fortunate as to fall into the hands of humane people at
every stage of their captivity, and their lot was far less severe
than that of most of their countrymen in the like situation.   At
the end of two years, having been transferred from Montreal to an
island some distance higher up the St. Lawrence, both father and
son, with several other prisoners, succeeded in effecting their
escape.*

The Mohawk Valley proper, during the Winter of 1780, had
enjoyed a period of comparative repose—interrupted only by the
common alarms incident to an unprotected border, at all times liable to invasion, and the people, as a consequence, feeling continually more or less insecure.   Still, there was not a single demonstration of the enemy in the lower part of the country, during
the cold season, worthy of note.   Among the prisoners taken by
the Tories who two years before had returned from Canada after
their families, and who had most unaccountably been suffered
to depart unmolested, was a very brave fellow by the name of
Solomon Woodworth.   He was entrusted to a party of Indians,
acting in concert with the Tories on their arrival at the Sacondaga, from whom he effected his escape on the following day.
These Indians, it appears, mortified at his successful flight, had
resolved either upon his recapture or his destruction.   Woodworth, in the Winter or Spring of 1780, was occupying, alone,

* Captain Snyder lived until the year 1827, and his narrative, taken from his own
lips, was written by Charles H. De Witt, Esq.

a block-house situated about eight miles north of Johnstown
While thus solitary, his castle was attacked in the dead of night,
by a small party of Indians, who set fire to it. Regardless of
danger, however, he ran out amidst a shower of bullets, extinguished the fire, and retreated within the walls again, before the
Indians, who had withdrawn some distance from the block-
house, could re-approach sufficiently near to seize him. As the
night was not very dark, Woodworth saw a group of the savages through the port-holes, upon whom he fired, not without
effect—one of their number, as it subsequently appeared, being
severely wounded. This disaster caused the Indians to retire.
But Woodworth was not satisfied. Collecting half a dozen kindred spirits, the next morning he gave chase to the intruders,
and after following their trail three days, overtook them—they
having halted to dress the wound of their companion. The
pursuers came so suddenly upon them, as to succeed in despatching the whole number without allowing them time to offer
resistance. The little band returned to Johnstown in triumph;
and their leader was immediately commissioned a lieutenant in a
regiment of nine months men—in which service he had again
an opportunity of showing his prowess, as will be seen hereafter.*

It was at about the same time that a party of Tories and In·
dians made a descent upon the small settlement at the Little
Falls of the Mohawk, for the purpose of destroying the mills
erected at that place by Alexander Ellis. This gentleman was
a Scotch merchant, who, under the favor of Sir William Johnson, had obtained a patent of the wild mountain gorge through
which the Mohawk leaps from the upper into the lower section
of the valley. He had himself returned to his own country;
but his mills were particularly important to the inhabitants, and
also to the garrisons of Forts Dayton and Herkimer,—more
especially since the burning of the mills at the German Flatts
by Thayendanegea two years before. Hence the present expedition for their destruction, which was easily accomplished—the
enemy having stolen upon the settlement unawares, and the
flouring mill being garrisoned by not more than a dozen men.
Only a few shots were exchanged, and but one man was killed
—-Daniel Petrie. As the Indians entered the mill, the occu-

---

* Information from the Rev. John I. Shew, of Northampton, N. Y., residing near
the place where the block-house stood.

pants endeavored to escape as fast as they could—some leaping from the windows, and others endeavoring to conceal themselves below.   It was night, and two of the number, Cox and Skinner, succeeded in ensconcing themselves in the race-way, beneath the water-wheel—Skinner having previously made fight hand to hand, and been wounded by a cut from a tomahawk.   Two of their companions, Christian Edick and Frederick Getman, leaped into the race-way above the mill, and endeavored to conceal themselves by keeping as much under water as possible. But the application of the torch to the mills soon revealed the aquatic retreat, and they were taken.   Not so with Cox and Skinner, who survived the storm of battle, and the mingled elements of fire and water ; the showers of coals and burning brands being at once extinguished as they fell around them, while the water-wheel served as an effectual protection against the falling timbers.   The enemy retired after accomplishing their object, carrying away five or six prisoners.*

A few incidents of the more distant border operations of the opening season will close the present chapter.   The Shawanese and their immediate allies continued to be exceedingly troublesome along the Ohio.   Among the single captives taken by them, by stratagem, early in the Spring, was a man named Alexander McConnel, of the Kentucky settlers.   He found his captors, five in number, to be pleasant tempered and social, and he succeeded in winning their confidence, by degrees, until they essentially relaxed the rigors of his confinement at night.   His determination was of course to escape.   At length his fastenings were so slight, that while they were asleep he succeeded in the entire extrication of his limbs.   Still he dared not to fly, lest escape from so many pursuers should be impracticable, and his life, should he be re-taken, would surely be required in payment for the rash attempt.   To strike them successively with one of their own tomahawks would be impossible.   His next plan was cautiously to remove three of their loaded rifles to a place of concealment, which should, nevertheless, be convenient for his own purpose.   Then placing the other two at rest upon a log, the muzzle of one aimed at the head of one Indian, and the other at the heart of a second, with both hands he discharged the rifles together, by which

* Conversations of the author with John Frank, Esq., of German Flatts.

process two of his enemies were killed outright. As the three others sprang up in amazement, McConnel ran to the rifles which he had concealed. The work was all but of a moment. Seizing another rifle, and bringing it in range of two of the three remaining savages, both fell with the discharge, one dead and the other wounded. The fifth took to his heels, with a yell of horror which made the forest ring. Selecting the rifle which he liked best, the subtle hunter pursued his way back at his pleasure.

On the 23d of June, Colonel Bird, at the head of five hundred Indians and Canadians, or American refugees, with six pieces of light artillery, fell upon the Kentucky settlement at the forks of the Licking river. Taken by surprise, the inhabitants seem to have made little, if any, resistance. Only one man was killed outright, and two women. All the others were taken prisoners, the settlement plundered, and the inhabitants marched off, bending beneath the weight of their own property for the benefit of the spoiler. Those who sank under their burdens by the way, were tomahawked. This outrage was promptly and severely avenged by Colonel Clarke, commanding at the falls of the Ohio, who immediately led his regiment into the heart of the Shawanese country—laying their principal town on the Great Miami in ashes, and taking seventy scalps. with the loss of only seventeen of his own men.*

---

* Adventures of Colonel Daniel Boon. The British account of Colonel Bird's expedition, as published in New-York, stated that he destroyed several small forts, and made a number of prisoners. "Most of the inhabitants of these new settlements," it was added, "from the extraordinary mild treatment of the Colonel, accompanied him, preferring to settle in the countries under the King to those of the Congress. Several of them have gone to Detroit, Niagara, &c."—*Vide Almon's Remembrancer, Part II.* 1780, *page* 347.

CHAPTER III.

ALTHOUGH the struggle had now been maintained more than five years, still the people of the lower section of the Mohawk Valley, severely as they had experienced the calamities of the war, had not yet by any means received the full measure of their suffering. Harassed by perpetual alarms, and oppressively frequent calls to the field—their numbers reduced by death and desertion, and by removals from a country so full of troubles—their situation was far from being enviable. Though unconscious of immediate danger from a formidable invasion, they were nevertheless in more peril than at any former period, from their diminished ability of self-protection. Hitherto, with the exception of small forays upon the outskirts, the lower valley, containing by far the largest amount of population, had not been traversed by an invading enemy. But it was their lot, in the course of the present season, repeatedly to experience the tender mercies of an exasperated enemy, armed with knife, and tomahawk and brand, and to see their fairest villages laid waste, their fields desolated, and their dwellings reduced to ashes.

The first blow was as sudden as it was unexpected—especially from the quarter whence it came. On Sunday the twenty-first of May, at dead of night, Sir John Johnson entered the north part of Johnstown at the head of five hundred men, composed of some British troops, a detachment of his own regiment of Royal Greens, and about two hundred Indians and Tories. Sir John had penetrated the country by way of Lake Champlain to Crown Point, and thence through the woods to the Saconda- ga river ; and so entirely unawares had he stolen upon the sleeping inhabitants, that he arrived in the heart of the country undiscovered, except by the resident loyalists, who were proba- bly in the secret. Before he reached the old Baronial Hall at Johnstown—the home of his youth, and for the recovery of which he made every exertion that courage and enterprise could put forth—Sir John divided his forces into two detachments, leading one in person, in the first instance, directly to the Hall, and thence through the village of Johnstown ; while the other was sent through a more eastern settlement, to strike the Mo- hawk river at or below Tripe's Hill, from whence it was direct ed to sweep up the river through the ancient Dutch village of Caughnawaga,* to the Cayadutta Creek—at which place a junction was to be formed with Sir John himself. This disposi tion of his forces was made at the still hour of midnight—at a time when the inhabitants were not only buried in slumber, but wholly unsuspicious of approaching danger. What officer was in command of the eastern division is not known, but it was one of the most stealthy and murderous expeditions—murderous in its character, though but few were killed—and the most disgrace- ful, too, that marked the progress of the war in that region. Dur ing the night-march of this division, and before reaching the river, they attacked the dwelling-house of Mr. Lodowick Put nam, who, together with his son, was killed and scalped. The next house assailed was that of a Mr. Stevens, which was burnt, and its owner killed. Arriving at Tripe's Hill, they mur dered three men, by the names of Hansen, Platts, and Aldridge. Hansen, who was a captain of militia, was killed by an Indian to whom he had formerly shown great kindness, and who had in return expressed much gratitude. The houses of all, it is believed, were plundered before the application of the torch. Proceeding toward Caughnawaga, about day-light they arrived at the house of Colonel Visscher—occupied at the time by him-

---

* More anciently still, the residence of the Caughnawaga clan of the Mohawk Indians, who at an early day moved into Canada, and established themselves on the St. Lawrence above the Lachine rapids.

self, his mother, and his two brothers. It was immediately assaulted. Alarmed at the sounds without, the Colonel instantly surmised the cause, and being armed, determined, with his brothers, to defend the house to the last. They fought bravely for a time, but the odds were so fearfully against them, that the house was soon carried by storm. The three brothers were instantly stricken down and scalped, and the torch applied to the house. Having thus completed their work, the enemy proceeded on their way up the river. Fortunately, however, the Colonel himself was only wounded. On recovering from the shock of the hatchet, he saw the house enveloped in flames above and around him, and his two brothers dead by his side. But, grievously wounded as he was, he succeeded in removing their mangled bodies from the house before the burning timbers fell in. His own wounds were dressed, and he lived many years afterward. Mrs. Visscher, the venerable mother of the Colonel, was likewise severely wounded by being knocked on the head by an Indian; but she also survived. The slaughter along the Mohawk, to the village of Caughnawaga, would have been greater, but for the alertness of Major Van Vrank, who contrived to elude the enemy, and by running ahead, gave the alarm, and enabled many people to fly as it were *in puris naturalibus* across the river.*

---

* The Visschers were important men among the Whigs of Tryon county.— There were four brothers of them at the commencement of the war, viz. Frederick, (the Colonel,) John, William Brower, and Harmanus. William B. died of scarlet fever in the Winter of 1776. A very bitter hostility existed against this family among the loyalists, having its origin in an unpleasant altercation between Colonel Visscher and Sir John Johnson, in the Autumn of 1775. The circumstances of this affair, as recently communicated to the author by the venerable Judge De Graff, of Schenectady, a near connection of the family, were substantially these:—In the year 1775, the Colonial Congress, having full confidence both in his principles and discretion, appointed Frederick Visscher a Colonel in the militia, furnishing him at the same time commissions in blank to complete the organization of his regiment. One of the commissions of captain thus confided to his disposal, he conferred on his brother John. In the Autumn of that year the Colonel directed his regiment to parade for review on an elevated plain near the ancient inn of Peggy Wymples, in Caughnawaga. It happened that while the regiment was on parade, Sir John Johnson, with his lady, drove along the river road. On descrying the regiment under arms, he ordered his coachman to drive up the hill to the parade ground. He then demanded of the first person to whom he had an opportunity to speak, who had called the assemblage together, and for what purpose? The reply was, that Colonel Visscher had ordered his regiment to parade for review. The Baronet thereupon

Meantime Sir John proceeded with his division through the village of Johnstown, stopping before it was yet light at what was once his own hall, where he made two prisoners. There was a small stockade, or picket fort, in the village, which, under favor of darkness and sleeping sentinels, was passed silently and unobserved. Directing his course for the confluence of the Cayadutta with the Mohawk, Sir John arrived at the residence of Sampson Sammons, whose name, with those of two of his sons, has appeared in the earlier portion of the present work. There was a third son, Thomas, a youth of eighteen. They all inherited the stanch Whig principles of their father, and the whole family had rendered the State efficient service in the course of the war.*

The particulars of the attack upon the family of Mr. Sammons are of sufficient interest to warrant the giving them somewhat in detail. Mr. Sammons, the elder, was well known to Sir John, between whom and himself very friendly relations had existed ; and in the early stage of the war, the former had exerted himself with some degree of success to protect the Baronet from the violence of the people. Soon after passing Johns-

---

stepped up to the Colonel, and repeated the question. The Colonel of course gave a similar reply. Sir John then ordered the regiment to disperse, but the Colonel directed them to keep their ranks—whereupon the Baronet, who was armed with a sword-cane, raised his weapon to inflict a blow upon Visscher, but the latter grasped the cane, and in the scuffle the sword was drawn—Visscher retaining the scabbard. Sir John threatened to run him through the body, and the Colonel told him if he chose to make the attempt he might act his pleasure. Sir John then asked for the scabbard of his blade, which was restored to him. Stepping up to his carriage, he directed Lady Johnson to rise that he might take his pistols from the box. Her ladyship remonstrated with him, but to no purpose, and having obtained his pistols, the Baronet again demanded that the regiment should be dismissed, for they were rebels. If not, he declared in a tempest of passion that he would blow the Colonel through. " Use your pleasure," was again the reply of Visscher. At this moment, a young Irishman, in the domestic service of the Colonel, who was in the ranks, exclaimed—" By J——s, if ye offer to lift hand or finger against my master, I will blow you through." The Baronet now saw that an unpleasant spirit was kindling against himself, whereupon he returned to his carriage, and drove away in great wrath.

* Sampson Sammons was of German extraction, a native of Ulster County, whence he had emigrated to Tryon County a few years before the war. In the first stages of the war he was a member of the Committee of Safety. In 1777, a corps of Exempts was organised under Colonel Jelles Fonda ; Fonda himself acting as Captain. Of this company, Sampson Sammons was the Lieutenant. In 1779 the corps was re-organised and enlarged. On the muster-roll of this year, Sammons was entered as an Ensign.

town, Sir John detached those of the Indians yet remaining with him in other directions, being desirous of making captives of Sammons and his sons, but wishing, at the same time, to do them no personal injury.   On arriving in the neighborhood of the house, Sir John halted his division, and directed a small detachment to move with the utmost stillness and caution, and fall upon the house by surprise—observing that Sammons had some stout sons, well armed, and unless they were very careful, there would be trouble.   The eldest of Mr. Sammons's sons was then the lessee of the Johnson farm at the hall, which had been sold by the Committee of Sequestrations, and which he was then cultivating ; and Thomas, the youngest, had risen at an unwonted hour, in order to feed his horses, and go over to the hall to work with his brother.   On coming down stairs, however, and stepping out of doors half-dressed, to take an observation of the weather—it being yet dark, though day was just breaking—the thought occurred to him, that should any straggling Indians be prowling about, he would stand but a poor chance if fallen upon alone.   While standing thus in doubt whether to proceed or wait for more light, he was startled by a noise of heavy steps behind, and, as he turned, by the glitter of steel passing before his eyes.   At the same instant a hand was laid upon his shoulder, with the words—" You are my prisoner !"   In such perfect stillness had the enemy approached, that not the sound of a footstep was heard, until the moment when the younger Sammons was thus arrested, and the house immediately surrounded.   One of the officers, with several soldiers, instantly entered the house, and ordered the family to get up, and surrender themselves as prisoners.   Jacob and Frederick, who were in bed in the second story, sprang upon their feet immediately, and seized their arms.   The officer, who was a Tory named Sutherland, and acquainted with the family, hearing the clatter of arms, called to them by name, and promised quarter on condition of their surrender.   Jacob inquired whether there were Indians with them ; adding, that if there were, he and his brother would not be taken alive.   On being assured to the contrary, the brothers descended the stairs and surrendered. The old gentleman was also taken.   While the soldiers were busied in plundering the premises, the morning advanced, and Sir John Johnson came up with the remainder of the division.

The females were not taken as prisoners, but the father and sons were directed to make ready to march immediately. Thomas here remarked to the soldier who yet stood sentinel over him, that he could not travel to Canada without his clothes, and especially without his shoes, which he had not yet put on— requesting liberty to repair to his chamber for his raiment. The sentinel sulkily refused permission ; but Thomas persisted that he must obtain his shoes at least, and was stepping toward the door, when the barbarian made a plunge at his back with his bayonet, which had proved fatal but for the quick eyes and the heroism of a sister standing by, who, as she saw the thrust at her brother, sprang forward, and seizing the weapon, threw herself across its barrel, and by falling, brought it to the ground. The soldier struggled to disengage his arms, and ac· complish his purpose. At the same instant an officer stepped forward, and demanded what was the matter. The girl informed him of the attempt upon her brother, whereupon he rebuked the soldier by the exclamation—"You d——d rascal, would you murder the boy ?" Immediate permission was then given him to procure whatever articles he wanted. The work of plunder having been completed, Sir John, with his troops and prisoners, proceeded onward in the direction of the river— about three miles distant.

For the purpose of punishing the old gentleman for his whig gish activity, some of the officers caused him to be tied to a negro, who was likewise a prisoner ; but the moment Sir John discovered the indignity, he countermanded the order. The hands of the young men were all closely pinioned, and they, with their father, were compelled to march between files of soldiers, and behold the cruel desolation of their neighborhood. Their course thence was direct to the river, at Caughnawaga, at which place they met the other division of Indians and rangers, who, among others, had murdered and scalped Mr. Douw Fonda, a citizen of great age and respectability. The whole army now set their faces westward, traversing the Mohawk Valley several miles, burning every building not owned by a loyalist, killing sheep and black cattle, and taking all the horses that could be found for their own use. Returning again to Caughnawaga, the torch was applied to every building excepting the church ; a number of prisoners were made, and several persons killed. Nine aged men were slain in the course of this march, of whom four were upward of eighty. From Caughnawaga, Sir John retraced his steps to Johnstown, passing the premises of Mr. Sammons, where the work of destruction was completed by applying the brand to all the buildings, leaving the females of the family houseless, and taking away the seven horses which were in the stables.

On the arrival of Sir John back to the homestead in the afternoon, he halted upon the adjacent grounds for several hours —establishing his own quarters in the hall of his father. The prisoners were collected into an open field, strongly guarded, but not in a confined space ; and while reposing thus, the Tory families of the town came in large numbers to see their friends and relatives, who for the most part constituted the white troops of the invading army. Thomas Sammons, during the whole morning, had affected to be exceedingly lame of one foot; and while loitering about the Hall he attracted the attention of the widowed lady of Captain Hare, one of the British officers who had fallen in the battle of Oriskany. Mrs. Hare, since the death of her husband, had occupied an apartment of the Hall ; and she now exerted herself successfully with Sir John for the release of several of her personal friends among the captives ; and on going into the field to select them, she adroitly smuggled young Sammons into the group, and led him away in safety.

It has already been mentioned that there was a small guard occupying the little fort in the village, which had been avoided by Sir John in his morning march. Toward night the militia of the surrounding country were observed to be clustering in the village, and Sir John thought it advisable to resume his march. He had collected a number of prisoners, and much booty, besides recruiting his ranks by a considerable number of loyalists, and obtaining possession of some eighteen or twenty of his negro slaves, left behind at the time of his flight in the Spring of 1776. While they were halting, on the next day, the elder Sammons applied to Sir John for an interview, which was granted in presence of his principal officers. On inquiring what he wanted, Mr. Sammons replied that he wished to be released. The Baronet hesitated ; but the old man pressed his suit, and reminded Sir John of former scenes, and of the efforts

of friendship which he himself had made in his behalf. " See
'what you have done, Sir John," said the veteran Whig : " You
'have taken myself and my sons prisoners, burnt my dwelling
"to ashes, and left the helpless members of my family with no
"covering but the heavens above, and no prospect but desolation
"around them. Did we treat you in this manner when you
"were in the power of the Tryon County Committee ? Do you
"remember when we were consulted by General Schuyler, and
"you agreed to surrender your arms ? Do you not remember
"that you then agreed to remain neutral, and that upon that con-
"dition General Schuyler left you at liberty on your parole ?
"Those conditions you violated. You went off to Canada ;
"enrolled yourself in the service of the King ; raised a regi-
"ment of the disaffected, who abandoned their country with
"you ; and you have now returned to wage a cruel war against
"us, by burning our dwellings and robbing us of our property.
"I was your friend in the Committee of Safety, and exerted
"myself to save your person from injury. And how am I re-
"quited ? Your Indians have murdered and scalped old Mr.
"Fonda at the age of eighty years : a man who, I have heard
"your father say, was like a father to him when he settled in Johns-
"town and Kingsborough. You cannot succeed, Sir John,
"in such a warfare, and you will never enjoy your property
"more !"

The Baronet made no reply ; but the appeal was effectual,
and the old gentleman was set at liberty. He then requested
the restoration of a pair of horses. Sir John replied that this
should also be done, if the horses were not in the possession of
the Indians, from whom he could not safely take them. On
making the inquiry, a span of his horses were found and restored
to him. A Tory officer, named Doxstadter, was seen by Mr.
Sammons to be in possession of one of his horses, but he would
not relinquish it, pretending that he was merely entrusted with
the animal by an Indian.* The two sons, Jacob and Frederick,
were carried into captivity, and suffered a protracted and severe
imprisonment, interesting accounts of which will presently be
given. Several of the aged prisoners, besides Mr. Sammons,

* After the war was over, Doxstadter returned from Canada upon some business,
was arrested in an action at law by Mr. Sammons, and made to pay the value of
the horse.

were permitted to return, one of whom, Captain Abraham
Veeder, was exchanged for Lieutenant Singleton, who had been
taken at Fort Schuyler by Colonel Willett, and was then in
Canada on his parole.*

The immediate object of this irruption by Sir John Johnson,
was to procure his plate, which had been buried at the time of
his flight in 1776, and not recovered with the iron chest. This
treasure was not indeed buried with the chest, but in the cellar,
and the place of deposite was confided to a faithful slave. While
Sir John was in the hall, in the afternoon, the slave, assisted by
four soldiers, disinterred the silver, which filled two barrels,
brought it to the Baronet, and laid it down at his feet.† It was
then distributed among about forty soldiers, who placed it in
their knapsacks—a quarter-master taking an account of the
names of the soldiers, and the articles confided to each—by whom
't was to be carried to Montreal. The irruption, however, was
one of the most indefensible aggressions upon an unarmed and
slumbering people, which stain the annals of the British arms.
As the commanding officer, Sir John is himself to be held responsible in a general sense. How far he was directly and
specially responsible for the midnight murders committed by
his barbarians, is a question which may, perhaps, bear a somewhat
different shade. Still, from the success which attended the expedition, and the unaccountable inaction of the people against
him, it is sufficiently obvious that he might have recovered his
plate without lighting up his path by the conflagration of his
neighbors' houses, or without staining his skirts with innocent
blood.‡ But the most remarkable circumstances attending this

* The present narrative of this irruption has been prepared almost entirely from
the manuscripts of and conversations with Major Thomas Sammons, the lad who was
taken prisoner—after a diligent comparison of his statement with other authorities.
The author has also the written narratives of Jacob and Frederick Sammons before
him, together with an account written by the Rev. John I. Shew. Major Thomas
Sammons is yet, (February, 1838,) well and hearty. He has formerly, for several
years, represented Montgomery (late Tryon county) in Congress.

† This faithful domestic had lived long with Sir William Johnson, who was so
much attached to him, that he caused him to be baptized by his own name, William.
When the estate was placed in the hands of Sammons by the Committee, William
was sold, and Sammons was the purchaser. He lived with him until retaken by
Sir John, but never gave the least hint either as to the burial of the iron chest, or the
plate, although both had been hidden in the earth by him.

‡ It is quite probable that Sir John's private papers, or correspondence, if the

expedition are, that the inhabitants were so completely taken by surprise, and that Sir John was so entirely unopposed in his advance on the morning of the 22d, and altogether unmolested on his retreat. The inhabitants, who had so often proved themselves brave, appear to have been not only surprised, but panic-stricken. True, as has already been incidentally stated, before Sir John commenced his return march, the militia had begun to gather at the village, a mile distant from the hall. They were led by Colonel John Harper, who was beyond doubt a very brave man. With him was also Colonel Volkert Veeder. But they were not strong enough to engage the enemy; and when Thomas Sammons arrived among them after his release, this opinion was confirmed by his report that the forces of Sir John exceeded seven hundred men. Colonels Harper and Veeder thereupon marched back to the river, and the invaders retired unmolested,* save by Captain Putnam and four men, who hung upon their rear, and observed their course to the distance of twenty-five miles.

Governor Clinton was at Kingston at the time of the invasion. Hastening to Albany on the first rumor of the intelligence, he collected such militia and other forces as he could obtain, and moved to Lake George with a view to intercept Sir John. It was supposed that the course of the enemy might possibly lie in the direction of Oswegatchie, and for the purpose of striking him upon such a march, Colonel Van Schaick, with eight hundred men, followed him by the way of Johnstown. Descending Lake George to Ticonderoga, the Governor was joined by a body of militia from the New Hampshire grants. But all was of no use; the invaders escaped—taking to their batteaux, probably, at Crown Point, whence they proceeded down the lake to St. John's. The captives were thence transferred to the fortress of Chamblee.

The prisoners at this fortress numbered about forty. On the day after their arrival Jacob Sammons, having taken an accurate survey of the garrison and the facilities of escape, con-

---

have been preserved, might place this and other dark transactions in a more favorable light. The author has exerted himself in vain to discover any such papers. They are believed to have been scattered, on the Baronet's decease at Montreal, some half a dozen years since.

* MS of Major Thomas Sammons.

ceived the project of inducing his fellow-prisoners to rise upon the guards and obtain their freedom. The garrison was weak in number, and the sentinels less vigilant than is usual among good soldiers. The prison doors were opened once a day, when the prisoners were visited by the proper officer, with four or five soldiers. Sammons had observed where the arms of the guards were stacked in the yard, and his plan was, that some of the prisoners should arrest and disarm the visiting guard on the opening of their door, while the residue were to rush forth, seize the arms, and fight their way out. The proposition was acceded to by his brother Frederick, and one other man named Van Sluyck, but was considered too daring by the great body of the prisoners to be undertaken. It was therefore abandoned, and the brothers sought afterward only for a chance of escaping by themselves. Within three days the desired opportunity occurred, viz. on the 13th of June. The prisoners were supplied with an allowance of spruce beer, for which two of their number were detached daily, to bring the cask from the brew-house, under a guard of five men, with fixed bayonets. Having reason to suppose that the arms of the guards, though charged, were not primed, the brothers so contrived matters as to be taken together to the brewery on the day mentioned, with an understanding that at a given point they were to dart from the guard and run for their lives—believing that the confusion of the moment, and the consequent delay of priming their muskets by the guards, would enable them to escape beyond the ordinary range of musket shot. The project was boldly executed. At the concerted moment, the brothers sprang from their conductors, and stretched across the plain with great fleetness. The alarm was given, and the whole garrison was soon after them in hot pursuit. Unfortunately for Jacob, he fell into a ditch and sprained his ancle. Perceiving the accident, Frederick turned to his assistance; but the other generously admonished him to secure his own flight if possible, and leave him to the chances of war. Recovering from his fall, and regardless of the accident, Jacob sprang forward again with as much expedition as possible, but finding that his lameness impeded his progress, he plunged into a thick clump of shrubs and trees, and was fortunate enough to hide himself between two logs before the pursuers came up. Twenty or thirty shots had previously been fired upon them, but without effect. In consequence of the smoke of their fire, probably, the guards had not observed Jacob when he threw himself into the thicket, and supposing that, like his brother, he had passed round it, they followed on, until they were fairly distanced by Frederick, of whom they lost sight and trace. They returned in about half an hour, halting by the bushes in which the other fugitive was sheltered, and so near that he could distinctly hear their conversation. The officer in command was Captain Steele. On calling his men together, some were swearing, and others laughing at the race, and the speed of the "long-legged Dutchmen," as they called the flying prisoners. The pursuit being abandoned, the guards returned to the fort.

The brothers had agreed, in case of separation, to meet at a certain spot at 10 o'clock that night. Of course Jacob lay ensconced in the bushes until night had dropped her sable curtains, and until he supposed the hour had arrived, when he sallied forth, according to the antecedent understanding. But time did not move as rapidly on that evening as he supposed. He waited upon the spot designated, and called aloud for Frederick, until he despaired of meeting him, and prudence forbad his remaining any longer. It subsequently appeared that he was too early on the ground, and that Frederick made good his appointment.

Following the bank of the Sorel, Jacob passed Fort St. John's soon after day-break on the morning of the 14th. His purpose was to swim the river at that place, and pursue his course homeward through the wilderness on the eastern shore of Lake Champlain; but just as he was preparing to enter the water, he descried a boat approaching from below, filled with officers and soldiers of the enemy. They were already within twenty rods. Concealing himself again in the woods, he resumed his journey after their departure, but had not proceeded more than two or three miles before he came upon a party of several hundred men engaged in getting out timber for the public works at the fort. To avoid these he was obliged to describe a wide circuit, in the course of which, at about 12 o'clock, he came to a small clearing. Within the enclosure was a house, and in the field were a man and boy engaged in hoeing potatoes. They were at that moment called to dinner, and supposing them to be French, who he had heard were rather friendly to the American cause than other-wise—incited, also, by hunger and fatigue—he made bold to present himself, trusting that he might be invited to partake of their hospitality. But, instead of a friend, he found an enemy. On making known his character, he was roughly received. "It is by such villains as you are," replied the forester, "that I was obliged to fly from Lake Champlain." The rebels, he added, had robbed him of all he possessed, and he would now deliver his self-invited guest to the guard, which, he said, was not more than a quarter of a mile distant. Sammons promptly answered him that "that was more than he could do." The refugee then said he would go for the guard himself; to which Sammons replied that he might act as he pleased, but that all the men in Canada should not make him again a prisoner.

The man thereupon returned with his son to the potatoe field, and resumed his work; while his more compassionate wife gave him a bowl of bread and milk, which he ate sitting on the threshold of the door, to guard against surprise. While in the house, he saw a musket, powder-horn and bullet-pouch hang-ing against the wall, of which he determined, if possible, to possess himself, that he might be able to procure food during the long and solitary march before him. On retiring, therefore, he travelled only far enough into the woods for concealment—re-turning to the woodman's house in the evening, for the purpose of obtaining the musket and ammunition. But he was again beset by imminent peril. Very soon after he entered the house, the sound of approaching voices was heard, and he took to the rude chamber for security, where he lay flat upon the irregular floor, and looking through the interstices, saw eleven soldiers enter, who, it soon appeared, came for milk. His situation was now exceedingly critical. The churlish proprietor might inform against him, or a single movement betray him. But neither circumstance occurred. The unwelcome visiters departed in due time, and the family all retired to bed, excepting the wife, who, as Jacob descended from the chamber, refreshed him with another bowl of bread and milk. The good woman now earnestly entreated her guest to surrender himself, and join the ranks of the King, assuring him that his Majesty must certainly conquer in the end, in which case the rebels would lose all their property, and many of them be hanged into the bargain. But

to such a proposition he of course would not listen. Finding
all her efforts to convert a Whig into a Tory fruitless, she then
told him, that if he would secrete himself two days longer in the
woods, she would furnish him with some provisions, for a supply of which her husband was going to the fort the next day, and
she would likewise endeavor to provide him with a pair of shoes.

Disinclined to linger so long in the country of the enemy,
and in the neighborhood of a British post, however, he took his
departure forthwith. But such had been the kindness of the
good woman, that he had it not in his heart to seize upon her
husband's arms, and he left this wild scene of rustic hospitality
without supplies, or the means of procuring them. Arriving
once more at the water's edge at the lower end of Lake Champlain, he came upon a hut, within which, on cautiously ap
proaching it for reconnoisance, he discovered a party of soldiers
all soundly asleep. Their canoe was moored by the shore,
into which he sprang, and paddled himself up the lake under
the most encouraging prospect of a speedy and comparatively
easy voyage to its head, whence his return home would be unattended with either difficulty or danger. But his pleasing anticipations were extinguished on the night following, as he approached the Isle au Noix, where he descried a fortification,
and the glitter of bayonets bristling in the air as the moon-
beams played upon the burnished arms of the sentinels, who
were pacing their tedious rounds. The lake being very narrow at this point, and perceiving that both sides were fortified,
he thought the attempt to shoot his canoe through between them
rather too hazardous an experiment. His only course, therefore,
was to run ashore, and resume his travels on foot. Nor, on
landing, was his case in any respect enviable. Without shoes,
without food, and without the means of obtaining either—a long
journey before him through a deep and trackless wilderness—it
may well be imagined that his mind was not cheered by the
most agreeable anticipations. But without pausing to indulge
unnecessarily his "thick-coming fancies," he commenced his
solitary journey, directing his course along the eastern lake shore
toward Albany. During the first four days of his progress he
subsisted entirely upon the bark of the birch—chewing the twigs
as he went. On the fourth day, while resting by a brook, he
heard a rippling of the water caused by the fish as they were

stemming its current. He succeeded in catching a few of these, but having no means of striking a fire, after devouring one of them raw, the others were thrown away.

His feet were by this time cruelly cut, bruised, and torn by thorns, briars, and stones; and while he could scarcely proceed by reason of their soreness, hunger and fatigue united to retard his cheerless march. On the fifth day his miseries were augmented by the hungry swarms of musquetoes, which settled upon him in clouds while traversing a swamp. On the same day he fell upon the nest of a black duck—the duck sitting quietly upon her eggs until he came up and caught her. The bird was no sooner deprived of her life and her feathers, than he devoured the whole, including the head and feet. The eggs were nine in number, which Sammons took with him; but on opening one, he found a little half-made duckling, already alive. Against such food his stomach revolted, and he was obliged to throw the eggs away.

On the tenth day he came to a small lake. His feet were now in such a horrible state, that he could scarcely crawl along. Finding a mitigation of pain by bathing them in water, he plunged his feet into the lake, and lay down upon its margin. For a time it seemed as though he could never rise upon his feet again. Worn down by hunger and fatigue—bruised in body and wounded in spirit—in a lone wilderness, with no eye to pity, and no human arm to protect—he felt as though he must remain in that spot until it should please God in his goodness to quench the dim spark of life that remained. Still, he was comforted in some measure by the thought that he was in the hands of a Being without whose knowledge not a sparrow falls to the ground.

Refreshed, at length, though to a trifling degree, he resumed his weary way, when, on raising his right leg over the trunk of a fallen tree, he was bitten in the calf by a rattlesnake! Quick as a flash, with his pocket-knife, he made an incision in his leg, removing the wounded flesh to a greater depth than the fangs of the serpent had penetrated. His next business was to kill the venomous reptile, and dress it for eating; thus appropriating the enemy that had sought to take his life, to its prolongation. His first meal was made from the heart and fat of the serpent. Feeling somewhat strengthened by the repast, and finding, moreover, that he could not travel farther in his present condition, he determined to remain where he was for a few days, and by repose, and feeding upon the body of the snake, recruit his strength. Discovering, also, a dry fungus upon the trunk of a maple tree, he succeeded in striking a fire, by which his comforts were essentially increased. Still he was obliged to creep upon his hands and knees to gather fuel, and on the third day he was yet in such a state of exhaustion as to be utterly unable to proceed. Supposing that death was inevitable and very near, he crawled to the foot of a tree, upon the bark of which he commenced inscribing his name—in the expectation that he should leave his bones there, and in the hope, that, in some way, by the aid of the inscription, his family might ultimately be apprised of his fate. While engaged in this sad work, a cloud of painful thoughts crowded upon his mind; the tears involuntarily stole down his cheeks, and before he had completed the melancholy task, he fell asleep.

On the fourth day of his residence at this place, he began to gain strength, and as a part of the serpent yet remained, he de termined upon another effort to resume his journey. But he could not do so without devising some substitute for shoes. For this purpose he cut up his hat and waistcoat, binding them upon his feet—and thus he hobbled along. On the following night, while lying in the woods, he became strongly impressed with a belief that he was not far distant from a human habitation. He had seen no indications of proximity to the abode of man; but he was, nevertheless, so confident of the fact, that he wept for joy. Buoyed up and strengthened by this impression, he resumed his journey on the following morning; and in the afternoon, it being the 28th of June, he reached a house in the town of Pittsford, in the New Hampshire Grants—now forming the State of Vermont. He remained there for several days, both to recruit his health, and, if possible, to gain intelligence of his brother. But no tidings came; and as he knew Frederick to be a capital woodsman, he of course concluded that sickness death, or re-capture, must have interrupted his journey. Procuring a conveyance at Pittsford, Jacob travelled to Albany, and thence to Schenectady, where he had the happiness of find-ing his wife and family.*

* MS. narrative of Jacob Sammons. He died about the year 1810.

Not less interesting, nor marked by fewer vicissitudes, were the adventures of Frederick Sammons. The flight from the fort at Chamblee was made just before sunset, which accounts for the chase having been abandoned so soon. On entering the edge of the woods, Frederick encountered a party of Indians returning to the fort from fatigue duty. Perceiving that he was a fugitive, they fired, and called out—" We have got him!" In this opinion, however, they were mistaken; for, although he had run close upon before perceiving them, yet, being like Asahel of old swift of foot, by turning a short corner and increasing his speed, in ten minutes he was entirely clear of the party. He then sat down to rest, the blood gushing from his nose in consequence of the extent to which his physical powers had been taxed. At the time appointed he also had repaired to the point which, at his separation from Jacob, had been agreed upon as the place of meeting. The moon shone brightly, and he called loud and often for his brother—so loud, indeed, that the guard was turned out in consequence. His anxiety was very great for his brother's safety; but, in ignorance of *his* situation, he was obliged to attend to his own. He determined, however, to approach the fort—as near to it, at least, as he could venture —and in the event of meeting any one, disguise his own character by inquiring whether the rebels had been taken. But a flash from the sentinel's musket, the report, and the noise of a second pursuit, compelled him to change the direction of his march, and proceed again with all possible speed. It had been determined by the brothers to cross the Sorel, and return on the east side of the river and lake; but there was a misunderstanding between them as to the point of crossing the river— whether above or below the fort. Hence their failure of meeting. Frederick repaired to what he supposed to be the designated place of crossing, below the fort, where he lingered for his brother until near morning. At length, having found a boat, he crossed over to the eastern shore, and landed just at the cock-crowing. He proceeded directly to the barn where he supposed chanticleer had raised his voice, but found not a fowl on the premises. The sheep looked too poor by the dim twilight to serve his purpose of food, but a bullock presenting a more favorable appearance, Frederick succeeded in cutting the unsuspecting animal's throat, and severing one of the hindquarters from the carcase, he shouldered and marched off with it directly into the forest. Having proceeded to a safe and convenient distance, he stopped to dress his beef, cutting off what he supposed would be sufficient for the journey, and forming a knapsack from the skin, by the aid of bark peeled from the moose-wood.

Resuming his journey, he arrived at the house of a French family within the distance of five or six miles. Here he made bold to enter, for the purpose of procuring bread and salt, and in the hope also of obtaining a gun and ammunition. But he could neither obtain provisions, nor make the people understand a word he uttered. He found means, however, to prepare some tinder, with which he re-entered the woods, and hastened forward in a southern direction, until he ascertained, by the firing of the evening guns, that he had passed St. John's. Halting for the night, he struck a light; and having kindled a fire, occupied himself until morning in drying and smoking his beef, cutting it into slices for that purpose. His knapsack of raw hide was cured by the same process. Thus prepared, he proceeded onward without interruption or adventure until the third day, when he killed a fawn and secured the venison. He crossed the Winooski, or Onion river, on the next day; and having discovered a man's name carved upon a tree, together with the distance from the Lake, (Champlain) eight miles, he bent his course for its shores, where he found a canoe with paddles. There was now a prospect of lessening the fatigue of his journey; but his canoe had scarce begun to dance upon the waters ere it parted asunder, and he was compelled to hasten ashore and continue his march by land.

At the close of the seventh day, and when, as he supposed, he was within two days' travel of a settlement, he kindled his fire, and lay down to rest in fine health and spirits. But ere the dawn of day, he awoke with racking pains, which proved to be an attack of pleurisy. A drenching rain came on, continuing three days; during which time he lay helpless, in dreadful agony, without fire, or shelter, or sustenance of any kind. On the fourth day, his pain having abated, he attempted to eat a morsel, but his provisions had become too offensive to be swallowed. His thirst being intense, he fortunately discovered a pond of water near by, to which he crawled. It was a stagnant pool, swarming with frogs—another providential circumstance, inasmuch as the latter served him for food. Too weak, however, to strike a light, he was compelled to devour them raw, and without dressing of any kind. Unable to proceed, he lay in this wretched condition fourteen days. Supposing that he should die there, he succeeded in hanging his hat upon a pole, with a few papers, in order that, if discovered, his fate might be known. He was lying upon a high bluff, in full view of the lake, and at no great distance therefrom. The hat, thus elevated, served as a signal, which saved his life. A vessel sailing past, descried the hat, and sent a boat ashore to ascertain the cause. The boatmen discovered the body of a man, yet living, but senseless and speechless, and transferred him to the vessel. By the aid of medical attendance he was slowly restored to his reason, and having informed the Captain who he was, had the rather uncomfortable satisfaction of learning that he was on board of an enemy's ship, and at that moment lying at Crown Point. Here he remained sixteen days, in the course of which time he had the gratification to hear, from a party of Tories coming from the settlements, that his brother Jacob had arrived safe at Schenectady and joined his family. He was also apprised of Jacob's sufferings, and of the bite of the serpent, which took place near Otter Creek, close by the place where he had himself been so long sick. The brothers were therefore near together at the time of the greatest peril and endurance of both.

Frederick's recovery was very slow. Before he was able to walk, he was taken to St. John's, and thence, partly on a wheelbarrow and partly in a calash, carried back to his old quarters at Chamblee—experiencing much rough usage by the way. On arriving at the fortress, the guards saluted him by the title of " Captain Lightfoot," and there was great joy at his re-capture. It was now about the 1st of August. As soon as his health was sufficiently recovered to bear it, he was heavily ironed, and kept in close confinement at that place, until October, 1781—fourteen months, without once beholding the light of the sun. Between St. John's and Chamblee he had been met by a British officer with whom he was acquainted, and by whom he was informed that severe treatment would be his portion. Compassionating his situation, however, the officer slipped a guinea and a couple of dollars into his hands, and they moved on

No other prisoners were in irons at Chamblee, and all but Sammons were taken upon the parade ground twice a week for the benefit of fresh air. The irons were so heavy and so tight, as to wear into the flesh of his legs ; and so incensed was Captain Steele, the officer of the 32d regiment, yet commanding the garrison at Chamblee, at the escape of his prisoner, that he would not allow the surgeon to remove the irons to dress the wounds, of which they were the cause, until a peremptory order was procured for that purpose from General St. Leger, who was then at St. John's. The humanity of the surgeon prompted this application of his own accord. Even then, however, Steele would only allow the leg-bolts to be knocked off—still keeping on the hand-cuffs. The dressing of his legs was a severe operation. The iron had eaten to the bone, and the gangrened flesh was of course to be removed. One of the legs ultimately healed up, but the other has never been entirely well to this day.*

In the month of November, 1781, the prisoners were transferred from Chamblee to an island in the St. Lawrence, called at that time Prison Island—situated in the rapids some distance above Montreal. Sammons was compelled to travel in his hand-cuffs, but the other prisoners were not thus encumbered. There were about two hundred prisoners on the island, all of whom were very closely guarded. In the Spring of 1782, Sammons organised a conspiracy with nine of his fellow prisoners, to make their escape, by seizing a provison boat, and had well-nigh effected their object. Being discovered, however, their purpose was defeated, and Sammons, as the ringleader, once more placed in irons. But at the end of five weeks the irons were removed, and he was allowed to return to his hut.

Impatient of such protracted captivity, Frederick was still bent on escaping, for which purpose he induced a fellow-prisoner, by the name of M'Mullen, to join him in the daring exploit of seeking an opportunity to plunge into the river, and taking their chance of swimming to the shore. A favorable moment for attempting the bold adventure was afforded on the 17th of August. The prisoners having, to the number of fifty, been allowed to walk to the foot of the island, but around the whole of which

* April, 1837—fifty six years ago ! Frederick Sammons is yet living, and otherwise well ; and was chosen one of the electors of President and Vice-President of the United States in November 1836.

a chain of sentinels was extended, Sammons and M'Mullen, without having conferred with any one else, watching an opportunity when the nearest sentinel turned his back upon them, quietly glided down beneath a shelving rock, and plunged into the stream—each holding up and waving a hand in token of farewell to their fellow-prisoners, as the surge swept them rapidly down the stream. The sentinel was distant about six rods when they threw themselves into the river, and did not discover their escape until they were beyond the reach of any molestation he could offer them. Three-quarters of a mile below the island, the rapids were such as to heave the river into swells too large for boats to encounter. This was a frightful part of their voyage. Both, however, were expert swimmers, and by diving as they approached each successive surge, both succeeded in making the perilous passage—the distance of this rapid being about one hundred and fifty rods. As they plunged successively into these rapids, they had little expectation of meeting each other again in this world. But a protecting Providence ordered it otherwise, and they emerged from the frightful billows quite near together. "I am glad to see you," said Sammons to his friend; "I feared we should not meet again." "We have had a merry ride of it," replied the other; "but we could not have stood it much longer."

The adventurous fellows attempted to land about two miles below the island, but the current was so violent as to baffle their purpose, and they were driven two miles farther, where they happily succeeded in reaching the land, at a place on the north side of the St. Lawrence, called by the Canadians "The Devil's Point." A cluster of houses stood near the river, into some of which it was necessary the fugitives should go to procure provisions. They had preserved each a knife and tinderbox in their waistcoat pockets, and one of the first objects, after arming themselves with substantial clubs, was to procure a supply of tinder. This was effected by boldly entering a house and rummaging an old lady's work-basket. The good woman, frightened at the appearance of the visiters, ran out and alarmed the village—the inhabitants of which were French. In the meantime they searched the house for provisions, fire-arms, and ammunition, but found none of the latter, and only a single loaf of bread. They also plundered the house of a blanket, blanket-coat, and a few other articles of clothing. By this time the people began to collect in such numbers, that a precipitate retreat was deemed advisable. M'Mullen, being seized by two Canadians, was only released from their grasp by the well-directed blows of Frederick's club. They both then commenced running for the woods, when Sammons, encumbered with his luggage, unluckily fell, and the loaf rolled away from him. The peasants now rushed upon them, and their only course was to give battle, which they prepared to do in earnest ; whereupon, seeing their resolution, the pursuers retreated almost as rapidly as they had advanced. This demonstration gave the fugitives time to collect and arrange their plunder, and commence their travels anew. Taking to the woods, they found a resting-place, where they halted until night-fall. They then sallied forth once more in search of provisions, with which it was necessary to provide themselves before crossing to the south side of the river, where, at that day, there were no settlements. The cattle fled at their approach ; but they at length came upon a calf in a farm-yard, which they captured, and appropriating to their own use and behoof a canoe moored in the river, they embarked with their prize, to cross over to the southern shore. But alas ! when in the middle of the stream their paddle broke, and they were in a measure left to the mercy of the flood, which was hurrying them onward, as they very well knew, toward the rapids or falls of the Cedars. There was an island above the rapids, from the brink of which a tree had fallen into the river. Fortunately, the canoe was swept by the current into the branches of this tree-top, among which it became entangled. While struggling in this predicament, the canoe was upset. Being near shore, however, the navigators got to land without losing the calf. Striking a fire, they now dressed their veal, and on the following morning, by towing their canoe along shore round to the south edge of the island, succeeded in crossing to their own side of the river. They then plunged directly into the unbroken forest, extending from the St. Lawrence to the Sacondaga, and after a journey of twelve days of excessive hardship, emerged from the woods within six miles of the point for which, without chart or compass, Sammons had laid his course. Their provisions lasted but a few days, and their only subsequent food consisted of roots and herbs. The whole journey was made almost in a state of nudity—both being destitute of pantaloons. Having worn out their hats upon their feet, the last three days they were compelled to travel bare-footed. Long before their journey was ended, therefore, their feet were dreadfully lacerated and swollen. On arriving at Schenectady the inhabitants were alarmed at their wild and savage appearance—half naked, with lengthened beards and matted hair. The people at length gathered round them with strange curiosity; but when they made themselves known, a lady named Ellis rushed through the crowd to grasp the hand of Frederick, and was so much affected at his altered appearance that she fainted and fell. The welcome fugitives were forthwith supplied with whatever of food and raiment was necessary; and young Sammons learned that his father and family had removed back to Marbletown, in the county of Ulster, whence he had previously emigrated to Johnstown.

A singular but well-attested occurrence closes this interesting personal narrative. The family of the elder Sammons had long given up Frederick as lost. On the morning after his arrival at Schenectady, he despatched a letter to his father, by the hand of an officer on his way to Philadelphia, who left it at the house of a Mr. Levi De Witt, five miles distant from the residence of the old gentleman. The same night on which the letter was thus left, Jacob dreamed that his brother Frederick was living, and that there was a letter from him at De Witt's announcing the joyful tidings. The dream was repeated twice, and the contents of the letter were so strongly impressed upon his mind, that he repeated what he believed was the very language, on the ensuing morning—insisting that such a letter was at the place mentioned. The family, his father in particular, laughed at him for his credulity. Strong, however, in the belief that there was such a communication, he repaired to the place designated, and asked for the letter. Mr. De Witt looked for it, but replied there was none. Jacob requested a more thorough search, and behold the letter was found behind a barrel, where it had fallen. Jacob then requested Mr. De Witt to open the letter, and examine while he recited its contents. He did so, and the dreamer repeated it word for word!*

* The facts contained in this account of the captivity of Frederick Sammons, have been drawn from the narrative written by himself immediately after his return. In regard to the dream, which I have thought of sufficient interest to record

Returning from these digressions, the chain of historical events to be recorded will be resumed in their order.   Sir John Johnson having made good his retreat, as heretofore described, no other transaction of consequence occurred in the Mohawk Valley until the 2d of August, when the dreaded Thayendanegea was again among the settlements on the river. Colonel Gansevoort had been directed by General Clinton, on the 6th of June, to repair to Fort Plank, with his regiment, to take charge of a quantity of stores destined to Fort Schuyler. In his instructions to that officer, General Clinton referred to the alarming situation of the Mohawk country, and enjoined the most vigilant watchfulness against surprise.   The stores were of course to be transported in batteaux, carefully guarded the whole distance.   Aware of the movement of these stores, Brant had caused the valley to be filled with rumors of his intention to capture them, and even to take Fort Schuyler itself.   In order to prevent either occurrence, the militia of the county were sent forward to strengthen the convoy, and repair to the defence of the Fort.   Having thus diverted the public attention, and caused the militia to be drawn from the lower section of the valley, the wily Mohawk passed round in their rear, and on the day above mentioned, made a sudden descent upon Canajoharie and its adjacent settlements.*   There were several small stockades among the different neighborhoods invaded, but the principal work of defence, then called Fort Plank, and subsequently Fort Plain, was situated upon an elevated plain overlooking the valley, near the site of the village yet retaining the latter name of the fortress.†   A small garrison had been left in this fort, but not of sufficient strength to warrant a field engagement with the forces of Brant, while the latter, being unprovided with artillery, had no design of assaulting the fort.

On the first approach of Brant in Canajoharie, a few miles

in the text, Major Thomas Sammons, who was at home at the time, has repeatedly assured me of the fact, in conversations ; and Mr. De Witt, when living, always confirmed the circumstances related as occurring at his house.   Jacob Sammons himself says at the conclusion—" I write this to satisfy that class of people who say there is nothing revealed by dreams."—*Author.*

* Annals of Tryon County.

† For a drawing of Fort Plank, or Fort Plain, and a more particular description, see Appendix, No. I.   To a modern engineer, its form must present a singular spectacle as a military structure.   The drawing has been preserved, as a specimen of the forts and block-houses of that frontier during the war of the Revolution.

eastwardly of the fort, the alarm was given by a woman, who
fired a cannon for that purpose. But as the able-bodied men
were absent, as already stated, the chief met with no immediate
opposition, and before the militia could be rallied from Schenectady and Albany, he had ample time to effect the object of the
enterprise. The settlements on the south side of the river, for
several miles, were entirely laid waste. All the moveable property that could be taken off was secured as plunder; but no
outrages were committed upon the defenceless women and children, other than carrying them into captivity—a circumstance
that has been attributed to the absence of the Tories in this expedition, and also to the fact that there was no divided command—Brant being himself the sole leader. Be that as it may,
the Mohawk chief is entitled to the benefit of this instance of
humanity, in forming a final judgment of his character.

But the strength of the main fort did not deter the chief from
leading his warriors directly into its vicinity, where the church,
distant about a quarter of a mile, and the parsonage, together
with several other buildings, were burnt. Sixteen of the inhabitants were killed, between fifty and sixty persons, mostly
women and children, were taken prisoners, fifty-three dwelling-
houses, and as many barns were burnt, together with a grist-
mill, two small forts, and a handsome church. Upward of three
hundred black cattle and horses were killed or driven away,
the arms of the people, their working-tools and implements of
husbandry destroyed, and the growing crops swept from the
fields.* Indeed, the fairest district of the valley was in a single
day rendered a scene of wailing and desolation; and the
ravages enacted in the Indian country by General Sullivan the
preceding year, were in part most unexpectedly re-enacted by
the Indian chieftain himself in the heart of the country of his
invaders.†

The first admonition of the invasion in the neighborhood of
Johnstown, fifteen miles from Canajoharie, was by the ascending
columns of smoke from the burning buildings. The people
were employed harvesting in the fields, but they turned out im-

---

* MS. letter of Colonel Clyde to Governor George Clinton.

† A detachment from this expedition was sent by Brant, at the same time, against
the settlement on the Norman's Kill, in the very neighborhood of Albany, where
they succeeded in burning twenty houses.—*Macauley.*

mediately, and joining Colonel Wemple, who advanced from below with the Schenectady and Albany militia, proceeded to the scene of conflagration. But their movements were not sufficiently expeditious to arrest the destroyer or to intercept his retreat. Indeed, it is intimated, by good authority, that although the Colonel's forces were superior to those of Brant, the former was, nevertheless, by no means anxious to arrive in the immediate vicinity of the Indians too soon.* The Colonel lodged his men that night in the fort. The next morning, while the troops, regular and irregular, were on parade, some buildings were discovered on fire at a distance, which had escaped the flames the day before. The attention of Colonel Wemple being directed to the fact, he remarked, that if any volunteers were disposed to go in pursuit, they might. Major Bantlin, with a few of the Tryon County militia, who had arrived that morning, immediately turned out. " We hastened to the place as soon as we " could. The enemy discovered us and ran off. It was a small " party sent out by Brant. We pursued them, but they reached " their main body before we came up. We ucceeded, however, " in rescuing a little girl, whom they had taken and painted."†

The forts destroyed by Brant at Canajoharie, were built by the people themselves, but had not yet been garrisoned. The inhabitants had complained bitterly that they were thus compelled to leave their own firesides unprotected, to assist the Government in re-opening the communication with Fort Schuyler. But being assured that their town could be in no danger, they submitted to the order, and their militia marched to the upper section of the valley. The result was deplorable enough ; while the success of his stratagem added another plume to the crest of " the Great Captain of the Six Nations."‡

* Major Thomas Sammons, who was in the wheat-field when the smoke was seen, and who immediately repaired to the scene of action.

† MSS. of Major Sammons.

‡ According to the British account of this irruption, as published in New-York on the 6th of September, Sir John Johnson was in the expedition with Captain Brant. But this could hardly have been the fact, and all other authorities be silent upon the subject. The same account claimed that in the Canajoharie settlements 57 houses and 42 barns were burnt; 17 persons killed, and 52 taken prisoners. At the same time, it was stated that in one of the Schoharie settlements 27 houses were burnt; 7 persons killed; and 21 taken prisoners. At Norman's Kill, 20 houses burnt. Total, 140 houses and barns burnt; 24 people killed; and 73 made prisoners.—Almon's Remembrancer, Part II.—1780.

CHAPTER IV.

THE active operations of the war, during the open months of the present year, with the exception of the successive invasions of the Mohawk Valley by Sir John Johnson and Captain Brant at the head of the loyalists and Indians, were chiefly confined to the Southern states. True, indeed, in anticipation of the arrival of another French fleet, with an army under the Count de Rochambeau, for the land service, an attack had been meditated by the Commander-in-chief upon New-York, and various preliminary measures were adopted for that object. But, in order to cover the real design, an attempt was made, after the return of the Marquis de Lafayette from France, in the Spring, to divert the attention of the British Commander by inducing a belief that Canada was again to be invaded by a combined movement of the Americans and their allies. For this purpose, proclamations, addressed to the Canadian people, were prepared, one of which was written in French, and signed by Lafayette. These proclamations were printed with great secrecy, but at the same time for the express purpose of allowing copies of them to fall into the hands of the enemy, to mislead Sir Henry Clinton. The printing was confided by Washington to General Arnold; and as the stratagem was unsuccessful, subsequent events induced a belief that the treasonable practices of that officer had then already commenced. The letter from Washington to Arnold, respecting the printing of those proclamations, was dated June 4th. It was afterward satisfactorily ascertained, that " for several " months previously Arnold had endeavored to recommend him-" self to the enemy, by sending intelligence concerning the " movements and plans of the American army."[*] Various untoward circumstances concurred in frustrating the design of the intended combined movement upon New-York. In the first place, although Congress had made large promises to France, of efficient co-operation, in the event of assistance from that quarter, yet the backwardness of many of the States in furnish-ing their respective quotas of men, and the continued deficiency of supplies, were serious discouragements to the Commander-in-chief, and he almost began to despair of the undertaking be-fore the arrival of his allies. In the second place, the fleet of the Chevalier Ternay, with the army of the Count de Rocham-beau, did not arrive so early by several weeks as was intended. In the third place, Sir Henry Clinton having returned to New-York from the south, instead of entering the harbor of New-York direct, the French admiral was constrained to put into the harbor of Rhode Island, where the army was landed ; and before dispositions could be made for a combined movement thence upon New-York, the British Admiral Graves arrived off Rhode Island with a superior force, so that the Chevalier Ternay was blockaded. The result of all these occurrences was a re-linquishment, for the time, of the enterprise against New-York ; and the French and American armies were doomed to compara-tive inactivity at the north the whole season.

Not so, however, at the south. After the fall of Charleston, in the Spring, the British troops, under those able and active officers, Cornwallis, Tarleton, Lord Rawdon, and others, almost entirely over-ran the Southern States. Tarleton's first achieve-ment was the cutting up of Colonel Buford, with about four hundred men, at the Waxhaws. In South Carolina all ideas of farther resistance seemed to be abandoned, until Sumpter re-turned, and revived their spirits by proving at Williamson's plantation that the invaders were not invincible. But in July, after General Gates had assumed the command in the Southern

---

* Sparks's Life and Correspondence of Washington, vol. vii. Vide several letters from Washington to Lafayette, Arnold, and others, during the month of May, 1780.

Department, to which the brave Baron De Kalb had opened the way, the severe disaster at Camden, where the militia ran away, as usual, at the beginning of the battle, rendered all again gloomy as before.* The Baron De Kalb fell in this action, covered with wounds. Close upon the heels of this defeat, followed the surprise and all but annihilation of Sumpter's forces, by Tarleton, at the Wateree. But the splendid affair at King's Mountain, on the 7th of October, in which Ferguson, with a body of twelve or fifteen hundred loyalists, and about one hundred British regulars, was defeated and taken by Campbell, Shelby, and Cleaveland, at the head of the hardy mountaineers of Virginia and North Carolina, with the re-appearance of Sumpter in the field at the head of a body of volunteers—defeating Major Wemys at Broad river, on the 12th of November, and repulsing Tarleton himself at Black-stocks near the Tiger river, on the 20th,—contributed not a little to revive the spirits of the Americans in that quarter. At the north, the only considerable movement by the enemy was the expedition of the Hessian General Knyphausen into New Jersey, during which he burnt thirteen houses and the church at Connecticut Farms, and fifty houses at Springfield. Fighting a battle at that place without achieving a victory, he returned to Elizabethtown, and thence back to New-York.

But the great event of the Summer at the north, was the capture of the British Adjutant General, Major André, in the character of a spy, and the consequent detection of the treason of General Arnold. The annals of war furnish not a more flagrant instance of treachery than that. Arnold was a brave man, who had shared largely in the confidence of Washington during the earlier years of the war; and although events had subsequently occurred which must seriously have shaken the faith of the Commander-in-chief in his private virtue and integrity, still he could not have entertained the slightest suspicion of his patriotism, or his integrity to the country; ignorant, probably, of the fact which will appear a few pages ahead, that even that *had* been questioned, during the Canadian campaign of 1776. But, aside from Arnold's thirst for military fame, which

---

* From the time of his leaving the command at Providence in the beginning of the preceding winter, General Gates had been residing at his own home in Virginia. He was unanimously appointed by Congress, on the 13th of June, to take command in the southern department.—*Sparks.*

certainly cannot be denied to him, his ruling passion was avarice. During his residence in Philadelphia, with the command
of which he was invested after its evacuation by the British
troops in 1778, he had lived in a style of splendor altogether
beyond his means. Embarking largely in privateering and
other speculations, he had suffered heavy losses; and to supply
an exchequer which had been exhausted by an almost boundless
prodigality, he had resorted to acts of oppression and base dishonor. Another device to obtain the means of indulging his
extravagance, was the exhibition of accounts against the public,
so enormous as to demand an investigation by a Board of Commissioners. Many of these accounts being disallowed by the
Commissioners, Arnold appealed to Congress. A committee of
re-examination was appointed; the report of which was, that
the Board of Commissioners had already allowed too much. He
was shortly afterward brought to answer for his peculations,
and other malpractices, before a General Court-martial; and he
only escaped being cashiered, by the death of one witness and
the unaccountable absence of another. Still, his conduct was
pronounced highly reprehensible by the Court, for which he was
subjected to a reprimand from the Commander-in-chief. The
impression, however, was strong, and very general, that he
ought to have been dismissed from the army. Stung to the
quick at these censures of the Congress, the Court, and of his
commander—hating that commander now, if he had not done so
before, for the high-souled honor of his sentiments, and the exalted virtue and moral purity of his life—hating him the more bitterly because of his own fall—and stimulated to the foul purpose,
like the Thane of Cawdor, by his wife, who was a traitress
before him*—Arnold had almost consummated his long-medi-

---

* It is well known that, on the detection of Arnold's treason and his flight, Mrs.
Arnold was apparently deeply affected—tearing her hair, and seeming almost frantic. So great was her agony, that the feelings of Washington, Hamilton, and other
officers, were greatly excited in her behalf. The author has long been aware, through
the confidential friends of the late Colonel Burr, that Mrs. Arnold was only *acting a
part* when she exhibited her distress. She was the daughter of Chief Justice Shippen,
of Pennsylvania, and had been married to Arnold at Philadelphia in 1779. She
had corresponded with Major André, during the Summer, under a pretext of obtaining supplies of millinery, &c. Her habits were extravagant, and had doubtless con
tributed to involve her husband more deeply in pecuniary difficulties. Having
obtained from General Washington a passport, and permission to join her husband

tated treachery,* when the arrest of the unfortunate André saved not only the citadel of the army, but probably the cause of the country itself.

With a seeming desire of active service, Arnold had urged forward his trial, that, as he protested, he might be enabled the earlier to take the field.   But in pursuance, no doubt, of his understanding with Sir Henry Clinton, his great anxiety was to obtain the command of West Point.   With this view he wrote to General Schuyler, who was then in camp, as one of a Committee of Congress; and it is supposed that he likewise corresponded with Robert R. Livingston upon the subject.   At all events, Mr. Livingston applied to General Washington for that station in behalf of Arnold.   The application was successful, though not immediately.   On the first of August Arnold was assigned to the command of the left wing of the army.   Complaining, however, that his wounds were yet too painful to allow him to act with efficiency in the field, on the 3d of the same month he was directed to repair to West Point, and take the command of the post.†

It would be foreign to the main design of the present work, to recapitulate the history of this memorable instance of the blackest treachery.   Suffice it to say, that, after his arrest, the conduct of André was characterised by candor, manliness, and honor.   He was tried by a board of officers, and convicted on

in New-York, Mrs. Arnold stopped on the way at the house of Mrs. Provost, at Paramus, the lady of a British officer, and afterward the wife of Colonel Burr, where she stayed one night.   Here the frantic scenes of West Point were re-enacted while there were strangers present; but as soon as they were alone, she became tranquilised, and assured Mrs. Provost that she was heartily sick of the theatrics she was playing.   She stated that she had corresponded with the British commander—that she was disgusted with the American cause, and those who had the management of it; and that, through great precaution and unceasing perseverance, she had ultimately brought the General into the arrangement to surrender West Point to the British, &c. &c.   For farther particulars upon the subject, see Davis's Life of Burr, pp. 219, 220.   In his letter in her behalf to General Washington, Arnold of course entirely exculpated his wife.   The public vengeance, he said, "ought alone to fall on me.   She is as good and as innocent as an angel, and is incapable of doing wrong."

   * Eighteen months before the consummation of his treason, General Arnold commenced writing to Sir Henry Clinton anonymously, and from time to time communicated to him important intelligence.—*Sparks.*

   † Letter of Washington to General Arnold, August 3, 1780.   See, also, note of Sparks to the same, and other antecedent letters.

his own frank confessions, without the testimony of a single witness. His main object, after he saw his destiny was inevitable, was to relieve himself from the reproach of having been guilty of any act of personal dishonor ; and to show that in fact he had been compelled to assume the disguise in which he was taken, by Arnold himself. And when he had expiated his error by his life, the feeling was almost universal, that the iron hand of the law-martial had fallen upon the wrong individual. For, although, in regard to André himself, it was doubtless right, under the circumstances of the case, that justice should be inexo rable ; yet humanity cannot but weep over the hard fate of the victim, while it marvels that an inscrutable Providence did not so order events as to bring Arnold to the gibbet on which the youthful stranger so nobly died. " Never, perhaps, did a man suf- " fer death with more justice, or deserve it less," was the remark of a gallant soldier who was in attendance upon him during his imprisonment ; and the account of his character, written by that officer, and his demeanor during the trying scenes inter vening between his arrest and execution, cannot be read with- out exciting emotions of high admiration and profound regret.*
Happy, however, was his fate, compared with that of the arch- traitor, whose moral leprosy, like the plague-spot, caused him to be shunned through life by all honorable men—an object of loathing and scorn, to fill—unregretted by any one—a dishonor· able grave !

Resuming, again, the Indian relations of the North, the first occurrence to be noted is a visit made by several of the Oneida, Tuscarora, and Caughnawaga Indians to the French army in Rhode Island. The Caughnawaga Indians, residing at the Lachine rapids near Montreal, had been altogether in the interest of France down to the time of the conquest of Canada by the British and Provincial arms ; and it was supposed that the ancient attachment of other branches of the Six Nations to the French had not been entirely lost. It was also recollected, that " when M. de Vaudreuil surrendered Canada to the En-

---

* The document referred to is a letter published in the Pennsylvania Gazette o October 25th, 1780, written, as was supposed, by Alexander Hamilton, at that time an Aid-de-camp to the Commander-in-chief. There is, either in the library or the picture gallery of Yale College, New-Haven, a likeness of Major André, sketched upon paper, by himself, during his confinement, and but a short time before his execution.

"glish, he gave to the Indians, as tokens of recognizance, a " golden crucifix and a watch ; and it was supposed that a re- " newal of the impressions, which had been in some degree pre- " served among them by these emblems of friendship, might " have the effect to detach them from the influence of the En- " glish, and strengthen their union with the Americans and " French."* That the British officers were apprehensive that an influence adverse to the cause of the King might be awakened among the Indians by the alliance of the French with the Americans, was rendered highly probable, from the pains taken by the former to impress them with a belief that no such alliance had been formed.† Hence it was judged expedient by General Schuyler, who was then at Albany, that a delegation of the Indians should be sent to Rhode Island, where conviction of the fact might be wrought upon their senses by the substantial evidence of the fleet and army.‡ Thirteen Oneidas and Tuscaroras, and five Caughnawagas, were accordingly despatched to Rhode Island, under the conduct of Mr. Deane the Interpreter. They arrived at Newport on the 29th of August, and were received with distinguished marks of attention by the French commanders. " Entertainments and military shows were pre- " pared for them, and they expressed much satisfaction at what " they saw and heard. Suitable presents were distributed among " them ; and to the chiefs were given medals representing the " coronation of the French King. When they went away, a " written address was delivered to them, or rather a kind of pro- " clamation, signed by Count Rochambeau, copies of which " were to be distributed among the friendly Indians." It was in the following words :—

" The King of France, your father, has not forgotten his children. As a token of remembrance, I have presented gifts to your deputies in his name. He learned with concern, that many nations, deceived by the English, who were his enemies, had attacked and lifted up the hatchet against his good and faithful allies, the United States. He has desired me to tell you, that he is a firm and faithful friend to all the friends of America, and a decided enemy to all its foes. He hopes that all his

---

* Sparks.
† Letter from Washington to Count de Rochambeau.   ‡ Idem.

children, whom he loves sincerely, will take part with their father in this war against the English."

The Caughnawagas being more conversant with the French than with the English language, the address was written in both languages, and signed and sealed in due form.* It is doubtful, however, whether either good or ill came from the movement. The Oneidas and Tuscaroras were already sufficiently true in their alliance with the Americans. The Caughnawagas had made friendly advances to the Americans before, which resulted in nothing. And as for the other and greater divisions of the Six Nations, their hostility, it will soon be perceived, was not abated.

But even yet the desire of vengeance, on the part of the savages, had not been satisfied. Smarting from the devastations of Sullivan's expedition, neither the irruption of Sir John Johnson to Johnstown and Caughnawaga, nor the invasion and destruction of Canajoharie by Thayendanegea, was deemed by them a sufficient retaliatory visitation. Another and yet more extensive expedition, both as to the numbers to be engaged, and the object to be accomplished, was therefore planned and carried into execution, under the auspices of Sir John Johnson, Joseph Brant, and the famous Seneca warrior, the *Corn-Planter*.† This latter chief was a half-breed, his father being a white man, living in the Mohawk country, named John O'Bail.‡

The Indian portion of this expedition was chiefly collected at Tioga Point, whence they ascended the Susquehanna to Unadilla, where a junction was formed with Sir John Johnson, whose forces consisted, besides Mohawks, of three companies of his own regiment of Greens ; one company of German Yagers ; a detachment of two hundred men from Butler's rangers ;§ and one company of British regulars, under the immediate command

---

* Note in the Life and Correspondence of Washington by Sparks, and also a letter from the Count de Rochambeau, cited by him.

† This is the first time that the name of this chief, afterward celebrated in our Indian annals, occurs in the history of the revolution, although he was in the field with his tribe against General Sullivan. There is some doubt as to the orthography of his parental name. It has been written Abeel, O'Beal, and O'Bail. The latter is the name according to Mary Jemison. He was, for a considerable period, the rival of the eloquent Keeper-Awake, Red Jacket, by whom his influence was ultimately destroyed and himself supplanted.

‡ Mary Jemison.　　　　　§ MSS. of Major Thomas Sammons.

of Captain Richard Duncan, the son of an opulent gentleman residing, previous to the war, in the neighborhood of Schenectady.* The troops of Sir John were collected at Lachine, near Montreal, whence they ascended the St. Lawrence to Lake Ontario and Oswego. From this point they crossed the country to the Susquehanna, where they were joined by the Indians and Tories from Tioga. Sir John had with him two small mortars, and a brass three-pounder, called a grasshopper, from the circumstance of its being mounted upon iron legs instead of wheels. These pieces of ordnance were transported through the woods upon pack-horses. Every soldier, and every Indian, was provided with eighty rounds of cartridges.†

The Indians never breathed more fiercely for vengeance than at this time, and they went forth upon the war-path with a determination that nothing should impede their march or prevent their depredations.‡ Their numbers have been variously estimated at from eight hundred to fifteen hundred and fifty—all descriptions of troops included. The latter estimate is probably the nearest to the truth, judging from the results of the campaign.

Their course was by their old route, along the Charlotte river, (sometimes called the eastern branch of the Susquehanna,) to its source, and thence across to the head of the Schoharie-kill, for the purpose of making thorough work in the destruction of the continuous chain of settlements through that beautiful valley to its junction with the Mohawk. The enemy had designed to keep the movement a profound secret, until proclaimed by his actual presence. Two of the Oneidas, in their service, having deserted, frustrated that design by giving information of their approach to the settlements.§ Whether from weariness of continual alarms, or from ignorance or doubt as to the quarter where the blow was to be struck, or from criminal negligence, cannot be told ; but it is certain that the surprise was as complete as the success of the campaign was discreditable to those who did not prevent it.

The plan of Sir John and Captain Brant was to enter the valley by night, pass, if possible, the upper fort unobserved, and then, by silently destroying the intervening settlements, attack

---

* Giles F. Yates, Esq.   † Major Sammons.
‡ Mary Jemison, who seems to have been present at the gathering.
§ Letter of General Haldimand to Lord George Germaine.

the middle fort, at Middleburgh, early in the morning. This fort was garrisoned by about one hundred and fifty state troops, called three months men, exclusive of some fifty militia-men— the whole under the command of Major Woolsey,* who, from all accounts, appears to have been an inefficient officer, and by some writers has been represented as the most miserable of poltroons.† The design of passing the upper fort unperceived, was in part successful ; nor was the enemy's approach to the middle fortress discovered until just at break of day, on the morning of the 16th of October, when a sentinel, named Philip Graft, standing upon the parapet of a mud wall, discovered a fire kindling in some buildings not more than a quarter of a mile distant. Calling to the sergeant of the guard, he communicated the discovery through him to the commanding officer. The drums at once beat to arms, and Major Woolsey requested forty volunteers to sally forth and discover the cause of the alarm. Every man on duty promptly responded to the invitation, and the complement was thereupon counted off from the right, and sent out in charge of Lieutenant Spencer. The little band proceeded with alacrity in the direction of the burning buildings, until they suddenly encountered the enemy's advance. Three shots were exchanged, when Spencer retreated, and brought his detachment back into the fort without the loss of a man.‡ At this moment the concerted signal of three guns from the upper fort came rolling down the gorge of the mountains, from which it was evident that the enemy had passed that fortress without molesting it. A proper degree of vigilance, however, ought certainly to have enabled the sentinels of that garrison to observe the advance of the invading army, instead of merely catching a glimpse of its rear. The moment the enemy had thus been discovered, front and rear, concealment of his approach being no longer possible, the torch was indiscriminately applied to such houses and barns as came in his way. The season had been bountiful, the rich alluvial

---

* MS. statement of Philip Graft, in the author's possession.

† "Woolsey's presence of mind forsook him in the hour of danger. He concealed himself at first with the women and children in the house, and when driven out by the ridicule of his new associates, he crawled round the intrenchments on his hands and knees, amid the jeers and bravos of the militia, who felt their courage revive as their laughter was excited by the cowardice of their major."—*Campbell's Annals*.

‡ MS. statement of Philip Graft.

bottoms of the Schoharie-kill producing an unusually abundant
harvest that year. The barns were therefore well stored with
the earlier grains, while the fields were yet heavily burdened
with the autumnal crops. But the husbandmen in the neighborhood, or those lodging for greater security in the little apology
for a fortress, looked abroad at sunrise to behold the produce
of their industry in flames.

Soon after sunrise the main forces of the enemy had arrived,
and the fort was completely invested. A column of troops, with
the pieces of light artillery heretofore mentioned, passed round the
north-east side of the fort, and planted their guns upon an eminence commanding the American works. An officer with a flag
was now despatched toward the garrison, and from the moment
he was seen, an order was given to cease firing. All was silent
until he had approached to within the distance of fair rifle shot,
when the reader's old acquaintance, Murphy, recently of Morgan's rifle corps, but now making war on his own responsibility,
expressed a determination to shoot down the officer by whom the
flag was borne. He was instantly ordered by the officers of the
regular troops to forbear. But the militia irregulars encouraged
him to persist in his mutinous determination. He did so; but
for once his rifle was untrue, and the flag-officer immediately
faced about and retired to his own ranks.

Sir John thereupon opened his artillery upon the fort, while
the Indians and rangers kept up a brisk fire of musketry—both
without much effect. The enemy's field-pieces were probably
of too small calibre for the distance, and the shells were thrown
with so little skill, for the most part, as either to fall short, or fly
over the works, or to explode in the air. Two shells, however,
fell upon the roof of the house within the fort, one of which was
precipitated down into a room occupied by two sick women.
It sank into a feather bed, and exploded—but without inflicting
farther injury. Fire was communicated to the roof of the
building by the other shell, and was extinguished with a
single pail of water carried up and applied by Philip Graft.
Unfortunately the garrison was unable to return the fire with
spirit, for the want of powder. The regular troops had only a
few rounds each, and the militia were but little better provided
in that respect. Messengers had been despatched to Albany on
the preceding day for ammunition, and also for reinforcements;

but neither had yet been received, so that the fort was but ill prepared for protracted or efficient resistance. But of this destitution the enemy was of course ignorant; and the shooting at his flag-officer may have been, and probably was, construed by Sir John as evidence of a determination to make no terms. Expecting a desperate resistance, therefore, the Baronet may, from that circumstance, have proceeded with the greater caution.

It was indeed a singular siege. The enemy, spreading over the whole of the little plain, were now occupied in feeble attacks upon the fort, and now dispersing in small detachments, to plunder another farm-house and burn another corn-stack. There was one large barn, situated near the fort, and around which stood a circle of stacks of wheat. These the enemy attempted several times to fire, but Lieut. Spencer sallied forth with his little band of forty, and so gallantly protected the property, that the enemy reluctantly abandoned his design upon that point. Spencer was fired upon briskly in this sortie, but lost only one of his men.

In the course of the forenoon, another flag was despatched toward the fort by Sir John, which Murphy again determined to shoot down the moment the officer came within range of his trusty rifle. Major Woolsey and the officers interposed, but the militia again rallied round Murphy; and although one of the officers drew his sword, and threatened to run the offender through if he persisted, yet the rifleman coolly replied that he had no confidence in the commanding officer, who he believed intended to surrender the fort; that, if taken, he knew well what his own fate would be, and he would not be taken alive. As the flag approached, therefore, he fired again, but happily without effect; and the flag officer once more returned to the head-quarters of Sir John.* When the officers of the regular troops remonstrated against such a barbarous violation of the usages of honorable war, the militia soldiers replied that they were dealing with a foe who paid no regard to such usages; and, however strictly they might observe the rules of war and of etiquette themselves, the besiegers would be the last men to exhibit a corresponding course of conduct in the event of their success. The wailings of plundered and murdered families without the fort, and the columns of

* Statement of Philip Graft.

smoke and flame then ascending to the heavens, afforded ample
testimony of the truth of their position. " The savages, and their
" companions, the Tories, still more savage than they, had
" shown no respect to age, sex, or condition; and it was not
" without force that the question was repeated, are we bound to
" exercise a forbearance totally unreciprocated by the enemy ?"
" Besides," it was added, " let us show that we will neither take
" nor give quarters; and the enemy, discovering our desperation,
" will most likely withdraw."*

The desultory battle was again renewed—small parties of the
garrison occasionally watching opportunities to sally forth and
do what mischief they could to the enemy, retreating within
the gates again when likely to be borne down by superior numbers. Sir John, perceiving at length that neither shot nor shells
made any impression upon the garrison, formed his disciplined
troops under shelter of a small building more immediately in
the neighborhood of the fort, and prepared for an attempt to
carry it by assault. A flag again approached, and Murphy
brought up his rifle to fire upon it the third time. He was admonished, as before, to desist, and an effort was made to arrest
him. But he was a universal favorite, and the soldiers would
not allow the procedure. A white flag was then ordered to
be raised from the fort, but Murphy threatened instant death to
any one who obeyed the direction; and as the enemy's flag
continued to approach, he was again preparing his piece, when
an officer once more interposed. Captain Reghtmeyer, of the
militia, standing by the side of Murphy, gave him the order to
fire. The continental officer made a demonstration toward Reghtmeyer, by attempting to draw his sword; but immediately desisted as the latter clubbed his fusee, and gave an impressive
motion with its breech, of an import not to be misunderstood;
whereupon the Major stepped back, and there the matter ended.†
The officer bearing the flag, having been thus a third time repulsed, Sir John convened a council of war, and after a brief
consultation, abandoned the siege, and proceeded on his Vandal
march down the valley. The reason of this hasty change of
purpose has never been known. Some have asserted that a
pretended loyalist gave the Baronet an exaggerated account of

* The Sexagenary.   † Ibid.

the strength of the garrison and its means of resistance.*
Others have said that rumors of approaching reinforcements
induced him to hasten forward, lest his projected march of desolation should be interrupted.   But it is likely that the repeated
violations of the flag had created an impression that such an
indomitable garrison might not prudently be engaged steel to
steel and hand to hand, by assailants not to be relied upon with
much confidence in such emergencies.

The march of the invaders was rapid in the direction of Fort
Hunter, at the confluence of the Schoharie-kill with the Mohawk
river, in the course of which they destroyed the buildings and
produce of every agricultural description.†   On arriving in the
vicinity of the Lower Fort at Old Schoharie, Sir John divided his
forces—the regulars continuing down on the bank of the creek
to the left of the fort, while the Indians skirted the meadows
half a mile distant on the right.   Having thus gained the north
side of the fort, they made a stand for a brief space of time,
and a few shots were interchanged.   Some sharp-shooters having been stationed in the tower of the church, the enemy
brought one of their field-pieces to bear upon it.   A single shot
only struck, which lodged in the cornice, and a discharge of
grape from the fort drove the invaders back,‡ whereupon their
march was resumed and continued to Fort Hunter ; at which
place they arrived in the night without interruption.   In their
course the whole valley was laid in ruins.   The houses and
barns were burnt, the horses and cattle killed or taken ; and
those of the inhabitants who were not safely within the walls of
their little fortifications, were either killed or carried into captivity.   Not a building, known by the Indians and Tories to
belong to a Whig, was saved.   Sir John had ordered his forces
to spare the church at the upper Fort, but his mandate was dis-
obeyed, and the structure was laid in ashes.   The houses of
the loyalists were passed unmolested ; but, exasperated by the destruction of their own habitations, the Whigs soon caused these

---

* Campbell.

† The destruction of grain was so great as to threaten the most alarming consequences, in respect to the forming of magazines for the public service at the North.
But for that event, the settlement of Schoharie, alone, would have delivered eighty
thousand bushels of grain.—*Letter of Washington to the President of Congress,*
Nov. 7, 1780.

‡ Campbell's Annals.

to be numbered in the common lot.* Thus was the whole valley of the Schoharie-kill made desolate.

The loss of the Americans at the forts was very trifling. Only two were killed, and one wounded, at the middle Fort, and none at the lower. But of the unprotected inhabitants, numbers—according to some accounts, one hundred—were killed. There were some individual occurrences during the day, moreover, which are worthy of being specially noted. It happened early in the morning, that John Vrooman and two of his neighbors were upon a scout in the woods, about eight miles from the fort, when they discovered an Indian. Vrooman fired, and the Indian fell. At the same instant another Indian was discovered through the bushes, who was also brought down by one of Vrooman's companions. A third savage was now seen ; but as Vrooman's third companion hesitated about firing, Vrooman himself snatched his rifle from him, and brought that warrior also to the ground. At the same instant—for it was all the work of a moment—up rose from the ground a group of Indians and Tories, who set upon them with a terrible yell. Vrooman and his companions fled in different directions at the top of their speed, and succeeded, by reason of their wind and bottom, and their zigzag flights, in making their escape. It was noon when the former reached his own home,—only to behold his house in flames. His wife and her mother were made captives by an Indian named Seth Hendrick, who had formerly resided in Schoharie ; but they were released and sent back on the following day, by Captain Brant, together with a letter, written upon birch bark, explaining his reasons for allowing their return.†

One of the farmers, on that day, while engaged with his boys in unloading a wagon of grain at the barn, hearing a shriek, looked about, and saw a party of Indians and Tories between

---

* The Indians spared one house, from the consideration that it had formerly been occupied at one of their treaties.

† The Sexagenary. The Vroomans were an extensive family in the Schoharie settlements, and were severe sufferers. In the last preceding chapter but one, the boastings of Becraft, who had murdered one entire family of that name, have been noted. During the present expedition, the following persons, among others, were murdered, viz :—Tunis Vrooman, his wife and son ; while at the same time Ephraim Vrooman and his two sons, Bartholomew and Josias, John Vrooman, Martin Vrooman, Bartholomew Vrooman, Jun., Simon Vrooman, his wife and his son Jacob, were taken prisoners and carried to Canada.—*Giles F. Yates.*

himself and the house. "The enemy, my boys!" said the father, and sprang from the wagon, but in attempting to leap the fence, a rifle ball brought him dead upon the spot. The shriek had proceeded from his wife, who, in coming from the garden, had discovered the savages, and screamed to give the alarm. She was struck down by a tomahawk. Her little son, five years old, who had been playing about the wagon, ran up to his mother, in an agony of grief, as she lay weltering in blood, and was knocked on the head, and left dead by the side of his parent. The two other boys were carried away into Canada, and did not return until after the war.*

The family of Ephraim Vrooman was also particularly unfortunate. He was at work in the field when he first discovered a straggling party of the enemy approaching. He started at full speed for his house, in order to obtain his arms, and sell his life as dearly as possible. But in climbing a fence he was seized, and taken prisoner. His wife, in endeavoring to escape by flight, was shot dead before his eyes. As she fell, her little daughter, aged eleven years, ran up, and cast herself down by the side of her dying parent, as clinging to her for protection, when an Indian came up, and added to the agony of the father and the crimes of the day, by crushing her head with a stone.†

There was an aged man in the middle Fort, who performed a bold exploit. He was the owner of a mill about two miles distant, at which his son had passed the night. Knowing that some one or more of the enemy's plundering parties would assuredly visit the mill, at the instant Lieutenant Spencer's party encountered Sir John's advance guard in the morning, the old

---

* The Sexagenary. "Ephraim Vrooman himself was carried away by Seth Hendrick, who treated him with much kindness by the way. There were two or three other Indians in the immediate party with Seth. These, before they arrived at their place of destination, grew tired of their prisoner, and proposed to despatch him. Mr. Vrooman overheard the conversation, which was conducted in a whisper, and repeated it to Hendrick. Hendrick assured him, in the most positive manner, that ' not a hair of his head should be touched,' and gave his companions a severe reprimand for their ungenerous conspiracy. After the termination of the revolutionary contest, Hendrick paid Mr. Vrooman a visit, and apologized for his conduct during the war, in the strong metaphorical language of his nation. The tomahawk, said he, is used only in war; in time of peace it is buried—it cuts down the sturdy oak as well as the tender vine; but I (laying his hand on Mr. V's shoulder,) I saved the oak."—*Giles F. Yates.*

† The Sexagenary.

man sallied out and hastened to the rescue of his son. Mounting each a horse to return to the fort, they found it already invested by the enemy on their arrival. Nothing daunted, however, they passed within a hundred yards of the enemy at full speed, dashed up to the rear of the Fort, and were received in safety.*

There was another incident transpiring at the fort, which stands in happy contrast with the conduct of the commanding major. The females within the fortress are said to have displayed a degree of heroism worthy of commendation and of all praise. Being well provided with arms, they were determined to use them in case of an attempt to carry the works by storm. One of them, an interesting young woman, whose name yet lives in story among her own mountains, perceiving, as she thought, symptoms of fear in a soldier who had been ordered to a well without the works, and within range of the enemy's fire, for water, snatched the bucket from his hands, and ran forth for it herself. Without changing color, or giving the slightest evidence of fear, she drew and brought bucket after bucket to the thirsty soldiers, and providentially escaped without injury.†

Sir John remained in the neighborhood of Fort Hunter on the 17th, continuing the work of destruction in every possible direction. On the evening of that day Captain Duncan crossed the river with three companies of the Greens and some Indians. On the morning of the 18th, all that had been left standing of Caughnawaga at the time of the irruption of Sir John in the preceding Spring, and all that had been rebuilt, was ruthlessly destroyed by fire. A simultaneous and most desolating march up the river was then commenced by Sir John and the main body of his forces on the south side of the river, and by Captain Duncan's division on the north. As at Schoharie, the march of both was one of entire devastation. Rapine and plunder were the order of the day, and both shores of the Mohawk were lighted up by the conflagration of every thing combustible; while the panic-stricken inhabitants only escaped slaughter or captivity by flight—they knew not whither.‡ Conspicuous among the sufferers was Major Jelles Fonda, a faithful and confidential officer under the father of Sir John; but who, having turned his

---

* The Sexagenary.   † Idem.   ‡ MSS. of Major Thomas Sammons.

back upon the royal cause, was singled out as a special and signal mark of vengeance. His mansion at "The Nose," in the town of Palatine, was destroyed, together with property to the amount of sixty thousand dollars. The Major was himself absent.* His wife escaped under the curtain of a thick fog, and made her way on foot, twenty-six miles, to Schenectady.† Sir John encamped with his forces on the night of the 18th nearly opposite, or rather above the Nose. On the following morning he crossed the river to the north side, at Keder's Rifts. The greater part of the motley army continued its progress directly up the river, laying waste the country as before. A detachment of one hundred and fifty men was, however, dispatched from Keder's Rifts against the small stockade called Fort Paris, in Stone Arabia, some two or three miles back from the river, north of Palatine. But, after marching about two miles, the main body also wheeled off to the right, to assist in attacking the fort. The work of devastation was continued also in this direction, as at other places.

The small fort just mentioned was at this time in command of Colonel Brown, with a garrison of one hundred and thirty men. An unfortunate occurrence induced him to leave his defences, and resulted in his discomfiture and fall. The circumstances were these:—the moment tidings that Sir John had broken into the settlements of the Schoharie reached Albany, General Robert Van Rensselaer, of Claverack, at the head of the Claverack, Albany, and Schenectady militia, pushed on by forced marches to encounter him, accompanied by Governor Clinton. Having arrived at Caughnawaga on the 18th, and having likewise ascertained that Fort Paris was to be assaulted on the morning of the 19th, Van Rensselaer dispatched orders to Colonel Brown to march out and check the advance of the enemy, while at the same time he would be ready to fall upon his rear. Brown, faithful to the hour designated, sallied forth, and gave Sir John battle near the site of a former work, called Fort Keyser. But General Van Rensselaer's advance had been impeded, so that no diversion was created in Brown's favor; and his forces were too feeble to withstand the enemy, or even to check his progress. Colonel Brown fell gallantly at the head of his

---

* In the State Senate, the legislature being then in Session at Poughkeepsie.

† Antiquarian Researches, by Giles F. Yates.

little division, of which from forty to forty-five were also slain. The remainder of his troops sought safety in flight.

Colonel Brown, who fell on this occasion, was a soldier of great courage and high moral worth. He was early in the service, and was engaged in the memorable and ultimately disastrous campaign in Canada. While the American army was at Sorel, he detected, or believed he detected, a design on the part of General Arnold then to play the traitor. Arnold was about making a mysterious night movement of the flotilla of light vessels belonging to the Americans, then with the army in the St. Lawrence, which Colonel Easton, suspecting all was not right, prevented—but not until he had ordered two or three pieces of ordnance to bear upon the vessels, threatening to fire upon them if they proceeded. The conviction upon the minds of Easton and Brown was, that it was the purpose of Arnold to run off with the flotilla, and sell out to Sir Guy Carleton.

After the close of the Canadian campaign, during the winter of 1776-77, while Arnold and many of the officers were quartered in Albany, some difficulty occurred between Brown and the former, which resulted in ill-feeling between them. Arnold was at the head of a mess of sixteen or eighteen officers, among whom was Colonel Morgan Lewis. Colonel Brown, having weak eyes, and being obliged to live abstemiously, occupied quarters affording greater retirement. In consequence of the misunderstanding referred to, Colonel Brown published a handbill, attacking Arnold with great severity; rehearsing the suspicious circumstances that had occurred at Sorel; and upbraiding him for sacking the city of Montreal while he was in the occupancy of that place. The handbill concluded with these remarkable words:—"MONEY IS THIS MAN'S GOD, AND TO GET ENOUGH OF IT, HE WOULD SACRIFICE HIS COUNTRY."

Such a publication could not but produce a great sensation among the officers. It was received at Arnold's quarters while the mess were at dinner, and read aloud at the table—the accused himself sitting at the head. Arnold, of course, was greatly excited, and applied a variety of epithets, coarse and harsh, to Colonel Brown, pronouncing him a scoundrel, and declaring that he would kick him wheresoever and whensoever he should meet him. One of the officers present remarked to the General, that Colonel Brown was his friend; and that, as the remarks just applied to him had been so publicly made, he presumed there could be no objection to his repeating them to that officer. Arnold replied, certainly not; adding, that he should feel himself obliged to any officer who would inform Colonel Brown of what had been said. The officer replied that he should do so before he slept.

Under these circumstances no time was lost in making the communication to Colonel Brown. Colonel Lewis himself called upon Brown in the course of the evening, and the matter was the principal topic of conversation. The Colonel was a mild and amiable man, and he made no remark of particular harshness or bitterness, in respect to Arnold; but, toward the close of the interview, he observed—" Well, Lewis, I wish you would invite me to dine with your mess to-morrow." " With all my heart," was the reply; " will you come?" Brown said he would, and they parted. The next day, near the time of serving dinner, Colonel Brown arrived, and was ushered in. The table was spread in a long room, at one end of which the door opened directly opposite to the fireplace at the other. Arnold was at the moment standing with his back to the fire, so that, as Brown opened the door, they at once encountered each other face to face. It was a moment of breathless interest for the result. Brown walked calmly in, and turning to avoid the table, passed round with a deliberate step, and advancing up close to Arnold, stopped, and looked him directly in the eye. After the pause of a moment, he observed: " I UNDERSTAND, SIR, THAT " YOU HAVE SAID YOU WOULD KICK ME: I NOW PRESENT MY- " SELF TO GIVE YOU AN OPPORTUNITY TO PUT YOUR THREAT " INTO EXECUTION !" Another brief pause ensued. Arnold opened not his lips. Brown then said to him—" SIR, YOU " ARE A DIRTY SCOUNDREL." Arnold was still silent as the sphinx. Whereupon Brown turned upon his heel with dignity, apologised to the gentlemen present for his intrusion, and immediately left the room.

This was certainly an extraordinary scene, and more extraordinary still is the fact, that the particulars have never been communicated in any way to the public. Arnold certainly did not lack personal bravery; and the unbroken silence preserved by him on the occasion, can only be accounted for upon the supposition that he feared to provoke inquiry upon the subject, while at the same time he could throw himself upon his well-attested courage and his rank, as excuses for not stooping to a controversy with a subordinate officer.   But it must still be considered as one of the most extraordinary personal interviews to be found among the memorabilia of military men.*

In the year following, during the campaign of Burgoyne, owing to the intrigues of Arnold, Brown was left without any command.   But he was too much of a patriot to remain idle in such a moment of his country's peril.   He raised a corps of volunteers on his own account, and performed one of the most daring exploits of the whole war.   While Burgoyne was yet in the full career of victory, Brown dashed into his rear, and proceeding down to the north end of Lake George, fell upon a small post, which he carried without opposition.   The surprise was complete.   He also took possession of Mount Defiance, Mount Hope, the landing-place, and about two hundred batteaux.   With the loss of only three killed and five wounded, Colonel Brown liberated one hundred American prisoners, and captured two hundred and ninety-three of the enemy.   He made an attempt on Mount Independence and Ticonderoga; but, too weak for the investment of those works, he returned through Lake George to Diamond Island, containing the enemy's *depot* of provisions.   He attacked the works upon this island, but being repulsed, burnt the vessels he had captured, and returned to his former station.   This brilliant affair by Colonel Brown took place at the time when Arnold had the ear of General Gates; and the consequence was, that in giving an account of the expedition, Gates carefully avoided even naming the gallant officer who had planned and achieved it.   It was an instance of neglect for which that officer ought for ever to have been ashamed.   Colonel Brown was a gentleman of education, bred to the bar, and greatly respected by those who enjoyed the pleasure of his acquaintance.   But to return.

After the fall of Colonel Brown, and the defeat of his troops, Sir John dispersed his forces in small bands, to the distance of five or six miles in all directions, to pillage and destroy.   Late in the afternoon he reunited his troops, and leaving Stone Ara-

* The particulars of this interesting story were derived by the author from the lips of General Lewis himself.

bia a desert, marched back to the river road, east of Caroga Creek. The detachment of Captain Duncan having come up, Sir John again moved toward the west. There was a small defence not far from the mouth of the creek, called Fox's Fort. Avoiding this work by diverging from the road to the margin of the river on the left, Sir John continued his course three miles farther, to a place called Klock's Field, where, from the fatigue of his troops, and the over-burthens of provisons and plunder with which they were laden, it became necessary to halt.

General Van Rensselaer was now close in pursuit of Sir John, with a strong force. Indeed, he ought to have overtaken him in the early part of the day, since he had encamped the night before on the south side of the river, at Van Eps's, nearly opposite Caughnawaga, while Sir John himself was encamped opposite the Nose, only two or three miles farther up the river. Sir John's troops, moreover, were exhausted by forced marches, active service, and heavy knapsacks, while those of Van Rensselaer were fresh in the field. On the morning of the same day, while continuing his march on the south side of the river, Van Rensselaer was joined by Captain M'Kean, with some eighty volunteers, together with a strong body of Oneida warriors, led by their principal chief, Louis Atayataronghta, who, as stated in a former chapter, had been commissioned a lieutenant colonel by Congress. With these additions, the command of General Van Rensselaer numbered about fifteen hundred—a force in every way superior to that of the enemy.

Sir John had stationed a guard of forty men at the ford, to dispute its passage. On approaching this point, General Van Rensselaer halted, and did not again advance until the guard of the enemy had been withdrawn. Continuing his march still upon the South side of the river, while the enemy was actively engaged in the work of death and destruction on the North, Van Rensselaer arrived opposite the battle-ground where Brown had fallen, before the firing had ceased, and while the savage war-whoop was yet resounding. This was at 11 o'clock in the morning, and the Americans came to a halt, about three miles below Caroga Creek, still on the south side. While there, some of the fugitives from Colonel Brown's regiment came running down, and jumping into the river, forded it without difficulty. As they came to the south bank, the General inquired whence

they came. One of them, a militia officer named Van Allen,
replied that they had escaped from Brown's battle. "How has
it gone ?" "Colonel Brown is killed, with many of his men.
Are you not going there ?" "I am not acquainted with the
fording place," said the General. He was answered that there
was no difficulty in the case. The General then inquired of
Van Allen if he would return as a pilot, and the reply was
promptly in the affirmative. Hereupon Captain M'Kean and
the Oneida chief led their respective commands through the
river to the north side, expecting the main army immediately
to follow. At this moment Colonel Dubois, of the State levies,
rode up to the General, who immediately mounted his horse,
and instead of crossing the river, accompanied the Colonel to
Fort Plain, some distance above, to dinner as it was understood.
Meantime the baggage wagons were driven into the river, to
serve in part as a bridge for the main body of Van Rensselaer's
forces, and they commenced crossing the stream in single files.
The passage in this way was not effected until four o'clock in
the afternoon, at which time the General returned and joined
them, just as the last man had crossed over. Governor Clinton
remained at the fort. As the General arrived at the water's
edge, Colonel Louis, as the Oneida chieftain was called, shook
his sword at him, and denounced him as a Tory. Arrived on
the north side, Colonel William Harper took the liberty of remon-
strating with the General at what he conceived to be a great and
unnecessary delay, attended with a needless loss of life and property, on the part of the inhabitants who had been suffered thus
long to remain unprotected. From that moment Van Rensselaer
moved with due expedition. The troops were set in motion,
and marched in regular order, in three divisions, with the exception of the Oneida warriors and the volunteers under M'Kean,
who regulated their own movements as they pleased—showing
no disposition, however, to lag behind. The advance was led
by Colonel Morgan Lewis.

Anticipating that he should be compelled to receive an attack,
Sir John had made his dispositions accordingly. His regular
troops, Butler's rangers, and the Tories less regularly organized,
were posted on a small alluvial plain, partly encompassed by a
sweeping bend of the river. A slight breast-work had been
hastily thrown across the neck of the little peninsula thus

formed, for the protection of his troops, and the Indians, under Thayendanegea, were secreted among the thick shrub oaks covering the table-land of a few feet elevation, yet farther north. A detachment of German Yagers supported the Indians.*

It was near the close of the day when Van Rensselaer arrived, and the battle was immediately commenced in the open field. Two of the advancing divisions of State troops, forming the left, were directed against the regular forces of Sir John on the flatts, commencing their firing from a great distance with small arms only—the field-pieces not having been taken across the river. Colonel Dubois commanded the extreme right, which was so far extended that he had no enemies to encounter. Next to him were M'Kean's volunteers and the Oneida Indians, whose duty it was to attack Thayendanegea's Indians and the Yagers. These were supported by a small corps of infantry, commanded by Colonel Morgan Lewis. The American left was commanded by Colonel Cuyler of Albany. Sir John's right was formed of a company of regular troops. His own regiment of Greens composed the centre, its left resting upon the ambuscaded Indians. The latter first sounded the war-whoop, which was promptly answered by the Oneidas. Both parties eagerly rushed forward, and the attack, for the instant, was mutually impetuous. Dubois, though too far extended, brought his regiment speedily to the support of M'Kean's volunteers, who were following up the attack of the Oneidas. The hostile Indians manifested a disposition to stand for a few moments; but Dubois had no sooner charged closely upon them, than they fled with precipitation to the fording place near the upper Indian Castle, about two miles above—crossing the road in their flight, and throwing themselves in the rear of the Greens as a cover. The Mohawk chief was wounded in the heel, but not so badly as to prevent his escape.

The enemy's regular troops and rangers, however, fought with spirit, although Sir John himself was reported by some to have fled with the Indians.† On the flight of the Indians, Major

---

* These Yagers were a sort of rifle corps—using short rifles.

† Major Thomas Sammons, from whose manuscripts the author has chiefly drawn the facts of this portion of the narrative—i. e. after the arrival of Gen. Van Rensselaer at Van Eps's—is positive in his declarations, that the British Command-

Van Benschoten, of Dubois's regiment, hastened to the General for permission to pursue the flying enemy. It was just twilight; and the indications were not to be mistaken, that the best portion of the enemy's forces were in confusion, and on the point of being conquered. The disappointment was therefore great, when, instead of allowing a pursuit of the Indians, or charging upon the feeble breast-work on the flatts, and thus finishing the battle, General Van Rensselaer ordered his forces to retire for the night. His object was to obtain a better position for a bivouac, and to renew and complete the battle in the morning—for which purpose he fell back nearly three miles, to Fox's Fort. His troops were not only disappointed, but highly incensed at this order, believing that the contest might have been victoriously ended in a very few minutes. Indeed, the brave Colonel Louis, of the Oneidas, together with Colonel Clyde and Captain M'Kean, refused to retreat, but sheltered themselves in the adjacent buildings—hanging upon the enemy's lines several hours, and making some prisoners. In the course of the evening Clyde, with a handful of Schoharie militia, succeeded in capturing one of the enemy's field-pieces. The Americans were still more chagrined on learning from one of the prisoners that the troops of Sir John were on the point of capitulating at the very moment of Van Rensselaer's order to retreat. And from the fact that the river was alike too rapid and too deep, where it curved round the battle-field, to admit of an escape in that direction, no doubt can be entertained that the enemy had been entirely within their power. But it was now too late. The golden opportunity had been lost. On the morrow's dawn there was no enemy in the field to encounter. Under cover of darkness the Royal Greens and Butler's Rangers had followed the example of the Indians, and made good their escape.

Louis with his warriors, and M'Kean with his volunteers, crossed the river early in the morning, in pursuit. General Van Rensselaer also arrived on the battle-ground between 8 and 9 o'clock, for the purpose of completing the work of the preceding day. While he was crossing the river and preparing to follow on, some of M'Kean's volunteers, who were waiting for the main army, in strolling about, came upon a little block-house, in which

er was among the first to flee. Other accounts speak differently. Major Sammons was in the battle, among the volunteers of M'Kean.

they found nine of the enemy who had been made prisoners
during the night.   One of the party making the discovery was
Thomas Sammons, and among the prisoners was a Tory who
had been his near neighbor in Johnstown.   On being asked how
they came there, this man, whose name was Peter Cass, replied
—" Why, I am ashamed to tell.   Last night, after the battle, we
" crossed the river.   It was dark.   We heard the word, ' lay
" down your arms.'   Some of us did so.   We were taken, nine of
" us, and marched into this little fort by seven militia-men.   We
" formed the rear of three hundred of Johnson's Greens, who
" were running promiscuously through and over one another.
" I thought General Van Rensselaer's whole army was upon us.
" Why did you not take us prisoners yesterday, after Sir John
" ran off with the Indians and left us?   We wanted to sur-
" render."

When Sir John fled from the field with the Indians and Yagers, he doubtless supposed all was lost.   He laid his course
direct for the Onondaga lake, where his boats had been concealed, pursuing the main road, and making only a slight deviation
to the south of the German Flatts, to avoid the forts at that place.
His Greens and Rangers followed closely upon his heels, and
overtook him at Oneida.   Van Rensselaer pressed forward in
pursuit, with all his forces, as far as Fort Herkimer, where he
was overtaken by Governor Clinton, who did not, however,
interfere with the command.   Louis and M'Kean were now
pushed forward in advance, with orders to overtake the fugitive
army if possible, and engage them—Van Rensselaer promising to
continue his march with all possible rapidity, and be at hand
to support them in the event of an engagement.   On the next
morning the advance struck the trail of Sir John, and took one
of his Indians prisoner.   Halting for a short time, Colonel Dubois came up, and urged them forward, repeating the assurances
of the General's near approach and sure support.   The march
of the advance was then resumed, but they had not proceeded
far before they came upon the enemy's deserted encampment—
the fires yet burning.   The Oneida chief now shook his head,
and refused to proceed another step until General Van Rensselaer should make his appearance.   There was accordingly a halt
for some time, during which a Doctor Allen arrived from the
main army, informing the officers that the pursuit had already

been abandoned by the General, who was four miles distant on his return-march !

The expedition was of course at an end. But fortune had yet another favor in store for Sir John Johnson—to be won without the bloodshed that had attended his desolating course through the Mohawk Valley. Having ascertained where Sir John's boats were concealed, General Van Rensselaer had despatched an express to Fort Schuyler, ordering Captain Vrooman, with a strong detachment, to hasten forward in advance of the enemy, and destroy them. Vrooman lost no time in attempting the execution of his orders ; but one of his men falling sick, or feigning himself to be so, at Oneida, was left behind. Sir John soon afterward came up ; and being informed by the treacherous invalid of Vrooman's movement, Brant and his Indians, with a detachment of Butler's rangers, were hastened forward in pursuit. They came suddenly upon Vrooman and his troops while they were engaged at dinner, and every man was captured without firing a gun.*

The last obstacle to his escape having thus been removed, Sir John reached Oswego without farther molestation. By this third and most formidable irruption into the Mohawk country during the season, Sir John had completed its entire destruction above Schenectady—the principal settlement above the Little Falls having been sacked and burnt two years before. General Van Rensselaer has always been censured for his conduct in this expedition. Indeed his behavior was most extraordinary throughout. On the night before the battle of Klock's Field, Sir John was not more than six miles in advance—having left Van Eps's just before dark, where Van Rensselaer arrived and encamped early in the evening ; and it was obvious to all that no extraordinary share of energy was required to bring the enemy to an engagement, even before the encounter with Colonel Brown. Major Sammons, at the close of his account of the expedition, remarks with emphasis—" When my father's buildings were burnt, and

---

* Major Sammons ; also statement of John More, yet living, who was one of Sir John's soldiers. According to the official returns of Sir John Johnson, this affair of the capture of Captain Vrooman and his detachment took place on the 23d of October, at a place called Canaghsioraga. Two captains and one lieutenant were taken, together with eight non-commissioned officers and forty-five privates. Three privates and one lieutenant were killed.

" my brothers taken prisoners, the pain I felt was not as great as
" at the conduct of General Robert Van Rensselaer."*

But Sir John's escape, after all, was rather a flight than a retreat ; and had it not been for the capture of Vrooman's detachment—a most unexpected conquest—the visible trophies of his
expedition would have been few and dearly purchased. Indubitable evidences were discovered by the pursuers, that he was
reduced to a most uncomfortable situation ; and from the Baronet's own letter to General Haldimand, it appears that there
were many missing, who it was hoped would find their way
to Oswego or Niagara. General Haldimand wrote to his government that Sir John " had destroyed the settlements of Scho-
" harie and Stone Arabia, and laid waste a great extent of coun-
" try," which was most true. It was added :—"He had several
" engagements with the enemy, in which he came off victorious.
" In one of them, near Stone Arabia, he killed a Colonel Brown,
" a notorious and active rebel, with about one hundred officers
" and men." "I cannot finish without expressing to your Lord-
" ship the perfect satisfaction which I have, from the zeal, spirit,
" and activity with which Sir John Johnson has conducted
" this arduous enterprise."†

While General Van Rensselaer was pushing forward in pursuit of Sir John Johnson, an incident occurred at Fort Hunter,
which speaks volumes in favor of the character of Joseph Brant.
The plundered and distressed inhabitants of the Schoharie settlements, the day after the enemy had departed from Fort Hunter, crowded about the fort, each his tale of loss or grief to relate. Among them was a woman, whose husband and several

---

* "With regard to the battle on Klock's Farm, and the facts stated in these papers, I would say that I joined with Captain M'Kean as a volunteer, and met Gen.
Van Rensselaer on the south side of the river, opposite Caughnawaga, early in the
morning ; and of my own knowledge I know most of the facts to be as they are
stated. I staid with the volunteers after the battle, and held the conversation with
the prisoners found in the little block-house the next morning, as stated. I was
with Capt. Kean when he had orders to advance and overtake Sir John, and a
short time after saw Dr. Allen, who came to inform us that Van Rensselaer was returning. With regard to the route of Sir John, I received my account from those
of his own party who are now living, and men of undoubted veracity."—*Note of
Major Sammons*—1836.

† Letter of Sir Frederick Haldimand to Lord George Germaine, New Annual
Register 1781.

other members of the family were missing. She was in an agony
of grief, rendered more poignant by the loss of her infant, which
had been snatched from the cradle. Early the next morning,
while the officers at Van Rensselaer's head-quarters were at breakfast, a young Indian warrior came bounding into the room like
a stag, bearing an infant in his arms, and also a letter from
Brant, addressed "to the commanding officer of the rebel army."
General Van Rensselaer not being present at the moment, the
letter was opened by one of his suite, and read substantially as
follows :—

" Sir : I send you by one of my runners, the child which he
" will deliver, that you may know that whatever others may do,
" *I* do not make war upon women and children. I am sorry to
" say that I have those engaged with me in the service, who
" are more savage than the savages themselves."

Among those thus referred to, he proceeded to name several
of the leading Tories, including the two Butlers, and others
whose names are not recollected.* It was very speedily ascertained that the infant was none other than that of the disconsolate mother of whom mention has just been made. Her sensations on again clasping her infant to her bosom need not be
described ; nor could they be.†

There was yet another adventure connected with this expedition, which was alike interesting and amusing. The Senecas,
it has already been stated, were led by the Corn-Planter, whose

---

* The bitter hostility of the Tories of the Mohawk country toward their former
neighbors, was at times exhibited in acts of such fiend-like ferocity as to defy explanation and stagger belief. In a former chapter the case of an infant murdered
in its cradle by a Tory, after the refusal of an Indian to kill it, has been stated.
There was another like instance in the neighborhood of the Little Falls, marked,
if possible, by still greater brutality. An Indian having refused to kill an infant
as it lay smiling in the cradle, the more savage loyalist, rebuking the compassion of
the red man, thrust it through with his bayonet as a fisherman would spear a
salmon, and held it writhing in its agonies in triumph above his head. A gentleman of the Bar, late of Little Falls, has assured the author, that to his knowledge
the wretch who committed that diabolical act had the effrontery a few years since to
present himself as a candidate for a pension, under one of the acts of Congress for
rewarding the surviving soldiers of the revolution. The fact just related was fortunately elicited before his papers were completed, and the result need not be
stated.

† The author has received the account of this interesting occurrence from
General Morgan Lewis, who was present at the time, a spectator of all the particulars.

father, as it has also been stated, was a white man named O'Bail. According to Mary Jemison, the residence of the Corn-Planter's father was in the vicinity of Fort Plank, and, of course, not far from the battle-ground of Klock's Field. He had formerly been in the habit of travelling back and forth from Albany through the Seneca country, to Niagara, as a trader. Becoming enamored of a pretty squaw among the Senecas, in process of time the Corn-Planter became one of the living evidences of his affection. Whether the father was aware that a chief of so much eminence was his own son, history does not tell; but the son was ignorant neither of his parentage, nor of the residence of his sire; and being now in his close vicinity, he took a novel method of bringing about an acquaintance with him. Repairing with a detachment of his warriors to his father's house, he made the old man a prisoner, and marched him off. Having proceeded ten or twelve miles, the chief stepped up before his sire, and addressed him in the following terms :—

" My name is John O'Bail, commonly called Corn-Planter. I am your son ! You are my father ! You are now my prisoner, and subject to the customs of Indian warfare. But you shall not be harmed. You need not fear. I am a warrior ! Many are the scalps which I have taken ! Many prisoners I have tortured to death ! I am your son ! I am a warrior ! I was anxious to see you, and to greet you in friendship. I went to your cabin, and took you by force : but your life shall be spared. Indians love their friends and their kindred, and treat them with kindness. If now you choose to follow the fortunes of your yellow son, and to live with our people, I will cherish your old age with plenty of venison, and you shall live easy. But if it is your choice to return to your fields, and live with your white children, I will send a party of my trusty young men to conduct you back in safety. I respect you, my father. You have been friendly to Indians : they are your friends."*

* Life of Mary Jemison. In a letter written by Corn-Planter to the Governor of Pennsylvania, in 1822, complaining of an attempt made by the officers of that State to impose taxes upon him and the Senecas residing on the Alleghany, he began as follows :—" When I was a child, I played with the butterfly, the grasshopper, and the frogs. As I grew up, I began to pay some attention, and play with the Indian boys in the neighborhood, and they took notice of my skin being a different color from theirs, and spoke about it. I inquired of my mother the cause, and she told me that my father was a resident of Albany. I ate still my victuals out of a bark

The old gentleman, however, had sown his wild oats. His days of romance were over. Preferring, therefore, the produce of his own fields, the company of his white children, and the comforts of his own house, to the venison, the freedom, and the forests of the western wilds, he chose to return. His son, fulfilling his word, bowed to the election, and giving his father in charge to a suitable escort, he was enabled to reach his own dwelling in safety. The proud Seneca and his warriors moved off to their own wilds.

Simultaneously with the movements of Sir John Johnson through the Schoharie and Mohawk country, the enemy had been actively engaged against the settlements at the North of Albany, between the Hudson and Lake Champlain, and likewise against some of the upper settlements on the Connecticut river. In order to create a diversion in favor of Sir John, Major Carleton came up the lake from St. John's, with a fleet of eight

dish: I grew up to be a young man, and married me a wife, but I had no kettle or gun. I then knew where my father lived, and went to see him, and found he was a white man, and spoke the English language. He gave me victuals while I was at his house, but when I started to return home, he gave me no provision to eat on the way. He gave me neither kettle nor gun, neither did he tell me that the United States were about to rebel against the government of England," &c. &c. By this statement it appears that he must have seen his father several years before the Mohawk campaign. This may very well have been, and yet the anecdote related by Mary Jemison be true also. In every instance in which the author has had an opportunity of testing the correctness of her statements by other authorities, they have proved to be remarkably correct. Corn-Planter lived to a great age, having deceased within the last eight or ten years. He was an able man—distinguished in subsequent negotiations. He was eloquent, and a great advocate for Temperance. He made a very effective and characteristic speech upon that subject in 1822. "The Great Spirit first made the world, and next the flying animals, and found all things good and prosperous. He is immortal and everlasting. After finishing the flying animals, he came down on earth, and there stood. Then he made different kinds of trees, and woods of all sorts, and people of every kind. He made the Spring, and other seasons, and the weather suitable for planting. These he did make. But stills to make whiskey to give to Indians, he did not make." * * * * * * * "The Great Spirit told us there were three things for people to attend to. First, we ought to take care of our wives and children. Secondly, the white people ought to attend to their farms and cattle. Thirdly, the Great Spirit has given the bears and deers to the Indians." * * * "The Great Spirit has ordered me to quit drinking. He wishes me to inform the people that they should quit drinking intoxicating drink." In the course of the same speech, he gave evidence that he was not overmuch pleased with the admixture of his own blood. * * * "The different kinds the Great Spirit made separate, and not to mix with and disturb each other. But the white people have broken this command, by mixing their color with the Indians. The Indians have done better by not doing so."

large vessels and twenty-six flat-bottomed boats, containing upward of one thousand men, regular troops, loyalists and Indians.
Fort George and Fort Anne were both taken by surprise, and
their garrisons, which were not large, were surrendered prisoners of war.* The party directed against the upper settlements
of the Connecticut river, was commanded by Major Haughton
of the 53d regiment, and consisted almost entirely of Indians, of
whom there were two hundred. This marauding incursion
was likewise successful. In addition to the booty taken, thirty-
two of the inhabitants were carried away prisoners. Several of
the militia, who turned out in pursuit of Major Haughton, were
killed. In regard to Major Carleton's expedition, sad tales of
cruelty were reported. One of these was a relation. by a deserter named Van Deusen, of a horrible case of torture inflicted
upon a soldier of Colonel Warner's regiment, taken by Carleton
in the action near Fort George. Van Deusen was a deserter from
the American army to the enemy; but having stolen back into
his own country, was apprehended and executed. Colonel Gansevoort, however, then in command at the North, wrote to Major
Carleton upon the subject on the 2d of November. stating the
particulars of the story. Carleton repelled the charge in the
most positive and earnest manner, as will presently appear.†

The correspondence between Gansevoort and Carleton, however, was not confined to this particular transaction. Indeed,
that was altogether an incidental affair, and the correspondence
with Carleton himself was also incidental, being part only of
a more extended negotiation with other and higher officers of
the British army in Canada, the object of which was the settlement of a cartel for an extensive exchange of prisoners at the
North. The story will be best told by the introduction of a

---

* Forts Anne and George were taken by Major Carleton on the 10th and 11th of
October. In his official report, Major Carleton stated his own loss, on both occasions, at four officers and twenty-three privates killed. The number of prisoners
taken is stated at two captains, two lieutenants, and one hundred and fourteen privates.

† Speaking of Carleton's expedition, Sir Frederick Haldimand, in a letter to Lord
George Germaine, observes :—" The reports assiduously published on all occasions
by the enemy, of cruelties committed by the Indians, are notoriously false, and propagated merely to exasperate the ignorant and deluded people. In this late instance
Major Carleton informs me, they behaved with the greatest moderation, and did not
strip, or in any respect ill use, their prisoners." Sir John Johnson had less control
over *his* Indians at Schoharie.

portion of the correspondence itself, while at the same time
several other points will receive satisfactory illustration.

GENERAL POWELL TO COLONEL VAN SCHAICK.

"*St. John's, Sept.* 22*d*, 1780.

" SIR,

" Agreeable to the promise made in my letter of the 15th of
last March, I send by your returning flag of truce, Mrs. Campbell, Mrs. Moore, and their families, together with Matthew Cannon, and five others, made prisoners by the Indians on the
Mohawk river, whose advanced time of life and earnest solicitations to return to their families, have induced General Haldimand to grant them that permission ;* as also Mr. Williams of
Detroit, who desires to go to his relatives ; and Mary and Betsey
Lewis, who beg to go to their father near Albany. His Excellency is sorry that the breach of faith on the part of the colonists,
in the cartel of the Cedars, has put it out of his power to enter
upon an exchange of prisoners, and, notwithstanding their repeated attempts to escape, many throughout the province are
enlarged upon their parole. They have all a plentiful allowance of wholesome provisions, and those whom it is thought
necessary to keep in confinement, are accommodated in the most
comfortable manner circumstances will admit of. They have,
besides, received money to the amount of the within accounts ;
and if this last indulgence is to be continued, it is but reasonable it
should be remitted in coin ; to which I am to desire your attention, as very heavy bills are every day presented from our troops
who are prisoners in the colonies.

" The attention which has been shown to Mrs. Campbell,
and those in her unfortunate circumstances, as well as the good
treatment of the prisoners, which it is hoped they will have the
candor to acknowledge, is referred to for comparison, to those
by whose orders or permission His Majesty's subjects have
experienced execution, the horrors of a dungeon, loaded with
irons, and the miseries of want.

" The families specified in the enclosed list have been long
in expectation, and many of them promised permission, to join

* The prisoners above-mentioned, it will be recollected, were taken at Cherry
Valley in 1778. See Mrs. Campbell's Narrative, sketched in Vol. I.

their husbands and relatives in this province : it is therefore
requested they may be sent to your advanced post on the
Skenesborough communication, and a flag of truce shall be
sent from hence, in the course of three weeks, in order to receive them.

" I am, Sir,

" Your most obedient,

" Humble servant,

" H. WATSON POWELL,

"*Brigadier General*

" *To Colonel Van Schaick.*"

COLONEL GANSEVOORT TO GENERAL POWELL.

" *Saratoga, Nov. 2d,* 1780.

" SIR,

" Your letter of 22d September last, directed to Colonel Van
Schaick, it becomes my duty to answer, as commanding this de
partment until the arrival of General McDougall, who is daily
expected.* The prisoners whom you noticed, I am informed,
have taken the route to Albany, through Bennington.

" The families specified in your list,† whom I believe to be

---

* This reference to the expected arrival of General McDougall was not exactly
true, and was made as a *ruse de guerre* to mislead the British General as to the
strength of the Northern Department. The truth was, that Colonel Gansevoort
was so weak in point of troops, that he was apprehensive of a second visitation from
St. John's should Powell and Carleton obtain information of his actual means of resistance. Hence he threw in the name of McDougall, in order to create an impression at
St. Johns that there was at least a General's command of troops at Saratoga. Colonel
Gansevoort wrote to General Washington upon the subject, and gave this explanation
for the deception he had practised in his letter to General Powell. There was, indeed,
good cause for apprehension at that time. After Carleton had captured forts George and
Anne, and returned down the lakes to St. John's, he had suddenly returned with reinforcements. The leaders in Vermont were also at the same time holding a correspondence with the British Commanders in Canada, of which semi-treasonable conduct
Ethan Allen himself was at the head, as will appear hereafter. General Schuyler
had obtained some knowledge upon the subject, which he lost no time in communicating to the Commander-in-chief. The consequence was, the ordering of several
regiments to the North, and the appointment of General James Clinton to the command of the Department at Albany.—*Washington's Letters—Sparks.*

† The following is the list referred to, as enclosed by General Powell, viz :—
"Names of the different families belonging to the following men of the 84th Reg't.
residing at Saratoga: John McDonell's family ; Donald McGrewer's family ; Duncan McDonell's family ; John McIntosh's ditto ; Duncan McDonell's ditto ; Donald
McDonald's ditto ; Kenneth McDonell's ditto ; John McDonell's father and mother.

all in the vicinity of this place, were to have been sent to the British shipping in Lake Champlain in the beginning of last month. Major Carleton's incursion prevented their being forwarded then, and as all the batteaux in Lake George were carried off by that gentleman, it may have been impracticable to send them on since, if even it had been proper, while he remained at Ticonderoga and Crown Point. I have written Major Carleton, and requested him to send batteaux to Fort Anne or Fort George, if he can, for their conveyance. As soon as I am advised of his determination, the necessary measures will be taken. The accounts of cash advanced to the prisoners in Canada, I shall do myself the honor to transmit to his Excellency, General Washington.

" It affords me great satisfaction to learn that the British have at length found it prudent to follow the generous example exhibited to them by the Americans, in the mild treatment with which the prisoners in the power of the latter have been invariably indulged during the war.

" It is, however, a justice due to General Carleton and his successors to declare that, from all accounts, the prisoners immediately in their power have been treated with much lenity.

" But you, Sir, suppose that British subjects in our possession have experienced executions, the horrors of a dungeon, loaded with irons, and the miseries of want. It is true some spies have been executed, and amongst these Major André, Adjutant General of the British army under the command of Sir Henry Clinton. And even his death, although justice required it, and the laws of nations authorised it, was and is lamented by us with a feeling of generosity which does honor to human nature. None have experienced the horrors of a dungeon, or been loaded with irons, excepting a few on whom it was thought proper to retaliate for the many, the very many, indeed, of ours, whom British cruelty and inhumanity could suffer to perish for want in dungeons and prison-ships, loaded with irons and with insults. If you are ignorant of these facts, I can excuse your observations. If not, give me leave to tell you they are unworthy the gentleman and the officer, and evince a degree of disingenuousness unbecoming either.

" If General Haldimand considers the governing powers of these States to have been guilty of a breach of faith with regard to the cartel of the Cedars, he ought to apply to them in regard to that matter. Barely to mention it to a subordinate officer, was indelicate and improper. But as you have ventured to accuse, I will venture to deny the justice of the charge; and, as far as my memory of that transaction serves, I think I can do it with propriety.*

" The newspapers announce that a general exchange of prisoners is settled below. Whether it extends to Canada, is not specified.

" I am, Sir,

" Your most obedient,

" Humble servant,

" PETER GANSEVOORT,

" Col. 3d N. Y. Reg't.

" *To Brigadier General Powell.*"

COLONEL GANSEVOORT TO MAJOR CARLETON.

" *Saratoga, Nov.* 26, 1780.

"SIR,

" This will be delivered you by Major Rosecrantz, of my regiment, who, together with the persons named in my pass of this day's date, goes as a flag to carry the letters he is charged with, and to return with your answer.

" General Powell's letter of the 22d September last, Captain Monsell's of the 19th, and your's of the 24th ultimo, were delivered me about noon to-day.

" I have left the letter for General Powell under flying seal for your perusal, that you may learn my determination respecting the families he requested to have sent. Should you conclude to send batteaux for them, they must come as far as Fort Anne, as the roads to Skenesborough are impassable for carriages, or to the farther end of Lake George, which would be much easier for the women and children. Their number amounts to nearly three hundred; and I believe ten batteaux will be neces-

---

* The maxim of Colonel Gansevoort was, " his country, right or wrong." He would have found it a difficult undertaking, however, to justify the course adopted by Congress touching the cartel agreed upon by General Arnold at the Cedars. Indeed, the violation of the stipulations made on that occasion, had created difficulties in regard to exchanges of prisoners during the whole war. It was frequently a source of embarrassment, and even of mortification, to General Washington, during the course of nearly the whole war.

sary to carry them all at once. You will please to give directions to the officer whom you may send with your flag, to pass his receipt for the number of men, women, and children which shall be delivered. Pray advise me on what day you think the batteaux will arrive at the place you may intend to send them, that I may so arrange matters as to cause the least delay.

"A certain James Van Deusen, who deserted from our service to you, and who, since you were on this side the lake, has stolen back into the country, has been apprehended, and will suffer death as a deserter. He confesses that after the rencontre near Fort George, with some of Colonel Warner's men and your party, in which one of our Indians was killed, your Indians, in cool blood, scalped one of Warner's men alive, tormented him a considerable time. and afterward cut his throat—and all this in your presence. Your character, Sir, suffers greatly on this account. It has hitherto been marked by conduct the reverse of this sad catastrophe; and men of honor are unwilling to believe Van Deusen. I wish you to explain yourself to me on the subject.

"I am, Sir,
"Your most obedient and
"Humble servant,
"PETER GANSEVOORT,
"Col. 3d N. Y. Reg't.

"Major Carleton."

MAJOR CARLETON TO COLONEL GANSEVOORT.

"Mile Bay, Nov. 6th. 1780.

"SIR,
"By your flag I have this moment received your letter of the 2d instant, with one directed to Brigadier General Powell. Respecting the families intended to be sent in, I answer to both. Being entirely ignorant of the purport of Brigadier Powell's letter to you on the subject, and having no instructions from General Haldimand respecting that business, I can only say that such persons as are specified in the Brigadier's list will be received, provided the number of boats mentioned in my postscript can contain them. Should there be room to spare, the names contained in the enclosed list, or as many of them as can be taken on board, will be received. My boats shall be at Skenesborough on

the 9th, where they shall remain till the 14th at night, and then return to me, as I could not take upon me the risk of their being frozen up there.

"I should have expected Captain Chapman would have given a flat contradiction to James Van Deusen's confession. No prisoner was scalped, or tortured alive. I saved the lives of several of the prisoners, who were neither stripped nor insulted in the smallest degree after the affair was over. I heard of one man being killed after he was taken during the firing, owing to a dispute between the two Indians, of different villages, who had taken him. He was either a negro or a Stockbridge Indian I believe, and he would not suffer himself to be conducted to the British guard by a loyalist officer. The attention of the officer was necessarily directed to the care of his own men; and after the action I heard of the man being killed."

"I am, Sir,

"Your most obedient, and

"Most humble servant,

"CHR. CARLETON,

"*Major 29th Reg't.*

"*Colonel Gansevoort.*

"P. S. There being no idea of this business, the shipping went down some days ago. I find it will not be in my power to furnish more than five boats. Could not the boat I gave to carry up the last families, be sent down with these?"*

No farther outrages were committed on the northern and western frontiers during that Autumn. The next information received of Brant and his associates, was brought to Fort Schuyler by a family of Oneidas who had been released from Niagara. They arrived at the Fort on the 6th of December. Colonel Weisenfeldts, then in command, caused the head Indian of the party, whose name was Jacob Reed, to be examined; and the whole examination was transmitted, as taken down by question and answer, to General Clinton. From this statement it appeared that Joseph Brant, Colonel Butler, and Colonel Guy

---

* These letters are contained among the Gansevoort papers, and have been copied from the originals by the author. The same papers, together with a letter from General Haldimand to Lord George Germaine, are likewise the author's authorities for the brief sketch of the expeditions of Carleton and Major Haughton.

Johnson, were then in their old winter-quarters at Niagara. Of the Oneida warriors only thirty-seven had been persuaded to join the royal cause; one of whom had been killed, and five others had returned with Reed. The forces at Niagara at this time were stated to be sixty British regulars, commanded by a captain; four hundred loyalists commanded by Colonel Butler, and twelve hundred Indians (including women and children,) commanded by Brant and Guy Johnson. One of the objects of the late expedition to the Mohawk was stated by Reed to be the destruction of Schenectady; but as they had not penetrated so far, Brant and Johnson were meditating another campaign. The prisoners taken from Stone Arabia, after reaching Niagara, had been shipped for Buck Island in the river St. Lawrence; but from the long absence of the vessel, and the fragments of a wreck, drums, furniture, &c., which had been washed ashore, it was believed that she had been lost, and that all on board had perished. Reed farther stated, that as soon as the snow was hard, Brant, with five or six hundred warriors, was coming to the Oneida country, in order to keep within a convenient distance for sending scouts down the Mohawk. One of their objects was to be at all times prepared for cutting off the supplies proceeding for the garrison of Fort Schuyler. The Indians at Niagara, according to Reed's account, were well provided with every thing they could desire.* But it was far otherwise with Fort Schuyler at this time. The letters of General Schuyler were full of complaints, not only of the difficulty of procuring provisions, but also of forwarding them to the outposts. In one of his letters, written at that period, he said there was not flour enough in Fort Schuyler to suffice for a single day's consumption.†

Thus ended the Indian campaigns of the North for the year 1780. There were, indeed, other petty occurrences on the outskirts, alarms, and now and then a few shots exchanged with a straggling Indian or Tory scout. But no other occurrence of importance within the range of the present history, marked the winter then closely advancing. And never did winter spread his mantle over a scene of greater desolation than lay beneath it in the Valley of the Mohawk.

---

* General Clinton's Manuscripts.   † MSS. of General Schuyler.

THE sun of the new year was veiled by a cloud of deeper gloom than had previously darkened the prospects of the American arms at any period of the contest. The whole army, in all its divisions, at the North and in the South, was suffering severely both for clothing and provisions. Indeed, the accumulated sufferings and privations of "the army constitute a large "and interesting portion of the history of the war of American "independence. At the date now under review, Winter, with- "out much lessening the toils of the soldiers, was adding to "their sufferings. They were perpetually on the point of starv- "ing, were often entirely without food, were exposed without "proper clothing to the rigors of the season, and had, moreover, "now served almost twelve months without pay."* Such was the general fact. The Pennsylvania troops had still farther grievances of which to complain. They had been enlisted in ambiguous terms—to "serve three years, or during the war." At the expiration of the stipulated period, "three years," the soldier claimed his discharge, while the officers insisted upon holding him to the other condition of the contract. The consequence was great dissatisfaction, increased, of course, by the much higher bounties subsequently paid for enlistments.

The Pennsylvania line, consisting of six regiments, was cantoned at Morristown, under the immediate command of Briga-

* Marshall's Life of Washington.

dier General Wayne. So long had they been brooding over
their wrongs, so intense had become their sufferings, and so discouraging were the prospects of remedy or redress, that the discontents which, down to the last day of the preceding year, had
only been nurtured, broke out into open mutiny on the evening
of the next. The spirit of insubordination was from the first so
decided, and the evidences of revolt were so general, as at once to
jeopard the cause. An effort was made to quell the mutiny, in
the course of which several of the turbulent soldiers were
wounded, as also were some of the officers, who were endeavoring to repress the disorder. One of the officers, Captain Billings,
was killed. But the cause of the revolt was too deeply seated,
and the disaffection too extensive, to be easily overcome. Even
Wayne himself, the favorite of the Pennsylvanians, was without
power. Drawing a pistol and threatening one of the most turbulent of the revolters, a bayonet was presented at his own bosom.* In a word, the authority of the commissioned officers
was at an end. The non-commissioned officers were generally
engaged in the mutiny, and one of their number being appointed
Commander-in-chief, they moved off in the direction of Philadelphia, with their arms and six pieces of artillery—deaf to the
arguments, the entreaties, and the utmost efforts of their officers
to change their purposes.† As a last resort, Wayne and his officers attempted to divide them, but without effect. Those who
at first appeared reluctant, were soon persuaded to unite with
their comrades, to march upon Philadelphia and demand a redress of their wrongs at the doors of Congress.

* Marshall.

† Letter of Washington to President Weare of New Hampshire. This was a
letter urging upon the government of New Hampshire to make some exertion to relieve the distresses of the army. A circular was sent to all the New England States
to the same effect, and confided to General Knox, as a special agent to enforce the
appeal. To President Weare, the Commander-in-chief said, plainly :—" I give it
decidedly as my opinion, that it is in vain to think an army can be kept together
much longer under such a variety of sufferings as ours has experienced ; and that unless some immediate and spirited measures are adopted to furnish at least three
months' pay to the troops in money, which will be of some value to them, and at the
same time provide ways and means to clothe and feed them better than they have
been, the worst that can befall us may be expected." The Legislatures of Massachusetts and New Hampshire nobly responded to the call, and immediately voted a
gratuity of twenty-four dollars in hard money to each of the non-commissioned officers and soldiers belonging to those States, who were engaged to serve during the
war.--*Sparks.*

The number of the revolters was about thirteen hundred—a loss that would have been severe of itself. But the most unpleasant apprehensions arose from the danger, not only that the spirit of insubordination might spread to other corps of the army, but that the mutineers might fall away in a body to the enemy, who would, of course, lose not a moment in availing himself of such a diversion in his favor. Coercive measures having failed to bring the revolters back to the path of duty, Wayne, with his principal officers, determined to follow close upon their rear, and after the first transports of their passion should subside, try what virtue might be found in the arts of persuasion. The General overtook them at night in the neighborhood of Middlebrook, but being advised in their present temper not to venture among them, he invited a deputation of one sergeant from each regiment to meet him in consultation. The deliberations were amicable, and the General suggested a mode of obtaining redress of their grievances, which satisfied the delegates, who, on retiring, promised to exert their influence in bringing the men back to duty. But the attempt was ineffectual; and on the day following the mutineers marched to Princeton—the few who were well disposed and willing to separate from the mutineers, continuing with the majority at the request of their officers, in the hope that their exertions might "moderate the violence of "their leaders, and check the contagion of their example."

The crisis was most critical. The Commander-in-chief, on receiving the first advices of the revolt, was disposed to repair at once to the camp of the mutineers; but on advisement and reflection, this course was relinquished. The complaints of the Pennsylvania line, in regard to destitution of provisions and clothing, were common to the whole army, and it was doubtful how far the contagion of disaffection might already have spread. Nor could the Commander-in-chief, whose head-quarters were at New Windsor, venture upon a visit to the mutineers, without taking with him a sufficient force to compel obedience to his commands should the exertion of force become necessary. But a sufficient body of troops for such an object could not be spared without leaving the fortresses in the Highlands too weak to resist an attack from Sir Henry Clinton, who would be sure to strike upon those important works at the first favorable moment. The river being free from ice, Sir Henry would possess every facility for such a movement the instant the back of Washington should be turned upon the North. Under all the circumstances of the case, therefore, the Commander-in-chief remained at his post, neglecting, however, no measure of justice within his power to heal the discontents, or of precaution to prevent their farther extension.

Meantime the mutineers remained several days at Princeton, refusing to proceed to the Delaware and cross into Pennsylvania, while Sir Henry Clinton made every disposition to avail himself of the revolt, and lost not a moment in despatching emissaries to their camp, with tempting offers to induce them to join the armies of the King. But, mutineers as they were, they nevertheless spurned the proposition ; and retaining the emissaries in custody, handed the communications, of which they were the bearers, over to General Wayne. Though in rebellion against their officers, the soldiers were nevertheless indignant at the idea of turning their arms, as Arnold had done, against their own country; and those about them who were well disposed, availed themselves of the occasion, with much address, to impress upon their minds the magnitude of the insult conveyed in propositions made to them in the character of traitors.*

News of the revolt had no sooner reached Philadelphia, than a committee was appointed by Congress, consisting of General Sullivan,† and two other gentlemen, in conjunction with President Reed on behalf of the Council of Pennsylvania, to meet the revolters, and attempt to bring them back to reason. The demands of the mutineers were exorbitant, but were in the end acceded to with some unimportant modifications. They then moved forward to Trenton, and in the end, although better things were anticipated from the stipulations agreed upon, the Pennsylvania line was almost entirely disbanded. A voluntary performance, by Congress, of much less than was yielded

---

* Five days after their arrival among the mutineers, viz. on the 11th of January, Sir Henry's emissaries were tried by a court-martial, and executed.

† Very soon after he left the army, at the close of the Seneca campaign, General Sullivan was elected to Congress, of which body he was an efficient and patriotic member. Afterward, in the years 1786, 1787, and 1788, he was President of New Hampshire, in which situation, by his vigorous exertions, he quelled the spirit of insurrection which exhibited itself at the time of the troubles with Shays in Massachusetts. It 1782 he was appointed a District Judge. He died in 1795, aged 54.

by the committee, would have averted the evil, and saved the division.*

The success of the Pennsylvania mutineers induced the New Jersey line, then stationed at Pompton, to follow the bad example; and on the night of the 20th of January a large portion of the brigade rose in arms. Their claims were precisely the same as those which had been yielded to the Pennsylvanians. By this time, however, the Commander-in-chief had satisfied himself that he could rely upon the eastern troops; and, chagrined as he had been by the result of the Pennsylvania revolt, he determined, not only that nothing more should be yielded to the spirit of insubordination, but that such an example should be made as would operate as a check to the like proceedings in future. A strong detachment of troops was accordingly led against the insurgents by General Howe, with instructions to make no terms whatsoever while they continued in a state of resistance. General Howe was farther instructed to seize a few of the ringleaders, and execute them on the spot. The orders were promptly complied with, and the insurrection was crushed at a blow. The mutinous brigade returned to its duty; and such vigorous measures were taken by the States to supply the wants of the army, as effectually checked the progress of discontent.† But it was only by the strong process of impressment that those supplies could be wrung from the people, whose discontents, though less immediately alarming, were, nevertheless, as great as had been those of the army.

The first active demonstration of Sir Henry Clinton, on the opening of the new year, was the expedition against Virginia, under the conduct of General Arnold. The arch-traitor had, in fact, sailed from New-York toward the close of December, but he did not enter the Capes of Virginia until the beginning of January—landing at Westover on the 5th. He marched to

---

* Although the Pennsylvania line was thus dissolved, the evil was surmounted much sooner than had been anticipated. Before the close of January, Wayne wrote to Washington that the disbanded soldiers were "as impatient of liberty as they had been of service, and that they were as importunate to be re-enlisted as they had been to be discharged." A *reclaimed* and formidable line was the result in the Spring.

† Sir Henry Clinton endeavored to avail himself of this New Jersey insurrection, in like manner as he had attempted to tamper with the Pennsylvanians. But his emissary, who was in the American interest, delivered his papers to the first American officer with whom he met.

Richmond, and after some trifling skirmishes on the way, destroyed the stores at that place, and also at Westham; whereupon he retired to Norfolk. This was a mere predatory expedition, attended by no important result. Farther south, events were continually occurring of greater moment. General Greene having been assigned to the command of that department, after the signal discomfiture of Gates, affairs soon wore a brighter aspect. The loss of the battle of Camden, a few months before, was balanced, and, in its moral effect, more than balanced, by the decisive victory over Tarleton, achieved by General Morgan at the Cowpens on the 17th of January. And although Greene was defeated at Guilford on the 15th of March, yet the victory was too dearly won by Earl Cornwallis to render it a just occasion of triumph. So likewise in the repulse of Greene by Lord Rawdon at Camden, owing to the misconduct of the militia, the British commander was nevertheless so roughly handled that, although he received a reinforcement in the course of the following night, he deemed it expedient to destroy the town, and retire farther down the Santee. But these apparent disadvantages were amply compensated by the masterly manœuvres of Greene, and the brilliant succession of victories over the smaller works and detachments of the enemy. In these latter affairs, Forts Watkinson, Orangeburgh, Motte, Silver Bluff, Granby, and Cornwallis were successively taken, and the enemy was compelled to evacuate other forts. Lord Rawdon was likewise obliged to fall back upon Charleston, while Cornwallis was pursuing a doubtful march into Virginia. The great disadvantage labored under by General Greene, was the necessity of depending in a great measure upon the militia—not having regular troops sufficient to cope with the veterans from Europe. But, though not always victorious in battle, he was invariably so in the results. And his masterly movements proved him far in advance of any of his antagonists, in all the requisites of an able commander.

But while events thus propitious to the American arms were occurring at the South, the aspect of affairs, as has already been seen, was sadly discouraging at the North. In addition to the destitution of the main army, causing the insurrections in the Pennsylvania and New-Jersey lines, so wretchedly supplied were the small garrisons from Albany northward and westward, both in respect to food and clothing, that it was only with the utmost difficulty that the officers could keep the soldiers upon duty. Ravaged as the whole Mohawk country had been the preceding Summer and Autumn, no supplies could be drawn from the diminished and impoverished inhabitants remaining in those settlements; while it was equally difficult to procure supplies, either at Albany or below, or eastwardly beyond that city. It is painful to read the private correspondence of General Schuyler, and Governor and General Clinton upon this subject. Orders for impressing provisions were freely issued, particularly against the disaffected portion of the people, who had greatly increased in numbers in that section of the country; but some of the supplies thus taken were returned, from the knowledge of General Schuyler that they had nothing more for their own support. Meantime, emboldened by his successes the preceding year, the enemy hung around the skirts of the settlements, approaching almost beneath the very guns of the forts, cutting off all communication with them, unless by means of strong escorts, so that it was difficult and often impossible even to throw such scanty supplies into the garrisons as could be obtained.

The Oneidas having been driven from their country the preceding year, even the slight barrier against irruptions from the more western tribes, who were all hostile, into the Mohawk country, afforded by that slender people, was gone. On the 15th of January, the scouts of Thayendanegea appeared openly in the German Flatts, and attacked some of the inhabitants. During the months of February and March, Brant was hovering about the Mohawk, ready to spring upon every load of supplies destined for Forts Plain, Dayton, and Schuyler, not too strongly guarded, and cutting off every straggling soldier or inhabitant so unfortunate as to fall within his grasp.

On the 6th of March, Major Nicholas Fish wrote to General Clinton, from Schenectady, informing him that a party of fifteen of Colonel Van Cortlandt's regiment, at Fort Schuyler, had fallen into the hands of Brant's Indians; and on the 2d of April, in moving to the neighborhood of that fort, to cut off another escort of supplies, the same lynx-eyed chieftain made prisoners of another detachment from that garrison of sixteen men. The difficulty of transporting the provisions, however, the unbeaten snow lying to a great depth, had so greatly retarded the progress of the scouts, that the intrepid warrior was disappointed in this portion of the spoils, having, as it subsequently appeared, attempted to strike too soon.

But the hunted Oneidas, notwithstanding the neutrality of the greater part of them, were not altogether safe in their new position near Schenectady. It seems to have chafed both Brant and his employers, that a single tribe of Indians had been detached from their influence or service; and their destruction was again seriously meditated, with the sanction of Sir Frederick Haldimand, as will more fully appear by the annexed letter from Colonel Daniel Claus, the brother-in-law of Sir John Johnson, to Captain Brant.

COLONEL CLAUS TO CAPTAIN BRANT.

"*Montreal, 3d March,* 1781.

" DEAR JOSEPH,

" Captain John Odeserundiye, about a month ago, showed me a letter he received from you, with a proposal to him about the Oneidas, telling me he had answered you that he would join you with his party about the 20th of this month, desiring me at the same time to keep it a secret from the Mohawk Indians and others, for fear of being made public; he then asked me where the Oneidas now lived, which then I could not tell him; but since that I was informed that the rebels had posted themselves at a place called Palmerstown, about twelve or fifteen miles west of Saraghtoga, of which I acquainted His Excellency General Haldimand, together with your intentions and plan; whereupon I received His Excellency's answer enjoining the utmost secrecy to me, and which I hereby give you in the words of his letter, by Captain Mathews his secretary, and is the occasion of this express.

" His Excellency, General Haldimand, commands me to ac-
" quaint you that Captain Brant's intention meets highly with
" his approbation, and wishes to assist it; which might be done
" from this place in the following manner, but the General de-
" sires you will keep it inviolably secret. He has for some time
" intended sending a party of about sixty chosen loyalists, under
" the command of Major Jessup, toward Fort Edward: this party
" might join Joseph against Palmerstown could he ascertain the
" time and place, which might be nearly done by calculating the

" time his express would take to come from Carleton Island—his
" march from thence, and Major Jessup's from Point au Fez,
" alias Nikadiyooni. If Joseph wishes to have this assistance,
" he must confer with Major Ross, who will send off an active
" express; otherwise, if Joseph should prefer aid from that quar-
" ter, Major Ross and Captain Robertson are directed to afford
" it; and, indeed, the delays and uncertainty of the parties join-
" ing punctually, incline the General to think it more eligible."

" Should you upon this adopt the General's offer and opinion,
and proceed from Carleton Island to Palmerstown, which place
I am sure several of Major Ross's men and others at the island
are well acquainted with, I wish you the aid of Providence with
all the success imaginable; in which case it will be one of the
most essential services you have rendered your king this war,
and cannot but by him be noticed and rewarded; your return
by Canada will be the shortest and most eligible, and we shall
be very happy to see you here. As I received the General's
letter this afternoon only, I could not speak with Odeserundiye,
but have wrote to him by express to let you know the precise
time he intends meeting you. Mrs. Claus and all friends are well
here, and salute you heartily; also your sister and daughters;
the others here are well, and desire their love and duty. I hope
she received the things safe which I sent lately by Anna.
Adieu. God bless and prosper you.

" Yours most sincerely,
" DAN'L. CLAUS.

" *Captain Brant.*

" P. S. The great advantage of setting out from Carleton
Island, is the route, which is so unexpected a one, that there is
hardly any doubt but you will surprise them, which is a great
point gained. Whereas, were you to set out from Canada, there
are so many friends, both whites and Indians, to the rebel cause,
that you could not well get to the place undiscovered, which
would not do so well. D. C."

Happily, from some cause now unknown, this project, so well
devised, and apparently so near its maturity, was never executed.
The narrative is therefore resumed.

So great, and so universal, was the distress for provisions, already adverted to, that, on the 29th of March, General Clinton wrote to the Governor, " I am hourly under apprehensions that " the remaining different posts occupied for the defence of the " frontiers of this State, will be abandoned, and the country " left open to the ravages of the enemy." Such continued suffering of course produced disaffection in this department also ; and the greatest possible prudence was required, on the part of the officers, to prevent desertions of whole bodies. So critical was their situation, that in a letter to the Governor, of May 3d, General Clinton mentions the fact, that a small scout, commanded by a corporal, in the neighborhood of Fort George, having captured a party of the enemy, " with a packet, had been bribed to " release them for a guinea each and two silk handkerchiefs." Still worse than this was the fact that the General was afraid to proceed openly to punish the delinquency. On the 5th General Clinton again wrote to the Governor—" From the present ap- " pearance, I am convinced that the troops will abandon the " frontier. It is absurd to suppose they can or will exist under " the present circumstances. However, let what will be the " consequences, I have nothing to reproach myself with. I have " repeatedly called for assistance from every quarter, but could " obtain none." On the 8th of May, General Schuyler, writing from Saratoga, said—" I wrote you this morning, since which, " finding the troops exceedingly uneasy, Colonel Van Vechten " and I turned out each one of the best cattle we had ; the meat " proved better than was expected, but the soldiers still continue " troublesome ; they have hung part of it on a pole with a red " flag above a white one, and some of them hold very alarming " conversation. I dread the consequences, as they can so easily " join the enemy. If a body of nine-months men were here, it " would probably deter the others from going off to the north- " ward, [the enemy meaning,] if they should have such an in- " tention."

Great blame was imputed to Congress, and likewise to the State governments, for allowing the commissariat to come to such a deplorable pass. The resources of the country were known to be abundant for the comfortable sustenance of a much larger army than was at that time in the field ; but the efficient action of Congress was fettered by its want of power. The States, jealous of their own sovereignty, had withholden from

the central government powers which were essential to the vigorous prosecution of the war, while it was but seldom that they
could be brought into a simultaneous and harmonious exertion
of those powers themselves.   Hence the frequent and keen distresses of the army, and the complicated embarrassments under
which the officers were compelled to struggle during the whole
war.   Still, the blame did not rest wholly with the States.
There were jealousies, and heart-burnings, and intrigues, in the
Congresses of that day, as in later times ; and their conduct was
often the subject of bitter complaint in the letters of the Commander-in-chief.   The following letter from General Schuyler
bears hard upon the officers of the federal government, while at
the same time it depicts the extreme destitution of the country
at the north, at the period under consideration :—

GENERAL SCHUYLER TO GENERAL CLINTON.

" *Saratoga, May* 13th, 1781.

" DEAR SIR,

" Your favor of the 8th instant, Captain Vernon delivered me
last evening.   The distress occasioned by the want of provisions in every quarter is truly alarming, but was the natural
consequence of such a system as was adopted for supplying the
army.   It is probable, if we should be able to continue the war
ten years longer, that our rulers will learn to conduct it with
propriety and economy ; at present they are certainly ignoramus-
es.   Not a barrel of meat or fish is to be had in this quarter
if an equal weight of silver was to be offered for it, and as there
is not above a quarter of the flour or wheat sufficient for the
use of the inhabitants, it would be needless to appoint persons
here to impress those articles.   I therefore return the blank
warrants.

" It is probable that some flour may be obtained in the neighborhood of Schaghticoke, and *I am certain* that a very considerable quantity of both wheat and flour is lodged in Albany.
Major Lush could employ his assistant at the former place, and
he might impress all at the latter *without much trouble.*   A
small collection of meat has been made at Stillwater for the
troops here, but that is already expended.   If there is any beef
at Richmond, or Barrington, I think it would be well to send a
party of nine-months men under an active spirited officer, to im-

press a number of wagons at Kinderhook and Claverack, and to attend them to the former places, and back again to the respective landings of the latter on Hudson's river. If an opportunity offers, pray send me some paper, as this is my last sheet. Captain Arson is not yet returned from Jessup's.

"I am, dear Sir,

"Yours sincerely, &c. &c.

"PH. SCHUYLER.

"*Gen. Clinton.*"

It was, indeed, a trying situation for brave and patriotic officers to find themselves in command of troops, driven, by destitution, to the very point of going over to the enemy almost in a body. But another disheartening occurrence was at hand. The works of Fort Schuyler, having become much out of repair, sustained great injury by the swelling of the waters in the early part of May. A council of officers was convened by Lt. Colonel Cochran, then in command, on the 12th of that month, to inquire and report what should be done in the premises. The council represented that more than two-thirds of the works had been broken down by the flood, and that the residue would be in the same condition in a very few days; that the only remaining strength of the fort was to be found in the outside pickets on the glacis; and that the strength of the garrison was altogether inadequate to attempt to rebuild or repair the works, for which purpose five or six hundred men, with an engineer, artificers, &c. would be indispensably necessary.

But even if the works were not altogether indefensible on the 12th, they were rendered so on the following day, when all that had been spared by the deluge was destroyed by fire. Intelligence of this disaster was received by General Clinton at Albany, on the 16th, in a letter from Colonel Cochran. The following is an extract from General Clinton's reply to that officer, from which it appears a strong suspicion was entertained that the conflagration was the work of design—a suspicion that was never removed:—"I have just received your favors of the 13th "and 14th instants, with the disagreeable intelligence contained "in them. I cannot find words to express my surprise at the "unexpected accident, or how a fire should break out at noon- "day, in a garrison where the troops could not possibly be ab-

"sent, after a most violent and incessant rain of several days,
"and be permitted to do so much damage. I am sorry to say
"that the several circumstances which accompanied this melan-
"choly affair, afford plausible ground for suspicion that it was
"not the effect of mere accident. I hope, when it comes to be
"examined in a closer point of view, such lights may be thrown
"upon it as will remove the suspicion, for which there appears
"too much reason. I have written to his Excellency on the sub-
"ject, and requested his farther orders, which I expect in a few
"days; in the meantime I would request that you keep pos-
"session of the works, and endeavor to shelter the troops in the
"best manner possible."

In his letter to the Governor, enclosing the dispatches of
Colonel Cochran, General Clinton suggested the expediency,
under the circumstances of the case, of abandoning the post
altogether, and falling back upon Fort Herkimer. On the following day he again wrote to his brother, renewing and re-en-
forcing this suggestion :—

GENERAL CLINTON TO THE GOVERNOR.

"*Albany, May 17th,* 1781.

"DEAR SIR,

"Since my last to you of yesterday, another letter, by express,
has been received from Fort Schuyler. Copies of the contents
I enclose for your information, under cover, which I wish you
to seal and forward to the Commander-in-chief. I informed you
yesterday of the general prevailing opinion among the better
part of the people in this quarter respecting Fort Schuyler.
The recent loss of the barracks, and the ruinous situation of the
works, have confirmed them in the propriety and even necessity
of removing it to the German Flatts near Fort Herkimer, where
they are disposed to afford every assistance in their power to
build a formidable work, confident that it will be able to afford
more protection, not only in that particular quarter, but also to the
whole western frontier in general. I must confess that I have
long since been of this opinion. I have not mentioned this circumstance to the General, [Washington,] as I conceive it will
come better from yourself, as you are acquainted with every
particular circumstance respecting it, and the numberless difficulties which we shall labor under in putting it in any considera-

ble state of defence. As I have directed the troops to remain in possession of the works until I shall receive instructions from head-quarters, I wish that you might have it in your power to have a conference with the General on the subject, and transmit to me the result of it without delay.

"I am, Sir, &c.

"JAS. CLINTON.

"*Governor Clinton.*"

This suggestion was adopted, and the post so long considered the key to the Mohawk Valley was abandoned.*

In addition to this disheartening state of affairs at the westward of Albany, intelligence was received that another storm was about breaking upon the northern frontier. In a letter from General Schuyler to General Clinton, from Saratoga, May 18th, after speaking of the "chagrin" he felt at the destruction of the fort, Schuyler proceeds :—

"Last evening Major McCracken of White Creek came here, and delivered me a copy of a paper which had been found *there*, in the same hand-writing as one that was put in the same place last year, announcing the approach of Major Carleton with the troops under his command. This contains in substance— 'That the writer had received a letter from a friend in Canada, ' to give him notice of the danger which threatened these parts ; ' that 1500 men were gone to Ticonderoga, from whence they ' were to proceed to Fort Edward and White Creek ; that they ' are to be down in this month, and from what he could learn, ' they were to desolate the country.' The Major thinks he knows the channel through which this intelligence is conveyed, and that it may be depended upon ;—as it in some degree corroborates that given by Harris, and the person I had sent to Crown Point, it ought not to be slighted. Please to communicate it to the Governor and General Washington.

"Fourteen of the nine months men have already deserted, two of whom are apprehended. There are now at this post only thirty-nine of them. As the Continental troops here are without shoes, it is impossible to keep out the necessary scouts. Can-

---

* After the war the fort was rebuilt, and the ancient name of Fort Stanwix restored. The works were repaired and essentially strengthened, as being an important post, during the administration of the elder Adams.

not a parcel of shoes be obtained at Albany, and sent up to them?
It will be of importance to give the earliest intelligence if the
party discovered by Colonel Lewis should appear on the Mohawk river, that we may with the troops here, and what militia
we may be able to collect, try to intercept them."

In a postscript to a letter of the 21st, General Schuyler observed :—" Since the above I have been informed *from very*
" *good authority,* that the enemy's morning and evening guns
" at Ticonderoga have been distinctly heard near Fort Anne
" for three or four days past." And on the 24th the General
wrote more confidently still of the enemy's approach. " Captain
" Gray is returned. He has not been near enough to deter-
" mine the enemy's force, but sufficiently so to discover, by the
" fires, that they are numerous. Is it not strange, and subject
" of suspicion, that the Vermonters should not afford us any
" intelligence of the enemy's approach, as they must certainly
" know of his arrival at Crown Point and Ticonderoga?"*

This was alarming intelligence, more especially when taken
in connexion with the reports simultaneously coming in from
the west, of an expedition meditated against Pittsburgh, to be
led by Sir John Johnson and Colonel Connelly ; while other
reports were rife, at the same time, of more extensive combina-
tions among the hostile Indians than had previously marked
the war. But even this was not all—nor by any means the
worst of the case. Treachery was at work, and from the temper of great numbers of the people, the carriage of the disaffected, and the intelligence received by means of spies and
intercepted despatches, there was just cause to apprehend that,
should the enemy again invade the country, either from the
north or the west, his standard would be joined by much larger
numbers of the people than would have rallied beneath it at
any former period. The poison was actively at work even
in Albany. On the 24th of May, General Schuyler announced
to General Clinton the return of a confidental agent from the

---

* This ambiguous conduct of Vermont was the consequence of the quarrel between the settlers of the grants from New Hampshire, which were within the chartered limits, and the government of New-York. Colonel Allen, not long before,
had been in Albany upon the business of the settlers, and had gone away dissatisfied
—having uttered a threat on his departure. He was at this time, as General Schuyler was informed, at the Isle Au Noix—sick—as was pretended.

north, "where he met with five of the enemy, whose confi-
" dence he so far obtained as to be entrusted with letters written
" on the spot to persons at Albany, whose names I forbear to
" mention," (says Schuyler,) " for fear of accidents. They con-
" tained nothing material, except the arrival of the enemy in
" force at Crown Point and Ticonderoga, with this expression
" in one,—' We shall make rare work with the rebels.' " But
other, and more " material" despatches were soon afterward intercepted, from the tenor of which the conclusion was irresist-
ible, not only that a powerful invasion was about taking place
from the north, but that very extensive arrangements had been
made in Albany, and the towns adjacent, for the reception of
the invaders, whose standard the disaffected were to join, and
whose wants they were to supply. Among the papers thus intercepted, was the following letter, supposed to have been addressed to General Haldimand :—

" *Albany, 9th May,* 1781.

" Your Excellency may learn from this that when I received
your instructions, &c., I was obliged at that time to put myself
into a place of security, as there were heavy charges laid against
me. I thank God I have baffled that storm. Your commands are observed to the letter, part of them faithfully executed, the particulars of which I hope in a short time to have
the honor to acquaint you verbally. Now is the season to strike
a blow on this place, when multitudes will join, provided a considerable force comes down. The sooner the attempt is made
the better. Let it be rapid and intrepid, carefully avoiding to
sour the inhabitants' tempers by savage cruelties on their defenceless families. If a few handbills, intimating pardon, protection, &c. &c. were sent down, and distributed about this part of
the country, they would effect wonders ; and should your Excellency think proper to send an army against this den of per-
secutors, notice ought to be given ten days before, by some careful and intelligent person, to a certain Mr. McPherson in Ball's
Town, who will immediately convey the intention to the well-
affected of New Scotland, Norman's Kill, Hillbarack's, Nes-
kayuna, &c., all in the vicinity of Albany. The plan is already
fixed, and should a formidable force appear, I make no doubt provisions and other succors will immediately take place. A few lines

of comfort, in print, from your Excellency to those people, would make them the more eager in prosecuting their designs ; and if the Vermonters lie still, as I have some hopes they will, there is no fear of success.   No troops are yet raised.   There is a flag from this place shortly to be sent ; perhaps I may go with it ; I expected before this time I would ' be removed from my present situation,' &c.

" 25th May. N. B. This I expected should reach you before now, but had no opportunity.   Excuse haste." *

Accompanying this letter were several pages of memoranda, in the same hand-writing, giving particular information upon every point which the enemy could desire.   The deplorable situation of Albany, and the whole Mohawk country, was described ; the temper of the people in the towns around Albany and elsewhere set forth ; the strength of the main army in the Highlands given with all necessary accuracy ; and the mission of Ethan Allen to Albany, and the probable defection of Vermont, announced.   Indeed, the character of these communications showed but too plainly that treason was deeply and extensively at work, and that the enemy was, beyond doubt, correctly advised of the true situation of the country.†

Under all these circumstances of internal and external danger—with but slender garrisons at the points of greatest exposure, and those so miserably provided that the soldiers were deserting by dozens, showing dispositions not equivocal of going over to the enemy—without provisions or the means of procuring them, and scarcely knowing whom to trust among their own people, lest the disaffection should prove to be even more exten-

---

* This document has been discovered by the author among the papers of General Clinton. It is endorsed as follows :—" A copy of a letter in Doctor Smyth's hand-writing, supposed to General Haldimand. Intercepted 27th of May, 1781." The author has not been able to ascertain who Doctor Smith was, farther than that he has been informed at Albany, that he was a brother to Smith the historian of New-York, afterward Chief Justice of New Brunswick.   Some time afterward Governor Clinton transmitted a special message to the legislature, then sitting at Poughkeepsie, containing important information respecting the designs of the Vermonters, by which it appears that Dr. Smith was actively engaged in fomenting disaffection in that quarter, and had held interviews with Ethan Allen upon the subject in Albany, &c.   Smith is spoken of in that message as having been appointed a Commissioner by the British officers to treat with the Vermonters.

† See Apendix, No. II.

sive than recent disclosures had taught the officers to suppose,—the Spring of 1781 may well be counted as the darkest period of the revolution. Had it not been for the gleams of light shooting up from the south, all indeed would have been sullen blackness, if not despair. But the truth of the homely adage, that the darkest hour is always just before day, received a glorious illustration before the close of the year. "Accustomed to contem- "plate all public events which might grow out of the situation "of the United States, and to prepare for them while at a dis- "tance, the American chief was not depressed by this state of "affairs. With a mind happily tempered by nature and im- "proved by experience, those fortunate events which had occa- "sionally brightened the prospects of his country, never relaxed "his exertions or lessened his precautions ; nor could the most "disastrous state of things drive him to despair."* Fortunately, in the Clintons and their associate officers at the north, the American Commander had subordinates possessing in no small degree the same great characteristics. Every possible precaution against lurking treason within, was taken, and every practicable means of preparation and defence against invasion from abroad, was adopted.

Anticipating, from the presence of the enemy at Ticonderoga, that Tryon county might again be attacked from that direction by the way of the Sacondaga, Captain John Carlisle was despatched into the settlements of New Galway, Peasley, and Ballston, accompanied by Captain Oothout and a small party of Indians, to make prisoners of certain persons suspected of disaffection to the American cause, and to remove all the families from those towns to the south side of the Mohawk river. About sixty families were thus removed, and all the suspected persons arrested. The Captain, in his report of the expedition, gave a deplorable account of the poverty of the people. He could scarcely procure subsistence for his party during his mission. On arriving at Ballston, however, he drew more liberally upon the stores of the disaffected, and then arrested them. But their disposition, Captain Oothout was glad to inform the Commission- ers, was such as to "prevent his setting fire to their houses agreeably to the letter of his orders."† Happily these measures

* Marshall.

† Manuscripts of Gen. Clinton. Indeed, the materials for this whole section of

of precaution, and the other preparations, were for that time unnecessary—the enemy, if he was in actual force at Crown Point or Ticonderoga, not then venturing another invasion from that quarter.

But the Mohawk Valley was continually harassed by the Indians and Tories—even to the very precincts of the stockades and other small fortifications. The spirit of the people had in a great measure been crushed, and the militia broken down, during the repeated invasions of the preceding year. The Rev. Daniel Gros,* writing to General Clinton from Canajoharie, upon the importance of having at least a small detachment of regular troops at Fort Rensselaer, observed—" It would serve to bring " spirit, order, and regularity into our militia, where authority " and subordination have vanished. If it should last a little " longer, the shadow of it will dwindle away ; and perhaps the " best men in the state will be useless spectators of all the havoc " the enemy is meditating against the country. The militia ap- " pears to me to be a body without a soul. Drafts from the " neighboring counties, even of the levies under their own com- " manders, will not abate the fatal symptoms, but rather serve to " produce a monster with as many heads as there are detach- " ments." Having no other defenders than such as are here described, with the exception of a few scattered companies, or rather skeletons of companies, at the different posts extending along the Valley, the prospect of the opening Summer was indeed gloomy—more especially when men's thoughts reverted to the sufferings of the past. Nor were the inhabitants encouraged to expect any considerable reinforcements from head-quarters, since the Commander-in-chief, in concert with the Count de Rochambeau, was again evidently preparing for some enterprise of higher moment than the defence of those remote settlements against any force that could be brought down upon them from the north.

Still, there was one officer whose name, among the people of that district, was a tower of strength. That man was Colonel Marinus Willett ; who, at the consolidation of the five New-York

the northern history of the Spring of 1781, have principally been drawn from the Clinton papers, so often referred to.

* Afterward a Professor in Columbia College, and author of a work on Moral Philosophy.

regiments into two—an event happening at about the same time—was induced by the strong solicitation of Governor Clinton to take the command of all the militia levies and State troops that might be raised for the protection of the country. It was only with great reluctance that Colonel Willett was persuaded to leave the main army, and enter upon this difficult and hazardous service. But the appeal of Governor Clinton was so strong, and enforced with so much earnestness, that he could not resist it. The Governor urged the high confidence reposed in him by the people of Tryon county—and reminded him of the cruelties of the Indians and Tories—speaking of the latter with great emphasis, as " cruel monsters worse than savages ;"* and Colonel Willett, feeling a hearty good-will to chastise such an enemy—the Tories especially—repaired to the north, and assumed the command. He arrived at Fort Rensselaer (Canajoharie), where he established his head-quarters, toward the close of June. The country he was to defend embraced all the settlements west of the county of Albany, including Catskill and the Hudson river. A fortnight after his arrival he ascertained that the following skeleton detachments composed the full complement of the forces under his command : one hundred and thirty levies, including officers, and Captain Moody's artillery, numbering twelve men, at the German Flatts ; at Schoharie he stationed a guard of twenty men ; at Catskill about the same number, and about thirty men at Ballston. Exclusive of these diminutive fragments of corps, stationed at great distances apart, the levies of the county amounted to no more than ninety-six men. In a letter to Governor Clinton, making known the paucity of his numbers, Colonel Willett added :—" I confess myself not a little dis-" appointed in having such a trifling force for such extensive " business as I have on my hands ; and also that nothing is done " to enable me to avail myself of the militia. The prospect of " a suffering country hurts me. Upon my own account I am " not uneasy. Every thing I can do, shall be done ; and more " cannot be looked for. If it is, the reflection that I have done my " duty, must fix my own tranquillity."†

Depressed, however, as were the people, and inefficient as, from the preceding descriptions, the militia must have become,

---

* Willett's Narrative.   † Idem.

these circumstances were, no doubt, in a great degree attributable to the want of officers in whom the people could repose confidence.   Colonel Willett had very soon an opportunity to make trial of their spirit, and he found them " a people who, having " experienced no inconsiderable portion of British barbarism, " were become keen for revenge and properly determined."* The occasion was the following :—On the 30th of June, several columns of smoke were discovered by the garrison of Fort Rensselaer, ascending as from a village on fire, in the direction of Currietown, lying eleven miles down the river, near the estuary of the Schoharie-kill.   Having previously sent forth a scout of thirty men, commanded by Captain Gross, to patrol the country south as far as a settlement called Durlagh,† an express was despatched to overtake that officer, with information of the probable presence of the enemy below, and with instructions, if possible, to fall upon his trail.   Meantime Captain M'Kean was ordered to Currietown, with sixteen levies only, but with instructions to collect as many of the militia in his way as possible.   Such was the celerity of M'Kean's movements, that he arrived at Currietown so soon after it had been ravaged and deserted by the enemy, as to enable him to assist in quenching the fires of some of the yet unconsumed buildings.   Colonel Willett was himself actively employed during the day in collecting the militia, while, through the vigilance of Captain Gross, not only the trail of the Indians was discovered, but the place of their encampment. Having reason to suppose they would occupy the same encampment that night, and being joined before evening by the detachments of Gross and M'Kean, the Colonel determined, with these forces, and such few militia-men as he had been able to collect, to march directly for the encampment, and, if possible, take them by surprise before morning—perhaps while asleep.   This encampment was in a thick cedar swamp, five or six miles to the north-east of Cherry Valley, and of course to reach it by a march through the woods, during an exceedingly dark night, and without any better road than a bridle-path, was no small undertaking.   It had been ascertained that the Indians numbered between two and three hundred, commanded by a Tory named John Doxstader, in connexion with an Indian

* Letter of Colonel Willett to General Washington.
† Sometimes spelt Turlock.   Now the town of Sharon, Schoharie County.

chief named Quackyack.   Colonel Willett's strength, levies and
militia included, did not exceed one hundred and fifty rank and
file.   The plan of falling upon the enemy while asleep did
not exactly succeed, in consequence of the difficulties of the
march—occasioned by the darkness, the thickness of the woods,
and, worse than all, the losing of his way by the guide.   It was
therefore nearly six o'clock in the morning when they arrived
in the vicinity of the encampment ; and, instead of falling upon
the enemy by surprise, they found him occupying a more favorable situation, and awaiting their reception.   Immediate dispositions were made to engage the enemy, with a view to which
a stratagem was laid to draw him from the advantageous situation which he had chosen.   For this purpose, before the Indians had become fully aware of Willett's near approach, Jacob
Sammons, now a lieutenant in the New-York levies, was detached with ten resolute men, to steal as near to them as possible, give them one well-directed fire, and retreat.   The *ruse*
succeeded.   Sammons and his men turned their backs on the
first yell of the Indians, and the latter sprang forward in pursuit.*   They were soon met by Colonel Willett in person, advancing at the head of his main division, which consisted of one
hundred men, while Captain M'Kean was left with fifty more
as a reserve, to act as occasion might require, on the right.   The
enemy did not wait an attack, however, but, with great appearance of determination, advanced with their wonted shouts
and yells, and began the fire.   The onset of the Indians was
furious ; but they were received with firmness, and in turn the
Americans advanced upon them with loud huzzas, and such
manifestations of spirit as soon caused them to give way.   Simultaneously with their attack upon the main body in front, the
Indians had made an equally desperate rush upon the right
wing, which might have been attended with disaster, but for
the destructive fire poured in upon them by the reserve of
M'Kean.   The Indians, thus driven back, now betook themselves to their old game of firing from behind the trees ; but
Willett's men understood that mode of fighting as well as themselves.   They did not, however, practise it long.   Willett
pressed forward waving his hat and cheering his men—calling

* MS. narrative of Jacob Sammons.

out that he could catch in his hat all the balls that the enemy might send ; and in the same breath exclaiming, " the day is our's, my boys !"   These inspiriting demonstrations being followed up by a timely and efficient use of the bayonet, the whole body of the enemy was put to flight in half an hour after the commencement of the action.   They retreated upon their old path down the Susquehanna, and were pursued to a considerable distance.   Their camp was, of course, taken, and the plunder they had gathered recaptured.   The loss of the Indians was severe—nearly forty of their dead being left on the field.   Colonel Willett's loss was five killed, and nine wounded and missing.   Among the wounded was the brave Captain M'Kean, fatally.   He received two balls early in the engagement, but kept at his post until it was over, and the rout of the enemy complete.*

There was one very painful circumstance attending this battle.   In their excursion to Currietown, the day before, Doxstader and his Indians had made nine prisoners, among whom were Jacob and Frederick Diefendorff, Jacob Myers and a son, a black boy, and four others.   The moment the battle commenced, the prisoners, who were bound to standing trees for security, were tomahawked and scalped by their captors, and left as dead.   The bodies of these unfortunate men were buried by Colonel Willett's troops.   Fortunately, however, the graves were superficial, and the covering slight—a circumstance which enabled Jacob Diefendorff, who, though stunned and apparently dead, was yet alive, to disentomb himself.   A detachment of militia, under Colonel Veeder, having repaired to the field of action after Willett had returned to Fort Rensselaer, discovered the supposed deceased on the outside of his own grave ; and he has lived to furnish the author of the present work with an account of his own burial and resurrection.†

Captain M'Kean died, greatly lamented, a few days after the detachment had returned to the fort, as will be seen by the annexed letter, addressed by Colonel Willett to the commanding officer at Albany :—

* Willett's Narrative—Campbell.

† Statements of Jacob Diefendorff and Jacob Sammons, in the author's possession.

COLONEL WILLETT TO GENERAL CLINTON.

" SIR :—I have just sent some of the wounded levies to Schenectady, there being no surgeon here. Doctor Petrie, the surgeon of the levies, is at German Flatts, where he has several
sick and wounded to attend ; and the intercourse between here
and there is too dangerous to allow travelling without a guard.
I could wish, therefore, to have a surgeon from the hospital posted
in this quarter.

" This place does not afford a gill of rum to bathe a single
wound. The two barrels designed for this quarter a few days
ago, met with a regular regiment passing down the country, who
very irregularly took away from the person that had them in charge
those two barrels of rum. I need not mention to you, Sir, that
the severe duty and large portion of fatigue that falls to the lot
of the troops in this quarter, make rum an article of importance
here, and that I should be glad to see some in the County of
Tryon.

" This morning Captain M'Kean died of the wound he received yesterday. In him we have lost an excellent officer. I
feel his loss, and must regret it."*

Shortly after the irruption of Doxstader, there was another
descent of Indians and Tories upon Palatine, which was an
event of more singularity than importance. A son of Colonel
Jacob Klock, with several of his Tory friends, went off to Canada. He returned in about four weeks with a band of Indians
and Tories to fall upon the settlement, and encamped for one
night in the vicinity of his own neighborhood. During the
night, one of the number, Philip Helmer, having discovered that
a part of their object was to plunder and murder the family of
his relative, John Bellinger, determined to save that family.
Taking a young Indian with him, therefore, under the pretext
of reconnoitring the settlement, he proceeded so near to some of
the houses, that the Indian, becoming suspicious, ran back to
his comrades. Helmer's object was to surrender himself, and
cause the Indian to be taken prisoner ; and he accordingly delivered himself up to Judge Nellis. Expresses were immediately
sent to Fort Plain and Stone Arabia for assistance ; and the
enemy, finding themselves betrayed, took to the woods. Lieu-

* Clinton papers.

tenant Sammons, with twenty-five men, was ordered by Colonel Willett to go in pursuit; and so rapid were they of foot, as to arrive at the enemy's encampment before his fires had gone out. William Feeter, with six other volunteers, was sent forward to keep his trail. In about two miles after entering the woods, most luckily they discovered a number of the Indians lying flat upon the ground. The latter no sooner discerned Feeter's approach, than they rose and fired; but one of their number having fallen grievously wounded by the return fire of Feeter's party, while they were stooping down to re-load, they sprang to their feet and fled—Tories and all—leaving their provisions, knapsacks, and some of their muskets. They ran down a steep hill, and were measurably shielded from Feeter's fire by the thickness of the shrubbery and trees. One of them gave himself up as a prisoner; three more were wounded, and died on their way to Canada. The poor Indian first wounded, was put to death by Helmer, who ran up and despatched him while he was begging for quarter!*

Colonel Willett took early occasion to make the Commander-in-chief acquainted with the deplorable situation to which this fine region of country had been reduced by the repeated visitations of the enemy. In his letter to General Washington upon the subject, he describes the beauty, the productiveness, and the natural advantages of the country with a glowing pen. From this communication it appears, that at the commencement of the war, the number of enrolled militia in Tryon county amounted to not less than two thousand five hundred; but at the date of the letter, (July 6, 1781,) the number of inhabitants liable to pay taxes, or to be assessed to raise men for the public service, was estimated at no more than twelve hundred; while the number liable to bear arms did not exceed eight hundred. To account for so large a reduction of the population, it was estimated that one-third had been killed or made prisoners; one-third had gone over to the enemy; and one-third, for the time being, had abandoned the country. The situation of those that remained, the Colonel described as so distressing as to provoke sympathy from even the most unfeeling heart. Those who could afford

---

* Narrative of Colonel William Feeter, in the author's possession, and also of Jacob Sammons. Colonel Feeter is yet living, (1837.)

the expense, or perform the labor, had erected block-houses on their own farms, for the protection of their families. Each neighborhood had been compelled to erect a fortification for itself, within which their families resided for safety—from ten to fifty families crowding together in a fort. Of these works there were twenty-four between Schenectady and Fort Schuyler. At the time of writing this letter—or rather memoir, for the communication was extended through several sheets—Colonel Willett stated that the whole number of men then under his command, exclusive of the militia, did not exceed two hundred and fifty. But he, nevertheless, kept up a good heart, and in the course of his anticipations of bringing about a better state of things, added—" Nor shall I exceed my hopes, if, in the course of less " than twelve months, I shall be able to convince the enemy that " they are not without vulnerable quarters in these parts." The following quotation will illustrate alike the wisdom, the activity, and the skill of the dispositions made by Willett, for the purpose not only of bringing order out of confusion, but of displaying his strength before an invisible foe, lurking stealthily about in every place of concealment, on all sides and every hand. After stating that he had fixed his head-quarters at Canajoharie, on account of its central position, he proceeds :—" My intention is " to manage business so as to have an opportunity of acquainting " myself, as well as possible, with every officer and soldier I may " have in charge. In order the better to do this, I propose, as far as " I can make it any way convenient, to guard the different posts " by detachments, to be relieved as the nature of the case will " admit. And as the relieved troops will always return to Fort " Rensselaer, where my quarters will be, I shall have an oppor- " tunity of seeing them all in turn. Having troops constantly " marching backward and forward through the country, and " frequently changing their route, will answer several purposes, " such as will easily be perceived by you, sir, without mention- " ing them. This is not the only way by which I expect to be- " come particularly acquainted with the troops and their situa- " tion. I intend occasionally to visit every part of the country, " as well to rectify such mistakes as are common among the kind " of troops I have at present in charge, as to enable me to ob- " serve the condition of the militia, upon whose aid I shall be " under the necessity of placing considerable reliance."

The effect of Colonel Willett's presence and example was very soon perceptible. The people reposed the most unlimited confidence in him; and so rapidly did he infuse something of his own fire and energy into the bosoms even of the dispirited and broken militia, that they presently appeared like a different race of men. An illustration of this fact occurred one night early in July. The Colonel was informed, at the hour of one o'clock in the morning, of the presence of fifty or sixty Indians and Tories in the neighborhood, at only about six miles distance. Having barely troops enough in the fort to guard it, he sent immediately for a Captain of the militia, and in one hour's time that officer was in search of the enemy at the head of seventy men. It is not often that much good results from the employment of militia. Few officers can do any thing with them. Most commanders nothing. But Willett was an exception in those days, as General Jackson has been since. Willett, like Jackson, possessed the faculty, by looking into the eyes of his men, of transfusing his own native fire into their bosoms in spite of themselves.

Fortunately, however, less trouble was experienced from the enemy during the Summer, in the lower section of the Mohawk Valley, than had been anticipated. The summary and severe chastisement inflicted upon Doxstader and his party had a powerful effect upon that irritating branch of the enemy's service; and for more than three months afterward the inhabitants were only troubled occasionally, and then merely by small flying parties of the enemy, who accomplished nothing worthy of record.

But in the upper section of the Valley, the German Flatts, it was otherwise, and several spirited affairs occurred in that neighborhood, attended by great bravery, though not by important consequences. The name of Solomon Woodworth has twice or thrice occurred in the preceding pages; once, as having been taken a prisoner and making his escape, and again as alone defending a block-house north of Johnstown, and repulsing the enemy from his fortress. In the year 1781 he was commissioned a captain, for the purpose of raising a company of rangers to traverse the wooded country north of Fort Dayton and the German Flatts. He succeeded in enlisting a company of forty brave and kindred spirits; at the head of whom, well armed and provided, he marched from Fort Dayton, striking in the direction of the Royal Grant,* for purposes of observation. After a few hours' march, one of Woodworth's men, being a short distance in advance, discovered an Indian, evidently in ambuscade, upon whom he immediately fired. Instantly the forest resounded with the war-whoop, and Woodworth with his little band was surrounded by double his own number. A furious and bloody engagement followed, in which the Rangers and Indians fought hand to hand with great desperation; and, for the numbers engaged, there was cruel slaughter. A fiercer engagement, probably, did not occur during the war. Woodworth fell dead. The savages were the victors; and of the rangers, only fifteen escaped to tell the melancholy fate of their comrades. Several were taken captive, and subsequently exchanged.†

Another affair, as an individual exploit, was as remarkable for its coolness and bravery, as for the singular incident occurring in the course of the battle, or rather siege, by which the leader of the enemy was made to supply ammunition to be used against his own troops. There was, and is to this day, a wealthy German settlement about four miles north of the village of Herkimer, called Shell's Bush. Among those of the settlers who had built block-houses of their own, was John Christian Shell. His stockade was large and substantial, and well calculated for defence. The first story had no windows, but small loop-holes, through which the inmates could fire upon any persons venturing to assail them. The second story projected two or three feet over the first, so constructed that the garrison could either fire upon those who approached too near, or cast down missiles upon their heads. Shell had a family of six sons, the youngest two of whom were twins and but eight years old. In the afternoon of the 6th of August, Donald M'Donald, one of the Scotch refugees who fled from Johnstown, made an attack upon Shell's Bush at the head of a band of sixty-six Indians and Tories, among the latter of whom were two celebrated traitors, named Empie and Kassellman.‡ Most of the inhabitants of Shell's Bush, however, had taken refuge in Fort Dayton—four miles distant; but John Christian Shell, being a sturdy believer in the doctrine

---

* A large tract of land, so called from the fact that it was a grant from the King, under his own sign manual, to Sir William Johnson.

† Manuscripts of the Rev. John I. Shew.

‡ MS. notes of Lauren Ford.

that every man's house is his castle, refused to quit his own domicil. He and his sons were at work in the field when M'Donald and his party made their appearance; and the children were unfortunately separated so widely from their father, as to fall into the hands of the enemy. Shell and his other boys succeeded in reaching their castle, and barricading the ponderous door. And then commenced the battle. The besieged were well armed, and all behaved with admirable bravery; but none more bravely than Shell's wife, who loaded the pieces as her husband and sons discharged them. The battle commenced at two o'clock, and continued until dark. Several attempts were made by M'Donald to set fire to the castle, but without success; and his forces were repeatedly driven back by the galling fire they received. M'Donald at length procured a crow-bar and attempted to force the door; but while thus engaged he received a shot in the leg from Shell's blunderbuss, which put him *hors du combat*. None of his men being sufficiently near at the moment to rescue him, Shell, quick as lightning, opened the door, and drew him within the walls a prisoner. The misfortune of Shell and his garrison was, that their ammunition began to run low; but M'Donald was very amply provided, and to save his own life, he surrendered his cartridges to the garrison to fire upon his comrades. Several of the enemy having been killed and others wounded, they now drew off for a respite. Shell and his troops, moreover, needed a little breathing time; and feeling assured that, so long as he had the commanding officer of the besiegers in his possession, the enemy would hardly attempt to burn the citadel, he ceased firing. He then went up stairs, and sang the hymn which was a favorite of Luther during the perils and afflictions of the Great Reformer in his controversies with the Pope.* While thus engaged, the enemy likewise ceased firing. But they soon afterward rallied again to the fight, and made a desperate effort to carry the fortress by assault. Rushing up to the walls, five of them thrust the muzzles of their guns through the loop-holes, but had no sooner done so, than Mrs. Shell, seizing an axe, by quick and well-directed blows ruined every musket thus thrust through the walls, by bending the barrels! A few

---

* A literal translation of this hymn has been furnished the author by Professor Bokum of Harvard University, which will be found in No. III. of the Appendix.

more well-directed shots by Shell and his sons once more drove the assailants back. Shell thereupon ran up to the second story, just in the twilight, and calling out to his wife with a loud voice, informed her that Captain Small was approaching from Fort Dayton with succors. In yet louder notes he then exclaimed—"Captain Small, march your company round upon this side of the house. Captain Getman, you had better wheel your men off to the left, and come up upon that side." There were, of course, no troops approaching; but the directions of Shell were given with such precision, and such apparent earnestness and sincerity, that the stratagem succeeded, and the enemy immediately fled to the woods, taking away the twin-lads as prisoners.* Setting the best provisions they had before their reluctant guest, Shell and his family lost no time in repairing to Fort Dayton, which they reached in safety—leaving M'Donald in the quiet possession of the castle he had been striving to capture in vain. Some two or three of M'Donald's Indians lingered about the premises to ascertain the fate of their leader; and finding that Shell and his family had evacuated the post, ventured in to visit him. Not being able to remove him, however, on taking themselves off, they charged their wounded leader to inform Shell, that if he would be kind to him, (M'Donald,) they would take good care of his (Shell's) captive boys. M'Donald was the next day removed to the fort by Captain Small, where his leg was amputated; but the blood could not be stanched, and he died in a few hours.† The lads were carried into Canada. The loss of the enemy on the ground was eleven killed and six wounded. The boys, who were rescued after the war, reported that they took twelve of their wounded away with them, nine of whom died before they arrived in Canada.‡

At a subsequent day, Shell, being at work in the field with his two sons at no great distance from the fort, was fired upon by a party of Indians concealed in the standing wheat, and

* One of Shell's neighbors lay in ambush during the battle, and heard Shell's directions to Small and Getman.

† M'Donald wore a silver-mounted tomahawk, which was taken from him by Shell. It was marked by thirty scalp-notches, showing that few Indians could have been more industrious than himself in gathering that description of military trophies.

‡ Among the slain was a white man, who had two thumbs on one hand. One of Shell's sons is yet living in Canada, being a member of the Dunkard's Society, in the neighborhood of Toronto.

severely wounded. He called to his sons not to allow the Indians to scalp him ; and neither of the brave boys would retreat until a guard came from the fort to their relief. But in the discharge of this filial duty, one of them was killed and the other wounded. John Christian Shell himself died of his wound, in the fort. His deeds were commemorated in one of the most rude and prosaic of ballads. But his memory is yet green in the remembrance of the German population of Herkimer.*

The policy of the enemy at the north, during the whole season, was to divide their own forces into small detachments, and harass the border settlements at as many different points as possible—thus distracting the attention of the people, and by allowing them neither a sense of security nor repose, rendering them disgusted with the protracted struggle. The most formidable movement of the Indians and Tories during the Summer months, was the descent of Captain Cauldwell, from Niagara, upon the border of Ulster County, at the head of about four hundred Indians and Tories. The first intelligence of this irruption was received in Albany by General Gansevoort,† by letter, as follows :—

GOVERNOR CLINTON TO GENERAL GANSEVOORT.

"*Poughkeepsie, August* 14, 1781

" SIR,

" Last Sunday, a body of the enemy, to the amount of about three hundred Indians and ninety Tories, appeared on the frontiers of Ulster County. They took a small scout Colonel Paul-

---

* This account of John Christian Shell's exploit has been drawn chiefly from the MS. statement of the venerable Col. William Feeter, yet living in that town, [Feb. 1838,] and from the ballad mentioned in the text, which contains a pathetic and particular recitation of the facts. This use of contemporaneous ballads as authority for facts is well sustained by precedent. Thierry makes bold use of English Norman ballads for his history of the Norman Conquest; and Prescott, in his late invaluable history of the reigns of Ferdinand and Isabella, has done the like with the ancient Castilian romance and Moorish ballad.

† In the re-organization of the army, at the close of the year 1780, Colonel Gansevoort was left out of service in the line, by seniority in rank of other officers. Being a brigadier general of the militia, however, stationed at Albany, his services were in continual requisition, since, in the absence of regular troops, his brigade was the chief dependence of the northern section of the State. His activity in the State service was incessant, and his correspondence with the Governor and the general officers of the regular army at the north, heavier than at any former period. See Appendix, No. IV.

ing had sent out, and from them it is supposed obtained information of the disposition of the levies in that quarter, whom they passed by, and were first discovered at the settlement of Warwasing. From the last accounts they had retired; but how far, is not known. The militia have been collected and marched to oppose or pursue them, as circumstances may render expedient. From their force, it is not probable they will leave the country without attempting farther mischief in that or some other quarter. I conceive it necessary, therefore, to give you this information that you may take proper steps with your militia in case this party should take their route toward the frontier of your county; and I would particularly recommend that a part of your brigade be immediately marched to Schoharie, for the protection of that settlement until this party shall entirely have gone off. The account of the enemy's strength is from one Vrooman, who deserted them; which is confirmed from their appearance to a small party of levies, who saw them paraded at a house they attacked, and which the party defended. By a more particular account received this morning, (and which was the first that demanded credit,) they have burnt and destroyed about a dozen houses, with their barns, &c., among which are those of John G. Hardenburgh, Esq. They killed only one of the inhabitants, the rest having made a timely escape from their houses. The levies stationed there were by no means sufficient to turn out and oppose them; but those who were in the house defended themselves with spirit against the assaults of the enemy, by which means several of them are said to have fallen, and many houses were saved.

"I am, with great esteem,

"Sir, your most obd't serv't,

"GEO. CLINTON.

"*Brig. Gen. Gansevoort.*"*

Captain Cauldwell was an officer in Butler's rangers. Who

---

* Colonel Vrooman, at Schoharie, having heard of the invasion of Ulster County by Cauldwell, wrote a pressing letter to General Gansevoort, for assistance, on the same day that the Governor wrote from Poughkeepsie. Colonel Henry Van Rensselaer was forthwith ordered to Schoharie with his regiment, and Colonel Wemple was directed to send a detachment of his regiment thither, from Schenectady, together with as many of the Oneida Indians as he could engage. Fortunately, their services were not required in action.

was the Indian leader on the occasion, is not known. Their route from Niagara had been by way of the Chemung, and thence, after crossing the Susquehanna, by the Lackawaxen to the Delaware. The stockade forts at the north of the Lacka-waxen, and at Neversink, had been passed unobserved. Luck-ily, however, for the inhabitants, shortly before Cauldwell reached the settlements, a scouting party had descried his ad-vance, and, eluding the enemy's pursuit, had succeeded in com-municating the alarm to the people, who at once fled with their most valuable effects to the picket forts erected for exactly such emergencies.

It was just at the first blush of morning that Cauldwell passed the small fortress on the frontier of Warwasing. Being fired upon by the sentinel, the report alarmed Captain Hardenburgh, who, with a guard of nine men, was stationed at a point about three miles distant from the fort. Proceeding immediately in the direction of the sound, Hardenburgh and his little band met the enemy on his way, directing their course toward the ad-joining settlement of Mombackus—now called Rochester. No-thing daunted, the Captain gave the enemy battle; but being closely pressed, he soon discovered that his retreat had been cut off by a party of Indians, who had gained his rear. In this dilem-ma, it being yet not quite light, Hardenburgh with his party took refuge in a small stone house near by, owned by a Mr. Kettle, which had probably not been observed by the enemy. Here they found six militia-men more—making sixteen in all; and being well armed, they gave the invaders a warm reception. The latter advanced several times to carry the house by assault, but as some of their number were each time doomed to fall, they as often gave way, and in the end relinquished the undertaking—leaving thirteen dead upon the field. In marching forward two miles to Hardenburgh's house, the enemy fell in with Kettle, the owner of the premises where they had been so roughly handled. He, poor fellow, was killed and scalped.*

Captain Henry Pauling, with a detachment of the regiment of State levies commanded by Colonel Albert Pauling, was sta-tioned at a point about six miles distant from the scene of the action just described. He hastened forward, but arrived too

* MS. statement of Captain Valentine Davis, in the author's possession.

late to have a brush with the enemy, and only in season to capture one straggling prisoner who was lingering for fruit in an apple orchard.* Finding his reception rather warm, and perceiving indications of farther and more powerful opposition to his advance, Cauldwell was already in full retreat. Nor did he commence retracing his steps a moment too soon for his own safety. The news of his advance having reached the west bank of the Hudson, where Colonel Pauling, of the State levies, and Colonel John Cantine, with a body of militia, were stationed, those officers marched immediately to the relief of the invaded settlements. They arrived at the outskirts in time to catch a glimpse of the enemy's rear, and to relieve some of the inhabitants, among whom were a man and his wife, who had conducted themselves with distinguished bravery. His house was constructed of unhewn logs, in the woods, and in advance of all others. On the appearance of the foe, he fled to his castle with his wife, and securing it in the best manner he could, gave battle to a party of the Indians who laid siege to his fortress. Being well armed, he defended himself with so much spirit, that they recoiled with loss. Finding, after several attempts, that they could not force an entrance, the Indians collected a heap of combustibles, and set fire to the premises. Retiring a short distance to see the result, the man watched his opportunity, and rushing out with a couple of buckets, he procured water, which was close at hand, and extinguished the fire. The Indians, of course, ran down upon him; but not being quick enough of foot to prevent his gaining the door, hurled their tomahawks at his head—happily without effect. He entered his castle, made fast his sally-port, and re-commenced his defence. Just at this moment Colonel Pauling with his troops appeared in sight, whereupon the Indians raised the siege and departed. Colonel Pauling was absent in pursuit seven days, but did not overtake them. The enemy suffered severely. They lost a goodly number of their men; took only two prisoners and but little plunder; and were so near starvation, that they were compelled to devour their dogs before they reached their head-quarters.†

* MS. of Major Thomas Sammons, who was at this time serving in the corps of Captain Pauling. The prisoner taken from the enemy was recognized as an old neighbor of his father's at Johnstown, who had served in the company of which Jacob Sammons was the lieutenant.   † Major Sammons.

The Shawanese and other western Indians seem to have remained comparatively quiet during the Spring and Summer of 1781. The Kentucky settlements were for the most part unmolested, save by a feeble attack upon M'Afee's station near Harrodsburgh. The assailants, however, were but a straggling party of Indians, who hung about the stockade, and were ultimately punished severely for their temerity. Two of them were killed by an equal number of the M'Afees, whom, having left the fort for some purpose, the Indians attempted to cut off on their return. The Indians then commenced an attack upon the fort, but a party of cavalry arriving suddenly from Harrodsburgh, the garrison sallied forth, and the savages were quickly dispersed, with a loss of six killed outright, and several others, whom they bore away, wounded. A few days afterward, Bryant's station, which was yet more exposed, was visited by the Indians. Bryant, who was a brother-in-law of Colonel Boon, having arranged a large hunting party of twenty men, left his fort on an expedition down the Elk-horn. Having divided his company in order to sweep a broader extent of country for game, by reason of a fog, and other untoward circumstances, they failed of uniting at the points designated. Meantime the Indians were hanging about both divisions, and by stratagem succeeded in defeating both. In one of their skirmishes Bryant was mortally wounded, and another man severely. It was reported that the hunters, taken by surprise, were deficient in firmness, when Bryant fell. On the following day they encountered the Indians again, and defeated them.

CHAPTER VI.

EMBOLDENED by the feeble state of the country, and by the increased numbers of the disaffected in the neighborhood of Albany, especially at the north of that city, in consequence of the equivocal indications in Vermont, the scouting parties of the enemy were exceedingly active and audacious in their incursions. Their chief object was to seize the persons of the most conspicuous and influential inhabitants, for transfer into Canada as prisoners. Among the notable leaders in this species of warfare were two bold partisans, named Joseph Bettys and John Waltermeyer. The daring misdeeds of Bettys, if collected, would of themselves furnish materials for a small volume. Waltermeyer was perhaps equally daring, but less savage in his disposition. In the month of April, a party of fifteen or sixteen of the enemy broke in upon the town of Coxsackie and the contiguous settlements, carrying off several prisoners; among whom were David Abeel and his son, residing a few miles south of Catskill.

At the north of Albany several active citizens were seized and carried away in the course of the season; among whom was Mr. John J. Bleecker, of Tomhanic, whose family had been broken up on the approach of Burgoyne, four years previous. After the surrender of Burgoyne, Mr. Bleecker returned to his sylvan plantation, where he had lived in tranquility until the month of August of the present year; at which time he was surprised in the field, while assisting his laborers in the wheat harvest, and carried away with two of his men. The enemy having stolen upon him in silence, and seized him without permitting an alarm, Mrs. Bleecker was ignorant of the occurrences. But, her husband not returning, as he was wont, on the approach of night, her suspicions were awakened that all was not right. When she sent to the field, he was not there, nor could trace of him or his laborers be found. But as such sudden disappearances were not unusual, his fate was not difficult of conjecture. The neighborhood was alarmed, and search for him made, but in vain. Mrs. Bleecker, overwhelmed with grief, gave him up as lost, and once more set her face for Albany. Fortunately, however, the captors of her husband fell in with a party of militia-men from Bennington, who rescued the prisoners; and Mr. Bleecker had the happiness to rejoin his wife after six days' absence.[*]

An attempt was also made, during the same season, to seize the person of General Gansevoort. Although, as has already been stated, General Gansevoort was no longer in the regular service, yet, as an experienced officer, and the commander of the militia in that part of the state, his services and his counsels were in continual requisition; nor was there a more active officer in the service, regular or irregular, or one more burdened with duties. It was therefore an object with the enemy to remove him from his post if possible. A scheme was therefore devised to seize him at one of the ferries which he was about to cross; the execution of which was entrusted to a hostile partisan named Tanckrey. By some means, however, Colonel Henry Van

---

[*] The joy experienced by Mrs. Bleecker on again beholding her husband, so far overcame her as to bring on a fit of sickness, so severe as nearly to prove fatal. Indeed, the events of 1777, particularly the loss of her daughter, made so deep an impression upon her mind, that she never recovered her happiness. Hence the pensive character of her writings. She died at Tomhanic in 1783, at the early age of 31.

Rensselaer, at Half Moon, obtained information of the project, and lost no time in admonishing the General of his danger by letter. Having also heard of the rendezvous of Tanckrey and his gang, Van Rensselaer despatched a detachment of troops under Major Schermerhorn, for their apprehension. They were found at the house of a Mr. Douglass; but before Schermerhorn's troops had surrounded the house, their approach was discovered, and they were fired upon by the marauders; all of whom, with a single exception, succeeded in getting off through the rear of the house. Two of Schermerhorn's militia were wounded.*

But the boldest enterprise of the kind was the projected abduction of General Schuyler from his residence in Albany, or rather in the suburbs of that city, in the month of August. Schuyler was not at that time in the army, having exchanged the military for the civil-service of his country two years before.† Still, his military exertions were almost as great, and his counsels were as frequently sought and as highly valued, as though he were yet in command of the department. Added to which, he had been specially charged by the Commander-in-chief with the prosecution of all practicable measures for intercepting the communications of the enemy.‡ Aside from this circumstance, the acquisition of a person of his consideration as a prisoner, would have been an important object to Sir Frederick Haldimand, the British Commander in Canada. A desperate effort was therefore resolved upon for his capture. For this purpose John Waltermeyer, the bold and reckless Tory partisan already mentioned,

* MS. Letter of Col. Henry Van Rensselaer to General Gansevoort.

† "It was not until the Autumn of 1778 that the conduct of General Schuyler, in the campaign of 1777, was submitted to the investigation of a court-martial. He was acquitted of every charge with the highest honor, and the sentence was confirmed by Congress. He shortly afterward, upon his earnest and repeated solicitations, had leave to retire from the army, and devoted the remainder of his life to the service of his country in its political councils. He had previously been in Congress, and on his return to that body, after the termination of his military life, his talents, experience, and energy, were put in immediate requisition ; and in November, 1779, he was appointed to confer with General Washington on the state of the southern department. In 1781 he was in the Senate of this state; and wherever he was placed, and whatever might be the business before him, he gave the utmost activity to measures, and left upon them the impression of his prudence and sagacity."—*Chancellor Kent.*

‡ Letter from Washington to General Schuyler, May 14, 1781.

was despatched to the neighborhood of Albany, at the head of a gang of Tories, Canadians, and Indians. He had, as it subsequently appeared, been lurking about the precincts of Albany for eight or ten days, sheltered by the thick growth of low pines and shrub-oaks, which yet spread over much of the common lands appertaining to that city ; and some dark intimations had been conveyed to General Schuyler that his person was in danger. These premonitions, it is believed, came first from a Dutch rustic who had fallen into the hands of Waltermeyer, and been examined as to the means of defence and the localities of the General's house, and who had been released only after taking an oath of secrecy. A similar caution had also been con veyed to him by a loyalist to whom the intention of Waltermeyer was known, but who was General Schuyler's personal friend. Of course the General and his family were continually on the *qui vive,* since the frequency with which leading citizens had been decoyed into ambush and taken, or snatched away by sunden violence, afforded ample cause for the exercise of all possible vigilance and caution. In addition, moreover, to his own household proper, the General had a guard of six men ; three of whom were on duty by day, and three by night.

It was in the evening of a sultry day in August, that the General was sitting with his family, after supper, in the front hall of his house, all the doors being open, when a servant entered to say that a stranger waited to speak with him at the back gate. Such an unusual request at once excited suspicion. The evening was so exceedingly warm that the servants had dispersed. The three sentinels who had been relieved for the night, were asleep in the cellar ; and the three who should have been on duty, were refreshing themselves at full length on the grass-plot in the garden. Instead, however, of responding to the invitation to meet the stranger at the back gate, the doors of the house were instantly closed and fastened. The General ran to his bed-chamber for his arms ; and having hastily collected his family in an upper apartment, and discovered from the windows that the house was surrounded by armed men, a pistol was discharged for the purpose of alarming the neglectful guards, and perchance the people of the city. At the same moment Mrs. Schuyler perceived that her infant child had been left in their bustle, in the cradle below, two flights of stairs. In

an agony of apprehension she was flying to its rescue, but
the General would not permit her to leave the apartment.
The third daughter, Margaret,* instantly rushed forth, and descending to the nursery, which was upon the ground floor, snatched the child from the cradle, where it was yet lying unmolested.
As she was leaving the room to return, a tomahawk was hurled
at her by an unseen hand, but with no other effect than slightly
to injure her dress. On ascending a private stairway, she was
met by Waltermeyer himself, who exclaimed—" Wench ! where
is your master ?" She replied, with great presence of mind—
" Gone to alarm the town." The villains had not, indeed, entered the house unopposed, for, on hearing the noise when they
were breaking in the doors, the three men in the cellar sprang
up, and without stopping to dress, rushed up stairs to the back
hall, where their arms had been left standing for convenience if
wanted, and into which the assailants were forcing their way.
Most unluckily, however, the arms of the guards were not at hand.
Mrs. Church,† who had lately returned from Boston, perceiving
that her little son‡ was playing with the muskets, and not entertaining the slightest suspicion that they would be wanted, had
caused them to be removed a few hours before the attack, without informing the guard of the circumstance. The brave fellows
had therefore no other means of resistance, after the yielding
of the doors, than by dealing blows as soundly as they could
with their fists, and also by embarrassing the progress of the
enemy otherwise as they might, while the General was collecting his family aloft.

But to return : Miss Margaret had no sooner informed Waltermeyer that her father had gone abroad for reinforcements,
than the traitor recalled his followers from the dining-room—
where it appeared they were at the moment engaged in bagging
the plate, from which work of plunder he had in vain urged
them to desist, that they might. perform the more important object of their mission—for consultation. Just at that moment, the

---

* Afterward the first lady of the present venerable and excellent General Stephen
Van Rensselaer.

† Another daughter of General Schuyler, married to John B. Church, Esq., an
English gentleman, contractor for the French army in America, and afterward a
member of Parliament. He died in 1818. [The venerable widow of Alexander
Hamilton is also a daughter of General Schuyler.]

‡ The present Captain Philip Church, of Alleghany county, (N. Y.)

General threw up a window, and with great presence of mind called out—" Come on, my brave fellows, surround the house and secure the villains who are plundering."* The stratagem succeeded, and the party made a precipitate retreat, carrying with them the three men who had vainly, and without arms, opposed their entrance,† one of whom had been wounded in defending the passage, while Waltermeyer himself was slightly wounded by one of the shots of Schuyler from the window. Thus, providentially, was the third conspiracy against the person of General Schuyler defeated.‡ The alarm was heard in the city, for the General had fired several shots during the affray ; but before any of the citizens arrived at the scene of action, the enemy had fled.

From Albany, Waltermeyer directed his course to Ballston, where he arrived at about day-break on the next morning. Taking General Gordon, of that place, a prisoner from his bed, the Tory leader pursued his journey back to Canada—having failed in the principal object of his expedition.

It may well be imagined that the situation of a people dwelling in such perpetual insecurity, was exceedingly unpleasant. Nor were they in dread only of a most subtle and wary foe from without. The disaffected were more numerous than ever among themselves, and the inhabitants scarcely knew who among their own neighbors could be trusted. Early in September it was represented to General Gansevoort that the disaffected had not only become formidable in numbers in the western and south western parts of the County of Albany, but were harboring and administering comfort to parties of the enemy sent from Canada, for the farther prosecution of the species of warfare already described in the present chapter—adding to the seizure of those men who were most active in the cause of their country, the destruction of their dwellings, and the murder of their women

---

* Letter of Schuyler to General Washington, Aug. 1781.

† The names of the guard were, John Tubbs, John Corlies, and Hans (John) Ward. They were carried to Canada, and when exchanged, the General gave them each a farm in Saratoga County. Ward is still, or was very lately, living, (Dec. 1837.)

‡ The particulars of this interesting adventure have been chiefly derived by the author from Mrs. Cochran, of Oswego, the infant who was rescued from the cradle by her sister Margaret.

and children.* Under these circumstances, Colonel Philip P. Schuyler, with a strong detachment of militia from Gansevoort's brigade, was despatched into the settlements designated, particularly to the Beaver Dams, where the family of Captain Deitz had been so cruelly murdered in 1777, with orders to arrest the disaffected, and bring them to Albany, together with their families and effects. The orders of General Gansevoort were issued on the 9th of September. On the 16th, Colonel Schuyler reported that he had executed his commission. From seventy to a hundred families " of the most notoriously disaffected," were arrested and brought into the city, where they were placed under a more vigilant surveillance than could be exercised over them in their own township.

But while these summary proceedings were rendering the country about Albany more secure in its internal relations, the inhabitants at the north were for several months kept in a state of ceaseless inquietude and alarm, by the movements of the enemy on Lake Champlain. General Heath was at that time invested with the command of the Northern Department, his head-quarters being in the Highlands. At Saratoga General Stark was in command, and Lord Stirling was also at the north. But as the Commander-in-chief had drawn the main army to Virginia, there were but few regular troops at the disposal of those officers. The consequence was, that with every alarm from Lake Champlain, (and the mysterious movements of the enemy rendered those alarms most inconveniently frequent,) General Stark was making pressing applications to General Gansevoort for assistance. The conduct of the enemy in the lake was indeed passing strange. It was ascertained that he had more than once ascended the lake from St. John's, with a force sufficiently strong, in the then exposed situation of the northern frontier, to make a formidable inroad upon the settlements; and the inhabitants of the New Hampshire Grants, then arrogating to themselves the character of citizens of the *State* of Vermont—not being in the secrets of their leaders—were as frequently alarmed as were those of the settlements *admitted* by the Vermontese to belong to New-York. Still the enemy attempted nothing beyond landing at Crown Point and Ticonderoga, and

---

* MS. order of General Gansevoort.

making a few occasional and inexplicable manœuvres with his flotilla upon the lake. These questionable movements were no less annoying than perplexing to the American generals. That a descent upon some point was intended, there seemed little reason to doubt. It was most likely to come from the north; but whenever the fleet was withdrawn down the lake, the idea prevailed that the movements there were intended to create a diversion, while the actual blow might be anticipated from the west. In support of the latter opinion was positive information, by a party of returning prisoners from Montreal, on the 19th of September, of the movements of between two and three hundred of Sir John Johnson's regiment, who were evidently preparing for an expedition in some direction.*

There was yet another source of distraction to the state authorities, civil and military, threatening nothing short of hostilities between New-York and the occupants of the New Hampshire Grants. A brief sketch of the cause and progress of the difficulties here referred to, though apparently foreign to the main subject of the present work, is nevertheless deemed essential to a just understanding of the situation of affairs in the Northern Department. Those who are versed in the early history of New-York and Vermont, cannot be ignorant of the fact, that for many years anterior to the war of the Revolution, a controversy had existed between the Governors of New Hampshire and New-York respecting the jurisdiction of the territory now constituting the State of Vermont. This controversy was begun in 1749, and continued fifteen years; during which period the Governor of New Hampshire was in the practice of making grants of lands and townships in the disputed territory. In 1764 the question was carried up to the King in council, and a decision rendered in favor of New-York, confirming her claim to the territory north of Massachusetts, as far east as the Connecticut river. Under this decision, the Colonial Government of New-York unwisely gave the Order in Council a construction of *retrospective* operation, involving the question of title. The grants from the Governor of New Hampshire were declared void, and the settlers were upon this ground called on either to surrender their charters, or to re-purchase their lands

* MSS. and correspondence of General Gansevoort.

from New-York. This demand they resisted, and with this resistance the controversy was renewed in another form, and continued with great vehemence, and with but little interruption, for many years.* About the year 1770 the celebrated Ethan Allen became conspicuous as a leader of "the Green Mountain Boys" in these proceedings. A military organization was adopted, and the mandates of the courts of New-York were disregarded, and its officers and ministers of justice openly set at defiance. When the sheriff of Albany appeared with his *posse comitatus,* the Green Mountain Boys opposed force to force, and drove them back. Lord Dunmore was then at the head of the colonial government of New-York, and exerted himself actively to maintain its territorial claim. An act of outlawry against Allen and several of his most prominent associates was passed, and a reward of fifty pounds offered for Allen's head. Lord Dunmore issued a proclamation, commanding the sheriff of Albany county to apprehend the offenders, and commit them to safe custody, that they might be brought to condign punishment;† but the friends of Allen were too numerous, resolute, and faithful, to allow of his arrest, or in any manner to suffer his personal safety to be compromised.‡

Governor Tryon, who succeeded Lord Dunmore, endeavored, both by force and by conciliation, to pacify the people of the Grants, and bring them back to their fealty to New-York. But in vain. Within the boundaries of the disputed territory, the laws of New-York were inoperative. It was to no purpose that civil suits, brought by the New-York grantees, were decided in their favor ; process could not be executed ; the settlers who had purchased farms under the New-York grantees, were forcibly driven away ; surveyors were arrested, tried under the *Lynch code,* and banished under the penalty of death should they ever again be caught within the bounds of the interdicted territory ;§ and those who presumed to hold commissions of the peace under the authority of New-York, were tried by the same courts, and inhumanly chastised with rods on their naked backs, to the extent of two hundred stripes.‖

* Slade's Vermont State papers, Introduction, p. 17.
† Sparks's Life of Ethan Allen.
‡ President Allen's Biographical Dictionary.   § Sparks—Life of Allen.
‖ By way of indicating their feelings toward the New-Yorkers, there was an inn at Bennington, called the "*Green Mountain Tavern,*" the sign of which was the

Such was the posture of affairs between New-York and the people of the New Hampshire Grants, at the commencement of the Revolution. But the battle of Lexington produced a shock which, for the time being, arrested the prosecution of the controversy. New-York was called to nerve her arm for a higher and nobler conflict, in the early stages of which she was gallantly assisted by the recusant settlers of the Grants. Ethan Allen himself struck the first blow at the north, by the capture of Ticonderoga; and his martial companion in resisting the authorities of New-York, Colonel Seth Warner, rendered efficient service at the battle of Bennington. Still, the Vermontese did not forget, while New-York was exerting her energies elsewhere, to prosecute their own designs for an entire alienation from New-York, and a separate state organization.* To this end all the energies of the chief men of the Grants were directed ; and the result was, that the Declaration of Independence of the British crown, by Congress, on the behalf of the twelve United Colonies, of July 4th, 1776, was followed by a convention of the people of the disputed territory ; which convention, on the 15th of January, 1777, declared the New Hampshire Grants to be a free and independent State,† and forwarded a memorial to Congress, praying for admission into the Confederation.

Indignant at this procedure, the state of New-York sought the interposition of Congress. The justice of the claim of New-York was fully recognised by that body ; and the memorial from the Grants was dismissed, by a resolution " that the independent " government attempted to be established by the people of Ver-" mont, could derive no countenance or justification from any " act or resolution of Congress." But the people of the Grants persisted in their determination to assert and maintain their independence. Nothing daunted, therefore, by the adverse action

skin of a catamount, stuffed, and raised on a post twenty-five feet from the ground, with its head turned toward New-York, giving defiance to all intruders from that quarter. It was at this tavern that that powerful and inexorable though ideal personage, *Judge Lynch*, was wont to hold his courts before he took up his abode at the South. Sometimes the delinquents, who were so unfortunate as to be obliged to answer in his court for the crime of purchasing lands of the real owners, or for acknowledging the government to which by law they belonged, were punished by being suspended by cords in a chair, beneath the catamount, for two hours. This was a lenient punishment. The more common one, was the application of the "*beech seal*" to the naked back—or, in other words, a flagellation with beechen rods.

* Slade's Vermont State Papers—a valuable work.   † Idem.

of Congress, they proceeded to form a constitution and to organise a State Government; the machinery of which was fully set in motion in the following year, 1778.

The Legislature of New-York still attempted to assert its right of jurisdiction, but made liberal proffers of compromise in regard to titles of lands—offering to recognise and confirm all the titles which had previously been in dispute. A proclamation to this effect, conceived in the most liberal spirit, was issued by Governor Clinton, in February, 1778; avowing, however, in regard to the contumacious, "the rightful supremacy of New-"York over their persons and property, as disaffected subjects."* But, like every preceding effort, either of force or conciliation, the present was of no avail. Ethan Allen issued a counter-proclamation to the people of the Grants, and the work of their own independent organization proceeded without serious interruption.† They were the more encouraged to persevere in this course, from an impression that, although Congress could not then sanction proceedings in regard to New-York that were clearly illegal; the New England members, and some of the Southern also, would, nevertheless, not be very deep mourners at their success. Roger Sherman maintained that Congress had no right to decide the controversy, and was supposed to countenance the proceedings of which New-York complained. Elbridge Gerry held that Vermont was *extra-provincial*, and had a perfect right to her independence.‡ But so thought not New-York and Governor Clinton; and the organization of a state government revived the heart-burnings that had subsided, and re-enkindled the fires of discord which had been inactive during the first three or four years of the war. The causes of irritation became daily more frequent and exasperating, until, during the Summer and Autumn of the present year, the parties were again on the verge of open hostilities. The people of the Grants, as they had grown in strength, had increased in their arrogance, until they had extended their claims to the Hudson river; and it was no diminution of the perplexities of New-

* Slade's Vermont State Papers.

† Respecting this manifesto, John Jay wrote to Gouverneur Morris—"Ethan Allen has commenced author and orator. A phillippic of his against New-York is handed about. There is quaintness, impudence, and art in it."

‡ Life of Gouverneur Morris.

York, that strong indications appeared in several of the northern towns, to which the people of the Grants had previously
interposed not even the shadow of a claim, of a disposition to
go over to Vermont.

Meantime Governor Clinton, inflexibly determined to preserve
the disputed jurisdiction, was exerting himself to the utmost
for that object; and in order, apparently, to bring the question to a test, several persons were arrested in the course
of the Summer of 1781, within the territory of the Grants, under the pretext of some military delinquency. This procedure
was the signal for another tempest.   Governor Chittenden wrote
to officers of New-York, demanding the release of the prisoners
taken from the Grants—asserting their determination to maintain the government they had "set up,"* and threatening that,
in the event of an invasion of the territory of New-York by the
common enemy, unless those prisoners were given up, they
would render no assistance to New-York.   This letter also contained an admonition, "that power was not limited only to New
York."† Nor was this all.   While the country was threatened
by invasion both from the north and the west, the spirit of the
Vermont insurgents began to spread among the militia in the
northern towns east of the Hudson, belonging to General Gansevoort's own brigade.   Thus, on the one hand, General Stark
was calling upon him for assistance against the enemy apparently approaching from Lake Champlain, at the same time that
Governor Clinton was directing him to quell the spirit of insubordination along the line of the New Hampshire Grants; and
both of these duties were to be discharged, with a knowledge that
a portion of his own command was infected with the insurgent
spirit.   Added to all which was, the necessity of watching, as
with an eagle's eye, the conduct of the swarms of loyalists within the bosom of Albany and in the towns adjacent; while for
his greater comfort, he was privately informed that the Green
Mountain Boys were maturing a plot for his abduction.   Meantime the government of the Grants had effected an organization
of their own militia, and disclosures had been made to the

* MS. Letter from Thomas Chittenden to Captain Van Rensselaer, among the
Gansevoort papers.

† This dark and rather awkward saying was full of meaning, as will appear in a
subsequent portion of the present chapter.

government of New-York, imputing to the leading men of the
Grants a design, in the event of a certain contingency, of throwing the weight of their own forces into the scale of the Crown.
The following letter may be considered important in this con
nexion :—

GOVERNOR CLINTON TO GENERAL GANSEVOORT.

"*Poughkeepsie, Oct.* 18. 1781.

" DEAR SIR,

"Your letter of the 15th instant was delivered to me on the
evening of the 16th. I have delayed answering it, in hopes that
the Legislature would ere this have formed a quorum, and that
I might have availed myself of their advice on the subject to
which it relates ; but as this is not yet the case, and it is uncertain when I shall be enabled to lay the matter before them, I
conceive it might be improper longer to defer expressing my
own sentiments to you on this subject.

" The different unwarrantable attempts, during the Summer,
of the people on the Grants to establish their usurped jurisdiction, even beyond their former claim, and the repetition of it
(alluded to in your letter,) in direct opposition to a resolution of
Congress injurious to this State and favorable to their project of
independence, and at a time when the common enemy are advancing, can only be accounted for by what other parts of their conduct have given us too much reason to suspect—disaffection to
the common cause. On my part, I have hitherto shown a disposition to evade entering into any altercation with them, that
might, in its most remote consequence, give encouragement to
the enemy, and expose the frontier settlements to their ravages ;
and from these considerations alone I have submitted to insults
which otherwise would not have been borne with ; and I could
have wished to have continued this kind of conduct until the
approaching season would have secured us against the incursions of the common enemy. But as from the accounts contained in Colonel Van Rensselaer's letter, it would appear that
the militia embodying under Mr. Chittenden's orders are for the
service of the enemy, and that their first object was to make you
a prisoner, it would be unjustifiable to suffer them to proceed.
It is therefore my desire that you maintain your authority
throughout every part of your brigade, and for this purpose, that

you carry the laws of the State into execution against those who shall presume to disobey your lawful orders. I would only observe that these sentiments are founded on an idea that the accounts given by Col. Van Rensselaer in his letter may be relied on ; it being still my earnest desire, for the reasons above explained, not to do any thing that will bring matters to extremities, at least before the close of the campaign, if it can consistently be avoided.

" In my last, I should have mentioned to you that it was not in my power to send you a supply of ammunition ; but, as I had reason to believe you were gone to Saratoga, I conceived it improper to say any thing on the subject lest my letter might miscarry. You may recollect that of the whole supply ordered by General Washington, last Spring, for the use of the militia, five hundred pounds is all that has been received in the state magazine, which you will easily conceive to be far short of what was necessary for the other exposed parts of the state. With respect to provisions, it is equally out of my power to furnish you with any, but what the state agent, who is now with you, may be able to procure.

" I am, with great respect and esteem,

" Dear Sir,

" Your most obed't serv't,

" Geo. Clinton.

" *Brig. Gen. Gansevoort.*"

But the controversy with the people of the Grants was suddenly interrupted, just at this juncture, though for a short period only, by the most formidable invasion of the Mohawk Valley which had taken place during the present year. Indeed, it was the last irruption of the enemy into that section of the country, of any importance, during the struggle of the revolution.

It has been seen, from the commencement of the contest, that the Johnsons, and those loyalists from Tryon County most intimate in their alliance with them, appeared to be stimulated by some peculiar and ever-active principle of hostility against the former seat of the Baronet, and the district of country by which it was environed. Another expedition against Johnstown was therefore secretly planned in the Summer of 1781, and executed with such silent celerity, that on the 24th of October " the Phi-

listines " were actually "upon" the settlements before their approach was suspected. This expedition was organized at
Buck's Island, in the river St. Lawrence, a few miles below the
foot of Lake Ontario, and consisted of four companies of the second battalion of Sir John Johnson's regiment of Royal Greens,
Colonel Butler's rangers, under the direction of Major Butler,
his son, and two hundred Indians—numbering in all about one
thousand men, under the command of Major Ross.* Proceeding from Buck's Island to Oswego, and thence through the
Oneida Lake, they struck off through the south-eastern forests
from that point, and traversed the woods with such secrecy as
to break in upon Warrensbush,† near the junction of the Schoharie-kill with the Mohawk river, as suddenly as though they
had sprung up from the earth like the warriors from the dra-
gon's teeth of Cadmus, full grown, and all in arms, in a single
night. This was on the 24th of October.‡ Warrensbush was
about twenty miles east from Fort Rensselaer, the head-quarters
of Colonel Willett; so that Ross and Butler had ample time for
the work of havoc and devastation on the south side of the river,
and to cross over to the north side, before the former could rally his
forces and dispute their farther progress. Not a moment was
lost by Colonel Willett, on hearing the news, in making such
dispositions to repel the unexpected invaders, as were within
his limited means. With such forces as were in the garrison,
together with such additional recruits from the militia as could
be collected in the neighborhood, Willett marched for Fort
Hunter on the same evening—simultaneously despatching orders for the militia and levies in contiguous posts and settle-

* Such is the estimate of the manuscript accounts which have been furnished to
the author. It is, however, too high, unless Major Butler carried an erroneous statement in his pocket. According to a memorandum found in his pocket-book, after
his fall, the force of Major Ross was made up as follows :—Eighth regiment, twenty-
five; thirty-fourth ditto, one hundred; eighty-fourth ditto, Highlanders, thirty-six;
Sir John's, one hundred and twenty; Lake's Independents, forty; Butler's rangers,
one hundred and fifty; Yagers, twelve; Indians, one hundred and thirty.—Total
six hundred and seventy.—*Vide Letter of Colonel Willett to Lord Stirling, Almon's
Remembrancer.*

† A settlement planted by Sir Peter Warren, the uncle of Sir William Johnson—
and the first place of residence of the latter gentleman after his arrival in America.

‡ Campbell states that this invasion was in August. Major Sammons dates it
the 22d of that month. Colonel Willett gives the date of Oct. 24—which was obviously correct, since the second part of the battle was fought in a snow-storm.

ments, to follow and join him with all possible expedition. By marching all night, the Colonel reached Fort Hunter early in the following morning, where he learned that the enemy were already in the occupation of Johnstown. The depth of the river was such that floats were necessary in crossing it, and although Willett had but four hundred and sixteen men all told— only half the enemy's number, exclusive of the Indians—yet it was afternoon before the crossing was effected. Ross and Butler had crossed the river some distance below Tripe's Hill the preceding day, and moved thence directly upon Johnstown— killing and taking the people prisoners, and destroying buildings, and cattle, and whatsoever came in their way. Soon after ascending the hill just mentioned, the enemy came upon a small scouting party commanded by Lieutenant Saulkill, who was on horseback. He was fired upon by the enemy's advance, and fell dead to the ground. His men sought safety in flight, and succeeded.* This was early in the morning of the 25th The advance of the enemy being slow, they did not arrive at the village of Johnstown until past 12 o'clock at noon. Even then, the main body of their forces, avoiding the town, marched round to the west, halting upon the grounds of the Baronial hall. The enemy's baggage wagons, however, passed through the village, and their conductors were fired upon from the old jail—then serving the purpose of a fortress. One man only was wounded by this consumption of ammunition.

Having effected the passage of the river, Colonel Willett pushed on in pursuit with all possible expedition. But deeming it unwise, where the disparity of their respective forces was so great, to hazard an attack in front with his whole force, the position of the enemy was no sooner ascertained with certainty, than Major Rowley, of Massachusetts, was detached with a small body of the Tryon County militia, and about sixty levies from his own state, for the purpose, by a circuitous march, of outflanking the enemy, and falling upon his rear—thus attacking in front and rear at the same time. These, and other necessary dispositions having been adjusted, Willett advanced upon the enemy at the head of his column. Entering an open

---

* In one of the manuscript accounts of this battle, the fruit of my researches in the Mohawk Valley, it is stated that Saulkill was not connected with the scout, but was passing at the moment on his way to Albany.

field adjoining to that occupied by the enemy, Willett displayed
his right into line, and pressed Major Ross so closely as to compel him to retire into the fringe of a neighboring wood.   Here
a skirmishing was kept up while the remainder of the Americans were advancing briskly in two columns, to bear a part.
The battle became spirited and general ; and although the only
field-piece belonging to the Americans was taken, it was speedily re-taken, and for a time the action proceeded with a promise
of victory.   But just at the crisis, the militia of Willett were
seized with one of those causeless and unaccountable panics,
which on most occasions render that description of troops worse
than useless in battle, and without any cause the whole of the
right wing turned about and fled.*   The field-piece was abandoned and the ammunition wagon blown up.   The former, of
course, fell into the hands of the enemy.   Colonel Willett did
his utmost to rally his men, but to no purpose.   They ran in
the utmost confusion to the stone church in the village.   Here,
having induced them to make a halt, the Colonel commenced
bringing them again into such order as best he might.   But the
defeat would still have been complete, had it not been for the
precautionary disposition previously made of Major Rowley.
Most fortunately, as it happened, that officer emerged from the
woods, and arrived upon the field, just in time to fall upon the
enemy's rear in the very moment of their exultation at their
easy victory.   Rowley pressed the attack with great vigor and
intrepidity, while the enemy were engaged in making prisoners
of the stragglers, and the Indians were scalping those who fell
into their hands.   The fight was now maintained with equal
obstinacy and irregularity for a considerable time.   Major
Rowley was early wounded by a shot through the ankle, and
carried from the field ; and the enemy were engaged in different
bodies, sometimes in small parties separated nearly a mile from
each other.   In some of these contests the advantage was on
the side of the enemy, and in others the Americans were the
temporary victors.   The battle continued after this fashion
until near sunset, when, finding such to be the fact, and that
Rowley's detachment alone was holding the enemy at bay,
Willett was enabled to collect a respectable force, with which

* Letter of Colonel Willett to Lord Stirling.

he returned to the field, and again mingled in the fight. The battle was severely contested until dark, when the enemy, pressed upon all sides, retreated in discomfiture to the woods— nor stopped short of a mountain top, six miles distant. Among the officers who signalised themselves on this occasion, in addition to the two leaders, Willett and Rowley, was the brave Captain Gardenier, who fought with such desperation at the battle of Oriskany, and was so severely wounded in the death-struggle with one of the M'Donalds. After the enemy had retired, Colonel Willett procured lights, and caused the wounded of the enemy, as well as his own, to be collected, and their wounds carefully dressed. The loss of the Americans was about forty. The enemy lost about the same number killed, and some fifty prisoners. The Tryon County militia, under Major Rowley, behaved nobly.

Knowing the direction from which Ross and Butler had approached, and that their batteaux had been left at the Oneida Lake, Colonel Willett lost not a moment in making arrangements to cut off their means of retreat by the destruction of their boats, while he likewise determined, if possible, to throw himself into their front. Having been apprised by some of Ross's prisoners, who had made their escape in the night, that it was his intention to strike at the frontiers of Stone Arabia, in order to obtain a supply of provisions, Willett marched to that place on the following morning, and encamped there that day and night, pushing forward a detachment of troops, with instructions to proceed by forced marches to the Oneida Lake and destroy the boats. Ascertaining, on the morning of the 27th, that Ross had avoided Stone Arabia by striking deeper into the wilderness, Willett hastened forward to the German Flatts, where he had the mortification, on the 28th, to learn that the party ordered to the lake had returned without performing their duty.*

While at Stone Arabia, a scouting party had been sent upon the enemy's trail by Willett, to ascertain whether he had laid his course in the anticipated direction, or whether he might not have inclined farther to the north, with a view of returning directly through the wilderness to Buck's Island. The scouts having satisfied themselves that the latter course would be taken

* Willett's Letter to Lord Stirling.

by Ross, hastily returned; and the result of their observation was communicated to Willett by express.*

Immediately on the receipt of this intelligence, Willett determined, if possible, to strike another blow. Having been joined by about sixty warriors of the Oneida tribe, together with some additional levies and militia-men, the Colonel selected about four hundred of his choicest troops, and furnishing them with provisions for five days, on the 29th struck off to the northward, along the course of the West Canada Creek. They marched the whole of that day through a driving snow-storm, halting at night in a thick wood on the Royal Grant. Supposing it probable that the enemy could not be far distant, Jacob Sammons was detached with two Oneida Indians to advance yet farther into the wilderness, and, under cover of the darkness, make such discoveries as might be in their power. " It was with much reluctance," says Sammons in his narrative, " that I undertook this business." They had not proceeded far before the Indians discovered the prints of footsteps. Having knelt down and scrutinised them closely, they pronounced them fresh, and refused any longer to advance. Taking Sammons by the arm, they entreated him to return; but he declined, and they separated. The intrepid scout soon descried fires kindling amid the deep forest-gloom, toward which he cautiously approached until he was enabled to take a survey of the enemy's camp. Having obtained all necessary information, and narrowly escaped detection withal, he returned to the camp of the Americans. Willett had kept his troops under arms awaiting the return of Sammons; but learning from the latter that the enemy were well provided with bayonets, of which his own men were deficient, a night attack upon the camp was judged imprudent, and he bivouacked his forces on the spot.†

Willett lost no time in advancing on the following morning, with a view of bringing the enemy to an engagement. But the latter had been as early on foot as himself, so that it was not until one o'clock in the afternoon that the Americans came up with a small party of the enemy's rear, consisting of about forty men, together with a few Indians, who had been detached from his main body for the purpose of obtaining provisions. A smart

---

* This scouting party was composed of Captain John Little, William Laird, and Jacob Shew.

† Narrative of Jacob Sammons.

brush ensued, during which some of the enemy were killed, others were taken prisoners, while the residue fled. Among the prisoners was a Tory lieutenant named John Rykeman. Pursuing on the enemy's trail, the Americans came up with his main body in a place called Jerseyfield, on the north side of the Canada Creek. A running fight ensued, but the enemy made a very feeble resistance—exhibiting symptoms of terror, and attempting to retreat at a dog-trot by Indian files. Late in the afternoon, as they crossed the Creek to the west or south-western side, Butler attempted to rally his forces and make a stand. A brisk engagement ensued, the parties being on opposite sides of the Creek; during which about twenty of the enemy fell. Among them was their bold and enterprising but cruel leader, Walter N. Butler. He was brought down by the rifle of an Oneida Indian, who, happening to recognize him as he was looking at the battle from behind a tree, took deliberate aim, and shot him through his hat and the upper part of his head. Butler fell, and his troops fled in the utmost confusion. The warrior, who made the successful shot, sprang first across the Creek in the general rush, and running directly up to Butler, discovered that he was not dead, but sorely wounded. He was in a sitting posture near the tree, and writhing in great agony. The Indian advanced, and while Butler looked him full in the face, shot him again through the eye, and immediately took his scalp. The Oneidas no sooner saw the bleeding trophy, than they set up the scalp-yell, and stripping the body, left it lying upon the face, and pressed forward in pursuit of the fugitive host. On coming to the guard, where Rykeman and the other prisoners were confined, the Indian attempted to flout the unhappy prisoner by slapping the scalp of his late commander in his face; but the lieutenant avoided the blow. The pursuit was closely followed up; but darkness and fatigue compelled the Colonel to relinquish it until morning. The enemy, however, continued their flight throughout the night.* And, truly, never were men reduced to a condition more deplorable. The weather was cold, and they had yet a

---

* "Strange as it may appear, it is nevertheless true, that, notwithstanding the enemy had been four days in the wilderness, with only half a pound of horse-flesh per man per day, yet in this famished situation they trotted thirty miles before they stopped. Many of them, indeed, fell a sacrifice to such treatment."—*Col. Willett's Letter to Lord Stirling.*

dreary and pathless wilderness of eighty miles to traverse, with
out food, and without even blankets—having been compelled to
cast them away to facilitate their escape.* But, scattered and
broken as they were, and having the start of one night, it was
judged inexpedient to give longer pursuit; especially as Willett's
own troops were supplied with provisions for but two days more.
The victory was, moreover, already complete. The Colonel
therefore wheeled about, and led his little army back in triumph
to Fort Dayton. The loss of the Americans in the pursuit was
only one man. That of the enemy was never known. In the
language of Colonel Willett's official despatches, "the fields of
" Johnstown, the brooks and rivers, the hills and mountains, the
" deep and gloomy marshes through which they had to pass,
" these only could tell; and, perhaps, the officers who detached
" them on the expedition."

In re-passing the battle-ground, the body of Butler was discovered as it had been left; and there, without sepulture, it was
suffered to remain.†

---

* "In this situation I left the unfortunate Major Ross; unfortunate I call him,
for he was surely so in taking charge of such a fine detachment of men to execute
so dirty and trifling a piece of business as he was sent on, at such immense hazard
and exquisite toil." * * * "We left them in a situation, perhaps, more suited
to their demerit than a musket, a ball, a tomahawk, or captivity."—*Col. Willett's
Letter to Lord Stirling.*

† Various statements of the circumstances attending the death of Walter N. Butler have been published. Marshall, in his Life of Washington, states it thus—"In
the party at Canada Creek, was Major Walter Butler, the person who perpetrated
the massacre at Cherry Valley. His entreaties for quarter were disregarded; and
he fell a victim of that vengeance which his own savage temper had directed
against himself." According to Colonel Willett's account, he was shot dead at
once, having no time to implore for mercy. President Dwight, in his travels, gives
an account corresponding with the following, by Campbell:—"He was pursued by
a small party of Oneida Indians; when he arrived at West Canada Creek, about
fifteen miles above Herkimer, he swam his horse across the stream, and then turning round, defied his pursuers, who were on the opposite side. An Oneida immediately discharged his rifle and wounded him, and he fell. Throwing down his rifle
and his blanket, the Indian plunged into the Creek and swam across; as soon as he
had gained the opposite bank, he raised his tomahawk, and with a yell, sprang like
a tiger upon his fallen foe. Butler supplicated, though in vain, for mercy; the Oneida, with his uplifted axe, shouted, in his broken English,—' Sherry Valley! remember Sherry Valley!' and then buried it in his brains." It is apprehended that neither
of these statements is exactly correct. The account in the text has been drawn by
the author from the manuscript statements of Philip Graft, who was a spectator of
the transaction, then attached to the company of Captain Peter Van Rensselaer,

So perished Walter N. Butler, one of the greatest scourges, as he was one of the most fearless men, of his native county. No other event of the whole war created so much joy in the Mohawk Valley as the news of his decease. He is represented to have been of a morose temperament, possessing strong passions, and of a vindictive disposition. He was disliked, as has already more than once appeared, by Joseph Brant, who included him among those whom he considered greater savages than the savages themselves. It is quite probable, however, that Walter Butler may have possessed other and better qualities, his friends being judges, than have been awarded to him by his enemies. It has been asserted, that after the massacre of Cherry Valley General Haldimand refused to see him. But this fact may well be questioned, inasmuch as Haldimand not only approved but encouraged the despatching of a similar expedition against the scarcely offending Oneidas, who had removed, and were living peaceably in the neighborhood of Schenectady.

This expedition of Ross and Butler closed the active warlike operations at the north for that year ; but while the events traced in the few preceding pages were in progress, others were occurring in a different quarter of the country, both in themselves and in their results of far greater moment. In the bird's-eye glance taken of the progress of the war in other parts of the confederacy during the first quarter of the year, Arnold was left at Portsmouth, contiguous to Norfolk. He afterward made various movements of the character heretofore described ; visiting Richmond again, and committing outrages there and elsewhere. On the death of the British Major General Phillips, the traitor succeeded to the command of the King's troops in Virginia, and maintained himself there against the Baron Steuben, and afterward against the Marquis de Lafayette,* until Lord Cornwallis, having traversed North Carolina, and entered Virginia, formed a

---

who was stationed at Fort Herkimer, and was engaged in this expedition. The statement of Jacob Sammons corresponds with that of Graft, though less circumstantial.

* On succeeding to the command of Phillips, Arnold addressed a letter to the Marquis de Lafayette ; but the latter informed the officer who bore it, that he would not receive a letter from the traitor. Indeed, Arnold was despised by the officers in the British service ; and how could it be otherwise ? Even Sir Henry Clinton had no confidence in him : and in detaching him to the south, had taken special care to send Colonel Dundas and Colonel Simcoe, two experienced officers, with him, with

junction with him, and assumed the command; sending Arnold from his presence to Portsmouth as soon as possible. After his return to New-York, Arnold led another piratical expedition, early in September, against New London and Groton. The former town was burnt, and Fort Griswold, on the opposite side of the river, having been carried by assault, was the scene of a bloody massacre; the brave Ledyard, who commanded, being thrust through with his own sword.*

Meantime, the American Commander-in-chief was meditating a blow, which, if successful, could not but have an important, and perhaps a decisive, bearing upon the great question of his country's final emancipation. While the Marquis de Lafayette was circumventing and perplexing Cornwallis in Virginia, Washington was preparing for an attempt upon the citadel of the British power in the United States—New-York. This design, as has been formerly stated, had been projected the season before, immediately after the arrival of the Count de Rocham-beau with the French army of alliance, in Rhode Island. But so many difficulties arose, and so many supervening obstacles were to be overcome, that, in obedience to stern necessity, the project was for that year abandoned. With the opening of the Spring of the present year it was revived, and after the respec-tive commanders had held another personal consultation, the French army moved from Rhode Island across the country to the Hudson. But other obstacles arose, which compelled an en-tire change in the plan of the campaign. Fortunately, however, the British commander in New-York was not quick to discover the change, and the demonstration served to divert his attention from the right object until it became too late to repair his error. The combined French and American forces, by an unsuspected but effectual basis of operations, had been tending as upon a central point toward Virginia, until, before he was aware of se-rious danger, Earl Cornwallis found himself shut up in York-

instructions to Arnold to consult them in regard to every measure and every opera-tion he might desire to undertake.

* "It has been said, that Arnold, while New London was in flames, stood in the belfry of a steeple and witnessed the conflagration; thus, like Nero, delighted with the ruin he had caused, the distresses he had inflicted, the blood of his slaughtered countrymen, the agonies of the expiring patriot, the widow's tears, and the orphan's cries. And, what adds to the enormity, is, that he stood almost in sight of the spot where he drew his first breath."—*Sparks.*

town. The event was fatal to him and to the cause of his master. The post was completely invested by the 30th of September. On the 9th of October the French and Americans opened their batteries. And on the 19th, his two advanced redoubts having been carried by storm a few days before, despairing of receiving the promised succors from Sir Henry Clinton, and having, moreover, failed in a well-concerted attempt to evacuate the fortress by night, Lord Cornwallis, submitting to necessity, absolute and inevitable, surrendered by capitulation. The loss of the enemy during the siege was five hundred and fifty-two, killed, wounded, and missing; and the number of prisoners taken, exclusive of the seamen, who were surrendered to the Count de Grasse, was seven thousand and seventy-three, of whom five thousand nine hundred and fifty were rank and file.

It would have been perfectly natural, and in fact no more than even-handed justice, had the recent massacre at Fort Griswold been avenged on this occasion. But, happily, it was otherwise ordered; and the triumph was rendered still more memorable by the fact, that not a drop of blood was shed save in action. "Incapable," said Colonel Hamilton, (who led the advance of the Americans in the assault,) "of imitating examples of barbarity, and forgetting recent provocation, the soldiers spared "every man that ceased to resist."*

The joy at this surrender of a second army was as great as universal. The thanks of Congress were voted to the Commander-in-chief, to the Count de Rochambeau, and the Count de Grasse, and to the other principal officers of the different corps, and the men under them. It was also resolved by Congress to erect a marble column at Yorktown, with designs emblematic of the alliance of France and the United States—to be inscribed with a narrative of the event thus commemorated. But, like all other monumental structures by Congress, it yet exists only on paper.

The Commander-in-chief availed himself of the occasion to pardon and set at liberty all military offenders under arrest. Ever ready and forward to acknowledge the interposition of the hand of Providence in the direction of human events, this truly

---

* Colonel Alexander Hamilton's report—Marshall.

great commander closed his orders in reference to this event, in the following impressive manner: " Divine service shall be per- " formed to-morrow in the different brigades and divisions. The " Commander-in-chief recommends that all the troops not upon " duty, do assist at it with a serious deportment, and that sensi- " bility of heart, which the recollection of the surprising and par- " ticular interposition of Divine Providence in our favor claims."

Recurring, again, to the progress of events at the North, the enigmatical conduct of the British commander in Canada, and the mysterious movements of his forces upon Lake Champlain, remain to be explained. On the 9th of November, General Heath, commanding the department, issued the following gene- ral order; a copy of which has been preserved among General Gansevoort's papers :—

" *Head-Quarters, Continental Village, Nov.* 9, 1781.

" The General has the pleasure of acquainting this army, that the enemy have been completely disappointed in their designs on the northern frontiers of this State, in consequence of the measures adopted to receive them in the vicinity of the lakes, in which the General is much indebted to Major General Lord Stirling, Brigadier General Stark, and the other officers and sol- diers, both of the regular troops and the militia, who, with great zeal and alertness, pressed to meet the enemy. That part of their force which was coming by way of the lakes has not dared to land on this side of them.

" Major Ross, who had advanced from the westward as far as Johnstown, with a body of between six and seven hundred regu- lar troops, Rangers, Yagers, and Indians, was met by Colonel Willett, defeated, and pursued into the wilderness, where many of them probably must perish ; the number of the enemy killed is not known. Major Butler, who has frequently distressed the frontiers, is among the slain. A number of prisoners, chiefly British, have been taken and sent in.

" The General presents his thanks to Colonel Willett, whose address, gallantry, and persevering activity exhibited on this oc- casion, do him the highest honor ; and while the conduct of the officers and soldiers in general, who were with Colonel Willett, deserves high commendation, the General expresses a particular approbation of the behavior of Major Rowley, and the brave levies and militia under his immediate command, who, at a critical moment, not only did honor to themselves, but rendered a most essential service to their country.

" Transcript from general orders:

" THOS. FRED. JACKSON,

" *Aid-de-camp.*"

General Heath, and many others, doubtless supposed that the anticipated invasion had been averted by the dispositions of Lord Stirling, and Generals Stark and Gansevoort, as set forth in the first paragraph of these general orders; but the facts of the case, without detracting an iota from the distinguished merits of those officers, will inevitably lead to a different conclusion.

A summary view of the controversy between New-York and the people of the New Hampshire Grants, has already been given—in addition to which several incidental allusions have been made to the equivocal movements and intentions of Ethan Allen. Reference was also made, by way of a note in the preceding chapter, to a special message from Governor Clinton to the Legislature of New-York, communicating important information respecting the designs of Allen and his associates, which had been derived from two prisoners who had escaped from Canada in the Autumn of the present year—John Edgar and David Abeel. The substance of the statements of these men was, that several of the leading men of the New Hampshire Grants were forming an alliance with the King's officers in Canada. Among these leaders were Ethan and Ira Allen, and the two Fays. A man named Sherwood, and Doctor Smith of Albany, whose name has already been mentioned, were the agents of the negotiation on the part of Great Britain, and their consultations were sometimes held at Castleton, on the Grants, and sometimes in Canada. According to the statement of Edgar, it was understood that the Grants were to furnish the King with a force of two thousand men. Mr. Abeel's information was, that fifteen hundred was the number of men to be furnished, under the command of Ethan Allen. Mr. Abeel also stated that Ethan Allen was then in Canada upon that business, and that he had seen Major Fay at the Isle au Noix, on board of one of the King's vessels; and that he, Fay, had exchanged upward of thirty Hessians, who had deserted from Burgoyne's army, delivering them up to the British authorities. The statements of Edgar and Abeel, the latter of whom had been taken a prisoner at Catskill the preceding Spring, were given under the sanction of an oath ; and although they were not fellow-prisoners, and had derived their information from different sources ; and although escaping at different times, under dissimilar circumstances, and by routes widely apart, yet there was a strong coincidence between them. A third account submitted to the Legislature by the Governor was somewhat different, and more particular as to the terms of the proposed arrangement. In this paper it was stated, first, that the territory claimed by the Vermontese should be formed into a distinct colony or government. Secondly, that the form of government should be similar to that of Connecticut, save that the nomination of the Governor should be vested in the crown. Thirdly, that they should be allowed to remain neutral, unless the war should be carried within their own territory. Fourthly, they were to raise two battalions, to be in the pay of the crown, but to be called into service only for the defence of the Colony. Fifthly, they were to be allowed a free trade with Canada. General Haldimand had not deemed himself at liberty to decide definitively upon propositions of so much importance, and had accordingly transmitted them to England for the royal consideration. An answer was then expected. Such was the purport of the intelligence ; and such was the weight of the testimony, that the Governor did not hesitate to assert that they " proved a " treasonable and dangerous intercourse and connexion between " the leaders of the revolt in the north-eastern part of the State, " and the common enemy." *

The fact is, according to the admissions, and the documents published by the Vermont historians themselves,† that the people of Vermont, though doubtless for the most part attached to the cause of their country, nevertheless looked upon New-York " as a more detested enemy" than Great Britain ;‡ and the officers of the latter were not slow in their efforts to avail themselves of the schism. Accordingly, Colonel Beverley Robinson sought to

---

* These and other documents may be found in Almon's Remembrancer, Vol. ix. —for 1782.

† Slade's State Papers.   ‡ Idem.

open a correspondence with Ethan Allen as early as March, 1780. The first letter was handed to Allen in Arlington, but was not answered.   A second letter from Robinson was received by Allen in February, 1781, which, with the first, he enclosed to Congress in March, accompanied by a letter plainly asserting the right of Vermont to agree to a cessation of hostilities with Great Britain, provided its claims, as a State, were still to be rejected by Congress.   It does not appear, however, that the threat had any effect upon that body.

In the months of April and May following, the Governor and Council of Vermont commissioned Colonel Ira Allen, a brother of Ethan, to proceed to the Isle au Noix, to settle a cartel with the British in Canada, and also, if possible, to negotiate an armistice in favor of Vermont.   The arrangements for this negotiation were conducted with the most profound secrecy ; only eight persons being cognizant of the procedure.*   Colonel Allen, accompanied by one subaltern,† two sergeants, and sixteen privates, departed upon his mission on the first of May ; and having arrived at the Isle au Noix, entered at once upon his business—negotiating with Major Dundas, the commander of that post, only on the subject of an exchange of prisoners, but more privately with Captain Sherwood and George Smith, Esq. on the subject of an armistice.   The stay of Allen at the island was protracted for a considerable time, and the conferences with the two commissioners, Sherwood and Smith, on the subject of the political relations of Vermont, were frequent, but perfectly confidential ; Allen carefully avoiding to write any thing, to guard against accidents.   But from the beginning, it seems to have been perfectly understood by both parties that they were treating " for an armistice, and to concert measures to establish " Vermont as a colony under the crown of Great Britain."‡   In the course of the consultations, Allen freely declared " that such was " the extreme hatred of Vermont to the state of New-York, that " rather than yield to it, they would see Congress subjected to the " British government, provided Vermont could be a distinct colo- " ny under the crown on safe and honorable terms."   He added,

* Thomas Chittenden, Moses Robinson, Samuel Safford, Ethan Allen, Ira Allen, Timothy Brownson, John Fassett, and Joseph Fay.

† Lieutenant Simeon Lyman.

‡ Political History of Vermont, published by Ira Allen in London, in 1798.

" that the people of Vermont were not disposed any longer to assist
" in establishing a government in America which might subject
" them and their posterity to New-York, whose government was
" more detested than any other in the known world."* These were
encouraging representations in the ears of his Majesty's officers;
and, after a negotiation of seventeen days, the cartel was arranged,
and an armistice verbally agreed upon, by virtue of which hostilities were to cease between the British forces and the people under the jurisdiction of Vermont, until after the next session of the
Legislature of Vermont, and even longer, if prospects were satisfactory to the Commander-in-chief in Canada. Moreover, as
Vermont had then extended her claims of territory to the Hudson river, all that portion of New-York lying east of the river,
and north of the western termination of the north line of Massachusetts, was included in the armistice. It was also stipulated
that, during the armistice, the leaders in Vermont were to prepare the people by degrees for a change of government, and that
the British officers were to have free communication through the
territory of the new State—as it claimed to be.†

But, notwithstanding the veil of secrecy drawn over the proceedings, dark suspicions got afloat that all was not right. The
sincere Whigs among the people of the Grants became alarmed,
and were apprehensive that they might be sold ere yet they were
aware of it. When the Legislature met, the people whose
jealousies had been awakened, flocked to the place of meeting
to ascertain whether all was well; and it was only by much
dissimulation on the part of those in the secret, that the friends
of the Union were pacified. There were also other spectators
present, from different States, who felt an equal interest to ascertain whether the great cause of the nation was not in danger of
being compromised. The result was, that the agents succeeded
in throwing dust into the eyes of the people; and so adroit was
their management, that the Allens held communication with the
enemy during the whole Summer without detection. On more
than one occasion, British guards, of several men, came to the
very precincts of Arlington, delivering and receiving packages
in the twilight.

In September the negotiations were renewed, the commission-

* Allen's Political History of Vermont.   † Idem.

ers of both parties meeting secretly at Skenesborough, within the territory of New-York, and farther progress was made in the terms of the arrangement, by which Vermont was in due time to throw herself " into the arms of her legitimate sovereign." Sir Frederick Haldimand, however, was becoming impatient of longer delay; and a strenuous effort was made for an immediate and open declaration on the part of Vermont. To this proposition the Vermont commissioners, Ira Allen, Joseph Fay, and a third person, whose name is not given, pleaded that there had not yet been time to prepare the people for so great a change, and that they should require the repose of the approaching Winter for that object. It was at length stipulated, however, that inasmuch as the royal authority had been received by Sir Frederick Haldimand for that purpose, an army might ascend the lake, with proclamations offering to confirm Vermont as a colony under the crown, upon the principles and conditions heretofore indicated, on the return of the people to their allegiance; the commissioners interposing a request, that the General commanding the expedition would endeavor to ascertain the temper of the people before the proclamation should be actually distributed.

The Legislature of the Grants assembled at Charlestown in October. Meantime General St. Leger, agreeably to the arrangement with Allen and Fay, ascended the lake to Ticonderoga with a strong force, where he rested. In order to save appearances, the Vermontese had stationed a military force on the opposite shore, under the command of General Enos, to whom was necessarily confided the secret. But on neither side would it answer to entrust that secret to the subordinates. *They* must, of course, regard each other as enemies in good faith; and the fact that they did so consider themselves, was productive of an affair which placed the Vermontese in a peculiarly awkward predicament. The circumstances were these: In order to preserve at least the mimicry of war, scouts and patrols were occasionally sent out by both parties. Unluckily one of these Vermont patrols happened one day to encounter a similar party from the army of St. Leger. Shots were exchanged with hearty goodwill; the Vermont sergeant fell, and his men retreated. The body was decently interred by order of General St. Leger, who sent his clothes to General Enos, accompanied by an open letter apologizing for the occurrence, and expressing his regret at the result.

It was hardly probable that an unsealed letter would pass through many hands, and its contents remain unknown to all save the person to whom it was addressed. Such, certainly, was not the fact in regard to the letter in question. Its contents transpired; and great was the surprise at the civility of General St. Leger in sending back the sergeant's clothes, and deploring his death. A messenger was despatched by General Enos to Governor Chittenden at Charlestown, who, not being in the secrets of his employers, failed not, with honest simplicity, to proclaim the circumstances of the sergeant's death, and the extraordinary message of General St. Leger. The consequence was excitement among the people assembled at Charlestown, attended with a kindling feeling of distrust. "Why should General St. Leger send back the clothes?" "Why regret the death of an enemy?" were questions more easily asked by the people, than capable of being safely and ingenuously answered by their leaders. The consequence was, a popular clamor unpleasant to the ears of the initiated. Major Runnels confronted Colonel Ira Allen, and demanded to know why St. Leger was sorry for the death of the sergeant? Allen's answer was evasive and unsatisfactory. The Major repeated the question, and Allen replied that he had better go to St. Leger at the head of his regiment, and demand the reason, for his sorrow, in person. A sharp altercation ensued, which had the effect, for a short time, of diverting the attention of the people from the dispatches which they had been clamoring to have read. These were precious moments for the Governor and the negotiators with the enemy. The Board of War was convened, the members of which were all in the secret, and a set of pretended letters were hastily prepared from such portions of General Enos's dispatches as would serve the purpose in hand, which were read publicly to the Legislature and the people; and which had the effect of allaying the excitement and hushing suspicion into silence.

Meantime a rumor of the capture of Cornwallis and his army at Yorktown was wafted along upon the southern breeze; the effect of which was such upon the people, as to induce Allen and Fay to write to the British commissioners with St. Leger, that it would be imprudent at that particular conjuncture for him to promulgate the royal proclamation, and urging delay to a more auspicious moment. The messenger with these despatches had

fed, unclothed, unpaid and deserting army ;* extensive disaffection among the people immediately at home ; continual irruptions of hostile partizan bands in every quarter ; mobs of insurgents setting the laws at defiance in one direction ; the militia
regiments in the district thus lawless, more than half disposed to
join the disorganizers ; with an actual and somewhat formidable
invasion from the west; it must be conceived that both civil
and military authorities were laboring under a complication of
evils, requiring for their control all that prudence and energy,
discretion, perseverance and courage, combined, could accomplish.

With the discomfiture and retreat of Major Ross on the one
hand, and the return of St. Leger to St. John's on the other,
all active operations ceased with the enemy at the north.   But
the difficulties of the state Government with the New Hampshire Grants were on the increase; and the controversy ran so
high, that by the 1st of December an insurrection broke out in
the regiments of Colonel John Van Rensselaer and Colonel
Henry K. Van Rensselaer, in the north-eastern towns of the
State ; while the regiment of Colonel Peter Yates—also belonging to the brigade of General Gansevoort—was in a condition
not much better.   These disturbances arose in Schaghticoke,
Hoosic, and a place called St. Coych, and parts adjacent, belonging then to the county of Albany ; but being on the east side of
the Hudson, north of the parallel of the northern line of Massachusetts, the Government of the New Hampshire Grants had extended its ægis over that section of country, claiming jurisdiction,
as heretofore stated, to the Hudson river.   General Gansevoort
was apprised of the insurrection on the 5th.   He immediately
directed Colonels Yates and Henry K. Van Rensselaer, whose
regiments, at that time, were the least affected with the insurgent spirit, to collect such troops as they could, and repair to St.
Coych, to the assistance of Colonel John Van Rensselaer.   An
express being dispatched to the Governor, at Poughkeepsie,
with the unwelcome information, and a request for directions

* "From the post of Saratoga to that of Dobbs's Ferry inclusive, I believe there is
not at this moment one day's supply of meat for the army on hand.   Supplies, particularly of beef cattle, must be speedily and regularly provided, or our posts cannot
be maintained, nor the army kept in the field much longer."—Letter of Washington
to President Weare of New Hampshire.

what course to pursue in the emergency, the return of the messenger brought very explicit orders from the indomitable chief magistrate :—"I perfectly approve of your conduct," said the Governor ; " and have only to add, that should the force already " detached prove insufficient to quell the insurrection, you will " make such addition to it as to render it effectual. I have " transmitted to General Robert Van Rensselaer the information, " and have directed him, in case it should be necessary, on your " application, to give assistance from his brigade."* Although the fact had not been stated in the dispatches forwarded to Governor Clinton, that the movement was beyond doubt sympathetic with, or instigated from, the Grants, yet the Governor was at no loss at once to attribute it to the " usurped government of that pretended State ;"† and it was his resolute determination to oppose force to force, and, in regard to the Grants themselves, to repel force by force.

Gansevoort did not receive his instructions from the Governor until the 15th. Meantime Colonels Yates and Henry Van Rensselaer had made no progress in quelling the insurrection ; the insurgents, on the other hand, being on the increase, and having thrown up a block-house for defence. On the 16th General Gansevoort took the field himself, repairing in the first instance to the head-quarters of General Stark at Saratoga, in order to obtain a detachment of troops and a field-piece. But the troops of Stark were too naked to move from their quarters ; and it was thought improper for him to interfere without an order from General Heath.‡ Gansevoort then crossed over to the east side of the river, in order to place himself at the head of such militia as he could muster in Schaghticoke and Hoosic ; but was soon met by Colonel Yates, in full retreat from the house of Colonel John Van Rensselaer. He had been able to raise but eighty men to put down the insurgents of John Van Rensselaer's regiment ; and on arriving at St. Coych, he discovered a force of five hundred men advancing from the Grants to the assistance

* MS. letter of Governor Clinton to General Gansevoort, Dec. 11, 1781.
† Idem.
‡ In his official report upon the subject, Gansevoort rather distrusted whether Stark assigned the true reason for withholding his aid on this occasion, Governor Chittenden, of the Grants, having just addressed him a letter requesting him not to interfere with his troops.

of the rebels. Gansevoort retired five miles farther, in order to find comfortable quarters for his men, and then attempted, but without success, to open a correspondence with the leader of the insurgents. Calls had been made upon four regiments, viz. those of Colonels Yates, and Henry K. Van Rensselaer, as heretofore stated, and upon Colonel Van Vechten and Major Taylor. But from the whole no greater force than eighty men could be raised. Of Colonel Van Vechten's regiment, only himself, a few officers, and one private could be brought into the field. Under these discouraging circumstances, the General was compelled to relinquish the expedition, and the insurgents remained the victors, to the no small terror of those of the inhabitants who were well-disposed, inasmuch as they were apprehensive of being taken prisoners and carried away, as had been the case with others, should they refuse taking the oath of allegiance to the government of Vermont.* Thus terminated the military events of the north, of all descriptions, for the year 1781.

There yet remain a few occurrences, connected with the Indian operations of the year, to be noted before closing the present chapter. It was in the Spring of this year that what was called the Coshocton campaign of Colonel Brodhead was performed, and was attended by circumstances that cannot be re-

---

* The materials for this rapid sketch of the insurrection of Dec. 1781, at the north-east of Albany, have been drawn from the Gansevoort papers, which are broken and imperfect. The controversy with Vermont was continued, with greater or less force, and in different ways, for several years. But a calm and powerful letter from General Washington to Governor Chittenden, written early in January, 1782, had great influence in causing the government of the Grants to relinquish the territory of New-York, twenty miles broad, upon the eastern side of the Hudson, upon which they had seized. The leaders who had entered upon the correspondence with the enemy in Canada, continued an interchange of communications during several months of the following year; but the course of things soon stripped that strange negotiation of its danger, and rendered it of no importance. Meantime, although Governor Clinton was fully determined to subdue the refractory spirits of the Green Mountains, the latter continued to gain strength and friends, and as their local government became settled, it was for the most part wisely and efficiently administered. Time and again the question was brought before Congress, where nobody cared to act upon it definitively. Hamilton, Jay, and Governeur Morris, all seemed to think it the part of wisdom to allow the secession and independence of Vermont. Things remained in an unsettled state, however, until after the adoption of the federal constitution by New-York in 1788, after which the controversy was amicably adjusted; Vermont agreeing to pay thirty thousand dollars as a full indemnification to persons in New-York holding titles to lands within its boundaries.

called with other than painful emotions.* It had at different times been the purpose of the Commander-in-chief that Colonel Brodhead should penetrate through the Ohio territory to Detroit; but that design was never accomplished. The expedition now under review was led by Brodhead against the villages of the unfriendly Delaware Indians at the forks of the Muskingum. In passing through the settlement of the Moravian Indians at Salem, under the religious care of the Rev. Mr. Heckewelder, some of Brodhead's men manifested a hostile disposition toward those inoffensive noncombatants; but their hostile feelings were repressed by Brodhead, whose exertions were seconded by Colonel Shepherd, of Wheeling. The towns against which the Americans were proceeding were under the control of Captain Pipe, who had espoused the cause of the crown at the instigation of M'Kee, Elliott, and Girty. On approaching Coshocton, Brodhead's forces were divided into three divisions; and so secret and rapid was their march, that the villages on the eastern bank of the river were fallen upon, and all the Indians who were at home taken, without firing a gun.† The immediate object of this visitation was to punish, as it was alleged, the Indians of those towns for some recent cruelties of unwonted atrocity. They had made a late incursion upon the frontiers of Virginia, in the course of which a considerable number of prisoners were taken; but, having been disappointed in the measure of their success, in a moment of rage they bound all the adult male captives to trees, and put them to death by torture, amidst the tears and lamentations of their families.‡ It was now Colonel Brodhead's design to inflict summary vengeance for those murders. He had with him a friendly Delaware chief, named *Pe-killon*, who pointed out sixteen of the captive warriors, upon whom he charged the murders in question. A council of war was convened in the evening, which decided that those sixteen warriors should be put to death. They were therefore bound, and despatched with tomahawk and spear, and scalped.§

A heavy rain had swollen the river, so that Colonel Brodhead could not cross over to the villages upon the opposite side. On the following morning an Indian presented himself upon the

---

* Doddridge, in his Indian Wars, dates the expedition referred to in 1780. Drake, who follows Heckewelder, states that it occurred in 1781.

† Doddridge.   ‡ Drake.   § Doddridge.

other side, and called for an interview with the "Great Captain," meaning the commander of the expedition. Colonel Brodhead presented himself, and inquired what he wanted. "I want peace," was the reply. "Send over some of your chiefs," said the Colonel. "May be you kill," rejoined the Indian. "They shall not be killed," was the answer. A fine-looking sachem thereupon crossed the river, and while engaged in conversation with Colonel Brodhead, a white savage, named Wetzel, stole treacherously behind the unsuspecting warrior, and struck him dead to the earth.*

Some ten or twelve prisoners were taken from another village farther up the river; and Brodhead commenced his return on the same day, committing the prisoners to a guard of militia. They had not proceeded far, however, before the barbarian guards began to butcher their captives; and all, save a few women and children, were presently despatched in cold blood.†

Glancing yet farther south, the Cherokee Indians having again become troublesome, and made an incursion into South Carolina, massacring some of the inhabitants and burning their houses, General Pickens proceeded into their own country, and inflicted upon them severe and summary chastisement. In the space of fourteen days, at the head of less than four hundred men, he killed upward of forty of the Indians, and destroyed thirteen towns. His troops were mounted men, who charged rapidly upon the Indians, cutting them down with their sabres with great effect. Unused to this mode of warfare, they sued immediately for peace.

The fall of Cornwallis was, in fact, the last important act of that great drama—THE AMERICAN REVOLUTION. Although the British were yet in considerable force in New-York, and were likewise in the occupancy of various posts in the southern states, still the season for active operations was past; and after the loss of the army of Cornwallis, they were not in sufficient force in the north to resist the troops that could now be directed against them. The campaigning of the year 1781, and in fact of the war of the Revolution, were therefore at an end. Still, there were other belligerent incidents occurring for months afterward, the record of which will require another chapter.

* Doddridge.   † Idem.

AMONG the minor, but yet not unimportant events of the border war at the north and west of Albany, was the capture, some time in the Winter of 1781—'82, of the celebrated loyalist marauder, Joseph Bettys, whose name has occurred in connexion with that of John Waltermeyer in the preceding chapter. Bettys, or "Joe Bettys" as he was commonly called, was a man of uncommon shrewdness and intelligence. Bold, athletic, and of untiring activity; revengeful and cruel in his disposition; inflexible in his purposes; his bosom cold as the marble to the impulses of humanity; he ranged the border settlements like a chafed tiger snuffing every tainted breeze for blood, until his name had become as terrific to the borderers, as were those of Kidd and Pierre le Grande upon the ocean in the preceding century. At the commencement of the war, Bettys was an inhabitant of Ballston. He early took the field in the cause of the republic, and a sergeant's warrant was conferred upon him in Colonel Wynkoop's regiment. But he had a proud, independent spirit, that could ill brook the severity of military discipline; and for some act of contumacy, he was reduced to the ranks. Still, knowing well his determined character and unflinching courage, and unwilling that his country should lose his services, the same gentleman* who had obtained his first warrant, procured him another, and a transfer to the fleet under the command of General Arnold on Lake Champlain, in the Summer of 1776.

* The late Colonel Ball, of Ballston.

In the severe naval engagement fought on that lake between
Arnold and Sir Guy Carleton, on the 11th of October of that
year, Bettys exhibited great bravery, and was of signal service
during the battle, which lasted four hours. He fought until
every commissioned officer on board his vessel was either killed
or wounded. Assuming the command then himself, he continued the fight with such reckless and desperate intrepidity, that
General Waterbury, Arnold's second in command, perceiving
that his vessel was about to sink, was obliged to order Bettys
and the survivors of his crew on board his own vessel. Having thus observed his good conduct, General Waterbury stationed
him by his side on the quarter-deck, and gave orders through
him, until his own vessel in turn became entirely crippled—the
crew mostly killed—the General himself wounded—and only
two others, exclusive of Bettys, left in fighting condition—when
his colors were struck to the enemy. General Waterbury afterward spoke in the most exalted terms of the high courage of
Bettys, adding, that the shrewdness of his management showed
that his conduct was not inferior to his courage.

While a prisoner in Canada, the arts of the enemy subverted
his principles. He was seduced from the service of his country,
and entered that of the enemy with the rank of ensign—proving himself an enemy equally subtle and formidable. From his
intimate knowledge of the country and his artful address, he
was frequently employed, sometimes as a messenger, at others
as a spy, and at others, again, in the double capacity of both.
During one of his missions of this nature, he was captured,
tried, and condemned to the gallows. But the entreaties of
his aged parents, and the solicitations of influential Whigs,
induced General Washington, on a promise of reformation, to
grant him a pardon. Yet if honor, generosity, and gratitude, had
ever been qualities of his soul, they had taken their departure.

Losing no time in rejoining the ranks of the enemy, he became alike reckless of character and the dictates of humanity;
and instead of suitably requiting the kindness which had successfully interposed to save him from an ignominious death, he
became the greatest scourge of his former friends and neighborhood. Ballston, in particular, had long reason to deplore the
ill-judged lenity. He returned, and recruited soldiers for the
King in the midst of the settlements; he captured and carried

off the most zealous and efficient Whigs, and subjected them to the severest sufferings; and those against whom he bore the strongest hate, lost their dwellings by fire or their lives by murder. No fatigue weakened his resolution—no distance was an obstacle to his purpose—and no danger appalled his courage. No one of the borderers felt secure. Sometimes in the darkness of the night he fell upon them by stealth; and at others, even at mid-day, he was seen prowling about, as if scorning disguise, and unconscious of danger. Indeed, he boldly proclaimed himself a desperado—carrying his life in his hand—equally careless of it as he said he should be of the lives of others were any again to attempt his arrest. His liberty, he declared, would only be yielded with his life; and whoever should attempt to take him, might rest assured that their heart's blood would in the same moment be drunk by the earth. His threats were well understood to be no unmeaning words; and, what added to the apprehension of the people, was the well-known fact, that he had always at his beck, openly or in concealment, according to the nature of the purpose immediately in hand, a band of refugees partaking of his own desperate character.

His adventures while engaged in this species of warfare were many and hazardous. Nor did he always confine his operations to the border-settlements, since he at one time entered the precincts of Albany, and made a similar attempt to that of Waltermeyer to abduct General Schuyler from the mansion of the Patroon, where he was then lodged.*

It must not be supposed, however, that all hearts quailed before Joe Bettys. Far from it; and many were the ineffectual attempts made for his arrest before the measures undertaken for that purpose were again crowned with success. But in the course of the Winter now under consideration his wonted vigilance was at fault. A suspicious stranger having been observed in the neighborhood of Ballston, upon snow-shoes, and well-armed, three men of that town, named Cory, Perkins, and Ful-

---

* This account of Joe Bettys has been written from a Fourth-of-July speech delivered by the late Colonel Ball some ten or twelve years ago. Among the prisoners made by Bettys and Waltermeyer from Ballston, in the Spring of 1781, were the following persons, viz: Samuel Nash, Joseph Chard, Uri Tracy, Ephraim Tracy, Samuel Patchin, Epenetus White, John Fulmer, and two men named Bontas, who were brothers. They were all taken to Canada, and roughly used.

mer, little doubting as to the identity of the man, immediately
armed themselves and went in pursuit. He was traced by a
circuitous track to the house of a well-known loyalist, which
was fortunately approached with so much circumspection as to
enable the scouts to reach the door unobserved. Breaking the
barrier by a sudden effort, they sprang in upon the black and
doubly-dyed traitor, and seized him before he had opportunity
of resistance. He was seated at dinner when they entered, his
pistols lying upon the table, and his rifle resting upon his arm.
He made an attempt to discharge the latter ; but forgetting to
remove the deer-skin cover of the lock, did not succeed. Powerful and muscular as he was, the three were an over-match for
him, and he was immediately so securely pinioned as to render
resistance useless and escape morally impossible.

Apparently resigning himself to his fate, Bettys now requested
permission to smoke, which was readily granted. While taking
the tobacco from his box, and making the usual preparations,
he was observed by Cory adroitly to cast something into the
fire. It was instantly snatched from thence with a handful of
coals, and proved to be a small leaden box, about the eighth of
an inch in thickness, and containing a paper in cipher, which
the captors could not read ; but it was subsequently ascertained
to be a despatch addressed to the British commander in New-
York. It also contained an order for thirty guineas, provided
the despatch should be safely delivered. Bettys pleaded hard
for permission to burn the paper, and offered a hundred guineas
for the privilege. But they refused his gold, and all his prof-
fered bribes for the means of escape, with the most unyielding
firmness. He then exclaimed—" I am a dead man !" It was
even so. He was taken to Albany, where he was tried, convicted, and executed as a spy and traitor.

If the conduct of the three captors of Major André was patriotic,
that of the three captors of Joe Bettys was both patriotic and
brave. André was a gentleman, and without the means of defence ; Bettys was formidably armed, and known to be a desperado. The capture of André was by accident ; that of Bettys,
by enterprise and design. The taking of the former was without danger ; that of the latter a feat of imminent peril. André
was a more important man, by rank and station, than Bettys ;
but not more dangerous. Both tempted their captors by gold,

and both were foiled.* The captors of Andre were richly rewarded, and the achievement hâs been emblazoned in history, and commemorated by monumental granite. The captors of Bettys have, until now, never been known to history; and their only visible reward was the rifle and pistols of their terrible captive. With such partial hand are the honors and rewards of this world bestowed!

As already remarked, the substantial fighting of the war was ended by the surrender of Cornwallis. It is true, there were affairs of outposts occurring afterward, and some partial fighting took place at the south early in the season of 1782, between General Wayne and sundry small British posts, after General Greene had detached the former into Georgia. The most serious of these affairs was a smart brush with a party of Creek Indians, near Savannah, on which occasion the British garrison sallied out to their assistance, but were repulsed. For the most part, however, the year 1782 was rather a period of armed neutrality than of active war. The news of the catastrophe at Yorktown at once and materially strengthened the opposition to the farther prosecution of the contest in the House of Commons, by which a resolution was soon afterward passed, declaring " That the House would consider as enemies to his Majesty and " the country, all who should advise or attempt the farther prose- " cution of offensive war on the Continent of North America." Sir Henry Clinton was superseded in the chief command by Sir Guy Carleton, who was specially instructed to use his endeavors to effect an accommodation with America. Commissioners for the negotiation of a treaty of peace were soon afterward appointed, viz. John Adams, Benjamin Franklin, John Jay, and Henry Laurens on the part of the United States, and Mr. Fitzherbert and Mr. Oswald on that of Great Britain. On the 30th of November these commissioners had agreed on provisional articles of peace, as the basis of a treaty by which the Independence of the United States was acknowledged in its fullest extent.

As the surrender of Earl Cornwallis was the last important military event between the main armies, so was the disastrous expedition of Majors Ross and Butler the last attempt of any magnitude upon the Valley of the Mohawk. True, indeed, that beautiful region of country had been so utterly laid waste, that

* Colonel Ball.

there was little more of evil to be accomplished.   But the chastisement of Major Ross, equally severe and unexpected, had
discouraged the enemy from making any farther attempt in that
quarter.   Not, however, that the Indians were entirely quiet.
On the contrary, they hung around the borders of the settlements in small parties, sometimes causing serious alarms, and
at others great trouble and fatigue, and likewise inflicting considerable injury.   On one occasion a party of thirty-five Indians crossed over from Oswegatchie to Palatine.   Falling in
with a scouting party, consisting of Jacob Timmerman and five
others, the Indians fired upon them.   Timmerman was wounded, and with one of his comrades taken prisoner.   Two of the
party were killed, and the other two succeeded in making their
escape.   The prisoners were taken to Oswegatchie, and thence
down to Montreal, where they were confined until the peace.
In consequence of exposures of this description, a vigilant watchfulness was necessary at all points; and Colonel Willett, who
retained the command, was exactly the officer for the station.
He had frequent occasion to despatch considerable bodies of
troops against the straggling parties of Indians and Tories; but
their lightness of foot, and dexterity in threading the mazes of
the forests, generally, if not always, enabled them to escape.   So
that no important event transpired in that section of country
during the year.

But while there was so little active warfare on the frontiers of
New-York during the Summer of 1782, the Indians of the
remoter west were more active along the Kentucky frontier than
in the preceding year.   In May they ravished, killed, and scalped a woman and her two daughters near Ashton's station.*   The
Indians perpetrating this outrage were pursued by Captain Ashton, at the head of a band of twenty-five men.   Being overtaken,
a battle ensued, in which the Indians were victorious.   The
Captain was killed, together with eight of his men, and four
others were mortally wounded.   In the month of August another
Kentucky settlement, called Hoy's Station, was visited by the
Indians, by whom two lads were carried into captivity.   This

---

* Adventures of Colonel Daniel Boon.   There is strong reason to doubt whether
the Indians abused the persons of the women.   If true, it was the only instance
of the kind that is believed to have occurred during the war.   It is a proud characteristic of the Indians, that they never violate the chastity of their female prisoners,

band was also pursued by Captain Holder, with a party of seventeen men, who, coming up with the Indians, were likewise defeated with a loss of seven killed and two wounded.

On the 15th of August, the post at Briant's station, five miles from Lexington, was invested by a far more considerable party of the enemy, numbering five hundred Indians and Canadians. After killing all the cattle in the neighborhood, they assaulted the post on the third day, but were repulsed with a loss of about eighty killed and numbers wounded;—how many, was not known. They were pursued on their retreat by Colonels Todd, Trigg, and Boon, and Major Harland, at the head of one hundred and seventy-six men, well armed and provided. The Indians drew the pursuers into an unfavorable position on the 19th, when a severe battle ensued, in which the Kentuckians were beaten with the loss of seventy-six men; among whom were Colonels Todd and Trigg, Major Harland, and a son of Colonel Boon. The battle lasted only fifteen minutes. The retreat from the field was yet more disastrous than the battle itself. It was fought on the banks of the main fork of the Licking river, at the great bend, forty-three miles from Lexington. The Kentuckians were pursued across the river, some on horseback and others on foot. Some were killed in the river, and others while ascending the cliffs beyond. The arrival of the fugitives at Lexington with the melancholy tidings, occasioned a scene of weeping and deep lamentation, since a large portion of the male population had fallen. Being reinforced a few days afterward, Colonel Boon returned to bury the dead, which he represents as an affair of a most painful description. So mangled and disfigured were the bodies, that their identity could not be ascertained. The Colonel was afterward informed that when the Indians discovered their own loss to have been four more than that of the Kentuckians, four of the seven prisoners they had taken were handed over to their young men to be put to death by torture.

On hearing of this disastrous affair, General Clark, who was at the Falls of the Ohio, directed a pursuit of the Indians to their own towns of Old and New Chilicothe, Peccaway, and Wills Town. Colonel Boon seems to have led this expedition, although the fact is not expressly stated in his narrative. Failing in an attempt to fall upon the Indians by surprise, the Colonel took possession of their deserted towns, which were burnt with fire. Seven prisoners and fifteen scalps were taken by the Kentuckians, whose own loss was but four men ; two of whom were killed by accident, not by Indians. With these incidents closed the Indian war of the Revolution on the Kentucky border.

But there yet remains a tale of murderous character to be recorded, which, in its black and inexcusable atrocity, transcends any and every Indian massacre which marked that protracted and unnatural contest. It is a tale of blood, too, in which the white men—not the Indians—are to be branded as the savages.

On the banks of the Muskingum resided several communities of Indians, who had embraced the peaceable tenets of the Moravians. They were of the Delaware nation, and had removed to the Muskingum from Friedenshutten on the Big Beaver, and from Wyalusing and Sheshequon on the Susquehanna, in the year 1772. Notwithstanding the annoyance experienced by them in consequence of the Cresap war, in 1774, their settle· ments, which were named Schoenbrunn, Salem, and Gnaden· huetten, rose rapidly in importance, and in a short time numbered upward of four hundred people. Among their converts was the celebrated Delaware chief *Glickhickan*, famous alike for his bravery on the war-path, his wisdom in council, and his eloquence in debate. Their location, being a kind of half-way station between the white settlements and the hostile Indians of the lakes, was unpleasant after the war of the Revolution came on, and subjected them to difficulties alternately arising from the suspicions of both or all of the belligerent parties, against whose evil intentions toward them they were occasionally admonished. Still, their labors, their schools, and their religious exercises were conducted and practised as usual.

Their spiritual guides, at the period now under discussion, were, Michael Jung, David Zeisberger, and John Heckewelder, known in later times as the Indian Historian. These people looked upon war with abhorrence ; maintaining that "the " Great Being did not make men to destroy men, but to love and " assist each other." They had endeavored to dissuade some of their own race from taking any part in the contest, and had likewise given occasional information to the white settlements when threatened with Indian invasions.

The hostile Indians frequently hovered around their settlements, and sometimes threatened their destruction, under the pretext that their neutrality was equivocal, and that they were secretly in alliance with the Americans, to whom they were in the practice of giving timely notice of the hostile advances of the Indians in the service of the King.* In 1777 they were visited by the noted Huron chief, *Half King*, at the head of two hundred of his warriors, on his way to attack some of the frontier settlements of Virginia. Half King at first menaced the Moravian non-combatants; but Glickhickan appeased his ire by a timely supply of refreshments, and diverted him from his purpose by an opportune speech, declaring their religious sentiments and praising their missionaries.

The British authorities at Detroit were by no means friendly to these Moravian towns; early in the year 1781 they applied to the Great Council of the Six Nations, assembled at Niagara, to remove them out of the country. A message was accordingly sent by the Iroquois to the Ottawas and Chippewas to this effect: "We herewith make you a present of the Christian Indians to make soup of;" a figurative Indian expression equivalent to saying—"We deliver these people to you to be killed." But neither the Ottawas nor Chippewas would receive the message, which was returned with the laconic reply—"We have no cause for doing this." The same message was next sent to the Wyandots, but they at that time were equally indisposed to make war upon their inoffensive brethren.† But in the Autumn of the same year, under the influence of M'Kee and Elliott, who had now become captains in the ranks of the crown connected with the Indian service at Detroit, and by reason of the more immediate persuasions of Simon Girty, the bloodthirsty refugee associate of M'Kee and Elliott, who was living among the Wyandots, over whom he had acquired great influence, the poor Moravians, with their pious and self-denying ministers, were forcibly removed, or rather compelled, by the hostile Indians, at the instigation of those men, to remove to Sandusky. The leaders of the Wyandots compelling this emigration, were Girty, Half King, and the celebrated Captain Pipe. The sachem-convert, Glickhickan, was also carried to Sandusky; and a young female relation of his, by her courage and gene-

---

* Doddridge.   † Heckewelder.

rosity, had well-nigh cost him his life. Apprehending that evil
would befall her friends, she stole a fine horse belonging to Captain Pipe, and rode to Pittsburgh, to give the alarm in regard
to the captive missionaries and their congregations. In revenge
for this courageous action, Glickhickan was seized by a party of
the Wyandot, or Huron warriors, who raised the death-song,
and would have put him to death but for the interference of
the Half King in his favor. Glickhickan was subsequently examined by his captors, and his innocence of all participation in
the mission of the heroic squaw fully made to appear.

It was at a great sacrifice of property and comfort that these
Indians were torn thus from their homes. They had more
than two hundred heads of black cattle, and upward of four hun
dred swine, of which they were deprived, together with large
stores of corn, and three hundred acres more just ripening for
the harvest. They arrived at Sandusky on the 11th of October—a distance of one hundred and twenty-five miles from their
homes. They were treated with great harshness on their march,
especially by Girty, who, in the course of the Winter subsequent
to their removal, caused their missionaries to be arrested by order of the commandant at Detroit, to which place they were
transferred.*

While the meek and pious missionaries, amid the tears and
other manifestations of grief of their people, were preparing for
the journey to Detroit, intelligence of a most painful character
was received. Being pressed by hunger at Sandusky, a considerable number of the Moravian Indians, with some of their
families, had been allowed to return to their former habitations
on the Muskingum, to secure their corn, and such other provi
sions as they could find, and forward the same from time to
time to their suffering brethren. Unhappily, while this peaceable party were thus engaged at Salem and Gnadenhuetten, the
weather being favorable for the operations of scalping parties, a
few hostile Indians of Sandusky had made a descent upon the
Pennsylvania frontier, and murdered the family of Mr. William

---

* These good men, after many trials and vexations, were ultimately released, and
Half King charged all the blame upon Girty, whose iniquity in the premises the
Indian prince indignantly exposed and denounced. The British Government also
censured the conduct of its officers in regard to the proceedings, especially the
harsh treatment of the missionaries.

Wallace, consisting of his wife and five or six children. A man named John Carpenter was taken prisoner at the same time.

Enraged at these outrages, a band of between one and two hundred men, from the settlements of the Monongahela, turned out in quest of the marauders, thirsting for vengeance, under the command of Colonel David Williamson. Each man provided himself with arms, ammunition, and provisions, and the greater number were mounted. They bent their course directly for the settlements of Salem and Gnadenhuetten, arriving within a mile of the latter place at the close of the second day's march. Colonel Gibson, commanding at Pittsburgh, having heard of Williamson's expedition, despatched messengers to apprise the Indians of the circumstance, but they arrived too late.

It was on the morning of the 7th of March that Williamson and his gang reached the settlement of Gnadenhuetten, the very day on which the Indians, having accomplished their labors, were bundling up their luggage for retracing their steps to Sandusky. Some of their number, however, were yet in the fields gathering corn, as were many others in the town of Salem, at no great distance thence. The party of Williamson divided themselves into three detachments, so disposed as to approach the settlements from as many different points at once. The Indians had indeed been apprised of Williamson's approach by four Delaware Indians on the day before ; but, conscious of their own innocence, and least of all anticipating harm from the Americans, they continued in their pacific occupations without suspicion of danger.

When within a short distance of the settlement, though yet in the woods, the advance guard of one of Williamson's divisions met a young Indian half-blood, named Joseph Shabosh, whom they murdered in the most cruel and wanton manner. The youth was catching horses, when he was shot at and wounded so badly that he could not escape. He then informed them who he was; stated that his father was a white man and a Christian; and begged for his life. But they regarded not his entreaties. His arm had been broken by the first shot. He was killed by a second, tomahawked and scalped, and cut into pieces with the hatchets of his murderers. Another Indian youth, a brother-in-law of young Shabosh, who was engaged in binding corn, about one hundred and fifty yards from the town, saw the white men approaching. Knowing some of them, however, and supposing them to be friends, he addressed them as such. But he was soon undeceived. He saw them shoot one of his Indian brethren who was crossing the river in a canoe, and immediately ran away in affright. Unfortunately, in his panic he ran from the village instead of toward it, so that no alarm was given until the Americans had quite proceeded into the heart of the town.

Many of the Indians were scattered over the fields at work, and were hailed by Williamson's men representing themselves as " friends and brothers, who had come purposely from Fort Pitt " to relieve them from the distress brought upon them by the ene- " my, on account of their being friends to the American people." The Indians, not doubting their sincerity, gave credence to their professions, and walking up to them, thanked them for their kindness. Their treacherous visiters next persuaded them to cease work and go into the village ; as it was their pur- pose to take them to Fort Pitt, in order to their greater security from the Wyandots, where they would be abundantly supplied with all they might want. Delighted with such an unexpected friendly visitation, the Indians mingled with the strangers with the utmost cordiality, walking and conversing with them like old acquaintances. They delivered up their arms, and began with all alacrity to prepare food for their refreshment. Mean- time a messenger was despatched to Salem, " to inform the breth " ren and sisters there of what had taken place at Gnadenhuetten ; " the messenger giving it as his opinion that perhaps God had " ordained it so, that they should not perish upon the barrens of " Sandusky, and that those people were sent to relieve them."

Pleased with the communication, and yet unwilling to act precipitately, the party at Salem deputed two of their number to confer with their brethren and the white men at Gnadenhuetten. Communications were interchanged, which were mutually satisfactory. The dissembling of Williamson and his men was so complete as to win the entire confidence of the simple-mind- ed people ; and at the solicitation of the party at Gnadenhuetten, those at Salem came over and joined their insidious visitors, for the purpose of removing to the white settlements, where, as they were farther assured, all their wants would be supplied by the Moravian brethren at Bethlehem. A party of Williamson's men

were detached to Salem to assist in bringing all the Indians and
their effects to Gnadenhuetten ; and, still farther to win upon the
easy confidence of their victims, this precious collection of assas-
sins made zealous professions of piety, and discoursed to the Indians, and among each other, upon religious subjects.   On leaving Salem, the white men applied the torch to the houses and
church of the village, under the pretext of depriving the hostile
Indians of their benefit.

Having, like their brethren at Gnadenhuetten, delivered up all
their arms, their axes, hatchets, and working-tools, under the
stipulation that they were all to be returned to them at Pittsburgh, the party from Salem set out with light hearts to enjoy the
white man's kind protection.   But on approaching the other
village, their apprehensions were awakened, by marks in the
sand, as though an Indian had recently been weltering there in
his blood.   They, nevertheless, proceeded to the village to join
their brethren ; but on their arrival thither a sad change came
over their waking dream of happiness.   Instead of being treated
as Christian friends and brothers, they were at once roughly designated as warriors and prisoners ; and already, previous to their
arrival, had their brethren, sisters, and children at Gnadenhuetten, been seized and confined for the purpose of being put to
death.   The party from Salem were now completely within the
toils of their enemies.   They could neither fight nor fly.   Besides that their religious creed forbad them to do the one, they
had no weapons of defence, and they were surrounded by armed
men, who would not suffer them to escape.

As a pretext for this usage, Williamson and his men now
charged them with having stolen their horses, and all their working tools and furniture—charges not only untrue, but known to
be so by their accusers.   A more humble, devout, and exemplary community of Christians, probably, was not at that day to
be found in the new world.   Under the untiring instructions of
their missionaries, they had been taught the dress and practices
of civilized life.   They were tillers of the soil, and had become
so well acquainted with the usages of society, and were so well
furnished with the necessaries and some of the luxuries of life,
that they could set a comfortable table and a cup of coffee before
a stranger.   All the animals and articles charged upon them as
having been stolen, were their own private property, honestly

acquired.   But their protestations of innocence, and their entreaties, alike were vain.   Their betrayers were bent upon shedding
their blood.

Still, the officers were unwilling to take upon themselves the
exclusive responsibility of putting them to death, and the solemn
farce of a council was held upon the subject.   By this tribunal
it was determined that the question of life or death should be
decided by a vote of the whole detachment.   The men were
thereupon paraded, and Williamson put the question, " whether
the Moravian Indians should be taken prisoners to Pittsburgh,
or put to death ?" requesting all in favor of saving their lives to
advance in front of the line.   Only sixteen or eighteen of the
whole number were by this process found to be inclined to
mercy, and the poor trembling prisoners were immediately admonished that they must prepare to die.

Some, indeed, there were among the blood-thirsty gang eager
to commence the work of death *instanter ;* but as the victims
united in begging a short delay for their devotions, the request
was granted.   " Then, asking pardon for whatever offence they
" had given or grief they had occasioned to each other, the In
" dians kneeled down, offering prayers to God their Saviour—
" and kissing one another under a flood of tears, fully resigned
" to his will, they sang praises unto Him, in the joyful hope
" that they would soon be relieved from all pains, and join their
" Redeemer in everlasting bliss.   During the time of their devo
" tions, the murderers were consulting on the manner in which
" they would put them to death."   Some were for setting fire to
the houses, and dispatching them as by an *auto da fé ;* others
were for killing them outright, and bearing their scalps as
trophies back to their homes ; while those who had opposed the
execution yet protested against " the deep damnation of their
taking off," and withdrew.   Impatient of delay, the blood-thirsty
wretches interrupted the last hymn they could sing in this
world, and demanded if they were not ready for death.   They
were answered in the affirmative—the victims adding : " That
" they had commended their immortal souls to God, who had
" given them the assurance in their hearts that he would receive
" their souls."   Then seizing a mallet from a cooper's shop, one
of the ruffians commenced the work of murder by knocking the
Indians on the head.   Having killed fourteen successively in

this manner, he desisted, and handing the weapon over to
another, remarked—"Go on in the same way: I think I have
done pretty well!" Those who had opposed the murder stood
at a distance, wringing their hands, and calling God to witness
"that they were innocent of the lives of these harmless Christian Indians."

The first victim in the other slaughter-house—for such both
in which the Indians were confined became—was an aged Indian
woman named Judith, a widow, of great piety. In a few
minutes the work of death was completed. Ninety Indians,
Christians and unarmed—unoffending in every respect—were
murdered in cold blood. Among them were old men and ma-
trons, young men and maidens, and infants at their mothers'
breasts. Sixty-two of the number were grown persons, one
third of whom were women, and the remaining thirty-four were
children. Five of the slain were assistant teachers, two of
whom had been exemplary members of the pious Brainard's
congregation in New Jersey. The convert chief, Isaac Glickhickan, was also among the slain. Only two of the captives escaped this shocking massacre. They were both young. One
of them eluded the murderers by creeping unobserved into a
cellar, from whence he stole into the woods; and the other,
having been knocked down and scalped, feigned death, and escaped after the murderers left the place. This they did not do,
however, until they supposed all were dead. On completing
the work, they retired for a short distance to recruit their
strength; but, as though resolved that not a living soul should
have the remotest chance of escape, they returned to take
another look at the dead; and observing a youth, scalped and
bloody, supporting himself with his hands upon the floor in order to rise, the monsters dispatched him with their hatchets!
As night drew on, they set fire to the buildings, and thereupon
departed for their own homes, singing and yelling with demoniac
joy at the victory they had achieved. According to the accounts of the American newspapers of that day, this massacre
was a very commendable transaction; it was represented that
the attack of Williamson was made upon a body of warriors,
who had been collecting a large quantity of provisions on the
Muskingum, for supplying their own warriors and other hostile
savages. It was stated, as the cause of their destruction having

been so complete, that they were surprised and attacked in their cabins at night; and it was exultingly added, that "about eighty "horses fell into the hands of the victors, which they loaded "with the plunder, the greatest part furs and skins—and re- "turned to the Ohio without the loss of a man !"*

If through the whole extent of the voluminous records of savage wars in America, a deed of darker treachery, or of deeper atrocity, than this massacre of the Moravian Indians, is to be found, it has thus far escaped the research of the author of the present work.   The uncivilized and unchristianized savages themselves were amazed at the enormity of the bloody deed. But the construction they put upon the transaction, as a provi- dential occurrence, was curious and striking.   They said they had envied the condition of their relations, the believing In- dians, and could not bear to look upon their happy and peace- ful lives in contrast with their own lives of privation and war.   Hence they had endeavored to take them from their own tranquil homes, and draw them back into heathenism, that they might be reduced again to a level with themselves.   But the Great Spirit would not suffer it to be so, and had taken them to himself.†

After this massacre, the Indians at Sandusky—not only those who were Christians, but the Wyandots, and others who were hostile, watched the movements of the whites along the Ohio with ceaseless vigilance.   Two months having expired after the destruction of the Moravians, another expedition was or- ganized to go against the Wyandots and other Indian tribes in the Sandusky country.   The number of men volunteering for the campaign, was four hundred and eighty.   They were mus- tered at the old Mingo towns on the western bank of the Ohio. An election was held for the office of Commander-in-chief of the expedition—Colonels Williamson and William Crawford being the candidates.   The choice devolved upon the latter, who was an unwilling candidate, and accepted the post with re-

---

* Pennsylvania Gazette, April 17, 1782.   The author will add, in this place, that the preceding account of this unparalleled case of wholesale murder has been chief- ly prepared from the accurate and laborious Heckewelder, together with extracts from Doddridge's Notes on the Indian Wars, and Loskiel, as quoted in Drake's Book of the Indians.

† Heckewelder—Nar. Moravian Missions.

luctance. The same men who had murdered the Moravians, composed the present army in part, and the march was commenced with a determination that not the life of an Indian, friend or foe, should be spared. The expedition had been organized with great secrecy, as it was supposed ; and as the men were mounted, the intention was by a rapid march to fall upon the Wyandot towns by surprise. Arriving, however, at the Moravian towns where the murders had been committed, three Indians were discovered by Crawford, who fled at a pace too rapid to be overtaken. The pursuit of them was disorderly ; and from the conduct of his men on that occasion, their commander lost confidence in them, and from that moment entertained a presentiment of defeat. So far from the advance of Crawford being a secret, it ultimately appeared that the Indians had been narrowly watching his progress at every step. They saw the gathering at the Mingo towns, and counted their numbers. They had also been apprised of the resolve that "no quarter was in any instance to be given."* It was to be expected, then, that at some point they would be prepared for Crawford's reception.

Crawford and Williamson had intended first to strike upon the Moravian town on the Sandusky ; but on arriving at that place, they discovered that the Indians had seasonably withdrawn, so that the brave Williamson had no non-combatants to vanquish. The town was, in fact, covered with tall grass, the Indians having removed to the Scioto some time before. Crawford and Williamson then directed their course for several towns of the hostile Indians—by whom they were unexpectedly drawn into an engagement upon an open prairie, the Indian warriors themselves being concealed by the shrubbery upon its margin. Night came on before the battle was terminated ; and the Indians, expecting a reinforcement from the Shawanese before morning, made their dispositions for surrounding the Americans at daylight. But when morning came, the white man was not there. The Americans, indeed, had not acquitted themselves like soldiers during the engagement of the preceding afternoon, and they availed themselves of the darkness to escape—greatly to the mortification of the Indians and their daring leader, Captain Pipe. They had encamped upon the prairie ; and so silent

* Doddridge.

was their flight, that some of them, not aware of the retreat, were found by the Indians in the morning still sleeping amid the tall prairie-grass, where they had laid themselves down.

An active pursuit of the fugitives took place, and many straggling parties were overtaken and cut to pieces. Upward of a hundred were thus either killed outright or taken. Among the latter were Colonel William Crawford, his son, and Doctor M'Knight. The former of these gentlemen had rendered himself particularly offensive to the Indians by his successful campaigns against them, so that his capture was a triumph. It was still more unfortunate for him that he was taken while serving with such a commander as Williamson—against whom, for his cruel treachery at Gnadenhuetten, the savages were cherishing the bitterest feelings of revenge. Crawford, however, had not been engaged in that shameful affair, but being found among the same men who had murdered their friends and relations in March, the Indians could not draw the distinction. They had anxiously sought for Williamson, but on being informed that he was among the first to escape, they called out " revenge !" " revenge !" on whomsoever they had in their power.

Crawford would probably have made good his retreat but that he lingered behind in anxiety for his son, whom he supposed yet to be in the rear. After wandering two days in the woods with Dr. M'Knight, both were taken by a party of Delawares, and conducted to the Old Wyandot town. Here Captain Pipe, with his own hands, painted the prisoners black, a certain premonition of the doom that awaited them. From thence they were taken to the New Wyandot town, passing on the way the mangled remains of a number of their fellow-captives. At the new town, the place appointed for the execution of Crawford, they found the noted Simon Girty. It had been decided that Crawford should die by the most aggravated torture, to atone in some degree for the murders by Williamson and his men at Gnadenhuetten. After he was bound to the fatal post, the surviving Christian Indians were called upon to come forth and take vengeance on the prisoner ; but they had withdrawn, and their savage relations stepped forward in their stead. Before the work of torture was commenced, Captain Pipe addressed the Indians at some length, and in the most earnest manner, at the close of which they all joined in a hideous yell, and prepared for the work in hand. The fire was kindled, when it occurred to poor Crawford, that among the sachems he had a particular friend, named Wingemund. "Where is my friend Wingemund?" he asked, "I wish to see him." It is true that this chief had been the warm friend of Colonel Crawford, by whom he had been entertained at his own house. Under these circumstances Crawford indulged a faint degree of hope, that if he could see the chief, his life might yet be saved. Wingemund was not far distant, having, in fact, retired from the place of execution, that he might not behold what he could not prevent. He was sent for, however, and an interesting and even affecting conversation ensued between himself and the prisoner. This conversation was commenced by Crawford, who asked the chief if he knew him. He replied that he believed he did, and asked—"Are you not Colonel Crawford?" "I am," replied the Colonel; and the conversation was thus continued—the chief discovering much agitation and embarrassment, and ejaculating—"So!—Yes!—Indeed!"

"*Colonel Crawford.* Do you not recollect the friendship that always existed between us, and that we were always glad to see each other?

"*Sachem.* Yes, I remember all this; and that we have often drunk together, and that you have been kind to me.

"*Col. C.* Then I hope the same friendship still continues.

"*Sachem.* It would, of course, were you where you ought to be, and not here.

"*Col. C.* And why not here? I hope you would not desert a friend in time of need; now is the time for you to exert yourself in my behalf, as I should do for you were you in my place.

"*Sachem.* Colonel Crawford, you have placed yourself in a situation which puts it out of my power, and that of others of your friends, to do any thing for you.

"*Col. C.* How so, Captain Wingemund?

"*Sachem.* By joining yourself to that execrable man, Williamson, and his party. The man who, but the other day, murdered such a number of the Moravian Indians, knowing them to be friends; knowing that he ran no risk in murdering a people who would not fight, and whose only business was praying.

"*Col. C.* But, I assure you, Wingemund, that had I been

with him at the time, this would not have happened. Not I alone, but all your friends, and all good men, reprobate acts of this kind.

"*Sachem.* That may be, yet these friends, these good men, did not prevent him from going out again to kill the remainder of those inoffensive yet foolish Moravian Indians. I say *foolish,* because they believed the whites in preference to us. We had often told them that they would one day be so treated by those people who called themselves their friends. We told them there was no faith to be placed in what the white men said ; that their fair promises were only intended to allure, that they might the more easily kill us, as they have done many Indians before they killed those Moravians.

"*Col. C.* I am sorry to hear you speak thus. As to Wil liamson's going out again, when it was known that he was de· termined on it, I went out with him to prevent him from committing fresh murders.

"*Sachem.* This the Indians would not believe, were I to tell them so.

"*Col. C.* And why would they not believe it ?

"*Sachem.* Because it would have been out of your power to prevent his doing what he pleased.

"*Col. C.* Out of my power ? Have any Moravian Indians been killed or hurt since we came out ?

"*Sachem.* None. But you went first to their town, and finding it empty and deserted, you turned on the path toward us. If you had been in search of warriors only, you would not have gone thither. Our spies watched you closely. They saw you while you were embodying yourselves on the other side of the Ohio. They saw you cross that river ; they saw where you encamped at night ; they saw you turn off from the path to the deserted Moravian town ; they knew you were going out of your way ; your steps were constantly watched ; and you were suffered quietly to proceed until you reached the spot where you were attacked.

"*Col. C.* (With emotion.) What do they intend to do with me ?

"*Sachem.* I tell you with grief. As Williamson, with his whole cowardly host, ran off in the night at the whistling of our warriors' balls, being satisfied that now he had no Moravians to deal with, but men who could fight, and with such he did not wish to have any thing to do; I say, as he has escaped, and they have taken you, they will take revenge on you in his stead.

"*Col. C.* And is there no possibility of preventing this? Can you devise no way to get me off? You shall, my friend, be well rewarded, if you are instrumental in saving my life.

"*Sachem.* Had Williamson been taken with you, I and some friends, by making use of what you have told me, might, perhaps, have succeeded in saving you; but as the matter now stands, no man would dare to interfere in your behalf. The King of England himself, were he to come to this spot with all his wealth and treasure, could not effect this purpose. The blood of the innocent Moravians, more than half of them women and children, cruelly and wantonly murdered, calls aloud for *revenge.* The relatives of the slain, who are among us, cry out and stand ready for *revenge.* The Shawanese, our grand-children, have asked for your fellow-prisoner; on him they will take *revenge.* All the nations connected with us cry out, *revenge! revenge!* The Moravians, whom you went to destroy, having fled instead of avenging their brethren, the offence has become national, and the nation itself is bound to take *revenge.*

"*Col. C.* My fate is then fixed, and I must prepare to meet death in its worst form.

"*Sachem.* Yes, Colonel. I am sorry for it, but I cannot do any thing for you. Had you attended to the Indian principle, that good and evil cannot dwell together in the same heart, so a good man ought not to go into evil company, you would not have been in this lamentable situation. You see now, when it is too late, after Williamson has deserted you, what a bad man he must be. Nothing now remains for you but to meet your fate like a brave man. Farewell, Colonel Crawford! They are coming. I will retire to a solitary spot."*

On turning away from his friend, whom it was not in his power to assist, it is said the old Sachem was affected to tears, and could never afterward speak of the incident without deep emotion. The moment the chief had left the Colonel, a number of the executioners rushed upon him, and commenced the work of torture, which was in progress three hours before the

---

* Heckewelder's Indian Nations.

victim fell upon his face and expired with a groan.   During the proceedings against him, he was continually and bitterly upbraided for the conduct of the white men at Gnadenhuetten.   If not himself a participator in that atrocious affair, they reproached him for having now come against them with the worst kind of murderers—such as even Indians had not among them. " Indians," said they, " kill their enemies, but not their friends. " When once they have stretched forth their hand, and given " that endearing name, they do not kill.   But how was it with " the believing Indians on the Muskingum ?   You professed " friendship for them.   You hailed and welcomed them as such. " You protested they should receive no harm from you. And what " did you afterward to them ?   They neither ran from you, nor " fired a single shot on your approach.   And yet you called them " warriors, knowing they were not such !   Did you ever hear war- " riors pray to God, and sing praises to him, as they did ?   Could " not the shrieks and cries of the innocent little children excite " you to pity, and to save their lives ?   No ! you did not !   You " would have the Indians believe you are Christians, because " you have the Great Book among you, and yet you are mur- " derers in your hearts!   Never would the unbelieving Indians " have done what you did, although the Great Spirit has not put " his Book into their hands as into yours !   The Great Spirit " taught you to read all that he wanted you to do, and what he " forbade that you should do.   These Indians believed all that " they were told was in that Book, and, believing, strove to act " accordingly.   We knew you better than they did.   We often " warned them to beware of you and your pretended friendship; " but they would not believe us.   They believed nothing but " good of you, and for this they paid with their lives."[*]

It was, indeed, most unhappy for Colonel Crawford, that he

---

[*] Heckewelder's Narrative of the Moravian Missions.   " There was farther a circumstance much against this unfortunate man, which enraged the Indians to a high degree.   It was reported that the Indian spies sent to watch their movements, on examining a camp which Crawford and Williamson had left, west of the Ohio, had found on trees peeled for the purpose, the words, written with coal and other mineral substances—' *No quarters to be given to an Indian, whether man, woman, or child.*'   When the Indians find inscriptions on trees or other substances, they are in the habit of making exact copies of them, which they preserve until they find some one to read or interpret them.   Such was the fact in the present case, and the inscription was sufficient to enrage them."—*Idem.*

had been captured in such company; but never were reproach-
es more righteously heaped upon the heads of the guilty than
on this occasion.   Never was the scorpion lash of satire more
justly inflicted—could but the really guilty have been there to feel
its withering rebuke.   The son of Colonel Crawford, himself
doomed to the same fate, was present with Dr. Knight, and
obliged to behold the torture, and listen to the agonising ejacu-
lations of his parent, without being able to render assistance or
offer a word of consolation.*   The sufferings of the son followed close upon those of the father ; but with Dr. Knight it was
otherwise.   He was reserved for sacrifice by the Shawanese,
and while on his way thither contrived to escape, and, after
twenty-one days of hardship and hunger in the wilderness, succeeded in gaining Fort M'Intosh.

The defeat of Colonel Boon at the Blue Licks in August, the
massacre of the Moravian Indians, and the fate of Crawford and
his expedition, are the last tales of blood connected with the
American Revolution.   It is true that in September following,
a large body of Indians laid siege to the fort at Wheeling, but
the siege was raised without farther bloodshed than the death of
one man in the fort and of three or four without.   A barn was
burnt at Rice's fort, which was also invested, but not seriously,
and the Indians withdrew to their own wilds.   Should the details of the last few pages be considered rather too ample for the
general plan of the present work, it must be remembered that
the awarding of justice to the Indian character also entered
largely into its design.   The transaction on the Muskingum
forms one of the darkest pages in the records of civilized war ;
unsurpassed, certainly, if not unparalleled, in the history, written or unwritten, of the whole aboriginal race.   The victims
were not only innocent and harmless, but, obedient to the pre-
cepts of their religion, offered no resistance to their hypocritical
murderers, and poured out their blood like water—crimson liba-
tions in sacrifice to the white man's rapacity and hate.   Nor can
the Indians be censured for the fate of Crawford.

With the exception of the Indian details in the present chapter, the year 1782 passed away without furnishing any military

* Withers's Chronicles, quoted by Drake in his Book of the Indians.   Dr. Ramsay says it was Colonel Crawford's son-in-law who was present, and subsequently
underwent the same fate.

operations of moment, under the immediate direction of the respective Commanders-in-chief. Sir Guy Carleton had probably been restrained from offensive war by instructions conforming to the pacific vote of the House of Commons, cited in the early part of the present chapter ; while the condition of the American army, had Washington been otherwise disposed, disabled him from making any attempt on the posts in possession of the British.* Generals Greene and Wayne had reconquered the south ; and Sir Guy Carleton had directed the officers of his Majesty in the north to send out no more Indian expeditions and to recall those already on foot. Still, notwithstanding all these conciliatory indications, there remained a possibility that the conflict was not yet ended. A change of ministers in England might produce a change of policy. In view of this uncertainty, the Commander-in-chief relaxed none of his efforts during the year to preserve the discipline of the army, and keep the country in an attitude of defence. In pursuance of this policy, in the month of January, 1783, news of the signing of a treaty of peace not having yet been received, the Commander-in-chief conceived the project of surprising and obtaining possession of the important fortress of Oswego. It was the occupation of this post which gave the British such ready facilities for intriguing with the Six Nations on the one hand, and for pouring their motley battalions down upon the American settlements; and the Commander-in-chief judged wisely, that in the event of another campaign the possession of that fortress would be of the first consequence to the Americans, being then one of the most formidable military defences on the Continent.

Having determined to attempt its capture by surprise, the execution of the project was confided to Colonel Willett. With the utmost secrecy therefore, as to destination, the troops of his command were suddenly assembled at Fort Herkimer on the eighth of February. Commencing their march immediately, on the night of the 9th they crossed the Oneida lake, and arrived at Oswego Falls, a few miles only from the fortress, by two o'clock P. M. on the following day. With the small force under his command, and without the means of prosecuting a siege, it was of course necessary to carry the works by escalade if at all.

* Marshall.

Halting, therefore, at the Falls, the necessary ladders were constructed and the march was resumed. At 10 o'clock in the evening they were within four miles of the fort. After which, having marched about two hours, and not coming in sight of the point of destination, an investigation of the cause was undertaken, when, to the astonishment and mortification of the Commander, and to the vexation of the whole corps, it was ascertained that, by diverging from the river, their guide, a young Oneida Indian, had lost his way. The situation was, indeed, awkward and perplexing. They had been at one time nearly within speaking distance of the works, and the shout of victory was almost raised in anticipation, when suddenly they discovered that they were lost in a deep forest, in the depth of winter, and amid mountains of snow. It was too late to prosecute the enterprise any farther that night. They could not remain in the vicinity of the fortress over the ensuing day without being discovered. And the instructions of the Commander-in-chief were peremptory, that if they failed in surprising the fort, the attempt would be unwarrantable. The only alternative, therefore, was to relinquish the enterprise, and reluctantly retrace their steps. It was a sad mistake of the poor Indian, but not an error of design. The march had been one of great severity and fatigue. The guide had led them into a swamp, and while they were standing still, after discovering themselves to be lost, so cold was the weather, that the feet of some of the men froze into the mire. The return march was even more painful still, because of the lameness of some and the varied sufferings of others. One man was frozen to death. But all happened well in the end, for on Colonel Willett's return to Fort Rensselaer, and thence to Albany, he arrived at the ancient Dutch capital just in season to hear the welcome news of peace proclaimed by the Town Clerk at the City Hall, and to mingle his rejoicings with those of the inhabitants.

An agreement for the cessation of hostilities between the United States and Great Britain was signed by the respective commissioners of the two powers on the 20th of January, upon the basis of the articles stipulated in Paris on the 30th of the preceding November. And on the 24th of March, a letter was received from the Marquis de Lafayette, announcing a general peace. On the 11th of April Congress issued its proclamation, declaring the cessation of arms by sea and land.

In regard to the failure of Colonel Willett's last expedition, no possible censure was imputable to him.   In reply to the Colonel's official account of the affair, General Washington wrote a characteristic letter, approving of his conduct, and consoling him for his disappointment.   " Unfortunate as the circumstance " is," said the Commander-in-chief, "I am happy in the persuasion " that no imputation or reflection can justly reach your charac- " ter ; and that you are enabled to derive much consolation " from the animated zeal, fortitude, and activity of the officers " and soldiers who accompanied you.   The failure, it seems, " must be attributed to some of those unaccountable events " which are not within the control of human means, and which, " though they often occur in military life, yet require, not only " the fortitude of the soldier, but the calm reflection of the philo- " sopher to bear.   I cannot omit expressing to you the high " sense I entertain of your persevering exertions and zeal on this " expedition ; and beg you to accept my warm thanks on the " occasion ; and that you will be pleased to communicate my " gratitude to the officers and men who acted under your com " mand, for the share they had in that service."

Thus ends the history of the border wars of the American Revolution—the principal theatres of which were in the districts north and west of Albany.   The vale of the Mohawk, including its intersecting valley of the Schoharie-kill, was among the most thickly populated and wealthy agricultural districts of the country at the commencement of the war.   The produc tiveness of its soil, and the riches of its people, rendered it ever an inviting object of plunder to the enemy—especially to the savages, and the swarms of refugees who had fled from the country, and were sharing a precarious livelihood among the Indian wig-wams and in the wilds of Canada.   Its geographical position, moreover, rendered it the most easily assailable of any well-peopled section of the whole Union ; while at the same time the larger armies of the enemy were employed elsewhere, and of course required the greatest portion of the physical strength of the country elsewhere to oppose them.   The consequence of these, and other circumstances that might be enumerated, was, that no other section or district of country in the United States, of the like extent, suffered in any comparable degree as much from the war of the Revolution as did that of the

Mohawk. It was the most frequently invaded and overrun ; and that, too, by an enemy far more barbarous than the native barbarians of the forest. Month after month, for seven long years, were its towns and villages, its humbler settlements and isolated habitations, fallen upon by an untiring and relentless enemy, until, at the close of the contest, the appearance of the whole district was that of wide-spread, heart-sickening, and universal desolation. In no other section of the confederacy were so many campaigns performed, so many battles fought, so many dwellings burnt, or so many murders committed. And those who were left at the return of peace, were literally a people " scattered and peeled." It was the computation, two years before the close of the war, that one third of the population had gone over to the enemy, and that one third had been driven from the country, or slain in battle and by private assassination. And yet, among the inhabitants of the other remaining third, in June, 1783, it was stated, at a public meeting held at Fort Plain, that there were three hundred widows and two thousand orphan children. But with the news of peace the dispersed population began to return to the sites of their former homes.* Their houses were rebuilt, and their farms once more brought into cultivation ; while different and not less enterprising occupants, deriving their titles from the state, took possession of the confiscated lands of those who had adhered to the cause of the crown. The spirit of industry and enterprise, so characteristic of the American people, was not long in imparting a new aspect to the scene ; and Tryon County, exchanging her name for that of the patriot MONTGOMERY, soon smiled through her tears.

Other scenes and other wars will afford materials for the remaining chapters of the present volumes, as connected with the subsequent life and career of JOSEPH BRANT—THAYENDANE-GEA.

---

* Along with the returning patriots, as Satan was wont in the olden time occasionally to present himself in better company, some of the Tories began to steal back into the country they had forsaken, and assisted to drench in tears of blood. But the Whig population would not endure their presence. The preceding narrative of events has shown that the Tryon County loyalists, who had taken arms in company with the Indians, were far more revengeful and bloody than were the Indians themselves. It is no marvel, therefore, that a feeling of peculiar bitterness against them existed in the bosoms of those who had suffered so keenly at their hands. These feelings were embodied and declared at two public meetings held in different sections of Tryon County, in June, 1783 ; for which, see Appendix, No. V.

CHAPTER VIII.

The treaty of November, 1782, restoring peace between the
United States and Great Britain, and recognising the uncondi
tional independence of the former, was such as to gratify every
reasonable wish of the American people. In regard to questions
of boundary and the fisheries, it was, indeed, more liberal than
their allies, France and Spain, desired. Professedly, France
had drawn the sword in behalf of the United States; but the
negotiations for peace presented the singular fact, that but for
the diplomacy of the former, the treaty of peace would have
been sooner completed. The negotiation was a work of intrica-
cy, requiring skill, penetration, judgment, and great firmness on
the part of the American commissioners—qualities which their
success proved them to possess in an eminent degree. But,
although the American treaty was first definitively concluded,
less than two months elapsed before preliminary articles of peace
were agreed upon and signed between Great Britain, France, and
Spain; France having the satisfaction of seeing her great rival
dismembered of the fairest portion of her American possessions, as she herself had been by that very power twenty years
before.

In the treaty with the United States, however, Great Britain
had made no stipulation in behalf of her Indian allies. Notwithstanding the alacrity with which the aboriginals, especially
the Mohawks, had entered the service of the crown—notwith-

standing their constancy, their valor, the readiness with which they had spilt their blood, and the distinguished services of their Great Captain, Thayendanegea, the loyal red man was not even named in the treaty; while " the ancient country of the Six " Nations, the residence of their ancestors from the time far be- " yond their earliest traditions, was included within the bounda- " ry granted to the Americans."*   What with the descent of Co- lonel Van Schaick upon the Onondagas, and the expedition of General Sullivan into their territory farther west, their whole country had been ravaged with fire and sword; and the Mo- hawks, in particular, had sacrificed the entire of their own rich and beautiful country.   It appears, however, that when the Mo- hawks first abandoned their native valley to embark in his Ma- jesty's service, Sir Guy Carleton had given a pledge, that as soon as the war was at an end they should be restored, at the ex- pense of the government, to the condition they were in before the contest began.   In April, 1779, General Haldimand, then Captain General and Commander-in-chief in Canada, ratified the promise of his predecessor, pledging himself, under hand and seal, as far as in him lay, to its faithful execution " as soon as that happy time should come."†

At the close of the war the Mohawks were temporarily residing on the American side of the Niagara river, in the vicinity of the old landing-place above the fort.   The Senecas, who had been in closer alliance with the Mohawks during the war than any other of the Six Nations, and who had themselves been chiefly induced by the former to take up the hatchet against the United States, offered them a tract of land in the valley of the Genesee.   But, as Captain Brant long afterward said in one of his speeches, the Mohawks were determined " to sink or swim" with the English; and besides, they did not wish to reside within the boundaries of the United States.   The generous offer of the Senecas was therefore declined, and the Mohawk Chief proceeded to Mon- treal to confer with the Superintendent General of Indian Affairs, Sir John Johnson, and from thence to Quebec, to claim from Ge- neral Haldimand, the Commander-in-chief, the fulfilment of his pledge.   The General received the warrior with great kindness,

---

* MS. memorial of the Six Nations, presented to Lord Camden by Teyonin- hokarawen, commonly called John Norton.

† MS. order of General Haldimand, among the Brant papers.

and evinced every disposition to fulfil the pledge in the most
honorable manner.   The tract upon which the chief had fixed
his attention was situated upon the Bay de Quinte, on the north
side of the St. Lawrence, or rather of Lake Ontario ; and at his
request General Haldimand agreed that it should be purchased
and conveyed to the Mohawks.

On the return of Thayendanegea to Niagara, the Senecas
were disappointed at the arrangement, and pained at the idea
that their friends were to be located at so wide a distance from
them.   They were apprehensive that their troubles with the
United States were not yet at an end ; and were, therefore, exceedingly desirous that the Mohawks should reside so near as to
assist them in arms if necessary, or afford them an asylum should
they be obliged to flee from the oppression of the United States.
Under these circumstances Captain Brant convened a council of
his people, and it was resolved that he should make a second
visit to Quebec, and, under the peculiar circumstances of the
case, request another and more convenient territory.   The country upon the Ouise, or Grand River, flowing into Lake Erie
some forty miles above the Falls of Niagara, was indicated to
General Haldimand as a location every way convenient, not only
for maintaining a ready intercourse with the residue of the Six
Nations, but also as affording facilities for corresponding with
the nations and tribes of the upper lakes.   His Excellency approved of the suggestion, and promptly ordered a second purchase to be made in conformity with the request.   On inquiring
the extent of the territory expected by the Mohawks, the Captain replied, " Six miles on each side of the river, from the mouth
to its source."   With assurances that the grant should be formally secured in fee, in due season, the chief returned once
more to Niagara, and shortly afterward entered into possession
of the lands allotted for the new home of his people.*

In the Autumn of 1784, having learned that General Haldimand was about returning to England, the vigilant chief repaired
to Quebec a third time upon this business, in order to make
sure of the title deed.   The result of this visit was a formal
grant by Sir Frederick Haldimand, in the name of the crown,

---

* This narrative of facts is derived from a long speech of Captain Brant, made
in council, to Gov. Simcoe, in 1795, a copy of which is preserved among the Brant
papers.

of a tract of land "upon the banks of the river Ouise, commonly "called Grand River, running into Lake Erie, of six miles "breadth from each side of the river, beginning at Lake Erie, "and extending in that proportion to the head of said river; "which the Mohawks, and others of the Six Nations who had "either lost their possessions in the war, or wished to retire from "them to the British, with their posterity, were to enjoy for-"ever."* The course of the river Ouise is about one hundred miles, so that the grant embraced a territory of that extent in length by twelve miles in width. "This tract, though much "smaller than that which they had been obliged to forsake with-"in the United States, amply satisfied these loyal Indians, who "preferred living under the protection of His Britannic Majesty, "(ready to fight under his standard again, if occasion should re-"quire,) to a more extensive country."† The district of coun-try thus granted, is said to be alike beautiful and fertile. The Grand River rises in the interior of the country toward Lake Huron, and winds its way to Lake Erie through a long and pic-turesque course. It is navigable for small vessels many miles upward, and for large boats a much greater distance still. The land along its whole course is uncommonly productive.

The policy to be observed by the United States toward the Indians residing within their borders, was a question of grave and weighty importance, and early arrested the consideration of American statesmen. Very soon after the English came into possession of the Colony of New-York, the Six Nations relin-quished their own primitive right of absolute sovereignty, and placed themselves and their lands under the protection of the government of New-York,‡ reserving to themselves a kind of qualified sovereignty. The immediate object of this act, on the part of the Indians, was to secure the alliance of the English in their wars with the French, and the Huron and Algonquin In-dians in Canada.§ Subsequently, during the Colonial adminis-tration, the Indians were considered as separate but dependent nations.‖ Aside from this circumstance, however, by the treaty of peace the sovereignty of all the Indian countries within the

---

* Copy of the Grant, among the Brant papers.
† Norton's Memorial to Lord Camden.
‡ Kent's Commentaries, vol. iii. p. 392.   § Colden's Canada.
‖ Kent's Commentaries.

prescribed limits granted to the United States by Great Britain, became vested in the former, to the same extent, of course, as it had been exercised by Great Britain.   With that sovereignty, moreover, the exclusive right of pre-emption to all the Indian lands lying within the territory of the United States also became vested in them—subject to the possessory right only of the natives.*   These rights had been acquired by England by discovery, which, under the practice of the European nations, was held to be equivalent to conquest ; and although the natives were admitted to possess a just and legal claim, as the original occupants of the soil, to retain and use it according to their own discretion, still they were not allowed to dispose of the soil at their own will, except to the government claiming the right of pre-emption.†   Such was the practice of Spain, France, Holland, and England ; and as early as 1782, Mr. Jay, then the American Minister at the Court of Madrid, in his correspondence with the Count d'Aranda, asserted the adoption of the same principle on the part of the United States.‡   But while the right of sove-reignty, as it had been exercised by England, passed over to the United States by virtue of the treaty, under the complicated system of the confederacy, the pre-emptive right to the soil became vested in the respective States within whose boundaries or grants they were situated—the States themselves being so many sovereign powers in all matters of national import which had not been specially conceded to the Government of the Union under the Articles of Confederation.

The treatment of the Six Nations by the Dutch Colonial Government had been kind and liberal.   So, also, had it been under the Colonial Government of England—the Indians, in no instance, being dispossessed of a rood of ground, except by purchase.   Immediately on the conclusion of the war, however, England having made no stipulation in behalf of the Indians, a disposition was manifested by the Legislature of New-York to expel the Six Nations from all the country within the bounds of that state, which had not been ceded by them previous to the war.§   This disposition, which seems, likewise, to have been entertained to some extent in other states, was viewed with great

---

* Kent's Commentaries, vol. i. p. 257.   † Idem, vol. iii. p. 379.
‡ Life and Writings of John Jay.
§ Letter of Washington to James Duane, Sept. 7, 1783.

concern by Generals Washington and Schuyler, who united in the opinion that such a line of policy would be alike injudicious, inhuman, and unjust.   General Schuyler addressed a memorial to Congress upon the subject in July.   Coinciding entirely in the sentiments of Schuyler, Washington followed up that communication by a long letter to James Duane, then in Congress, in September.   The views of these gentlemen were, that the most liberal and humane policy should be adopted in respect to the Indians.   True, they had taken up the hatchet in favor of the crown, and by a rigid construction of the laws of conquest, they might be dispossessed of their lands, and driven, with their allies, north beyond the lakes.   But General Washington strongly urged, that while the Indians should be informed of the strict right of the United States to deal thus severely with them, and compel them to share the same evil fortune with those whom they had chosen for their allies, nevertheless, looking upon them as a people who had been deluded into the service of the crown, they should be allowed honorable terms of peace, and to retain the possession of lands and hunting grounds, to be designated by treaty, within the boundaries of which they should not be molested.   It was the desire of Washington, that with regard to these children of the forest, a veil should be drawn over the past, and that they should be taught that their true interest and safety must henceforward depend upon the cultivation of amicable relations with the United States.   In regard to the Six Nations, he thought the course which the Legislature of New-York seemed desirous of pursuing would involve the country in another Indian war, since the Indians would never surrender their whole territory without another struggle ; while he justly held that all the territory that was actually wanted by the people of the United States might be obtained by negotiation and compromise.   As a general principle, moreover, it was held that, in all time to come, it would be much cheaper to obtain cessions of land from the Indians, from time to time, as they should be required for the extension of settlements, by purchase, than to acquire them by conquest—to say nothing of the sufferings, the evils, and the guilt of war.   Upon this whole subject of Indian policy there was an entire coincidence of opinion between Washington and Schuyler.   Most happily it prevailed ; and the subsequent cession by the states of their Indian lands to the general government, facilitated the benevolent action of the latter under that system; the wisdom of which, irrespective of its justice and humanity, has become every year more apparent since.

It was while the Mohawk chief was occupied in making his final arrangements with the Canadian Commander-in-chief, as has been seen a few pages back, that the sachems and warriors of the Six Nations were holding a treaty with the United States at Fort Stanwix. At this negotiation, the Mohawks, Onondagas, Senecas, Oneidas, Cayugas, Tuscaroras, and Seneca-Abeal* nations were represented. The Commissioners on the part of the United States were Oliver Wolcott, Richard Butler, and Arthur Lee. The records of this treaty, containing the speeches interchanged on the occasion, seem not to have been preserved, as has been usual in diplomatic matters with the Indians. No thing appears upon the subject among the Indian state-papers at the seat of Government, save the naked result of the council, in the form of a very brief treaty, signed by the nations repre sented instead of the several chiefs. It is known, however, that among the leading chiefs who took an active part in the negotiations, were the Corn-planter and Red Jacket; and enough is to be gathered from the records of subsequent transactions with the Indians, to afford a general idea of the course of these proceedings. Beyond doubt the representatives of the Six Nations at that council were opposed to a separate negotiation with the United States. Their desire was, that no definitive treaty of peace and boundaries should be concluded, unless the whole ground was covered at once; and, as a consequence, they strenuously urged that the Hurons, Ottawas, Shawanese, Chippewas, Delawares, Pottawattamies, the Wabash Confederates, and the Cherokees, should be represented, in order that the whole question of boundaries, on all the Indian borders, might be determined.† But the Commissioners on the part of the United States would listen to no such delay. The Six Nations, as such, had taken up the hatchet in favor of the crown, and it was determined to punish them by a dismemberment of their territory. Red Jacket, a somewhat younger chief than the

* The clan of the Senecas residing with the Corn-planter on the Alleghany.

† Speech of the united Indian nations at a confederate council, holden at the mouth of the Detroit River, November and December, 1786.

Corn-planter, was opposed to a burial of the hatchet, and spoke with great eloquence and vehemence in favor of a continuance of the war by the Indians on their own account. " His speech " was a masterpiece, and every warrior who heard him was " carried away with his eloquence."* The Corn-planter was a wiser man than his junior associate. He saw the folly of a war to be waged by the Indians single-handed against the United States, and he exerted himself with all his power in favor of peace. He saw that the only alternative of his people was the relinquishment of a portion of their territory by compromise, or the loss of the whole by force. His efforts were in the end successful, and on the 22d of October a treaty was signed, by which the United States gave peace to the Mohawks, Senecas, Onondagas, and Cayugas—the four hostile nations of the confederacy —and received them under their protection on condition that all the prisoners, white and black, in the possession of the said nations, should be delivered up ; the Oneidas and Tuscaroras were secured in the possession of the lands then in their occupation ; the Six Nations at the same time relinquishing all claims to the country west of a line beginning at the mouth of the Oyonwayea Creek, flowing into Lake Ontario four miles east of Niagara ; thence southerly, but preserving a line four miles east of the carrying path, to the mouth of the Tehoseroron, or Buffalo Creek ; thence to the north boundary of Pennsylvania ; thence west to the end of that boundary ; and thence south along the Pennsylvania line, to the river Ohio. All the Six Nations were to be secured in the possession of the lands they were then occupying ; and six hostages were to be delivered to the United States, to remain in their possession until all the prisoners, whose liberation was stipulated, should be surrendered by the Indians.† There was likewise a stipulation that the

---

* Drake, who translates from Levasseur's Lafayette in America. The Marquis de Lafayette was present at the treaty, and, when visited by Red Jacket at Buffalo, during his tour through the United States in 1824—25, the General was reminded by the venerable chief of the circumstance of their former meeting at Fort Stanwix. This is the earliest account given of the eloquence of the man of the woods who afterward became so renowned for his oratory.

† Vide the treaty itself, American State Papers, Indian Affairs, vol. i. Originally the Five Nations claimed " all the land not sold to the English, from the mouth of Sorel River, on the south side of Lakes Erie and Ontario, on both sides of the Ohio until it falls into the Mississippi ; and on the north side of these lakes, that whole

Indians should deliver up certain persons of their own people, who were considered very great offenders, to be tried by the civil laws of the United States. Two persons were surrendered under this stipulation; but the Indians afterward complained, that, instead of being tried according to law, they were wrested from the hands of the magistrate by some of the lowest of the white people, and immediately put to death.*

The result of this negotiation gave great dissatisfaction to the Indians generally; and the crafty Red Jacket afterward availed himself of the advantages of his position, in stealing the hearts of the Senecas from the Corn-planter to himself. The Mohawk chief, Thayendanegea, was likewise highly displeased with the conditions of the treaty, the more so, doubtless, from the circumstance that Captain Aaron Hill, a subordinate chief of the Mohawk nation, was detained as one of the hostages under the treaty. When he heard of the proceedings, the old chief was at Quebec. He had completed his business with Sir Frederick Haldimand, and was on the point of embarking for England, to adjust the claims of his nation upon the crown for their sacrifices during the war. The design of going abroad was immediately relinquished for that season, and Captain Brant hastened back to his own country, to look after the welfare of his own people at home. He arrived at Cataraqui on the 27th of November, and two days afterward addressed a long letter to Colonel James Monroe,† in which, after expressing a wish that the letter may find the Colonel in health, and thanking him for some recent personal civilities, he says—

"I was at Quebec, getting ready to set off from thence for England (you know my business there perfectly well.) About the same time I received an account that our chief, Capt. Aaron Hill,‡ was detained, and kept as a prisoner at Fort Stanwix by

territory between the Ottawa river and Lake Huron, and even beyond the straights between that and Lake Erie."—*Smith's History.*

* Speech of Big Tree, Corn-planter, and Half-Town, to President Washington, in 1790.

† Whether the Colonel Monroe, to whom this letter was addressed, was the late President of the United States, the author has not ascertained: and if so, it does not appear how he was connected with the Fort Stanwix treaty.

‡ This chief was connected with the family of Thayendanegea. Aaron Henry Hill married one of his daughters, and is spoken of by Captain Brant, fifteen years afterward, in his correspondence with Thomas Morris, Esq.

the commissioners of Congress, and understood that he was to be kept until all the American prisoners returned to their own places, from the different nations of Indians, who are still remaining amongst them. When I received this disagreeable news, I immediately declined going any farther from there. It did alarm me very much of hearing this, because it was me that encouraged that chief to come and attend that meeting at Fort Stanwix.

"I never did expect that it should be the cause of detaining chiefs in the matter; for I thought the affair was too far gone to happen any such things. The Congress have past their words to us that they wish to be friends with all the Indians; and we likewise did the same to them. However, suppose the commissioners of Congress did find it necessary for them to detain some of the chiefs, I should have thought they could reasonably have excused our chief, and let him gone, and kept other right persons, who ought to be detained, because we are clear from keeping prisoners since peace. As soon as the word came, peace, we let all our prisoners go, except one or two children which could not help themselves. Captain Aaron Hill had no conveniences to take with him when he went to Fort Stanwix. We also all along advised the other tribes of Indians, since peace, that the prisoners should go to their homes; and have during the war always favored the prisoners, especially women and children; and likewise did push the matter forward since, to promote peace, and to renew the friendship with you again as we formerly had, in honestly manner. We mean to go through with it and be done with it, that every body should mind their own business and be happy. This is our customs and manners of the Mohocks, whenever engaged any thing. They are allways active and true;—no double faces at war, or any other business. All this makes me think the commissioners should consider this, and our chief should [have] gone home, for we have been a generous enemy to you during the war, and very active in forwarding the matters of settling peace with you all last Summer. I believe the commissioners must have some spite against the Mohocks of using them so, through the advice of Priest Kertland and the Oneidas, and he did likewise even to the Senekas, who were our friends. He tried all he could that they should themselves be against the Mohocks; all this I am well

informed.   Sir, these low-live tricks (it is very odd to me why
it should be so,) confuses me very much.   I believe we shall be
at last prevented of becoming good friends with you.   If it
should be the case, the fault shall not be ours, which I hope you
will find so.   It would relieve me many points if you would be
so kind as to answer me this letter, as far as you will understand
my English, and please to explain me at once of your sentiments
concerning this kind of complaint of mine, let it be what it will,
because whatever must be done its no help for it, it must be so.
If I could see you, and talk with you, I could explain myself better than a letter half English half Indian.   You remember I told
you that I should be happy to be present if any council-fire of
yours should be held in the Spring ; I mean about the Indian
affairs ; and I wanted to see you in New Jersies if I had time.
But, my dear sir, I begin to be backward about going there, since
my chief is detained.   Perhaps I should be served the same, and
be kept from my different sweethearts, which would be too hard
for me.   It is the very thing which will deprive me from having the pleasure to see you, and attending your council in the
Spring—except the affairs change in different footing.   But
believe me this, let the affairs turn out what it will, I should
be always very happy to see you.   I shall winter here, myself
and family ; early in the Spring I shall leave this, and go to my
new country at Grand River.

" I am your well-wisher,

" And humble servant,

" JOS. BRANT, or

" THAYENDANEGEA.*

" *To Col. James Monroe.*"

What effect was produced by this letter, or how just were the
complaints set forth therein, is not known ; but the probability is,
that the difficulty in regard to the detention of Hill was satisfactorily adjusted.   In any event, Captain Brant accomplished
his purpose of visiting England at the close of the year following, (1785.)   Before his embarkation, however, he seems to have

---

* The MS. of this letter, preserved among the papers of Capt. Brant, is probably
the first rough draft.   It was evidently written in great haste, and the author has
made a very few corrections where the errors seemed clearly to be the effect of carelessness.   Otherwise, it stands as it was written.   Captain Brant improved in his
English composition very much and very rapidly in after years.

formed a plan somewhat analogous to that entertained, and in part accomplished, twenty years before, by Pontiac—that of combining all the great north-western Indian nations into a single grand confederacy, of which he was to be chief. In furtherance of this design, he visited the country of the upper lakes, and held councils with the nations. It is not known whether, like Pontiac, he meditated war upon the United States, unless in the event of being attacked. Still, he could not but look upon hostilities, in the event of the formation of his confederacy, as more than probable. Ostensibly, his visit to England was undertaken for the purpose of adjusting the claims of the loyal Mohawks upon the crown, for indemnification of their losses and sacrifices in the contest from which they had recently emerged. And such, probably, was the sole design of the visit, when originally projected, the preceding year. But the dissatisfaction existing in regard to the treaty of Fort Stanwix, and other indications among the Indians, had probably increased the objects of his mission. At all events, it soon appeared that, coupled with the special business of the Indian claims, was the design of sounding the British government, touching the degree of countenance or the amount of assistance which he might expect from that quarter, in the event of a general Indian war against the United States.

Sir John Johnson, who visited England immediately after the war, had returned to Canada during the Summer of 1785. He seems likewise to have been charged with the claims of the Mohawks, but accomplished nothing to their satisfaction. Still, he was opposed to the mission of Captain Brant, and wrote on the 6th of November, strongly dissuading him from undertaking the voyage. Sir John thought the claims in question might be adjusted to mutual satisfaction before the lapse of another year; and he hinted to his friend that his own interest required his attention at home. "I need not, I am sure," said the Baronet, "endeavor by many words, to point out to you the "critical situation of your own affairs; I mean those of your "confederacy; and how much the aid of every man of weight "and influence among you is wanting at present, to guard "against the designs of your enemies, who, by calling meetings "at this time in every quarter, mean to spare no pains to divide "and separate your interests, thereby to lessen your consequence

" and strength, and to answer their designs upon your country
" and liberty."*

But the chief was not to be diverted from his purpose. Embarking immediately, and having a short passage, he was received by the nobility and gentry with great consideration and respect. His arrival at Salisbury was thus noted in a letter from that place, dated December 12, 1785, and published in London.
" Monday last, Colonel Joseph Brant, the celebrated King of the
" Mohawks, arrived in this city from America, and after dining
" with Colonel De Peister, at the head-quarters here, proceeded
" immediately on his journey to London. This extraordinary
" personage is said to have presided at the late grand Congress
" of confederate chiefs of the Indian nations in America, and to
" be by them appointed to the conduct and chief command in
" the war which they now meditate against the United States of
" America. He took his departure for England immediately as
" that assembly broke up ; and it is conjectured that his embassy
" to the British Court is of great importance. This country
" owes much to the services of Colonel Brant during the late
" war in America. He was educated at Philadelphia ; is a very
" shrewd, intelligent person, possesses great courage and abili
" ties as a warrior, and is inviolably attached to the British
" nation."

What particular Indian council is referred to in the preceding quotation, is unknown. Most likely it was connected with the ambitious project of Thayendanegea already indicated ; and it is, moreover, very likely that the discontents of the north-western Indians, chiefly in relation to questions of boundary, which ultimately produced the war of 1789–'95—may, even thus early, have been at work in the bosoms of the Indians. Undoubtedly, if such a council was held, " the Great Captain of the Six Nations" was present. Certain it is, that while prosecuting the just claims of the Mohawks at the British Court, he did not fail, with great adroitness, though indirectly, to present the other subject to the consideration of Lord Sidney, then Secretary for the Colonies. Indeed, it appears from a passage in the letter of Sir John Johnson, already quoted, that that gentleman had previously been sounding the government on the same question. " With

* MS. Letter of Sir John Johnson, among the Brant papers.

regard to the assistance required or expected in case of war,"
said the Baronet in the letter referred to, " I think I explained
that to you also, and shall more fully when I see you."

The reception of the distinguished Mohawk in the British
capital was all that the proudest forest king, not unacquainted
with civilized life, could have desired. In the course of the war
he had formed many acquaintances with the officers of the army,
upon whom he must have made a highly favorable impression,
since all who met him in London recognised him with great
cordiality. Some of these he had met in the *salons* of Quebec,
as well as been associated with them in the field. His visits to
the Canadian capital had been frequent during and subsequent
to the war. On one of these occasions the Baroness Riedesel
met him at the provincial court, which gave her occasion to
speak of him thus in her memoirs :—" I saw at that time the
" famous Indian chief, Captain Brant. His manners are polish-
" ed ; he expressed himself with fluency, and was much esteem-
" ed by General Haldimand. I dined once with him at the
" General's. In his dress he showed off to advantage the half
" military and half savage costume. His countenance was manly
" and intelligent, and his disposition very mild."* Aside, therefore, from the novelty of gazing upon an Indian prince in the
British capital, his education and associations, his rank as a warrior, and his bravery, were so many substantial reasons why
he should be received with kindness and courtesy. Sir Guy
Carleton, afterward Lord Dorchester, who was then on the point
of embarking for America to relieve Sir Frederick Haldimand
in the government of the Canadas, was well acquainted with
the Chief. Earl Moira, afterward Marquis of Hastings, who had
served in America as Lord Rawdon, had formed a strong
attachment to Captain Brant, and gave him his picture set in
gold.† The late General Sir Charles Stuart, fourth son of
the Earl of Bute, who, while serving in America, had often
slept under the same tent with him, had the warmest regard for
him,‡ and cordially recognised him as his friend in London.

* Letters and memoirs of the Baroness de Riedesel.

† Now in possession of the lady of Colonel William J. Kerr, the daughter of
Thayendanegea.

‡ Letter of Thomas Campbell to the late John Brant, or Ahyonwaeghs, the son
of Thayendanegea ; of whom more hereafter.

With the late Duke of Northumberland, then Lord Percy, he had likewise formed an acquaintance in America, which ripened into a lasting attachment, and was maintained by a correspondence, continued at intervals until his death. With the Earl of Warwick, and others of the nobility and gentry, he had become acquainted during his first visit, ten years before. His acquaintance was also sought by many of the distinguished statesmen and scholars of the time ; among whom were the Bishop of London, Charles Fox, James Boswell, and many others. He sat for his picture for Lord Percy, as he had done for the Earl of Warwick and Boswell when first in England ; and Fox presented him with a silver snuff-box, bearing his initials.* With the King and royal family he was a great favorite—not the less so on the part of his Majesty, for having proudly refused to kiss his hand on his presentation. The dusky Chief, however, in declining that ceremony, with equal gallantry and address remarked that he would gladly kiss the hand of the Queen. George the Third was a man of too much sterling sense not to appreciate the feelings of his brother chief, and he loved his Queen too well not to be gratified with the turning of a compliment in her Majesty's favor, in a manner that would have done no discredit to the most accomplished cavalier of the Court of Elizabeth—Sir Walter Raleigh.

Equally well did he stand in the graces of the Prince of Wales,† who took great delight in his company ; sometimes inviting him in his rambles to places " very queer for a prince to go to," as the old chief was wont to remark in after-life. He was also, it is believed, an occasional guest at the table of the Prince, among that splendid circle of wits, orators, and scholars, who so frequently clustered around the festive board of the accomplished and luxurious heir apparent. It has been asserted, likewise, that these associations, and the freedom with which the leading Whigs were accustomed to speak of the King, had an unhappy effect upon the mind of the warrior, by lessening his reverence for the regal office, if not for his Majesty's person.

But, amidst all the attractions of the metropolis, and the hospitalities in which he was called to participate, the Chief did not neglect the special object, or *objects,* of his mission. He had left his nation suffering from their losses of property and

* Still in the possession of Mrs. Kerr.   † His late Majesty George IV.

other sacrifices, by which, as well as their arms, they had proved their loyalty, or rather their good faith to the King as allies, during the late war, and his first object was to obtain relief. The claims of his people had previously been presented to the consideration of his Majesty's Government, as already stated, by Sir John Johnson ; but, apparently receiving no attention, on the 4th of January, 1786, Captain Brant addressed the following letter to Lord Sidney, his Majesty's Secretary for the Colonial Department :—

CAPTAIN BRANT TO LORD SIDNEY.

" My Lord,

" The claims of the Mohawks for their losses having Leen delivered by Sir John Johnson, His Majesty's Superintendent General for Indian affairs, to General Haldimand, and by him laid before your Lordship, who cannot but be well informed that their sufferings, losses, and being drove from that country which their forefathers long enjoyed, and left them the peaceable possession of, is in consequence of their faithful attachment to the King, and the zeal they manifested in supporting the cause of His country against the rebellious subjects in America.

" From the promises made by the Governor and Commander-in-chief of Canada, that their losses should be made good, and that soon, when I left them, I was desired to put His Majesty's ministers in mind of their long and sincere friendship for the English nation, in whose cause their ancestors and they have so often fought and so freely bled,—of their late happy settlements, before the rebellion, and their present situation,—and to request their claims might be attended to, and that orders may be given for what they are to receive to be paid as soon as possible, in order to enable them to go on with the settlement they are now making ; in some measure stock their farms, and get such articles and materials as all settlements in new countries require, and which it is out of their power to do before they are paid for their losses.

" On my mentioning these matters, since my arrival in England, I am informed orders are given that this shall be done ; which will give great relief and satisfaction to those faithful Indians, who will have spirit to go on, and their hearts be filled with gratitude for the King, their father's, great kindness, which

I pray leave, in their behalf, to acknowledge, and to thank your Lordship for your friendship.

"JOSEPH BRANT, *Captain, or*

"THAYENDANEGEA.

" *London, 4th January,* 1786."

On the same day Captain Brant was honored by an interview with the Secretary, on which occasion he addressed his Lordship in the following speech, a copy of which was delivered in writing .—

SPEECH OF CAPTAIN BRANT TO LORD SIDNEY.

" MY LORD,

" I am happy at the honor of being before your Lordship, and having an opportunity of delivering the following speech to you, in behalf of the Five United Nations of Indians, and their con federates in North America.

" The cause of my coming to England being of the most serious consequence to the whole Indian Confederacy, I intreat your Lordship patiently to hear and listen to what I am going to say.

" We hope it is a truth well known in this country, what a faithful part we took in their behalf in the late dispute with the Americans : and though we have been told peace has long since been concluded between you and them, it is not finally settled with us, which causes great uneasiness through all the Indian nations.

" When we heard peace was made between his Majesty and the Americans, we made application to General Haldimand at Quebec, to know our situation, delivering him a speech at the same time, which we requested might be sent to the King—a copy of which I now deliver to your Lordship.

" Having in that speech, in as few words as possible, pointed out what friendship we had shown to the English from the earliest time of their arrival in America, and being conscious of the active part our forefathers and we had taken in their favor in every dispute they have had with their enemies, we were struck with astonishment at hearing we were forgot in the treaty. Notwithstanding the manner we were told this, we could not believe it possible such firm friends and allies could be so neglected by a nation remarkable for its honor and glory, whom we had served with so much zeal and fidelity. For this reason we applied to the King's Commander-in-chief, in Canada in a friendly and private way, wishing not to let those people in rebellion know the concern and trouble we were under. From the time of delivering that speech, near three years, we have had no answer, and remain in a state of great suspense and uneasiness of mind. This is well known to the officers who commanded at the upper posts in America, as is also our zeal for His Majesty's service during the war.

" Our trouble and distress is greatly increased by many things the Americans have said, to whom we have avoided giving any direct answers, or entering into any engagements with, before we have an answer. On the arrival of Sir John Johnson, our Superintendent-General, in Canada, we hoped to have received it ; in full expectation of which, several of our first and principal chiefs came down the country to meet him and hear it, and were very much mortified and sorry at being disappointed. It was then resolved that I should come to England, and I hope the necessity we are under of getting this answer will plead my excuse for the trouble I give your Lordship.

" It is, my Lord, the earnest desire of the Five United Nations, and the whole Indian Confederacy, that I may have an answer to that speech ; and from our present situation, as well as that of the American States, who have surveyed and laid out great part of the lands in our country, on our side of the boundary line fixed at Fort Stanwix in 1765, the last time we granted any territory to the King, (at which time some of the governors attended in person, and where they did not, commissioners, vested with full powers, appeared on their behalf ; so that we had all the reason to hope that the transaction was binding with respect to all parties,) but through their encroaching disposition, we have found they pay little regard to engagements, and are therefore apprehensive of immediate serious consequences. This we shall avoid to the utmost of our power, as dearly as we love our lands. But should it, contrary to our wishes, happen, we desire to know whether we are to be considered as His Majesty's faithful allies, and have that support and countenance such as old and true friends expect.

" I beg liberty to tell your Lordship, that your answer to these

matters will be the means of relieving all our nations from that
very troublesome and uneasy suspense they now labor under,
and this they all hope for on my return.

" JOS. BRANT, Captain, or

" <i>London,</i> 4th <i>Jan.</i> 1786.   " THAYENDANEGEA.
" <i>The Right Hon. Lord Sidney.</i>"

The forest chief was not an unsuccessful envoy, as will appear by the subjoined communication from Lord Sidney—so
far at least as relates to the indemnification claimed by the Mohawks and their allies of the Six Nations :—

LORD SIDNEY TO CAPTAIN BRANT.

" Whitehall, 6th April, 1786.

" SIR,

" The King has had under his royal consideration the two
letters which you delivered to me on the 4th of January last, in
the presence of Colonel Johnson and other officers of the Indian
Department ; the first of them representing the claims of the
Mohawks for losses sustained by them and other tribes of Indians, from the depredations committed on their lands by the
Americans during the late war ; and the second, expressing the
desire of the confederacy to be informed what assistance they
might expect from this country in case they should be engaged
in disputes with the Americans relative to their lands, situated
within the territory to which His Majesty has relinquished his
sovereignty.

" Were the right of individuals to compensation for losses
sustained by the depredations of an enemy to be admitted, no
country, however opulent it might be, could support itself under
such a burthen, especially when the contest happens to have
taken an unfavorable turn.   His Majesty, upon this ground, con-
ceives that, consistently with every principle of justice, he might
withhold his royal concurrence to the liquidation of those demands ; but His Majesty, in consideration of the zealous and
hearty exertions of his Indian allies in the support of his cause,
and as a proof of his most friendly disposition toward them, has
been graciously pleased to consent that the losses already certified by his Superintendent-General shall be made good ; that a
favorable attention shall be shown to the claims of others, who

have pursued the same system of conduct; and that Sir Guy Carleton, his Governor General of his American dominions, shall take measures for carrying his royal commands into execution immediately after his arrival at Quebec.

"This liberal conduct on the part of His Majesty, he trusts, will not leave a doubt upon the minds of his Indian allies that he shall at all times be ready to attend to their future welfare; and that he shall be anxious, upon every occasion wherein their happiness may be concerned, to give them such farther testimonies of his royal favor and countenance, as can, consistently with a due regard to the national faith, and the honor and dignity of his crown, be afforded to them.

"His Majesty recommends to his Indian allies to continue united in their councils, and that their measures may be conducted with temper and moderation; from which, added to a peaceable demeanor on their part, they must experience many essential benefits, and be most likely to secure to themselves the possession of those rights and privileges which their ancestors have heretofore enjoyed.

"I have the honor to be,

"With great truth and regard,

"Sir,

"Your most obedient humble servant,

"SIDNEY.

"*To Captain Joseph Brant,*
          "*Thayendanegea.*"

It appears, that during his negotiations with the ministers, conversations had been held touching his claim to half-pay; but from the loss of papers, it is difficult to arrive at the precise circumstances of the case. Captain Brant held His Majesty's commission during the war as a Captain. But it was probably a special commission, not in the regular line of the army, and consequently there may have been doubts as to his title to half-pay on the reduction which followed the war. No matter, however, for the exact circumstances of the case, such doubts were entertained, and were the occasion of the following magnanimous letter from the chief to one of his Majesty's under Secretaries, a copy of which was preserved among the private papers of the warrior:—

CAPTAIN BRANT TO SIR EVAN NEPEAN. (No Date.)

" SIR :—

"Since I had the pleasure of seeing you last, I have been thinking a great deal about the half-pay, or pension, which you and I have talked about.

"I am really sorry that I ever mentioned such a thing to you. It was really owing to promises made to me by certain persons several times during the late war, that I should always be supported by the government, at war or peace. At that time I never asked any body to make me such a promise. It was of their own free will.

"When I joined the English at the beginning of the war, it was purely on account of my forefathers' engagements with the King. I always looked upon these engagements, or covenants, between the King and the Indian Nations, as a sacred thing. Therefore I was not to be frighted by the threats of the rebels at that time. I assure you I had no other view in it. And this was my real case from the beginning.

"However, after this, the English gave me pay and a commission from the Commander-in-chief, which I gladly received as a mark of attention, though I never asked for it; and I believe my trouble and risques was of equal value to the marks of attention I received : I am sure not too much in the eyes of the Indians, or I should not have accepted them, as I should be sorry to raise jealousies. My meaning for mentioning those things to you, is because I saw there was some difficulty on your part how to act on this head relative to half-pay or pension ;— and when it does not seem clear, I should be sorry to accept it. Therefore I beg of you will say no more about it ;—for was I to get it when there were doubts about the propriety of it, I should not be happy. For which reason I think it is best to go without it.

"I am now, Sir, to beg you will return my best thanks to Government for what they [have] done for me, and am, Sir,

" Your most obedient,

" Humble servant,

" JOSEPH BRANT.

" *To Sir Evan Nepean, Under Secretary, at Home.*"

There are a frankness and manliness of tone and spirit in this letter, which will illustrate a striking feature in the character of the writer, and are worthy of high approbation. It is the only paper of any consequence connected with the Captain's mission to England, in addition to those already cited, that remains.

The chieftain's visit must have been most agreeable, since, in addition to the success which crowned his labors in regard to the claims of the Indians, no pains were spared to render his residence in London one of uninterrupted gratification. He was caressed by the noble and the great, and was alike welcome at court or at the banquets of the heir apparent—who, with all his faults, was " the first gentleman in the realm ;"—a fine classical scholar himself, and a lover of genius and intellect—of letters and men of letters—of sparkling wit, as well as wine. Among his most frequent guests were Fox, Burke, and Sheridan, and others of that splendid galaxy of eloquence and intellect— the master spirits of the opposition in the House of Commons— who were at that time basking in the sunshine of the Prince's favor, and living in the hope of more substantial things to come. Though deficient in his literary acquisitions, Brant, with great strength of mind and shrewdness of observation, had, moreover, sufficient taste and cultivation to appreciate society, even of this elevated and intellectual character. The natural reserve of the Indian temperament he could assume or throw off at pleasure, and with a keen sense of the ludicrous, he could himself use the weapons of humor and sarcasm with a good share of skill and dexterity.

Several anecdotes have been preserved in well-authenticated tradition, illustrative of these traits of character. One of these is the following :—Among the gentlemen of rank with whom Brant was acquainted, was a nobleman of whom it was scandalously reported that his place was purchased by the illicit favors bestowed upon another by his beautiful wife. On one occasion his Lordship undertook to rally the forest chief upon the subjects of the wild and rude manners and customs of the Indians, to which they pertinaciously adhered notwithstanding all the attempts made to improve them by the arts of civilization. Some of their absurd practices, of which the English, as his Lordship remarked, thought very strange, were particularised. Brant listened very patiently until it became his turn to speak, when he replied that there were customs in England, also, of which the Indians thought very strange. "And pray what are they?" inquired his Lordship. "Why," answered the chief, "the Indians have heard that it is a practice in England for men who are born chiefs to sell the virtue of their squaws for place, and for money to buy their venison!" The Mohawk occupied a position which enabled him to say what he pleased with impunity. But in the present instance the rebuke was doubly withering,—from the gravity and assumed simplicity with which it was uttered, and the certainty that the titled gentleman could not mistake the direction of the arrow, while he could neither parry nor avoid, nor appear to notice it.

During his stay in London, a grand fancy ball, or masquerade, was got up with great splendor, and numerously attended by the nobility and gentry. Captain Brant, at the instance of Earl Moira, was also present, richly dressed in the costume of his nation, wearing no mask, but painting one half of his face. His plumes nodded as proudly in his cap as though the blood of a hundred Percies coursed through his veins, and his tomahawk glittered in his girdle like burnished silver. There was, likewise, in the gay and gallant throng a stately Turkish *diplomat* of rank, accompanied by two houris, whose attention was particularly attracted by the grotesque appearance of the chieftain's singular, and, as he supposed, fantastic attire. The pageant was brilliant as the imagination could desire; but among the whole motley throng of pilgrims and warriors, hermits and shepherds, knights, damsels, and gipsies, there was, to the eye of the Mussulman, no character so picturesque and striking as that of the Mohawk; which, being natural, appeared to be the best made up. He scrutinised the chief very closely, and mistaking his *rouge et noir* complexion for a painted visor, the Turk took the liberty of attempting to handle his nose. Brant had, of course, watched the workings of his observation, and felt in the humor of a little sport. No sooner, therefore, had Hassan touched his facial point of honor, under the mistaken idea that it was of no better material than the parchment nose of the Strasburgh trumpeter, than the Chieftain made the hall resound with the appalling war-whoop, and at the same instant the tomahawk leaped from his girdle, and flashed around the astounded Mussulman's head as though his good master, the Sultan, in a minute more, would be relieved from any future trouble in the matter of taking it off Such a piercing and frightful cry had never before rung through that *salon* of fashion ; and breaking suddenly, and with startling wildness, upon the ears of the merry throng, its effect was prodigious. The Turk himself trembled with terror, while the female masquers—the gentle shepherdesses, and fortune-telling crones, Turks, Jews and gipsies, bear-leaders and their bears, Falstaffs, friars, and fortune-tellers, Sultans, nurses and Columbines, shrieked, screamed and scudded away as though the Mohawks had broken into the festive hall in a body. The matter, however, was soon explained ; and the incident was accounted as happy in the end as it was adroitly enacted by the good-humored Mohawk.*

But neither the pleasures of society, nor the follies of the Prince of Wales, nor the special business of his mission, nor the views of political ambition which he was cherishing, made him forgetful of the moral wants of his people. Notwithstanding the ceaseless activity of his life, he had found time to translate the Gospel of Mark into the Mohawk language ; and as most of the Indian Prayer and Psalm Books previously in use had been either lost or destroyed during the war, the opportunity of his visit was chosen by the Society for the Propagation of the Gospel in Foreign Parts, to bring out a new and superior edition of that work, under Brant's own supervision, and including the Gospel of Mark as translated by him. This was the first of the Gospels ever translated entire into the Mohawk language. The book was elegantly printed in large octavo, under the immediate patronage of the King. It was printed in alternate pages of English and Mohawk ; and the volume contained the psalms and occasional prayers before published, together with the services of communion, baptism, matrimony, and the burial of the dead. It was embellished with a number of scriptural engravings, elegant for the state of the arts at that day ; the frontispiece representing the interior of a chapel, with portraits of the King and Queen, a bishop standing at either hand, and groups of Indians receiving the sacred books from both their Majesties.†

---

* This incident was somewhat differently related by the British Magazine, which represented that the weapon was raised by Brant in sober earnest ; he having taken the freedom of the Turk for a real indignity: But such was clearly not the fact. His friends never so understood it.

† A handsome copy of this valuable book, in morocco gilt, has been loaned to

It is not known at what time of the year 1786 Captain Brant turned his back upon the gay metropolis of England, to bury himself once more in the deep forests toward the setting sun. It must, however, have been soon after receiving Lord Sidney's dispatch of April 6th, since, among the papers of the chief, there is a letter addressed to him after his return, by Major Matthews, who was attached to the military family of Sir Guy Carleton, dated at Montreal, July 24, 1786. Early in the month of December following he will also be found attending an Indian Council far in the country of the Great Lakes.

the author by Mrs. Kerr. It belonged to the widow of the old chief, and contains the record of his death.

CHAPTER IX.

UNHAPPILY the treaty of peace did not bring the United States and Great Britain immediately to so good an understanding with each other as could have been desired. Several important questions remained for subsequent arrangement. The treaty proposed a general restoration of confiscated property to all such loyalists as had not actually borne arms in the service of the King. The American Congress passed a resolution recommending the fulfilment of this clause of the treaty by the several states; but it was not considered binding, and South Carolina alone approached to a compliance therewith. There was, likewise, an explicit provision in the treaty, respecting the payment of debts due by Americans to British subjects, not resting upon a recommendation only; the fulfilment of which was sadly neglected. Indeed, the states in which those debts chiefly lay, showed but too plainly an indisposition to aid in carrying the stipulation into effect. On the other hand, the negroes belonging to American citizens who were in the possession and service of the officers of the British army, were not restored; and, contrary to all expectation, Great Britain refused to surrender the military posts upon the American side of the great lakes. The surrender of those posts was expected with the utmost con-

fidence, as one of the most immediate consequences of the rati-
fication of the treaty. To this end, Congress instructed the Commander-in-chief to make all the necessary arrangements to receive
and occupy the posts in the Summer of 1783; and in July of
that season, the Baron Steuben was despatched by General
Washington on a mission to Sir Frederick Haldimand at Quebec, to concert the necessary dispositions, and proceed along the
frontiers as far as Detroit, to examine the different posts, and
report in regard to their condition, and how many and which of
them it would be expedient for the United States permanently to
occupy.* The Baron met General Haldimand at Sorel, on his
way to visit the country of the lakes himself. But on making
known his business, the British commander informed him that
he had received no instructions for the evacuation of the posts,
or for any other objects than a cessation of hostilities, with
which he had complied. He did not consider himself at liberty
to enter into any negotiations with the Baron upon the subject,
and even refused him the necessary passports for visiting Niagara and Detroit.† In addition to this, under the pretext that the
government of the United States had not sufficient power to enforce the observance of a commercial treaty, Great Britain refused to join in the negotiation of such an instrument.‡ Thus
situated—the government and people of each nation complaining of the other—crimination and recrimination ensued, until
the public feeling became irritated almost to exasperation.

The Indians, in the mean time, brooding over the real or fan
cied wrongs they had sustained at the treaty of Fort Stanwix,
and irritated at the onward current of the white population
pressing in their own direction, were becoming restiff; particularly the more distant tribes at the south-west; and their movements indicated any thing but pacific intentions. Indeed, along
some portions of the western frontier, particularly on the Ohio
river, it could scarcely be said that they had been at peace. Both
in 1785 and in 1786, acts of individual hostility were not unfre

* Letter of Washington to General Haldimand, July 12, 1783   Also, Instructions of the same to Baron Steuben.   † Sparks.
‡ The fact was but too true. After the common danger of the war had ceased to
bind the States together, the articles of the Confederation were but a rope of sand.
The government was, indeed, but a ricketty concern until the formation of the Constitution of 1787.

quent on the banks of the Ohio and on the Kentucky border; and in both of those years larger parties had repeatedly attacked the crews of boats descending the river. It was likewise certain that two years only had elapsed after the close of the war before a hostile combination of the great north-western nations was supposed to have been formed; and documentary proof has been adduced in the preceding pages that a powerful and influential messenger, in the person of Captain Brant, had been instructed by those nations to ascertain prospectively the measure of assistance they might, in the event of hostilities, expect to receive from Great Britain. It is true that Lord Sidney, in his reply to the message of Thayendanegea, had avoided committing himself either way upon this point. But the message of the Mohawk chief, and the reply of the minister, were alike unknown to the public at that day. Still, it was to the detention of the posts on the lakes that the hostile temper manifested by the Indians, and their frequent outrages on the frontier, were ascribed; with more justice, as will hereafter appear, than Great Britain would be willing to allow.

The conduct of Captain Brant, moreover, when illustrated by his private correspondence as well as his public actions, will presently appear very mysterious, if not equivocal. By retiring with his own nation into Canada, the Mohawks had not withdrawn from the Confederacy of the Six Nations, nor had Thayendanegea relinquished his official rank as the principal or superior chief of the whole, though five of them remained within the United States. The differences which thus early sprang up between the United States and the Indians, arose upon a question of boundary; the latter maintaining that the Ohio river was not to be crossed by the people of the former. Captain Brant espoused the cause of the Indians at large upon this question, and had early and strenuously exerted himself to compass a grand confederation of all the north-western tribes and nations, of which, it is believed, he intended to be the head. The incipient steps to the formation of such a confederacy, the reader has already seen, had been taken in 1785, previous to his departure for England. On his return in the following year, his efforts for that object were renewed.* In December, 1786, a

* Letter of General Knox, Secretary of War—11th May, 1791.

grand confederate council of the Indians north-west of the Ohio, including the Six Nations, was held at Huron Village, near the mouth of the Detroit River.   This council was attended by the Six Nations, and the Hurons, Ottawas, Twitchtwees, [Miamis,] Shawanese, Chippewas, Cherokees, Delawares, Pottawattamies, and the Wabash Confederates.   On the 18th of that month, an address to the Congress of the United States was agreed upon, the tone of which was pacific—provided the United States made no encroachments upon their lands beyond the Ohio.   After a declaration of their surprise that they were not included in the treaty of peace, they observed that they had nevertheless received a message from the King, advising them to remain quiet.   They had likewise received two very agreeable messages from the thirteen States, from the tenor of which they had anticipated a period of repose.   But while they were devising the best measures to secure this result and form a lasting reconciliation—while they had " the best thoughts in their minds, mischief had happened."   Still, they were anxious to prevent farther trouble, as a principal means of which they recommended that no treaties should be formed by the United States with separate Indian tribes or nations; but that all treaties for lands should be negotiated openly and above board, in the most public manner, and by the united voice of the Confederacy.   They attributed the " mischief and confusion " that had arisen, to the fact that the United States would have every thing their own way—that they would " kindle the council-fires wherever they thought pro- " per, without consulting the Indians."   At the treaty of Fort Stanwix in 1784, they had urged a different policy; and they believed that, had the course then recommended, of treating only in a general conference of the nations, been pursued, all would have continued peace and concord between them.   Notwithstanding the mischiefs that had happened, the council professed their strong desire of peace.   " This," they said, " is the deter- " mination of all the chiefs of the Confederacy, now assembled, " notwithstanding that several Indian chiefs were killed in our " villages, even when in council, and when absolutely engaged " in promoting peace with you, the thirteen United States."   In order to ensure this desirable result, they proposed a grand confederate council, to be holden at some half-way place in the ensuing spring—recommending to the United States, in the mean time to prevent their surveyors and other people from crossing to the Indian side of the Ohio. This important address con cluded in the following words :—" BROTHERS : It shall not be " our faults, if the plans which we have suggested to you should " not be carried into execution. In that case the event will be " very precarious, and if fresh ruptures ensue, we hope to be ' able to exculpate ourselves, and shall most assuredly, with our " united force, be obliged to defend those rights and privileges " which have been transmitted to us by our ancestors ; and if " we should be thereby reduced to misfortunes, the world will " pity us when they think of the amicable proposals we now " make to prevent the unnecessary effusion of blood. These " are our thoughts and firm resolves, and we earnestly desire " that you would transmit to us, as soon as possible, your an- " swer, be it what it may."

This address, the ultimatum antecedent to the general war that afterward arose, was not signed by individual chiefs, but by the nation, the name of the nation being written, and the bird or animal adopted as the national emblem rudely marked upon the paper. Thayendanegea was present and active at this council, as will appear by the annexed letter, found among his papers, from the American Secretary of War, General Knox :—

GENERAL KNOX TO CAPTAIN BRANT.
" *War Office, July 23d,* 1787.

" SIR :—

" On the 17th instant, and not before, I received the favor of your letter, dated 'Huron Town, Dec. 18th, 1786,' enclosing the original speech by the several nations of Indians met at the same time and place, to the United States in Congress assembled.

" It appears from the information of General Butler, the Superintendent, that the Shawanese neglected to forward the above despatches at the time it was expected they would ; and it appears by a letter from Captain Pipe, of the Delawares, and the Half-King of the Wyandots, dated at Sandusky the 3d of June, that they forwarded the despatches finally to Fort Pitt—at which place, and at the same time also, your messengers arrived with your letters to General Butler, dated Buffalo Creek, the 16th of May, 1787, enclosing a copy, or translation, of the speech of the chiefs, transmitted by Captain Pipe and the Half-King of the Wyandots.

" I mention these circumstances, to convince you that the result of your council, at the Huron village, in December, has been a long time in travelling to this city.

" On the receipt of your papers, they were submitted to Congress, who have taken the same into consideration, and will soon come to some decision thereon, which will be communicated to the Superintendant, in order to be transmitted to you.

" I have the honor to be,

" Sir,

" Your most obedient,

" Humble servant,

" H. KNOX.

" COLONEL JOSEPH BRANT,
   " *One of the Chiefs of the Mohawk Nation.*"

Neither the preceding letter, nor that in reply to which it was written, has been preserved in the archives of the American Department of War. The signature of " *The Five Nations,*" however, stood at the head of the list, and from the rank and superior intelligence of Thayendanegea, there can be little doubt that the address to the Government of the United States was dictated, if not written, by him. That it was in entire accordance with his views, appears most fully by the following letter from Sir John Johnson. This letter is worthy of preservation, as affording the first authentic evidence of the equivocal attitude Great Britain was assuming in regard to the Indian relations of the United States.

SIR JOHN JOHNSON TO CAPTAIN BRANT.
" *Quebec, March* 22d, 1787

" DEAR SIR,

" I have received your letter of the 14th of February. I am happy to find things turned out as you wished at your several meetings in the Indian country near Detroit, and I hope it may have the effect you wish in preventing the Americans from incroaching on your lands. Your conduct, I hope, for your own sake, will always be such as to justify the good opinion that has been entertained of you by your friends the English, and such as will merit the continuance of their friendship. I hope in all your decisions you will conduct yourselves with prudence and moderation, having always an eye to the friendship that has so long subsisted between you and the King's subjects, upon whom alone you can and ought to depend. You have no reason to fear any breach of promise on the part of the King. Is he not every year giving fresh proofs of his friendship? What greater could you expect than is now about to be performed, by giving an ample compensation for your losses, which is yet withheld from us, his subjects? Do not suffer bad men or evil advisers to lead you astray; every thing that is reasonable and consistent with the friendship that ought to be preserved between us, will be done for you all. Do not suffer an idea to hold a place in your mind, that it will be for your interests to sit still and see the Americans attempt the posts.* It is for your sakes chiefly, if not entirely, that we hold them. If you become indifferent about them, they may perhaps be given up; what security would you then have? You would be left at the mercy of a people whose blood calls aloud for revenge; whereas, by supporting them, you encourage us to hold them, and encourage the new settlements, already considerable, and every day increasing by numbers coming in, who find they can't live in the States. Many thousands are preparing to come in. This increase of his Majesty's subjects will serve as a protection for you, should the subjects of the States, by endeavoring to make farther encroachments on you, disturb your quiet. At present I think there is little to apprehend from any but the Southern States; those to the eastward are already opposed to each other in arms, † and have shed blood, and the disorder seems to be spreading throughout. Men of character are coming in here to see if no assistance will be given them; and the people of New England, who were the most violent at the commencement of the war, are now the most desirous of returning under the British government, should Great Britain incline to receive them, which many think they would not.

"Remember me in the most friendly manner to Mrs. Brant all your family, and to all my brothers in your settlement, and

---

* Oswegatchie, Oswego, Niagara, Detroit and Mackinaw—withheld from the United States, as heretofore stated in the text.

† This allusion refers to the memorable insurrection of Captain Shays, in Massachusetts.

tell them to be patient, and that they will find that all that has
been promised them, coming within my knowledge, will be performed.   I hope to see you in the course of the summer; in
the mean time, I remain with truth,

" Dear Sir,

" Your friend and

" Humble servant,

" JOHN JOHNSON." *

The object of this communication will be seen at a glance.
It is unfortunate that the letter of Thayendanegea, giving the
private history of the great Amphictyonic council of the Indians,
has not been discovered.   Still, enough can be learned from the
scattered correspondence that remains, to show that Great Britain was by no means an indifferent observer of the storm gathering in the north-west.   It is also evident that the officers of
the crown in Canada were rejoicing in the insurrection of Captain Shays in Massachusetts; which, though at one moment of
threatening importance, had been crushed but a few days before the Baronet's letter was written, of which result he had
not then been apprised.   That insurrection was a consequence,
in the main, of the weakness of the government of the confede
racy.   Fortunately, however, instead of working farther detriment to the republic, its influence was not inconsiderable in
binding the states more firmly together, by means of the Constitution, which arose from the ruins of the old Articles of
Confederation in the course of the same year.   There is another
feature in the letter of Sir John deserving to be noted.   It dis-
closes the fact, that already, even so early as the year 1787,
had the British authorities imbibed the absurd notion that the
people of New England, who had been first in raising the standard of revolt, wearied with their freedom, were seeking a dismemberment of the Union, that they might throw themselves
back into the arms of their former sovereign.   Nor was this idea
eradicated until after the failure of a miserable intrigue, under
the Canadian administration of Sir James H. Craig, with a worthless fellow named John Henry, in 1810.

Great Britain not only continued to retain possession of the
north-western posts, but added to their strength.   Upon this sub-

* Copied from the original, among the Brant papers.

ject, and the policy by which she was governed in regard to it, the following letter reflects additional light. It was addressed to Captain Brant by Major Matthews, whose name has already occurred as an officer in the suite of Sir Guy Carleton—who had now become Lord Dorchester. Matthews had been assigned to the command of Detroit, and was on his way thither when the letter was written :—

MAJOR MATTHEWS TO CAPTAIN BRANT.

"*Niagara,* 29th *May,* 1787.

"My Dear Friend,

" A few days before I left Quebec, I had the pleasure to re· ceive your letter of the 3d April, and was happy at the prospect I had of so soon answering it in person, and once more shaking hands together upon our old ground. On my arrival yesterday, I was much disappointed to hear that you had left this place, and gone by a route which, for the present, prevents our meeting ; for though there is nothing I wish more than to pay you a visit in your settlement, and to have a conversation with you, the despatch which I am under the necessity of making to Detroit, renders it impossible. I therefore sit down to thank you for the information in your last, and to renew our old agreement of communicating freely to each other whatsoever we may know or think is for the mutual advantage and well-being of that cause, which has always been common, and which, I am persuaded, is equally dear to us both ; and being better informed of what relates to the situation of affairs in this quarter than when I last wrote to you, I shall begin by informing you of what his Excellency, Lord Dorchester, desired I would, should I chance to fall in with you. His Lordship wishes you should be acquainted that, when he arrived at Quebec last fall, it was too late to forward any thing more than a few provisions necessary for the posts and Indians, a part of which even could not proceed on account of the ice ; but that he did not forget the presents intended for the Indians ; and had, as soon as the communication opened, ordered them to be sent up from Montreal. At the same time his Lordship was sorry to learn, that while the Indians were soliciting his assistance in their preparations for war, some of the Six Nations had sent deputies to Albany to treat with the Americans, who, it is said, have made a treaty

with them, granting permission to make roads for the purpose
of coming to Niagara; but that, notwithstanding these things, the
Indians should have their presents, as they are marks of the
King's approbation of their former conduct.   In future his
Lordship wishes them to act as is best for their interest; he cannot begin a war with the Americans, because some of their people encroach and make depredations upon parts of the Indian
country; but they must see it is his Lordship's intention to defend the posts; and that while these are preserved, the Indians
must find great security therefrom, and consequently the Americans greater difficulty in taking possession of their lands; but
should they once become masters of the posts, they will surround the Indians, and accomplish their purpose with little trouble. From a consideration of all which, it therefore remains with
the Indians to decide what is most for their own interest, and to
let his Lordship know their determination, that he may take his
measures accordingly; but, whatever their resolution is, it should
be taken as by one and the same people, by which means they
will be respected and become strong; but if they divide, and act
one part against the other, they will become weak, and help to
destroy each other.   This, my dear Joseph, is the substance of
what his Lordship desired me to tell you, and I request you
will give his sentiments that mature consideration which their
justice, generosity, and desire to promote the welfare and happi
ness of the Indians, must appear to all the world to merit.

" In your letter to me, you seem apprehensive that the English are not very anxious about the defence of the posts.   You
will soon be satisfied that they have nothing more at heart, provided that it continues to be the wish of the Indians, and that
they remain firm in doing *their* part of the business, by prevent
ing the Americans from coming into their country, and conse
quently from marching to the posts.   On the other hand, if the
Indians think it more for their interest that the Americans
should have possession of the posts, and be established in their
country, they ought to declare it, that the English need no
longer be put to the vast and unnecessary expense and inconvenience of keeping posts, the chief object of which is to protect
their Indian allies, and the loyalists who have suffered with
them.   It is well-known that no encroachments ever have or
ever will be made by the English upon the lands or property of

the Indians in consequence of their possessing the posts, how far that will be the case if ever the Americans get into them, may very easily be imagined, from their hostile perseverance even without that advantage, in driving the Indians off their lands and taking possession of them.

" In regard to myself, I have to acquaint you, that in consequence of the reports which reached Quebec from the upper country respecting the intentions of the Americans against the posts, Lord Dorchester has been pleased to permit me to take the command of Detroit, which is garrisoned by the regiment I am in, and has ordered that another regiment be sent up for the protection of the posts in general, two companies of which, under the command of your acquaintance, Captain Malcolm, arrived with me in the Seneca, and I am to take two companies of the 53d from hence, to reinforce Detroit; so that I think we shall have but little to apprehend from any thing in the power of the Americans to attempt. I confess to you I have no idea they have any serious intention of the kind, the few troops they can muster not being sufficient to support their government; they are, besides, in rebellion, and cutting each others' throats. A people in this situation are but ill able to march considerable armies with artillery and the necessary stores, (which they must have to be successful,) through a distant and difficult country.

" Inclosed I send you a letter from Sir John Johnson. It will probably inform you that the presents mentioned by Lord Dorchester are sent up; they crossed the lake in the ship with me, and are stored here, waiting the arrival of Sir John for the distribution of them.

" On your way to the Southern Council, I shall hope for the satisfaction of seeing you at Detroit; in the meantime I remain, with very sincere regard,

    " My dear friend,
     " Your faithful and obedient servant,
       " R. MATTHEWS.

" If Mrs. Brant is with you, I beg you will recommend me in the kindest manner to her."

There can be no misunderstanding touching the purport of this letter. Lord Dorchester would no more commit himself on the question of a direct participation, in the event of actual declared hostilities between the Indian Confederacy and the Americans, than Lord Sidney had done. Captain, now Major Matthews, was anxious to confer with Captain Brant "for the "mutual advantage and well-being of *that cause,* which had "always been common, and equally dear," &c. His Lordship wished the Indians to act as was best for their own interest—"he "could not *begin* a war with the Americans," but "they must "see that it was his Lordship's intention to defend the posts; and "while these were preserved, the Indians must find great secu- "rity therefrom, and the Americans greater difficulty in taking "possession of their lands," &c. Indeed, the whole tenor of the letter was to promote a feeling of hostility in the bosoms of the Indians against the United States, with a mutual understanding that the British government was maintaining the posts for the benefit of the Indians; while the Indian hostilities, should they ensue, would serve to check or prevent the Americans from ob taining possession of them.

There are neither printed nor written records, from which any additional information can be drawn respecting the conduct and movements of Captain Brant during the residue of the year 1787. The delay in the transmission of his despatches to the government of the United States, as mentioned in the letter of General Knox, had of course disappointed the Indians in their expectation of an early reply from Congress. In consequence of this delay, another grand council was determined upon by the western Indians, of which, among the papers of Captain Brant, is the following notification to his nation :—

MESSAGE FROM THE HURONS OF DETROIT TO THE FIVE NATIONS.

"*January* 21*st*, 1788.

"BRETHREN,

"Nothing yet has reached us in answer to the messages sent to the Americans on the breaking up of our General Council, nor is it now probable we shall hear from them before our next meeting takes place; a circumstance that ought to expedite us in our business. The nations this way have adhered hitherto to the engagements entered into before we parted, at least as far as has come to our knowledge; and we intend immediately to call them to this council-fire, which shall be uncovered at the time appointed; that without farther delay some decisive measures may be finally fixed upon for our future interest, which must govern hereafter the conduct of all the nations in our alliance; and this we intend to be the last council for the purpose; therefore it is needless for us to urge farther the indispensable necessity of all nations being present at the conclusion of affairs tending so much to their own future welfare and happiness. And we do in a particular manner desire you, the Five Nations, to be strong and punctual in your promise of being with us early and in time; and that not only the warriors, but the chiefs of your several nations attend on this occasion. We shall therefore endeavor to have as many of the western and southern Indians as possible collected.

"Strings of Wampum."

Accompanying this address to the Five Nations, was another of similar import, (save only that it expressed the dissatisfaction of the Hurons at the proceedings of the former grand council,) directed to the other tribes of Canadian Indians, and summoning them to appear at the great council-fire of the Confederacy in the Spring.

It will appear by the three letters next successively to be introduced, that Captain Brant was preparing in March to attend the proposed council, and that, having attended the said council, his views became more pacific. He had, however, begun to distrust all the nations of his own confederacy, excepting only the Mohawks—and probably not without reason. The Congress of the United States, in the Autumn of the preceding year, had given instructions to Major General St. Clair, then Governor of the North-western territory, to inquire particularly into the temper of the Indians, and if he found it still hostile, to endeavor to hold as general a treaty with them as he could convene; and although the purchase of the Indian right to the soil was not to be considered a primary object, yet he was instructed if possible to extinguish their title as far westward as the Mississippi river. It will be seen presently, that Brant had, even thus early, reason to suppose, that in a war with the United States the majority of the Five Nations would not be found in arms. The gentleman to whom two of these letters were addressed, was Patrick Langan, Esq. private secretary to Sir John Johnson:—

CAPTAIN BRANT TO LIEUTENANT LANGAN.[*]

" Grand River, March 20th, 1788.

"DEAR SIR,

" I hope you have enjoyed your health since I had the pleasure to see you last. We have had no particular news here from
the southward, only they are preparing to have another great Council in that country early in the Spring, and I am obliged to attend myself there. As for the Five Nations, most of them have
sold themselves to the Devil—I mean to the Yankeys. Whatever they do after this, it must be for the Yankeys—not for the
Indians or the English. We mean to speak to them once more.
We must, in the first place, get the Mohawks away from the Bay
of Quinte. As soon as we can get them here, we shall begin to
argue to the Five Nations, and will show our example of getting together ourselves ; also, we shall know who is for the Yankeys and who is not. I forgot to mention to Sir John I wanted very much to have the papers here. I mean the list of our
losses and claims, and our names. I should be much obliged to
you if you would be so kind as to send me those papers, or the
copies of them, as there are some disputes here concerning those
lists. I should be exceeding happy if you could get me a quarter of a pound of sewing thread, of silk, of different colors, and
send me the account and the money I owed you before. Also, I
wish you could get me a pipe tomahawk. Please to get the best,
if you can.

" Sir, I remain

" Your most obedient, humble servant,

" JOSEPH BRANT.

" *To Lieutenant Langan.*"

There is no farther information of Brant or his movements
until the closing week of August, at which time he was in the
neighborhood of Detroit, preparing to mingle in the deliberations
of the great council spoken of in the preceding letter. The following is a copy of a letter found among his papers, written
at this time :

* Copied from the original by the author.

CAPTAIN BRANT TO SIR JOHN JOHNSON.

"*Huron Village, mouth of the Detroit.*
28th August, 1788.

"SIR,

"I am happy to inform you of our having arrived at Detroit the 10th inst. The party with Capt. David who went by water, and those with myself who went by land, being so lucky as to arrive the same inst. And wishing to lose as little time as possible, the next day we met the principal men of the Hurons, Chippewas, Ottawas, and Pottawattamies. As they had lost three of their Chiefs, we went through our ancient custom of condoling with them, by giving about 10,000 wampum, as we could not proceed with our public business till such time as that ceremony was over; when, upon examining into the business we came about, I plainly foresaw numberless difficulties, owing to the people here not being so unanimous as the situation of affairs requires. The Wyandots do not wish to attend at the place that was last Fall agreed upon, but wish to have the Council at this place; but that we strenuously opposed, and have got them to consent to meet at the Miamis; their reason is, I believe, that they would wish to have a private and separate meeting with the Americans to settle matters for themselves. On the other hand, the Twightwees or Miamis are quite the reverse,—wishing by no means to fall in with the Hurons in their way of thinking, but would wish to be at open war with the Americans. Thus are matters here situated. However, I have some reason to think that if we can get them at the appointed place of rendezvous, we will be able to point out to them their error, and get them again to adopt the measures that the whole of us agreed upon, and cause that unanimity to subsist among us, which is so requisite in our situation, and without which we cannot expect the business will terminate so much to our satisfaction as it otherwise would. In case that they should be headstrong, and not wish to fall in with our plan of operation, I shall scarcely know how to act upon it, but shall take every necessary precaution to prevent the minds of those who are unanimous being any ways inflamed by those nations in opposition and wavering. Still I hope to have the pleasure of writing to you a more favorable account after we have had a meeting. Capt. McKee has given us every assistance that he could towards forwarding our business, and I expect will attend the Council at the Miamis, which I sincerely hope will now be soon.   Upon leaving Niagara, I found from the multiplicity of business which we should have, that it would be highly requisite to have a man with us who understood the English language, and capable of transacting business, for which purpose we have thought proper to appoint Ralph Clement, and will make him some allowance out of the money we are to receive next summer for the lands sold the Americans.   In the meantime I have to request you will be so kind as to allow him something towards defraying his necessary expenses out of the Indian store at Niagara.   Upon application made to Col. Butler, he did not think proper to advance him any thing without he should have your order for it.   As to the news from the Southern Indians and American Commissioners, we have some accounts, but must refer you to Capt. McKee, who writes you by this vessel, for the particulars.   This is the fourth letter I have written you since I had the pleasure of seeing you last.

" Your most obedient servant,
" JOSEPH BRANT.

" *Sir John Johnson.*"

From the nomadic habits of the Indians, and the long distances most of their nations were obliged to travel, the gathering of their great council was a work of time.   Thus it will be seen that six weeks more elapsed, before the kindling of the council-fire, and how much longer it is impossible to tell, from the brokenness of the correspondence of the chief, who was probably the only writer among them.   On the 7th of October the Captain wrote as follows :—

CAPTAIN BRANT TO LIEUTENANT LANGAN.

" *Miamis River*, 7th *October*, 1788.

"DEAR SIR,

" The business I have been obliged to attend to since I had the pleasure of seeing you, had so much taken up my attention, and kept me so busily employed, that I have scarcely had time to write any of my friends.   And, indeed, nothing worth communicating has occurred, or otherwise I should have strained a point to have dropt you a line, as my intention always was to correspond with you, who, I am certain, would at any time spare a moment to acknowledge the receipt. I have done myself the pleasure of writing four letters to Sir John, who, I hope, has received them,* as I would wish to give him every information affecting our proceedings. Probably his time is too busily employed to attend to them, and that it would be more agreeable to him if I corresponded with you on public business. I should be happy to hear from time to time whether my conduct met with his approbation, as I would not wish to act in any manner that he would not approve; he being at the head of the department, is the one we look to for advice.

" Upon my arrival at Detroit I found the nations there. All had forgot our last Fall's agreements, and were averse to attend the council at this place. However, we talked over matters with them, and convinced them of the necessity there was for our being unanimous, and determining the business that has been so long in agitation, and after some time, I prevailed, and have got them all here. After waiting at this place, for near five weeks, the arrival of the Shawanese, Miamis, Onias, and the rest of the nations westward of this, are at last arrived; so that I am in hopes in a few days to be able to give you the particulars of our meeting. I have still my doubts whether we will all join or not, some being no ways inclined for peaceable methods. The Hurons, Chippewas, Ottawas, Pottawattamies, and Delawares, will join with us in trying lenient steps, and having a boundary line fixed; and, rather than enter headlong into a destructive war, will give up a small part of their country. On the other hand, the Shawanese, Miamis, and Kickapoos, who are now so much addicted to horse-stealing that it will be a difficult task to break them of it, as that kind of business is their best harvest, will of course declare for war, and not giving up any of their country, which, I am afraid, will be the means of our separating. They are, I believe, determined not to attend the treaty with the Americans. Still I hope for the best. As the major part of the nations are of our opinions, the rest may be brought to, as nothing shall be wanting on my part to con-

* One only of these has been discovered—that of the 25th of August, on the preceding page. The author has made many efforts to obtain the papers of Sir John Johnson, where these letters, probably, may yet be found—but without success. They are either scattered and lost, or have been taken to England.

vince them of their error. I sincerely hope our business may terminate to our general interest and satisfaction. We have not as yet entered upon public matters, as the Shawanese have a great feast, which will take up a couple of days, after which we will have a general meeting, and then we will be certain of each other's opinions. Till then, I am, with compliments to Sir John and Mrs. Claus,

" Your most obed't friend,

" And very humble serv't,

" Jos. Brant.

" *P. Langan.*"

The tone of the three immediately preceding letters, is more pacific than might have been anticipated. Indeed, they seem to indicate a change in the intentions of the writer, which it will be found somewhat difficult to reconcile with portions of his subsequent conduct. He is in these letters—particularly the last addressed to Lieutenant Langan, though intended more especially for the information of Sir John Johnson—the friend of peace—perhaps being compelled to assume that attitude by the force of circumstances—having reason to anticipate the success— temporary, as it proved—which was to crown the Indian diplomacy of General St. Clair. In his first letter to Langan, Brant had declared that " the Six Nations had sold themselves to the devil," or, in other words, " to the Yankees," which in his opinion was equivalent thereto—and the result was shortly afterward such as to sustain his sagacity.

No records of the proceedings of the grand council so long assembling in the Autumn of 1788, have been discovered, although it appears by a letter from Captain Brant to his friend Matthews, who had returned once more to Quebec, written in March, 1789, that all the proceedings and speeches had been forwarded—by Captain M'Kee probably—to Lord Dorchester. The presumption is, that the council came to no harmonious conclusion, inasmuch as a treaty was shortly afterward held with the Americans at Fort Harmar, which was attended by only a part of the Indians, while its proceedings were subsequently disavowed by other and the larger portions of the nations.

Be these things, however, as they may, on the 2d of May following, (1789,*) General St. Clair wrote to President Washington from New-York, announcing that on the 9th of the preceding month of January, he had concluded two separate treaties with the Indians assembled in council at Fort Harmar ; the first with the sachems and warriors of the Five Nations, the Mohawks excepted—and the second with the sachems and warriors of the Wyandot, Delaware, Ottawa, Chippewa, Pottawattame and Sac Nations. The reason of these separate negotiations, as explained by General St. Clair, was found in the Roman maxim—" *Divide et impera.*" " A jealousy," says the General, " subsisted between them, which I was not willing to " lessen by appearing to consider them as one people. They " do not so consider themselves ; and I am persuaded their ge-" neral confederacy is entirely broken. Indeed, it would not be " very difficult, if circumstances required it, to set them at deadly " variance."† This Machiavelian policy of dividing to conquer —of poising nations, tribes, and factions against each other, that all may the more easily be crushed at will—is an ancient mode of war, and has been practised by every government having the opportunity. Its morality, however, cannot be defended—more especially in regard to the simple children of the American forests, against whom it has been prosecuted with the greatest success. Still, there was an approximation to justice, in a pecuniary point of view, toward the Indians, in these negotiations of General St. Clair, which had not been previously countenanced by Congress. From the date of the peace with England, to the reception of the address of October, 1786, from the Grand Council at Huron Village, Congress had acted upon the principle that the treaty with Great Britain invested them with the fee of all the Indian lands within the boundaries of the United States. The address of the Indian Council, of December, 1786, written, as has been assumed, by Captain Brant, asserted a contrary principle—viz : that the Indians were the only rightful proprietors of the soil. And this principle was acceded to in the instructions of Congress to General St. Clair, of October, 1787, and July, 1788.‡ However greatly the Indians may have

---

* Erroneously dated, May 2d, 1788, in the State Papers, as will be seen by the dates of the treaties, and by the Report of the Secretary of War, July 7, 1789.

† St. Clair's letter, Am. State Papers, Vol. IV. p. 10.

‡ Vide State Papers, Vol. IV. p. 9 ; and report of the Secretary of War, July 15, 1789—same vol. p. 13.

been defrauded since that date, such has at least been the basis of all subsequent negotiations with them for lands.

Although the Mohawks were not parties to the treaty of Fort Harmar, yet it appears that they, at least their chief, Thayenda-negea, must have been present at its negotiation. This fact is disclosed in a passage in his letter to Major Matthews, already referred to : " You'll hear by this opportunity the result of our "jaunt to the southward, as Captain M'Kee has sent down all "the proceedings of our councils with the American Commis-"sioners, speeches, and answers. Our proceedings have been "such as I hope will be approved of. I must farther mention "that much may yet be done, if we meet with necessary assist-"ance, as business cannot be carried on in the upper country to "advantage without the attendance of the Five Nations, which "they cannot do without being more amply supplied than hereto-"fore with ammunition, provisions, &c. I have ever been forward "in pointing out what I thought would tend to the good of our "service, and which has ever been attended to, notwithstanding "that my friends below seem to credit these reports. Still, my "attachment to government is such, that personal injury will "not have sufficient weight to make me swerve from the duty I "owe my King."*

There is an allusion, in the closing sentences of this quotation, to certain "private griefs" of the writer, requiring an explana-tion. Captain Brant was no more exempt than other men from the ill-will and evil machinations of the envious and jealous. "Great honors are great burdens" as well among the red men as the white ; and it was the fate of the noble Mohawk to en-counter his full share of trials of this description. Difficulties had already sprung up in the administration of his affairs, not only with the Provincial Government, in regard to the nature of the title which the Mohawks were to receive of the lands

* Letter from Joseph Brant to Capt. Matthews, March 8, 1789, among the Brant papers. Writing to Governor Clinton respecting the conduct of Captain Brant touching St. Clair's proceedings at Fort Harmar, President Washington said— "Captain Brant has not been candid in his account of General St. Clair, nor done justice in his representation of matters at Muskingum. It is notorious that he used all the art and influence of which he was possessed to prevent any treaty being held; and that, except in a small degree, General St. Clair aimed at no more land by the treaty of Muskingum than had been ceded by the preceding treaties."—*Let-ter from President Washington to Governor Clinton, Dec. 1, 1790.*

granted them on the Ouise or Grand River, but also between the chief and some of the Indians themselves; not Mohawks, but stragglers from other tribes of the Iroquois Confederacy. During the protracted absence of the Captain to the councils of the preceding year, in the country of the great lakes, it appears that a council of disaffected Indians had been held at Montreal ; the object of which was to denounce the conduct of Brant, but in what respects does not exactly appear. Strong complaints were preferred against him, however, at that council, "not only "in the name of the Five Nations. but by some of his relations "and intimate friends," under circumstances, and with an air so imposing, as to give serious alarm to his friends at the castle of St. Lewis.

On the 3d of January, 1789, Major Matthews addressed a long letter to his Mohawk friend, on the subject of that council, and the charges then and there preferred against him. This letter was written by Matthews with the knowledge and approbation of a distinguished personage, who, although his name is not given, must have been Lord Dorchester. Major Matthews did not specify the charges made against his friend, and they can only be vaguely surmised from the following extract: " The " circumstances which have been alleged against you, you have " no doubt been minutely informed of. It is therefore unneces- " sary, and would be painful to me, to recapitulate them. Your " friend* wishes you to reflect seriously upon the fatal conse- " quences that must attend a misunderstanding and disunion of " your nation, and of those Indians who might make the settle- " ment upon the Grand River a happy retreat for themselves and " their posterity, by a cordial and friendly union. How materi- " ally the contrary must weaken their interest, and yours in par- " ticular, in the great scale of the Indian Confederacy ; and how " heavy the blame must fall upon whoever shall be considered " the promoter of so great a calamity. He therefore recom- " mends to you, as the safest and surest road to consequence and " fame, to effect, without loss of time, a perfect reconciliation " with your friends and fellow-settlers ; convincing them, by your " mildness and generosity, and still more by a strict attention to " justice, that you are worthy of their confidence ; exert all your " powers in establishing perfect union and friendship among

* Lord Dorchester doubtless, meaning.

"your own nation, and you will convince those at a distance
"that you are capable and worthy of cementing a general union
"for good purposes.

"Having thus far given you the sentiments of a hearty well-
"wisher, I cannot conclude without adding from myself, in the
"language and with the heart of an old and sincere friend, that
"I feel more sensibly than I can find words to express, for the
"critical situation in which every person who was present at the
"Council must consider you to stand with your nation. For
"my own part I could scarce believe my own eyes and ears,
"when I saw and heard our old friends, whose hands and
"hearts have been so long joined together in one common cause,
"pour out complaints against you; and they did it at the same
"time with such reluctance and concern, that it was the more
"affecting. It is impossible that men who were born, brought
"up, who have so oft fought by each others' sides, and bled to-
"gether, can seriously disagree. The whole must be a misun-
"derstanding, and must be explained with reconciliation. It is
"noble and generous to acknowledge an error, and mutually to
"forgive injuries; and, my dear Joseph, listen to mine, and to
"the voice of your friends, who wish your happiness by seeing
"you so firmly re-united with your own flesh and blood as to
"resist any power on earth that would separate you from
"them." *

It is from the reply of Captain Brant to this communication,
that the brief reference to the proceedings of the western councils has been quoted. In regard to the proceedings at Montreal
to which his attention had been so earnestly invited by his correspondent, the answer of Captain Brant was full and frank,
manifesting on his own part, a feeling of dignified and conscious rectitude. The charges themselves were not specified by
the chief in his defence, but the inference deduced from his language is, that his integrity had been impeached in regard to
their lands, and his loyalty questioned to the King; and farther,
that he had been censured for introducing a few white settlers
upon the Indian lands—his object in so doing, being to benefit
the Indians by the better examples of the whites in husbandry,
and also by the introduction of some of the mechanic arts

* Extracted from the original letter of Capt. Matthews, among the Brant papers.

among them. He regrets that his enemies, few in number, as he says, had availed themselves of his absence to assail his character, at a moment, too, when in a distant country he was exerting all his energies for the benefit of his people ; and regrets still more that his friends in Montreal had listened to the charges for a moment, until after he could have a hearing. If he had erred at all, he maintained that it could only have been in the warmth of his ardour in promoting the substantial interests of his nation. In the course of his letter, he pointed with modest exultation to the proceedings of a full Council of the Five Nations, held at Niagara, in presence of the agent and the commanding officer, subsequent to the denunciation at Montreal, by which his conduct had been approved. Should the proceedings of this council be insufficient to remove " the censure thrown up-" on him by a seditious and discontented few, and make the " complainants appear in their proper light," the Captain suggested that he should make application to the agents at Detroit and Niagara for certificates of his conduct during the war and since the peace ; and thus provided, he would repair to head-quarters with all the principal men, both sachems and warriors,* of all the nations settled in that country, and let them speak freely. After which, he hoped to stand better with " the great men below" than he had reason to suppose he did at that time.

With the conclusion of the treaties of January, 1789, by General St. Clair, the purpose of forming a grand Indian Confederacy, to include the Five Nations, which should be lasting, was defeated, at least for that time ; and although peace had not been restored to the south-western settlements on the Ohio, yet the name of Captain Brant does not again appear in connexion with the affairs of the western Indians during the residue of the year 1789 and the two succeeding years. It appears, however, by the copy of a letter found among his papers, addressed by him to Colonel M'Donnell, in September, that the Shawanese

---

* "Both Sachems and warriors." " A Sachem is considered a civil magistrate, who takes precedence of all war-chiefs in time of peace, and is hereditary. Not so the war-chiefs. They, as by all the rest of the world, are made by the voice of the nation for their gallantry in the field. In time of war, the war-chiefs take the command, and direct all the movements,—what is called in civilized life,---martial law." *Letters to the author from Colonel William J. Kerr.* The distinction is scarcely ever observed in writing of Indian affairs, since sachems, warriors, chiefs, are most usually written indiscriminately, as it happens.

had then just sent an embassy, "inviting the Five Nations very
" strongly to a grand council of the different nations, to be held at
" the Wyandot Town, near Detroit, for the purpose of RENEW-
" ING and STRENGTHENING the Confederacy." " We left it,"
the letter continues, " entirely to the Buffalo Creek people to
" determine how to act, because they are in general backward
" and dilatory; but for our parts, we can always be ready at
" the shortest notice. I, however, think, myself, that it cannot
" take place until next Spring, since by this time the young men
" have begun to scatter in the woods for hunting; and it would
" be necessary to have them present to hear what is agreed upon
" by the chiefs; and by that means whatever may be agreed on
" will more firmly effect and unite the different nations. The
" larger number present from the different nations the better."
Whether the proposed council was held, or whether, if held,
Captain Brant participated in its deliberations, is not known.

But while Thayendanegea had successfully vindicated himself from the aspersions of the disaffected of his own people, as
has been seen, and while he was pondering upon the invitation
of the Shawanese to attempt the assembling of another great
council in the west, he was admonished of the rumored existence of a plot against the English garrison at Detroit, and also
against himself and his own people in their new location, con
certed by his recent *quasi* confederates, the Hurons, Pottawatta
mies, and Chippewas. The inauspicious rumor was communi
cated to him in writing by Sir John Johnson.

SIR JOHN JOHNSON TO CAPTAIN BRANT.

" *Montreal, 4th Nov.* 1789.

" DEAR JOSEPH,

" I do not think I should be justifiable in not acquainting you
(though perhaps you may have heard the report,) that an account has been received at Detroit, upon the oath of one the
party concerned, that the Hurons, Pottawattamies, and Chippewas are concerned in a plot to cut off the garrison at Detroit,
and your settlement, this Winter, or as soon as the navigation of
the lakes is shut up. Though this information wants farther
confirmation, and I give very little credit to it, I think you had
better be on your guard, and try to find out the real situation,
designs, and disposition of those nations, by sending some trusty,

unsuspected persons among them. I should imagine that you had some friends among the Hurons that you could rely upon to give you all the information you want, and that some trusty Messissagoes might be got to go among the other nations to watch their motions; any recompense for these services will be readily granted, if you think them necessary, upon producing this letter to Lieut. Col. Butler, or Mr. M'Kee.

"I have your letter to Langan of the 23d of September. As to the business of Aaron and Isaac, so much has been said on that already, and, in fact, it is so trifling, that nothing farther is necessary to be said in answer to that part of your letter; but I must acknowledge that I am a little hurt at the other queries you put to him, as they are the offspring of an ungenerous suspicion, and ill-founded doubts of the conduct and sincerity of your best and only friends. Rest assured that we know nothing of the intentions of government to relinquish or give up the posts; so far from any appearance of it, I am well informed that the post of Niagara is put, or putting, into the best state of defence the nature of the works will admit of, as I believe all the others are likewise; and I am confident no such step will ever be taken without some previous notice given to all interested. As to the department I have the honor to superintend, I have no reason to think any change or alteration will take place in it, that can in any manner affect the interests of the Indians.

"You wish to know our news. All we have that can be interesting to you is, that one of the most wonderful revolutions has happened in France that ever was known in so short a time. The people have been made, by the more enlightened part of the nation, to view their situation in its proper light, and to throw off the yoke of bondage, slavery, and oppression, under which they have for ages groaned, and have compelled their grand monarch to yield to a Constitution similar, in most respects, to the happy one under which we live. They have abolished all their monks and nunneries, and have made such changes as are wonderful to relate. With my best regards to Mrs. Brant, &c. and to all at the village, I remain, as ever,

"Your friend and faithful servant,

"JOHN JOHNSON."*

* Respecting the rumor which elicited this letter, there is no farther information. Indeed, the letter of Sir John itself has been inserted in the text, more for the pur-

Relieved, temporarily at least, from the cares and labors of diplomacy among the nations of the more distant lakes, Brant was enabled, early in the year 1789, to direct his attention more closely to other matters of business; not forgetting the pursuits of literature, so far as under the disadvantages of his situation he was enabled to attend to its cultivation. He was ever anxious for the moral and intellectual improvement of his people; and as a primary means of such improvement, he now earnestly sought for the settlement of a resident clergyman among them. Visiting Montreal for that purpose, he wrote to Sir John Johnson, who was absent (probably at Quebec) at the time, and through him appealed to Lord Dorchester to procure the removal of the Rev. Mr. Stuart from Kingston to the neighborhood of Grand River. Many of the Indians, he said, wished to be near a church where there should be a proper minister; and nowhere, as he thought, could one be found who would suit their dispositions so well, and exert such a desirable influence over the morals of the young people, as Mr. Stuart, who had been a missionary among them in the Valley of the Mohawk. " This " good thing," he said in his letter to Sir John, " I know must " be done by his Lordship, and through your kind interposition : " which, be assured, I would not mention, if I was not very well " convinced of the good that would arise from it."† He wrote other pressing letters to the same purport; but the transfer of Mr. Stuart was not effected.

He is believed at about the same time to have resumed the labor of translating devotional books into the Mohawk language. In addition to the work published in England in 1786, as already mentioned, he translated the entire liturgy, and also a primer; a copy of each of which works was presented to Harvard University. The donation was acknowledged by a vote of thanks, which was enclosed in the following letter from the President of that institution :—

PRESIDENT WILLARD TO CAPTAIN BRANT.

" *Cambridge, July* 20th, 1789.

SIR,

" I have the pleasure of enclosing you a vote of thanks of the

pose of disclosing the liberal spirit in which the Baronet hailed the beginning of the French Revolution, (as all the civilized world did at first,) as the dawn of liberty in France, than for any other purpose.   † MS. letters among the Brant papers.

Corporation of the University in this place, for your present of books to the library, which were received but a little while before the date of the vote.* To the vote of thanks from the whole corporate body for this acceptable present, give me leave, Sir, as head of the University, to add my thanks in particular.

"I am pleased to hear, from the Rev. Mr. Kirkland, that you are writing a history of the natives of this country. I hope, when you have finished it in your own language, you will give us a translation in English, as I doubt not we shall have many curious and important things contained in it, respecting the various Indian nations, that we are now unacquainted with.

"Mr. Kirkland is so obliging as to take charge of this letter, and I doubt not will convey it to you as soon as possible.

"I am, Sir,

"With sentiments of great esteem,

"Your very humble servant,

"JOSEPH WILLARD.

"*Colonel Joseph Brant.*"

The historical work mentioned in the preceding letter, it is believed, was never commenced, although it had been projected, or rather, Captain Brant had designed writing a history of the Six Nations. But he had, probably, too many demands upon his time, and cares upon his mind, to allow of the execution of his plan. The work of translating the New Testament was continued by Captain Brant's friend and fellow-chief, John Norton, alias Teyoninhokaraven, which was his Indian name. This chief translated the Gospel of John, which was printed by the British and Foreign Bible Society; and he intended to proceed with the Gospels of Matthew and Luke, but probably the work was not completed.†

But, aside from the cultivation of letters, Captain Brant had

---

* See Appendix, No. VI.

† Norton's name will appear frequently hereafter. He was a half-breed, his father being an Indian, and his mother a Scotch woman. He received a classical education at an English school. Next to Thayendanegea, Teyoninhokaraven was the most distinguished of the modern Mohawks. His observations were said to be acute, and his language in conversation strong and elegant. He was well versed in ancient and modern history, and particularly well informed in geography. On every subject connected with his own country and people his knowledge was minute. In his person he was tall and muscular, with a large and expressive eye.

ample employment, for both mind and body, in regulating his domestic Indian relations.   The planting of his own nation upon their new territory at Grand River, and the exertions necessary to bring them into order, and persuade them to substitute the pursuits of husbandry for the chase, were labors of no small moment. The grant of land on the Grand River was doubtless intended solely for the Mohawks, who had been dispossessed of their own native valley ; but other Indians of the Six Nations intruded upon them, even some of those who had borne arms against the crown and the Mohawks. Jealousies and heart-burnings were the consequence, which occasionally called for the interposition of the chief, sometimes to the injury of his popularity, as has already appeared.

Nor was his attention alone required to regulate the affairs of the Indians on the British side of the line.   Difficulties sprang up as early as 1789 among the Oneidas, Onondagas, Cayugas, and Senecas, in consequence of the intrusion of the whites upon their lands, and the unlawful purchases effected by some of them, from Indians not authorized to sell. All the weight of these troubles seemed to fall upon the shoulders of Captain Brant, between whom and Governor George Clinton an active correspondence took place upon the subject, in 1789 and the following year. The Governor made every possible effort to cause justice to be done to the Indians ; for which purpose, several councils were held at Fort Stanwix, and at least one special interview was held between the Governor and the chief in relation to it. The result was an amicable arrangement. In his letters, Governor Clinton treated the Indian chieftain not only with marked respect, but with evident personal kindness and regard. The following letter will serve as a specimen of this correspondence on the part of that distinguished man :—

GOVERNOR CLINTON TO CAPTAIN BRANT.

" *New-York*, 1st *September*, 1790.

" SIR,

" I was favored with your letter of the 21st of July yesterday, and am happy to hear of your health and safe arrival at your place of residence.

" A rumor of a Spanish war also prevails among us. It is

certain, that both that and the British nation are equipping powerful naval armaments ; the ostensible object of which is the settlement of a dispute which has taken place between them, with respect to their possessions on the north-west part of this Continent, and the right of fishery in that quarter. It is, however, probable that all this political bustle may terminate in negotiation, by one conceding and the other accepting of what neither have any well-founded pretensions to, farther than mere discovery and the displaying of a national flag by the permission of the hospitable and unsuspecting natives.

" The gentlemen who are appointed commissioners of Indian affairs, and whom you saw with me at Fort Stanwix, chiefly reside in the country, and are now so dispersed that it is not practicable to confer with them. I perfectly recollect the conversation which passed between you and me relative to the land you was to have had from Doctor Benton, and I communicated the import of it at the time, to the commissioners ; and you will remember I afterward informed you that, however strong their dispositions were to serve you, yet they could not consent to any thing that would give the least sanction or countenance to any part of Benton's transactions, as they considered them not only contrary to law, but committed by him in open defiance of the authority of the State. They expressed, at the same time, sentiments of the warmest friendship for you ; and I considered the present which they directed me to make you, as the only way they had in their power to evince the sincerity of their professions.

" I shall be happy to see you here next Summer, and will endeavor to make your visit agreeable to you. Colonel Varick and your brother, the sachem, are the only two of the gentlemen who were at Fort Stanwix, now in town. They request you to accept of their best respects. I will not fail to communicate your expectations to Mr. L'Hommedieu, that he may stand prepared to discharge the tribute.

" I am

" Your most obed't servant,

" GEO. CLINTON.

" *Captain Joseph Brant.*"

CHAPTER X.

Continued troubles with the Indians—English emissaries in Kentucky—Mission of Antoine Gamelin—Preparations for war—Campaign of General Harmar—Successive defeats of Colonel Hardin—Conduct of the militia—Retreat of Harmar—Indian deputation to Lord Dorchester—Letter of Sir John Johnson—Colonel Gordon—Letter of Brant to Colonel M'Kee—Pacific views of Lord Dorchester—Renewed efforts of the United States to bring the Indians to peace—Interposition of Corn-planter—Mission of Corn-planter and Colonel Proctor—British officers wish a mediation—Letter of Colonel Gordon—Colonel Pickering holds an Indian Council at the Chemung—Red Jacket's course—Brant interferes—Indian Councils at Buffalo—Influence of Colonel John Butler and Brant—Mission of Colonel Proctor and Corn-planter frustrated—Important position of Brant—Correspondence between the Secretary of War and Governor Clinton—Colonel Pickering's Council with the Indians at Painted Post—Mission of Hendrick, the Stockbridge chief—Renewal of hostilities—Campaign of General St. Clair—His defeat—Thayendanegea among the Indian captains—The panic that followed—Clamor against St. Clair—His resignation—Wayne appointed his successor—Refusal of Colonel Willett to embark in an Indian war.

NOTWITHSTANDING the treaties of peace concluded by General St. Clair with all the Six Nations, the Mohawks excepted, and with several of the great north-western tribes, the tranquility of the frontier settlements, now extending four hundred miles along the Ohio, had not been secured. The Shawanese, Miamis, and Wabash Indians* still kept up a bloody war, ravaging the settlements of Kentucky, and the territory now known as Ohio, and causing serious apprehensions in the frontier settlements of Virginia. The President had made every possible effort to conciliate the Indians by just and pacific overtures, but in vain.† Even the Indians with whom one of the treaties had

---

* Such were the statements of the accounts of that day. In the early part of the present year, however, Captain M'Kee, the active (British) Indian Agent at Detroit, wrote to Captain Brant—"The Indians of the Miamis, I understand, have been "more quiet than usual this year, few hostilities having been committed, and those "by that nation alone." In the same letter Captain M'Kee stated that a quarrel had arisen between the Miamis and Delawares respecting the lands occupied by the latter, who were so much offended as to be preparing to retire across to the Spanish side of the Mississippi. The Captain added:—"Their withdrawing themselves at "this time will be extremely detrimental, not only to the Indian confederacy, but to "the country in general, as it will draw a number of others after them who do not "consider the consequences." M'Kee invoked Captain Brant to send the disaffected Delawares a speech, to prevent their separation. But if this request was complied with, it failed of the desired effect. The Indians in question carried their design of a removal into execution.

† "The basis of our proceedings with the Indian nations has been, and shall be, justice, during the period in which I have any thing to do with the administration of

been formed, could not all of them be restrained from the war-path. There was, moreover, another angry cloud lowering in the western sky. The governments of the United States and Spain were at issue on the question of the navigation of the Mississippi, respecting which strong solicitude was felt by the people of the west—especially of Kentucky. Not satisfied with fomenting discontents among the Indians at the north, the English government, availing itself of the Spanish question, and hoping, should the mouth of the Mississippi be ultimately closed against the commerce of the United States, that disaffection might ensue in the west, was believed to have despatched secret agents into Kentucky, with propositions to test the fidelity of the people to the Union. Among these emissaries was Lieutenant Colonel Connolly, of Detroit, a loyalist formerly of Fort Pitt, who had espoused the cause of the crown in the Revolution. He held several confidential conferences with some of the most influential citizens of Kentucky, and attempted to seduce them into a project for making a descent upon New Orleans, seizing the city, and securing the navigation of the Mississippi by force, as a necessary consequence. Information of these secret proceedings was transmitted to the President, who, looking upon the intrigue as an attempt to divide the Union, was prompt in concerting measures to detect any farther machinations of the kind.* What progress was made in sowing the seeds of disaffection, or whether any, does not appear.

In the Spring of 1790, Antoine Gamelin, an experienced Indian merchant, was despatched to visit all the principal tribes of

this government."—*Letter of President Washington to the Marquis de Lafayette,* *Aug.* 1790.

* Sparks's Life and Correspondence of Washington, vol. ix. pages 473, '76. Letter of President Washington to Mr. Innes, and Notes. These attempts upon the fidelity of Kentucky were made in 1788 and 1789. In the following year, in the prospect of a war between Great Britain and Spain, apprehensions of trouble between the United States and the former arose from the same quarters, but upon a very different question. From certain circumstances which came to the knowledge of the President, it was believed that Lord Dorchester, in the event of a war with Spain, had it in contemplation to send an expedition from Detroit for the invasion of Louisiana. This could not be done without marching an army across the whole breadth of the territory of the United States. On the 25th of August, President Washington communicated his apprehensions to the members of his cabinet, the Vice-President, and the Chief Justice, (Jay,) requiring their opinions in writing upon the course proper to be pursued by the Government of the United States in such an emergency.

the west, as a messenger of peace, with a view of ascertaining
the general temper of the Indians.   Among the tribes who had
entered into the treaty, he found the old chiefs and warriors generally well disposed, and by no means hostile.   But with these
exceptions, the war feeling was almost universal.   Of the spirit
that prevailed, an idea may be formed from the following notes
of Gamelin, of his interview with the Ouiatanons and Kickapoos :—" After my speech, one of the head chiefs got up and
" told me : ' You, Gamelin, my friend and son-in-law, we are
" pleased to see in our village, and to hear by your mouth the
" good words of the Great Chief.   We thought to receive a few
" words from the French people, [traders,] but I see the contrary :
" None but the Big Knife is sending speeches to us.   You know
" that we can terminate nothing without the consent of our elder
" brethren, the Miamis.   I invite you to proceed to their village,
" and to speak to them.   There is one thing in your speech I
" do not like.   I will not tell of it.   Even was I drunk, I would
" not perceive it ; but our elder brethren will certainly take no-
" tice of it in your speech.   You invite us to stop our young
" men.   It is impossible to do it, being constantly encouraged
" by the British.' "   Another chief said : " The Americans are
" very flattering in their speeches : many times our nation went
" to their rendezvous.   I was once there myself.   Some of our
" chiefs died on the route, and we always came back all naked ;
" and you, Gamelin, you came with a speech, but with empty
" hands."   Another chief said : " Know ye that the village of
" Ouiatanon is the sepulchre of our ancestors.   The chief of
" America invites us to go to him, if we are for peace ; he has
" not his leg broke, being able to go as far as the Illinois.   He
" might come here himself, and we should be glad to see him
" in our village.   We confess that we accepted the axe, but it
" was by the reproach that we continually receive from the En-
" glish and other nations, which received the axe first, calling
" us women : at the same time they invite our young men to
" war.   As to the old people, they are wishing for peace."[*]

All the endeavors of the President to give security to the parties by peaceful arrangements having proved unavailing, vigorous offensive measures were determined upon, and an expedi

* Gamelin's Journal, Am. State Papers, Vol. IV. p. 93.

tion against the hostile tribes was entrusted to General Harmar,
a veteran of the revolution. His force consisted of fourteen
hundred and fifty men, three hundred and twenty of whom
were regular troops, and the residue levies of the Pennsylvania
and Kentucky militia. The object was to bring the Indians to
an engagement, if possible ; if not, in any event to destroy their
settlements on the waters of the Scioto and Wabash.* The expedition left Fort Washington on the 30th of September, 1790,
The Indians at first abandoned their principal town, after applying the torch to it, but rallied subsequently upon a detachment of two hundred and ten men, commanded by Colonel Harden, thirty of whom were regulars, and gave battle. At the first
fire Harden's militia all ran away. The regulars maintained their
ground for a time, and fought bravely until but seven of their
number were able to escape. On the next day Col. Harden, at
the head of three hundred and sixty men, sixty of whom were
regulars, undertook to retrieve their disgrace. They were met
by the Indians, and a bloody conflict ensued near the junction of
the St. Joseph and St. Mary rivers. The militia, for a miracle,
fought bravely on this occasion. Overpowered by numbers, however, they were defeated, with the loss of several gallant officers,
and one hundred and eighty-three men—seventy-five of whom
were regulars. Among the former were Majors Fontaine and
Wyllys, and Lieutenant Frothingham. Ten militia officers were
also among the slain. The Indians lost about one hundred
and twenty warriors. The battle was severely fought, and ended in the flight of the Americans. General Harmar thereupon returned to Fort Washington and claimed the victory—
with what propriety has never been ascertained.†

* Holmes—Marshall.

† A letter to Captain Brant, written from Detroit, gave a still more disastrous account of this affair than was admitted by the American authorities. The following
is an extract :—" I have to inform you that there have been two engagements about
" the Miami towns, between the Americans and the Indians, in which, it is said, the
" former had about five hundred men killed, and that the rest have retreated. The
" loss was only fifteen or twenty on the side of the Indians. The Shawanese, Mia-
" mis, and Pottawattamies were, I understand, the principal tribes who were engag-
" ed ; but I do not learn that any of the nations have refused their alliance or as-
" sistance, and it is confidently reported that they are now marching against the
" frontiers on the Ohio. As Mr. McKee writes to the chiefs at the Grand River, he
" will be able to state circumstances more particularly than I can. The gentlemen of
" the garrison beg their compliments."—MS. Letter of John Smith to Captain Brant.

Flushed and emboldened by their success, the depredations of the Indians became more frequent, and the condition of the frontier was more deplorable than it had been previous to this ill-fated expedition.* Nor were their aggressions confined to the settlements along the Ohio and the Kentucky border. Two of the Seneca Indians having been murdered by the whites, that nation, with others among the warriors of the Six Nations, were becoming more hostile ; and the consequence was, that early in the Spring of 1791, the Pennsylvania settlements along the Alleghany river, above Pittsburgh, experienced repeated and fearful visitations of Indian retribution. Several stations of the settlers were entirely broken up. The murders of women and children were frequent, and were often attended with circumstances of undiminished inhumanity, while many people were carried into captivity.†

News of the disastrous victory of General Harmar having reached the seat of government, a regiment was added to the permanent military establishment, and the President was authorised to raise a body of two thousand men for six months, to appoint a major and a brigadier general to continue in command so long as he should think their services necessary.‡ No time was lost in calling this augmented force into the field, and Major General Arthur St. Clair, Governor of the territory north west of the Ohio, was appointed Commander-in-chief, and charged with the conduct of the meditated expedition ; the immediate objects of which were to destroy the Indian villages on the Miamis, to expel the Indians from that country, and to connect it with the Ohio by a chain of posts which would prevent their return during the war. §

It appears that on the repulse of Harmar, the confederated nations of the Chippewas, Pottawattamies, Hurons, Shawanese, Delawares, Ottawas, Tustans, and Six Nations—after a consultation at the foot of the Miami Rapids with Capt. McKee,—deputed a representation of chiefs and warriors to visit Lord Dorchester

---

* "It appears, from the most indubitable testimony, that from 1783, when peace was made, to October, 1790, when the United States commenced offensive operations against them, on the Ohio and the frontiers, the Indians killed and wounded, and took prisoners, about fifteen hundred men, women, and children; besides taking away two thousand horses and a large quantity of other property."—*Narrative and Sufferings of Massy Harbison.*   † Idem.
‡ Marshall's life of Washington.   § Holmes's Annals.

at Quebec, for the purpose of consultation, and also to ascertain whether any, and if any, what, assistance might be expected from the British or provincial government. Lord Dorchester's views were doubtless at that time pacific, as also were those of Captain Brant—provided always that the United States would establish the Ohio as the boundary, and relinquish all claims of jurisdiction beyond that river. On the 22d of February, 1791, Sir John Johnson addressed a letter to Captain Brant, from Montreal, enclosing a copy of a letter from Lord Dorchester to himself, and another copy of the same to Captain McKee, the purport of which can only be inferred from the letter of the Baronet. It is accordingly inserted :—

SIR JOHN JOHNSON TO CAPTAIN BRANT. (Private.)

" Montreal, 22d Feb'y, 1791.

"DEAR JOSEPH,

" As I think the Six Nations much interested in the business proposed by the inclosed copy of a letter from Lord Dorchester, (another copy of which I transmit to Mr. McKee,) I could not think of withholding it from you, that you may take such steps, in concert with Mr. McKee and the western nations, as you may judge most conducive to their interest and honor. As you certainly are all free and independent, I think you will have a right to insist upon disposing of whatever lands you judge fit to reserve for the General Confederacy, in whatever manner, and to whomsoever you please. The idea of the States claiming a jurisdiction up to the line of separation settled between Great Britain and them, must arise from a supposition that the Indians, at some time or other, allowed that power to our Provinces for the better government of their subjects. Whether or not that is the case, I know not, nor can I at present find out ; but certain I am that without such a cession of power on the part of the Indians, no just right or claim to such a power can be supported beyond the line of 1768, and to the western line of the land ceded or sold by the Indians to the States since the war. This is certainly a nice point, and may not be proper to insist upon too positively ; but in justice I believe it is as I have stated. When the Indians allowed the English and French to build forts for the protection and support of their subjects and trade, they no doubt had a right to a certain jurisdiction or com-

mand round those places, but I never believe it extended farther, or that the Indians meant it should. Upon the whole,
you understand your own rights better than I do. I shall therefore say no more than to recommend coolness and a manly firmness in whatever you may determine on. As I mean this letter
as entirely private, I shall acquaint you that I believe this measure has been thought of by Lord Dorchester, in consequence of
my writing to him on receiving the account of the expedition
carried on last Fall by the Americans against the Miamis, at
which time I took the liberty of saying that the Americans had
no claim to any part of the country beyond the line established
in 1768, at Fort Stanwix, between the Indians and the Governors and agents of all the Provinces interested, and including the
sales made since the war; and that I therefore thought, as we
could not afford them assistance in arms, we should at least afford them our mediation to bring about a peace between them
and the States, on terms just and honorable, or something to
that purpose. You may converse with, or write freely to Mr.
McKee upon the subjects of this letter, but let it be as from
yourself—perhaps I may say something similar to him if time
will permit. I have wrote Lord Dorchester that an answer
might be had to his inquiries by some time the beginning of
May, but I fear not; a great deal will depend on you, however,
in forwarding the packet to Mr. McKee, which let me intreat
you to lose no time in doing. My best wishes attend you all,
and believe me as ever sincerely yours,

" JOHN JOHNSON.

   " *Captain Brant.*"

Colonel Gordon, commanding the British post at Niagara, was
also at that time and afterward, a friend of peace. On the 4th
of March he addressed a letter to Captain Brant, from which
the following is an extract:—" I hope you will embrace the pre-
" sent opportunity of the meeting of the chiefs of the Five Na-
" tions in your neighborhood, to use your endeavors to heal the
" wounds between the Indians and Americans. I dare say the
" States wish to make peace on terms which will secure to the
" Indians their present possessions in the Miami country, pro-
" vided the young men are restrained from committing depre-
" dations in future." The temper of the chief himself, at this

period, can best be determined by the following extracts from a letter addressed by himself to Captain M'Kee, three days after the letter from Colonel Gordon was written, and probably immediately on its receipt :—

CAPTAIN BRANT TO CAPTAIN M'KEE. (EXTRACTS.)

" *Grand River, March* 7, 1791.

*   *   *   *   *   *

" I have received two letters from the States, from gentlemen who have been lately in Philadelphia ; by which it appears the Americans secretly wish to accommodate the matter—which I should by all means advise, if it could be effected upon honorable and liberal terms, and a peace become general."

*   *   *   *   *   *   *

" I am happy to see in Sir John's last letter to me, that he has suggested to his Lordship the necessity of their interference in bringing about a peace between the Indians and the United States ; by which it appears he has an idea of recommending the line settled in 1768 [qu ? 1765] between the Indians and government, as the northern and western boundary of the States in that quarter. I expect to hear more from him in the Spring on that subject, as I have pressed him hard to give me his sentiments on the utility of my interference in the present dispute."

Lord Dorchester's speech in reply to the deputation already mentioned, was of a similar tenor to the preceding letter of Sir John Johnson. His Lordship informed them that he should be glad to be instrumental in restoring peace. He informed them that the line marked out in the treaty of peace with the United States, implied no more than that beyond that line the King their father would not extend his interference ; and that the King had only retained possession of the posts until such time as all the differences between him and the United States should be settled. In regard to the questions of the deputation, whether it was true that, in making peace with the States, the King had given away their lands, his Lordship assured them that such was not the fact, inasmuch as the King never had any right to their lands, other than to such as had been fairly ceded by themselves, with their own free consent, by public convention and sale. On this point, his Lordship likewise referred to the treaty with Sir William Johnson, at Fort Stanwix, in 1765. In conclusion, he assured the deputation, that although the Indians had their friendship and good-will, the Provincial Government had no power to embark in a war with the United States, and could only defend themselves if attacked. He also informed them that the command of the province was about to devolve upon General Clarke; and that Prince Edward,* who had just arrived with a chosen band of warriors, would be the second in command. His Lordship himself was on the eve of embarking for England, where it would afford him great pleasure to hear that peace had been established between the Indians and United States upon a just and solid foundation.†

This speech afforded but small encouragement to the Indians, and most likely but ill corresponded with the expectations that had been raised by M'Kee, and other subordinate officers in the British Indian Department at the remote posts—of whom several, like M'Kee, were refugee Americans, indulging bitter hatred toward the country which they had deserted in the hour of its peril. Indeed, there is no reason to distrust the manly and honorable conduct of Lord Dorchester during the greater part of this singular border contest, the progress of which was marked by so many vicissitudes of feeling and action on the part of many of the Provincial authorities. And besides, the attitude of the two nations was at that moment less seemingly belligerent than it shortly afterward became.

During these side negotiations in Canada, and while the preparations for another campaign by the American government, as already mentioned, were in progress, no relaxations of efforts to prevent the farther effusion of blood were allowed to take place. Captain O'Bail, or the Corn-planter as he was usually called, the principal chief of the Senecas, being in Philadelphia in the month of December, after the defeat of General Harmar, was induced not only to use his influence to prevent the warriors of the Six Nations from taking a part in the contest, but also to undertake a mission with other friendly Indians to the country of the Miamis, to persuade them to peace, also, if possible. In March following, the Corn-planter, with whom Colonel Proctor, an active officer in the (American) Indian Department had been

* The late Duke of Kent, father of the present young Queen of England.

† Journal of Major General Lincoln, which will be more particularly referred to hereafter.

associated, set out upon the mission. Meantime, measures were adopted to draw the Indians of the Six Nations to a general conference at a distance from the theatre of war, in order, not only to prevent their joining the war, but, if necessary, to obtain some of their young warriors for the service against the Miamis and the other hostile tribes. This attempt to create a diversion of the Six Nations, however, was looked upon with displeasure by the Provincial authorities in Canada, as will be seen by the annexed letter from Colonel Gordon to Captain Brant. It also appears from this letter, that these Provincials were ambitious of being appealed to by the government of the United States as mediators in the controversy. Nor was this an individual conceit of Colonel Gordon, inasmuch as Sir John Johnson had hinted the same thing, as was evident from his letter, after consultation with Lord Dorchester. It will farther appear by the address of the letter, that the ever-vigilant Brant was already once more in the country of the Miamis, although but a very few days previous he had been assisting at a private council at Buffalo. His movements in all these matters, as in the war of the Revolution, seem to have been as rapid as the light.

COLONEL GORDON TO CAPTAIN BRANT.

" Niagara, June 11th, 1791.

" DEAR SIR,

" I was glad to find by your letter, from the foot of the Rapids, to Colonel Butler, that you was in good health ; and I very sincerely hope the business you are engaged in, will be attended with success.

" From the inconsistent proceedings of the Americans, I am perfectly at a loss to understand their full intentions. Whilst they are assembling councils at different quarters with the avowed purpose of bringing about a peace, the Six Nations have received a speech from General St. Clair, dated at Pittsburgh, 23d April, inviting them to take up the hatchet against their brothers the western nations.

" Can any thing be more inconsistent ? or can they possibly believe the Indians are to be duped by such shallow artifices ? This is far from being the case; the Indians at Buffalo Creek saw the business in its proper light, and treated the invitation

with the contempt it deserved. It must strike you very forcibly, that in all the proceedings of the different Commissioners
from the American States, they have cautiously avoided applying for our interference, as a measure they affect to think perfectly unnecessary ; wishing to impress the Indians with ideas
of their own consequence, and of the little influence, they would
willingly believe, we are possessed of. This, my good friend,
is not the way to proceed. Had they, before matters were
pushed to extremity, requested the assistance of the British Government to bring about a peace on equitable terms, I am convinced the measure would have been fully accomplished long
before this time.

" I would, however, willingly hope they will yet see the propriety of adopting this mode of proceeding ; and that peace, an
object so much to be desired, will at length be permanently settled.

" I am the more sanguine in the attainment of my wishes, by
your being on the spot, and that you will call forth the exertion
of your influence and abilities on the occasion. Let me hear
from time to time how matters are going forward, and with my
wishes for your health, believe me

" Your friend,

" A. Gordon.

" *Captain Brant.*"

The Council of the Six Nations, always excepting the Mo
hawks, was successfully held by Colonel Timothy Pickering,
in the Chemung country, in the month of June. But the Corn-
planter and Colonel Proctor met with insurmountable difficulties in the prosecution of their mission. The special object of that
mission, after traversing the country of the Six Nations, and
exerting such wholesome influence upon them as might be in
their power, was to charter a vessel at Buffalo Creek, and proceed to Sandusky, and if possible induce the Miamis to meet
General St. Clair in council on the Ohio. They were every
where well received on the route from Alleghany to Buffalo
Creek, at which place a grand Council was called in honor of
their arrival, and attended by Red Jacket and other chiefs. After
having been welcomed by a speech from Red Jacket, Colonel
Proctor opened to them the message from General Washington,

the great chief of the Thirteen Fires. Red Jacket replied, that many persons had previously at different times been among them, professing to come by the authority of the Thirteen Fires, but of the truth of which declarations they were not always convinced. In the course of the conversation, it was ascertained that at a private council held at that place one week before, at which Captain Brant and Colonel Butler, of the British Indian department, were present, these officers had uttered the same doubts now started by Red Jacket. Brant had advised the Indians to pay no attention to Proctor and O'Bail, of whose approach and purpose he was aware, and to render them no assistance in their projected visit to Sandusky, assuring them it should do no good; but that Colonel Proctor, and all who would accompany him to the country of the Miamis, would be put to death. They also ascertained, that while holding the said private council, in anticipation of their visit, Captain Brant had received secret instructions from "head-quarters,"* to repair to Grand River, and from thence to Detroit. It was believed by a French trader who gave the information, and also by Captain Powell of the British service, who confirmed it, that the Mohawk chief had been sent to the Indians hostile to the United States with instructions of *some* kind; and the Indians at Buffalo Creek had been charged by Brant to conclude upon nothing with Proctor and O'Bail before his return.

Colonel Proctor and O'Bail continued at Buffalo from the 27th of April to the 22d or 23d of May. The Indians collected in large numbers, and many councils were held. On the 8th of May, the Fish-carrier, one of the principal Cayuga chiefs, and the right hand man of Captain Brant, declared in a speech that O'Bail had taken a course that was not approved by them—that more than one half of the Indians there, *were not for peace*,† and that Captain Brant had been sent to the council-fire of the Miamis. "We must, therefore," he added, "see his face, for "we can't determine until we know what they are about. So "we beg you to grant our request, to keep your mind easy; for "we, who do this business, look on you, and hold ourselves to

---

* The words used in Col. Proctor's narrative; but whether he meant the British or Indian head-quarters, the author cannot say. Probably the former.

† Proctor's Journal.

" be slaves in making of peace.   Now, we all say you must look
" for Captain Brant's coming, to hear the words that come from
" his mouth, for then we can say to you, what towns will be
" for peace : and this is all that we have to say to you for this
" time." *

An effort was made by Red Jacket to induce Proctor and
O'Bail to go down to the British fortress at Niagara to hold a
consultation with Colonel Butler ; but Colonel Proctor declined
the adoption of any such course.   The Indians thereupon despatched a messenger for Colonel Butler to meet them at Buffalo Creek, which he accordingly did—but previously called a
separate council at Fort Erie.   He afterward h. d an interview
with Proctor, and endeavored to dissuade him from visiting the
country of the hostile Indians,—proposing that the negotiations
for a peace should be left to Captain Brant and McKee, who, Colonel Butler thought, could best manage the business.   Of course
a proposition going to clothe British subjects with power to negotiate for the government of the United States, was promptly
rejected.

One of the leading objects of Colonel Proctor in meeting the
Six Nations at Buffalo, was to induce as many of their sachems
and warriors as he could, to accompany the Corn-planter and
himself to the Miamis country, to aid, by their influence, in
bringing the hostile Indians into a more pacific temper ; but
from the whole cast of the deliberations, it was perfectly evident
that the majority of the leading chiefs were under the direct influence of the British officers, who, it was obvious, had now
suddenly become less pacific than they had very recently been.
Colonel Proctor met with but little success in persuading a portion of the warriors to accompany him to the Miamis ; and on
applying to Colonel Gordon, commanding at Niagara, for permission to charter a British schooner on Lake Erie, to transport
himself and such Indians as might feel disposed to accompany
himself and Corn-planter to Sandusky, the request was peremptorily refused.   The expedition was thus abruptly terminated,
and Colonel Proctor returned to Fort Washington.

Before leaving Buffalo, however, according to an entry in his
journal, Colonel Proctor seems to have been apprised of the fact,

---

* **American State papers—Indian Department.**

which will subsequently appear, that Captain Brant had not gone to the Miamis as a messenger, or an observer merely, but that he had actually gone to join them with his warriors :—

"*May* 21st. Being in private conversation this evening "with Captain O'Bail, and sitting between him and the New-"Arrow sachem, I hinted to Captain O'Bail that if he would go "and join General St. Clair with thirty-five or forty of his war-"riors, as well equipped as he could make them, purely to coun-"terbalance the force that Brant had taken with him to the un-"friendly Indians, I would use endeavors with the Secretary of "War to procure him a commission that should yield to him "and his people a handsome stipend. He replied, that the Sene-"cas had received a stroke from the bad Indians, by taking two "prisoners, a woman and a boy, from Conyatt ; and that, should "the hatchet be struck into the head of any of his people hereaf-"ter, he would then inform me what he would undertake to do."

The natural import of this entry in Proctor's journal is, that Captain Brant had at that time actually joined the Miamis in hostile array against the United States. It is possible, however, that such was not *at that time* the fact ; and it is certain that General Knox, the Secretary of War, after the return of Colonel Proctor to Philadelphia, did not so construe it. In writing to Colonel Pickering respecting the council which he was then preparing to hold at the Painted Post on the 13th of June, the Secretary speaks of Brant's journey to the western Indians as having probably been undertaken for pacific purposes, under the direction of the British officers, who were using him with a view to a peace, of which they intended to claim the merit at some future time. And this construction would comport with the idea of a British intervention, as heretofore suggested by Colonel Gordon and Sir John Johnson.

But it is, nevertheless, a curious fact, which speaks largely of the talents and address of Brant, and the high importance which was attached to his influence, that if the British authorities were then thus using his services, the American government was at the same time seeking his assistance for the same object. Colonel Pickering was instructed to treat him with "great kindness" if he could be persuaded to attend the council at the Painted Post ; and on the 12th of April, the Secretary of War addressed a letter to Governor Clinton, from which the following is an extract:

"Aware of your Excellency's influence over Captain Joseph
"Brant, I have conceived the idea that you might induce him,
"by proper arrangements, to undertake to conciliate the western
"Indians to pacific measures, and bring them to hold a general
"treaty.   This measure would be abundantly more compatible
"with the feelings and interest of the United States than to ex-
"tirpate the Indians, which seems to be the inevitable consequence
"of a war of long continuance with them.   You are entirely
"able to estimate Brant's talents, and the degree of confidence
"that might be placed in him on such an occasion.   Perhaps
"Colonel Willett, of whose talents in managing the minds of
"men I have a high opinion, might accept of an agency on this
"occasion, as it might respect Brant.   If your Excellency should
"entertain the opinion strongly that Brant might be employed
"with good effect, I earnestly request that you would take the
"necessary measures for the purpose, according to your own
"judgment."

Other topics were embraced in the Secretary's letter, to all of
which Governor Clinton replied on the 27th of April.   The
following extract relates to the subject of this biography :—

"I have communicated to Colonel Willett your confidence in
"his talents and desire for the interposition of his influence
"with Brant, but have it not in my power to inform you of his
"explicit answer."   *   *   *   "I had, in June last, appointed an
"interview with Brant, contemplating the danger you appear to
"apprehend from his address and his influence with several of
"the Indian nations, (which, I am persuaded, is very considera
"ble,) and from different letters I have since received from him,
"I have reason to hope he will give me the opportunity of a
"personal conference with him at this place, (New York,) the
"beginning of the ensuing summer, if the proposed convention,
"to which I will not venture to say he may not be opposed,
"should not prevent it.   But the good understanding between
"us, and the friendly and familiar intercourse I have successful-
"ly endeavored to preserve, will, I doubt not, predominate over
"any transient disgust that the measures of the Union may have
"heretofore excited in his mind, and enable me to procure an
"interview with him at any time and place not particularly in
"convenient.   To accomplish this, however, with certainty, it

" may require the personal application of some one expressly
" delegated, and in whom he will confide."

Captain Brant has been charged with great vanity, and with at-
taching undue importance to his position and influence. But how
few are the men, Indians or whites, who would not have stood
in danger of being somewhat inflated, on finding two such nations as Great Britain and the United States, apparently outbid-
ding each other for his services and friendship ? Still, he was
looked upon with no inconsiderable distrust by the American
Secretary of War. In his letter of reply to Governor Clinton,
dated May 11th, the Secretary, after speaking of the hostility of
Brant to the Corn-planter, refers to the former design of the Mohawk chief to place himself at the head of the great Indian
confederacy, so often spoken of, north-west of the Ohio, the Six
Nations included ; and cites a letter which he had just received
from the Rev. Mr. Kirkland, the Indian missionary, intimating
that he had not yet abandoned that project. Indeed, Brant himself had then just written to Mr. Kirkland that he should yet
like to compass that measure, should he find it practicable. The
United States could not, of course, be favorable to the formation
of any confederacy, by which the whole of the then vast body
of Indians might be moved by a single impulse ; and with a
view of diverting him from such a purpose, and of securing his
friendship to the United States, Governor Clinton was requested,
if possible, to effect the interview of which he had spoken, with
Captain Brant. Authority was also given the Governor to enter into any pecuniary engagements which he should judge necessary, to make sure of his attachment to the United States.

It has already been observed that the council held with the
Six Nations by Colonel Pickering, at the Painted Post, in June,
had been to a great extent successful. Although the chiefs at
Buffalo were for the most part under the influence of the British
officers in Upper Canada, and of course not very friendly to the
United States at that time, yet the warriors in general were more
amicably disposed. The women, moreover, were anxious for
peace, and addressed Colonel Proctor upon the subject. Before
that officer left Buffalo, the Indians began to draw off to meet
Colonel Pickering, and the council with him was well attended—serving, if no other good purpose, to divert the attention
of the Indians, and by the distribution of presents to keep the

young warriors from indulging their favorite propensity, by stealing away and joining the Miamis. Colonel Pickering had also induced Captain Hendrick Aupamut, the justly celebrated chief of the Muhheconnuck,* to undertake the mission to the Miamis, which Colonel Proctor and Corn-planter had been prevented from performing. Captain Brant, it was also reported to the War Department, about the 1st of August, had returned to Niagara from the Miami town, accompanied by some of the western chiefs. The Indians at Pickering's treaty had asserted that, after all that had transpired, Brant's designs were still pacific; and since Lord Dorchester, as already stated, had expressed himself favorable to a pacification of the Indian tribes, and Sir John Johnson was about to assemble the Six Nations again at Buffalo, strong hopes were entertained by the American government, that the border difficulties would soon be adjusted without the necessity of another appeal to arms.

But, notwithstanding these favorable indications, the preparations for another offensive campaign were not relaxed. And it was well that they were not. The movements of Brant, beyond doubt the most influential warrior of his race, were yet mysterious, and his designs too cautiously veiled to be penetrated. The unlimited power with which the President had been clothed, the preceding year, to call mounted militia into the field, had been exercised by General Washington as far as was deemed necessary, and two expeditions had been conducted against the villages on the Wabash,—the first led by General Scott, in May, and the second by General Wilkinson. These desultory excursions, however, were unattended by any beneficial results. A few warriors had been killed, and a small number of old men, women, and children captured. But such results were not calculated to make any serious impression upon the savages, or to have any particular influence on the war. It was likewise well known that the Indians had received from the British posts large supplies of provisions and ammunition, immediately after the defeat of General Harmar the preceding Autumn. This fact, it is true, was disclaimed by Lord Dorchester, but it was nevertheless certain; and it was also certain that, in addition to the unfriendly influence of the British officers on the frontiers

* The Stockbridge Indians, who had removed from Massachusetts to the Oneida country in 1785.

the English and French traders, scattered among the Indian towns, were constantly inciting them to acts of hostility.

Under these circumstances, all the efforts of the United States to bring the hostile Indians to a friendly council having failed, the conquest of the Miami country and the expulsion of the Indians became necessary. The most vigorous measures within the power of the Executive had failed in raising the troops and bringing them into the field until the month of September. On the 7th of that month General St. Clair moved from Fort Washington, north, toward the Miamis—establishing, on his way, two intermediate posts, at the distance of more than forty miles from each other, as places whence to draw supplies should the army be in need, or upon which to fall back in the event of disaster. At the farthest of these posts, called Fort Jefferson, reinforcements of militia, to the number of three hundred and sixty, were received—augmenting the army to about two thousand men. With this force St. Clair moved forward, but the necessity of opening a road through the forests rendered his progress slow. The Indians hung in small scattered parties upon the flanks, and by the skirmishing that took place, were somewhat annoying. Added to these vexations, the militia began to desert ; and as the army approximated more nearly to the enemy's country, sixty of them went off in a body. It was likewise reported to be the determination of those " brave defenders of their country's soil " to fall upon the supplies in the rear ; to prevent which act of moral treason, it was judged necessary to detach Major Hamtramck in pursuit.

After these reductions, the effective force of St. Clair that remained did not exceed fourteen hundred men—including both regulars and militia. Moving forward with these, the right wing commanded by General Butler and the left by Lieutenant Colonel Darke, both, like the Commander-in-chief, veterans of Revolutionary merit, on the 3d of November they had approached within about fifteen miles of the Miamis villages. The army encamped for the night on the margin of a creek, the militia crossing in advance, to encamp on the other side. Here a few Indians were discovered ; but these fleeing with precipitation, the army bivouacked for the night—the situation, and the dispositions both for defence and to guard against surprise, being of the most judicious character.

This position had been selected with a view of throwing up a slight defence, and awaiting the return of Major Hamtramck with the first regiment. Both designs were anticipated and circumvented by the Indians. About half an hour before sunrise on the morning of the 4th, just after the soldiers were dismissed from parade, the militia, who were about a quarter of a mile in front, were briskly attacked by the Indians. Like most militiamen, their first impulse was to run—and that impulse was obeyed in the greatest terror and wildest confusion. Rushing through the main encampment, with the enemy close upon their heels, no small degree of confusion was created there also. The lines had been formed at the firing of the first gun ; but the panic-stricken militia broke through, and thus opened the way for the enemy—an advantage which was not lost upon him. The officers endeavored to restore order in vain, although, for a time, the divisions of Butler and Darke, which had encamped about seventy yards apart, were kept in position. But the Indians charged upon them with great intrepidity—bearing down upon the centre of both divisions in great numbers. The artillery of the Americans was of little or no service, as the Indians fought in their usual mode, lying upon the ground and firing from behind the trees—springing from tree to tree with incredible swiftness, and rarely presenting an available mark to the eye even of the rifleman. Having, in the impetuosity of their pursuit of the fugitive militia, gained the rear of St. Clair, they poured a destructive fire upon the artillerists from every direction—mowing them down by scores, and with a daring seldom practised by the Indians, leaping forward, and completing the work of death at the very guns. General St. Clair was himself sick, having been severely indisposed for several weeks. He assumed his post, however, and though extremely feeble, delivered his orders in the trying emergency with judgment and self-possession. But he was laboring under the disadvantage of commanding militia upon whom there was no reliance, and having few, if any, but raw recruits among his regulars. These, too, had been hastily enlisted, and but little time for drill or discipline had been allowed. Hence, though brave, and commanded by officers of the highest qualities, they fought at great disadvantage. General Butler fell early in the action, mortally wounded, and was soon afterward killed outright, under circum-

stances of deep atrocity. Among the Indian warriors were considerable numbers of Canadians, refugees from the United States,
and half-breeds—young men born of Indian mothers in the remote Canadian settlements.* These motley allies of the savages
were even more savage than their principals. Among them
was the noted and infamous Simon Girty, whose name has occurred in a former part of the present work. After the action,
Girty, who knew General Butler, found him upon the field,
writhing from the agony of his wounds. Butler spoke to him,
and requested him to end his misery. The traitor refused to do
this, but turning to one of the Indian warriors, told him the
wounded man was a high officer; whereupon the savage planted
his tomahawk in his head, and thus terminated his sufferings.
His scalp was instantly torn from his crown, his heart taken out,
and divided into as many pieces as there were tribes engaged in
the battle.

The Indians had never fought with such fury before. The
forest resounded with their yells, and they rushed upon the
troops, under their favorite shelter of trees, until they had partially gained possession of the camp, artillery and all. Ascertaining that the fire of their troops produced no perceptible effect
upon the Indians, recourse was had to the bayonet. Colonel
Darke made an impetuous charge at the head of the left wing,
and drove the enemy back about four hundred yards, with some
loss. But not having a sufficient number of riflemen to maintain his advantage, he gave over the pursuit—being instantly
pursued in turn under a deadly fire. The same gallant officer
was subsequently ordered to make a second charge, which he
performed with equal bravery—clearing for the moment that
portion of the camp to which his attention was directed. But
the Americans were now completely surrounded; and while
he was driving the Indians in one direction, clouds of them
were seen to fall, " with a courage of men whose trade is

---

* "A great many young Canadians, and, in particular, many that were born of
Indian women, fought on the side of the Indians in this action; a circumstance
which confirmed the people of the States in the opinion they had previously formed,
that the Indians were encouraged and abetted in their attacks upon them by the
British. I can safely affirm, however, from having conversed with many of these
young men who fought against St. Clair, that it was with the utmost secrecy they
left their homes to join the Indians, fearful lest the government should censure their
conduct."—*Weld's Travels in Canada.*

war," upon another point—keeping up a most destructive
fire from every quarter. The use of the bayonet was always
attended with temporary success, but each charge was also
attended by severe loss, especially of officers; nor in a single
instance were the Americans able to retain the advantage
thus severely gained. Finally, a large proportion of the best
and bravest officers having fallen, nearly all that had been preserved of order disappeared. The men huddled together in
groups, and were shot down without resistance. Having done
all, under the circumstances, that a brave man could do, and
finding that the day was lost past recovery, General St. Clair
directed Colonel Darke, with the second regiment, to charge a
body of Indians who had gained the road in the rear, and thus
open a door of retreat. The order was promptly and successfully executed, and a disorderly flight ensued. The victorious
Indians followed up their advantage to the distance of only four
miles, when, leaving the pursuit, they directed their attention to
the plunder, and ceased fighting to revel in "the spoils of the
vanquished." The fugitives continued their flight thirty miles,
to Fort Jefferson. Here they met Major Hamtramck with the
first regiment; but it was not deemed advisable to make a stand,
and the remains of the army fell back to Fort Washington, as
Harmar had done the year before. The retreat was indeed most
disorderly and cowardly. "The camp and the artillery," says
General St. Clair in his narrative of the campaign, "were
"abandoned; but that was unavoidable, for not a horse was
"left to draw it off, had it otherwise been practicable. But the
"most disgraceful part of the business is, that the greatest part
"of the men threw away their arms and accoutrements, even
"after the pursuit had ceased. I found the road strewed with
"them for many miles, but was not able to remedy it; for, hav-
"ing had all my horses killed, and being mounted upon one
"that could not be pricked out of a walk, I could not get for-
"ward myself, and the orders I sent forward, either to halt the
"front, or prevent the men parting with their arms, were unat-
"tended to."

This was one of the severest battles ever fought with the Indians—the latter being unaided by any other description of force,
excepting the wild half-breed Canadians already mentioned.
The loss of the Americans, in proportion to the number engaged,

was very severe. Thirty-eight commissioned officers were killed on the field, and four hundred and ninety-three non-commissioned officers and privates killed and missing. Twenty-one commissioned officers were wounded, several of whom mortally, and two hundred and forty-two non-commissioned officers and privates were also wounded. General Butler, who fell early in the action, was a brave man; and with many other excellent officers who fell, " had participated in all the toils, the dangers, " and the glory, of that long conflict which terminated in the in- " dependence of their country."*

The loss of the Indians was about one hundred and fifty killed and a considerable number wounded. Their immediate booty was all the camp equipage and baggage, six or eight field-pieces, and four hundred horses. As the contest was one for land, the Indians, in their mutilations of the dead, practised a bitter sarcasm upon the rapacity of the white men, by filling their mouths with the soil they had marched forth to conquer. †

General St. Clair imputed no blame to his officers. On the contrary, he awarded them the highest praise for their good conduct; and of those who were slain, he remarked,—" It is a " circumstance that will alleviate the misfortune in some mea- " sure, that all of them fell most gallantly doing their duty." From the fact of his being attacked at all points as it were at the same moment, it was the General's opinion that he had been overwhelmed by numbers. But from subsequent investigation it appeared that the Indian warriors counted only from a thousand to fifteen hundred. But they fought with great desperation. Their leader, according to the received opinion, was *Meshecun-nayua*, or, the *Little Turtle*, a distinguished chief of the Miamis. He was also the leader of the Indians against General Harmar the year before. It is believed, however, that though nominally the commander-in-chief of the Indians on this occasion, he was greatly indebted both to the counsels and the prow-

* Marshall's Life of Washington. For a ballad giving an account of this disastrous battle, see Appendix, No. VII.

† Two years afterward, when the battle-ground was re-occupied by the army of Wayne, its appearance was most melancholy. Within the space of about three hundred and fifty yards square were found five hundred skull bones, the most of which were collected and buried. For about five miles in the direction of the retreat of the army, the woods were strewn with skeletons and muskets. Two brass field-pieces were found in a creek not far distant.—*Drake's Book of the Indians.*

ess of another and an older chief. One hundred and fifty of the Mohawk warriors were engaged in this battle; and General St. Clair probably died in ignorance of the fact, that one of the master-spirits against whom he contended, and by whom he was so signally defeated, was none other than JOSEPH BRANT--THAYENDANEGEA.* How it happened that this distinguished chief, from whom so much had been expected as a peace maker, thus suddenly and efficiently threw himself into a position of active hostility, unless he thought he saw an opening for reviving his project of a great north-western Confederacy, is a mystery which he is believed to have carried in his own bosom to the grave.

The news of the decisive defeat of General St. Clair spread a gloom over the whole country—deepened by the mourning for the many noble spirits who had fallen. The panic that prevailed along the whole north-western border, extending from the confines of New-York to the estuary of the Ohio, was great beyond description. The inhabitants feared that the Indians, emboldened by success, and with greatly augmented numbers, would pour down upon them in clouds, and lay waste all the frontier settlements with the torch and the tomahawk, even if some modern Alaric of the forest did not lead his barbarians to the gates of Rome. Nor were these apprehensions by any means groundless. During the twelve months that followed the rout of St. Clair, the depredations of the savages became more furious and ferocious than ever before; and some of the most tragical scenes recorded in history took place on the extended line of the frontiers.†

* This interesting fact has been derived by the author from Thayendanegea's family. He has in vain sought for it in print. It is the circumstance of Brant's having been engaged in this battle, that prompted the author to give so full a narrative of the event, and the incidents attending it, in this place. It would seem that the government of the United States was sadly at fault as to the numbers and tribes of the Indians who fought this battle; and when, in the month of January, 1792, Captain Peter Pond and William Steedman were sent into the Indian country as messengers, it was a part of their instructions to obtain information upon these points—Vide Indian State papers, vol. iv. p. 227.

† Thatcher's Lives of the Indian Chiefs--Little Turtle. As an example, the author cites a well-authenticated case, occurring in what was then perhaps the most populous section of the west. The proprietor of a dwelling-house in Kentucky, whose name was Merrill, being alarmed by the barking of his dog, on going to the door received a fire from an assailing party of Indians, which broke his right leg and arm. They attempted to enter the house, but were anticipated in their move-

There was another cause of disquietude. It was feared that, flushed with this defeat of a second expedition, even the five of the Six Nations who had concluded treaties with the United States, but of whose ultimate fidelity many grains of distrust had been entertained, would now grasp their hatchets, and rush to the ranks of the Miamis and their western allies. The most earnest appeals to the government for protection were therefore sent forward by the inhabitants of the border towns, to which a deaf ear could not be turned.

The popular clamor against St. Clair, in consequence of his disastrous defeat, was loud and deep. With the great mass of the people, it is success only that constitutes the general, and St. Clair had been unfortunate. The surrender of Ticonderoga in 1777, was an event which had occasioned great disappointment and dissatisfaction at the time, and the recollection was revived, in connection with this signal reverse. But in neither instance did the fault lie at the door of the commanding General ; Ticonderoga was evacuated because indefensible, and the battle lost by the cowardice of the militia. Fully conscious, himself, that no blame was justly attributable to him, General St. Clair applied to the President for an investigation by a court of inquiry. The request was denied, only for the reason that there were not officers enough in the service, of the requisite rank, to form a legal court for that purpose.† Aware of the prejudices excited against

ment by Mrs. Merrill and her daughter, who closed the door so firmly as to keep them at bay. They next began to cut their way through the door, and succeeded in breaking an aperture, through which one of the warriors attempted to enter. The lady, however, was prepared for the event, and as he thrust his head within, she struck it open with an axe, and instantly drew his body into the house. His companions, not knowing the catastrophe, but supposing that he had worked his way through successfully, attempted one after another, to follow. But Mrs. Merrill dealt a fatal blow upon every head that pushed itself through, until five warriors lay dead at her feet. By this time the party without had discovered the fate of their more forward companions, and thought they would effect an entrance by a safer process— a descent of the chimney. The contents of a feather-bed were instantly emptied upon the fire, creating a smoke so dense and purgent, as to bring two more warriors headlong down upon the hearth in a state of half-suffocation. The moment was critical, as the mother and daughter were guarding the door. The husband, however, by the assistance of his little son, though sorely maimed, managed to rid himself of those two unwelcome visitors by a billet of wood. Meantime the wife repelled another assault at the door---severely wounding another Indian ; whereupon the assailants relinquished the siege. For another highly interesting narrative of border sufferings in the Spring of 1792, see Appendix, No. VIII.

† Letter of President Washington to General St. Clair, March 28, 1792.

him in the public mind, the unfortunate General spontaneously announced his intention of resigning his commission, suggesting, however, that he should prefer retaining it until his con·duct could be investigated in some way ; but as the military establishment at that time allowed only one Major General, and as the service required the speedy designation of a successor, this request was also denied, though with reluctance, by the President.* Complaints, it is true, were poured into the ears of the President against him. Among others, General John Armstrong, the hero of Kittaning, and an experienced Indian fighter in Pennsylvania, addressed a letter to the President, censuring the generalship of St. Clair.† It is believed, however, that the veteran Governor of the North-western Territory continued in the full enjoyment of the President's confidence to the last.

The appointment of a successor to St. Clair as Commander in-chief of the army, was a source of no little perplexity to the President. His own inclinations were in favor of Governor Henry Lee of Virginia ; but it was apprehended that difficulties would arise in procuring the services of officers who had been his seniors in the army of the Revolution, as subordinates under him. There appear to have been several candidates, among whom were Generals Morgan and Scott, and Colonel Darke, who had served under St. Clair during the last campaign. Ultimately the appointment was conferred upon General Anthony Wayne. The selection was most unpopular in Virginia ; but the result demonstrated its wisdom.‡

* Letter of the President to General St. Clair, April 4, 1792.

† Sparks's Life and Correspondence of Washington, Vol. X, p. 223.

‡ Governor Lee wrote to President Washington on the 15th of June, respecting the selection of a successor of General St. Clair at large, and on the subject of Wayne's appointment in particular, he said :—"You cannot be a stranger to the "extreme disgust which the late appointment to the command of the army excited "among all orders in this state." To this letter the President replied at length. The following paragraph contains the answer to the remark of Governor Lee given above:—"How far the appointment of General Wayne is a popular or an unpopu-"lar measure, is not for me to decide. It was not the determination of the moment, "nor was it the effect of partiality or of influence ; for no application (if that in any "instance could have warped my judgment) was ever made in his behalf from any "one who could have thrown the weight of a feather into his scale; but because, un-"der a full view of all circumstances, he appeared most eligible. To a person of "your observation and intelligence it is unnecessary to remark, that an appoint-"ment, which may be unpopular in one place and with one set of men, may not be "so in another place or with another set of men, and *vice versa;* and that to attempt

Rufus Putnam, a son of the veteran of Bunker Hill, who had served with credit in the war of the Revolution, and who had settled in the North-western Territory soon after the close of that contest, was appointed a brigadier-general, to serve with Wayne. This appointment was tendered to Colonel Willett of New-York, but declined by that gentleman upon the ground of conscientious scruples with regard to fighting the Indians. " It " has been uniformly my opinion," said the Colonel in a letter to the President, " that the United States ought to avoid an In- " dian war. I have generally conceived this to be our wisest " policy. The reasons alleged in support of the present Indian " war have never-brought conviction to my mind. From my " knowledge and experience of these people, I am clear that it is " not a difficult thing to preserve peace with them. That there " are bad men among them, and that these will at times do acts " which deserve punishment, is very clear. But I hold, that to " go to war is not the proper way to punish them. Most of the " Indians that I have had any knowledge of, are conceited and " vain. By feeding their vanity, you gain their good opinion ; " and this in time procures their esteem and affection. By con- " ciliating their good-will, you will render them susceptible of " almost any impression. They are credulous, yet suspicious. " They think a great deal ; and have in general good notions of " right and wrong. They frequently exhibit proofs of grateful " minds ; yet they are very revengeful. And though they are " not free from chicanery and intrigue, yet if their vanity is pro- " perly humored, and they are dealt justly by, it is no difficult " matter to come to reasonable terms with them. The inter- " course I have had with these people, the treatment I have my- " self received from them, and which I have known others to " receive, make me an advocate for them. To fight with them, " would be the last thing I should desire. And yet, Sir, I de- " clare, from the experience I have had, I do not conceive it dif- " ficult to beat them when brought to action. When in small " parties they scatter themselves along a frontier, they have al-

" to please every body is the sure way to please nobody ; because the attempt would " be as idle as the exertion would be impracticable. General Wayne has many " good points as an officer, and it is to be hoped that time, reflection, good advice, " and, above all, a due sense of the importance of the trust which is committed to " him, will correct his foibles or cast a shade over them."

" ways been found exceedingly troublesome and dangerous. This
" kind of warfare is their forte ; and in it they are found to be
" truly tremendous.   But when they attempt any thing in large
" bodies, I have found, notwithstanding their great dexterity in
" the wilderness, and the advantage they usually derive from
" the admirable position they take, that they are easily beat.
" In marching through woods, where troops are exposed to at-
" tacks from Indians, particular attention should be paid not
" only to the mode and line of march, but also to extend small
" parties and single men far on the flanks in front and in rear.
" But whenever a serious attack is made, which is usually fu-
" rious, an instantaneous charge, with huzzaing sufficiently loud
" to drown the noise the Indians make, will never fail to repel
" them.   And this stroke repeated and pursued, will, I am well
" convinced, terminate in victory.   And yet victory even over
" Indians is generally paid for : but defeats are terrible.   The
" honour, however, of fighting and beating Indians, is what I do
" not aspire after.   If in any way I could be instrumental in ef-
" fecting and maintaining peace with them, it would be a source
" of great gratification."

CHAPTER XI.

Preparations for an Indian Consultation at Philadelphia—Captain Brant invited to attend—His objections—Letter of the Rev. Mr. Kirkland to Captain Brant—Letter of the Secretary of War to the same—Letter of Colonel Gordon to the same—Letter of Captain Brant to the Secretary of War—The Secretary of War to Captain Brant—Attempts from Montreal to prevent Brant from going to Philadelphia—His journey—Feelings against him in the Mohawk Valley—His arrival at New-York and Philadelphia—Liberal offers made him—Letter to the Count de Puisy—The offers rejected—Undertakes a Mission of Peace to the Miamis—Returns to New-York—Pursued by a German from the German Flats bent on taking his life—Discovered in New-York—Brant returns to Niagara—Murder of Colonel Harden and Major Trueman—Letters of Brant to the Secretary at War—Feelings of the Western Nations—Correspondence between Brant and McKee—Great Indian Council at the Au Glaize—Sickness of Captain Brant—Hostilities deferred until Spring and a treaty with the United States ordered—Return of the Delegates of the Six Nations—Address to President Washington—Separate organization of Upper Canada—Arrival of Governor Simcoe—Letter to Brant from the Duke of Northumberland—Preparations for the Great Council of 1783—Fresh dissatisfaction of the Indians—Private Councils—They send their ultimatum in anticipation—The American Commissioners depart for the Indian country—Their arrival at Niagara—Friendly conduct of Governor Simcoe—Celebration of the King's Birth-day—The Commissioners start for the West—Their progress interrupted—Conduct of General Wayne—Brant suddenly returns from the West with a Deputation—Council held at Fort Erie—Commissioners return to Niagara—Council there—Speech of Captain Brant—Reply of the Commissioners—Speech of Cat's-Eyes—Rejoinder of Brant—Arrival of the Seven Nations—Brant proceeds to the Miami Rapids—Followed by the Commissioners—Arrival at the Detroit River—Their progress interrupted—Unexpected turn of affairs—Explanations with Deputies from the Great Council—Long Debates in the Indian Council—Brant speaks strongly for peace—Governor Simcoe declines advising the Indians—The negotiations suddenly terminated by the Indians—Their address—And sine qua non.

At the treaty with the Six Nations, except the Mohawks, holden by Colonel Pickering at the Painted Post,* in the preceding month of June, an arrangement was made with certain of their chiefs to visit Philadelphia, then the seat of government of the United States, during the session of Congress to ensue in the winter of 1791—92. The motive for this invitation was threefold. First, if possible, to attach them more cordially to the interests of the United States. Secondly, to consult as to the best methods of extending to them the advantages and blessings

---

* From the earliest knowledge the white men have possessed of the country of western New-York, the Painted Post has been noted as a geographical landmark. When first traversed by the white men, a large oaken post stood at the spot, which has retained the name to this day. It was painted in the Indian manner, and was guarded as a monument by the Indians, who renewed it as often as it gave evidence of going to decay. Tradition says it was a monument of great antiquity, marking the spot of a great and bloody battle, according to some statements. According to others, it was erected to perpetuate the memory of some great war-chief.

of civilization. Thirdly, to impress them with just opinions as to the physical and moral strength of the country, that they might see with their own eyes how futile must be every war-like effort of the Indians against the United States. The improvement of the moral and social condition of the Indians was an object dear to the heart of the President, and he lost no opportunity, on all proper occasions, of impressing upon their minds the desire of the United States to become the protectors, friends, and ministers of good to all the sons of the forest peaceably disposed. From the great influence of Captain Brant, not only with the Six Nations, but over all the Indian nations, it was deemed an important point to persuade him to attend the anticipated Council at Philadelphia. Great efforts were accordingly made for the attainment of that object.

The first invitation was given by Colonel Pickering by letter. Apprehending, however, that a mere invitation would not be a sufficient inducement for the veteran chief to undertake the journey, the Secretary of War, on the 20th of December, wrote to the Rev. Mr. Kirkland, the well-known Indian missionary, requesting him to repair from Oneida to Genesee, to meet the chiefs of the Six Nations who were going to Philadelphia, and conduct them thither. Arriving at that place, Mr. Kirkland was instructed to write to Captain Brant in his own name, and dispatch messengers, assuring him of his welcome reception by the government of the United States, and pledging himself for his personal safety. These steps were promptly taken by Mr. Kirkland, to whom Captain Brant wrote a reply, declining the invitation—for what reasons, as this letter seems not to have been preserved, can only be inferred from the subsequent correspondence of the Secretary of War and Mr. Kirkland. By a letter from the former, it appears that the chief thought the invitation not sufficiently formal. By a letter from Mr. Kirkland, also addressed to the chief himself, it would seem that the latter was apprehensive that, should he undertake the journey, the American government would expect him to travel like the common herds of Indians who frequently, as now, were in the habit of visiting the capital of the Republic,—and who are usually led through the country in a drove by a single conductor Such, however, was not the intention of the government, as will more fully appear by the following correspondence :—

Rev. Mr. Kirkland to Captain Brant. (Extract.)

"*Genesee, February* 17, 1792.

*   *   *   *   *   *   *

" My dear and worthy friend, it is not in my power, at this instant, even to attempt such a reply to your letter by Dr. Allen as it justly merits. Suffice it to say, it was not in my idea that you should be crowded into the company of all the old chiefs, and dragged along promiscuously with them through the proposed tour to Philadelphia. No, Sir; the respect I have for your character and happiness would have spurned at the thought. Dr. Allen was apprised of this, and directed to acquaint you with my instructions relative to the same. You need, Sir, be under no apprehensions of any neglect, or want of proper attention on my part, in the proposed tour, or of a cordial reception upon your arrival at the seat of government. Pardon me, if I say you will have occasion much more to fear the opposite extreme. There are so many matters of importance relative to the Indians upon which I have a desire to converse with you, that I cannot willingly relinquish the idea of a personal interview.

" Believe me, my dear friend, that your honor and happiness, as well as the cause of humanity, have a share of my affection and concern. It is very possible I may be partial in your favor by reason of your rescuing my life at the beginning of the late war, which instance I can never forget, and have thousands of times mentioned to your praise. I cannot but flatter myself, from the sensibility of soul you possess, that you will so adjust your domestic affairs as to honor me with a short visit in this vicinity next Spring, should I return here at that season; and should you, upon mature deliberation, conclude to come down sooner, General Chapin and Dr. Allen will be ready to wait on you wherever you please to go. Excuse the abruptness with which I close, being much crowded—wishing you every form of happiness, believe me to be, in great truth and esteem,

" Dear Sir, your affectionate friend

" And very humble serv't.

" S. Kirkland.

" *Col. J. Brant.*

" P. S. Please remember me respectfully to Dr. Kerr and

his lady. I am exceedingly sorry for the detention of my former letter, which deprived me of the happiness of a personal interview. I hope this will be delivered by the bearer's own hand, your friend, Captain Hendrick."

Nearly at the same time that Mr. Kirkland was thus endeavoring to persuade the chief to comply with the request of the government in this matter, the Secretary of War addressed directly to him a letter as full, courteous, and formal, as the most fastidious diplomatist could have desired :—

The Secretary of War to Captain Brant.
"*Philadelphia, February 25th,* 1792.

Sir,

" Colonel Pickering, who had some communications with the Senecas and others of the Six Nations, during the last two years, was duly authorised to invite you to visit this city, in order to consult you upon the best means of civilizing and advancing the happiness of the Indians. Some information has been re cently received from Mr. Kirkland, intimating your disposition to perform the visit, but declining to do it upon the former invitation, as not being sufficiently explicit.

" I now repeat to you this invitation, accompanied with a wish that you would repair to this city, being the seat of the American government; and I *can* assure you that the President of the United States will be highly gratified by receiving and conversing with a chief of such eminence as you are, on a subject so interesting and important to the human race.

" This invitation is given to you from the fairest motives. The President of the United States is conscious of the purest disposition to promote, generally, the welfare of the Indians ; and he flatters himself that proper occasions only are wanting to impress them with the truth of this assertion. He considers your mind more enlightened than theirs, and he hopes that your heart is filled with a true desire to serve the essential interests of your countrymen. The United States, much against the inclination of the government, are engaged in hostilities with some of the western Indians. We, on our parts, have entered into it with reluctance, and consider it as a war of necessity ; and not, as is supposed, and industriously propagated, by many, for the purpose of accumulating more land than has been ceded by the treaty with the Indians, since the peace with Great Britain. We are desirous of bringing it to a conclusion, not from any apprehension as to a favorable result, because, by a comparison of forces and resources, however troublesome a perseverance therein may be to us, it must be utter destruction to the hostile Indians. We are desirous, for the sake of humanity, of avoiding such a catastrophe.

"This is the main business which will be mentioned to you on the part of the United States; and it is an object worthy of the best cultivated head and heart. If you should enter into this view, Mr. Kirkland has directions to concert with you the most satisfactory mode of your performing the journey. The nature of the case will show the necessity of your coming without delay, if you incline to accept the invitation.

"I am, Sir,
"H. Knox.

" *To Capt. Joseph Brant.*"

This letter was enclosed by General Knox to Mr. Kirkland, who was assured that the "presence of Captain Brant in Philadelphia was considered of great importance." Mr. Kirkland was accordingly enjoined "to spare no pains in endeavoring to in- "duce him to come," and "to arrange with him the most satis- "factory mode of travelling—to make it as flattering to him as "might be, and to accompany him." Mr. Kirkland despatched the letter of the Secretary immediately to Colonel Gordon, at Niagara, by the hand of Dr. Allen, with a request that it might be transmitted by the Colonel to its place of destination—Grand River. But Mr. Kirkland's messenger disclosed to Colonel Gordon the contents of the package, thereby enabling that officer to exert an immediate influence upon the mind of the chief, if he chose to do so. The result was, that, accompanying the Secretary's letter, Captain Brant received the following communication :—

COLONEL GORDON TO CAPTAIN BRANT.

" *Niagara, 20th March,* 1792.

"My Dear Friend,

"The packet which I now send you was brought here by a Doctor Allen, from Canadasago. I do not know the contents, farther, than the bearer tells me it is a letter from the Secretary at War of the United States, inviting you to Philadelphia on business of consequence.

" Your own good sense will best dictate the answer vou ought to give.

" Should it have a reference to the bringing about a peace with the Western Indians, I cannot conceive that Philadelphia is the place where a conference of so much moment ought to be held ; as it is evident none of the Western Indians, whose dearest interests are concerned in the event, can be present ; and if any steps are taken by the Six Nations without their concurrence, it is much to be feared it will give rise to jealousies, which may be attended with disagreeable consequences hereafter.

" If the United States have at length seriously determined to do justice to, and make peace with, the Western Indians, a general council should be convened in some convenient situation, where deputies from all the nations concerned, as well as commissioners on the part of Great Britain and America, can be assembled. The views of all parties would then be clearly defined ; an accurate boundary ascertained ; past acts of hostility be buried in oblivion ; and such measures adopted as would tend to establish permanent peace and friendship on a solid and equitable basis.

" In the many conversations we have had on this subject, we have generally agreed, that from the line of conduct the United States have hitherto pursued, it did not appear that they had this object seriously in view ; and I am sorry to observe, from the mode of proceeding on the present occasion, there is too much reason to suspect they have not yet seen their error.

" In almost every transaction they have had with the Six Nations during the course of the last two years, there has appeared a duplicity and inconsistency, on which it is impossible to put a liberal construction.

" The Six Nations, in the present critical situation of affairs with their western brethren, ought to be exceedingly cautious how they involve themselves either one way or another. Great Britain is at peace with the United States, and it is therefore anxiously wished that her friends, the Indians in general, should be so likewise ; every advice which has been given to them had that object in view ; and I still hope the period is at no great distance, when this desirable event will be accomplished on equitable terms, and to the mutual satisfaction of all parties.

" I have thus, my dear friend, been induced to give you my private opinion on the present occasion, and I am fully persuaded you will pursue a line of conduct that will deserve the approbation of your brethren and friends.

" Accept my sincere good wishes, and believe me, with much regard, your friend,

"A. GORDON.

" P. S. I understand some of the Senecas from Buffalo Creek are gone to Philadelphia on Colonel Pickering's former invitation, which, I am told, causes much uneasiness in the village.

"A. G.

" *Captain Joseph Brant, Grand River.*"

This was certainly an artful communication. His Majesty's commander at Niagara was desirous that peace should be restored between the Indians and the United States, but takes care not to omit the oft-repeated insinuations of injustice and bad faith on the part of the latter toward the former. In one word, notwithstanding his pacific protestations, Colonel Gordon was desirous of peace only through the agency of British intervention, and his present purpose was, to prevent the influential chief of the Mohawks from visiting the seat of the American government. Notwithstanding the Colonel's letter, however, the chief addressed the following conditional acceptance of the invitation to the Secretary of War :—

CAPTAIN BRANT TO GENERAL KNOX.

" *Nassau, March 27th,* 1792.

" SIR :—

" Yours of the 25th of February I have the pleasure of acknowledging the receipt of, and entertain the highest sense of the honor done me by the invitation and flattering compliment contained therein. It is a visit I have long been desirous of making, and the time now seems not to be far distant when that desire will be accomplished. Visiting you as an individual, would be by no means tending to the accomplishing any good end, as those meetings must show that have hitherto been held with people not deputized by the nation in general to transact business. I should therefore wish to visit you, vested with some power that will enable me to speak with certainty as to what I may assert, and not assert what I, at the same time, must well know would be by no means approved of. This has been too much the case of late years, and in my opinion is principally the cause of the present disturbances. An explanation of grievances it is absolutely necessary should be made, and that to the head of the United States, from whom I entertain not the smallest doubt but justice will be given where due. To accomplish such desirable ends as civilization and peace-making, no exertions on my part shall be wanting; and though circumstances render it impossible for me to do myself the honor of accepting the invitation at present, as I cannot say whether the western nations would approve of it, I shall nevertheless despatch messengers immediately to the Miamis, with your invitation, to have the opinion of the people there, who, I have no great reason to suppose otherwise than that they'll approve of my going, and very possibly invest me with such powers as will give energy to what I may do.

"My messengers, I suppose, will return here in about thirty days, until when, I shall remain at home. If visiting you after that would not be too late to answer the good end intended, I shall endeavor to accomplish my wished-for journey—at least if I may hear from you in answer to this, ere that period.

"I am, Sir,

"With esteem,

"Yours, &c.

"JOSEPH BRANT.

"*The Secretary of War.*"

Immediately on the receipt of this letter at the War Department, General Israel Chapin, of Genesee, was appointed a Deputy Indian Agent by the President, with instructions to transmit the following communication to Captain Brant, and make all needful preparations for his journey:—

THE SECRETARY OF WAR TO CAPTAIN BRANT

"*April* 23d, 1792.

"SIR: I have received your letter of the 27th of March, post-

poning your visit to this city until a period of thirty days after that date.

" I regret exceedingly the existence of any circumstance which
suspended your visit. But as the dispositions of the President
of the United States remain the same, as to the objects mentioned
in my former letter, I can with great truth assure you that your
visit at the time you have proposed, will be cordially received.

" General Chapin, who is appointed an agent of the Five Nations, will either accompany you to this city, or he will obtain
some other person for that purpose, as shall be agreed upon between you and him.

" I am, &c. &c.

" H. KNOX.

" *To Captain Joseph Brant.*"

Pending this correspondence, however, the proposed conference with a deputation of the Six Nations, referred to in the
postscript of Colonel Gordon's letter, took place in Philadelphia.
It was begun on the 13th of March, and protracted until near
the close of April. Fifty sachems were present, and the visit
resulted to the mutual satisfaction of the parties. In addition
to arrangements upon other subjects, the delegations agreed to
perform a pacific mission to the hostile Indians, and endeavor
to persuade them to peace. But such were their dilatory movements, that they did not depart from Buffalo for the Miamis until the middle of September. At the head of this embassage was
that fast friend of the United States, the Corn-planter.

In regard to the mission of Captain Brant, in addition to
the dissuasions of Colonel Gordon, strenuous efforts were made
by the official friends of the chief at Montreal, to prevent his
visit to the federal capital. On the 1st of May he was addressed
by Mr. Joseph Chew, an officer under Sir John Johnson, expressing much satisfaction at the refusal of the first invitation
by Captain Brant, and advising the chief of the preparations the
Americans were making for another Indian campaign. The
following passage occurs in this letter:—" I see they expect to
" have an army of about five thousand men, besides three troops
" of horse. By the advertisements for supplies of provisions,
" &c., it seems this army will not be able to move before the
" last of July. What attempts Wilkinson and Hamtramck may

" make with the militia, is uncertain. *Our friends ought to
" be on their guard.* I long to know what they think in Eng-
" land of the victory gained over St. Clair's army."* On the
23d of May, Brant advised Mr. Chew that he had accepted the
invitation ;† and on the 19th of June, the latter gentleman replied—expressing his regrets that several of his letters to the
Chief had not been received prior to his taking that resolution.
Mr. Chew, who doubtless expressed the views of Sir John Johnson and the Executive government of the province, thought the
Captain should not have accepted such an invitation without
previously knowing the wishes of the King, in regard to the
means of bringing about a peace between the Americans and
the Indians. In the same letter he also announces to " his
namesake," as he calls the Captain, that a Mr. Hammond was
on his way to the Indian country, charged with an offer of his
Majesty's mediation.‡

The necessary arrangements having been adjusted, the journey was commenced early in June. General Chapin not being
able to accompany the Chief to the seat of government, he was
attended by the General's son, and by Doctor Allen, and two
body servants of his own—all mounted. Their route from
Niagara to Albany was taken through the Mohawk Valley. At
Palatine, by previous invitation, the Captain visited Major James
Cochran, who had then recently established himself in that
place. But the feelings of the inhabitants had become so embittered against him during the war of the Revolution, and such
threats were uttered by some of the Germans, of a determination to take his life, that it was deemed prudent for him privately
to leave the inn, where his friend Major Cochran was then at
lodgings, and sleep at the house of Mrs. Peter Schuyler in the
neighborhood, where he would be less likely to be assailed. He
did so, and the next morning pursued his journey.§ With this
exception, he was well received at every point of his journey.
His arrival in New-York was thus announced in the newspapers :—" On Monday last arrived in this city, from his settle-
" ment on Grand River, on a visit to some of his friends in this
" quarter, Captain Joseph Brant of the British army, the famous
" Mohawk chief who so eminently distinguished himself during

---

* Original letters among the Brant papers.   † Idem.   ‡ Idem.
§ Letter of Major Cochran to the author.

" the late war as the military leader of the Six Nations. We
" are informed that he intends to visit the city of Philadelphia,
" and pay his respects to the President of the United States."

He arrived in Philadelphia on the 20th of June, where he was
announced in terms very similar to the above, and received by
the Government with marked attention. But few memorials of
this visit have been preserved. The President announced his
arrival in respectful terms, on the 21st of June, in a letter addressed to Gouverneur Morris ; and he speaks of the circumstance
again in a subsequent letter, but makes no allusion to the result
of his interviews with him. No doubt, strong efforts were made,
not only to engage his active interposition with the Indians to
bring about a peace, but likewise to win him over permanently
to the interests of the United States. In a letter subsequently
addressed by Captain Brant to the Count de Puisy,* in regard to his
difficulties with the British government touching the title to the
Grand River territory, while pleading the claims of his Indians
to the favorable consideration of the Crown, and repelling certain charges of selfishness which had been bruited respecting
himself, the following passage occurs on the subject of the proposals made to him by the American Executive :—" I am sorry
" to find that my perseverance in endeavoring to obtain our
" rights, has caused unjust surmises to be formed of my inten-
" tions, notwithstanding the many evident proofs I have shown
" of my integrity and steady attachment to the British interest.
" Had I not been actuated by motives of honor, and preferred
" the interests of his Majesty, and the credit of my nation, to my
" own private welfare, there were several allurements of gain
" offered me by the Government of the United States when I
" was at Philadelphia, during the time the Shawanese and other
" tribes maintained a war against them, I was offered a thou-
" sand guineas down, and to have the half-pay and pension I
" receive from Great Britain doubled, merely on condition that I

* The Count de Puisy was one of the French nobles driven into exile by the revolution of 1789. He subsequently held a commission as Lieutenant General in
the British service, and commanded a detachment of the emigrants in the Quiberon
expedition. Receiving a grant of land in Canada from the British crown, as did several of the exiles, the Count came over, and resided for a time near Niagara. During this period he formed an intimate acquaintance with Captain Brant, who corresponded with him after his return to England. The Count resided somewhere in the
neighborhood of London until his death, which happened many years afterward.

" would use my endeavors to bring about a peace. But this I
" rejected.   I considered it might be detrimental to the British
" interests, as also to the advantage and credit of the Indian na-
" tions, until the Americans should make the necessary conces
" sions.   Afterward I was offered the pre-emption right to land
" to the amount of twenty thousand pounds currency of the
" United States, and fifteen hundred dollars per annum.   This
" I considered as inconsistent with the principles of honor to re-
" ceive, as by accepting of any of these offers, they might
" expect me to act contrary to his Majesty's interest and the
" honor of our nations ; and from the repeated assurances of
" his Majesty's representatives, I had full confidence his bounty
" would never fail."

But notwithstanding his refusal of these propositions, the result
of the interview seems at the time to have been mutual satisfaction.   The true causes of the war with the western Indians
were explained to him ; and great pains were taken by the President and Secretary of War to impress upon his mind the sincere desire of the United States to cultivate the most amicable
relations with the sons of the forest, of any and every tribe. In
the end, the Chief was induced to undertake a mission of peace
to the Miamis, for which purpose he was furnished with ample
instructions by the Secretary of War.   Most emphatically was
he enjoined to undeceive the Indians in regard to their apprehensions that the United States were seeking to wrest from
them farther portions of their lands.   On this point the Government solemnly disclaimed the design of taking a foot more than
had been ceded in the treaty of Muskingum in 1789.   The Chief
left Philadelphia about the 1st of July, on which occasion the
Secretary of War wrote to General Chapin, among other things,
as follows :—" Captain Brant's visit will, I flatter myself, be pro-
" ductive of great satisfaction to himself, by being made acquaint-
" ed with the humane views of the President of the United
" States."   To Governor Clinton the Secretary likewise wrote
as follows :—" Captain Brant appears to be a judicious and sensi-
" ble man.   I flatter myself his journey will be satisfactory to
" himself and beneficial to the United States."

The Chief returned by the same route, lingering a few days
in New-York, where he was visited by some of the most distinguished gentlemen in the city.   It has been mentioned, a few

pages back, that Brant was apprehensive of some attempt upon his life in the Mohawk Valley. Indeed, he had been informed that it would be unsafe for him to traverse that section of country, lest some real or fancied wrong, connected with the war of the Revolution, should be avenged by assassination. Nor were these apprehensions groundless; for while resting in New-York, he ascertained that he had not only been pursued from the German Flatts, but that the pursuer was then in the city watching for an opportunity to effect his purpose. The name of this pursuer was Dygert. Several members of his father's family had fallen in the battle of Oriskany, fifteen years before, and this man had deliberately determined to put the leader of the Indian warriors to death in revenge. Brant's lodgings were in Broadway,* where he was visited, among others, by Colonel Willett and Colonel Morgan Lewis, both of whom he had met in the field of battle in years gone by. While in conversation with these gentlemen, he mentioned the circumstance of Dygert's pursuit, and expressed some apprehensions at the result, should he be attacked unawares. Before his remarks were concluded, glancing his quick eye to the window, he exclaimed, " there is Dygert now !" True enough, the fellow was then standing in the street, watching the motions of his intended victim. Colonel Willett immediately descended into the street, and entered into a conversation with Dygert, charging his real business upon him, which he did not deny. " Do you know," asked Willett, " that if you kill that savage, you will be hanged ?" " Who," replied the ignorant German, " would hang me for killing an Indian ?" " You will see," rejoined the Colonel ; " if you execute your purpose, you " may depend upon it you will be hanged up immediately." This was presenting the case in a new aspect to Dygert, who, until that moment, seemed to suppose that he could kill an Indian with as much propriety in a time of peace as in war—in the streets of New-York as well as in legal battle in the woods. After deliberating a few moments, he replied to Colonel Willett, that if such was the law, he would give it up and return home.†

* The old wooden building where the City Hotel now stands.
† These particulars have recently been communicated to the author in a conversation with the venerable Governor, then Colonel Lewis, and confirmed by a letter from Major Cochran, with whom Brant conversed on the subject. Indeed the hostility of the Mohawk-Germans toward all Indians, after the close of the war, was deep and

He did so, and the Mohawk chief shortly afterward reached Niagara in safety.

Independently of the proposed mediation of Captain Brant, the Government of the United States, in its great solicitude to prevent the effusion of blood, had employed a large number of messengers of peace, among whom, in addition to the fifty chiefs of the Six Nations already mentioned, were the Rev. Mr. Heckewelder, General Rufus Putnam, Colonel Hardin, Major Trueman, and a man named Freeman. The celebrated Hendrick, chief of the Stockbridge Indians, was also employed upon the same service. It is possible that Captain Brant was not well pleased at the appointment of so large a number of pacificators—very naturally preferring the honor of being the sole agent of terminating the war. It would have been no inconsiderable subject of boasting, to be enabled to say " Alone I did it !" Hence, we may reasonably infer, the tone of the annexed letter, addressed to the Secretary of War by Captain Brant on his arrival at Niagara—a fitting occasion for writing it having been furnished by the murder of Major Trueman.*

universal. The author well remembers a pensioner living in the neighborhood of the village of Herkimer, named Hartmann, who, some years after the war, deliberately killed an Indian at the German Flatts, moved only by his revolutionary thirst for vengeance. Hartmann, it is true, had been grievously hacked and wounded by the Indians, so that he was disabled from labor for life. He was a very ignorant man, and thought it no harm to kill an Indian at any time. Happening one day, in after years, to fall in with a son of the forest, he persuaded the savage to let him examine his rifle. The moment he obtained the weapon, he dropped slowly behind, and shot his confiding companion. He was arrested and carried to Johnstown for trial, but the investigation was so managed as to produce an acquittal. The excuse of Hartmann for the commission of the deed, was, that he saw the Indian's tobacco-pouch,which was, as he said, made of the skin of a child's hand. It was, probably, a leather glove which the Indian had found.

* Three of the messengers of peace above mentioned, Messrs. Trueman, Freeman, and Hardin, were murdered by the Indians during that season. Formerly no nations on earth were wont to respect the sacred character of " the man of peace" more than the Indians. But they had now become treacherous even to them. They pleaded, however, the example of the whites, who, they alleged, paid no attention to treaties with the Indians, but treated them as a contemptible race, and had killed several of their own messengers of peace, some of whom were chiefs.—Vide Heckewelder's History of Indian Nations, chapter xxi. President Washington, who was then at Mount Vernon, announced the death of Hardin and Trueman, together with "the harbingers of their mission," in a letter to Mr. Jefferson, Secretary of State, on the 23d of August. Every thing then looked hostile at the west ; added to which were rising difficulties with the Cherokees, occasioned, as was supposed, by the intrigues of Spain. " If Spain is really intriguing with the Southern Indians,"

CAPTAIN BRANT TO THE SECRETARY OF WAR.

" *Niagara, 26th July,* 1792.

" SIR,

" Since my arrival here, I am sorry to have to say that intelligence respecting Major Trueman's being killed by an Indian boy, who met with him a hunting, has arrived. This will induce you to recollect what passed between us relative to messages being sent. The route by Presque Isle I again recommend as the most eligible ; from thence keeping along the lake to the Miamis, at which place the chiefs are aptest to be met with ; and when once there, they are safe. Sending such number of messengers rather makes the Indians suspicious of your intentions, and by any other route they are much more liable to meet with hunters. There are now great numbers of Indians collected, and, from all their councils, seem determined upon a new boundary line. In short, they are all sensible that what has hitherto been done, (which I fully explained to you,) was unfair ; and I am of opinion peace will not easily be established without your relinquishing part of your claim. The purchases were all made from men who had no right to sell, and who are now to be thanked for the present difficulties.*

" The Senecas and Seven Nations of Canada are now waiting at Fort Erie for a passage for Detroit, on their way to the Miamis. I shall be able to go up by the next trip of the vessel. My intention and wish is still for the accomplishing of peace. 'Tis a business will require time ; things too rashly or hastily agreed upon, seldom have the effect of those seriously and coolly reflected on ; knowing the foundation to be just, and the benefits that will arise therefrom, affords a greater space for forwarding the business.

said the President, " I shall entertain strong suspicions that there is a very clear understanding in all this business between the Courts of London and Madrid ; and that it is calculated to check, as far as they can, the rapid increase, extension, and consequence of this country ; for there cannot be a doubt of the wishes of the former, if we may judge from the conduct of its officers, to preclude any *éclaircissement* of ours with the Western Indians, and to embarrass our negotiations with them, any more than there is of their traders and some others, who are subject to their government, aiding and abetting them in acts of hostility."—*Letter of Washington to Jefferson, August* 23d, 1792.

* The writer here refers to the treaty of Fort Harmer, which the great majority of the Indians always maintained was unauthorized by their people, and therefore of no binding force upon them.

"After leaving your place until my arrival here, I had a tedious journey.   The fatigue is done away by the recollection of
the politeness and attention showed me by your officers of government, for which I cannot but return my warmest thanks,
and request you to communicate the same.   If any return should
be in my power to make, I shall think myself particularly happy.

"And am, Sir,

"Yours, &c.

"Jos. Brant.

"*The Secretary of War.*"

Apprehensive, from the opposition of his friends to his Philadelphia mission, that evil reports might have been circulated
concerning him, and distrust of his fidelity engendered among
the upper nations, on the 29th of July the Captain wrote to his
friend M'Kee, at Detroit, making inquiries as to that and various
other points, and also with a view of ascertaining whether his
presence would be acceptable at the then approaching council
at the Miamis.   In reply, Colonel M'Kee assured him that,
"whatever bad birds had been flying about," the opinions of the
western Indians respecting him were unchanged, and that they
were anxious for his presence among them, to aid in their consultations for the general welfare.   In regard to the murder of
the American messengers, Colonel M'Kee said they were killed
by a banditti, and the circumstance was regretted,—"although
"the Indians considered that the messengers had been sent more
"with a view to gain time, and lull the confederacy into a fa-
"tal security, than to effect a peace, since they have proposed
"no other terms than what the nations rejected at first; and
"you must be perfectly sensible," (added Colonel M'K.) "that
"after two successful general engagements, in which a great
"deal of blood has been spilt, the Indians will not quietly give
"up by negotiation what they have been contending for with
"their lives since the commencement of these troubles."   Captain Brant having expressed an opinion that the hostile nations
would not be likely to move again until the effect of farther negotiation should be known, M'Kee replied, that the Indians did
not look upon "the hostile preparations" of the Americans,
"such as forming posts and magazines in the heart of their
"country, as indicating much sincerity on their part; nor do
"they [the Indians] think that such establishments would tend

" to conciliate or convince them that the Americans wish for
" peace on any reasonable terms, or on the terms proposed by
" the confederacy the beginning of last year. A great council
" is soon to be held at the Au Glaize—the chiefs not judging it
" proper to move lower down at present, on account of the Ame-
" rican force collecting at Fort Jefferson." In regard to the
treaty of Muskingum, (Fort Harmar,) Colonel M'Kee said—
" Duintate, the Chief who conducted that business, is dead ; but
" he always declared that he, and all the chiefs who were with
" him there, were imposed upon—imagining that what they
" signed was a treaty of amity, and not a cession of country ; and
" were not undeceived until they had been some time returned
" to their respective villages, and had their papers explained to
" them. Some messengers are arrived at the Glaize from the
" westward of the Mississippi, announcing that large bodies of
" their nations are collected, and will shortly be here to give
" their assistance to the general confederacy ; so that, in all pro-
" bability, more nations will soon be assembled here than at any
" former period." *

The letter from which the preceding extracts have been made,
was dated from the " Foot of the Miami Rapids, September 4th,
1792." The council of which it speaks, was held at the Au
Glaize, on the Miami of Lake Erie, in the course of the Autumn.
A fit of sickness, however, prevented the attendance of Thayendanegea. The Corn-planter, and forty-eight of the chiefs of the
Six Nations, residing within the boundaries of the United
States, repaired thither, together with about thirty chiefs and
warriors of the Mohawks, and other Canada Indians. But they
were not well received, in their character of peace-makers, by
the hostiles, who were sturdily bent upon continuing the war.
The council was numerously attended on the part of the
western tribes ; the Shawanese were the only speakers in favor
of war, and Red Jacket from the Senecas was alone the orator
in opposition, or in behalf of the friendly Indians. The Shawanese taunted the Six Nations with having first induced them to
form a great confederacy, a few years before, and of having come
to the council now " with the voice of the United States folded
" under their arm."† There were indications of an angry pas-

---

* Correspondence among the Brant papers.
† Alluding to the belt by which they were to speak.

sage between the two parties in the earlier stages of the council ; but after mutual explanations, harmony was restored. The result was, that the hostile Indians finally agreed to suspend belligerent operations for the winter, and to meet the United States in council at the Rapids of the Miami in the following Spring. The basis of the proposed armistice, however, was, that the United States should withdraw their troops from the western side of the Ohio. Nor did they hold out any prospect of treating in the Spring, upon any other principle than that of making the Ohio the boundary, and receiving payment for their improvements on the south-eastern side of that river. They insisted that the United States should allow them all the lands they possessed in Sir William Johnson's time, and that upon no other terms would they agree to a treaty of peace. The council was dissolved about the 10th or 12th of October ; and Captain Brant did not arrive at the Au Glaize until after it had broken up. It was a very large council. There were representatives in attendance from the Gora nations, whom it had taken a whole season to travel thither. There were also present, besides the Six Nations and the north-western tribes, twenty-seven nations from beyond the Canadian territory.

On the return of the friendly Indians to Buffalo, a grand council was called, at which the Indian agents of the Five Nations were present, and also Colonel Butler, and a number of other gentlemen from Niagara. At this council, the proceedings and speeches at the Au Glaize were rehearsed, and in conclusion of their mission, the Six Nations transmitted the following speech to the President of the United States ; from which it will appear that, though friendly to them, the Six Nations, after all, were yet more friendly to the Miamis, and their claim of the Ohio for a boundary :—

SPEECH FROM THE SIX NATIONS TO THE PRESIDENT.

" You sent us on to the westward, with a message of peace to the hostile Indians.

" We proceeded accordingly to your directions, and was protected, going and coming, by the Great Spirit.

" We give thanks to the Great Spirit, that we have all returned safe to our seats.

" While we was at the westward, we exerted ourselves to

bring about peace. The fatigues we underwent are not small. Now, it is our desire for your people on the Ohio to lay down their arms, or otherwise it is all in vain what we have done.

" Now, if you wish for peace, you must make every exertion, and proceed through this path we have directed for you. If peace does not take place, the fault must arise from your people.

" We now desire you, Brothers, to send forward agents, who are men of honesty, not proud land-jobbers, but men who love and desire peace. Also, we desire they may be accompanied by some friend, or Quaker, to attend the council.

" Wish you to exert yourself to forward the message to the western Indians as soon as possible ; and we are taken by the hand, and have agreed, next Spring, to attend the council at the Rapids of Miami, when we shall hear all that takes place there."

Notwithstanding the stipulations of the Shawanese and Miamis to call in their warriors, and commit no farther hostilities until the grand council should be held in the following Spring, the armistice was not very rigidly observed, and skirmishes were frequent along the border. On the 6th of November, Major Adair, commanding a detachment of Kentucky volunteers, was attacked by a large body of Indians in the neighborhood of Fort St. Clair. The battle was sharp and severe, and the Indians were rather checked than defeated. General Wilkinson, who was in command of the fort, could render no assistance, from the strictness of his orders to act only on the defensive. He bestowed high praise on the good conduct of Major Adair, as the latter did upon his officers and men.

It was at about this period that a change was made in the Canadian government, which, from the character and dispositions of the new officers introduced upon the stage of action, may not have been without its influence in the progress of Indian affairs. During the visit of Lord Dorchester to England of 1791, '93, what had previously been the entire province of Canada was divided, and an upper province with a lieutenantcy created. Colonel J. G. Simcoe was the first Lieutenant Governor assigned to the newly organized territory—an able and active officer, who, in the progress of events, though very friendly at first to the United States, was not long disposed to manifest any particular good-will for them, farther than courtesy to public officers and the discharge of indispensable duties required. He arrived at

Quebec in the Spring of 1792, but was detained in the lower province several months, while waiting for other officers from England, whose presence and assistance were necessary to the organization of the new government.   Colonel Simcoe established his head-quarters at Niagara, which was temporarily constituted the seat of government.   He was the bearer of a letter of introduction from the Duke of Northumberland to the Mohawk Chief, Thayendanegea.   The Duke, who had served in the Revolutionary war as Lord Percy, had been adopted by the Mohawks as a warrior of their nation, under the Indian name, conferred by Brant himself, of *Thorighwegéri*, or *The Evergreen Brake*.   The name involves the very pretty conceit that a titled house never dies.   Like the leaves of this peculiar species of the brake, the old leaf only falls as it is pushed from the stem by the new ; or rather, when the old leaf falls, the young is in fresh and full existence.   The following is the letter, which the character of the parties and the circumstances of the case render worthy of preservation :—

THE DUKE OF NORTHUMBERLAND TO CAPTAIN BRANT

" *Northumberland House, Sept.* 3d, 1791

" MY DEAR JOSEPH,

" Colonel Simcoe, who is going out Governor of Upper Canada, is kind enough to promise to deliver this to you, with a brace of pistols, which I desire you will keep for my sake.   I must particularly recommend the Colonel to you and the nation. He is a most intimate friend of mine, and is possessed of every good quality which can recommend him to your friendship.   He is brave, humane, sensible, and honest.   You may safely rely upon whatever he says, for he will not deceive you.   He loves and honors the Indians, whose noble sentiments so perfectly correspond with his own.   He wishes to live upon the best terms with them, and, as Governor, will have it in his power to be of much service to them.   In short, he is worthy to be a Mohawk.   Love him at first for my sake, and you will soon come to love him for his own.

" I was very glad to hear that you had received the rifle safe which I sent you, and hope it has proved useful to you.   I preserve with great care your picture, which is hung up in the Duchess's own room.

" Continue to me your friendship and esteem, and believe me
ever to be, with the greatest truth,

" Your affectionate

" Friend and Brother,

" NORTHUMBERLAND,

" *Thorighweg(ri.*

"CAPTAIN JOSEPH BRANT,

" *Thayendanegea.*"

Thus strongly and affectionately introduced, by the head of
the British peerage to the head chief of a nation, a close intimacy was formed between Governor Simcoe and Captain Brant, as
will more clearly be disclosed in the progress of these pages.
The regular chain of history will now be resumed.

On the 19th of February, 1793, pursuant to the arrangement
made by the Indians at the Au Glaize in the preceding Autumn,
General Benjamin Lincoln, Beverley Randolph, and Colonel
Timothy Pickering, were commissioned by the President, to
attend the great council at the Miamis, to be held in the course
of the ensuing Spring.

Meantime the Indians of the confederate nations, dissatisfied
with what they considered the evasive reply which had been
received from the President to the address on their behalf, transmitted by the Six Nations, held another council at the Glaize in
February, at which a very explicit address upon the subject was
framed, and transmitted to the Six Nations. They were apprehensive that the Six Nations had either not understood them, or,
that in communicating with the Executive of the United States
they had not made themselves understood. Reminding the Six
Nations that when in council they had understood them to be
of one mind with themselves touching the boundary question.
they now repeated that they would listen to no propositions from
the United States, save upon the basis of the Ohio for a boundary and the removal of the American forts from the Indian
territory. This was the irrevocable determination of the confederates, and they deemed it right and proper that the government of the United States should be fully apprised of the fact
before the commissioners should set out upon their journey.
They likewise advised the Six Nations, in this address, of their de

termination to hold a private council at the Miami Rapids before they would proceed to meet the American commissioners at San-dusky, that they might adjust their own opinions, so as to be of one mind, and speak one language in the public council. It was their farther determination, before they would consent to meet the Commissioners at all, to ascertain whether the Com-missioners had been clothed with authority to meet them upon the terms thus preliminarily prescribed. This letter, or message, was concluded thus :—" BROTHERS : We desire you therefore, to be " strong, and rise immediately to meet us at the Miami Rapids, " where we want the advice and assistance of our elder brethren " in the great work which we are about. The western nations " are all prepared and in daily expectation of the arrival of our " brothers, the Creeks, Cherokees, and other southern nations, " who are on their legs to join us, agreeably to their promise. " And we desire you will put the Seven Nations of Canada in " mind of their promise last Fall, to be early on their legs to join " us, and that you will bring them in your band." [*Four dou-* " *ble strings of black and white Wampum.*"] A postscript enjoined that the United States should send no messengers into their country, except through the Five Nations.*

The communication was dated February 27th. On the same day the Commissioners left Philadelphia for Buffalo Creek, ac-companied, as the Indians had requested, by several members of the society of Friends—so strongly had the nations become at-tached to the disciples of the beneficent Penn.† Colonel Picker ing and Mr. Randolph proceeded directly across the country, while General Lincoln took the route via Albany, to superin tend the forwarding of supplies. General Wayne, now in com-mand of the North-western army, had been instructed in the meantime to issue a proclamation, informing the people of the frontiers of the proposed treaty, and prohibiting all offensive

* Original document from among the Brant papers.

† The names of the Quaker gentlemen who went upon this benevolent errand were, John Parish, William Savory, and John Elliott, of Philadelphia ; Jacob Lindlay, of Chester County ; and Joseph Moore and William Hartshorn, of New-Jersey. It may be noted as a singular fact, that while the Quakers solicited the appointment on this pacific mission at the hands of the President, the Indians, at about the same time, and evidently without consultation or arrangement, requested of some of the American agents, that some Quaker might be appointed on the Commission to treat with them.

movements on the part of these people until the result of the council should be known.

Messrs. Randolph and Pickering arrived at the Queenston landing, (Niagara river,) on the 17th of May. Governor Simcoe, who was at home, had no sooner heard of their arrival in his vicinity, than he sent invitations insisting that they should consider themselves his guests during their stay at that place. He treated them with great hospitality, and at their request readily despatched a vessel to Oswego, to receive General Lincoln and the stores for the expedition. The latter gentleman did not reach Niagara until the 25th.

On their arrival at that place, the Commissioners were informed that Captain Brant, with a body of Mohawks, had set off for the west about the 5th of May. There was a preliminary council to be held at the Miami Rapids, which it was the purpose of that Chief to attend. The United States had fixed the 1st of June for the time of meeting; but Colonel M'Kee had written to Niagara, stating that that period would be quite too early, since the Indians were ever slow in such proceedings, and withal would not then probably have returned from their hunting. The Indians, however, were collecting at the Au Glaize, and Colonel M'Kee advised Governor Simcoe that the conference with the American Commissioners would probably be held at Sandusky. In the meantime it was proposed that the Commissioners should remain at Niagara until all things were ready for the conference.

Such being the position of affairs, the commissioners were detained with Governor Simcoe—occasionally visiting some of the Indian towns in that region—until near the middle of July. Every hospitable attention was bestowed upon them by the Governor, who spared no pains to render their sojourn with him agreeable. On the 4th of June, the King's birth-day was celebrated, on which occasion the Governor gave a *fète*, ending with a ball in the evening, which was attended by " about twenty well-" dressed and handsome ladies, and about three times that num-" ber of gentlemen. They danced from 7 o'clock until 11 " when supper was announced, and served in very pretty taste. " The music and dancing were good, and every thing was con-" ducted with propriety. What excited the best feelings of the " heart, was the ease and affection with which the ladies met

"each other, although there were a number present whose
" mothers sprang from the aborigines of the country.   They
" appeared as well dressed as the company in general, and in-
" termixed with them in a manner which evinced at once the
" dignity of their own minds and the good sense of others.
" These ladies possessed great ingenuity and industry, and have
" great merit; for the education they have received is owing
" principally to their own industry, as their father, Sir William
" Johnson, was dead, and the mother retained the manners and
" dress of her tribe."*

Thus far the deportment of Governor Simcoe was conciliatory, and in all respects indicative of any thing rather than a hostile spirit.   Reports having reached the ears of the Commissioners, that the Governor had qualified the expressions of his desire that the Indians might determine upon a peace with
the United States, by advising them that they should not
relinquish any of their lands to obtain it, those gentlemen
addressed him a note upon the subject.   The imputation was
promptly and satisfactorily disclaimed; and at the request of
the Commissioners, several British officers were detailed to accompany them to the council.   Colonel Butler, the British In
dian Superintendent of that station,† had already departed with
a large number of the Six Nations residing at the Buffalo Creek,
to attend with Captain Brant the preliminary council at Miami.

Advices from Colonel M'Kee, at Detroit, having communicated the fact that all was ready on the part of the Indians, and
urged them forthwith to repair to Sandusky and meet them, the
Commissioners took their departure from Niagara on the 26th
of June.   Reports had been bruited about, however, that, should
the council break up without making peace, it was the determination of the hostile Indians to fall upon the Commissioners and
sacrifice them.   In consequence of this intimation they were furnished with a letter from the Governor, expressed in the strongest
terms, enjoining the officers in the Indian Department at the west
to take care that they should be neither injured nor insulted by
the savages; adding, " that an injury to them would greatly af-

---

* Private Journal of General Lincoln—Massachusetts Historical Collections.
This incident has been preserved in the text by the author, as a curiosity; it being
the first *gala* of a representative of royalty in the western woods.

† The British commander at Wyoming.

" fect him, the Commander-in-chief, the British nation, and even " the King himself."*

The Commissioners were detained by contrary winds at Fort Erie, at which point they were to embark, until the 5th of July. Here another serious interruption to their progress took place. The extreme jealousy of the Indians naturally prompted them to magnify every thing bearing a hostile appearance ; and they had been watching with much suspicion, during the whole season, the movements of General Wayne, who was then occcupying the country about Fort Washington. It was understood that he was not to advance beyond that position pending the negotiations. But the Indians were nevertheless suspicious lest he should avail himself of the absence of their chiefs and warriors at the council, and fall upon their towns. Governor Simcoe had called the attention of the Commissioners to this subject, and they, in turn, had urged the consideration, through the Secretary of War, upon General Wayne. But, notwithstanding every precaution that could be adopted, the Indians at the preliminary council became alarmed ; and, greatly to the surprise of the Commissioners, while waiting to embark at Fort Erie, on the 5th of July a vessel arrived from Miami, having on board Captain Brant, Colonel Butler, and a deputation of about fifty Indians from the north-western tribes, attending the council, with instructions to have a conference with the American Commissioners in the presence of Governor Simcoe. The object of their visit was twofold ; first, they were desirous of being enabled " to possess their minds in peace " in regard to the movements of General Wayne with the army ; secondly, they were desirous of obtaining information whether the Commissioners were empowered to establish a new boundary line, or rather to stipulate that the American settlers should fall back upon the Ohio—since the great majority of the Indians had uniformly disclaimed the boundary specified in the treaty of Fort Harmar. An immediate interview between the deputation and the Commissioners was arranged, at the request of the former. at which a Shawanese chief, called Cat's-Eyes, addressed them as follows :—

" BROTHERS : We are sent by the nations of Indians assembled at the Rapids of Miami, to meet the Commissioners of the

* General Lincoln's Journal.

United States. We are glad to see you here. It is the will of the great chiefs of those nations that our Father, the Governor of this province, should be present, and hear what we have to say to you, and what you have to say to us.

"BROTHERS: Do not make yourselves uneasy that we did not meet you at the time you proposed, at Sandusky. The reasons thereof will be mentioned at another time."

Four strings of black and white wampum.

To which the Commissioners replied :—

"BROTHERS: The Commissioners are glad to see you. We will confer with you in presence of your Father, the Governor of this province, at any time and place which shall be convenient to you and him."   *Returned the four strings.*

The parties then separated ; but the Indian deputation, after a brief consultation, requested another interview, and proposed that the meeting with Governor Simcoe should be at his own house at Niagara. To this arrangement the Commissioners assented, and agreed to return thither on the following day Accordingly, on the 7th of July, a conference was held at the council-house at Niagara. The Governor and the Indians having arrived at the council-chamber a few minutes in advance of the Commissioners, Captain Brant addressed the former thus :—

"BROTHER: It being agreed at the Rapids that we should come and meet the Commissioners in our Father's presence, we return our thanks to the Great Spirit for seeing your Excellency well this day. Our intention and business is peaceable, and our inclination is to do what is right and just. We are all of one mind, and wished your Excellency to be present."

A belt of wampum

His Excellency replied :—

"BROTHERS: I am happy to see you so well. The Commissioners have expressed a wish to meet you in my presence, and I shall be happy to hear what they have to say."

Belt returned.

The Commissioners having arrived, the conference commenced, in the presence not only of the Governor, but also of a large number of the civil and military officers of that station. The proceedings were opened on the part of the Western deputation by Captain Brant, who rose with a belt and string of wampum, and said :—

"BROTHERS : We have met to-day our brothers, the Bostonians and English. We are glad to have the meeting, and think it by the appointment of the Great Spirit.

"BROTHERS OF THE UNITED STATES : We told you the other day, at Fort Erie, that at another time we would inform you why we had not assembled at the time and place appointed for holding the treaty with you. Now we inform you, that it is because there is so much the appearance of war in that quarter.

"BROTHERS : We have given the reason for our not meeting you, and now request an explanation of these warlike appearances.

"BROTHERS : The people you see here are sent to represent the Indian nations who own the lands north of the Ohio as their common property, and who are all of one mind—one heart.

"BROTHERS : We have come to speak to you for two reasons: one, because your warriors, being in our neighborhood, have prevented our meeting at the appointed place : the other, to know if you are properly authorized to run and establish a new boundary line between the lands of the United States and the lands of the Indian nations. We are still desirous of meeting you at the appointed place.

"BROTHERS : We wish you to deliberate well on this business. We have spoken our sentiments in sincerity—considering ourselves in the presence of the Great Spirit, from whom, in times of danger, we expect assistance." [*With this speech a belt of twelve rows, and thirty strings of wampum, in five bunches, were presented.*]

The Commissioners answered :—

"BROTHERS : We have attended to what you have said. We will take it into our serious consideration, and give you an answer to-morrow. We will inform you when we are ready."

Captain Brant rejoined :—

"BROTHERS : We thank you for what you have said. You say that you will answer our speech to-morrow. We now cover up the council-fire."

On the next day the Commissioners replied at length, in the Indian form of speech. In regard to the warlike indications of which the deputation complained, the Commissioners assured them that they might " possess their minds in peace ;" and stated to them the orders that had been transmitted to General Wayne, and the other precautionary measures adopted by the Great Chief, General Washington, to prevent any act of hostility during the negotiations. On the subject of the second query of the Indians, the Commissioners replied explicitly, that they had authority to run and establish a new boundary. This question, they were aware, was to be the great subject of discussion at the council, and they hoped that the result would be satisfactory to both parties. But, in saying this, they reminded the Indians, that in almost all disputes and quarrels there was wrong upon both sides, and consequently that in the approaching council both parties must be prepared to make some concessions. The Commissioners requested information as to the names of the nations, and the number of the chiefs as sembled at the Rapids of the Miami ; and in conclusion re-as sured the chiefs of the groundlessness of their apprehensions respecting the movements of General Wayne, and explained to them that they might place themselves perfectly at rest upon this point ; promising, moreover, immediately to send a messen ger on horseback " to the Great Chief of the United States, to " desire him to renew and strongly repeat his orders to his " head-warrior, not only to abstain from all hostilities against " the Indians, but to remain quiet at his posts until the event of " the treaty should be known." Having returned the Belt,

Cat's-Eyes, the Shawanese leader, replied :—

" BROTHERS, THE BOSTONIANS, ATTEND ! We have heard your words. Our fathers, the English people, have also heard them. We thank God that you have been preserved in peace, and that we bring our pipes together. The people of all the different nations here salute you. They rejoice to hear your words. It gives us great satisfaction that our fathers, the English, have also heard them. We shall for the present take up our pipes and retire to our encampments, where we shall deliberately consider your speech, and return you an answer tomorrow."

The conference was re-opened on the 9th, when Captain Brant arose, with the belt and strings in his hands which had been presented by the Commissioners on the preceding day, and addressing himself to the English and Americans, said :—

"BROTHERS : We are glad the Great Spirit has preserved us in peace to meet together this day.

"BROTHERS OF THE UNITED STATES : Yesterday you made an answer to the message delivered by us, from the great council at the Miami, in the two particulars we had stated to you.

"BROTHERS : You may depend on it that we fully understand your speech. We shall take with us your belt and strings, and repeat it to the chiefs at the great council at Miami."

[Laying down the belt and strings, the Captain took up a white belt, and proceeded :]

"BROTHERS : We have something farther to say, though not much. We are small, compared with our great chiefs at Miami : but, though small, we have something to say. We think, brothers, from your speech, that there is a prospect of our coming together. We, who are the nations at the westward, are of one mind : and if we agree with you, as there is a prospect that we shall, it will be binding and lasting.

"BROTHERS : Our prospects are the fairer, because all our minds are one. You have not spoken to us before unitedly. Formerly, because you did not speak to us unitedly, what was done was not binding. Now you have an opportunity to speak to us together ; and we now take you by the hand to lead you to the place appointed for the meeting.

"BROTHERS : One thing more we have to say. Yesterday you expressed a wish to be informed of the names of the nations and number of chiefs assembled at the Miami. But as they were daily coming in, we cannot give you exact information. You will see for yourselves in a few days. When we left it, the following nations were there, viz: Five Nations, Wyandots, Shawanese, Delawares, Munsees, Miamies, Ottawas, Chippewas, Pottawattamies, Mingoes, Cherokees, Nantikokes. The principal men of all these nations were there."

A white belt of seven rows.

The Commissioners then replied :—

"BROTHERS : Our ears have been open to your speech. It is agreeable to us. We are ready to proceed with you to Sandusky, where, under the direction of the Great Spirit, we hope that we shall soon establish a peace on terms equally interesting and agreeable to all parties."

While these deliberations were in progress, a deputation from the Seven Nations of Canada arrived at Niagara, to the number of two hundred and eighty. The proceedings were terminated with a confident expectation on all hands that the result of the mission would be a pacific arrangement. With the public dispatches transmitted to the Secretary of War from this place, however, General Lincoln addressed a private letter to that officer, advising him that if the reports in circulation were in any degree true, General Wayne must have violated the clearest principles of a *truce*, and expressing great solicitude for the result—less, however, on account of the personal safety of the Commissioners, whose lives would be thereby jeoparded, than for the apprehensions felt for the honor of the country. Captain Brant had given information as to the movements of Wayne, of the certainty of which there could be but little doubt ; and those movements caused the Commissioners as much uneasiness as they did the Indians ; being moreover viewed by the British officers at Niagara as unfair and unwarrantable.

Captain Brant and the Indian deputation proceeded on their return to Miami, in advance of the Commissioners, the latter embarking from Fort Erie on the 14th. On the 21st they arriv ed at the mouth of the Detroit river, where they were obliged to land—the British authorities at Detroit forbidding their approach farther toward the place of meeting. They were, however, hos- pitably entertained at the landing-place by Captain Elliot, Colo- nel M'Kee's assistant in the Indian Department. The latter officer was in attendance upon the council at the Rapids, to whom the Commissioners lost no time in addressing a note, ap- prising him of their arrival, and of their design to remain there until the Indians should be ready to remove the council to San- dusky. They also requested the good offices of Colonel M' Kee in expediting the proceedings of the Indians. This dis- patch was borne by Captain Elliot himself, who returned on the 29th, bringing an answer from the Colonel, and attended by a deputation of upward of twenty Indians from the different na- tions in council. An audience of these Indians was had on the day following, at which a Wyandot Chief, whose name in English was *Carry-one-about*, opened their business with the following unexpected address :—

"BROTHERS, LISTEN ! We are glad to see you here in peace, and thank the Great Spirit that has preserved us to meet again.

"BROTHERS : We were sent to speak with you some time ago at Niagara. Some chiefs are now here who were then present.

"BROTHERS : We did not explain ourselves to each other, and we did not rightly understand each other.

"BROTHERS : We desire that we may rightly understand each other. We have thought it best that what we had to say should be put into writing, and here is the meaning of our hearts.

Saying which, the Wyandot chief put a paper into the hands of the Commissioners, which read as follows :—

"To THE COMMISSIONERS OF THE UNITED STATES.

"BROTHERS : The Deputies we sent you did not fully explain our meaning. We have therefore sent others to meet you once more, that you may fully understand the great question we have to ask you, and to which we expect an explicit answer in writing.

"BROTHERS : You are sent here by the United States in order to make peace with us, the Confederate Indians.

"BROTHERS : You know very well that the boundary-line, which was run by the white people and us, at the Treaty of Fort Stanwix, was the river Ohio.

"BROTHERS : If you seriously design to make a firm and lasting peace, you will immediately remove all your people from our side of that river.

"BROTHERS : We therefore ask you, Are you fully authorised by the United States to continue and fix firmly on the Ohio river as the boundary-line between your people and ours ?

"Done in General Council, at the foot of the Miami Rapids, 27th July, 1793. In behalf of ourselves and the whole Confederacy, and agreed to in full council."

This missive was signed by the Wyandots, Delawares, Shawanese, Miamis, Mingoes, Pottawattamies, Ottawas, Connoys, Chippewas, and Munsees; but not by the Six Nations. The Commissioners replied to them at great length in the afternoon. They began, after the Indian custom, by repeating their speech, and then gave a succinct statement of the conferences at Niagara, and the perfect understanding then had, that some concessicns would be necessary on both sides, and of which they were to speak face to face. They had already been detained sixty days beyond the time appointed for the meeting, and were desirous of proceeding to business in council without farther delay. The Commissioners next recited briefly the history of all the treaties that had been formed with the north-western Indians, from the treaty of Fort Stanwix, held before the Revolution, to that which was commenced at the falls of the Muskingum, by General St. Clair, and completed at Fort Harmar. At this treaty the Six Nations renewed their treaty of Fort Stanwix, of 1784, and the Wyandots and Delawares renewed and confirmed the treaty of Fort M'Intosh. There were also parties to this treaty from the Ottawas, Chippewas, Pottawattamies and Sacs. Under these treaties the United States had acquired the territory, now claimed by the Indians, north of the Ohio ,and on the faith of these, settlements had been formed, that could not now be removed ; and hence the Commissioners replied explicitly to the first question, that the Ohio could not be designated as the boundary. After attempting to explain the impossibility of uprooting the settlements beyond the Ohio, and the great expenses incurred by the people in forming them, they spoke again of the promised " mutual concessions," and proposed, as the basis of negotiation, that the Indians should relinquish all the lands ceded by the treaty of Fort Harmar, and also a small tract of land at the Rapids of the Ohio, claimed by General Clark ; in return for which they proposed to give the Indians " such a large sum in money or goods as was never " given at one time for any quantity of Indian lands since the " white people set their foot on this inland." They likewise proposed a large annuity in addition to the amount to be paid in hand. Originally, under the treaty of peace with England, the American Commissioners had claimed the right to the soil of all the lands south of the great lakes ; but this claim, the Commissioners said they thought, was wrong ; and as a farther concession, if the lands already specified were relinquished by the Indians, the United States would relinquish all but the right of pre-emption to the vast tracts that remained. In conclusion, the Commissioners said :—

" BROTHERS : We have now opened our hearts to you. We are happy in having an opportunity of doing it, though we should have been more happy to have done it in full council of your nations. We expect soon to have this satisfaction, and that your next deputation will take us by the hand, and lead us to the treaty. When we meet and converse with each other freely, we may more easily remove any difficulties which may come in the way."

A white belt with thirteen stripes of black wampum.

The speech having been interpreted fully to the deputation, the council was adjourned until the next day, when, having re-assembled, the Wyandot chief rose, and replied as follows :—

"BROTHERS : We are all brothers you see here now. Brothers, it is now three years since you have desired to speak with us. We heard you yesterday, and understand well, perfectly well. We have a few words to say to you.

"BROTHERS : You mentioned the treaties of Fort Stanwix, Beaver Creek, and other places. Those treaties were not complete. There were but few chiefs who treated with you. You have not bought our lands ; they belong to us. You tried to draw off some of us.

"BROTHERS : Many years ago we all know that the Ohio was made the boundary ; it was settled by Sir William Johnson. This side is ours ; we look upon it as our property.

"BROTHERS : You mention General Washington. He and you know you have houses and people on our lands. You say you cannot move them off ; and we cannot give up our lands.

"BROTHERS : We are sorry that we cannot come to an agreement. The line has been fixed long ago.

BROTHERS : We do not say much. There has been much mischief on both sides. We came here upon peace, and thought you did the same. We wish you to remain here for an answer from us. We have your speech in our breasts, and shall consult our head warriors."

From the 1st to the 14th of August the Commissioners were detained at the place of their first landing, in the daily expectation of receiving an invitation to join the council at the Rapids They had information from thence several times, and on the 8th were informed that all the nations were disposed for peace, excepting the Shawanese, Wyandots, Miamies, and Delawares. The Six Nations, and the Seven Nations of Canada, exerted themselves strongly to bring about a pacification. It was un-

derstood, however, that the debates had been long and animated.   Captain Brant and the Corn-planter were unwearied in
their efforts to accomplish this desirable object, and both spoke
much in council.   The discussions being thus protracted, the
former availed himself of the time to endeavor to enlist the direct interposition of Governor Simcoe to bring the Indians into
a more pacific temper.   For that purpose the Captain dispatched messengers to York, at which place* the Upper Canadian
Government was about being established, with letters to the
Governor, informing him of the intractable disposition of the
Indians, and soliciting his influence to induce them to compromise the boundary question.   Governor Simcoe wrote back on
the 8th of August, declining any interference.   His Excellency
declared in this letter, that, as his correspondent (Brant) well
knew, he had always, both in private conversation and in public messages, endeavored to impress a disposition and temper
upon the Indians, that might lead to the blessing of peace.
Still, he thought the Indians were the best judges as to the
terms upon which a treaty of peace should be negotiated; and
at their request he had directed the Indian Agents to attend
their councils, and explain to them any circumstances which
they might not clearly understand.   There was another circumstance which Governor Simcoe thought would render it
improper for him to interfere, which will be best understood by
quoting his own words from the letter :—" Since the Govern-
" ment of the United States have shown a disinclination to con-
" cur with the Indian nations in requesting of his Majesty per-
" mission for me to attend at Sandusky as mediator, it would be
" highly improper and unseasonable in me to give any opinion
" relative to the proposed boundaries, with which I am not suffi-
" ciently acquainted, and which question I have studiously
" avoided entering into, as I am well aware of the jealousies en-
" tertained by some of the subjects of the United States, of the
" interference of the British Government, which has a natural
" and decided interest in the welfare of the Indian nations, and
" in the establishment of peace and permanent tranquility.   In
" this situation I am sure you will excuse me from giving to
" you any advice, which, from my absence from the spot, cannot

* Now Toronto, the capital of Upper Canada.

"possibly arise from that perfect view and knowledge which so "important a subject necessarily demands."*

This letter contains the only authority extant for the fact that Governor Simcoe himself had been proposed as the mediator, and rejected, and he may have been piqued thereat. Still, although he cautiously abstained from the remotest interference, there was nothing in this communication calculated to defeat a pacific determination of the council. The Commissioners were yet anxiously awaiting the result at the mouth of the Detroit River. On the 11th of August they were informed that the debates were still running high in council ; that the chiefs of the Six Nations had spoken twice, and were about to speak a third time. Indeed, so desirous were they now of effecting a pacific arrangement, that Thayendanegea was determined to transcend the ordinary rules of an Indian council, and speak a fourth time, should it become necessary.† It was added, that nearly half the four tribes, who were persisting for war, had been won over ; and hence, when the messengers left the council, they even anticipated that runners with pacific news would overtake them. Having waited, however, until the 14th, and receiving no farther news, the Commissioners proposed to repair to the council in person—but were prevented by the British authorities, who would not suffer them to move in that direction, unless by special invitation from the council. Impatient of longer delay, their next measure was to send a speech to the council, with a request to Captain Brant to bring it before them, urging upon them the necessity of a speedy determination of the question of peace or war, one way or the other. The conclusion of this address was thus :—

"BROTHERS : We have waited fourteen days, and no answer has arrived.

"BROTHERS : It is time to bring the business to a conclusion.

---

* From the original letter among the Brant papers.

† What a pity that at such an Indian Congress, where the great warriors and orators of so many nations were assembled to discuss subjects at once the most exciting and of the deepest moment to them, a bench of stenographers could not have been present! What bursts of thrilling eloquence—the unsophisticated language of nature—gathering all its metaphors fresh and glowing from her own rich storehouse—the flowers, the forests, and the floods—the sun, the stars, and the blue sky—the winds, the earthquake, and the storm—must there have been poured forth but to die away upon the ears that heard them !

The summer has almost passed away, and we do not yet even know whether we are to have a treaty.

" BROTHERS : You know that we came to treat with you of peace. We again tell you, that we earnestly desire to make peace ; and in the terms of peace we are disposed to do you ample justice. But if no treaty is to be held, if peace is not to be obtained, we desire immediately to know it, that we may go home."

But all the anticipations of a pacific adjustment of the difficulties proved fallacious. Two days after this address had been dispatched to the care of Captain Brant and the Corn-planter, the Commissioners received a long address from the council, in writing, in answer to their own speech of July 31st, which put an end to the negotiation. It was addressed,

" TO THE COMMISSIONERS OF THE UNITED STATES.

" BROTHERS : We have received your speech of the 31st of last month, and it has been interpreted to all the different nations. We have been long in sending you an answer, because of the great importance of the subject. But we now answer it fully, having given it all the consideration in our power."

In their address the council entered upon an extended review of the negotiations heretofore referred to, and the circumstances under which the treaties of Fort M'Intosh and Fort Harmar were made. They contended that these treaties had not been properly obtained, and were not binding upon the Indians, inasmuch as but few of their chiefs and warriors had been present at the councils, and those few were not empowered to cede away any of their lands. Of this fact they said they had apprised General St. Clair before the treaties were made, and admonished him not to proceed. But he persisted in holding councils in which their nations were not consulted, and in receiving cessions of an immense country, in which the few who, under constraint, had signed the treaty, were no more interested than as a mere branch of the General Confederacy, and had no authority to make any grant whatever. In reply to the remarks of the Commissioners respecting the impracticability of breaking up the settlements on the disputed territory, and their offers of large sums of money for a confirmation of the grant under the treaty of Fort Harmar, the speech of the Council was ingenious and forcible. Indeed, the residue of this document is worth transcribing entire :—

" BROTHERS : Money to us is of no value, and to most of us unknown ; and as no consideration whatever can induce us to sell our lands, on which we get ʀ istenance for our women and children, we hope we may be allowed to point out a mode by which your settlers may be easily removed, and peace thereby obtained.

" BROTHERS : We know that these settlers are poor, or they never would have ventured to live in a country which has been in continual trouble ever since they crossed the Ohio. Divide, therefore, this large sum of money which you have offered to us among these people ; give to each also a proportion of what you say you would give us annually, over and above this large sum of money ; and we are persuaded they would most readily accept of it in lieu of the lands you sold to them. If you add, also, the great sums you must expend in raising and paying armies with a view to force us to yield you our country, you will certainly have more than sufficient for the purposes of repaying these settlers for all their labor and improvements.

" BROTHERS : You have talked to us about concessions. It appears strange that you expect any from us, who have only been defending our just rights against your invasions. We want peace. Restore to us our country, and we shall be enemies no longer.

" BROTHERS : You make one concession to us by offering to us your money, and another by having agreed to do us justice, after having long and injuriously withheld it ; we mean, in the acknowledgment you have now made that the King of England never did, nor ever had a right to give you our country by the treaty of peace. And you want to make this act of common justice a great part of your concession, and seem to expect, that because you have at last acknowledged our independence, we should for such a favor surrender to you our country.

" BROTHERS : You have also talked a great deal about preemption, and your exclusive right to purchase the Indian lands, as ceded to you by the King at the treaty of peace.

" BROTHERS : We never made any agreement with the King, nor with any other nation, that we would give to either the exclusive right to purchase our lands ; and we declare to you, that we consider ourselves free to make any bargain or cession of lands whenever and to whomsoever we please. If the white people, as you say, made a treaty that none of them but the King should purchase of us, and he has given that right to the United States, it is an affair which concerns you and him, and not us. We have never parted with such a power.

" BROTHERS : At our general council held at the Glaize last Fall, we agreed to meet Commissioners from the United States, for the purpose of restoring peace, provided they consented to acknowledge and confirm our boundary line to be the Ohio ; and we determined not to meet you until you gave us satisfaction on that point. That is the reason we have never met.

" BROTHERS : We desire you to consider that our only demand is the peaceable possession of a small part of our once great country. Look back and view the lands from whence we have been driven to this spot. We can retreat no farther, because the country behind hardly affords food for its present inhabitants ; and we have therefore resolved to leave our bones in this small space, to which we are now consigned.

" BROTHERS : We shall be persuaded that you mean to do us justice, if you agree that the Ohio shall remain the boundary line between us. If you will not consent thereto, our meeting will be altogether unnecessary. This is the great point, which we hoped would have been explained before you left your houses ; as our message last Autumn was principally directed to obtain that information.

" Done in General Council at the foot of the Miami Rapids, on the 13th day of August, 1793."

This address was signed by the Wyandots, the Seven Nations of Canada, the Delawares, Shawanese, Miamis, Ottawas, Chippeways, Senecas (of the Glaize), Pottawattamies, Connoys, Munsees, Nantikokes, Mohegans, Missisaguas, Creeks, and Cherokees—the name of each nation being written, and its emblem or escutcheon rudely pictured opposite the name.* The

---

* Thus, according to the original communication in the author's possession :—

Wyandots,	A Bear.	Senecas of the Glaize,	A Turtle.
Seven Nations of Canada,	A Turtle.	Pottawattamies,	A Fish.
Delawares,	A Turtle.	Connoys,	A Turkey.
Shawanese,		Munsees,	
Miamis,	A Turtle.	Nantikokes,	A Turtle.
Ottawas,	A Fish.	Mohegans,	{ A Turtle.
Chippeways,	A Crane.		{ A Turkey.

Six Nations did not sign it.   Indeed, it is believed that Captain
Brant and the Six Nations " *held fast together* " in their efforts
to make peace, to the last ; and that the character of the final
answer of the council was not communicated to them previous
to its being sent off.   On the contrary, they were told that it was
a proposition to meet the Commissioners on the Miami instead
of Sandusky, about five miles below their then place of sitting ;
and so well assured were they of the fact, that they proposed
removing thither the day after the runners were dispatched from
the council-fire.

Nothing could be more explicit than this ultimatum of the
Indians.   Their *sine qua non* was the Ohio for the boundary.
To this proposition the Commissioners could never assent, and
they accordingly wrote to the chiefs and warriors of the council
at the Rapids, that "the negotiation was at an end."   So imperfect are the records of Indian history, preserved, as they are, for the
most part, only in the tablets of the brain, the memory being aided
by belts and other emblems—that it is a difficult matter to determine the precise merits of the controversy sought to be terminated
at this council.   Being the weaker party, belonging to a doomed
race, the law of the strongest was of course left to decide it in
the end, and the Indians were driven beyond the Mississippi.
But an impartial survey of the case, at the distance of only forty
years, presents strong reasons for believing that the Indians
were the party aggrieved.   Certainly, it would form an exception in the history of their dealings with the white man, if they
were not ; while it is very evident that they themselves solemnly believed they were the injured party.   And, thus believing,
nothing could have been more patriotic than the attitude assumed in their address, or more noble than the declarations and
sentiments it contained.

CHAPTER XII.

Suspected duplicity of the British authorities—Conduct of Simon Girty—Disclosures upon the subject by Captain Brant—Council at Buffalo, and Indian report of the doings of the Great Congress—Speech of Captain Brant respecting the Miami council—Mission of General Chapin to Philadelphia, with the speech—Answer unsatisfactory to the Indians—Red Jacket—Indian council—Speech of Captain Brant in reply to the answer of the United States—Troubles thickening between the United States and Great Britain—Inflammatory speech of Lord Dorchester—Question of its authenticity settled—Conduct of Governor Simcoe—Indignation of President Washington—His letter to Mr. Jay—Speech of Captain Brant against holding a council at Venango—The design frustrated—Affairs farther in the West—Singular message from the distant Indians under the Spanish and French influence—Their speech—Operations of General Wayne—Encroachments of Pennsylvania upon the Indian lands—Indian council upon the subject—Address to General Washington—Important letter of Brant to Colonel Smith—Pennsylvania relinquishes Presque Isle—Defeat of Major M'Mahon near Fort Recovery—Indians repulsed in their attack upon the fort—Letter to Brant giving an account of the battle—Advance of Wayne to the Au Glaize and Miamis of the Lakes—Little Turtle apprised of his movements and strength by a deserter—The Chief determines to give battle—Wayne makes one more effort for peace—Failure of the attempt—Advance of Wayne to the Rapids—Position of the Indians—Battle and defeat of the Indians—Little Turtle opposed to the hazard of a battle—Opposed by Blue-Jacket and overruled—Tart correspondence between Wayne and Major Campbell—Destruction of Indian property by fire, and burning of Colonel M'Kee's establishment—Disappointment of the Indians that Major Campbell did not assist them—Letter of Governor Simcoe to Brant—Aggression at Sodus Bay—Simcoe and Brant repair to the West—Interfere to prevent a peace—Indian council—The hostiles negotiate with Wayne—Simcoe's address to the Wyandots—Division in their counsels—Brant retires displeased—Letter of apology from the Chiefs—The distant Indians become weary of the war.

THE return of the Commissioners to the eastern extremity of Lake Erie was immediate ; from whence both the government of the United States and General Wayne were apprised of the failure of the negotiation, for which such long and anxious preparation had been made. It has been charged that, notwithstanding the apparent friendship of Governor Simcoe and his little court at Niagara, and their seeming desire of peace, this unpropitious result was measurably, if not entirely, produced by the influence of the British officers in attendance upon the Indian councils—Colonel M'Kee, Captain Elliot, and the notorious Simon Girty. The Rev. Mr. Heckewelder, at the request of General Knox, accompanied the Commissioners, and was present at the delivery of the last message from the council, refusing an interview, which, as delivered, both in matter and manner was exceedingly insolent. Elliot and Girty were both present when this message was delivered, the latter of whom supported his insolence by a quill, or long feather run through the cartilage of his nose cross-wise. He was the interpreter of the message; and Mr. Heckewelder states that he officiously added a sentence not transmitted from the council. Two Delaware chiefs, visiting the Commissioners from the council, while at Detroit River, on being questioned by Mr. Heckewelder why the Commissioners were not allowed to proceed to their quarters at the Rapids, replied:—"All we can say is, that we wish for "peace; but we cannot speak farther, our mouths being stopped "up when we left the council!" In other words, they had been forbidden to disclose any of its secrets.*

These circumstances, from the pen of such a witness, furnish strong presumptive testimony of duplicity on the part of the Canadian administration. But there is yet other evidence of the fact, so strong as to be indisputable. It is that of Captain Brant himself, who, of all others, participated most largely in the deliberations of those councils. In one of the speeches delivered by him in the course of his land difficulties with the Canadian government, some time subsequent to the war, the following passage occurs:—"For several years" (after the peace of 1783,) "we were engaged in getting a confederacy formed,† and the "unanimity occasioned by these endeavors among our western "brethren, enabled them to defeat two American armies. The "war continued without our brothers, the English, giving any "assistance, excepting a little ammunition; and they seeming "to desire that a peace might be concluded, we tried to bring it "about at a time that the United States desired it very much, so "that they sent Commissioners from among their first people, to "endeavor to make peace with the hostile Indians. We assem- "bled also for that purpose at the Miami River in the Summer "of 1793, intending to act as mediators in bringing about an "honorable peace; and if that could not be obtained, we re- "solved to join with our western brethren in trying the fortune "of war. But to our surprise, when on the point of entering "upon a treaty with the Commissioners, we found that it was "opposed by those acting under the British government, and "hopes of farther assistance were given to our western brethren,

---

* Heckewelder's Narrative of the Moravian Missions.

† In another portion of the same speech, Captain Brant stated that General Haldimand exhorted them to the formation of that union with the different nations.

" to encourage them to insist on the Ohio as a boundary between
" them and the United States."[*]

The deputation from the Six Nations and the Seven Nations
of Canada, (the Caughnawagas,) having returned from the Miami, a council was convened at the village of the Onondagas residing at Buffalo Creek, to hear their report—intended not only
for their own people, but for the information of the British and
American Superintendents, Colonel Butler and General Chapin.
The council-fire was kindled on the 8th of October.   The procedure, it will be seen, was characteristic and striking.   The
belts, pictures, and emblems used by the several nations represented in the Grand Council at the Miami Rapids, were forwarded to the Six Nations by the hands of their deputies, and
after the council had been regularly opened, these were produced, and the speeches with which their delivery had been accompanied, were repeated, in the form of a report, with incidental
explanations.   By this process, though tedious, the proceedings
of the Grand Congress were probably reported to the Buffalo
council, with as much accuracy as though they had been written out in form by a committee of the more civilized " Congress
of the Thirteen Fires."

All things being ready, the proceedings were commenced
by Clear-Sky, a chief of the Onondagas, who spoke as follows :—

" BROTHERS : We thank the Great Spirit for our happy meeting, that he has preserved us through all difficulties, dangers,
and sickness, and given us an opportunity of meeting together
at this place."

The ceremony of condolence for the loss of friends since the
last council, having been regularly performed and reciprocated
by all the tribes present, and also by the Superintendents, the
business of the council was resumed by the Farmer's Brother,
who delivered the speech of the Shawanese, Delawares, and
Twithuays, as follows :—

" BROTHERS : Colonel Butler and General Chapin, we wish
you to attend the Shawanese and other nations of Indians.   We
thank the Six Nations for their attention.   We were glad to see

---

* Quoted from the manuscript copy of the speech, contained among the Brant papers, in the hand-writing of the Chief himself.

them at the Great Council-fire which had been kindled some time at the Rapids of the Miami.*

" BROTHERS : You are acquainted with the friendship that once subsisted between you and our fathers, and the reason that the present fire is kindled, is to renew that friendship.

" BROTHERS : We mentioned this to you last Fall at a council at the Glaize, and we now repeat it to put you in mind of that friendship which once subsisted between you and our wise forefathers.

[A belt of white wampum was here presented, made in a circular form, representing their place of meeting, as in the centre, and crossed by four stripes of black wampum, representing all their confederates, East, West, North, and South.]

" BROTHERS : The ancient confederacy which subsisted between us and the Five Nations,† was, that if any of the Five Nations were in distress, we would take them to us ; we now see that you are in distress ; that you are surrounded by water, and have not any land to stand upon ; that a large white beast stands with open mouth on the other side, ready to destroy you. We have dry land for you to stand on ; and we now take you by the hand, and invite you to come, and bring your beds, and sit down with us." [*Belt of seven rows of black and white wampum.*]

The warriors here joined with the Chiefs, and repeated the ancient agreement, recommended a union of all the different nations, and asked them to follow what was recommended by the chiefs. Puck-on-che-luh, head warrior of the Delawares,‡ then spoke :—

" BROTHERS : I call you my uncles, and all the other Indians my grand-children. Them I have already united and bound together, and I now bind you all together with this string." [*A large bunch of black wampum.*]

---

* In order to understand the report, the reader must bear in mind that the speech of each belt is delivered by the bearer of it, as though he were in fact a delegate from the nation whose report he is making.

† In answer to a question by the Seven Nations of Canada, how long this confederacy had existed between the Shawanese, &c. the reply was, " *three lives.*"

‡ After the defeat of St. Clair, on which occasion the Delawares fought bravely, the Mohawks, who had formerly declared the Delawares to be women, or, in other words, degraded them from the rank of warriors, reversed the sentence of disgrace, and wiped out the stigma, by formally declaring the Delawares no longer *women*, but MEN.

The Sachems of the Delawares then spoke :—

"BROTHERS : You have heard the speech of the chief warriors. We join with them, and are glad to hear they have bound all their grand-children together, and that they have spoken with great respect to their uncles, and recommended to them to be of one mind." [*A large bunch of black wampum.*]

The Wyandots then spoke :—

"BROTHERS: You came to us one hundred and fifty years ago, when we lived above Detroit, with a speech from the Six Nations, assembled at their council-fire at Onondaga Hill, and recommended to us to be friends, and advised us not to listen to any bad report, or any thing that would disturb our minds.

" BROTHERS : Listen to a few words more we have to say to you. We hear the Virginians are near us : we shall not go to meet them ; but if they should come among us, we do not know what will be the consequence."

[The Wyandots spoke with a very large belt of wampum, with three pictures upon it, one in the middle, and one at each end, representing the Americans at one end, the Six Nations in the middle, and themselves at the other end, and expressed their sorrow that the Americans were gone before they had had an opportunity of speaking to them.]

The Chippewas and twenty-six other nations, their confederates, then spoke :—

" BROTHERS : We are sorry that the business for which the council-fire at the Rapids of the Miami was kindled has not been completed as we could wish. We were desired by the different nations which we represent, to attend the council, and use our efforts to bring about a general peace, and unite all nations."

The Chippewas, Ottawas, and Pottawattamies, deputies from twenty-seven nations, inhabiting along the lakes, and above Michilimackinack, then spoke :—

" BROTHERS : We are sorry that we have attended all Summer at the council-fire, and have not done any business as we expected.

" BROTHERS : We are now united with you, the Six Nations, and ask you to return to your seats, and let the United States know our determination, and return with an answer to us by the middle of winter, and not stop, as some nations may confuse you and make your minds bad."

To which the Six Nations replied :—

"BROTHERS : We thank you, and as soon as we get to our seats we will kindle our council-fire, and call Canadasago, an agent, appointed by the United States to meet with us, and through him will have our determination communicated to Congress."

The Six Nations then, addressing General Chapin and Colonel Butler, said :—

"BROTHERS : We have now made known to you our proceedings at the late proposed treaty at the Rapids of the Miami, and have informed you of the proposed line between the Indians and the United States, which if accepted, we shall assist the white people to make peace."

Captain Brant and the Mohawks were not present at the council on the 8th, a circumstance regretted by the deputation in making their report. The Farmer's Brother remarked that Captain Brant would be able to give fuller explanations than they had done of the proceedings at Miami, and the determination at which the nations there assembled had arrived. The Mohawk having arrived on the 9th, the council-fire was again raked open, when Captain Brant thus addressed Colonel Butler the British, and General Chapin the American Superintendant :—

"BROTHERS : You, the King, our father, and you, our brother, the United States, attend to what we have to say. We will now explain to you the material point upon which we have requested your attendance at this council, and which has not been fully explained. We wish to act openly, that the world may judge of our proceedings.

"BROTHERS : It is unnecessary to repeat what passed at the great council at the Miami Rapids, as we know that you are already acquainted therewith. We shall therefore point out the cause of our parting from the meeting in the manner we did.

"BROTHERS : When the first deputation from the confederate Indians met the Commissioners of the United States at Niagara, every thing seemed to promise a friendly termination of the treaty ; but before their return to the council-fire at the Rapids of the Miami, messengers from the Creek nation arrived there, and brought authentic information of the white people having encroached upon that part of the confederacy.

" This intelligence at once gave a change to the face of our proceedings, and, probably, was the sole cause of the abrupt termination of the negotiations for peace. Thus you see that claims upon our lands always have been, and still continue to be, the cause of war.

" BROTHERS : About five years ago we agreed upon a line of demarcation with the United States, which you know to be the Muskingum ; and, notwithstanding the various accidents that have since occurred, we will still adhere to that boundary.

" BROTHERS : We think the United States will agree to this line, which will show the sincerity and justice they always profess for the Indians ; should they agree to this, we sincerely hope that peace will still take place, and we think that the weight of our branch of the confederacy will be able to accomplish peace upon the reasonable line we have just mentioned, and we shall be exceeding sorry to find that this proposal should not be generally accepted by the confederacy. If it is rejected, we must be involved in difficulties in our own country

" BROTHERS : We will now proceed to explain the line upon which we hope peace will be made. We know that the lands along the Ohio are claimed by the Indians, but we propose to give up such part of these lands as are actually settled and improved, which settlements are to be circumscribed by a line drawn around them, and no farther claims are to be admitted beyond such line. The remainder of the boundary to be ex plained by General Chapin, for which purpose it is the general wish of the Six Nations that General Chapin, himself, will proceed with the speech to Congress." [*A belt of black and white wampum.*]

Agreeably to this request, General Chapin proceeded to the seat of government, to submit their speech to the President, and make the necessary explanations. The Secretary of War replied on the 24th of December, reiterating the desire of the United States to cultivate relations of friendship with the Indians, evading a decision upon the boundary recommended by Captain Brant, and proposing another Indian Council in the spring, to be held at Venango. But in the event of the Indians, hostile or otherwise, agreeing to meet in such council, they were distinctly told that the army would not in the mean time be restrained from hostile operations, as had been the case the preceding season. Farther to secure the good-will of the Six Nations, however, a supply of warm winter clothing was sent to them, with the letter from the Secretary containing the President's decision, which was delivered, and well received at a council holden at Buffalo Creek on the 7th of Februrary, 1794. This council had been convened expressly to receive the answer to the proposals of Captain Brant ; and the same having been read, it was soon perceived to be less acceptable to the Indians than they had anticipated. Red Jacket, after a long pause, replied to General Chapin :—

"BROTHERS (of the United States :) We have heard the speech that has been delivered to us with great attention, and shall now remove the council-fire to our castle, to take it into private consideration.

Two days afterward, the council was re-opened, when Red Jacket spoke :—

"BROTHERS : We have taken your speech into consideration, and our eldest brother, Captain Brant, is to relate the result of our meeting in private council yesterday."

Captain Brant then spoke as follows, with nine strings of white and black wampum :—

"BROTHERS : I now address to you, General Chapin of the United States, and to you, Major Littlehales* in behalf of the King, and thank the Great Spirit for bringing us again together in council, as what we are a going to relate we wish the world to know.

"BROTHERS : You have both heard the message we delivered to our brothers of the United States, last Fall, relative to a boundary line ; and we expected a positive answer from you, brothers of the United States, whether you would accept of it or not.

"BROTHERS : When we delivered the message to you last Fall for the United States, we had first taken it into serious consideration ; we spoke the language of our hearts, and the Great Spirit knew our minds ; all the Six Nations were of the same opinion, and we are well assured that, had the United

---

* Private Secretary of Governor Simcoe, attending the council in his absence.

States accepted our proposed boundary line, peace would certainly have taken place.

"BROTHERS: The speech you have brought us, has given us great uneasiness; we are greatly at a loss how to act; we expected a direct answer to our proposals of a boundary line; now we are much distressed that you have brought us but half an answer; the kindling a council-fire at a distant place is what we are not prepared to give a reply to.

"BROTHERS: Provided the United States had accepted our proposed boundary line, we should have sent immediately to our Western brethren, who know our sentiments, and we should have attended your council and confirmed it.

"BROTHERS: Make your minds easy; but, in consequence of the importance of your speech, we must have time to deliberate very seriously upon it; we cannot give you an immediate answer; we must have a general council of all the Chiefs; only a few are now present, and we should all be together. The reason of so much counselling at different times has proceeded from so small a number of our sachems and chiefs being assembled, and this has been the principal cause of the present trouble.

"BROTHERS: You, General Chapin, live near us; we have two months and a half to consider of your speech, and by that time we will give you a final answer. We pray the Great Spirit that these difficulties may terminate to the happiness of both parties.

"BROTHERS: You requested an answer as soon as was convenient, but in such very weighty business, it is impossible to give one immediately. With regard to provision, there is plenty in your country; and if we should agree to meet you, you need not be particular about what we shall consume, for we shall not expect any thing but provision.

"BROTHERS: We now conclude, and we pray the Great Spirit to protect you safe home, and we desire you will bear it continually on your minds, that you will soon receive an answer. [*The nine strings of wampum, delivered to General Chapin.*]

Notwithstanding the postponement of a definitive answer, on the part of the Indians, to the proposition for the assembling of another council at Venango, it was the opinion of General

Chapin, at the close of these proceedings, that they would yet accede to it.   Circumstances, however, arose during the intervening period, which materially changed the aspect of the border relations of the United States, and the tone and temper of the Six Nations.   The protracted and sanguinary wars between England and the French Republic had then commenced, as also had the invasions of the rights of neutrals by those powers, so frequent and so aggravated during that furious contest.   In order to cut off the supplies of bread stuffs from France, Great Britain had resorted to the strong and questionable measure of stopping all vessels loaded in whole or in part with corn, flour, or meal, bound to any port in France, and sending them in to the most convenient ports, where their cargoes were to be purchased for his Majesty's service, at a fair value, after making a due allowance for freight, &c.   The British government labored to justify this measure by citations from some modern writers upon national law, but it was nevertheless esteemed a violation of neutral rights, and produced much feeling among the American people, and strong remonstrances from the government. The assumption set up by Great Britain, of the right of impressing seamen, British subjects, from neutral vessels, by the exercise of which it was asserted that many American seamen had been seized, and carried forcibly into foreign service, was now producing farther and still greater irritation.   Added to all which were the incendiary machinations of Citizen Genet to undermine the administration of Washington, alienate from his government the affections of the people, and involve the United States in a war with Great Britain.   Party spirit was already running high, and from the blind zeal with which the anti-federalists had espoused the cause of revolutionary France, as against England, very serious apprehensions were entertained that another war between the latter power and the United States would be the result.

One of the consequences of the apparent probability of such an event, was a manifest change of temper on the part of the British officers in the Canadas, and at the posts yet in British occupancy along the north-western frontier of the United States. That during the whole controversy between the Indians and the United States, from 1786 to the defeat of St. Clair, the former had been countenanced and encouraged by English agents, and repeatedly incited to actual hostilities by the traders, there was no doubt.   Latterly, however, a better state of feeling had been manifested.   Lord Dorchester, previous to a visit to England at the close of the year 1791, had sent a speech to the Indians, of a complexion rather pacific ; and it has been seen, that in the Summer of the preceding year, (1793,) Governor Simcoe had displayed a better feeling than had previously been evinced by the officers of that nation, since the close of the Revolutionary contest.   But the difficulties between the two nations, already referred to, now daily becoming more serious, and threatening, at no distant day, a resort to the *ultima ratio regum*, had wrought a decided change in the views of the Canadian authorities respecting an Indian pacification.   In the event of a war, the Indians would again be found valuable auxiliaries to the arms of his Majesty, for the annoyance they would inflict upon the United States, if not by reason of any important victories they might gain.   Hence, instead of promoting a pacification, the efforts of the Canadian government were obviously exerted to prevent it.   *Meshecunnaqua*, or the *Little Turtle*, had made a visit to the province of Lower Canada, after the victory over St. Clair, for the purpose of engaging all the Indian forces he could, in that quarter, in the farther prosecution of the war. Lord Dorchester had now returned from England, and was waited upon by the Indians of the Seven Nations of Canada, as a deputation from all the Indians at the Grand Miami council of the preceding Autumn.   Their object was to ask advice, or procure countenance or assistance, in regard to the boundary for which they had been so long contending.   His Lordship answered the deputation on the 10th of February, in language, respecting the United States, far from conciliatory or pacific. After referring to the proceedings of a council with the Indians, held at Quebec, previous to his departure for Europe, two years before, and the expression in his speech on that occasion, of a hope that he should hear in England of a satisfactory adjustment of their difficulties with the United States, his Lordship proceeded :—

"CHILDREN : I was in expectation of hearing from the people of the United States what was required by them : I hoped that I should have been able to bring you together, and make you friends.

" CHILDREN: I have waited long, and listened with great attention, but I have not heard one word from them.

" CHILDREN: I flattered myself with the hope that the line proposed in the year eighty-three, to separate us from the United States, *which was immediately broken by themselves as soon as the peace was signed,* would have been mended, or a new one drawn, in an amicable manner. Here, also, I have been disappointed.

" CHILDREN: Since my return, I find no appearance of a line remains ; and from the manner in which the people of the United States rush on, and act, and talk, on this side ; and from what I learn of their conduct toward the sea, I shall not be surprised if we are at war with them in the course of the present year ; and if so, a line must then be drawn by the warriors.

" CHILDREN: You talk of selling your lands to the State of New-York.* I have told you that there is no line between them and us. I shall acknowledge no lands to be their's which have been encroached on by them since the year 1783. They then broke the peace, and as they kept it not on their part, it doth not bind on our's.

" CHILDREN: They then destroyed their right of pre-emption. Therefore all their approaches toward us since that time, and all the purchases made by them, I consider as an infringement on the King's rights. And when a line is drawn between us, be it in peace or war, they must lose all their improvements and houses on our side of it. Those people must all be gone who do not obtain leave to become the King's subjects. What belongs to the Indians will, of course, be secured and confirmed to them.

" CHILDREN: What farther can I say to you? You are witnesses that on our parts we have acted in the most peaceable manner, and borne the language and conduct of the people of the United States with patience. But I believe our patience is almost exhausted."†

* The Caughnawaga Indians, residing near Montreal, were about this time in treaty with Governor George Clinton for the sale of some of their lands lying within the boundaries of the state of New-York. The late Egbert Benson was a Commissioner on the part of the State.

† The authenticity of this speech of Lord Dorchester is denied by Chief Justice Marshall, and Mr. Sparks, in his Life and Correspondence of Washington, notes that denial without dissent. Hence it has been received as spurious, and Lord

There could be no doubt as to the effect of such an address upon the warlike tribes of the upper lakes, chafed, as they were, by what they really believed to be wrongs, and by the presence of a hostile army in the heart of their own country—buoyed up in their spirits, moreover, by the complete success which had crowned their arms in the two preceding campaigns. But the Governor General did not here cease his exertions to keep the Indians, the Six Nations not excepted, on the *qui vive* of the war feeling. Soon after the close of the council at Buffalo in the same month, his Lordship transmitted an inflammatory speech to those tribes, which was interpreted to them by Colonel Butler, and produced an obvious and decided change in their feelings toward the United States. Large presents were likewise sent up from Quebec, and distributed among them, and the British officers in the Indian Department took pains, on all occasions, to represent to them that a war between the two nations was inevitable.* Such was doubtless their opinion, for with the arrival of Lord Dorchester's speech, early in April, Governor Simcoe repaired over-land to Detroit, and with a strong detachment of troops proceeded to the foot of the Miami Rapids, and commenced the erection of a fortress at that place

Dorchester, with his Government, has escaped the responsibility of having uttered such an unwarrantable document. The first copy was forwarded to President Washington by Governor Clinton, who did not doubt its genuineness. Neither did the President ; since, in his letter to Governor Clinton acknowledging its receipt, he states his reasons at large for dissenting from the opinions of those who were proclaiming it to be spurious. On the contrary, he declared that he entertained "not a doubt of its authenticity." Equally strong was he in the opinion, that in making such a speech Lord Dorchester had spoken the sentiments of the British Cabinet, according to his instructions. [*See Letter of President Washington to Governor Clinton, March* 31, 1794.] On the 20th of May the attention of the British Minister, Mr. Hammond, was called to the subject by the Secretary of State, Edmund Randolph, who remonstrated strongly, not only against the speech, but against the conduct of Governor Simcoe, who was then engaged in measures of a hostile character. Mr. Hammond replied on the 22d of May rather tartly ; and, what renders the denial of the speech by Marshall and Sparks the more singular, is the fact that the British Minister said in that letter,—"I am willing to admit the authenticity of the speech." [*See T. B. Wait & Sons' Edition of American State Papers,* Vol. I. pages 449—453.] But if doubt has existed before, as to the genuine character of that document, it shall no longer exist. I have myself transcribed the preceding extracts from a certified manuscript copy, discovered among the papers of Joseph Brant in my possession.—*Author.*

* Letter from General Israel Chapin to the Secretary of War, April 29, 1794. See *Indian State Papers*—p. 480.

This movement caused fresh irritation among the American people, since the retention of the old posts had been a continual source of dissatisfaction, although the non-fulfilment of a portion of the treaty of peace by the United States still furnished the pretext for such occupancy. But the movement of Governor Simcoe into the Miami country, and the erection of a fortress there—the territory being clearly within the boundaries of the United States—awakened yet stronger feelings of indignation in the bosom of the President. Mr. Jay was at that time the American minister near the Court of St. James, and the President gave vent to his feelings in a private letter to that functionary, in the most decided terms of reprobation. "Can that government," asked the President in the letter to Mr. Jay, "or will
"it attempt, after this official act of one of their Governors, to
"hold out ideas of friendly intentions toward the United States,
"and suffer such conduct to pass with impunity? This may be
"considered as the most open and daring act of the British
"agents in America, though it is not the most hostile or cruel;
"for there does not remain a doubt in the mind of any well-in-
"formed person in this country, not shut against conviction,
"that all the difficulties we encounter with the Indians—their
"hostilities, the murders of helpless women and innocent chil-
"dren along our frontiers—result from the conduct of the agents
"of Great Britain in this country. In vain is it, then, for its ad-
"ministration in Britain to disavow having given orders which
"will warrant such conduct, whilst their agents go unpunished;
"whilst we have a thousand corroborating circumstances, and
"indeed almost as many evidences, some of which cannot be
"brought forward, to know that they are seducing from our
"alliance, and endeavoring to remove over the line, tribes that
"have hitherto been kept in peace and friendship with us at a
"heavy expense, and who have no causes of complaint, except
"pretended ones of their creating; whilst they keep in a state of
"irritation the tribes who are hostile to us, and are instigating
"those who know little of us or we of them, to unite in the
"war against us; and whilst it is an undeniable fact that they
"are furnishing the whole with arms, ammunition, clothing, and
"even provisions, to carry on the war; I might go farther, and
"if they are not much belied, add men also in disguise."

It was under these altered circumstances that General Chapin met the Six Nations again in council on the 21st of April, to receive their reply to the communication from the Secretary of War, General Knox, proposing the holding of another treaty at Venango, as heretofore mentioned. The proceedings were opened by the Onondaga chief, Clear Sky, who addressed the Superintendents as follows :—

"General Chapin : We are happy to see that you are ar rived safe at our council-fire, and that you have been preserved by the Great Spirit in good health :

"Colonel Butler : We are also very happy to see you at our council-fire, as representing the King."

Captain Brant thereupon rose, and addressed the two Super-. intendents as follows :—

"Brothers : You of the United States listen to what we are going to say to you ; you, likewise, the King.

"Brothers : We are very happy to see you, Colonel Butler and General Chapin, sitting side by side, with the intent of hearing what we have to say. We wish to do no business but what is open and above-board."

Then addressing himself exclusively to General Chapin, he proceeded :—

"Brother : You, of the United States, make your mind easy, on account of the long time your President's speech has been under our consideration ; when we received it, we told you it was a business of importance, and required time to be considered of.

"Brother : The answer you have brought us is not according to what we expected, which was the reason of our long delay ; the business would have been done with expedition, had the United States agreed to our proposals. We would then have collected our associates, and repaired to Venango, the place you proposed for meeting us.

"Brother : It is not now in our power to accept your invitation ; provided we were to go, you would conduct the busidess as you might think proper ; this has been the case at all the treaties held, from time to time, by your Commissioners.

"Brother : At the first treaty after the conclusion of the war between you and Great Britain, at Fort Stanwix, your Commissioners conducted the business as it to them seemed best ; they pointed out a line of division, and then confirmed it ;

after this they held out that our country was ceded to them by the King; this confused the Chiefs who attended there, and prevented them from making any reply to the contrary; still holding out, if we did not consent to it, that their warriors were at their back, and that we could get no farther protection from Great Britain. This has ever been held out to us by the Commissioners from Congress; at all the treaties held with us since the peace, at Fort M'Intosh, at Rocky River, and every other meeting held, the idea was still the same.

"BROTHER: This has been the case from time to time. Peace has not taken place, because you have held up these ideas, owing to which much mischief has been done to the southward.

"BROTHER: We, the Six Nations, have been exerting ourselves to keep peace since the conclusion of the war; we think it would be best for both parties; we advised the confederate nations to request a meeting, about half way between us and the United States, in order that such steps might be taken as would bring about a peace; this request was there proposed by us, and refused by Governor St. Clair, one of your Commissioners. The Wyandots, a few Delawares, and some others, met the Commissioners, though not authorized, and confirmed the lines of what was not their property, but common to all nations.

"BROTHER: This idea we all entertained at our council at Lower Sandusky, held for the purpose of forming our confederacy, and to adopt measures that would be for the general welfare of our Indian nations, or people of our color; owing to these steps taken by us, the United States held out, that when we went to the westward to transact our private business, that we went with the intention of taking an active part in the troubles subsisting between them and our western brethren; this never has been the case. We have ever wished for the friendship of the United States.

"BROTHER: We think you must be fully convinced, from our perseverance last summer, as your Commissioners saw, that we were anxious for a peace between you. The exertions that we, the Six Nations, have made toward the accomplishing this desirable end, is the cause of the western nations being somewhat dubious as to our sincerity. After we knew their doubts, we still persevered; and, last Fall, we pointed out methods to be taken, and sent them, by you to Congress ; this we certainly expected would have proved satisfactory to the United States ; in that case we should have more than ever exerted ourselves, in order that the offers we made should be confirmed by our confederacy, and by them strictly to be adhered to.

"BROTHER : Our proposals have not met with the success from Congress that we expected ; this still leaves us in a similar situation to what we were in when we first entered on the business.

"BROTHER : You must recollect the number of chiefs who have, at divers times, waited on Congress ; they have pointed out the means to be taken, and held out the same language, uniformly, at one time as another ; that was, if you would withdraw your claim to the boundary line and lands within the line, as offered by us ; had this been done, peace would have taken place, and, unless this still be done, we see no other method of accomplishing it.

"BROTHER : We have borne every thing patiently for this long time past ; we have done every thing we could consistently do with the welfare of our nations in general, notwithstanding the many advantages that have been taken of us by individuals making purchases of us, the Six Nations, whose fraudulent conduct towards us Congress never has taken notice of, nor in any wise seen us rectified, nor made our minds easy. This is the case to the present day ; our patience is now entirely worn out ; you see the difficulties we labor under, so that we cannot, at present, rise from our seats and attend your council at Venango agreeable to your invitation. The boundary line we pointed out we think is a just one, although the United States claim lands west of that line ; the trifle that has been paid by the United States can be no object in comparison to what a peace would be.

"BROTHER : We are of the same opinion with the people of the United States ; you consider yourselves as independent people ; we, as the original inhabitants of this country and sovereigns of the soil, look upon ourselves as equally independent, and free as any other nations. This country was given to us by the Great Spirit above ; we wish to enjoy it, and have our passage along the lake within the line we have pointed out.

"BROTHER : The great exertions we have made, for this number of years, to accomplish a peace, have not been able to obtain it ; our patience, as we have already observed, is exhausted, and we are discouraged from persevering any longer. We therefore throw ourselves under the protection of the Great Spirit above, who, we hope, will order all things for the best. We have told you our patience is worn out ; but not so far but that we wish for peace, and, whenever we hear that pleasing sound, we shall pay attention to it." [*The belt and speech sent by General Knox were then returned to General Chapin.*]

Thus was extinguished the hope of a council of pacification at Venango ; and not only that, but the altered temper of the Six Nations seemed to threaten an augmentation of the hostile Indian power at the west, by the desertion to their cause of the whole of the Iroquois Confederacy, under a leader whose prowess and wisdom had both often been tested. In the mean time all the accounts from the west concurred in the fact, that the distant tribes were gathering for a renewal of the conflict— encouraged as they were by promises of strong assistance from the English. The traders and the "mixed multitude" constituting the refugees and parti-colored inhabitants of Detroit, were doubtless active in promoting these hostilities, and very probably made promises to the credulous Chiefs as coming from Governor Simcoe, of which he himself was ignorant. Two Pottawattamies were taken prisoners on the 5th of June by the troops of General Wayne, who made a variety of disclosures upon this subject. They represented, and intelligence to that effect was dispatched to the interior tribes by their Chiefs, that Governor Simcoe was to march to their assistance with fifteen hundred men. He was giving them clothing and all necessary supplies, and "all the speeches received from him were red as "blood. All the wampum and feathers were painted red ; the "war-pipes and hatchets were red ; and even the tobacco was "painted red." Several Shawanese prisoners, however, were soon afterward captured, who were less confident of English assistance. They said "they could not depend upon the British "for effectual support ; that they were always setting the In-"dians on like dogs after game, pressing them to go to war and "kill the Americans, but did not help them."

Another influence was brought to bear upon the Indians of the west at this conjuncture, from a most unexpected quarter.

It was the arrival at the Miamis Rapids, early in May, of a messenger from the Spanish settlements on the Mississippi, charged with a spirited war-speech to the confederacy. This messenger was conducted to the Miamis by a deputation from the Delawares, who had emigrated beyond the Mississippi four years previous. He admonished the confederates of the gathering of the "Big-Knives," meaning the troops of the United States, and offered assistance from the Spanish and French settlements in the south-west, who, he said, were preparing to come to their help.

"CHILDREN!" said the Spaniard, "you see me on my feet, grasping the tomahawk to strike them. We will strike together. I do not desire you to go before me, in the front, but to follow me.

"CHILDREN: I present you with a war-pipe, which has been sent in all our names to the Musquakies, and all those nations who live towards the setting sun, to get upon their feet and take hold of our tomahawk: and as soon as they smoked it, they sent it back with a promise to get immediately on their feet, and join us, and strike this enemy.

"CHILDREN: You hear what these distant nations have said to us, so that we have nothing farther to do but put our designs into immediate execution, and to forward this pipe to the three warlike nations who have so long been struggling for their country, and who now sit at the Glaize. Tell them to smoke this pipe, and forward it to all the lake Indians and their northern brethren. Then nothing will be wanting to complete our general union from the rising to the setting of the sun, and all nations will be ready to add strength to the blow we are going to make."*   [*Delivered a war-pipe.*]

The Spaniard farther assured them that the Creeks, Cherokees, Choctaws and Chickasaws, had also charged him with a message, assuring them that their hearts were with the Confederacy, and that eleven nations of the southern Indians were then on their feet, with the hatchet in their hand, ready to strike their common enemy.

The Chiefs to whom these messages from the west and south were delivered at the Rapids, immediately convened a council,

* MS. among the Brant papers.

composed of the Wyandots, Ottawas, Chippewas, Mingoes, Munseys, and Nantikokes, before whom the intelligence was repeated. They were then addressed as follows :—

" BROTHERS : You have now heard the speeches brought to our council at the Glaize a few days ago from the Spaniards; and as soon as they heard them, and smoked the pipe, their hearts were glad, and they determined to step forward and put into execution the advice sent to them. They desire you to forward the pipe, as has been recommended, to all our northern brethren ; not doubting but as soon as you have smoked it, you will follow their example, and they will hourly expect you to join them, as it will not be many days before the nearness of our enemies will give us an opportunity of striking them."

[*Delivered the pipe.*]

Egouchouoy answered for all the nations present :—

" BROTHERS : I am happy at the good news you have told us, and we will immediately go and collect all our people, and be with you as soon as possible."*

There is mystery attached to this mission of the Spaniard, concerning which no farther information has been obtained. The Indians of the Confederacy were greatly encouraged by the assurances of assistance, and it will soon appear that some tribes came to their help from a very great distance. The employment of a Spanish Envoy, however, was a remarkable circumstance, and serves to strengthen the suspicions entertained by Washington two years before, that, even at that early day, the possessors of the estuary of the Mississippi, and of the vast Spanish territories above, had already become alarmed lest what has happened respecting that territory, would happen, unless the power of the United States should be crippled. But the promised Spanish and French assistance from that direction did not arrive, nor were the Confederates aided in their subsequent

---

* The reader must bear in mind that these speeches and proceedings of the Indian Councils, exclusively such, were written down by the British agents and officers among the Indians, who attended to assist them. The author finds many of them among the papers of Captain Brant—some from the Upper Lake tribes in French. The account of this Spanish writer, his message, and the consequent address to the Lake tribes, the author has found among these papers, signed by Colonel M'Kee *as Deputy Agent of Indian Affairs,* and the copy certified by Thomas Talbot. Several paragraphs of both addresses have been omitted, as not material to the history. See Appendix, No. IX.

operations by the Creeks, Cherokees, and Chickasaws, as promised.

The United States were not inactive during these hostile movements and preparations among the Indians. General Wayne, or *Sukach-gook* as he was called by the Indians,[*] was making the most vigorous preparations for opening the campaign with decision. Among other measures, it was determined, while he was approaching the Miami towns with a force sufficient, as it was hoped, to end the war at a blow, to occupy a station at Presqu' Isle, and fortify it. This movement not only gave great uneasiness to the confederates, but, in connexion with another, of a different description, adopted by the State of Pennsylvania, had well-nigh driven the whole of the more ancient alliance of the Six Nations at once into hostilities against the United States under their old leader Thayendanegea. Pennsylvania, it seems, claimed a district of country on the south shore of Lake Erie, including Presqu' Isle, under color of a purchase from the Corn-planter—which purchase the Six Nations, to whom the territory in question had belonged, held to be invalid. Regardless of the objections and remonstrances of the Indians, thus claiming proprietorship, the Corn-planter having, as they contended, sold it without authority, Pennsylvania was now planting settlers upon this territory and erecting an establishment at Presqu' Isle; at which aggression, as they esteemed it, Captain Brant and his nations were greatly incensed. A council was thereupon held, to take that and other subjects into consideration, at Buffalo, the sittings of which were commenced on the 24th of June. General Chapin was in attendance, at the urgent solicitation of the Indians, and Captain O'Bail (the Corn-planter) was the speaker. He complained first of the absence of several of their warriors, who were believed to have been killed by the Americans. One of their chiefs, Big Tree, he said, had some months before gone to the camp of the Americans in the most friendly manner, and had been put to death; while another of their warriors had been killed at Venango "while sitting easy and peaceable on his seat." He next entered upon the subject

---

[*] Sukach-gook is the Delaware name for black snake, which they called General Wayne by, saying that he possessed all the art and cunning of that reptile; which was known to be the greatest destroyer of the small birds and animals of the snake tribe.—*Heckewelder.*

of the Pennsylvania encroachments, of which he complained bitterly, insisting that the sale alleged to have been made by himself was not in any manner obligatory upon the Indians. The erection of the fort at Presqu' Isle was likewise a theme of complaint. The determination of the council was to send a delegation of their Chiefs into the disputed territory, to request a removal of the intruders; and General Chapin was solicited to accompany the deputation. He did so, but the mission was executed to no good purpose.

On the return of the delegation to Buffalo Creek, another council was held to receive the report. This convention was on the 4th of July. The report, being unfavorable, of course gave no satisfaction, and the Indians immediately manifested a still greater degree of alienation from the United States. The general boundary question was revived during the discussions, and an address from the council to the President, spoken by O'Bail, was written down, and transmitted by General Chapin. In this address the Indians re-asserted their determination to insist upon the Ohio and Muskingum boundary. The following is an extract :—

"GENERAL WASHINGTON, ATTEND! What gives us room for the making of so many speeches, is, because you relate all the former deceptions that have been used.

"GENERAL WASHINGTON: I depend upon you to gratify our request, and that will make my mind easy. Sometimes I hear that I am going to flee from my seat, for the injuries I have done. These reflections make me so unhappy, that I am almost tempted to die with the Six Nations.

"BROTHER: We are determined now, as we were before, that the line shall remain. We have fully considered on the boundary we have marked out. We know all that we have received from time to time, and we think if you establish this line, it will make us about even.

"BROTHER: If you do not comply with our request, we shall determine on something else, as we are a free people.

"BROTHER: We are determined to be a free people. You know, General Washington, that we, the Six Nations, have always been able to defend ourselves, and we are still determined to maintain our freedom.

"BROTHER: You must not suspect that any other nation corrupts our minds. The only thing that can corrupt our minds, is not to grant our request.

"BROTHER: If this favor is not granted, I wish that my son may be sent back with the answer, and tell me which side he means to join. If he wishes to join that side, he is at liberty."

Although the name of Brant does not often occur in the proceedings of the councils touching the movement of Pennsylvania upon Sandusky, yet he was by no means a passive spectator of passing events. There were no hours of idleness in his life, and when not engaged in the field, or in attendance upon councils, or upon foreign missions, his mind was occupied in the work of improving the minds and morals, and adding to the comforts, of his own people. In the Spring of the present year he was engaged in the erection of a council-house for his nation at Grand River. But the Sandusky affair called him again to the field; and while others were deliberating in council, and attempting to negotiate, the Chief was preparing to contest the disputed title by arms—directly aided, as will be seen from the following letter, by the Executive of Upper Canada:—

CAPTAIN BRANT TO COLONEL SMITH—("FOR GOVERNOR SIMCOE."*)

"*Grand River*, 19*th July*, 1794.

"SIR: I have to acknowledge the receipt of your favor of the 16th instant, enclosing the extracts his Excellency has been pleased to favor me with, for which I have to request you would have the goodness to thank his Excellency for me.

"I am much concerned to find that the Lake Indians think their belts completed.† I foresaw the event,‡ for which reason it has ever been my opinion that they should avoid coming to any considerable engagement, because it is a custom among the Indians, that after having struck a good blow, and having taken

---

* So filed in Brant's own hand, on the copy preserved among his papers.

† Captain Brant had just received a letter from Detroit, dated on the 5th of July, one paragraph of which explains the signification of this expression: "The Macki-"naw and Lake Indians, having *completed the belts* they carried, with scalps and "prisoners, seem resolved on going home again. The return of these people will "considerably weaken the defence expected from the collected sections of two thou-"sand Indians."

‡ Referring, doubtless, to an engagement between Little Turtle and Major M'Mahon, which will be more particularly noted a page or two onward.

prisoners and scalps, they return home.   Nevertheless I hope they will not go.

"In regard to the Presqu' Isle business, should we not get an answer at the time limited, it is our business to push those fellows hard, and therefore it is my intention to form my camp at Pointe Appineau ; and I would esteem it a favor if his Excellency the Lieutenant Governor would lend me four or five batteaux.   Should it so turn out, and should those fellows not go off, and O'Bail continue in the same opinion, an expedition against those Yankees must of consequence take place.

"His Excellency has been so good as to furnish us with a cwt. of powder, and ball in proportion, which is now at Fort Erie ; but in the event of an attack upon Le Bœuf people, I could wish, if consistent, that his Excellency would order a like quantity in addition to be at Fort Erie, in order to be in readiness : likewise I would hope for a little assistance in provisions.

" I would request that his Excellency would favor me with an answer by the bearer, Seth.   I would also trouble his Excellency in regard to those people who went with him to Detroit.   They were promised to be handsomely rewarded, which as yet has not been done ; and as they now expect to go upon service, they are rather impatient ; and if it was convenient that they could be satisfied, either by borrowing goods, or otherwise, as his Excellency would think fit, I would be extremely happy.

"I understand some new regiments are raising, or to be raised. In that case I would consider myself much favored should some of my relations, young men, have an equal chance of being provided for.

" A few days ago I sent seven men to Cadaragara, to remind O'Bail that he should watch any movement of those people* very narrowly ; and that he should be ready to march immediately after the expiration of the time, should they not then evacuate that place."

The insertion of this letter at length is deemed important, showing, as it does, and that, too, beyond the power of contradiction, that the Indians were supplied purposely, with their munitions of war, by the officers of the British crown.   The fact was denied by Great Britain, or at least it was argued, that

* The settlers at Presqu' Isle.

if the Indians drew their supplies from the Canadians, they were furnished by individuals, as such, over whose actions in the premises the government had no control. Independently of these circumstances, moreover, the detention of the boats, and the erection by Governor Sinclair of a new fortification, heretofore spoken of, on the Miamis of the Lakes, fifty miles South of Detroit, afforded strong evidence of a design on the part of Great Britain, to avail herself of the non-execution of that article in the treaty of peace stipulating for the payment of debts, for the purpose of establishing a new boundary line, by which the great lakes should be entirely comprehended in Upper Canada. An animated correspondence took place on the whole subject, between the American Secretary of State and Mr. Hammond, the diplomatic representative of Great Britain, in which a considerable degree of mutual irritation was displayed, and in which each supported the charges against the nation of the other much better than he defended his own.[*] Had the Secretary of State been in possession of the preceding letter from the Mohawk Chief, he would not have argued upon uncertainties—at least so far as a supply of powder and ball to the Indians by the Governor of Upper Canada would have sustained his case. In any event, the charge is now brought home with sufficient distinctness to put the question at rest. Captain Brant, however, found no occasion for a farther requisition upon his Excellency for ammunition at that time. The interposition of the President deterred Pennsylvania from the farther prosecution of her designs upon Presqu' Isle, and the projected expedition of the Six Nations was accordingly relinquished.

The desultory contest with the Indians, so long protracted, and at times so bloody, was now approaching its termination. On the 30th of June a sharp action took place under the walls of Fort Recovery—a fortress which had been thrown up by General Wayne on the battle-ground of St. Clair's defeat. The primary object of the Indians, who were the assailants, was the capture of a large number of pack-horses, recently arrived at that fort with provisions, which were returning to Fort Grenville, guarded by a company of cavalry under Captain Gibson, and a detachment of ninety riflemen, the whole under the com-

* Marshall.

mand of Major M'Mahon. Taken by surprise, and finding the Indians in great force, the Americans sought speedy refuge within the walls of the fort. The Indians were led by the distinguished Miami Chief, Little Turtle. Pressing close upon the garrison, with an evident design to carry it, the moment M'Mahon's troops had regained the fortress a fire was opened upon the assailants, which drove them back with great slaughter. They rallied again, however, and maintained the engagement through the day, but keeping at a more respectful distance. The night, which was thick and foggy, was employed by them in removing their dead by torch-light. On the next day the assault was renewed ; but the Indians were ultimately compelled to retreat, with loss and disappointment, from the field of their former triumph. Both in advance and retreat, in this expedition, the Indians marched with perfect order. Their encampments were square and regular, and they moved upon the fort in seventeen columns, at wide distances apart. Many white men were in their ranks, supposed to be the inhabitants and militia of Detroit. Officers in British uniform were likewise so near the scene of action as to be distinctly discerned. Several valuable officers of Major M'Mahon's corps fell at the first onset, among whom was the gallant Major himself. The total loss of the Americans was twenty-two killed and thirty wounded. The Indians suffered very severely. In their retreat it was ascertained that a large number of pack-horses were literally loaded with their slain. Such, at least, were the facts in regard to this affair, as derived from the most ample and apparently authentic accounts of the Americans. Nor did the Indian accounts differ from the American as widely as is often the case between opposite statements of antagonist parties. As an evidence of which, and to show how accurately and promptly Captain Brant was advised of the progress and events of the war, the following extract is given from his correspondence :—

EXTRACT FROM A LETTER TO CAPTAIN BRANT.

" Detroit, July 5, 1794.

" An attack was made on the 30th of June by the Indians, on three hundred pack-horses returning to Fort Grenville, from whence they came the day before with provisions. All of these, with the pack-horsemen, were either taken or killed close by

Fort Recovery, together with thirty bullocks   Captain Gibson, the officer commanding, on perceiving the attack made on his horses, ordered a troop of dragoons, or light-horse, to charge the Indians, and at the same time he drew up his garrison in front of the fort, as if with a design to sustain his cavalry. But they were all beaten back in a few minutes, and pursued to the gate of the fort, with the loss of about fifty men and upward of twenty-five horses. The loss of the Indians commenced from this period; for they kept up a useless attack upon the fort, while the troops within were firing at them through loop-holes. Seventeen were killed, and as many wounded.

"The *Mountain Leader* was killed two days before the action, by a scouting party of the Hurons. He was the chief of the Chickasaws. Wells, (a scout from Wayne's army,) was killed in the engagement; and May is reported to be so by one of three prisoners who were taken, together with two more Chickasaws. Captain Gibson and two other officers are also among the killed.

"My information states that these prisoners report there are sixty Chickasaws with their army, twenty of whom are at Fort Recovery and forty at Fort Grenville. They also say that the horses which are now taken and killed, were the only means General Wayne had of transporting provisions—that he was to commence his campaign about the middle of next month— waiting for an augmentation of his force of three thousand militia from Kentucky—and that he is to build a fort at the Glaize, and proceed from thence to Detroit.

"The Chiefs of several nations are now in council at the Glaize, adopting measures to re-unite their force if possible."

Taught by the unfortunate experience of Harmar and St. Clair, General Wayne moved not but with the utmost caution, and all the preparation which a prudent forecast required. He had not therefore advanced beyond Fort Recovery until sufficient strength had been concentrated, and such other dispositions made as would enable him not only to strike a decisive blow, but retain possession of the country he might conquer. The delays incident to these preparations carried the active prosecution of the campaign into midsummer. The richest and most extensive towns of the hostile Indians lay about the confluence of the Au Glaize and the Miamis of the Lakes. At this

place General Wayne arrived on the 8th of August, where some
works of defence were thrown up for the protection of the magazines.   It was thirty miles thence to the Rapids, where, as has
been already seen, Governor Simcoe had recently erected a strong
fortress, fifty miles within the stipulated and understood boundary, as between the British possessions and those of the United
States.   At this latter place, in the immediate neighborhood of
the fort, the Indian forces were collected to the number of
nearly two thousand.   The Continental legion under General
Wayne was of about equal strength, exclusive of eleven hundred mounted Kentuckians under General Scott.   Here the
BLACK SNAKE had intended to surprise the neighboring villages of the enemy ; and the more effectually to ensure the success of his *coup de main*, he had not only advanced thus far by
an obscure and very difficult route, but taken pains to clear out
two roads from Greenville in that direction, in order to attract
and divert the attention of the Indians while he marched upon
neither.   But his generalship proved of no avail.   The Little
Turtle was too wary a leader to be taken by surprise—to say
nothing of the desertion of a villain named Newman, an officer
in the Quarter-master General's department, who gave the
Indians warning of Wayne's advance.   Little Turtle thereupon retired to the Rapids ; and having been apprized by the
deserter of the strength of the Americans, determined to give
battle, and made dispositions for that object.

Having learned on the 12th, from Indian prisoners who were
brought in, the position of the enemy, in close proximity to the
British garrison at the Rapids, and being yet desirous of bring
ing the Indians to terms, if possible, without the farther effusion
of blood, the American commander despatched another messenger of peace.   The name of the envoy selected for the occasion
was Miller—a man who had been so long a captive among
the Indians as to have acquired their language.   He was exceedingly reluctant to undertake the hazardous enterprise.   But
being strongly urged upon the service, with an assurance from
the General that eight of the Indian warriors, who were prisoners, should be held as pledges of his safety, he at last assented—
taking two of the prisoners, a warrior and a squaw, along with
him.   He was received in a very hostile mood, and his life
threatened.   But addressing them in their own language, dis-

playing a flag, and explaining the object of his visit, the menacing blow was suspended, and he was placed in confinement while the Chiefs deliberated in council upon the letter from the General, of which he was the bearer. Assuring them that every prisoner in the American camp would be put to death unless he should be sent back in safety before the 16th, he was liberated on the preceding day—with a message to Wayne, that if he waited where he was ten days, they would then treat with him, but if he advanced at an earlier day they would fight. Impatient of delay, however, Wayne had taken up his line of march on the 15th—the day of Miller's release. The message which he met did not check his advance, and the General arrived in the vicinity of the Rapids on the 18th. The 19th was occupied in reconnoitring the positions of the enemy, and throwing up a slight fortification for the protection of the stores, which was appropriately named Fort Deposite.

The enemy had taken post behind a thick wood, rendered almost inaccessible by a dense growth of under-brush and fallen timber, marking the track of a tornado, and almost under the guns of the fort that had been erected by Simcoe. Their left was secured by the rocky bank of the river. The Americans advanced for the attack early on the morning of the 20th. At about ten o'clock, having proceeded nearly five miles, the advance guard, commanded by Major Price, received so brisk a fire from the enemy, who were secreted in the woods and the tall grass, as to compel it to fall back. The ground was most happily chosen by the enemy for their mode of warfare, so obstructed and difficult of access as to render it almost impossible for the cavalry to act. Immediately on the attack upon the corps of Major Price, the legion was formed in two lines and moved rapidly forward. The thick forest and old broken wood already described, extended to the left of the army several miles— the right resting on the river. The Indians were formed in three lines within supporting distance of each other, and extending for about two miles at right angles with the river. The American commander soon discovered, from the weight of his fire, and the extent of his lines, that it was the design of the enemy to turn his left flank. The second line was thereupon ordered to advance in support of the first, while, by a circuitous route, Scott was directed with his Kentuckians to turn the ene-

my's right.   In concert with this movement, the front line was
ordered by General Wayne to charge with trailed arms, and
rouse the Indians from their covert at the point of the bayonet.
Having started them up, the Americans were directed to fire,
and charge them so closely as to allow no time for re-load-
ing.   The open ground by the river permitted the movements
of cavalry, with which the right flank of the enemy was gained
and turned.   Indeed, such were the promptness of movement on
the part of the Americans, and the impetuosity of the charge of
the first line of infantry, that the Indians, together with the Detroit militia and volunteers, were driven from all their coverts in
so brief a space of time that the mounted men, though making
every possible exertion to press forward, were many of them
unable to gain their proper positions to participate in the action.
In the course of an hour, the enemy, notwithstanding all the
embarrassments of the ground already enumerated. were driven
more than two miles, by a force of less than half their numbers
actually engaged.   The victory was complete and decisive;
both Indians and their allies, composed of the "mixed multitude" already more than once referred to, abandoning themselves
to flight in terror and dismay,—leaving the field of battle in the
quiet possession of the Americans.   The commanding General
stated in his official report of the action, that " it was terminat-
" ed under the influence of the guns of the British garrison,"—
the pursuit having continued until they were within reach of
those guns.   The loss of the Americans in killed and wounded,
including officers, was one hundred and seven.   Among the
slain was Captain Campbell, commanding the cavalry, who fell
in the first charge.*

The loss of the Indians is not known.   It must, however, have
been very severe.   Seven Nations were engaged in the action,
viz : the Miamis, Wyandots, the Pottawattamies, Delawares,

* It was in this memorable action that Captain Solomon (now General Van Rensselaer) of Albany, an officer of dragoons, received a wound in the commencement
of the battle, by being shot through the lungs.   General Wilkinson, who was also
in the battle, states, in his Memoirs, that Van Rensselaer kept his horse, and continued fighting until the blood spurted from his mouth and nostrils.   General Van
Rensselaer was afterward dreadfully wounded in half a dozen places, at the daring
assault upon Queenston Heights in 1812.   He yet lives, and, after having served
the State of New-York several years as Adjutant General, and been repeatedly
elected to Congress, has for the last fifteen years held the office of Post-master in
Albany.

Shawanese, Chippewas, Ottawas, and a portion of the Senecas. All the Chiefs of the Wyandots engaged in the battle, being nine in number, were killed.* Great slaughter was made by the legionary cavalry in the pursuit, so many of the savages being cut down with the sabre, that the title of "*Long Knives*," years before given to the Americans, was brought again into general use among the Indians.† It was believed by many that the Indians would not have incurred this signal disaster had the advice of the *Little Turtle* been heeded. He was opposed to the policy of a general engagement at that time, and it has even been asserted that he was rather inclined to peace. During the night preceding the engagement, the Chiefs of the several tribes were in council, and a proposition was submitted to make a night attack upon the Americans in their encampment. The proposal was overruled, and a general engagement on the following morning was determined upon. *Little Turtle* alone was opposed to the plan, while *Blue Jacket*, a Shawanese warrior of high character and influence, strenuously supported the course adopted by the council. Colonel M'Kee was in the council, and is believed to have urged the Indians to fight. *Little Turtle* was inspired with a presentiment that they could not successfully encounter the Black Snake. "We "have beaten the enemy," said the *Turtle*, "twice, under sepa- "rate commanders. We cannot expect the same good for "tune always to attend us. The Americans are now led by a "chief who never sleeps. The night and the day are alike to him : "and during all the time that he has been marching upon our "villages, notwithstanding the watchfulness of our young men, "we have never been able to surprise him. Think well of it. "There is something whispers me it would be prudent to listen "to his offers of peace." For holding language like this, he was reproached by some of the Chiefs with cowardice, and that ended the conference. Stung to the quick by an imputation which he was conscious he had never merited, he would have laid the reviler dead at his feet ; but his was not the bravery of an assassin. Suppressing his resentment, he took part in the battle, and performed his duty with his wonted bravery. The event proved that he had not formed an erroneous estimate of the

---

* Drake's Book of the Indians.   † Thatcher's Lives of the Indian Chiefs.

character of Wayne; and that his rival, *Blue Jacket,* though equally brave, was less of a prophet than himself.*

Excepting the militia and refugees gathered about Detroit, the British or Canadian authorities took no part in the battle; but the direction in which ran their sympathies could not be mistaken, from the tone of a somewhat tart correspondence occurring after the battle, between General Wayne and Major Campbell, commanding the British garrison. On the day after the engagement, Major Campbell addressed a note to General Wayne, expressing his surprise at the appearance of an American force at a point almost within reach of his guns, and asking in what light he was to view such near approaches to the garrison which he had the honor to command. General Wayne, without questioning the propriety of the interrogatory, replied, that even were the Major entitled to an answer, " the most full and " satisfactory one was announced the day before from the muzzles " of his small arms, in an action with a horde of savages in the " vicinity of the fort, and which terminated gloriously to the " American arms." But, added the General, " had it continued " until the Indians were driven under the influence of the fort " and guns mentioned, they would not have much impeded the " progress of the victorious army under my command, as no " such post was established at the commencement of the present " war between the Indians and the United States." Major Campbell rejoined, complaining that men, with arms in their hands, were approaching within pistol shot of his works, where his Majesty's flag was flying, and threatened hostilities should such insults to that flag be continued. Upon the receipt of this letter, General Wayne caused the fort to be closely reconnoitered in every direction. It was found to be a strong and regular work, with two bastions upon the rear and most accessible face of it, mounting eight pieces of artillery upon that side and four upon the front facing the river. This duty having been discharged, General Wayne addressed a letter to the British commander, disclaiming, of course, as Major Campbell had previously done, any desire to resort to harsh measures; but denouncing the erection of that fortress as the highest act of aggression toward the United States, and requiring him to desist

* Schoolcraft's Travels. Thatcher. Drake.

from any farther act of hostility, and to retire with his troops to the nearest British post occupied by British troops at the peace of 1783. To this requisition, Major Campbell answered that he should not abandon the post at the summons of any power whatever, unless in compliance with orders from those under whom he served. He likewise again warned the American commander, not to approach within the reach of his guns without expecting the consequences that would attend it.

The only notice taken of this last letter was, by immediately setting fire to, and destroying every thing within view of the fort, and even under the muzzles of his Britannic Majesty's guns. But no attempt was made by Major Campbell to carry his threat into execution. Among the property thus destroyed were barns and fields of corn, above and below the fort, together with " the barns, stores, and property of Colonel M'Kee, the British " Indian Agent and principal stimulator of the war between the " United States and the savages."* The American army lay three days before the fort, when it returned to the Grand Glaize, arriving at that place on the 28th of August. A vast destruction of Indian property took place during this expedition. The Miamis and Grand Glaize ran through the heart of the country of the hostile Indians. " The very extensive and highly cul " tivated fields and gardens showed the work of many hands. " The margins of those beautiful rivers the Miamis of the lakes, " and the Au Glaize," wrote General Wayne, "appeared like one " continued village for many miles; nor have I ever before be- " held such immense fields of corn in any part of America, from " Canada to Florida."† All were laid waste for twenty miles on each side of the river, and forts erected to prevent the return of the Indians.

There is reason to believe that the Indians were grievously disappointed in the conduct of Major Campbell during the action. Among the papers of Captain Brant, is the copy of a letter addressed by him to Sir John Johnson, in April, 1799, wherein the Baronet is reminded of various wrongs alleged to have been suffered by the Indians, at the hands even of his Majesty's government. The following remarkable passage in this letter induces a belief that the Indians expected that, in the event of

---

* Letter of General Wayne. State Papers, Vol. IV.
† Letter of General Wayne to the Secretary of War.

defeat, the garrison would come to their succor, or, at least, that the gates of the fortress would be thrown open to them as a place of refuge on their retreat :—" In the first place," wrote the Mohawk Chief to Sir John, " the Indians were engaged in a war " to assist the English—then left in the lurch at the peace, to " fight alone until they could make peace for themselves. After " repeatedly defeating the armies of the United States, so that " *they* sent Commissioners to endeavor to get peace, the Indians " were so advised as prevented them from listening to any terms, " and hopes were given to them of assistance. A fort was even " built in their country, under pretence of giving refuge in case " of necessity ; but when that time came, the gates were shut " against them as enemies. They were doubly injured by this, " because they relied on it for support, and were deceived. Was " it not for this reliance of mutual support, their conduct would " have been different. I imagine that your own knowledge of " these things, and judgment, will point out to you the necessity " of putting the line of conduct with the Indians on a more " honorable footing, and come as nigh as possible to what it was " in the time of your father."

Considering the distance, and the difficulties of travelling at that time, intelligence of the disaster which had befallen his Indian friends was very rapidly conveyed to Governor Simcoe at Niagara, and by him communicated to Captain Brant in the following letter :—

GOVERNOR SIMCOE TO CAPTAIN BRANT.

" *Navy Hall,* 28*th August,* 1794.

" DEAR SIR,

" I understand that the Indians and Wayne had an action on the 20th near McCormack's ; that the Indians, who amounted to nine hundred, retreated with the loss of some principal chiefs of the Hurons, Ottawas, and Shawanese ; a deserter reports that the Americans lost an hundred men.

" The Wyandots, and a friend * of your's, most gallantly covered the retreat.

" The Indians having retreated to the Miami Bay, Major Campbell was summoned to deliver the post, which of course

---

* Although the fact does not appear, yet it is believed that a goodly number of the Mohawk warriors were in the battle against Wayne, and Brant was likewise to

he refused, and reports that he considered it tenable against Wayne's force.

" The Indians having placed their women and children in safety, have again moved forward to an advantageous position, I imagine Swan Creek, where they wait for reinforcements, and I hope will recover their spirits.

" All the militia on the La Branche are gone to Detroit.

" I shall proceed in the first vessel, and am, in great haste, your faithful humble servant,   " J. G. SIMCOE.

" *To Captain Brant.*"

The difficulties between Great Britain and the United States not having yet been adjusted, and a war between the two nations continuing still a probable event, it suited not the Canadian authorities to allow the Indians to conclude a peace, notwithstanding their signal overthrow. The north-western posts, moreover, within the territory not only of the far west, but within the boundaries of the State of New-York. were obstinately retained, while an attempt was made to grasp additional territory on the south side of Lake Ontario. It was during the Summer of this year, that Captain Williamson commenced a settlement on the Great Sodus Bay, about forty miles from Oswego ; and in this same month of August, Governor Simcoe despatched Lieut. Sheaff to that place, to demand by what authority such an establishment was forming, and that it should be immediately relinquished.* General Simcoe himself, pursuant to the intimation in his letter to Brant, hastened to the west, as also did the Chief,

have been in the field with them. Several years afterward, Brant stated these facts in a conversation with the venerable Jacob Snell, Esq. yet living (1837) in Palatine. The Chief stated to Mr. Snell that he obtained the ammunition used by the Indians, himself, at Quebec, and that he should have led his Mohawks in person but was detained by sickness.

* Marshall. Captain Williamson being absent from Sodus at the time of Lieut. Sheaff's visit, that officer left a written declaration of which the following is a copy :—" I am commanded to declare that, during the inexecution of the treaty of peace between Great Britain and the United States, and until the existing difficulties respecting it shall be mutually and finally adjusted, the taking possession of any part of the Indian territory, either for the purposes of war or sovereignty, is held to be a direct violation of his Britannic Majesty's rights, as they unquestionably existed before the treaty, and has an immediate tendency to interrupt, and in its progress to destroy, that good understanding which has hitherto subsisted between his Britannic Majesty and the United States of America. I therefore require you to desist from any such aggression."

attended by one hundred and fifty of his warriors—evidently for the purpose of continuing in the exercise of an unfriendly influence upon the minds of the Indians against the United States. The Governor was at the fort near the battle-field, on the 30th of September, as also were Captain Brant and Colonel M'Kee. The Indians had already made some advances to General Wayne toward a negotiation for peace ; but their attention was diverted by Simcoe and Brant, who invited a council of the hostile nations to assemble at the mouth of the Detroit river on the 10th of October. This invitation was accepted, as also was an invitation from General Wayne, who was met by a few of their Chiefs ; so that the wily savages were in fact sitting in two councils at once, balancing chances, and preparing to make peace only in the event of finding little farther encouragement to fight.

At the council on the 10th of October, the Wyandot Chiefs addressed Governor Simcoe as follows :—

" FATHER : We request of you to give your sentiments candidly : we have been these many years in wars and troubles : you have, from time to time, promised us your assistance. When is your promise to be fulfilled ?"

THEIR FATHER'S ANSWER.

" CHILDREN : Your question is very difficult to be answered. I will relate an ancient history, perhaps before any of you here were born. When I first came into this country, I found it in the possession of your fathers, the French. We soon became enemies of each other. In time, the Great Spirit above gave the conquest in my favor. In those days the United States were my subjects. We lived in this state for many years after. At last the Americans began to act independently, which caused a rupture between us. The contest lasted for a while. At last we made peace. From that period they have been encroaching upon your lands. I looked on as a spectator—never would say a word ; they have even named the rivers that empty themselves into the Ohio.

" CHILDREN : I am still of the opinion that the Ohio is your right and title. I have given orders to the commandant of Fort Miami to fire on the Americans whenever they make their appearance again. I will go down to Quebec, and lay your grievances before the great man. From thence they will be for-

warded to the King, your father.   Next Spring you will know
the result of every thing, what you and I will do."

The particulars of this council, and the labors of Governor
Simcoe and Captain Brant in otherwise tampering with the
Indians, transpired through some prisoners taken by General
Wayne, and also through the means of a confidential deputation
of the Wyandots of Sandusky, who were disposed to peace.   According to their statements, Governor Simcoe advised them not
to listen to any terms of pacification, which did not secure to
them their long-contested boundary.   He moreover proposed to
them to convey all their lands west of that river to the King, in
trust, that a pretext might be furnished for a direct interposition
of his Majesty's arms in their behalf.   In furtherance of this
object, he advised them to obtain a cessation of hostilities until
the Spring following ; when a great council of all the warriors
and tribes should take place, which might call upon the British
for assistance.   The English would at that time be prepared to
attack the Americans from every quarter, and would drive them
back across the Ohio, and compel the restoration to the Indians
of their lands.

Captain Brant's counsel was to the same effect.   He told them
to keep a good heart and be strong ; to do as their father advised ; that he would return home at present with his warriors,
and come again in the Spring with a stronger force.   They would
then have the whole Summer before them for operations, and
the Americans would not be able to stand before them.   He had
always been successful, and with the force they would then be
able to bring into the field, he would ensure them a victory.
He told them, however, that he could not attack the Americans
at that time, as it could do no good, but would bring them out
against the Indians with more troops in the Winter.   He therefore advised the Chiefs to amuse the Americans with a prospect
of peace until the Spring, when the Indians might be able to
fall upon and vanquish them unexpectedly.

There was considerable division of opinion in the council ;
the Wyandots being inclined to peace, and also portions of
the other tribes.   But large presents were given, and the counsels of Brant and Governor Simcoe prevailed—the Indians returning to their temporary homes, consisting of huts and tents
in the neighborhood of the fort at the Rapids.   Captain Brant,

however, left these councils under high displeasure toward the Chiefs of the three principal tribes, in consequence of some neglect which he construed into an insult. What was the precise nature of the circumstances, his papers do not disclose. But among those papers, is a letter from seven of the Chiefs of those tribes, couched in terms of humble apology. The following passages are cited from this letter :—

" The Chiefs of the three nations are very sorry, and in great trouble, that Colonel Brant was obliged to leave them so precipitately ; that it was their intention to be in the greatest friendship with him, and that they intended to hold council with him immediately after that with the Governor was finished.

" They sincerely hope Colonel Brant will take their apology for not waiting upon him when his messenger arrived with his pipe. They own themselves much in fault, but are willing by their future services to convince him that they esteem and honor him.

" In token of friendship they send Colonel Brant their Union belt of wampum, as a pledge that they now will, and their children in future generations will, be in peace and unity with him and the Six Nations, and wish a correspondence to commence immediately by express between them, on the most friendly terms.

" They have heard with grief that Colonel Brant departed hence with a heavy heart and full of sorrow for their negligence and misbehavior, and therefore send him an additional string of wampum to enlighten his heart, and renew friendship with him."*

Such was the posture of Indian affairs at the close of the year 1794 ; and the prospect then was, certainly, that another campaign of active hostilities must ensue. But it was otherwise ordered. The Indians themselves were growing weary of the contest, and becoming more and more convinced that they could not contend successfully against the Americans, of whose leader, General Wayne, they stood in great fear. Before the close of

---

* This letter, or "speech" as it was called, was signed as follows—the names being written in full by a gentleman named William Bailey, who subscribes the paper as a witness, and each Chief drawing his own mark rudely with the pen :— AQUSHUA, the mark of a *Fox :* SOWOSAY—a *Beaver :* QUAGEEWON—a *Crane :* CUCHEHWASKISEEGUA—a *Hatchet :* BOUEMAWCUTUS—a *Wolf :* GOWSOWAINSE—a *Turtle :* CLAPPUM—an *Arrow-head.*

the season, it was ascertained that the warriors from a distance were re-crossing the Mississippi, declaring that it was useless to attempt longer to fight. In March, the difficulties between the United States and Great Britain were adjusted by the treaty of Mr. Jay, which, despite the influence of France and the fierce clamors of the democratic opposition, General Washington had the sagacity and firmness to ratify; so that the Indians were deprived of even the expectation of farther assistance from the accustomed quarter. The restlessness of the Six Nations, the Mohawks excepted, had been quieted by the victory of Wayne; so that no farther support could be anticipated from that direction. The result of all these circumstances was, that by the treaty of Greenville, concluded with the hostile Indians by General Wayne, on the 3d of August, 1795, the long, expensive, and destructive war, which had for so many years desolated that frontier, was terminated in a manner perfectly satisfactory to the United States. In the language of Captain Brant in one of his speeches delivered long afterward, " the Indians, convinced by " those in the Miami fort, and other circumstances, that they " were mistaken in their expectations of any assistance from " Great Britain, did not longer oppose the Americans with their " wonted unanimity. The consequence was, that General " Wayne, by the peaceable language he held to them, induced " them to hold a treaty at his own head-quarters, in which he " concluded a peace entirely on his own terms." With this event closed the military career of Joseph Brant—Thayendanegea.

CHAPTER XIII.

THE termination of Brant's military life brought not therewith a state of inactivity. The proverbial indolence of his race in regard to all matters excepting the war-path and the chase, was not a characteristic of him. On the contrary, the history of man scarcely supplies a parallel instance of such active, unremitting, and unwearied public service, as well in the council as in the field, as was performed by this celebrated man, from the day when he first fleshed his youthful tomahawk at Lake George, until his death more than half a century afterward. The war of the American Revolution being ended, it has already been seen that he early thereafter directed his attention to the improvement of the moral and social condition of his nation. Nor did he lose sight of this object during the years of his active interposition in the complicated affairs of the western nations with the United States.

Mention has been made in a former chapter of the difficulties in which, subsequent to the Revolution, the Six Nations were involved, respecting their lands in the State of New-York, the adjustment of which repeatedly demanded the attention of Captain Brant. There were, likewise, similar difficulties to be adjusted with the purchasers of the Connecticut reservation in Ohio, respecting which formal negotiations were held.

Nor did these constitute all his troubles. But a few years had elapsed after the grant of the Grand River country had been obtained, before difficulties sprang up between the Indians and the Provincial Government, in regard to the nature of the title by which the former were to hold their new possessions. The Chief and his people supposed that the territory allotted to them had been conveyed in fee by a perfect title. But in this supposition they were disappointed. There is scarcely a finer or more inviting section of country in North America than the peninsula formed by Lake Ontario on the east, Lake Erie on the south, and Lake Huron on the west—through the heart of which flows the Grand River. The Indians, therefore, had not long been in the occupancy of their new country, before the white settlers began to plant themselves down in their neighborhood. To a man of Brant's sagacity, it was at once obvious that in such an attractive region of country the approach of the white man would soon circumscribe the hunting-grounds of his people, within the narrow boundaries of their own designated territory. He also saw, and without regret, that the effect would be to drive his people from the hunter to the agricultural state ; in which case, while his territory was too small for the former, it would be far larger than would be necessary for the latter condition of life. As a compensation for the loss of his game, therefore, he conceived the idea of making sales of portions of his lands, for the creation of an immediate fund for the benefit of the nation, and of leasing other portions in such manner as to ensure a perpetual revenue. There was no selfish design in this project, farther than may be found in the fact, that his own fortunes were identified with those of his people. However covetous Captain Brant may have been of honor and power, he was neither covetous nor mercenary in regard to property. In one of his speeches he declared, with all solemnity, that he had never appropriated a dollar of money, or its value in other property, belonging to his nation, to his own use. Nor had he ever charged his nation a dollar for his services, or even for his personal expenses, in all the journeys he had performed upon their business. All his personal wants, under all circumstances, had been supplied from his own private funds.

There was another consideration connected with his desire to make sales and leases of lands to white settlers. He was anxious to promote the civilization of his people; and in his first negotiations with General Haldimand, after the close of the war, he made provision for the erection of a church and school-house; and it is an interesting fact, that the first temple erected for the worship of the true God in Upper Canada, was built by the Chief of a people recently pagan; and the first bell which summoned the people to the house of prayer in that province on the Christian Sabbath, was carried thither by him. In the furtherance of his plans of civilization, the Chief knew very well that an increasing contiguous white population would be the means of introducing such of the common arts and employ-ments of life, as would materially contribute to the comfort and happiness of his people, while at the same time their progress in civilization would be greatly accelerated.

But he had no sooner commenced disposing of some small portions of land, than the colonial government raised objections. It was alleged that his title was imperfect—that a pre-emptive right to the soil had been retained by the government; and, as a consequence, that the Indians had no right to sell a rood of ground, since it was their's no longer than they themselves should occupy it. The question proved a fruitful source of disagreement between the parties, and of perpetual vexation to the old Chief until the day of his death. Council after council was holden upon the subject, and conference after conference; while quires of manuscript speeches and arguments, in Brant's own hand, yet remain to attest the sleepless vigilance with which he watched over the interests of his people, and the zeal and ability with which he asserted and vindicated their rights.

Even his friend Governor Simcoe was among the most strenuous opponents of the claim of the Indians to the fee of the soil, and in one instance attempted to curtail their grant by di-recting the land board to run a line due west from the head of Lake Ontario, which would have stripped the Mohawks of the fairest half of their possessions. On examining the grant from General Haldimand, however, the Governor desisted from this purpose; but still was determined that the Indians should neither lease nor sell any portion of their grant, nor make any manner of use of it, excepting such portions as they should cultivate with their own hands. By these proceedings, the situation of the Indians was rendered truly uncomfortable. Reduced to a nar-

row strip of land of only twelve miles in breadth, their hunting was of course seriously affected ; while their skill in agriculture was so imperfect, that some other resources were indispensable to their sustenance.

In order to define more clearly and explicitly the rights of
the Indians, two other deeds were successively framed and presented for their acceptance—both of which were promptly rejected, as being less favorable than their original grant. Finally, in 1795, Governor Simcoe visited Grand River with his
councillors, for the purpose of ascertaining, as he said, the real
wishes and condition of the Indians. A Council was holden,
and the Chief delivered an elaborate speech, containing the
whole history of the grant, the circumstances under which it
had been made, and the difficulties they had been called to encounter. Among other objections, it seems to have been alleged by the Provincial authorities, as a pretext for dealing
hardly by the Indians, that the government had been deceived
in regard to the location and value of the territory. General
Haldimand had supposed that the territory in question lay a long
distance from Niagara, and would not be approached by a white
population for an age to come. These assertions were sternly
denied by Brant, who declared that the Commander-in-chief,
at the time of making the grant, was thoroughly acquainted with
the situation, its peculiar advantages, and its value.

This conference with Governor Simcoe resulted in nothing
more than a promise that the speech of Thayendanegea should
be forwarded to Lord Dorchester. Governor Simcoe left the
province soon afterward, and a change was made in the admi
nistration of the Indian department, by the appointment of Captain Claus to the Indian agency at Niagara. It appears that
before his departure, the Governor had confirmed such sales
as had been previously made by the Indians ; but difficulties
arose on making the surveys, which once more placed every-
thing afloat. The consequence was, that another hearing took
place before Mr. Claus at Niagara, in October, 1796, at which,
in another written speech, the Chief gave a historical argument
of his case. From portions of this speech, it appears that Upper
Canada had already become infested with unprincipled land-
jobbers, who were the especial dislike of the Chief. " I cannot
" help remarking," said he, " that it appears to me that certain

" characters here, who stood behind the counter during the last
" war, and whom we knew nothing about, are now dictating to
" your great men concerning our lands. I should wish to
" know what property these officious persons left behind them
" in their own country, or whether, through their loyalty, they
' ever lost any ! I doubt it much. But 'tis well known that
" scarcely a man amongst us but what sacrificed more or less
" property by leaving our homes. I again repeat, that if these
" officious persons have made the smallest sacrifice of property,
" then I think they may in some measure be allowed to inter-
" fere, although it may be well known that personal interest
" prompts them to it, not the public good."

This speech, the Chief declared, should be his final effort to
obtain justice from the " great men below "—the provincial government meaning. If not successful there, he declared his
purpose of proceeding to England, and bringing his case in
person before the King. But this resolution was contingent,
and was not kept. On the departure of Governor Simcoe, the
Executive government of the colony devolved upon the Hon.
Peter Russell, President of the Executive Council of the province. For the more convenient administration of the Indian
affairs of the province, Mr. Russell was clothed with all the
powers upon that subject previously exercised by the General-
in-chief at Quebec, acting under the advice of the Superintendent-General of Indian Affairs, Sir John Johnson. Captain
Brant lost no time in bringing the subject of his land title before Mr. Russell, and he speedily succeeded in part. The sales
already made were confirmed, and the old Chief wrote to his
friend and correspondent, Thomas Morris, Esq., then a resident of Canandaigua, that their difficulties respecting lands
were nearly removed, and he had reason to believe that hence-
forth their affairs would go on to their satisfaction.* The
basis of the arrangement sanctioned by the acting Governor,
was, that the lands then sold, or intended to be sold, by the Indians, should be surrendered to the government, which, upon
the good faith of the agreement, was to issue grants to the per-

* Letter to Thomas Morris, Esq., July 30, 1797. [Mr. Morris has furnished the
author with a package of letters from Capt. Brant, written between the years 1796
and 1801, which, though chiefly upon private business, have nevertheless been
found of use in the present work.]

sons nominated as purchasers by the agent transacting the land business of the nation.   Captain Brant was acting in that capacity.   The lands were of course to be mortgaged as security for the payment of the principal and interest of the purchase money.   It was, moreover, the duty of the Agent to appoint three trustees, to receive the payments in trust for the Indians, and to foreclose the mortgages in cases of default—the lands to revert to the Indians.   Captain Brant fulfilled his part of the agreement to the letter ; but the government failed altogether to comply with its own corresponding duty.   Some of the purchasers had paid their interest for several years, but could not obtain their titles ; others died, and the heirs were in the like predicament, and the whole business became involved more than ever in difficulty.   Added to all which, as the Indians themselves improved in their agricultural labors, the system of possessing all things in common operated unequally, and interposed great embarrassments to individual industry.   But so long as the government refused to the Indians the privilege of disposing of the fee of the soil, the nation could not convey any portion of its own domain to its own people.*

There were other difficulties in the business, which it would be tedious to enumerate, the result of all which was, that the arrangement was in fact a nullity.   Not only so, but the Mohawks felt themselves to be an independent nation, and they, or perhaps more correctly speaking, their proud and indomitable Chief, could ill brook submission to such a species of guardianship.   The "satisfaction" arising from the arrangement under the auspices of President Russell, was consequently of but short continuance, and the Captain was compelled to fight his land battles over again.   Many were the councils and conferences which succeeded, in all of which Brant was the principal speaker and defender of the rights of his people to the fee of their lands.   The design of the British government was to hold the Indians in a state of pupilage, according to the practice of the United States ; and consequently to allow them merely the occupancy of lands of which the government claimed the title. But neither the Mohawks nor their indefatigable leader would listen to any such doctrine ; always, on all occasions asserting

* Memorial of John Norton to the Marquis of Camden.

their own complete and entire independence as a nation. They were an independent nation in the Valley of the Mohawk, argued the Chief in one of his speeches,* and were the undisputed owners of the soil of their country. Their right in this respect had never been questioned. On the breaking out of the war, they had relinquished their country—their all—because of their friendship and loyalty to the King. " In the year 1775," said the old Chief in the speech now referred to, " Lord Dorchester, " then Sir Guy Carleton, at a very numerous council, gave us " every encouragement, and requested us to assist in defending " their country, and to take an active part in defending his Ma- " jesty's possessions ; stating, that when the happy day of peace " should arrive, and should we not prove successful in the contest, " that he would put us on the same footing in which we stood pre- " vious to our joining him. This flattering promise was pleas- " ing to us, and gave us spirit to embark heartily in his Majesty's " cause. We took it for granted that the word of so great a " man, or any promises of a public nature, would ever be held " sacred." Again, in another part of the speech, the Captain remarked :—" We were promised our lands for our services, " and those lands we were to hold on the same footing with " those we fled from at the commencement of the American war, " when we joined, fought, and bled in your cause. Now is pub- " lished a proclamation, forbidding us leasing those very lands " that were positively given us in lieu of those of which we " were the sovereigns of the soil. This, brothers, is surely a " contradiction that the least discerning person amongst you " must perceive, and which we think wonderful. Of those " lands we have forsaken, we sold, we leased, and we gave " away, when and as often as we saw fit, without hindrance on " the part of your government; for your government well knew " we were the lawful sovereigns of the soil, and they had no " right to interfere with us as independent nations " In support of this assertion, the Chief proceeded to enumerate various sales and gifts of their lands ; among which he mentioned the large and celebrated tract to Sir William Johnson, commonly called

* Speech delivered at a meeting of the Chiefs and warriors at Niagara before Co- lonel Sheaffe, Colonel Claus, and others, in August, 1803, on the occasion of a government proclamation forbidding the sale or leasing of any of their lands by the Indians.

the Royal Grant, and for signing the conveyance of which the Captain asserted that he received a present of fifty pounds.

The history of the whole controversy was very clearly stated in the speech just cited, and the argument throughout exceedingly well put. The Captain, in some of his speeches, dwelt with emphasis upon another feature of his case, affording a farther example of the magnanimity of the Mohawks in their dealings with the government, and the want of that attribute as evidenced in the manner of their requital. The Indians never asked of the crown any compensation for the vast tracts of their hunting-grounds relinquished by adhering to the cause of the crown. In a letter written to Sir John Johnson at this stage of the controversy, the veteran Chief cut with a two-edged blade :—
" You know we demand nothing new. We have made no de
" mand for compensation for our hunting-grounds, which were
" very extensive, nor for our wood-lands adjoining our improve
" ments. All we ask is a confirmation of our just right to this
" very land, which we receive in lieu of those for which we re
" ceived no compensation. I presume few loyalists have omit
" ted charging, and receiving pay for their woodlands, as we
" did ; many of whom received lands who had never possessed
" one foot before."*

But the prospect of obtaining justice from the Provincial Government becoming less and less favorable by the lapse of time, the Chief again directed his attention to the parent government. Availing himself of the return to Europe of the Count De Puisy, whom he describes " as a brother soldier and fellow-sufferer in the cause of loyalty,"† the Captain placed in his hands a succinct history of the troubles he was laboring to remove, with

---

* In a letter subsequently addressed to Lord Dorchester, after the relinquishment by that officer of the Canadian Government, Captain Brant estimated those hunting grounds relinquished by his tribe at more than two millions of acres.

† In one of Captain Brant's speeches, dated October 28, 1800, this passage occurs :—" It had for some time been observed that the too large, uninhabited space " between York and the head of the Lake was a great inconvenience to the commu-" nication by land, we therefore thought it a fit occasion to remove the difficulty, by " presenting the Count de Puisy and his adherents a tract of land in this space—" sympathizing with them as having suffered in the cause of loyalty, and being "obliged to quit their native clime on that account, and seek an asylum in this un-"cultivated region. This was objected to," &c., &c. When the younger Brant visited London, twenty years afterward, he refers to the Count as then living in retirement in the neighborhood of that capital.

an urgent request that he would lay the same before his Majesty's ministers. By the same conveyance he likewise addressed a vigorous appeal to Lord Dorchester, then in England, enclosing to his Lordship a copy of his original promise to him (Brant) as written down in 1775, and also the subsequent confirmation of that promise by General Haldimand.* He was, moreover, in active correspondence upon the subject with the Duke of Northumberland, in whom the Mohawks had ever a constant friend.

These attempts to enlist the parent government in behalf of the Indian claim, were backed by the mission to England of Teyoninhokarawen, alias John Norton, who spread the case before the ministers in a strong and lucid memorial addressed to Lord Camden, then one of his Majesty's ministers. Among other considerations, it was urged by Norton, that in case their lands should be released from all incumbrances, and every tribe and family be allowed to have their just portion of land con firmed to them, the province would be strengthened by the emigration thither of the major part of the tribes of the Six Nations, who still remained in the United States. It had, doubtless, entered into the policy of Brant to bring the ancient confederacy of the Six Nations once more together, within the jurisdiction either of England or the United States. The removal of the Mohawks into Canada had not dissolved the union of those nations, although their separation, thrown, as they were, under the action of different superior laws, and obliged sometimes to hold their own councils within the boundary of one nation, and at other times within the limits of another, could not but be attended with many embarrassments. Indeed, so numerous were the difficulties they were obliged to encounter, and such was the conduct of the provincial government in regard to their lands, that the Mohawk Chief, notwithstanding his attachment to the crown, had at one period contemplated withdrawing from Canada with his people in disgust. That such a project was actually entertained, appears by the following lette to his friend Morris:—

* The copy of this letter to Lord Dorchester is not entire. Two foolscap pages have only been preserved, or rather, all but the first two pages has been lost.

CAPTAIN BRANT TO THOMAS MORRIS, ESQ.

(SECRET AND CONFIDENTIAL.)

" *Grand River, December* 26, 1800.

" DEAR SIR,

" From our friendship, and the regard you have continually shown to Indians in general, I flatter myself you will be so good as to assist in what I am about to communicate to you.

" There are numbers of our people scattered about in the westward at Sandusky, the Miami, &c. I wish to have them collected in one place, and for that purpose intend making a purchase of the Western Indians, so that any moving from here may also find a place to go to. We are certain that the Indians there will be very happy at the proposal, and that they even would give it for nothing; but we rather wish to buy, that it may be indisputably our own. The favor I have to ask of you is, that you would please to oblige us so far as to sound some of your friends in Congress if such a thing could be confirmed by them, for if we should move there, we would desire to be under the protection of the United States. What you may say on the subject to any one, I hope you will do it in a confidential manner; you may learn the general sentiments in the way of conversation, without making known our real intentions. The reason of my being so cautious, is the great jealousy of the British.

" Dear Sir,
" I am in truth,
" Your sincere friend
" And humb. serv't,
" JOS. BRANT.

" *Thomas Morris, Esq.*"

Nothing farther is disclosed among the manuscripts of Brant respecting this design of removal into the United States, and the suggestion was most likely owing to a momentary feeling of despondency and vexation. But it was his fortune soon afterward to encounter an annoying circumstance from another and most unexpected quarter—his long and well-tried friend, Sir John Johnson. The circumstance referred to was the receipt of a letter from the Baronet, then at Niagara, under date of September 1st, 1801, in which, after apologizing for his long delay in answering certain letters, from an apprehension that he could not so frame his communications as to avoid hurting the old Chief's feelings, the writer adverted to the difficulties respecting the lands. He spoke of some uneasiness prevailing at Grand River; and stated that he had given his views, as to these troubles, to Captain Claus, in writing, and advised the Chief to aid in getting up a council, and adjusting the matter upon the basis he had proposed. In regard to the claim of the Mohawks upon a portion of the Mississagua reservation, the Baronet advised the Chief to abandon it at once, admonishing him that the government was determined, under no circumstances whatsoever, to sanction that claim; but on the contrary would protect the Mississaguas in the quiet and peaceable possession of all their lands. The letter concluded as follows :—" Let me therefore once more " advise you to give up all concern in their affairs, and desist " from assembling the different nations in distant parts of the " country, and only attend to the business of your settlement, " except when called upon by government to do otherwise; as " it gives opening to the world to put unfavorable constructions " on your conduct, which must tend to lessen your consequence " in the opinion of those at the head of affairs; and I much fear " may do you serious injury. And as you can have no doubt " of my friendship for you and your fine family, I earnestly re- " quest you will maturely weigh what I now recommend to " you, and consider it as the result of serious reflection."

This missive kindled the indignation of Brant, and elicited some spirited letters in reply. Its burden was the existence of difficulties among the Indians themselves, arising, as the Baronet had left the Chief to infer, from their distrust of the proceedings of Brant himself. The council, which the Superintendent-General had directed his Deputy, Captain Claus, to convoke, had been held, but does not seem to have been attended by any other results than an entire exoneration, by the sachems, of their principal Chief from all censure.* The Captain, however, was not satisfied with allowing the matter to rest there; and he wrote the Baronet, in a tone of decision, demanding specific charges, if any could be produced against him, accompanied by the names of his accusers. He likewise severely upbraided the

* See Appendix, No. X.

officers of the government for their conduct toward him, charging the fact upon them, explicitly, of having not only sanctioned the great Indian Confederacy of which there has been occasion so frequently to speak, but of having caused the formation of that confederacy under their own immediate auspices. This letter, as a historical document, bearing upon other relations than those appertaining to the writer, as an individual, deserves preservation, and is accordingly transcribed :—

CAPTAIN BRANT TO SIR JOHN JOHNSON, BAR'T.

" *Grand River, November*, 1801.

" DEAR SIR,

" When I answered your favor of the first of September last, I promised to let you hear farther from me after the meeting should have taken place, which you then said Captain Claus was to hold for the purpose of satisfying the discontented, &c.

" He did not, however, do any thing in the business, as I expected, from your letter, he would have done ; but the Chiefs, on being made acquainted with the contents of it, became uneasy, and called a scrutiny to find who it was among the Indians on this river that had expressed dissatisfaction at my conduct respecting the public lands. The dissatisfied party was found to be only a few of the lower Mohawks, mostly women, and no real chief among them. Afterwards, the Chiefs unanimously expressed their general approbation of my conduct as their agent in land matters, in a speech to Captain Claus. They at the same time hinted at the almost impossibility of things being done in such a manner as to please every particular individual, which was also the case in the discharge of his own duty as Superintendent ; but assured him that they, the Chiefs, who had constituted me their agent in land affairs, were perfectly satisfied. Since that I hear no more of the discontented ; all seem quiet. Then I was prepared to give a full explanation of all my transactions, and also put them in mind of the trouble and expense I had been at on their business ; but this conduct of the Chiefs prevented me, thinking if I yet persevered it would be wantonly ripping up old grievances, &c.

" I hope you will do me the favor to let me know who informed you that there prevailed such an universal discontent among the Grand River Indians at my transactions, as you said was the case; and you will infinitely oblige me by making me acquainted with the author of this rumor, which has not a little hurt my feelings; and it would also give satisfaction to the greater part of the Chiefs here.

"Respecting your advice not to have more councils of other nations, &c., the Chiefs, both here and at Buffalo, cannot comprehend the meaning of it; and I have been particularly requested, by two messengers from the latter, to remain unshaken in my public capacity, and attend to their common interests as usual; I therefore hope you will do me the kindness to acquaint me with the reason why I should desist from attending any councils of the nations of the General Confederacy which we formed under the auspices of Great Britain; and if our friendly intercourse with each other is supposed to be detrimental to the interests of government, and in what measure; for, since the year 1760, I perfectly remember what has passed at most councils, and I never recollect an instance of government interfering to prevent our mutual correspondence, but, on the contrary, they have rather encouraged our uniting. Should it therefore be the case, that what formerly gave satisfaction, has now quite a different effect, it will be very difficult for me to act so as not to get censured, without I am well acquainted with the change of politics. Also, the serious consequences you mention, that the not complying with your advice may be of to me, I would be glad to know what it is. I hope that laws and customs are not so far changed, as that punishment is first to be inflicted, and the trial brought on afterwards, and you should give me no plainer hint of it than that. In short, your advice seems no other than a threat in disguise. Still, my dear friend, don't think that I suspect you to be the author of it; but rather that you have softened the original so as to save my feelings.

"During the war, although *I bore the commission of a captain*, I never received commands as such, but acted as War Chief, which I believe was of more utility than if I had been in the other capacity—generally having more men under my command than is customary for one of that rank. Since the peace, I have attended to our affairs as a sachem. I never supposed it to be wrong my so doing; if it is so, I could wish to have written instructions how I am to conduct myself, so as to prevent the serious consequences spoken of, by which, probably, may be meant the taking from me my half-pay or pension. I hope to have the pleasure to hear from you as soon as possible ; at the same time I remain

" Dear Sir,

" Your very humble

" And obed't servant,

" Jos. BRANT

" Sir John Johnson, Bar't."

Norton had been furnished by Brant with letters to his friends in England, and among them to the Duke of Northumberland, who interested himself warmly in behalf of the object of his mission. Such, moreover, were the zeal and ability with which he discharged the duties of his errand, that for a time there was a prospect of his mission being crowned with entire success. The decision of the ministers was favorable to the Indians, and letters to that effect were dispatched to the Provincial government. These, however, were met by an unexpected movement at home, which palsied the exertions of the agent, and caused his return with hopes at least deferred, if not blighted. The cause of this untoward change in the course of the parent government will be developed in a few succeeding pages.

It appears that in the course of the controversy violent disagreements had arisen between Captain Brant and the Deputy Superintendent, which were ultimately embittered by mutual allegations of pecuniary delinquency. A charge of this description had been made against Brant, a few years before, in connexion with a negotiation between the government of the State of New-York and the Caughnawaga and St. Regis Indians, calling themselves the Seven Nations of Canada. These nations, as the reader has been informed in a former part of the present work, were clans of the Mohawks, who had long before separated from the principal nation, and settled upon the banks of the St. Lawrence. In the year 1792, they sent a deputation to the government of the State of New-York, claiming a tract of land covering a large portion of the northern part of the state ; all, indeed, lying between Lake Champlain on the East, and the head waters of the Mohawk on the West, bounded north by the St. Lawrence, and south by a line to be drawn from a point between Fort Edward and Lake George to the junction of Canada Creek with the Mohawk River, in the neighborhood of the Little Falls. This extensive claim was resisted by the state upon several grounds. One of these was, that the Indian title had been extinguished to a portion of the territory in question by the French; another, that several patents from the English crown had extinguished their title to other portions of it; added to all which, it was held by the state that the Caughnawagas had never any just title to the land, inasmuch as it originally belonged to the Six Nations, of whom the claimants formed but a small number. As proof of this position, it was contended by the state that the Six Nations had themselves sold this same territory, together with a large additional tract, extending from the Mohawk River to the Pennsylvania line, to Colonel John Livingston. This sale to Colonel Livingston was first made by forty-five chiefs of the Six Nations in 1787, and was confirmed in the following year, by a second deed, signed by sixty-five of their chiefs, and witnessed by Colonel John Butler and Joseph Brant. The purchase by Colonel Livingston being unconstitutional, was annulled; but the fact that such a sale had been made by the Six Nations at large, was adduced against the claim of the Caughnawagas, by way of showing that it was unfounded. Still as the St. Regis and Caughnawaga Indians persisted in their claim, a commission, consisting of Egbert Benson, Richard Varick, and James Watson, was appointed to treat with their Chiefs upon the subject; and it was not until the Summer of the year 1796 that an arrangement was effected, by virtue of which the Seven Nations relinquished their claim, with the exception of the St. Regis reservation, for a small sum in hand paid, and a yet smaller perpetual annuity.

It was as a witness only to the deed of sale to Colonel Livingston, that the name of Captain Brant came to be involved in this controversy. The Commissioners maintained to the last that the Six Nations had sold the lands, and that their great chief, Brant, was a witness to the sale. In reply to which, the Caughnawagas insisted that the Six Nations had no more right to sell the lands they claimed than they had to dispose of the city of New-York.* The Caughnawaga Chiefs, probably, did not exactly understand the case of the sale to Colonel Living-

* Talk of the Seven Nations, delivered to the Commissioners at Albany, May, 1796.

ston, which was set aside as being contrary to the fundamental
law of the state, nor the position in which the name of Joseph
Brant stood upon the deed. On the contrary, they seem to
have been impressed with an idea that Brant and the Mohawks
had been selling *their* lands *to the state.* The consequence
was a controversy between the Caughnawagas and the Mohawks, which gave the old Chief an infinite deal of trouble—
even after the affair between the former and the State of New
York had been amicably closed. The charges of the Caugh
nawagas amounted to this—that Brant and the Mohawks had
sold their lands to the state, and pocketed the avails. Brant
repelled the charge with indignation. In regard to the deed of
sale to which he was a witness, he affirmed that not a foot of
the territory claimed by the Caughnawagas was embraced within
it, but that the sale was of a portion only of lands belonging to
the Senecas. He demanded of the Caughnawagas their authority for the charge against himself and the Grand River Indians. They replied, that their information was derived from
the representations of the officers of the State of New-York at
Albany. Brant opened a correspondence with George Clinton *
and Governor Jay upon the subject, the negotiations having
commenced under the administration of the former and been
concluded under the latter. But not satisfied with any thing
resulting from the correspondence, he caused a deputation of
his tribe to repair to Albany,† at the head of which was his

---

* See Appendix, No. XI.

† Brant had previously, in 1797, visited Albany on the same business, accompanied by Corn-planter and two or three other sachems. Arriving at Canajoharie
in the evening, Brant called with his party upon Major Hendrick Frey, who
had served in the cause of the crown during the war of the Revolution, but returned to his native county after the close of the contest. The meeting of Brant
with Frey was like that of two brothers. The party adjourned to a tavern, where
they had a merry time of it during the live-long night. Many of their adventures
during the war were recounted, among which was a duel that had been fought by
Frey, to whom Brant acted as second. In the course of those relations, Corn-planter acknowledged that he shot the girl who was gathering berries in the neighborhood of Fort Stanwix, as related by Colonel Willett and cited in the first volume of
the present work. Corn-planter said he was lurking about the fort in order to seize
a prisoner; but failing in that object, fired upon the girl. The landlord of the inn,
named Rolfe, had resided near Fort Stanwix at the time, and could hardly be restrained from doing violence upon Corn-planter on hearing the relation.—[*Conversations of the author with Dr. Jonathan Eights of Albany, who, being at the time a
resident with Major Frey, was one of the party.*]

adopted nephew, John Norton, to meet a similar deputation from the Caughnawagas, face to face, and to require his accusers connected with the government of the State of New-York, either to substantiate their charges or acquit him in the presence of both delegations. The papers of Captain Brant are pretty full in regard to this controversy, which seems to have affected him with the keenest sensibility. The result of this double mission to Albany, however, does not exactly appear, save that the Chief was not well satisfied with it. At least thus much is evident from the tone of the annexed letter to his friend, Thomas Morris, who was a member of the Legislature of New-York at that time, and to whom he had given his deputies letters of introduction :—

CAPTAIN BRANT TO THOMAS MORRIS, ESQ.
"*Grand River, April* 4, 1799.
" DEAR SIR,

" It is now some time since the return of Mr. Norton and the Cayuga Chiefs from Albany: they have acquainted me with their treatment there, and that of the business they went on ; and particularly of your friendship and assistance to them while there ; for which I could not omit taking the earliest opportunity of testifying to you my most hearty thanks for the friendship you showed them, and hope you will not find us unmindful of the favor.

" At the same time I cannot avoid expressing my surprise to you at the conduct of your government respecting the affair of the Caughnawagas. In the first place, it appears their Commissioners treated the business so mysteriously as to make these people believe we had sold their lands ; first having defrauded us by having all that country included in the confirmation of Mr. Livingston's deed to Mr. Oliver Phelps, to which the Senecas signed their names, only supposing that they sold part of their own country, and to which I signed as a witness. This was made use of to convince the Caughnawagas they had no right to the country they inhabit ; and I learn that it was not till after much argument that your Government owned that they never paid any money to me or the Five Nations on account of these lands, and that they never looked on any Indians to have a right to them, either Caughnawagas or Five Nations. Had they only said this at first, when they treated with the Caughnawagas, and not brought our name in question, they would have saved us immense trouble. And now I cannot imagine what good reasons they could have to refuse our Deputies to certify in writing that they never paid us any money on account of these lands claimed by the Caughnawagas, which it is certain they never did. It still appears they wish to make the affair mysterious, and evade, as much as they can, the thoroughly clearing up of the business, so as to keep the Caughnawagas from making farther claims on them ; for it now appears pretty clear to us that they have wronged these people. However, their conduct comports a good deal with the uncivilized character of Judge Benson, who, I find, was one of the Commissioners ; and now the Governor left the business mostly to him, who I know would skin a flint if it was possible, should it belong to the Indians.*

" I intend, for my own satisfaction, to have the whole affair, from the beginning to ending, published in the newspapers.

" Dr. Sir,

" I am your most humble and

Obd't. Serv't.

" Jos. Brant.

" *Thomas Morris, Esq'r.'*

In July of the same year, Brant proceeded to the Caughnawaga country in person, accompanied by a body of Chiefs of several of the tribes, for the purpose of a thorough investigation in General Council. Such a council was convened ; and the difficulties, from the reports of the speeches preserved in writing by Captain Brant, were fully discussed—and that, too, in the most amicable manner. From several intimations in these speeches, it appears that the whole difficulty had been caused " by chattering birds," and by the machinations against Captain Brant, of the old Oneida Sachem, Colonel Louis. The Council-fire was kindled on the 8th of July. On the 9th Captain Brant was satisfied by the explanations given, and remarked " that he had

---

* Judge Benson was only one of the Commissioners ; but it is probably true that the business was confided entirely to him. In the original account of the treaty with the Caughnawagas, of May, 1796, containing the speeches written out in full on both sides, found by the author among Brant's papers, Judge Benson's signature stands alone at the close of the whole.

"pulled up a pine, and planted down beneath it the small bird
"that tells stories;" on the 10th, the Caughnawaga Chief replied—"Brother, we return you thanks: we also join with you
"to put the chattering-bird under ground from where the pine
"was taken up, there being a swift stream into which it will
"fall beneath, that will take it to the Big Sea, from whence it
"never can return."

The result of the Council seems to have been satisfactory on
all hands. Indeed, as Brant himself wrote to a correspondent
"in the States,"* a short time afterward, he was rather surprised that he had so little to encounter at their meeting:—"We
"expected they would have had a great deal to say to us; but
"instead of that, they said they had never accused us of them-
"selves—that it was only from what the people of New-York
"said that they had inquired about the matter; and that now
"they hoped we would be so good as to agree to bury the
"whole affair under ground." To Sir John Johnson he subse-
"quently wrote in the following terms:—"Without doubt, long
"before this you have received an authentic account of our
"business with the Caughnawagas, which has convinced you
"and the world of our innocence. You know that I was sup-
"posed to be a leader in that business, and how often I have
"been falsely accused. But upon investigation my rectitude
"has ever been sufficiently proved. This groundless accu-
"sation of theirs created a great expense to government as
"well as us, and I should expect that, after being convinced of
"their error, some acknowledgment should be made for the
"great trouble they have put us to."

But the Caughnawaga difficulties were no sooner at an end,
than it was his lot to encounter others yet more nearly touching
his pecuniary integrity, which annoyed him not a little. There
were active spirits about him, official and unofficial, who, for
reasons of their own, looked with no favorable eye upon the
mission of Teyoninhokàràwen. So strongly indeed were these
men opposed to the claims of the Indians, that they were led to
the adoption of very unjustifiable means, not only to circum-
vent the negotiations of Norton, but to prostrate the power and

---

* The name of this correspondent is not given in the original draught of the letter preserved among Brant's papers.

influence of the old Chief himself. To this end, domestic dissensions were fomented, even among his own kindred, the Mohawks. The Chief was again accused of peculations; and although the grant of the Grand River territory had been notoriously made for the exclusive benefit of the Mohawk nation, yet the Senecas, and others of the Iroquois Nations, not residing in Canada, were stirred up to claim a voice in the disposition of those lands, and in the domestic relations of that nation, by virtue of their confederate league, which had never before been construed as clothing them with any such rights or powers. In furtherance of the design of prostrating Brant and thwarting the efforts of Norton in England, a Council of the Six Nations was held at Buffalo Creek, under the direction of the Seneca Chiefs, Red Jacket and the Farmer's Brother; at which all the proceedings of Brant and Norton were formally disavowed, and Brant himself deposed from the chieftainship of the Confederacy, at the head of which he had stood for more than a quarter of a century. His associate Mohawk Sachems were likewise removed, and others, taken, as Jeroboam selected his priests, from the lowest of the people, appointed in their stead. None of the Mohawk Chiefs were present at this Council, but only a few of the discontents, and of the more worthless members of the nation, who had been wrought upon by the white opponents of the principal Chief. The whole movement was illegal, according to the ancient usages of the Confederacy, in other respects. The Council was not convened at the National Council-fire, which had years before been regularly removed from Buffalo Creek to the Onondaga Village on the Grand River. Nor, aside from the fact that the Senecas, and others residing within the United States, had no right to a voice in regard to the domestic affairs or the lands of the Mohawks, was the General Confederacy properly or legally represented. Red Jacket, however, was both a ready and a willing instrument in the hands of Brant's opponents. In all the councils in which it had been the fortune of the two Chiefs to meet for the transaction of business, there had been little of cordiality between them, and much less of friendship. *Yau-go-ya-wat-haw*, or Red Jacket, was not a chief by birth, but had made himself such by his cunning. He was artful, eloquent, and ambitious. Aspiring to the rank of a chief, he availed himself of the superstitious dispositions of his people to attain his object. His first essay was, to dream that he was, or should be, a Chief, and that the Great Spirit was angry because his nation did not advance him to that dignity. These dreams, with the necessary variations, were repeated, until, fortunately for him, the small-pox broke out among the Senecas. He then proclaimed the loathsome infliction as a judgment of the Great Spirit, because of the ingratitude of the nation to him. The consequence, ultimately, was, that by administering flattery to some, and working upon the superstitious fears of others, he reached the goal of his ambition. Brant, however, had always, on all suitable occasions, pronounced him a coward—the greatest coward of his race. He used to say that Red Jacket was always valiant for fight with his tongue ; but that, although by his eloquence he persuaded many warriors to fight, he was ever careful not to get into personal danger himself. He also asserted as a fact, that having sent others upon the war-path, he would turn to, and steal and kill their cows for his own use.* Smarting under the contemptuous treatment of the Mohawk Chief, therefore, the eloquent demagogue of the Senecas was not backward in compassing, as he hoped, the overthrow of his enemy, if not his rival. Hence, for years antecedent to the council called clandestinely for the deposition of Brant, Red Jacket had labored, with all art and diligence, to create jealousies and distrust against him.†

The Chief himself was, of course, early apprised of what had taken place, and the manner of the conspiracy, of which he appears to have written a full account to his friend, the Duke of Northumberland. The copy of only a portion of that communication has been discovered. It is without date, but must have been written in A. D. 1805.

---

* Conversations of the author with Thomas Morris, Esq. This gentleman, during his residence in the western part of New-York, became intimately acquainted with the Senecas and Mohawks—especially with their Chiefs—having assisted at several treaties with them. He once entertained Brant, Red Jacket, and a number of other chiefs, at his own house in Canandaigua. At dinner, Brant was very amusing ; and among other stories, related the cow-killing exploits of *a* Seneca Chief, in such an arch manner as to direct the attention of the whole company upon Red Jacket, and yet compel Red Jacket himself to raise an affected laugh.

† See the certificate of Israel Chapin, as to the general character of Brant, and the unfounded jealousies excited against him by his opponents, Appendix, No. XII·

RED JACKET.

From the Original Painting in the possession of James Thail Esq.

CAPTAIN BRANT TO THE DUKE OF NORTHUMBERLAND.

" MAY IT PLEASE YOUR GRACE :

" As my nephew, Teyoninhokàràwen, has safe returned, gratitude prompts me to return you my most hearty thanks for the very kind reception and aid you gave him, and express the regret myself and the other Chiefs of the Five Nations inhabiting the Grand River feel, that after the trouble your Grace has taken in our affairs, he should have been frustrated in having them concluded to our satisfaction by the intrigues of the Agent for Indian affairs, (a Mr. Claus,) of which I shall take the liberty to give you a succinct account.

" When, in consequence of the warm support you gave my nephew, dispatches were received by the late Governor from England, in favor of the Indians, the Agent insinuated, through his instruments of intrigue, that he was about effecting something much to their detriment, should they not immediately prevent it. But finding that he could not succeed at the Grand River, a few of the common people went to Buffalo Creek, a village of the Five Nations within the American line, where they had a council, and then went to Niagara,* where Mr. Claus, the Agent, dictated to them what was sent to England. *   *   *   Several of the principal Chiefs from Buffalo, who signed, are pensioners to the Americans ; one of them, Red Jacket, or the *Cow-killer*, the speaker, and the greatest coward of all the Five Nations, at the Connecticut (in New-England) Assembly swore, or promised, kissing the portrait of General Washington, to be true to their interests. But to make their numbers appear more respectable, all the common people signed as Chiefs, from the villages on the American side, as did the few, with three or four petty chiefs, who went from the Grand River. The poor fellows, in consequence of the promises, and having signed together with the officers, have been long expecting to receive their commissions ; and even some of them have been expecting to receive tidings of them by Teyoninhokàràwen. The purport of the writing was, that the mission and proceedings of Teyoninhokàràwen should be disallowed of and disavowed ; that I should be displaced from being Chief ; and that a few settlers introduced by the Chiefs ——————."

* Vide certificate of Captain Leonard, and other American officers, then stationed at Niagara.—Appendix, No. XIII.

Here the copy of this communication abruptly breaks off. But although the proceedings referred to were transmitted to England by the opponents of the Chief, and followed by consequences fatal to the mission of Norton ; yet the failure, so far as the Chief himself was concerned, was as signal as the plot in all respects was indefensible and unjust. It was but a few months anterior to these proc_edings, founded, in the main, upon alleged embezzlements, or mal-appropriations, of the revenue of his nation, that a General Council had been holden at Grand River, which was attended by the chiefs and warriors, the Deputy and Superintendent-General, and the principal military officers of the province, and at which the pecuniary transactions of Captain Brant had been fully investigated—found to be accurate, and approved. The proceedings at this council appear to have been dictated in the most amicable spirit ; and from their complexion, nothing could have been more unlikely than the revival of charges, then so thoroughly shown to be without foundation in truth.[*]

But the old Chief did not remain passive under his persecutions. He took an early occasion to meet a council of the faction of his own nation who were opposing him, and to upbraid them in no very measured terms for their ingratitude. His address was written out in full, in the Mohawk dialect, and was afterward circulated in the form of an appeal to his nation.[†] After a spirited review of his life, and the services he had rendered them from the commencement of the war of the Revolution, the appeal proceeded :—

  *   *   *   *   " It astonishes me, therefore, after all that I have done for you, to hear almost all of you, young and old, joining your voices with Colonel Claus, and saying of me that I have embezzled your property, and such like hard speeches, which you know are false,—while you never so much as think of mentioning the many important services I have rendered you, the many privations I have suffered on your account, and the journies I have undertaken for your benefit—for the

---

[*] See Appendix, No. XIV.

[†] This document was never translated by Captain Brant. Portions of the manuscript are illegible ; but all that can be read has been translated for the use of the author.

time and expenses of which you have never paid me one penny.
* * * * * * * *　At Philadelphia
the Americans spoke in a very friendly manner to me, and
made me large offers of presents for myself and family if I
would prevent any farther attacks from the Indians. But I
positively refused to accept of any thing from them, lest I should
injure your good name as the Six Nation Indians. And again,
I knew that the King would not suffer me to be in want; and
had I accepted any thing at this time, it might have been
thought that I had been bribed, and become a traitor, which,
when made public, would have been disgraceful to me, and injurious to you as my people. I thought I could depend on our
white brethren, the King's subjects, should I at any time need
their assistance. * *　There was the Grand River
Tract, upon which I might have had a farm, and lived on its
produce. These considerations were more than sufficient to
deter me from receiving the valuable presents offered for my
acceptance. * * * * * * *　I think
the only way I could satisfy you, would be for me to pay out of
my own purse for every item that has to be expended for your
public uses. My only crime is, that I want to make you a
happy people, and for you to be enabled to call your land your
own forever; and not leaving it doubtful whether it is yours
or not. I say you would be well pleased if every thing could
be done for the general good of the Six Nations, without parting with a foot of land to pay for contingencies. Colonel Claus
asks you where your money is gone to? He never asks where
the proceeds of sales of your lands are gone to, else you might
tell him that it is gone to assist in building his splendid house.
Whenever I have had occasion to use any of your money, I
have never touched any but the interest, and have left the principal entire. But your friend Claus has devoted principal and
interest together; and yet you come to my house complaining. * * *　I ask again, what do you find in my
conduct to disapprove of? If you can point any thing out,
I should like to hear it. Or, will you say that every thing
that I have done has been for your injury and not for your benefit?

　　* * * * * * * * * *

"I say I cannot find, in all that I have done, that any thing has tended to your injury, or the injury of the King's cause. Yet you speak of me as one who is your enemy—as one who does what he can to injure you ; and I have no doubt that you, who are hearing me, feel so toward me in your hearts, although I have reiterated in your hearing many instances where what I did tended to raise your name as well as my own ; and in other instances, when I might have been enriched, I have refused receiving for fear of your name being tarnished. Still, you would almost brand me with the name of thief, although not one of you have ever subscribed a penny to pay my expenses when I have travelled on your public business."

The original manuscript of this address is much broken, especially in that portion of it containing a review of his services in connexion with the wars of the north-western Indians with the United States. The following fragments of sentences upon that subject, only, have been translated :—

*   *   *   " Every man of us thought, that by fighting for the King, we should ensure to ourselves and children a good inheritance.   *   *   *   *   *   *   At another time, at the last council we held, when the Americans were talking with the Indians, I spoke to Otsinarenta, and said, ' if the Americans fail in   *   *   *   *   *   I should like to go and surprise Wayne when he least expects it.' "

It was very soon manifest that the pretended deposition of the veteran Mohawk, at the instigation of white men, and through the immediate agency of Red Jacket, was no act of the great body of the Six Nations, much less of his own nation ; and the attempt to shake the faith of their " fathers in council," in the perfect integrity of the Chief who had so long been their leader in the cabinet and in the field, was a signal abortion. A meeting of the chiefs and warriors was soon afterward held, at which the whole controversy seems again, from the fragments of the proceedings yet in existence, to have been renewed. From one of the speeches, the following passages, connected immediately with the position and conduct of Brant, and the proceedings against him, are extracted :—

" BROTHER, LISTEN ! Is it not thus, when a present is given, that the bestower will not think of again grasping hold of it ? But it seems as if we were in that predicament—not being considered as real proprietors. We are grieved and ashamed that so much should have been said on the subject, without it being confirmed according to the first promise.

" BROTHER : We find divisions among us. The young men think to take the lead, who know nothing of our affairs nor what we suffered in the war. According to the first formation of our confederacy, the Mohawk was the leading nation. So it has been since our establishment at the Grand River. Therefore our leading Chief, Captain Brant, has stood foremost in our affairs, with which he is thoroughly acquainted.

" BROTHER : There have been rumors concerning our money, and the application made of it. We, that have been engaged in the public affairs, know where it is gone. He has not been always travelling, and employed on his own concerns—it has been on those of the public. He has been to the other side of the water, and several times to Quebec ; and always in these journies expended his own property, we never making any collection for him whatever. And now what he may have made use of is only the interest. Nothing has been taken from the principal. The payment for one township has been made without any delinquency whatever. We are perfectly satisfied with all his transactions.

" BROTHER, LISTEN ! That which was done at Buffalo, and which you have confirmed and sent to the other side of the water, was a thing that had never before taken place, in which they pretend to break our Chief, Captain Brant. But we assure you, brother, that this shall not be ; for we know not his having so transgressed as to merit such treatment. Neither is it proper that such a proceeding within the American line, and done by Indians inhabiting that territory, should be countenanced by you."

At the same setting, *Tchaosennoghts*, or *Duguoin*, a Seneca Chief, spoke as follows :—

" BROTHER : You see here a remnant of the warriors that ·fought last war, whose hearts are grieved that they have lived to see the present change of our treatment, and our situation. The divisions existing among us, and the attempts of the young men to put the Chiefs aside, have no other origin than the Indian store. It is there the young men receive from his Majesty's bounty that which was designed for those who fought and suffered in his cause, and who are now treated with neglect. It is from this they are led to imagine themselves men of ability and consequence. It is easy for them to say, now, there is nothing to be done, or no danger—that they are loyal, and side with government. We are no less loyal, we assure you, now; and when occasion required, we gave proofs of our attachment. But we know our Great Father is no less generous than opulent, and does not want our lands. Neither can we think ourselves departing from our duty in wishing to preserve them for our posterity, for we are poor. It is not Captain Brant who is the sower of dissension ; but it is what I just mentioned that causes the division amongst us.

" BROTHER : The right of being chief, according to our customs, arises either from hereditary line on the female side, or from having been distinguished by meritorious conduct, so as to be accepted as such. This has not been the case in the late appointment you sanctioned. One of them, to whom you pay great regard, we know has been distinguished in your opinion for some things which we have not been accustomed to pay that respect to."

Finally, at this, or a subsequent General Council, a speech, drawn up in the form of a declaration, was executed, under the sanction of the signatures and seals of sixteen of the most distinguished chiefs, residents upon the Grand River, and representing the Mohawks, Cayugas, Oghkwagas, Tuscaroras, and one Delaware chief; bearing the most unequivocal testimony to the integrity of Thayendanegea, and asserting their undiminished confidence in his faithful management of their business, as agent in the matter of their lands. It was stated in this paper that he had desired, of himself, some time before, to withdraw from that agency, and that he had only consented to remain therein at their urgent solicitation—he requiring that a board of twenty-four chiefs might be selected from the different tribes, to act as counsellors, and probably to determine all questions of doubt or controversy. " This," says the declaration, " has been done—but at the same time we desired that he might " continue at the head. And farther hearing that there are " many obstacles yet preventing the equitable conclusion of our " land business, we now unanimously renew and strengthen " him in quality of agent, which, from the confidence we have " in his integrity from what has already passed, we assure our-

" selves he will exert himself in that office, as far as lies in his
" power, to promote the general welfare. With these strings
" we therefore exhort him to continue with moderation and pa-
" tience, and flatter ourselves from the equity of our brethren,
" the British government, and his abilities, all difficulties will
" at last be surmounted."

Nothing could be more explicit than this testimony of exoneration, so far as the charges against the Chief were connected
with his management of the land concerns of his people. But
his vindication did not rest here. Soon after the return of
Teyoninhokârâwen to the Grand River, a general council of the
Six Nations was convened at Niagara, for the purpose of meeting the Deputy Superintendent-General, and entering a solemn
protest against the proceedings of the council at which Red
Jacket and the Farmer's Brother had pretended to depose
Thayendanegea. For several days the Deputy declined meeting the Council, upon the plea of waiting for the attendance of
Mr. Selby, a gentleman from Detroit. But as that gentleman
did not arrive, and it was uncertain when he would come, if
at all, the Chiefs determined to proceed with their business.
The Deputy, accompanied by Colonel Proctor, met the Chiefs
only to repeat his excuse, and to declare, that under existing
circumstances, he would not listen to what they had to say.
The Chiefs, however, resolved to proceed with their deliberations ; and their protest, yet existing in the chirography of Captain Brant, was read and sanctioned by the council, in presence
of several officers of the garrison, and also of several distinguished civilians. This paper contained a succinct review of
the controversy respecting the lands ; the object of Norton's mission to England ; the partial success of that agent—thwarted
only by the use that had been made of the proceedings of Red
Jacket's unauthorized and illegally-constituted council—a review of those proceedings ; and a protest against the whole.*
After the reading had been concluded, *Okoghsenniyonte*, a
Cayuga Chief, rose, and declared the general approbation of the
document by the council.

With these proceedings, it is believed, the efforts to prostrate
Brant, and deprive him of the chieftainship, ceased. In any
event they were not successful, and he remained at the head of

* See Appendix, No. **XV.**

the Mohawks, and consequently at the head of the Confederacy, until the day of his decease.

But, even under all these discouragements, it was not the design of the indefatigable Chief to relinquish his exertions to obtain justice for his people at the hands of the parent government. For this purpose another visit to England was determined upon, to be performed, either by himself, or Norton, or perhaps by both. This determination was announced to the Duke of Northumberland by letter, early in the year 1806:—

CAPTAIN BRANT TO THE DUKE OF NORTHUMBERLAND.

" *Grand River, January* 24*th*, 1806.

"MY LORD DUKE,

" The kind and affectionate letter I received from your Grace, has deeply penetrated our hearts with a sense of the honor you confer on the Five Nations in the sincere regard you express for their welfare ; and we hope that our future conduct, and that of our descendants, may never fail to cause such sentiments to be cherished in the noble hearts of the leaders of the British nation. For, however wounding to our feelings, or detrimental to our interests, may be the treatment we have received, and yet continue to receive, in this country, our reliance on the fatherly protection of his Majesty, and the confidence we have ever placed in the humanity, love of justice, and honor of your nation, is not weakened.

" The reason of my having delayed so long writing to your Grace, is, that from the arrival of a new Governor,* I received some hopes that what respects our land affairs might have been accomplished to our satisfaction in this country. But these hopes are now vanished—for appearances give me reason to apprehend that the old council, (principally composed of men influenced by an insatiable avarice for lands,) have so prejudiced his Excellency against us, as to disappoint what otherwise we might have expected from the innate benevolence of our father's representative. It is therefore the determination of the real chiefs and faithful warriors to comply with the brotherly advice of your Grace.† Therefore, either both of us, or Te-

---

* Sir Francis Gore.

† Contained, probably, in a letter from the Duke, which has not been found.

yoninhokârâwen,* shall make another attempt in England, invested with full powers from our nations, in writing, according to European customs, which your distance and our situation at present render absolutely necessary. Some small difficulties necessitate delay, or we would immediately be on the road.

" His Excellency has expressed that he will only hear from us through Mr. Claus, the head of the Indian Department, who is our implacable enemy ; and from what has already passed, we are well assured will do every thing in his power to thwart our success. Previous to receiving any speech, he requests that we give him a copy of it ; but himself, when he pretended, last of all, to make a defence to what we had expressed at Niagara in July, in reference to his having deceived the British ministry by the improper names sent to England to thwart the mission of Teyoninhokârâwen, he read his speech in such a low voice that it could only be heard by those who sat next to him, and afterwards refused to give us a copy of it. So we remain as ignorant of what he alleged in his defence, as if he had made no speech.

" The same confidence in the good faith of our allies, which animated my courage to persevere in the most trying situations during the war, and exhort to a similar perseverance those whom extraordinary difficulties, or American intrigue, might stagger, yet encourages me to hope for justice, notwithstanding the clouds that shade us from it.

" Mr. Wyatt, Surveyor General of this province, does me the favor to take this. The copy of the speech delivered at Niagara last July, Teyoninhokârâwen sent you several months ago ; so I hope you have received it by this time. With the sincerest respect and gratitude, I remain,

" Your Grace's

" Faithful friend and

" Brother warrior,

" Jos. Brant,

" *Thayendanegea.*

" His Grace the Duke of Northumberland,

" *Thorighwagèri.*"

---

* John Norton.

THE DUKE OF NORTHUMBERLAND TO CAPTAIN BRANT.

Northumberland House, 5th May, 1806.

" MY VERY GOOD FRIEND AND BROTHER WARRIOR :

" I have received safely your letter of the 24th January, which reached me on the 23d of last month, with all that pleasure which is naturally felt by one friend when he receives a letter from another friend. I am happy to find that the interest I took in the affairs of the Five Nations has been acceptable to their Board, as I am by being one of their community. They may rest assured I shall always be happy to assist them to the utmost of my power.

" I was very sorry that the zeal of my brother Teyoninhoka-râwâren failed of success ; but I can assure you and the Chiefs of the Five Nations, that it was not for want of constant attention and the most unremitting zeal on his part. No person could possibly execute the mission on which he was sent, with more ability than he did. It is only a piece of justice due to him, to desire you to mention this to the General Council when they meet.

" The names of those who gave credit to Mr. Claus's fictitious council, are washed out from the administration of this country, and a more sensible set of ministers are appointed in their room, and I think those who now fill the high offices of State in this kingdom, would listen to the wishes of our brethren in the Five Nations.* I shall be happy if I can be of service in procuring for them the accomplishment of their wishes. But before I attempt any thing, I must desire clearly to understand what are the wishes of the Five Nations. Do they desire to have a confirmation of the grant of Sir Frederick Haldimand and (if possible) to have it under the Great Thayendanegea, &c. with the Seal of the United Kingdom of Great Britain and Ireland ? Would they consent, (if such a thing is proposed) to have a clause inserted in the confirming grant declaring the

---

* The Duke, probably, referred to the dissolution of Mr. Addington's administration in 1804, and the return to power of Mr. Pitt. True, the ministry of the latter was dissolved by the decease of that incomparable premier, in January antecedent to the time the Duke was then writing ; but it must have been the Addington ministry which was in power at the time of Norton's mission, and which was "washed out" by dissolution after Pitt had abandoned it, and made a speech in opposition, even on the same side with Fox.—*Author.*

grant to be vacated, if the Five Nations should at any time part with the territory thus granted to them, either to the Americans, or to any other nation of Indians, or to any other person or persons not being of the Five Nations, or a British subject, without the consent of the crown of Great Britain? I mention this circumstance, because I think something of this kind was hinted at by Mr. Cooke, and the improper manner in which it was stated, gave reason to suppose that the Five Nations could not alienate it, or any part of it, from one Indian of the Five Nations to another Indian of the Five Nations, which never was intended to be prevented.

"I should, however, advise that either yourself, Teyoninhokâ-râwen, or some other chief, should come over, properly authorised by the chiefs, to transact and finally settle all this business.

"There are a number of well-meaning persons here, who are very desirous of forming a society to better (as they call it,) the condition of our nation, by converting us from hunters and war riors into husbandmen. Let me strongly recommend it to you, and the rest of our chiefs, not to listen to such a proposition. Let our young men never exchange their liberty, and manly exercises, to become hewers of wood and drawers of water. If they will teach our women to spin and to weave, this would be of use; but to endeavor to enervate our young men by doing nothing but tilling the earth, would be the greatest injury they could do the Five Nations. Nine hundred or a thousand warriors, enured to hardship by hunting, are a most respectable and independent body; but what would the same number of men become who were merely husbandmen? They would hardly rate a small parish, seeking for protection from others, scarcely heard of and known, and obliged tamely to submit to laws and regulations made by other people, and incapable of defending themselves. If you want an example of what the Five Nations would soon become, look only at the Stockbridge Indians. They, like us, were once a noble and formidable tribe; they now are less than women. Some of the persons who propose this plan, have their own private reasons. They wish to go over among you, and when they have collected you together in order to teach you to cultivate the ground, they will then show you how very small a part of the land granted you is sufficient for to supply your wants, and will next endeavor to prevail upon you to grant them the remainder, in gratitude for the trouble they have had in instructing you in agriculture. No, my dear friend and brother warrior, never suffer yourself, or your Chiefs, to be induced by their plausible arguments. If you do, remember I now foretell that you will become a poor, dependent, and insignificant body, instead of continuing a free, warlike, and independent nation as we now are. I wish to see the Christian religion, sobriety, and good morals, prevail among our nation; but let us continue free and independent as the air that blows upon us; let us continue hunters and warriors, capable of enforcing respect, and doing ourselves justice; but let us never submit to become the tillers of land, hewers of wood, and drawers of water, by the false and interested advice of those who, from being our pretended friends, would soon become our imperious masters. Accept this, my good friend and brother warrior, from one who wishes the Five Nations ever to continue a formidable nation, commanding respect from all its neighbors, and who interests himself most sincerely in their welfare. Say every thing proper for me to my brother Chiefs, and believe me,

" Your faithful friend and brother warrior,

" NORTHUMBERLAND,

" *Thorighwagéri*

" Dezonhighkor (Lord Percy) desires to return his thanks, and to offer his compliments to you and to Teyoninhokârâwen, (Norton,) to whom I desire you to give my compliments likewise. I have received his letter, and will write to him by this mail if I possibly can."

Pursuant to the suggestions of the preceding correspondence, the preparations were made for another mission to London, by Thayendanegea himself. He actually commenced his journey, and proceeded as far as Albany, with the design of embarking at New-York. Circumstances, however, occurred, which rendered it necessary for him to return to his own country. Afterward, owing to pecuniary difficulties, the undertaking was indefinitely deferred, as will be seen by the annexed communication to the Duke, which was probably the last ever addressed to that nobleman by his brother warrior of the forest:—

CAPTAIN BRANT TO THE DUKE OF NORTHUMBERLAND.

"*Head of Lake Ontario, June* 26, 1807.

"MY LORD DUKE,

"I wrote you last by the Surveyor General, Mr. Wyatt, acquainting your Grace that Teyoninhokàràwen or myself should again cross the sea on the subject of our land affairs, &c. Shortly after that we have been formally deputed, either jointly or separately, by a general council of the chiefs and warriors of the Grand River, held at the Onondaga Village, according to the ancient custom of the Five Nations.

"The want of money for the journey, and suspicions of new intrigues being attempted in our absence again to frustrate our endeavors for the public good, have deterred us for the present from undertaking the intended journey. But, confiding in the regard which we know that your Grace has for your brethren of the Five Nations and their interests; in the fatherly affection of his Majesty; and in the justice of the British nation; we send you the powers we have received; and beg that your Grace may grant us your aid to obtain from his Majesty a confirmation of General Haldimand's grant to the Five Nations under the Great Seal; and that the part we have surrendered to Government for sale, they shall guarantee to us and our heirs the regular payment of the purchase money stipulated, according to former representation.

"With the greatest respect and esteem, I have the honor to be

"Your Grace's humble servant, and
"Faithful brother warrior"

For a good and sufficient reason, which will appear in the closing pages of the present work, the claims of the Mohawks were prosecuted no farther by their old and vigilant Chief, Thayendanegea. Nor have their difficulties with the officers of the crown entirely ceased to this day.

CHAPTER XIV.

Exertions of Thayendanegea for the moral and social improvement of his people—His religious views—Efforts for the religious instruction of his people—Letter to Sir John Johnson upon the subject of obtaining a resident clergyman—Farther correspondence—Interview of Brant with the Bishop—Disappointment—Letter to the Chief Justice—Appeal of Brant to the Lord Bishop, but without success—Application to the American church—Letter to Colonel Burr—Succeeds in obtaining the ordination of Mr. Phelps—Estimate of Brant's character by the clergy—Letter of Rev. Dr. Mason—Rev. Elkanah Holmes—Letter of Brant to the Rev. Dr. Miller—Ardent spirits—Efforts of Brant to prevent their introduction—Letter to Sir John Johnson—Interposition of the women—Address of Brant in reply—Indian games and pastimes—National game of Cricket—Great game at Grand River, between the Senecas and Mohawks—Judge Woodruff's visit to Brant's residence—Description of his person—Indian funerals—Respect for the dead—Estimate of women—Their influence—Funeral speech of Seneca-George—Death of Mrs. Claus—Speech of condolence by Captain Brant—Captain Claus in reply Brant's visit to New-York, Philadelphia, and Hartford, in 1797—Attentions to him in Philadelphia—Dinner party of Colonel Burr—Talleyrand and other distinguished guests—Letter of introduction from Colonel Burr to his daughter—Dinner party in his honor by Miss Theodosia—His manners described by Dr. Miller and by General Porter—Designs upon his life in the Mohawk country—The late John Wells—Striking incident in Albany—Anecdotes—Brant and General Gansevoort—Brant and Colonel Van Courtlandt—Reasons of Brant for taking up arms for the King—His reasonings in defence of the Indian mode of warfare.

HAD no other subjects demanded the consideration, and required the active personal exertions, of Captain Brant, during the last twelve years of his career, than those already reviewed, his life must still have been considered one of uncommon industry. But the cares upon his hands were multitudinous in other respects. His desire for the moral and social improvement of his people led him to a vigilant oversight of all their domestic concerns. Rude as was their government, it was still to be administered, and a domestic police, of some kind, was to be observed. The administration of their government, moreover, was probably attended by none the less difficulty from the peculiar position in which the Mohawk Indians were placed at that particular period of their history. Their society was in a transition state—being neither the hunter nor the agricultural, but partaking in part of both ; while, notwithstanding the advice of the Duke of Northumberland, it was the strong desire of the Chief to draw them from the former to the latter course of life. Before their transplantation from their native valley, they had, many of them, made considerable advances in the pursuit of husbandry, Brant himself having cultivated an excellent farm in the neighborhood of General Herkimer's residence, near the Upper Mohawk Castle;* and though the vicissitudes of war had cast them once more into a primitive forest, entirely unsubdued, the Chief had no idea of relinquishing the certainty of agricultural competence for the precarious supplies of the chase.

Nor was he ignorant of what alone can form the basis of an industrious and truly moral community. Whether he was himself a man of experimental religion, in the evangelical sense of the term, is a question which it is not the province of the historian to decide. There is no doubt that he was a believer in the great and essential truths of revelation, and it is equally certain that after his return from Dr. Wheelock's school, he was the subject of deep religious impressions. But whether these impressions were entirely effaced during the long years of arduous and active public service in which he was subsequently engaged, both as a warrior and a politician—in the battle-field, in the council of war, and in the Indian Congress—threading the solitudes of his native forests, or amidst the splendid gaieties of the British metropolis—is not for the writer to affirm or deny. Be this, however, as it may, he was a man of too much sagacity not to perceive the importance of education and religion, as auxiliaries in carrying forward the moral and social improvement of his nation ; and the preponderance of testimony favors the opinion that he was never careless of the spiritual interests of his charge. It has been seen, that when quite a young man, he was engaged with the Episcopal and other Christian missionaries, assisting in translating the Church Prayer Book and the Holy Scriptures. And immediately after the close of the long conflict in which he had borne so active a part, he was again found recurring, of his own volition, to the same labors, and superintending the printing of the Gospel of Mark, and other religious works, in London. One of his first stipulations with the Commander-in-chief, on the acquisition of his new territory, was for the building of a church, a school-house, and a flouring mill ; and no sooner had the North-western Indian wars been brought to an end, than the religious principle was again in action, and his thoughts and exertions once more directed to the

* The author visited the plantation formerly belonging to Brant in the Autumn of 1836. Nothing of his domicil, save the cellar, remained. His orchard of apple-trees, however, was thrifty and in full bearing.

means of imparting to his people a knowledge of their relation to God, and the consequences flowing therefrom. In proof of this assertion, the following letter may be appropriately introduced :—

CAPTAIN BRANT TO SIR JOHN JOHNSON, BAR'T.

"*Grand River*, Dec. 15, 1797.

" DEAR SIR,

" Since writing the letter accompanying this, the Chiefs have conferred together respecting the state of religion among the Five Nations, which now appears to be a subject of more serious consideration among them than formerly. We are sensible, Sir, of the goodness of Government, among other benefits, in accommodating us with a church, and we have long been desirous of having a clergyman to reside constantly with us ; this, we apprehend, would be highly promotive of morality and the Christian virtues among our people. We do not complain, Sir, of the neglect of the society in this respect, as we are satisfied that their benevolent attention to mankind has been equal to their means ; for this reason we have hitherto omitted making application to them upon this head. Besides, we are sensible how difficult it must be for them to find a suitable character willing to settle among us in this rude and distant quarter.

" In order to discharge my duty in this important affair, and that I may rest in peace, I have conferred with a gentleman of a liberal education, Mr. Davenport Phelps, with whose character and family I have long been acquainted, who has ample testimonials respecting his literary and moral qualifications, and who, I believe, will consent to devote his life to the service of the Church among us, provided his Lordship, the Bishop of Quebec, shall think proper to ordain him to the sacred office. Mr. Phelps with great candor observes, that from his not having been so conversant with books for a number of years past as he could have wished, particularly classical ones, he is diffident of a critical examination in the dead languages. But, Sir, from his general, I may say almost universal, character among the discerning, I consider the prospect of his usefulness among us very great ; and assure you that it is the desire of the Chiefs in general, and my most ardent wish, that he may be ordained a missionary for the Five Nations on this river. And from your

official relation to us, I take the liberty of begging you to communicate our wishes to his Lordship the Bishop respecting this
gentleman, that we may be informed, if possible, before the
opening of the Spring, whether a character of Mr. Phelps's description will be approved by his Lordship, and deemed a proper
subject for ordination.

" I am, dear sir,

" Your most obedient

" And humble serv't,

" JOS. BRANT.

" Sir John Johnson, Bar't."

"P. S. I know you will excuse my observing that we shall be
glad to know what sum the society, and what government will
severally think proper to allow our missionary; since, should
their allowances be insufficient for his support, by other means
it must be made adequate."

The Baronet lost no time in bringing the subject before the
Bishop, but difficulties were interposed by his Lordship, and an
occasional correspondence of two or three years ensued, before
the wishes of the Indians, for the ordination of a spiritual teacher, were complied with. The first objection was that the candidate for orders had not been examined. In reply, Captain
Brant apologized for their ignorance as to the pre-requisites,
and urged that an examination might be undergone before the
Rev. Mr. Addison, "who, having gone through the forms him-
"self, must be acquainted with the business." Both the Chief
and his people were impatient of delay; and the Captain reminded the Bishop, through Sir John, of the pledge which the Arch-
bishop of Canterbury had made to him in the presence of the
King, that whenever the Indians, by the erection of a church,
should be ready for religious instruction, he would do all in his
power to supply their wants.

In the Spring of 1798, the Chief had an earnest correspondence with Mr. Russell, the provincial Governor, upon the subject, in the course of which, in one of his letters, he said :—
" With respect to any uncertainty or difficulty there may be in
" obtaining a salary from government, we would wish that that
" should not entirely restrain his Lordship; for, should govern-
" ment not be willing to grant an allowance for a clergyman,

"sooner than want one we would strain every point ourselves
"to procure a salary, and would be joined by several respecta-
"ble families of white people in the neighborhood."

In the Summer of the following year, on his return from a
visit to the lower province, the Captain met with the Lord
Bishop at Kingston, and again urged his attention to the subject ;
and, as he supposed, arranged matters for an examination of
Mr. Phelps at Niagara, to which place his Lordship was preparing to extend his visit. But there was again disappointment,
arising from a cause altogether unexpected. The following
spirited letter will disclose the motive of the delay :

CAPTAIN BRANT TO THE CHIEF JUSTICE.

" *Grand River,* —— ——*

"SIR,

"I feel myself under the necessity of representing to your
Honor, that from the consideration of the great importance of
having a missionary resident among the Indians, and that from
the knowledge I have long had of Mr. Davenport Phelps, and
my particular acquaintance with his family and connexions, I
have been earnestly desirous that he might be ordained to that
office. To this end, the Winter before last I wrote the Honorable Sir John Johnson, who communicated my wishes, and those
of the other chiefs, in this respect, to his Lordship the Bishop of
Quebec. No determinate answer was given, and in consequence the subject thus remained till the Summer past, when, on
my return from Lower Canada, at Kingston, in a conversation
with his Lordship, he was pleased to express the utmost readiness to do what was incumbent on him to carry what was desired into effect—manifesting a cheerful willingness to examine
Mr. Phelps, in order to his ordination.

"Thus circumstanced, I requested Mr. Phelps to accompany
me to Newark,† to offer himself for examination ; but to my
great disappointment found, that previous to our arrival his
Lordship had sailed for Quebec. I was, Sir, however, surprised
to learn, that he had left information pointedly against the ex-

---

* The date is wanting in the copy. It must have been, however, toward the
close of 1799.

† Formerly a town on the Niagara—now called Niagara.

pected examination; which, though then to me mysterious, I more fully understand since the arrival of his Excellency Governor Hunter, at that place, who has told me that he had been informed that Mr. Phelps had been at the head of a mob in the province. This charge, replete with odium, I have good evidence to believe was originally made by Mr. White, Attorney General, and as long ago as 1795. I must acknowledge, Sir, that it is unaccountable in my mind how a charge of this nature, made by one whose duty it is to prosecute seditious practices, should remain unnoticed until so late a period, and then be suggested, as I have too much reason to believe, to defeat a purpose earnestly desired by many friends to the cause of religion and morality.

" I cannot, in justice to truth, omit to observe that the proposal of Mr. Phelps's being ordained to the church did not originate with him, (nor has it since been solicited by him,) but by myself and others of respectability, who have long known his virtues and abilities; who have an indubitable claim to the honor of having defended this country against the King's enemies; and whose loyalty and discernment cannot with decency be disputed. If, however, a charge of this nature be proved, I shall remain silent. If not, I humbly conceive justice and humanity require that due reparation be made.

" Your Honor's love of justice makes me confident of your best advice, and wise interference in this affair.

" I cannot but farther observe, that, considering the nature and circumstances of this affair, I have a right to expect that Mr. White, or whoever else has made this charge, be called on to prove it without delay. I shall be much obliged by your answer to this by the bearer. I have the honor to be, &c."

It is manifest from this letter, that the government were entertaining political objections to the candidate. The conduct of the Attorney-General, however, would not stand the scrutiny to which the Mohawk was disposed to subject it. Nothing could be more apparent than that the charge was either frivolous, or adduced as a pretext, or that the Attorney General had been remiss in the performance of his own official duty. The Indians still adhered to Mr. Phelps; and such was the strength of their attachment to him, that Captain Brant subsequently prepared a formal memorial to the Lord Bishop, setting forth

his excellent qualities—his talents, his virtues, and his loyalty—
and urging his ordination, "as their choice had been, and still
"was, fixed on him, in preference to any other."* But every
effort to obtain the ordination of Mr. Phelps from the English
prelate was fruitless, and the attention of Captain Brant was
thereupon directed to the Episcopal Church of the United States,
through the interposition of General Chapin, the American
Indian Agent residing at Canandaigua, and Colonel Aaron Burr.
Mr. Phelps, the candidate for orders, visited the city of New-
York, and was the bearer of the following letter to Colonel
Burr upon the subject :—

CAPTAIN BRANT TO COLONEL BURR.

"*Grand River, May* 7, 1800.

"Sir,

"About three weeks since, I received a message from O'Bail
to attend a council at Buffalo, where I expected the pleasure of
seeing you. We attended, and waited a few days; but the

---

* The warmth of Brant's friendship for Mr. Phelps, and the strength of his
attachment to him, are explained by the circumstance that Mr. Phelps had married
the daughter of the elder President Wheelock, with whom the Chief had doubtless
become acquainted while at the Moor Charity School. As Mr. Phelps subsequently became the pioneer of the Episcopal Church in the western part of the State of
New-York, some farther notice of him will be proper in this place. He was a native of Hebron, (Connecticut,) where he was born in 1755. He was graduated at
Yale College, with high credit for his classical attainments, in 1775. Soon afterward he entered the army of the Revolution, in Colonel Beadle's regiment—was
made prisoner and taken to Montreal, where he remained so long that he acquired
the French language so as to speak it with elegance. He was married to Catharine
Wheelock in 1785, and was for a time engaged in the mercantile business, in company with his brothers-in-law, Ebenezer and James Wheelock, in Hartford (Conn.)
He afterward removed to New-Hampshire, where he practised law, and served as a
magistrate. In 1792 he visited Upper Canada in company with James Wheelock,
where they jointly obtained a grant of eighty-four thousand acres of land from Governor Simcoe. Soon afterward he removed his family to Upper Canada, and
settled for a time at Niagara, where he commenced the practice of the law, and established a printing-office. He also had a mercantile concern at that place, the business of which was chiefly conducted by an agent. He had a taste for agricultural
and horticultural pursuits, and paid much attention to husbandry and the cultivation
of fruit. A close intimacy subsisted between himself and Captain Brant, and
between their families. He appears to have been early a religious man, and had,
for some time anterior to Brant's application in his behalf for orders, a strong desire
to enter the Episcopal Church.—*MS. Life of Rev. Davenport Phelps, in preparation by the Rev. Dr. Rudd of Utica.*

chiefs there not being ready to meet us, and we having business that required our attendance at this place, were under the necessity of coming away. Had I been so fortunate as to have met you there, it was my intention to have conversed with you upon a subject which I have long considered as most important to the present and future well-being of the Indians on *both sides* of the lakes and at large; namely, their situation in a moral point of view, and concerning measures proper to be taken in order that regular and stated religious instruction might be introduced among them.

" You well know, Sir, the general state of the Indians residing on Grand River, as well as in other parts. A considerable number of some of these nations have long since embraced Christianity, and the conversion of others must depend, under the influence of the Great Spirit, on the faithful labors of a resident minister, who might visit and instruct both here and elsewhere, as ways and doors might from time to time be opened for him.

" The establishment and enlargement of civilization and Christianity among the natives must be most earnestly desired by all good men; and as religion and morality respect mankind at large, without any reference to the boundaries of civil governments, I flatter myself that you, Sir, will approve what many of the chiefs here, with myself, are so greatly desirous of.

" I have in view, as I have before suggested, the welfare of the Indians at large; being fully persuaded that nothing can so greatly contribute to their present and future happiness as their being brought into the habits of virtue and morality, which, I trust, may and will be gradually effected by instruction, if properly attended and enforced by example.

" I well know the difficulty of finding a gentleman suitably qualified, and willing to devote his life to the work of a missionary among them; and especially one of talents and manners to render him agreeable in a degree highly to favor his usefulness. And, in order to satisfy myself in this respect, I faithfully inquired and consulted, and am clearly of opinion, that Mr. Davenport Phelps, who is recommended as a gentleman of virtue and respectable accomplishments, is the most suitable character for this office of any one within my knowledge. My long acquaintance with his family, and particular knowledge of him, as well as the opinion and wishes of the most respectable characters among the white people in this vicinity, who earnestly wish, for themselves as well as for us, that he may be ordained a missionary, make me earnestly hope that you will officially recommend both the design and him to the Right Reverend Bishops in the United States, or to some one of them, and to such other characters as you may think proper.

"From the consideration that religion and politics are distinct subjects, we should not only be well satisfied to receive a Missionary from a Bishop in the United States, but, for various other reasons, would prefer one from thence.

"We shall be able here to do something considerable towards Mr. Phelps's support; and I doubt not but others, who have ability, will be disposed to assist in promoting so good a work. I will add no more than that I have great satisfaction in being confident of your friendly and influential exertions in this important affair, and that I am, with great sincerity, yours, &c.,

"JOSEPH BRANT."[*]

The application to the American Church was successful, and the Missionary was ordained.[†] But whether the measure was

---

[*] Brant had had some previous acquaintance with Colonel Burr and his family, as will appear in a subsequent page. This letter was enclosed by Colonel Burr to his daughter Theodosia, then Mrs. Alston, in December, 1801, with the following remark :--"Yesterday Mr. Phelps, mentioned in the enclosed, delivered to me two pair of moccasins, directed--" From Captain Joseph Brant to Mr. and Mrs. Alston." Your ship having sailed, I don't know how or when I shall forward them to you; but we will see. I send the original letter of Capt. Brant, merely to show how an Indian can write. It is his own hand-writing and composition. Upon this notice of his attention you should write him a letter of acknowledgment for his hospitality," &c. The author will here remark, that the orthography of Captain Brant was remarkable and almost invariably accurate.

[†] Mr. Phelps was ordained a Deacon in Trinity Church, in the city of New-York, by Bishop Benjamin Moore, on Sunday, December 13, 1801. He immediately returned to Canada, and entered upon the active duties of a missionary, holding frequent services, and travelling far and wide in the discharge of his duties. His residence then, and for several years before, was upon his farm about three miles from Burlington Bay. Captain Brant had repeatedly endeavored to induce him to accept a grant of land, probably with a view to his residence with, or near him, at Grand River, but without success—as the accumulation of wealth was not the desire of Mr. Phelps. In 1803 he was ordained as a priest in St. Peter's Church, Albany, also by Bishop Moore. Thenceforward he entered upon the life of a missionary in the western part of New-York, and in 1805 removed his family from Upper Canada to Onondaga. He subsequently removed to Geneva, where he died some years since.—*MS. Account of his life by Dr. Rudd.*

facilitated by the exertions of Colonel Burr, is not known. The subject has been treated thus at large, for the purpose of developing with more distinctness the religious bias of the Chieftain's character, as illustrated by the earnest perseverance with which he sought the Christian improvement of his people. From other letters and documents among his papers, it is farther rendered certain that several religious gentlemen of distinction in the United States were in occasional correspondence with him upon religious and other subjects connected with the history and condition of his people.   His house, likewise, seems to have been the free and open quarters of the Missionaries employed at that early stage of the modern missionary enterprise, among the borderers, both Anglo-Saxon and Aboriginal.*   As an example of this description of correspondence, the following letter is given—for the double purpose of showing the estimate placed upon the character of Captain Brant by the great and good of that day, and of embalming the name of one of the most devout and faithful pioneers of Christianity that ever made the wilderness ring with the Gospel trumpet—the Rev. Elkanah Holmes :

REV. JOHN M. MASON, D. D., TO CAPTAIN BRANT.
" *New-York, June* 16, 1801.

" SIR,
" The Directors of the New-York Missionary Society have instructed me to tender you their acknowledgments for your friendship to their missionary, the Rev. Elkanah Holmes.† This gentleman, in whose discretion and integrity they repose entire confidence, they have employed in a second mission to those tribes of Indians whom your influence particularly affects.

---

* Mr. Phelps had much intercourse with Captain Brant and his family.   When he preached in the vicinity of the family of Brant, that household formed a part, and a very attentive part, of his audience.—*MS. of the Rev. Dr. Rudd.*

† Mr. Holmes devoted many years to missionary labors among the Indians, of whom he took his leave about the year 1812. He lived many years afterward, and died at a very advanced age. Like Heckewelder, he imbibed the most enthusiastic admiration of the Indian character in its native unsophisticated state. In the course of his experience, however, he arrived at the painful conclusion that it is all but impossible to do any good to them while subject to the moral contagion of white men and strong drink. His appearance in the latter years of his life was truly patriarchal. His hair, long and white, fell down upon his shoulders ; his manner was remarkably impressive, and his whole demeanor that of one who was ripe for heaven. He was a Calvinistic Baptist.

The purity of their views, embracing the moral and religious interests of the Indians, induces them to believe that their attempts will not be unacceptable to you ; and your former kindness to Mr. Holmes emboldens them to ask for him such countenance and advice as your intimate knowledge of Indian affairs, and the weight of your opinion in directing them, render it expedient for you to give. For your farther satisfaction with regard to the missionary system, Mr. Holmes will present you with a volume containing the sermons preached before the Society, and the annual accounts of their procedure ; of which the directors do themselves the pleasure to request your acceptance.

" With respect, I am, Sir,

" Your obedient servant,

" JOHN M. MASON, *Secretary.*

" *Captain Joseph Brant.*"

The Chief was likewise in correspondence with the Rev. Samuel Miller of New-York, now Doctor Miller, of Princeton, as appears by the following letter :—

CAPTAIN BRANT TO THE REV. SAMUEL MILLER.

" *Grand River*, *Feb.* 9, 1801.

" SIR,

" I feel a particular satisfaction that I have now had an opportunity of answering your letter by the Rev. Mr. Holmes. I have explained, as far as in my power, the queries you have proposed. I hope you will excuse the long delay I have made since I received your letter, and not altogether attribute it to neglect or unwillingness to serve you ; for I have myself a strong inclination for searching into the antiquities of our nations and others, but the multiplicity of business I have always had on hand, has hitherto prevented me. Even now, what I have said on the subject is in haste, and as brief as possible. Should it so happen that I might have it in my power further to assist you, I shall do it with pleasure.*

---

* It is a matter of no small regret that the author has not been able to procure a copy of the letter referred to. At the time when the now venerable Dr. Miller opened a correspondence with Brant, he was projecting a *History of New-York*, and was then collecting materials for that object. Brant had also contemplated writing a

"I cannot omit acknowledging the satisfaction I feel from what the Rev. Mr. Holmes has acquainted me with, respecting the generous intentions of your society for diffusing religion and civilization among the Indian nations in general. I would be happy to hear from you, how far your society may propose to extend their goodness, with respect to the education of Indian youths that might be well recommended to them. And also, if they would be willing, and it might be consistent with their constitution, to assist some Indians who have yet claims on lands in the United States, such as the Nantikokes in Maryland, and the Munsees near Minisink, who have requested me to make the application. The Rev. Mr. Holmes can more particularly inform you on this subject."

Unfortunately the Mohawks, like all other primitive American nations with whom the white people have come in contact, were lovers of rum, and subject, of course, to the evils consequent upon that species of debasement. The prevalence of this vice seems to have been viewed with deep solicitude by Captain Brant, and a system of prevention early entered into his views on commencing the labor of building up his nation anew. But all experience has shown how futile are these attempts to keep the fire-waters from the lips of the Indian, so long as unprincipled white men are permitted to approach their borders with their alembics, or minister the ready-made liquor to their burning appetites. In like manner were the efforts of Captain Brant frustrated. In a letter to Sir John Johnson, dated June 30th, 1800, in reference to this subject, he said:—"The accidents "which have happened in the drunken frolics here, have princi- "pally proceeded from an opposition party to those chiefs who "wished to adopt some necessary regulations. Captain Claus

history of *The Six Nations;* and it is quite probable that his reply to the queries of Doctor Miller was both a valuable and a curious document. When Doctor Miller removed from New-York to Princeton, in the year 1813, he was just recovering from a fit of sickness, which disabled him from attending to his papers. The consequence was, that owing to the carelessness of others, his manuscripts and historical collections were greatly scattered, and many of them irrecoverably lost. Among the latter were the letters of Captain Brant, as the author has been informed by the Doctor himself, in reply to a letter addressed to him. After stating the circumstances attending the loss of his manuscripts, the Doctor says—"after the most diligent search that I can make, I cannot find a line of what I received from that remarkable man."

" seems very uneasy, and wishes to take some steps to prevent
" those mlancholy misfortunes.   He urges me to point out some
" mode in which it can be effected.   In answer I furnished him
" in writing with a detail of the plan, (of which I presume he
" will send you a copy,) which was adopted when we first set-
" tled here, and which could at that time have been carried into
' effect, but for the insurmountable impediments thrown in the
" way by the government.   I should be glad of your opinion
" on this unfortunate subject."

It must be reckoned among the mysteries in the economy of
Providence, that women, of every age, and hue, and clime, are
doomed to suffer more severely from the effects of intemperance
in the other sex than men.   The maddening poison of the intoxicating cup infuriates the stronger passions of the men, and im-
parts fiend-like energy to their already superior physical powers ;
and among savage as well as civilized men, those under its diabolical influence often wreak their senseless violence upon the
least offending and the least capable of resistance.   It was thus
among the Mohawks.   At least nothing less can be inferred
from the following memoranda of proceedings upon this subject,
among the papers of Captain Brant :—

" On the 22d of May, 1802, the women assembled in council,
to which they called the chiefs.   They then addressed them as
follows :

" UNCLES : Some time ago the women of this place spoke to
you ; but you did not then answer them, as you considered
their meeting not sufficient.   Now, a considerable number of
those from below having met and consulted together, join in
sentiment, and lament as it were with tears in our eyes, the many misfortunes caused by the use of spirituous liquors.   We
therefore mutually request that you will use your endeavors to
have it removed from our neighborhood, that there may be none
sold nigher to us than the mountain.   We flatter ourselves that
this is in your power, and that you will have compassion on
our uneasiness, and exert yourselves to have it done."

Strings of Wampum.

How like woman !   She discerned the cause of the evil she
saw and felt : yet she indulged no resentments—she complained not of her sufferings—but mildly entreated that the
cause might be removed.   Thus, ever forward to shield those

she loved from temptation and danger, by her influence and persuasions exerting might in her weakness, and rendering the strong man stronger by her anxious yet watchful guardianship of his virtue. But their counsel did not end here. There had been domestic feuds and collisions among their lords. The Seneca demagogue had sown dissensions between the warriors and their chiefs, and the Mohawk women appeared also in their own true and beneficent character of peace-makers. After the portion of their address quoted above had been delivered, " some others," (says the manuscript,) spoke thus :—

" Uncles : The division and separation of the warriors from the chiefs gives us much uneasiness ; we therefore entreat you, both chiefs and warriors, that you will bury all dispute, that our affairs may go on with the usual friendship and tranquility. As for our part, we have been in a great measure a principal cause in influencing our male relations ; but we now drop it, and promise to observe a quite different conduct, and we hope in future that no reports shall be able to rekindle the fire of contention."   *Strings of Wampum.*

The manner in which these rude females of the forest made their appeal, might serve as a pattern of delicacy to many of the sex of loftier pretensions. Nor was it without its effect upon the council of chiefs to whom it was addressed. After adjourning a short time for consideration, they returned, and Captain Brant delivered their reply to the following purpose :—

" Nieces : We are fully convinced of the justice of your request ; drinking has caused the many misfortunes in this place, and has been, besides, a great cause of the divisions, by the effect it has upon the people's speech. We assure you, therefore, that we will use our endeavors to effect what you desire. However, it depends in a great measure upon government, as the distance you propose is within their line. We cannot therefore absolutely promise that our request will be complied with.
                                        Strings.

" Nieces : With respect to your request to bury all differences, we heartily comply with it, and thank you for the wisdom you showed in here interfering. It was the custom of our ancestors for the women, by their moderation, to heal up all animosities. Be assured, therefore, that we bury every thing disagreeable that may have happened hitherto ; and in future we shall be upon our guard against tales, and also saying any thing thought-lessly ourselves; we only regret that the warriors are not here present, to concur with us in re-establishing unity and amity."

Strings.

If the proceedings of this female council appear rather too episodical for direct historical narrative, they are nevertheless illustrations of Indian manners and character. It is, moreover, a satisfaction thus to secure from oblivion, and preserve, a docu-ment bearing beautiful testimony, that even in a barbarous state of society, women are still found foremost in the conservation of virtue, and as persevering peace-makers in the midst of anarchy and strife. And besides, the females of no other race have had so little justice done to their character as those of the American Indian. While the women of every other people have been apotheosized, even down to the ebon daughter of Africa who moistened the parched lips of Mungo Park; who has ever ren-dered the just meed of homage to the patient, unostentatious virtues, and the noble qualities, of the tawny daughters of the American forest, save in the case of Pocahontas?

The reader has already seen that the religious tenets of Cap-tain Brant were Episcopalian. It came not within the requisi-tions of his creed, therefore, even had policy been out of the question, to discountenance the games and amusements of his people. On the contrary, he loved to encourage their pastimes and divertisements, and by so doing, gave evidence of his wis-dom. Indeed, it may well be doubted whether, in this respect, the ancients, and all uncivilized nations, have not been wiser in their generations than the modern Anglo-Saxons and their American children. Relaxation of mind and body is neces-sary alike to the health and elasticity of both. When the Puri-tans of New England banished the merry Christmas festival of Old England, they soon saw the necessity of creating a substi-tute, which was found in the feast of Thanksgiving. Still, the people of the United States have ever been so thoroughly util-itarian in the use of their hours, as really to deny themselves time for a suitable indulgence in rational amusements. Thus the harvest-home is forgotten; the rustic gambols of Christmas are almost unknown; no joyous groups dance around the May-pole, or twine the garland for the brow of its queen. The Ame-ricans have no seasons for reinvigorating their systems by wholesome athletic exercises, or dispelling care by rural sports among flowers, and groves, and fountains. The native sports of the Indians are less refined and poetical than were the pastimes and festivals of the Greeks and Romans; but they doubtless contribute as much to the enjoyment of the people, while they are no less rational, and are marked by a high degree of moral purity.

The neglect of athletic exercises, and games, by the white people, moreover, works positive injury. Contrast the tall, erect posture, the elastic tread of the Indian, with the plodding pace and inclining gait of the white man! Is it not obvious that the difference is attributable to the difference of physical training? The white laborer is generally worked too hard when young. His labors, whether in the field or the work-shop, are invariably such as to draw the body forward, while there is no exercise allowed the antagonistic muscles—those which sustain the body in an upright position. The consequence is, that while the Indian indulges in those sports which expand the chest, and throw back the shoulders, and impart agility and grace to the movements of the limbs, the white man, instead of looking upward to the heavens, is bowed down to the posture of the brute crea tion.

Among other amusements, in addition to their own native sports of running, wrestling, and leaping*—their dances and songs—their sacrifices, and other festivals of war and of thanksgiving—the Six Nations had adopted from the whites the popular game of ball, or cricket. Indeed, so much attached were they to this manly exercise, that the game had become national throughout the Confederacy; and it was no uncommon thing for one nation to challenge another to play a match—upon a much larger scale, beyond doubt, than was ever practised among the pale-faces.

A game of this kind was commenced on one occasion, in the year 1794, between the young Mohawks and Senecas, which was well nigh attended with fatal consequences. The Mohawks were the challengers. After the game had proceeded

---

* Mary Jemison states that these athletic games and exercises were practised, not only that their bodies might become more supple, or rather that they might not become enervated, but that they might be enabled to make proper selection of chiefs for the councils of the nation and leaders for war.

for a considerable time, one of the Mohawks, in a struggle with a Seneca for a stroke at the ball, struck his antagonist a sharp blow with his bat. The occurrence having been observed by the players, the Senecas dropped their bats instantly, to a man, and retired to their posts with silent, though evident resentment. Without speaking a word, but with bosoms heaving with indignation, they took up the stakes they had deposited, and retired to their own country, on the upper waters of the Genesee, toward the northern spur of the Alleghanies. About three weeks subsequent to the occurrence, a Seneca messenger arrived at the Mohawk village, dispatched thither by Red Jacket, the Cornplanter, and others, complaining of the insult, demanding satis· faction for the affront, and denouncing war in case of refusal. The Mohawks, feeling that they were in the wrong, were somewhat troubled at the message. Brant convened a council of his chiefs, and after consultation, a message was returned to the Senecas, proposing an amicable meeting of the chiefs of both nations, to confer upon the subject matter of complaint, with a view of healing the wound by compromise and explanation, and of course without bloodshed. The Senecas, anxious to avoid hostilities against a nation with which they had been in alliance so long, acceded to the pacific proposition, and a joint council was the consequence. Red Jacket, however, did all he could to prevent a reconciliation. He delivered an inflammatory speech, laboring with all his art and eloquence to aggravate the insult, and urging his nation to avenge the insult by an appeal to arms. But Captain O'Bail, and some others of the older Seneca chiefs, were for the adoption of a more conciliatory course. They were little moved by the exciting philippic of Red Jacket, and desired nothing more of the Mohawks than a reasonable and honorable atonement for the wrong done to their young warrior by the party offending. The proposition was met with equal magnanimity on the part of the Mohawks, and the result of the council was an adjustment of the difficulty. The calumet was smoked, and the chiefs—all save the disappointed demagogue, Red Jacket—separated upon the most amicable terms.*

Three years afterward, in the Summer of 1797, another match

* Notes of a visit to Captain Brant, and of conversations with him, by Samuel Woodruff, Esq. of Windsor, Con.

of cricket was played between the two nations. The Senecas were this time the challengers, but the game was played at the Mohawk village, on the Grand River, and was commenced during the visit of the gentleman to whom Captain Brant had related the particulars of the foregoing unpleasant occurrence. It was, in fact, the conversation naturally flowing from the pending match that led the Chief to speak of the incidents connected with the former. The playing was to commence at 9 o'clock in the morning, and the invitation of Captain Brant to see the amusement, was accepted by his guest.

The place selected for the trial of strength, agility, and skill, was a broad and beautiful green, of perhaps one hundred acres, perfectly level, and smooth as a carpet, without tree or shrub, or stone to encumber it. On one side of the green the Senecas had collected in a sort of irregular encampment—men, women, and children—to the number of more than a thousand. On the other side the Mohawks were actively assembling in yet greater numbers. The stakes deposited by each party were laid upon the ground in heaps, consisting of rifles, hatchets, swords, belts, knives, blankets, wampum, watches, beads, broaches, furs, and a variety of other articles of Indian utility and taste—amounting, in the whole, according to the estimate of Captain Brant, to upward of a thousand dollars a side. By the side of the stakes were seated a group of the aged Chiefs—" grave and reverend seignors," whose beards had been silvered by the frosts of many winters, and whose visages gave evidence of the toils of war and the chase.

The combatants numbered about six hundred upon a side, young and middle-aged men—nimble of foot, athletic and muscular. Their countenances beamed with animation and high hope. In order to the free and unfettered use of their sinewy limbs, their persons were naked with the exception of a single garment like an apron, or kilt, fastened around the waist, and descending nearly to the knee. The area of the play-ground was designated by two pair of "byes," placed at about thirty rods distant from each other, and the goals of each pair about thirty feet apart. The combatants ranged themselves in parallel lines on each side of the area, facing inward, and leaving a space between them of about ten rods in breadth. Their bats were three feet six inches in length, curved at the lower end somewhat in the form of a ladle, the broad part for striking the ball being formed of net-work, woven of thongs of untanned deer-skin, strained to the tension of tight elasticity. The ball, large as a middling-sized apple, was also composed of elastic materials.

On one side of the area, near the centre of the line, and in a conspicuous place, were seated a body of elderly sachems, of each nation, with knives and tally-sticks, to score the game. The rules governing the game were somewhat intricate. None of the players were allowed to touch the ball with hand or foot, until driven beyond the "byes" or land-marks. It was then thrown back by hand toward or into the centre of the area, when the game proceeded as before. Their mode of counting the game was peculiar, the tallies-men not being in all cases bound by arbitrary rules, but left to the exercise of a certain degree of discretionary power. Each passage of the ball between the goals, at the end of the play-ground, counted one, so long as the contest was nearly equal ; but, for the purpose of protracting the game, whenever one party became considerably in advance of the other, the tally-chiefs were allowed to check or curtail their count in proportion to the excess. For instance, if the leading party had run up a regular count to thirty, while their opponents had numbered but fifteen, the tallies-men, at their discretion, and by consent of each other, though unknown to the players, would credit the winning party with only two notches for three passages of the ball—varying from time to time, according to the state of the game. The object of this course was to protract the game, and to increase the amusement, while despondency upon either side was prevented, and the chance of ultimate victory increased. Frequently, by this discretionary mode of counting, the game was continued three or four days.

The game on this occasion was commenced by about sixty players on a side, who advanced from their respective lines with bats in their hands, into the centre of the play-ground. Of this number about twenty were stationed at the end land-marks, to guard the passage of the ball. The players who were to begin, were apparently mingled promiscuously together. All things being thus ready, a beautiful maiden, richly dressed in the native costume of her people, wearing a red tiara plumed with eagles' feathers, and glittering with bracelets and other ornaments of silver, came bounding like a gazelle into the area, with the ball. which she placed upon the ground in the centre. Instantly the welkin rang with the shouts of the whole multitude of spectators, and the play began ; while the bright-eyed maiden danced back, and joined her own circle among the surrounding throng. The match was begun by two of the opposing players, who advanced to the ball, and with their united bats raised it from the ground to such an elevation as gave a chance for a fair stroke ; when, quick as lightning, it was sped through the air almost with the swiftness of a bullet. Much depends upon the first stroke, and great skill is exerted to obtain it.

The match was played with great spirit, and the display of agility and muscular strength was surprising. Every nerve was strung ; and so great were the exertions of the players, that each set was relieved by fresh hands every fifteen or twenty minutes ; thus alternating, and allowing every player of the whole number to perform his part, until the game was finished. The scene was full of excitement and animation. The principal Chief entered fully into the enjoyment, and by his explanations to his guest heightened its interest, which of itself, the latter declared to have afforded him a greater degree of satisfaction than any game or pastime that he had ever beheld. The contest was continued three days, at the end of which, after a severe struggle, the Senecas were proclaimed the victors, sweeping the stakes, to the great mortification of the proud-spirited Mohawks— the head of the Confederacy.

Mr. Woodruff, from whose notes the preceding description has been derived, was highly gratified with his visit to the Chief, with whom he passed several days. In his person he said he was graceful and dignified—easy and affable in conversation. His stature was five feet eleven inches—of the finest form and proportions—robust and firm, and possessing great muscular power. His countenance was open, placid, and inviting—his eyes brilliant and expressive—in short, every thing in relation to his person was engaging and prepossessing.

No people are more particular in paying honors to the dead than the Indians, and their funerals are marked with deep and affecting solemnity. As among civilized nations, the pomp and pageantry of woe vary according to the rank of the deceased and the wealth of the family, or the ability and disposition of friends to defray the expenses of the funeral, the entertainment at the grave, and the presents to be distributed. But, however humble the deceased, the remains are never unhonored or unwept ; and among no people on earth are stronger evidences given of tender affection. Nor are funeral honors bestowed only upon the men. There is a mistaken idea generally prevalent, that the Indian woman is treated with contempt, arising from the well-known fact, that certain offices and labors, accounted as menial among the whites, or as improper to be imposed upon women, are always performed by them among the Indians. But the allotment of those duties to the women has arisen from their usages, and the peculiar structure of their society, time immemorial. Nor is the custom any evidence of disrespect or contumely. On the contrary, it may be doubted whether the females of the white people, even among nations of the most refinment, exercise a higher or more salutary degree of influence, than do the Indian women. Nor, when dead, are they treated with less respect than the warriors. " The greatest honors are paid to the " remains of the wives of renowned warriors and veteran chiefs, ' particularly if they were descended themselves of a high " family, which is by no means an indifferent thing among the " Indians, who love to honor the merit of their great men in the " persons of their relatives."* The funerals of chiefs and warriors, and of distinguished women, were attended by the heads of the tribe, and all the people, and their ceremonies were highly impressive. On the opening of all their councils, a ceremony of condolence was performed, and an appropriate speech delivered, in memory of those who had died, or been slain on the war-path, since their last meeting. These ceremonies were solemn, and their speeches often full of simplicity, tenderness, and pathos. Among the papers of Sir William Johnson is a manuscript of a speech of condolence, delivered at the opening of a council in 1761, by Seneca George, a few passages of which may be cited as an example :—

" BROTHERS : We suppose that in the late troubles you may have lost many of your people, either by sickness or war, since we were last together ; by this string, therefore, we wipe away the tears from your eyes, clear your throats, wash away the

---

* Heckewelder.

blood from your bodies, sweep the council chamber, and throw the dirt out of doors, that you may see and speak to us clearly at the present conference.   [*A String.*

"BROTHERS: We are sorry, from the bottom of our hearts, for the death of your men, women, and children, and by this belt we collect all their bones together, bury them in one grave, and cover them up.

[*A black belt, eight rows, streaked with white.*

"BROTHERS: We are at great loss, and sit in darkness as well as you, by the death of Conrad Weiser,* as, since his death, we cannot so well understand one another. By this belt we cover his body with bark.

[*A white belt of seven rows, with four black streaks.*

"BROTHERS: By the last belt, I mentioned to you that we both sat in darkness. Now, by this belt I remove the clouds from before the sun, that we may see it rise and set, and that your hearts may be eased from sorrow on account of what I mentioned before. [*Delivered a white belt of five rows, with three black bars.*] We pray the Great God above, who can enlighten our hearts, that we may live in love and peace until death."

From the manuscripts of Captain Brant, it seems frequently to have been his duty to perform the ceremony of condolence, and he sometimes speaks of making a journey to a considerable distance for that sole purpose. Only one of his speeches, however, on such an occasion, remains among his papers. That was delivered in the name of the Five Nations, on the 24th of February, 1801, at Fort George, (Niagara,) on the death of Mrs. Claus,† the mother of the Deputy Superintendent:—

SPEECH OF CONDOLENCE TO CAPTAIN CLAUS.

"BROTHER: We are here now met in the presence of the Spirit above, with intent to keep up the ancient custom of condolement. We therefore condole with you for your late loss of our well-beloved sister, whom now you have interred.

"BROTHER: We hope that this may not damp your heart so much as to make you forget us, who are your brothers—not only ourselves, but our wives and children.

---

* Celebrated in the Indian Annals, for many years, as an interpreter
† Daughter of Sir William Johnson.

"BROTHER: We say now again, that by our late loss, it seems our fire is somewhat extinguished. But we have now found a few brands remaining, and have collected them together, and have raised a straight smoke to the clouds.

" BROTHER : We therefore with this string of wampum wipe away the tears from your eyes, and would take away all sorrow from your heart. But that is impossible : still, it is the customary way of making the speech. We therefore mention it : and with the said wampum we wipe away all stains of whatever should remain on your seat, so that you may sit down in comfort.

" BROTHER : We say again with this string of wampum, as you seem to be all in darkness, we with the same string enlighten the skies above us, so that it may appear to us all as it formerly used to do.

" BROTHER : We say again with this string of wampum, as we have now made our speech of condolement, we hope to raise you upon your feet, as you formerly used to be ; for since our late loss, it seems you have been confined as one absent.*

" BROTHER : We hope you will not forget our calamities— hoping that this shock may not put us out of your memory entirely—and also that you may continue to help us, as you formerly used to do.

" BROTHER : This last string which now I give you, is given by the whole Six Nations, so as to strengthen your mind and body—that you may not be too much cast down by the occasion of our late loss."

An address was likewise transmitted to the council from the women, which was delivered by a sachem called Old Thomas ; but a copy has not been preserved. Only the last half sheet of Captain Claus's reply is now to be found. The conclusion was this :—

"   *   *   *   *   * She was good, and was a friend to you all, as far as she had it in her power, by speaking in your favor always. But was I to continue, I should again bring to my memory her great love for me, and fill my eyes and heart again, so that I could not attend to your affairs. Accept my

---

* Captain Claus had been so much affected by the death of his mother, as to be confined to his room ; and although he met the Chiefs in council on this occasion, he was unable to reply—but sent his speech afterward in writing.

grateful thanks for your condolence, and allow me to look upon you as my friends—wishing you, and all belonging to you, health and all happiness.

"BROTHERS, I now address myself again to you. As the business is now over, and you will be turning your faces toward nome, I pray to the Great Spirit that he will make your road smooth, and leave no obstacle in the way, that will either hurt or stop you; but that you may get safe home, and meet your friends all well; whom I beg you will salute for me. I shall always be happy to be numbered among your friends."

In private life, the character of Brant was estimable, and in the social circle often very agreeable. The testimony of the Baroness De Reidesel, who met him at the castle at Quebec, has already been cited in a former chapter. During the portion of his life now under review, being the last twelve years, he had many journies to perform,—to the lower province to look after the interests of his own immediate people ; to the upper lakes, to keep the chain of friendship with his old confederates from becoming rusty; and to Canandaigua, and elsewhere, to visit his friends, and upon matters of business. In addition to all these, early in the year 1797 he made another visit to Albany and Philadelphia, striking from New-York into New England on his return.* Judging from the tone of a letter which he wrote after his arrival home, to a friend among the upper Indian nations, he must have encountered some unpleasant circumstances during that journey. It was not, however, entirely divested of agreeable associations; and several incidents have been collected by the author, which will serve as better illustrations of his social character than any other in the entire history of his career. An extract from the letter just referred to follows :—

"Grand River, July 2, 1797.

"DEAR SIR,

"It is some time since I received your letter, and I have already answered it by way of Fort Erie ; but I did not in it mention the particulars of my jaunt to the States. In the first place,

---

* His quarters in the city of New-York, during that visit, were at Batton's Hotel, the old brick edifice yet standing on the south corner of Nassau and John streets. The Hon. Jeromus Johnson, of New-York, has furnished the author with an account of a visit made by him to the Chief in that hotel, in company with Dr. Dingley and the celebrated Dr. Priestley. See Appendix, No. XVI.

I met with a very cool reception, insomuch that I did not see any of the great men at Philadelphia. I suppose, by this, that they must have forgot that I was a Yankee when I was there before, and also at the last meeting we had at the foot of the Rapids, when it was reported among you, gentlemen of the Indian department, that I was favoring the Yankee interest. I expected they might have paid a little more attention to me, after the great service you supposed I had done them. I was greatly insulted on the road between Philadelphia and Jersey, by a Yankee colonel whose name I don't recollect, insomuch that the affair was nearly coming to blows. At New-York they were very friendly, and likewise in Connecticut, (in New England,) they were very civil. At Albany there were several people who threatened to kill me behind my back; so that the great men there thought it necessary to send a man with me, as a protector, to the end of the settlement at German Flatts. I suppose these people have also forgot that I was a Yankee."

By the term "great men at Philadelphia," the old Chief must have meant the heads of the administration, since he was most hospitably entertained by some distinguished gentlemen then at the seat of government. The attentions which he received from "the great men at Philadelphia," five years before, were bestowed under peculiar circumstances. He was there at that time in a semi-official capacity, and at the urgent solicitation of the government itself; and it was the duty of the government to render all those civilities which might contribute to the pleasure of his visit. The government, moreover, were hoping that important results might flow from that visit, and very marked attentions were the natural consequence. It is, indeed, too much the way of the world—especially of courts, whether republican or monarchical—to caress and flatter where they have a purpose to serve, as in turn the great are caressed and flattered by those hanging upon their favors. But, under the circumstances of this second visit of the Mohawk, divested, as it was, altogether of official character and importance, his expectations of particular official attentions were probably unreasonable. He had seen far too much of the world, and had mingled too much in society of all ranks and conditions, yet to retain the simplicity of unsophisticated nature, and he might therefore have understood his altered position, and spared his sarcasm. Certainly, though he

might not have breathed the air of the court, or been shouldered
by the factious bandyings of its favorites, he was treated with
marked attention by gentlemen at that time of high distinction,
and his society much courted.   Among others, the late Colonel
Burr, then a Senator in Congress, gave him a brilliant dinner
party.   The Senator had previously been in correspondence
with the Chief, and liked him much.   Indeed, it was upon the
Colonel's invitation that he visited Philadelphia at that time.
Among the guests from abroad assembled on that occasion, were
the minister of the French Republic ; Volney the traveller ; Tal
leyrand, and other distinguished gentlemen of that nation,
brought hither by the political troubles of their own country.
Knowing his colloquial powers to be very good, and that he had
the faculty of rendering himself not only agreeable but fascinating in conversation, the Colonel and his friends were somewhat
disappointed, in the earlier stages of the entertainment, at the
Chieftain's taciturnity.   All the cold reserve of his race seemed
to have come over him, and for a while every effort to draw him
out in discourse was ineffectual.   Meantime the Indians, their
character, history, and destiny, became the leading topics of conversation.   At length, after various suggestions had been made
as to the most feasible and effectual methods of their civilization,
Brant suddenly joined in the discussion ; treating the subject
with good sense, but with alternate gravity and humor.   He
avowed it as his settled conviction, however, that the only effectual process of civilizing his people, must be their amalgamation
with the blood of the whites ; that the Indian could only be
tamed by intermarriages.   Occasionally during his own partici
pation in this discussion, there was a drollery in his manner
that created great amusement.   During the residue of the evening he contributed his full share to the conversation, exhibiting
at all times sterling good sense, and enlivening the hours with
sallies of pleasantry and wit which " set the table in a roar."
The result was not only an agreeable, but highly intellectual
entertainment.*

On leaving Philadelphia for New-York, Colonel Burr gave
the Chief the following letter of introduction to his youthful
and gifted daughter Theodosia†—afterward Mrs. Alston :—

* Conversations of the author with Colonel Burr, noted down on the day they
were held.   † Miss Burr was then in her fourteenth year.

COLONEL BURR TO HIS DAUGHTER.

"*Philadelphia, Feb.* 28, 1797.

" This will be handed to you by Colonel Brant, the celebrated Indian Chief. I am sure that you and Nataliet will be happy in the opportunity of seeing a man so much renowned. He is a man of education—speaks and writes the English perfectly—and has seen much of Europe and America. Receive him with respect and hospitality. He is not one of those Indians who drink rum, but is quite a gentleman ; not one who will make you fine bows, but one who understands and practices what belongs to propriety and good breeding. He has daughters—if you could think of some little present to send to one of them—a pair of ear-rings, for example,—it would please him. You may talk to him very freely, and offer to introduce him to your friend Mr. Witbeck, at Albany. Vale, et ama,

" A. B.

" MISS THEODOSIA BURR,
          " *No.* 30 *Partition-street, New-York.*"

Miss Theodosia received the forest Chief with all the courtesy and hospitality suggested ; and, young as she was, she performed the honors of her father's house in a manner that must have been as gratifying to her absent parent as it was creditable to herself. Among other attentions, she gave him a dinner party, selecting for her guests some of the most eminent gentlemen in the city, among whom were Bishop Moore and Doctors Bard and Hosack. In writing to her father upon the subject, she gave a long and sprightly account of the entertainment. She said that, in making the preliminary arrangements she had been somewhat at a loss in the selection of such dishes as would probably suit the palate of her principal guest. Being a savage warrior, and in view of the many tales she had heard, of

> The Cannibals that each other eat,
> The anthropophagi, and men whose heads
> Do grow beneath their shoulders—

she added, sportively, that she had a mind to lay the hospital under contribution for a human head, to be served up like a

---

† Nataliè Delagiè, an adopted child of Colonel Burr, born in France, and subsequently married to a son of General Sumpter, of South Carolina.

boar's head in ancient hall barbaric. But, after all she found him a most christian and civilized guest in his manners.*

It has been seen from his own letter, that the Chief was well pleased during his visit in New-York. He had, indeed, reason to be gratified, for he was treated with marked kindness and consideration. His own deportment was, moreover, such as t) secure the respect and esteem of those with whom he came into association. The Rev. Dr. Miller, who became acquainted with him during that visit, in a letter to the author already referred to in a note, thus speaks of him:—" I have called Joseph Brant " 'a remarkable man.' He was, in my opinion, truly so. My " personal intercourse with him was not considerable ; but it " was quite sufficient to impress me with most respectful senti- " ments of his intellectual character, his personal dignity, and " his capacity to appear well in any society I met with him " repeatedly ;—was with him at a dining party—and listened " to his conversation in various situations—some of them rather " trying ; and was surprised at the simple, easy, polished, and " even court-like manners which he was capable of assuming ; " though, at the same time, I was assured that he was capable " of being as great a savage as any individual of his nation. I " remember, on one occasion, that when some very impertinent " and unseasonable questions were addressed to him by a gen- " tleman who ought to have known better, he evaded them with " perfect civility, and at the same time with an adroitness and " address which showed that he was fitted to be no mean diplo " matist."

Another gentleman, whose opportunities of studying the manners and character of Captain Brant were extended through several years of occasional intercourse with him, remarks :—" His " manners, which were greatly improved, if not formed, by a con- " stant intercourse, not only with the best society in the pro-

<hr/>

* Conversations of the author with Colonel Burr. The Colonel was anxious that this letter from his daughter should be found among his papers; but Mr. Davis, his biographer, after diligent search, has not discovered it—nor has he been able to find the correspondence between Brant and Colonel Burr. By the papers of Captain Brant, it appears that Miss Burr visited him at Grand River, after she became Mrs. Alston, in company with her husband. Seeing that when the Chief saw her in New-York " she was very young, and had since assumed a new name," Governor George Clinton gave the young married couple a cordial letter of introduction to the Chief.

"vince, but also in England—which he visited more than once,
"and was there received and caressed in the families of the no-
"bility and gentry—were remarkably easy and dignified. When
"among strangers, or in mixed company, he was reserved and
"taciturn ; but extremely affable and communicative when with
"friends in whom he could confide. Although not particularly
"distinguished as a public speaker, he was a man of strong
"mind, possessed a voice of surpassing softness and melody, a
"fascinating address, and great colloquial powers, which ren-
"dered him a most interesting companion. He lived in the
"style of a gentleman, and was punctilious in the observance
"of the rules of honor and etiquette practised among individuals
"of that caste in their social relations."*

From New-York, the Chief made a trip through Connecticut
and into Massachusetts, in the course of which he was well received, as appears from his own letter. At Northampton he
purchased an elegant horse, which, greatly to his regret, sick-
ened and died in Albany.†

It was during this visit in Albany, that he was again exposed
to some danger, by threats against his life. The sufferers of
the Mohawk Valley had neither forgotten nor forgiven the
ravagers of their country in the Revolutionary war ; and "the
monster Brant" was still held responsible for every act, either
of barbarity, or of death, or devastation, by the wonted usages of
war. The Mohawk Germans of that day were neither educated
nor discriminating ; and knowing that Brant was the great
leader of the Indians, they attributed every torch that had been
applied, and every butchery committed, to his own single hand.
Hence, as has been stated before, it was notoriously the purpose
of many in the valley to take his life if possible, during some of
his transits through that country. And it is not unlikely that
some persons from the valley might have been watching for an
opportunity to accomplish the purpose in Albany, as had been
designed by a Mohawk German in New-York, during his visit
in 1792.

---

* Letter to the author, from General Peter. B. Porter.

† My venerable friend Douw Fonda, now of Albany, says Brant was an excellent horseman, and remarkably fond of fine horses. After the death of his Northampton horse he purchased another in Albany, to pay for which Mr. Fonda loaned
him the money. The note for the amount was promptly met at maturity.—*Author.*

Added to these unpleasant designs, was an incident coming somewhat nearer to the point of action, which is worth record-ing as an illustration both of history and character. In the ac-count of the ravaging of Cherry Valley, the reader will doubtless recollect the massacre of the entire family of Mr. Wells, with the exception of John, then a lad at school in Schenectady. But that lad was now a member of the bar, of high spirit and uncommon promise. The tragedy by which his whole family had been cut off, had imparted a shade of melancholy to his character, deepening with the lapse of time, and descending with him to the grave. Nineteen years had elapsed since it was enacted ; but there was a feeling in the breast of young Wells, which only wanted awakening by opportunity, to prompt a strong desire of avenging the foul murders. He happened to be in Albany during the visit of the Chief, and erroneously looking upon him as the author of the murders, his feelings by proximity became exceedingly bitter and exasperated. In-deed, he could not restrain his desire of revenge ; and hastening to the tavern at which Brant had put up, he inquired furiously where he should find his enemy—declaring that he would slay him on the spot. Of course his friends remonstrated, and other-wise opposed his purpose ; but it was not without difficulty that he was persuaded to forego it. Brant, hearing the disturbance, asked what caused it ; and was told that a young man, whose father had perished at Cherry Valley, was below, and threaten-ing to take his life. His answer was brief, and given with a re-markably fine assumption of dignity and composure. Not a feature changed—not a muscle of his countenance was seen to move—but, slightly drawing himself up as he sat, and his eyes glittering for an instant more keenly, even than was their wont, he said, calmly and quietly, " Let him come on ;" and nothing more escaped him on the subject, until word was brought that Mr. Wells had left the house.*

It was in consequence of these unpleasant indications that Governor Jay directed a guard to accompany him through the Mohawk Valley on his return to Upper Canada. But, notwith-standing these drawbacks to the pleasure of his visit in Albany, there were circumstances and incidents contributing to render

---

* The particulars of this incident have been derived from William Inman, Esq. now of Leyden, N. Y. who was at the hotel at the time of its occurrence.

it otherwise than disagreeable on the whole. He was hospitably received and entertained by some of the most respectable citizens; and during that and a subsequent visit, made to Albany in 1805 or 1806, had opportunities of meeting at the festive board some of the veteran officers of the American army, whom he had met in the field, or rather in the forest fights of the frontiers; on which occasions, with the best feelings possible, the old soldiers "fought their battles o'er again," as old soldiers are wont to do. Dining with General Gansevoort, the hero of Fort Stanwix, their conversation turned upon the memorable campaign of Sullivan, and the march of Gansevoort with his regiment at the close of that campaign, through the wilderness from Seneca Lake to Fort Schuyler. Although Gansevoort had no idea that Brant was nearer to him than Niagara, Brant assured him that he was hovering about him during the whole march; and was so near that, to use his own words, "I roasted my venison by the fires that you left."*

He also met, on one of these occasions, with the late General Philip Van Courtlandt, who had served in the New-York line, and who was one of the expedition of Sullivan and Clinton to Chemung, and thence into the Seneca country. While conversing upon the subject of the battle at Newtown, Brant inquired— "General, while you were standing by a large tree during that battle, how near to your head did a bullet come, which struck a little above you?" The General paused for a moment, and replied—"about two inches above my hat." The Chief then related the circumstances. "I had remarked your activity in the battle," said he, "and calling one of my best marksmen, pointed you out, and directed him to bring you down. He fired, and I saw you dodge your head at the instant I supposed the ball would strike. But as you did not fall, I told my warrior that he had just missed you, and lodged the ball in the tree."

Another incident may be introduced in this connexion, illustrative at once of his sagacity, his strong sense of justice, and his promptness of decision and execution. Among the border settlers west of the Hudson, opposite the Manor of Livingston, was an opulent farmer named Rose. He was an Irishman; and having no child to inherit his wealth, had sent to the Emer-

---

* Conversations of the author with Gen. Peter Gansevoort, of Albany, who was present at the dinner, though a lad at the time.

ald Isle for a nephew, whom he had adopted.   In one of Brant's
hostile incursions upon the settlements, during the war of the
Revolution, Rose and his nephew, with others, were taken prisoners, and marched in the direction of Niagara.   During the
journey, Brant took Rose aside one morning, and admonished
him not to move far away from himself (Brant,) but at all times
on their march to keep within call.   " I have reason to believe,"
said the Chief, "that that nephew of your's is plotting your
"death.   He is endeavoring to bribe one of my Indians to kill
"you.   I shall keep an eye upon them, and if I find my suspi-
"cions true, I will execute him on the spot."   The caution was
observed by Rose, and no long time elapsed before Brant informed him that his suspicions were well-founded.   The
nephew, for the purpose of an earlier possession of his confiding
uncle's estate, had agreed upon the price of his murder with the
savage who was to do the deed.   Having full evidence of the
fact, the stern purpose of the Chief was executed upon the in-
grate by his own hand, and the life of the uncle was saved.*

His notions on the subject of public wars were founded, however, upon those of a savage.   The reader has already seen
that he was perfectly aware of the detestation in which his
name was held in different parts of the United States, and particularly among the inhabitants of the Mohawk and Susquehannah countries, where some of the most revolting scenes
of savage, Tory, and Indian barbarity were perpetrated during
the war of the Revolution, in which he bore so prominent a
part ; and he always seemed particularly anxious to justify, by
frank and gratuitous explanations to those who received him
as friends—for he was too proud to make explanations to his
enemies—the course he had taken in the commencement and
conduct of that war ; and his plausible statements and reasonings were well calculated to lessen the horror and execration
with which the public have been too prone to regard the Indian
character, in consequence of their atrocities in war.

The Indians, he said, engaged in that contest reluctantly, but
from necessity.   At the period of its commencement, the Americans, he said, as well as they, acknowledged the authority of
the British government, and were living under its protection ;

* Conversations of the author with General Morgan Lewis, of whose family con
nexions Rose had purchased his land.

that none of the inducements which led the colonies to revolt had any place with them, and that they fought against the colonies to protect their women and children, and to preserve the lands which God had given to them, and of which the British authorities threatened to deprive them unless they would join in their defence ; and it is apprehended that stronger or better reasons for going to war will rarely be found, even among civilized nations.

In justification of the savages' practices of Indian warfare, his course of reasoning was somewhat like the following : That the object of each party, when engaged in war, was to destroy his enemy, or to weaken and intimidate him so much as to force him into a reasonable peace. The Indians, he said, were destitute of many of the means and implements of war which the white people possessed. They could not successfully contend with them in the open field, man to man, because they had no artillery, so indispensable to, and so destructive in, a field fight. Besides, if they could, the Indians being generally inferior in numerical force to their white enemies, would soon be subdued by an equal sacrifice of man for man ; that the Indians had no forts to resort to for protection after a discomfiture in the field ; no battering trains to dislodge the enemy after they had retired to theirs ; and no depots or jails for securing the prisoners they might capture. The simple and necessary principle, therefore, of Indian warfare, was extermination—to destroy as many of the enemy, and save as many of themselves, as practicable ; and for this purpose, to resort to ambuscades, stratagems, and every species of deception, direct or indirect, to effect their object. Brant justified taking the lives of prisoners, but disapproved the practice, so common among savages, of torturing them ; and he always maintained that he had himself at different times, by great efforts, saved several, not only from torture, but death. As to taking life, he thought (and with some truth,) that in this respect there was but little practical difference between the red and white men ; for the death of an Indian prisoner was as certain a consequence of his capture, as that of a white man taken by the Indians.*

* Conversations of Brant with General Peter B. Porter.

CHAPTER XV.

Domestic relations of Brant—Account of his family—Bad character of his eldest son
—His death by the hand of his father—Condolence of the Chiefs—Grief of the
father at the event—Anxiety for the education of his sons—Proposed memorial to
the Duke of Portland—Letter of Brant to Colonel Smith—Correspondence with
the Wheelock family—Letter from Brant to James Wheelock—Two of his sons
sent to school at Dartmouth—Various letters from and to the Wheelocks—Correspondence upon other subjects—Reply to the question, whether the Indians have
beards—Letter from Bishop Peters—Views of Brant on imprisonment for debt—
Tu nu'i—Opinion of Brant touching their origin—Indian tradition of white settlements cut off in a single night—Investigations of Samuel Woodruff—Brant's
inquiries in Paris—The discoveries of the Northmen—Review of the life and
character of Brant—His death.

THE life and character of the Mohawk Chief in his domestic relations, remain to be considered.   These have never been
accurately illustrated or understood ; or rather, they have been
greatly misrepresented and misunderstood, from the circum
stance of a severe family affliction, the particulars of which have
never been truly set before the public.   Those even partially
acquainted with the domestic history of Brant will readily perceive that reference is here made to the death of one of his sons
by his own hands.   Several accounts of this unfortunate transaction have been published by travellers, missionaries, and
others , but most of them darkly shaded, and reflecting in a
greater or less degree upon the father.   In the preparation of
material for the present work, great efforts have been made to
arrive at the truth in regard to this painful incident.

Captain Brant, it will be recollected, was thrice married.   By
his first wife, the daughter of an Oneida Chief, he had two
children, Isaac and Christiana.   His great solicitude for the
well bringing up of those children has been noted in the early
history of his life.   By his second wife, the sister of his first, he
had no children.   By his third he had seven,* the eldest of
whom, Joseph, was born in 1783.

Isaac, the eldest of the children, was partly educated at a
school in the Valley of the Mohawk, and his education was
completed at Niagara.   His disposition, bad, from his youth,
grew worse as he increased in years, and was not improved by

* Joseph, Jacob, John, Margaret, Catharine, Mary, and Elizabeth, (the present
Mrs. Kerr).   Joseph, John, and Mary, are dead.

his associations at the military post of Niagara, after the war of the Revolution. Many of the officers on that station were free, sometimes to excess, in their living ; and in the progress of his intercourse with them he became addicted to strong drink. When in his cups, he was always quarrelsome, even toward his parents—forgetting the honor due from a son to a father, and particularly disrespectful to his step-mother. As the younger family grew up, he became jealous of them, imagining that they received a larger share of parental favor than his sister and himself. Nothing could have been more groundless than were his suspicions, since from the concurrent testimony of the survivors of the family, and the aged contemporaries of the old Chief yet living at Grand River, no parent was ever more scrupulous in the impartial bestowment of his affection among all his children than Captain Brant. As an evidence of this fact, it may be mentioned, that when in England, in 1786, he sat for his likeness in miniature, which he transmitted in a golden locket to Christiana, the sister of Isaac. Isaac himself, moreover, notwithstanding his untoward conduct, received the most indubitable evidence of parental affection. With a view of keeping him more immediately under his own eye, and if possible reclaiming him, his father had caused him to be married to a beautiful girl, the daughter of a chief of the Turtle tribe, and installed him in the capacity of his own secretary.* But all to no purpose. The demon of jealousy had gained possession of his bosom ; and during his drunken frolics, among his Indian associates, he often threatened to take the life of his father. Still, he was treated with kindness, and his step-mother invariably kept silent during his paroxysms of insult and abuse.

His career, however, in addition to his intemperance, without the circle of his own family, was marked by outrage and blood. On one occasion, long before the catastrophe fatal to himself, soon to be recorded, he grievously assaulted a young man, who was riding on horseback on the King's highway—killed the horse, and sadly maimed the young man himself. His father was obliged to pay a large sum of money by way of compensation for the outrage.

Subsequently to this brutal affair, and not long before the

---

* MS. notes of conversations with Brant, by Samuel Woodruff.

painful incident with his father soon to be noted, he killed
a white man at the Mohawk (Grand River) village, outright,
and in cold blood. The name of his victim was Lowell, a har-
ness-maker by trade. He was busily engaged in his shop at
work, when Isaac Brant entered, and said—"Lowell, I am going
to kill you." The man, supposing him to be jesting, at first
laughed at the threat; and then remarked—"Why should you
"kill me? I have never injured you, neither have we ever
"quarrelled." The savage then deliberately drew a pistol and
shot him.

But his reckless and cruel career was soon arrested, by a death
wound, received, under the highest degree of provocation, at the
hand of his father. The circumstances were these : At the time
of the occurrence there was an assemblage of the Six Nations at
Burlington Heights, near to the residence of Colonel Beasley, for
the purpose of receiving the annual bounty of the government,
consisting of presents of clothing and other articles. On this occasion Isaac, with some of his young Indian companions, again
drank to intoxication, and renewed his threats against the life of
his father, declaring his intention to kill him that night. The
Chief had that evening taken tea with Colonel and Mrs. Beasley, (who then lived near the margin of Burlington Bay,) and
afterward walked up to a small inn upon the hill, at a short distance from the Colonel's residence, to lodge for the night. Isaac
followed his father to the inn, entered an adjoining room, and
began abusing him to the people about, in language perfectly
audible to his parent, the two apartments being divided only by
a board partition. Becoming quite violent in his conduct, his
father entered his son's apartment, but had no sooner done so,
than the latter sprang toward him for the purpose of assault—
armed, as it was asserted by some, though the fact was denied
by others, with a sharp-pointed knife. Be that as it may, the
Captain was badly wounded by a cut across the back of his
hand. Young Brant had been seized around the waist by some
of the Indians, at the instant he was leaping upon his father;
while the latter, irritated by the wound, had also been seized in
like manner by some white men, to prevent farther injury. The
affray was the work of an instant, during which Captain Brant
had drawn a large dirk, which he always carried upon his
thigh, and with which he struck at his son. In the descent of

the blow, the point of the dirk fell upon the head of Isaac, and, cutting through his hat, inflicted a wound which would have been more severe had the position of the parties been that of closer proximity. The wound was by no means considered dangerous at the time it was inflicted, although, from excitement and intoxication, it bled profusely. But such were the rage and violence of the young man, that he resisted all attempts to dress the wound—tearing off the bandages as fast as they could be applied, until, ultimately, they were compelled to bind him fast for the return of sobriety. He then allowed his head to be dressed properly; but the next day he resumed his drinking, and tearing the dressings from his wound, caused it of course to bleed afresh. His perverse conduct continued several days; a severe fever of the brain ensued, and the result was a speedy termination of his life.*

This painful transaction took place in the year 1795. The afflicted father immediately surrendered himself to the civil authorities, and resigned the commission which he yet retained in the British service, and upon which he drew half pay. Lord Dorchester, however, would not accept the resignation; and the death of Isaac was universally regarded as in the main accidental, and in any aspect of the case justifiable homicide.† The Chief called a council of his elderly sachems and warriors on the occasion, to whom, when assembled, he related the circumstances of the melancholy catastrophe. After great deliberation—for the Indians never decide hastily upon questions of moment—the council delivered an opinion nearly in the following words:—

"BROTHER: We have heard and considered your case. We sympathise with you. You are bereaved of a beloved son.

---

* Such were the real facts of this unhappy affair, as collected, recently, for the use of the author, from the statements of the witnesses of the transaction, and the surviving contemporaries of Captain Brant. And yet Dr. Morse and Dr. Belknap, who in the year following the event were sent forth by the Board of Commissioners of the society established in Scotland for the propagation of Christian Knowledge, to visit the Oneida and Mohekunuh, or Stockbridge Indians, recorded the incident in their report as a murder:—"Last Summer, Joseph Brant, a Mohawk Chief, and a "captain in the British service, formerly one of Doctor Wheelock's scholars, mur-"dered his own son, who was, indeed, a bad fellow, and had attempted the life of "his father."

† Morse and Belknap's Report to the Scot's Society.

But that son raised his parricidal hand against the kindest of fathers. His death was occasioned by his own crime. With one voice we acquit you of all blame. We tender you our hearty condolence. And may the Great Spirit above, bestow upon you consolation and comfort under your affliction."*

But the affliction was a very severe one to the old Chief, not-withstanding the condolence of his people, the convictions of his own conscience that he had not done intentional wrong, and the acquittal of all. Doctor Allen, President of Bowdoin College, has stated, upon the authority of Joseph Brant, jun., that as his father lay upon his bed and looked at the dirk with which the wound was inflicted, and which hung up in his room, he was accustomed to cry in the sorrow of his heart.†

Taking all the circumstances of this trying event into con-sideration, notwithstanding the unfavorable impressions, arising from prejudice and an imperfect knowledge of the facts, that may have prevailed, no just conclusion can be drawn to the dis-advantage of the Chief as a parent. While, on the other hand, all the evidence that can be obtained, goes to establish the fact that both in husband and father, his own family circle was most happy. Certainly nothing could have been stronger than his desire for the education and moral culture of his children. Knowing his solicitude upon this subject, and appreciating the disadvantages of his position in that respect, several gentlemen, in the year 1800, suggested to him the expediency of an appeal to the parent government for the education of his sons at the expense of the crown. A memorial for that object, addressed

---

* The account of this proceeding I received from the Secretary of the Upper Pro-vince, at Newark, while at his office to obtain the copy of an Indian deed."—*Note by Samuel Woodruff.*

† Allen's Biographical Dictionary. Isaac Brant left a widow and two children. Judge Woodruff, in his notes, says—"The widow and two lovely children which he left, I saw in Brant's family." The eldest of these "lovely children," was Isaac, to whom his grandfather, the old Chief, left a just proportion of his real estate. He also devised an equal proportion of his real estate to his eldest daughter, Christiana. The younger Isaac, however, grew up with the same disposition, and walked in the footsteps of his father. He was nevertheless a brave fellow in the field, and exhibit-ed his prowess during the late war between the United States and Great Britain, 1812—15. He was afterward killed in a drunken frolic, at Brantford, by a blow with a gun-barrel, inflicted, as was supposed, by a white man. But so bad had his character become, that his poor mother, then living, seemed rather relieved than other-wise by the occurrence, being in constant fear that he would commit some dreadful act which would bring him to an ignominious end.

to the Duke of Portland, was drawn up by one of his friends in the Upper Canadian administration, and submitted for his consideration. In this document a strong case was made, arising from the peculiar services which the Captain had rendered to the Crown, and the policy of having his sons educated in sound principles of loyalty. But the Chief peremptorily declined making such an overture. The following is an extract from his letter announcing his determination :—

Captain Brant to Colonel Smith.

"*Grand River, September* 20, 1800.

"Dear Sir,

"I have very seriously considered the petition to his Grace the Duke of Portland, for the education of my sons. which your friendship for me prompted you to advise me to make, and must acknowledge the particular satisfaction I feel at this further instance of your inclination to serve me with your friendly advice. I am confident it must have been suggested to your mind from the most friendly motives, of which I have had sufficient proofs since our acquaintance. But I am sorry I cannot altogether comply with your opinion on this point; for, considering the many oppositions I have met with since the establishment of the government of this province, in obtaining what I only considered as our rights, and which indeed seems yet to be in some measure undetermined, I cannot flatter myself with any prospect of succeeding in asking such a particular favor. I therefore decline, purely from the apprehensions of having my feelings farther hurt by a refusal. Notwithstanding, I think such a thing being granted would be extremely for the good of my family, and give me heartfelt satisfaction, could it be obtained for me by my friends, without my running the risk of meeting with farther rebuffs."

The Chieftain's papers afford evidence that an occasional correspondence must have been maintained between Captain Brant and the family of his old preceptor, President Wheelock, for many years. The venerable founder of Moor's Charity School, and subsequently of Dartmouth College, had slept with his fathers, before the close of the Revolutionary war, being succeeded in the presidentship of the college by his eldest son, John Wheelock, Esq., who was recalled from active service in the army, to assume the duties of that station.   James Wheelock, another son, had resided near the Chief in Upper Canada, after the conclusion of the Indian wars, and there was a renewal of ancient acquaintance and friendship.   During this period, Mr. Wheelock had proposed taking charge of the eldest surviving son, Joseph ; and having relinquished the project of applying to the government for assistance in the premises, the Captain once more turned his attention to the land in which, and the friends with whom, forty years before, he had acquired the rudiments of his imperfect education.   With this view a correspondence was opened with James Wheelock, and his brother, the president, which was attended by the desired results.   Extracts from this correspondence will not be found uninteresting, affording, as they will, farther and very gratifying illustrations of the Chieftain's domestic character :—

CAPTAIN BRANT TO JAMES WHEELOCK, ESQ.

"*Niagara, 3d October,* 1800.

"DEAR SIR,

"Although it is long since I have had the pleasure of seeing or corresponding with you, still I have not forgot there is such a person in being, and now embrace the kind offer you once made me, in offering to take charge of my son Joseph, whom I certainly should at that time have sent out, had it not been that there was apparently a jealousy subsisting between the British and Americans ; however, I hope it is not yet too late.   I send both my sons, Joseph and Jacob, who, I doubt not, will be particularly attended to by my friends.   I could wish them to be studiously attended to, not only as to their education, but likewise as to their morals in particular ; this no doubt is needless mentioning, as I know of old, and from personal experience at your seminary, that these things are paid strict attention to. Let my sons be at what schools soever, your overseeing them will be highly flattering to me.   I should by this opportunity have wrote Mr. John Wheelock on the same subject, but a hurry of business at this time prevents me.   I shall hereafter take the first opportunity of dropping him a few lines ; until when, please make my best respects to him, and I earnestly solicit his friendship and attention to my boys, which be assured of, I shall ever gratefully acknowledge.   I am, dear Sir, wishing you and your family health and happiness,

" Your friend and well wisher,

" Jos. Brant.

" *Mr. James Wheelock.*"

The lads were sent to Dartmouth in charge of Colonel Benjamin Sumner, of Claremont, (N. H.) a gentleman who had resided fifteen months among the Canadian Indians.   Colonel Sumner gave Dr. Wheelock a very gratifying account of the surprising progress the Mohawks had made in the art of husbandry, and the conveniences of living, in consequence of the influence exercised over them by Captain Brant.   He also repeated to the Doctor the anxious charge which he had received from the Chief, that his sons should be educated not only in letters, but in piety and virtue.*   The lads arrived at Hanover safely, were well received by President Wheelock and his brother James, and domesticated in the family of the latter. Both the President and James Wheelock wrote to the Captain on the 3d of November, announcing the fact, and informing him of the arrangements that had been made.   These were highly satisfactory to the parent, as will appear from the subjoined letters :—

CAPTAIN BRANT TO PRESIDENT JOHN WHEELOCK.

" *Grand River, Feb.* 9, 1801.

" DEAR SIR,

" I have received your favor of the 3d of November last.   I have delayed answering it until the return of Captain Brigham.

" I receive an inexpressible satisfaction in hearing from you, that you have taken my sons under your protection, and also to find that you yet retain a strong remembrance of our ancient friendship.   For my part, nothing can ever efface from my memory the persevering attention your revered father paid to my education, when I was in the place my sons now are.   Though I was an unprofitable pupil in some respects, yet my worldly affairs have been much benefitted by the instruction I there received.   I hope my children may reap greater advantages under your care, both with respect to their future as well as their worldly welfare.

* M'Clure's Life of Wheelock.

"Their situation at your brother's meets my highest approbation. Your goodness, in having provided for them out of the funds, far exceeds my expectations, and merits my warmest thanks. The reason that induced me to send them, to be instructed under your care, is the assurance I had that their morals and education would be there more strictly attended to than at any other place I know of.

"I am much pleased at the kindness you show in pressing them to be familiar at your house. I beg you will be constant in exhorting them to conduct themselves with propriety. The character you give me of the worthy gentleman, their preceptor, is extremely pleasing. From the whole, I feel perfectly easy with respect to their situation, and the care taken of their education, and am fully convinced that all now depends on their own exertions. The steady friendship you do me the honor to assure me of, is what, from numberless obligations, I doubly owe your family on my part ; and I beg leave to assure you, that until death, I remain your sincere friend.

"Should there be any thing you might wish from these parts, curiosities or the like, I shall be happy to send them to you.

"Dear Sir, I am

"Your very humble serv't.

'Jos. Brant.

"*Hon. John Wheelock.*"

From same, to James Wheelock, Esq.

"*Grand River, Feb.* 9, 1801.

"Dear Sir,

"It is now some time since I had the pleasure of receiving your kind letter of the 3d of November, 1800. It gives me unspeakable satisfaction to find that my boys are with you, as I am fully confident they could not have a better or more agreeable situation. I am assured, from the known reputation of the President, that if they do not make a progress in their studies, it will be owing to themselves. I therefore hope you will shew me the kindness to make free, and be particular in exhorting them to exert themselves, and to behave in a becoming manner.

"I am happy to find you yet retain the same sentiments of friendship for me that you have ever testified. I was apprehensive the manner in which I disappointed you respecting my son, when you was here, would have too much affected you. The occasion of it then was, the too great jealousy showed by our government here.

"I yet add, that I should wish them to be learned that it is their duty to be subject to the customs of the place they are in, even with respect to dress, and the cutting of their hair.

"The reason I did not answer you sooner, is that I have expected Captain Brigham back this way, and thought him the safest opportunity to send by. Any thing you might want from this quarter, I should be happy to assist you in.

"Dear Sir, I am,

"With respect and esteem,

"Your friend and humble servant.

"Jos. BRANT.

"*James Wheelock, Esq.*"

JAMES WHEELOCK TO CAPTAIN BRANT.

"*Hanover May* 1, 1801.

"VERY DEAR SIR,

"I received your polite and very agreeable letter of February 9th some days ago, for which please to accept my sincere and cordial thanks.

"I am very happy in again gratifying your parental feelings, with the information that your very worthy sons conduct themselves still in a most agreeable manner; are quite attentive to their school, and make, I believe, very laudable progress in learning. By their amiable dispositions and manly behavior they are continually growing in our esteem; and I sincerely hope and trust that *your* and our *expectations* concerning their future *usefulness* and *respectability* in life, will be highly gratified. You may depend on my friendly freedom in advising and exhorting them whenever I may see occasion. But, Sir, (without flattery,) such occasions will be very rare.

"What has become of my old friend, Mr. Phelps? I want to hear from him; but I have written so often without return, that I have done. Please when you see him to remember and mention me to him with cordial affection, and ask him to think of our former friendly days.

"I wish we could have the pleasure of seeing you here—perhaps, some time or other, we may be indulged in this wish. Please to remember me, with Mrs. Wheelock, affectionately to your lady, and believe that I continue to be, with attachment and respect, very dear Sir,

" Your sincere friend,

" And humble servant,

" JAS. WHEELOCK.

" *Captain Joseph Brant.*"

PRESIDENT WHEELOCK TO CAPTAIN BRANT.

" *Dartmouth College, May* 6, 1801.

" DEAR SIR,

" Though I have but a moment now allowed me to write, yet I cannot omit embracing it to express my thanks for your kind favor of February 9th ult.

" I rejoice to hear of your good health ; and great also is my happiness to be able to inform you of the regular conduct, and steady application, and laudable improvements of your dear sons with me. I will do all I can for their good, and future usefulness ; and may God grant that they shall be, and long continue, great sources of comfort and assistance to you in the sublime business of enlightening and meliorating your nations. I will write longer when I may have a good opportunity, and can now only ask the favor that you will accept this as a token of my cordial respect, and perfect friendship ; I am,

" Dear Sir,

" Your most ob'dt serv't,

" JOHN WHEELOCK.

" *Capt. J. Brant, &c. &c.*"

CAPTAIN BRANT TO PRESIDENT WHEELOCK.

" *Buffalo Creek, July* 23, 1801.

" DEAR SIR,

" It gives me great satisfaction to hear that my sons have so conducted themselves as to merit your approbation. The hope you form of them, is pleasing beyond expression. When my sons went away, I promised they should remain only one year ; but as they seem to make progress, I hope you will begin by times to convince them it is their interest to remain another winter, and exert themselves in their studies. I intend going to England this Fall, and should I return safe in the Spring, I will see them, and they might then come out on a visit home.

"I am, Dear Sir,

" Your friend sincerely,

" Jos. BRANT.

" *Hon. John Wheelock.*"

THE SAME TO JAMES WHEELOCK, ESQ.

" *Buffalo Creek, July* 23, 1801.

" VERY DEAR SIR,

" Your kind letter gives me an extreme pleasure to find that you and family are well, and that my sons grow in your esteem. I hope sincerely they may continue to behave in such a manner as to deserve a continuance of it. I have not seen Mr. Phelps since I received your favor, but expect I shortly shall, and I will then mention what you desire. We are likely to succeed in getting him ordained for a minister.

" It is a long time since I sent any pocket money to the boys. I shall in a few days send by Mr. Gideon Tiffany, a note for a hundred pounds, N. Y. C. I would do it sooner, but have not had the opportunity of conveyance. My best respects to Mrs. Wheelock and family.

"I am, Dear Sir, sincerely,

" Your friend and

" Humble servant,

" Jos. BRANT.

" P. S. I send a letter of Captain Elliott's son, their cousin, who is much younger than they, to shew them how he improves.*

" *James Wheelock, Esq.*"

JAMES WHEELOCK TO CAPTAIN BRANT.

" *Marcellus, Sept.* 19th, 1801.

" VERY DEAR AND RESPECTED SIR,

" I am almost overjoyed at meeting your worthy son, Joseph, this morning, on his way homeward. By him I have only a moment to write to express my respect for you, and my attachment and regard for your dear and promising sons. They have

---

* The name of Captain Elliott has repeatedly occurred before, in connexion with the British-Indian affairs at Detroit and the Miamis. Captain Brant, in one of his letters to Sir John Johnson, complained that Elliott was dismissed from the public service, for some reason not stated, and without trial.

been so long in my family, that to see Joseph seems like meeting one of my own children ; indeed they are both, by their pleasing conduct, which has been uniform, highly esteemed by all their acquaintance with us. I sincerely hope that your expectations concerning them will be answered, and that they will both be *good, useful,* and *honorable* in the world.

" It is some weeks since I left home. I want much to see you, and Joseph mentions that by a letter from you since I left home, we may expect that pleasure next Spring, on your return from your intended European tour. I hope we shall not be disappointed. I wish I could have the pleasure of my friend Joseph's company on my return home, as I have mentioned to him. May every blessing and happiness constantly attend you and yours, is the sincere wish of,

" Dear Sir, your very

' Sincere friend, and

" Humble servant,

" JAS. WHEELOCK.

" *Capt. Joseph Brant.*"

CAPTAIN BRANT TO MR. WHEELOCK.

" *Grand River, 22d Oct.* 1801.

" MY DEAR SIR,

" I received your kind letter favored by my son Joseph, and am extremely happy to find they both give such great satisfaction to their friends, of their good conduct, as well as to me. I cannot express myself the great pleasure you give me by the great attention to my children. I would really wish you to take the opportunity to continue them as your own children, and give them every good advice, so they may be useful and honorable in the world. As for my European route, it is uncertain.

" I remain, Dear Sir,

" Your sincere friend,

" And very humble serv't,

" JOS. BRANT.

" *Jas. Wheelock, Esq.*"

Unfortunately, while thus happily situated, pursuing their studies with diligence, and so demeaning themselves toward their friends as to win golden opinions from all, some difficulty arose between the brothers themselves, which produced a separation; Joseph, the eldest, leaving the school and returning home. Jacob followed in the course of the Spring, on a visit only, returning to the school again in the Autumn. Two or three letters more will close all that can be found of this interesting correspondence.

CAPTAIN BRANT TO MR. JAMES WHEELOCK.

" *Grand River, March* 20, 1802.

" MY DEAR SIR,

" I received your favor of the 25th January, and I am sorry to learn by it that your friendly arguments had not the desired effect of dissuading Joseph from his determination of coming this way. I regret very much his leaving, so unreasonably, the advantageous situation he was in, for improvement; for I am fully confident he could not have been in a better place, and I shall ever remain thankful for your kind attention and that of the President, although the imprudence of youth has rendered it ineffectual. At the same time I must assure you that Joseph has a grateful remembrance of the civilities he received from you and family, and acknowledges to have been as happy and comfortable as he could wish to be; and perfectly at nome in your house.

" After the great care and attention the worthy President has been pleased to show to my sons, it doubly grieves me that any part of their conduct should have the least appearance of neglect, or disrespect to a character that it was their duty to revere, and to which they were so much indebted.

" The only reason Joseph can allege for his coming away, is the perpetual disagreement between him and his brother Jacob. Mrs. Brant joins me in thanks and best respects to you and Mrs. Wheelock, and be assured we think equally well of your kind endeavors as if they had had the desired effect.

" My best respects to the President, and in a short time I shall write him in answer to the letter I received.

" My Dear Sir,

" I remain, affectionately,

" Your friend and

" Humble servant,

" Jos. BRANT.

" *James Wheelock, Esq'r.*"

James Wheelock to Captain Brant.

"*Hanover, April* 19, 1802.

"Very Dear Sir,

"It is with much pleasure I acknowledge the receipt of your friendly and obliging letter of March 20th,—am glad to learn that Joseph arrived at home; for I assure you, I felt not a little anxious for him, on his setting out, horseback, at such a season of the year, so long a journey. I hope he, as well as Jacob, will somewhere complete his education, and that they both will have a disposition and abilities, to follow the example of their worthy parent, in promoting eminently the happiness, prosperity and advantage of their fellow men, *while you and I shall be asleep with our fathers.*

"My brother, the President. has mentioned particularly concerning the conduct, &c. of Jacob, which renders any thing from me in his praise unnecessary; however, I must just say, that from what I have seen and understood since he left our house, (not from our desire, but his own,) his conduct has been quite unexceptionable, amicable, and pleasing; and I shall always rejoice in an opportunity to shew him any mark of friendship, by advice, or otherwise, that may be in my power.

"My brother has likewise mentioned to him Captain Dunham,* the gentleman who will accompany Jacob. He is a gentleman we highly esteem and respect, and I doubt not but he will meet with your friendly notice and attention.

"I shall always be happy in an opportunity to render you, or any of yours, any services that may be in my power; but how happy should I be in an opportunity, especially at my own house, to see you, and to manifest that respect to which you are so justly entitled, and to which my own feelings so warmly would prompt me. Mrs. Wheelock joins me in cordial respects to yourself and Mrs. Brant.

"I am, very Dear Sir, &c. &c.

"Jas. Wheelock."

"*Capt. Joseph Brant, &c. &c.*"

---

* Captain Josiah Dunham, an officer in the American service—a gentleman of ta lents and letters. After the surrender of the Northwestern posts, so long retained by Great Britain, Captain Dunham was stationed at Michillimackinack. Subsequently, during the earlier part of Mr. Madison's administration, Captain D. edited a political paper with signal ability, in Vermont.

FROM CAPTAIN BRANT TO JAMES WHEELOCK.

" *Niagara, 17th December,* 1802.

" MY DEAR SIR,

" I received your very polite and friendly letter by my son Jacob, and am very much obliged to you, your brother, and all friends, for the great attentions that have been paid to both my sons ; likewise to Captain Dunham, for the great care he took of Jacob on the journey.

" My son would have returned to you long before this but for a continued sickness in the family for three months, which brought Mrs. Brant very low ; my son Jacob and several of the children were very ill.

" My son now returns to be under the care of the President, and I sincerely hope he will pay such attention to his studies, as will do credit to himself, and be a comfort to his parents. The horse that Jacob rides out, I wish to be got in good order after he arrives, and sold, as an attentive scholar has no time to ride about. Mrs. Brant joins me in most affectionate respects to you and Mrs. Wheelock

" I am, Dear Sir,

" With great respect, your sincere friend and

" Humble servant,

" Jos. BRANT.

" *James Wheelock, Esq.,*

" *Hanover.*"

The only remaining letter of this branch of Captain Brant's correspondence which has been obtained, was addressed to James Wheelock, in October, 1804. It relates to matters indifferent to the present work, save only the mention that by the bursting of a gun, his son Jacob's left hand had been shattered, and that he was " about marrying one of our Mohawk girls." *
The whole of this correspondence, however, speaks the old

---

* Joseph Brant, Jr. died several years ago. Jacob Brant is yet living, [July, 1837.] A daughter of Captain Brant married a Frenchman, who, in June, 1789, was killed by a party of Indians while peaceably travelling up the Wabash River. He was in company with nine others, four of whom were killed, and three wounded. When the hostile party came up to them, and discovered the son-in-law of the Mohawk Chief, they assisted in drawing the arrows from the wounded, and then went off.—*Carey's Museum—quoted by Drake.*

Chief exceedingly well in his domestic relations. No parent could have been more solicitous for the moral and intellectual training of his offspring. His letters are characterised by an amiable temper, and by good, sound, common sense—breathing a spirit of kindness and affection throughout. And such was his general character in his family.

In addition to his correspondence upon public affairs, upon the business of his own nation exclusively, and in regard to his private and domestic concerns, which must have been very extensive, Captain Brant wrote many letters upon miscellaneous subjects to which his attention was from time to time invited. His fame was co-extensive with England and the United States, and he must have had acquaintances in France. His personal friends were very numerous, and those to whom he was known, far more numerous still. The consequence of these friendships and this celebrity, was frequent applications analagous to those made by Doctor Miller, for information in regard to the history, condition, and polity of his own people, or for the purpose of eliciting his own views and opinions upon given subjects. Of these miscellaneous letters, but few have been preserved. The annexed is given as an example. It had long been contended by physiologists, both in Europe and America, that the American aboriginals naturally have no beards. Nor is the opinion uncommon at the present day. It was for a solution of this question that a Mr. M'Causeland wrote to Brant, soon after the close of the American war. The following was the Chief's reply :—

> "*Niagara, April* 19, 1783.

"The men of the Six Nations have all beards by nature ; as have likewise all other Indian nations of North America, which I have seen. Some Indians allow a part of the beard upon the chin and upper lip to grow, and a few of the Mohawks shave with razors, in the same manner as Europeans ; but the generality pluck out the hairs of the beard by the roots, as soon as they begin to appear : and as they continue this practice all their lives, they appear to have no beard, or, at most, only a few straggling hairs, which they have neglected to pluck out. I am however of opinion, that if the Indians were to shave, they would never have beards altogether so thick as the Euro-

peans ; and there are some to be met with who have actually
very little beard.

"JOSEPH BRANT,

" *Thayendanegea.*"

Among others, the late eccentric Samuel Peters, LL. D.,
either opened, or attempted to open, a correspondence with the
Chief, a few years before his decease. Dr. Peters was a native
of Hebron, (Conn.) He was graduated at Yale College in 1757,
and, taking orders in the Episcopal Church, had charge of the
churches at Hartford and Hebron, at the commencement of the
Revolutionary contest. Being a friend of the crown, he went
to England, where he remained many years, and in 1781 published his extraordinary, and in many respects fabulous, history
of his native state. In the year 1805, he returned to the United
States; and in 1817 or 1818, made a journey into the country
of the great northwestern lakes, to the Falls of St. Anthony;
claiming a large extent of territory in that region, under a grant
to the ancient traveller, Captain Carver.*

On the subject of imprisonment for debt, his views were those
of an enlightened philosopher and philanthropist, as will be
manifest from the following interesting letter discovered among
the papers of the late Thomas Eddy ; a name ever to be revered,
as among the most honorable, if not the brightest, adorning the
annals of humanity.† Mr. Eddy was at the period mentioned,
and for years afterward, directing his attention to the subject of
prison discipline, and his mind was much occupied on the
question of imprisonment for debt. The views of the Mohawk
Chieftain were coincident with his own. Both were more than
a quarter of a century in advance of public opinion in the United States, in that important feature of English and American

* A letter of Dr. Peters to Captain Brant, written in April, 1803, is so characteristic of its author that a place has been assigned to it in the Appendix, (No.
XVII,) as a curiosity. Doctor, or Bishop Peters, as he was called, died in the city
of New-York, April 19, 1826, at the advanced age of 90. His remains were interred
at Hebron.

† This letter was transcribed by Thomas Eddy, into a volume of Indian documents, speeches &c., collected by him while in the discharge of his duties as an Indian commissioner for certain purposes. He had much intercourse with the Oneida,
Stockbridge, and some other tribes of Indians, some forty years ago, and was led to
inquiries and exertions for their moral and social improvement.

jurisprudence ; and how much in advance of England, remains to be seen.

LETTER FROM JOSEPH BRANT TO * * * *

" My Dear Sir,

" Your letter came safe to hand. To give you entire satisfaction I must, I perceive, enter into the discussion of a subject on which I have often thought. My thoughts were my own, and being so different from the ideas entertained among your people, I should certainly have carried them with me to the grave, had I not received your obliging favor.

" You ask me, then, whether in my opinion civilization is favorable to human happiness ? In answer to the question, it may be answered, that there are degrees of civilization, from Cannibals to the most polite of European nations. The question is not, then, whether a degree of refinement is not conducive to happiness ; but whether you, or the natives of this land, have obtained this happy medium. On this subject we are at present, I presume, of very different opinions. You will, however, allow me in some respects to have had the advantage of you in forming my sentiments. I was, Sir, born of Indian parents, and lived while a child among those whom you are pleased to call savages ; I was afterward sent to live among the white people, and educated at one of your schools ; since which period I have been honored much beyond my deserts, by an acquaintance with a number of principal characters both in Europe and America. After all this experience, and after every exertion to divest myself of prejudice, I am obliged to give my opinion in favor of my own people. I will now, as much as I am able, collect together, and set before you, some of the reasons that have influenced my judgment on the subject now before us. In the government you call civilized, the happiness of the people is constantly sacrificed to the splendor of empire. Hence your codes of criminal and civil laws have had their origin ; hence your dungeons and prisons. I will not enlarge on an idea so singular in civilized life, and perhaps disagreeable to you, and will only observe, that among us we have *no* prisons ; we have no pompous parade of courts; we have no written laws ; and yet judges are as highly revered amongst us as they are among you, and their decisions are as much regarded.

" Property, to say the least, is as well guarded, and crimes are as impartially punished. We have among us no splendid villains above the control of our laws. Daring wickedness is here never suffered to triumph over helpless innocence. The estates of widows and orphans are never devoured by enterprising sharpers. In a word, we have no robbery under the color of law. No person among us desires any other reward for performing a brave and worthy action, but the consciousness of having served his nation. Our wise men are called Fathers; they truly sustain that character. They are always accessible, I will not say to the meanest of our people, for we have none mean but such as render themselves so by their vices.

" The palaces and prisons among you form a most dreadful contrast. Go to the former places, and you will see perhaps a *deformed piece of earth* assuming airs that become none but the Great Spirit above. Go to one of your prisons; here description utterly fails ! Kill them, if you please ; kill them, too, by tortures; but let the torture last no longer than a day. Those you call savages, relent ; the most furious of our tormentors exhausts his rage in a few hours, and dispatches his unhappy victim with a sudden stroke. Perhaps it is eligible that incorrigible offenders should sometimes be cut off. Let it be done in a way that is not degrading to human nature. Let such unhappy men have an opportunity, by their fortitude, of making an atonement in some measure for the crimes they have committed during their lives.

" But for what are many of your prisoners confined ?—for debt !—astonishing !—and will you ever again call the Indian nations cruel ? Liberty, to a rational creature, as much exceeds property as the light of the sun does that of the most twinkling star. But you put them on a level, to the everlasting disgrace of civilization. I knew, while I lived among the white people, many of the most amiable contract debts, and I dare say with the best intentions. Both parties at the time of the contract expect to find their advantage. The debtor, we will suppose, by a train of unavoidable misfortunes, fails ; here is no crime, nor even a fault ; and yet your laws put it in the power of the creditor to throw the debtor into prison and confine him there for life ! a punishment infinitely worse than death to a brave man ! And I seriously declare, I had rather die by the most severe tortures ever inflicted on this continent, than languish in one of your prisons for a single year. Great Spirit of the Universe!—and do you call yourselves Christians? Does then the religion of Him whom you call your Saviour, inspire this spirit, and lead to these practices? Surely no. It is recorded of him, that a bruised reed he never broke. Cease, then, to call yourselves Christians, lest you publish to the world your hypocrisy. Cease, too, to call other nations savage, when you are tenfold more the children of cruelty than they."

Few subjects of greater interest have been presented for the consideration of antiquaries in North America, than those monuments of an age and a people that are lost, found scattered over western New-York, through the state of Ohio, and in great numbers in the valley of the Mississippi. called Tumuli. These mounds, or barrows, as they are usually ter ed in older countries, have been objects of extensive inquiry and much speculation; but their origin, in America, and the purposes of their erection, are yet among those hidden mysteries which it is probable that even time itself will not unfold. Among the Greeks, on the steppes of Tartary, in the north of Europe, in England, Ireland, and New South Wales, in all which coun tries, and several others, they abound, it has been well ascertained that these tumuli were monumental heaps, of greater or less extent, raised over the remains of the dead. But in the United States, and in Mexico, where similar barrows are numerous, appearances, in regard to very many of them, have seemed to warrant a different opinion as to the object of their formation. Their magnitude in this country is much greater than in any other, some of the largest American tumuli being approached in dimensions only by the celebrated Irish barrow at New Grange, described by Governor Pownall;* while the form of very many of the American has induced at least a plausible conjecture, that

---

* The Irish barrow in New Grange, county Meath, covers two acres at the base, the circumference at the top being three hundred feet, and its height ninety. It consists of small pebbles, and has a gallery within, sixty-two feet long, leading to a cave. There is one near Wheeling, on the Ohio, between thirty and forty rods in circumference at the base, one hundred and eighty at the top, and seventy feet high. Near Cohokia there is a numerous group, stated at about two hundred in all—the largest of which is a parallelogram, about ninety feet high, and eight hundred yards in circuit. [*Ency. Americana.*] There are some very large and of evident military formation, in the Wyoming Valley.

they were the military defences of a people long since become extinct.

While, therefore, every inquiry of the white man concerning these remains in America has ended as it began, leaving the subject of investigation as deep in obscurity as before, the opinion of a man of Brant's information and sagacity, thoroughly conversant, as he was, with the traditions of his own people, may not be unacceptable to the curious reader. That opinion, or rather such information as the Chief had derived from the dim light of Indian tradition, has been supplied in the manuscript notes of Mr. Woodruff, already referred to several times in the preceding pages. A few extracts follow:—

'" Among other things relating to the western country," says Mr. Woodruff, " I was curious to learn in the course of my conversations with Captain Brant, what information he could give me respecting the *tumuli* which are found on and near the margin of the rivers and lakes, from the St. Lawrence to the Mississippi. He stated, in reply, that the subject had long been agitated, but yet remained in some obscurity. A tradition, he said, prevailed among the different nations of Indians throughout that whole extensive range of country, and had been handed down time immemorial, that in an age long gone by, there came white men from a foreign country, and by consent of the Indians established trading-houses and settlements where these tumuli are found. A friendly intercourse was continued for several years ; many of the white men brought their wives, and had children born to them ; and additions to their numbers were made yearly from their own country. These circumstances at length gave rise to jealousies among the Indians, and fears began to be entertained in regard to the increasing numbers, wealth, and ulterior views of the new comers ; apprehending that, becoming strong, they might one day seize upon the country as their own. A secret council, composed of the chiefs of all the different nations from the St. Lawrence to the Mississippi, was therefore convoked ; the result of which, after long deliberation, was a resolution that on a certain night designated for that purpose, all their white neighbors, men, women and children, should be exterminated. The most profound secrecy was essential to the execution of such a purpose ; and such was the fidelity with which the fatal determination was kept, that the conspiracy was successful, and the device carried completely into effect. Not a soul was left to tell the tale.

"The Captain expressed no opinion himself as to the truth of the tale, but added, that from the vessels and tools which had been dug up in those mounds, or found in their vicinity, it was evident that the people who had used them were French.

"In the year 1801, having occasion to travel through the States of New-York and Ohio, and a part of Pennsylvania," (continues Judge Woodruff,) "I had frequent opportunities of viewing these artificial mounds, as well as the entrenched plots of land contiguous to them. They are all placed upon small and handsome elevations of ground. The entrenched plots are of various dimensions, from six to ten rods square. The ditches and their banks are yet plainly visible. Their antiquity may be inferred from the size of the trees standing both in the ditches and on the banks—being as large as any of those in their vicinity. Many of these trees I saw which were more than two feet in diameter. Near one corner of each of these areas, is a space of twelve feet in width, where the ground appears never to have been broken. It is evident that these spaces were used for gate-ways. About ten or fifteen yards from these gate-ways, stand the mounds. These are of different dimensions, in different places, from ten to fifteen feet in diameter at the base, and from six to twelve feet elevation, being now much flattened down.

"Various have been the conjectures for what use these mounds were raised. Some have supposed they were made as depositories of the dead; others, for places in which to store provisions in winter; and others, for watch-towers, on which sentinels were posted to guard the garrisons from approaching danger. While in Ohio, I felt an anxiety to satisfy myself, if possible, for which of these uses, or for what other, these tumuli were designed. I employed a party of young men to dig down through one of them, beginning at the centre of the apex. When they had descended through to the natural surface of the ground, it appeared by the mould, or soil, that the earth had not *there* been broken. All we found there, were a few oaken chips, nearly sound, and bearing the mark of the axe. These circumstances, in my judgment, served greatly to strengthen the probability that the mounds had been designed and used only for watch-towers. Mr. Quimby, the owner of the land, shewed me a tinner's anvil, a pair of shears, and an adze, which he had found on the area within the lines of the entrenchment. All these were evidently of French origin. Many other tools and vessels, as I was well informed, had been found at other of these stations, in different parts of the western country, all of the same character.

"In farther conversation with Captain Brant, he informed me that he had ever entertained a strong desire to know something more decisive concerning those white people—their former neighbors—and that while in England, he made a visit to the French capital for the purpose of pushing his inquiries upon the subject. Letters of introduction were furnished by his friends in London, to some literary gentlemen in Paris, by whom he was received with great politeness and respect, and kindly assisted in making researches in the public libraries. Nothing, however, could be found in any of their histories, respecting the object of his inquiries, excepting, that about the year 1520, (if I rightly remember,) several ships were fitted out and sailed from L'Orient, bound to North America, freighted with goods suitable for that market, and carrying out a number of traders, and other enterprising individuals, with their families, to plant a colony in that part of the world. But nothing farther was recorded concerning the enterprize. Hence Captain Brant was induced to give additional credit to the tradition before mentioned." *

There seem to be many strong reasons for believing, that

* John Norton, the intelligent Mohawk Chief, heretofore repeatedly mentioned, gave a different version of the tradition upon this subject. Being at Albany, upon the business of the St. Regis Reservation, during the administration of Governor Jay, the Governor took occasion to ask Norton if he knew any thing concerning the origin of the Indian fortifications, as they were called, found in such numbers in many parts of the United States. He answered, that there was a tradition in his tribe that they were constructed by a people who in ancient times occupied a great extent of country, but who had been extirpated; that there had been long and bloody wars between this people and the Five Nations, in which the latter had been finally victorious. He added, that one of the last of the fortifications which was taken, had been obstinately defended; that the warriors of the other four nations of the Confederacy had assaulted it without waiting for the Mohawks, and had been repulsed with great loss, but that the latter coming to their assistance the attack was renewed, the place taken, and all who were in it destroyed.—*Letter to the author from the Hon. Peter Augustus Jay, who was present during the conversation.*

at some remote period of time, a race of men, different from the Indians found in occupancy by the English, farther advanced in civilization, and possessed of arts of which they were ignorant, must have been in possession of portions of this country. The Indians have various traditions upon the subject of such a lost race of men, differing, however, among different tribes, and often among individuals of the same tribes. Mary Jemison, who was raised among the Senecas, and spent a long life with them, states that the Indians held that the flatts of the Genesee were cleared, and had been cultivated, by another people, before the Indians came into possession. They were a people of whom they could give no account, because "their fathers had never seen them." By the sliding of a bank of Mary's farm into the river, a burial-place was discovered, of which the Indians had no knowledge, and they held that the bones were not those of Indians.[*] But of what race, nation, or complexion, were this ancient people, will probably never be known. That the continent of North America was discovered by the Normans, during the patriarchal government of the Colony of Greenland, by Erik the Red, five centuries before the voyages of Columbus, is no longer a matter of doubt. The shores of the Gulf of St. Lawrence, and the coast of New England, were visited by Lief and Thorwald, the sons of Erik, and colonies planted, as far back as the tenth century. These colonies, however, were soon lost or extirpated ; and from the Icelandic records, and the histories of the Northmen,[†] there is but faint reason for supposing that the few colonists of Vinland, as the new country was named, or their descendants, could have extended themselves from the estuary of the St. Lawrence across into the valley of the Mississippi.[‡]

The tradition recited by Brant, however, tends, especially in its details, to corroborate the well-known legend of the Welsh, concerning Prince Madog, or Madoc, which has occasioned so many stories of White and Welsh Indians, rather than any other tale of discovery and colonization with which the public is acquainted. According to the Welsh tradition, Madoc—if indeed there

[*] See Appendix, No. XVIII.

[†] Vide, History of the Northmen, by Henry Wheaton ; Voyages of Sebastian Cabot, &c. &c.

[‡] See Appendix, No. XIX.

was such a veritable personage—in consequence of some domestic dissensions, went to sea, with ten ships and three hundred men, in the twelfth century, and discovered land far to the west. He made several voyages to and from this unknown land, but finally, with all his followers, was lost to the knowledge of his countrymen. The tradition of Brant, that the white strangers made annual voyages to and from their own country for several years, corresponds with the story as related in the Welsh Triads, and by Hakluyt, who has given an account of the supposed voyages of the Prince. The cutting off of the colonists at one fell stroke, as related by Brant, also shows very satisfactorily why his fate was never known. Œdipus solved the riddle of the Sphinx ; but unless he was able to solve still greater mysteries, the origin and uses of the American tumuli present questions that would have baffled the wisdom even of the accomplished though unfortunate son and husband of Jocasta.

In bringing the life and actions of Joseph Brant—Thayendanegea, to a close, something in the form of a summary review of his character will doubtless be expected at the hands of the biographer. This task can be readily and expeditiously executed, from the method adopted in the composition of the work itself. Nor, after the record already given of his public life and conduct, and the occasional anecdotes and illustrations of character introduced in the regular progress of the narrative, will the reader be surprised to find the author disposed, not only to set aside, but to reverse the popular estimate, and all previous decisions of history, in relation to the character of that remarkable man.

His fine personal appearance in the full maturity of manhood has already been described from the notes of Mr. Woodruff and General Porter. His early advantages of education were limited, but of these he evidently made the best use. Probably, being connected by the alliance of his sister with Sir William Johnson, he may have attended some of the missionary schools in the Mohawk Valley previous to his being sent by the Baronet to the Moor charity school, under the care of the elder Doctor Wheelock. But as he had already, though at so early an age, been upon the war-path in two campaigns, his opportunities of study could not have been great,—to say nothing of the

reluctance with which an ardent youth, looking with delight upon the pride, pomp and circumstance of glorious war,
and impatient of military renown, might be expected to confine
himself to the dull and quiet pursuits of the school-room. Still,
he acknowledged in after life that he had derived great and lasting advantages from the instructions of Doctor Wheelock.
The wars of Pontiac a third time called him to the field; but the
campaign was no sooner ended, than he was again engaged in
literary pursuits under the direction of the missionaries. The
influence of his sister in the administration of the Indian department, called him more directly into active public life
on the death of Sir William Johnson, although he had been
much employed in the transaction of business with the Indians
previous to that event. These avocations had of course deprived him of much time which might otherwise have been
devoted to study; and when upon him had devolved the
chieftainship of the whole confederacy of the Six Nations,
it may well be imagined that the official claims upon his attention were in themselves sufficient to occupy, unremittingly, the
most active mind. Then followed the protracted conflict of the
American Revolution, requiring, from his position, and the side
he espoused, the exercise of all his energies, physical and intellectual. But his return to his books, the moment that the great contest was ended; the progressive improvement in the style of his
letters; and the fruits of his labors in the translations he produced,
are circumstances proving his perseverance amidst the most
harassing cares and perplexities of his after-life, and that he
had a natural taste for literature, and was zealous in the acquisition of knowledge. His solicitude was great for the thorough
education of his children; and he had himself not only projected writing a history of his own people, but had it in contemplation himself to acquire the knowledge of the Greek language,
that he might be enabled to read the New Testament in the
original, and thus make a more perfect translation of the Greek
Scriptures in the Mohawk tongue.

His character has been represented as savage and cruel; and
in the meagre sketches of his life hitherto published, although
an occasional redeeming virtue has been allowed by some, anecdotes of treachery and blood have been introduced, to sustain

the imputed disposition of relentless ferocity.* The causes of this general libel upon the native character of the Indians, and upon that of Brant in particular, have been indicated in the commencement of the present work. Such, however, was not the fact. On the contrary, making the necessary allowances for his position, his own blood, and the description of warriors he commanded, after the most diligent and laborious investigation, the author is free to declare his belief that Brant was no less humane than he is on all hands admitted to have been brave. He was an Indian, and led Indians to the fight, upon their own principles and usages of war. Bold and daring, sagacious and wily, he often struck when least expected; but the author has in vain sought for an instance of wanton cruelty—of treachery—or of the murder of prisoners, or others, by his own hand, or by his permission, in cold blood. At the first outbre.k of the American revolution, he interposed and saved the life of the Rev. Mr. Kirkland when on the point of becoming a victim to Indian fury, although not at that time on the very best terms with that gentleman. The first battle of the revolutionary war in which Brant was engaged, was that of the Cedars, on the banks of the St. Lawrence. Immediately after the fate of the day was decided, he interposed to save the prisoners, and actually, at his own private expense, appeased the Indians, and prevented the sacrifice of the brave Captain M'Kinstry. This gentleman was well known to the author, and he ever entertained a high regard for Captain Brant, by whom he was afterward visited on the

* As a specimen of these bloody anecdotes, take the following, related many years since by a traveller named Weld, from whom it has been universally copied since. And yet there is not a syllable of truth in its composition:—"With a considerable body of his troops, he joined the forces under the command of Sir John Johnson. A skirmish took place with a body of American troops; the action was warm, and Brant was shot by a musket ball in his heel; but the Americans in the end were defeated and an officer and sixty men were taken prisoners. The officer, after having delivered up his sword, had entered into conversation with Sir John Johnson, who commanded the British troops, and they were talking o ether in the most friendly manner, when Brant, having stolen slily behind them, laid the American officer low with a blow of his tomahawk. The indignation of Sir John Johnson, as may be readily supposed, was roused by such an act of treachery, and he resented it in the warmest terms. Brant listened to him unconcernedly, and when he had finished, told him that he was sorry for his displeasure, but that indeed his heel was extremely painful at the moment, and he could not help revenging himself on the only chief of the party that he saw taken. Since he had killed the officer, he added, his heel was much less painful to him than it had been before."

manor of Livingston. The Chieftain's efforts at the massacre of Cherry Valley, to stay the effusion of innocent blood, have been mentioned in the account of that tragic irruption. In addition to the circumstances there narrated, Doctor Dwight, who was as careful as he was diligent in the collection of his facts, relates, that on entering one of the houses in Cherry Valley, Walter Butler ordered a woman and child, who were in bed, to be killed ; but the Mohawk Chief interposed, and said— "What! kill a woman and child! No! That child is not an "enemy to the King, nor a friend to the Congress. Long be- "fore he will be big enough to do any mischief, the dispute "will be settled." At the affair of Wyoming, for which he has always received the severest condemnation, he was not present. His conduct to Captain Harper and his fellow-prisoners was any thing but cruel, in the Indian acceptation of the term, although the execution of the aged and weary prisoner, if done with his knowledge or by his direction, was indefensible. But at Minisink, according to his own relation of the circumstances, (and his veracity has never been questioned,) his conduct has been grossly misrepresented. He exerted himself in the first instance to avert the effusion of blood, and was fired upon while in the act of making pacific overtures. True, Colonel Wisner was finally killed by his own hand ; but the very blow was prompted by humanity, according to the reasoning of an Indian. The soldier was wounded past cure or removal ; and after reflection upon the painful case, to prevent his dying agonies from being aggravated by beasts of prey, the Chief put an end to his sufferings through an honest dictate of compassion. A thoroughly civilized warrior would neither have reasoned nor acted as he did under the circumstances. Still, the act was prompted by feelings of humanity, and was doubtless such in reality. Lieutenant Wormwood was killed at Cherry Valley by mistake, and after refusing to stand when hailed. Lieutenant Boyd and his companion were treated with humanity by Brant after the capture in the Genesee country, and the dreadful tragedy which ended their lives was not enacted until Brant had departed for Niagara. The reader cannot well have forgotten the touching and beautiful incident of the restoration of the infant to its mother, at Fort Hunter, as related to the author by Governor Lewis, an eye-witness of the transaction. To all which may be added, that his last act of the last battle he fought was the rescuing of an American prisoner from a savage Irish ally of his own Indians, who was about to murder him.*

In the course of his conversations with Major James Cochran and General Porter, long after the war, in regard to the alleged cruelty of his career, Brant assured those gentlemen that he had always spared in battle whenever it could be done without bringing upon himself the censure of his own people. In more instances than one, he said, he had been instrumental in preserving life when exposed to the fury of his warriors, and that he had winked at the escape of white prisoners, whose sufferings would not permit them to proceed on their march. He related one instance in particular, in which a young female prisoner had lagged behind, and whom he himself hid in the bushes that she might escape and return to her home. This account of himself was subsequently confirmed by Captain Philip Frey, son of Colonel Hendrick Frey, of Tryon county, of most respectable character and connexions, and an officer in the British army, who had served with Brant on several military expeditions, and shared with him the dangers of several battles.†

Having thus disposed of the principal events in his career during the war of the Revolution, in respect to which his conduct was certainly the opposite of savage and blood-thirsty, this point of his vindication may be appropriately closed by the fol-

* This incident was mentioned to me by Colonel Kerr, his son-in-law. The occurrence was at the defeat of St. Clair.

† Letter of Major Cochran to the author. In farther illustration of Brant's general desire to prevent the shedding of blood unnecessarily, the following incident has been communicated to the author while these sheets were passing through the press:—"The late Jonathan Maynard, Esq. of Framingham, (near Boston,) Massachusetts, formerly a member of the Senate of that State, was actively engaged in the war of the Revolution, and, as he was in the habit of relating to his friends, was taken prisoner at one time in the western part of New-York by a party of the enemy, composed chiefly of Indians, under the command of Brant. The savages were disposed to put him to death according to the exterminating mode of warfare practised in that section of the country by the combined Indians and Tories; and preparations were making to that effect, when, having been partially stripped, Brant discovered the symbols of Freemasonry marked upon the prisoner's arms, which led him to interpose and save his life. Mr. Maynard was then sent a prisoner to Canada, where, after remaining several months, he was finally exchanged, and returned home. He lived to an advanced age, universally respected in the town where he resided, as an upright man and faithful magistrate; and was favorably known throughout the county of Middlesex, which he represented in the Senate of the commonwealth."—*Letter to the author by George Folsom, Esq.*

lowing extract from a letter addressed to him in February, 1792, by the Rev. Mr. Kirkland, than whom none was more intimately acquainted with his general character and disposition :—

REV. MR. KIRKLAND TO CAPTAIN BRANT.—(Extract.)
"*Genesee, February 17th,* 1792.

"MY DEAR FRIEND,

"I was honored with your very polite and affectionate letter of the 1st inst. by Dr. Allen, last Saturday. The opportunity which now presents of addressing you, is very unexpected. Yes'erday I had the pleasure of a short interview with Captain Williamson, who had lately passed through Philadelphia, where he received a large packet for Colonel *Gordon,* commanding at Niagara, soliciting his aid in behalf of a disconsolate mother, to inquire after the fate of her son, *Captain Turner*—an unfortunate officer, who is supposed to be a prisoner among the *Miamis,* and taken in the action of last Fall. I told Mr. Williamson that no person would be more willing and ready on such an occasion to make inquiry, and perhaps no one under equal advantages, to obtain the much-desired information, than your self; and that, *notwithstanding all your martial fire and heroism, you possessed a sensibility of soul that would weep at the tale of woe.* He gave me a most affecting account of the situation of the afflicted mother—probably he was a darling son. Mr. Williamson has accordingly written you on the subject."

One of the distinguishing features of his character was his strong sense of justice. It will be recollected, in the narrative of the captivity of Alexander Harper and others, that during their long and fatiguing march, when his own warriors and himself were suffering almost the extremity of hunger, he saw with his own eyes the most rigid impartiality exercised in the distribution of such scanty supplies of food as they were able casually to procure. Every prisoner was allowed a full share with himself; and at the end of their march, it has been seen how adroitly he averted the torture of the gauntlet-running, which it was so customary with the Indians to inflict upon their prisoners. This same love of justice, moreover, marked his conduct during the Indian wars of 1789—'95, and pervaded his correspondence connected with those wars, and his own subsequent difficulties with the British Government touching the Grand River land title, and in all his negotiations with the State of New-York. He honestly thought the claim of the north-western Indians to the Ohio and Muskingum boundary a just one. Hence his untiring exertions, year after year, to adjust the difficulties between the Indians and the United States upon that basis. When he thought the Indians claimed too much, he opposed them; and so far as he thought them in the right, he was ready to fight for them. In a letter to General Chapin upon this subject, written in December, 1794, he says:

" Your letters from Kanandaigua are now before me. I have to say that our meetings during the whole of last summer, at all of which our thoughts were solely bent on fixing a boundary line, such as we thought would be the means of fixing a peace on a solid basis, for which reason we pointed out the line we did, well knowing the justness of it, and being certain that the whole Indian confederacy would ratify it.

" I must regret, as an individual, to find that this boundary has been abandoned, as I am well convinced a lasting peace would have ensued had it been adopted. I, therefore, ever have, to bring about this desirable end, exerted every nerve, wishing for nothing more than justice between us. This line, you will recollect, was offered to Governor St. Clair at Muskingum. Notwithstanding the two successful campaigns of the Indians, I still adhered to the same line, and still do. This, I hope, will satisfy you that my wish ever was for peace. The offer made was rejected by Mr. St. Clair, and what the consequences have been you well know. * * * * *

* * * * * You will recollect that I differed even with my friends, respecting the boundary,* and to the two last messages that you then received, my name was to neither, for the reason that I thought them [the Indians] too unreasonable. For this reason I was obliged to take more pains and trouble to bring the Indians and you to an understanding, than I was under any obligation to do, otherwise than having our mutual interests in view. As to politics, I study them not. My principle is founded on justice, and justice is all I wish for. Never shall I exert myself for any nation or nations, let their

---

* Captain Brant had proposed a compromise boundary line, of which he was here speaking. But neither the United States nor the Indians would listen to it.

opinions of me be what they will, unless I plainly see they are sincere and just in what they may aim at, and that nothing more than strict justice is what they want. When I perceive that these are the sentiments of a people, no endeavors ever shall be wanting on my part to bring nations to a good understanding."

These views are frank, manly, and honorable; and correspond with the whole tenor of his speeches and correspondence, as well upon that as all other questions of controversy in which he was called to participate.

His efforts for the moral and religious improvement of his people were indefatigable. In addition to the details already presented upon this point, the fact is no less interesting than true, that the first Episcopal church erected in Upper Canada was built by Brant, from funds collected by him while in England in 1786. The church was built the same year, and the first "church-going bell" that tolled in Upper Canada, was placed there by him.* The Rev. Davenport Phelps, in writing to President John Wheelock, November, 1800, upon the subject of the exertions of Captain Brant, and the progress his people were making in religious knowledge and the arts of civilized life, under his influence, remarks :—" I cannot, sir, but here observe, " that strong hopes may be entertained that we may yet see the " wilderness bud and blossom like the rose. There is already a " degree of civilization among a number of the Indians which " would surprise a stranger. And with some of them there is " such an appearance of Christianity, that many of the whites " who possess it, might well blush at a comparative view. Of " this great and important alteration, and of the present pleasing " prospect of success in extending the knowledge of the Redeem- " er among them, I am fully persuaded the labors of your vene- " rable predecessor, under God, have been the cause. Colo- " nel Brant greatly encourages civilization and Christianity. " Through his exertions and influential example among the " Indians, it is to be hoped their progress toward refinement " may yet be considerable."† His earnest desire, beyond a doubt, was to render himself a benefactor to his people.

* Letter to the author from Colonel W. J. Kerr.
† M'Clure's Life of Wheelock.

As a warrior, he was cautious, sagacious and brave ; watching with sleepless vigilance for opportunities of action, and allowing neither dangers nor difficulties to divert him from his well-settled purposes.   His constitution was hardy, his capacity of endurance great ; his energy untiring, and his firmness indomitable.   His character, in his social and domestic relations, has been delineated at length, and needs no farther illustration.   In his dealings and business relations he was prompt, honorable, and expert ; and, so far as the author has been able to obtain information from gentlemen who knew him well, he was a pattern of integrity.   The purity of his private morals has never been questioned, and his house was the abode of kindness and hospitality.

His manners in refined society have been described by Dr. Miller and General Porter.   Without divesting himself altogether of the characteristic reserve of his people, he could, nevertheless, relax as occasion required, and contribute his full share, by sprightly and intelligent conversation, to the pleasures of general society.   He was at once affable and dignified, avoiding frivolity on the one hand and stiffness on the other ; in one word, unbending himself just to the proper medium of the well-bred gentleman.   He has been described by some as eloquent in his conversation.   Others, again, deny him the attribute of eloquence, either in public speaking or in the social circle; asserting that his great power lay in his strong, practical good sense, and deep and ready insight into character.   Mr. Thomas Morris avers that his sagacity in this respect exceeded that of any other man with whom he has been acquainted.   His temperament was decidedly amiable ; he had a keen perception of the ludicrous, and was both humorous and witty himself—sometimes brilliant in this respect ; and his conversation was often fascinating, by reason of its playfulness and vivacity.*

* As an illustration of his shrewdness and sagacity, the following anecdote of Brant has been communicated to the author by Professor Griscom :—" When Jemima Wilkinson, (who professed to be, in her own person, the Saviour of the world in his second appearance on earth,) was residing on her domain in western New-York, surrounded by her deluded and subservient followers, she could not fail to attract the notice of Colonel Brant ; while the celebrity of the Chieftain must, in turn, have forcibly commended itself to her attention.   This led, of course, to a mutual desire to see each other, and Brant at length presented himself at her mansion, and requested an interview.   After some formality he was admitted, and she

The implacable resentments imputed to the American Indians were not characteristic of him. In a speech to a council of Misissaguas—a clan of the Hurons, located on the Bay of Quinte,—on the occasion of certain grievous personal insults, of which some of their people were complaining, he remarked: —" Brothers, I am very glad you suffer these abuses so pa-" tiently. I advise you to persevere in your patience and pru-" dence, never allowing yourselves to feel and exercise revenge, " until every regular step be taken to remove them."† In the whole course of his correspondence, positive hostility, of a personal character, seems only to have been cherished toward Colonel Claus, the Deputy Superintendent General of the Indian Department. The precise nature of this difficulty the author has not ascertained. It was connected, however, with the pecuniary affairs of the Indians, in regard to which Brant was exonerated from censure at every scrutiny. Still, perfection cannot be predicated of the Mohawk Chief more than other men, and the author has not discovered a particle of evidence, going to inculpate the moral or official conduct of Colonel Claus—save that he appears to have connived at the unsuccessful machinations of Red Jacket and other enemies of Brant, to effect the chieftain's deposition.

Like other men, Brant doubtless had his faults, but they were redeemed by high qualities and commanding virtues. He was charged with duplicity, and even treachery, in regard to the affairs of the Indians and the United States, in connexion with his first visit to Philadelphia. But the aspersion was grievously unjust. During the years of those wars, his position was trying

addressed to him a few words in the way of a welcome salutation. He replied to her by a formal speech in his own language, at the conclusion of which she informed him that she did not understand the language in which he spoke. He then addressed her in another Indian dialect, to which, in like manner, she objected. After a pause, he commenced a speech in a third, and still different American language, when she interrupted him by the expression of dissatisfaction at his persisting to speak to her in terms which she could not understand. He arose with dignity, and with a significant motion of the hand, said—'Madam, you are not the person you pretend to be. Jesus Christ can understand one language as well as 'another,' and abruptly took his leave." Since this striking and characteristic anecdote was received from Dr. Griscom, I have discovered that it has been attributed to Red Jacket. This Chief, however, was a Pagan—a disbeliever in Jesus Christ; and as Brant was the opposite, the anecdote is more charasteristic of him than of the Seneca orator.

† MS. speech among the Brant papers.

and peculiar. He had his own ulterior objects to consult in regard to the Indians of the upper lakes. He desired to see justice done to them, and also to the United States. And he likewise desired not 'to impair his own influence with those Indians. At the same time he had a difficult game to play, with the Colonial and British governments. The doubtful relations between England and the United States induced the former to keep the Indians in a very unpacific mood toward the latter for a series of years ; sometimes even pushing them into hostilities, by means and appliances of which policy required the concealment, and the means of diplomatic denial, if necessary. At the same time, while Brant was thoroughly loyal to the King, he was nevertheless resolved upon maintaining the unfettered independence of his own peculiar nation ; friendly relations with the Colonial government being also essential to his desire of a perfect title to his new territory.

Such a position must at all times have been full of embarrassment and difficulty, and at some conjunctures could not have been otherwise than deeply perplexing. And yet he sustained himself through the whole—proving himself above the influence of gold at Philadelphia, and passing the ordeal without dishonor. In letters, he was in advance of some of the Generals against whom he fought ; and even of still greater military chieftains, who have flourished before his day and since. True, he was ambitious—and so was Cæsar. He sought to combine many nations under his own dominion—and so did Napoleon. He ruled over barbarians—and so did Peter the Great.

A few years before his death, Captain Brant built a commodious dwelling-house, two stories high, on a tract of land presented him by the King at the head of Lake Ontario—directly north of the beach which divides the lake from the sheet of water known as Burlington Bay. The situation is noble and commanding, affording a glorious prospect of that beautiful lake, with a fruitful soil and a picturesque country around it. At this place, on the 24th of November, 1807, he closed a life of greater and more uninterrupted activity for the space of half a century, than has fallen to the lot of almost any other man whose name has been inscribed by the muse of history. He was a steadfast believer in the distinguishing doctrines of Christianity, and a member of the Episcopal church at the time of his decease. He bore his illness, which was painful, with patience and resignation. He died in the full possession of his faculties, and, according to the belief of his attendants, in the full faith of the Christian religion.* His age was sixty-four years and eight months. His remains were removed to the Mohawk Village, on the Grand River, and interred by the side of the church which he had built. The interests of his people, as they had been the paramount object of his exertions through life, were uppermost in his thoughts to the end. His last words that have been preserved upon this subject, were contained in a charge to his adopted nephew, Teyoninhokârâwen :—" Have " pity on the poor Indians : if you can get any influence with " the great, endeavor to do them all the good you can." With great justice the surviving Mohawks might have made a similar exclamation to that of King Joash at the bed of the dying prophet—" My father, my father, the chariot of Israel, and the horsemen thereof !"

* See Appendix, No. XX.

CATHARINE BRANT, the widow of Thayendanegea, was forty-eight years old at the time of his decease. According to the constitution of the Mohawks, which, like that of Great Britain, is unwritten, the inheritance descends through the female line exclusively. Consequently the superior chieftainship does not descend to the eldest male; but the eldest female, in what may be called the royal line, nominates one of her sons or other descendants, and he thereby becomes the chief. If her choice does not fall upon her own son, the grandson whom she invests with the office must be the child of her daughter. The widow of Thayendanegea was the eldest daughter of the head chief of the Turtle tribe—first in rank of the Mohawk nation. In her own right, therefore, on the decease of her husband, she stood at the head of the Iroquois Confederacy, alone clothed with power to designate a successor to the chieftaincy. The official title of the principal chief of the Six Nations, is TEKARIHOGEA; to which station JOHN, the fourth and youngest son, whose Indian name was AHYOUWAIGHS, was appointed.

Hoxie Pinxt.   Parker Sculpt.

Printed by J. Neale

Your very obt sevt
John Brant
Ahyonwaeghs

On the removal of the old Chief, Thayendanegea, to his new establishment at the head of Lake Ontario, he had adopted the English mode of living, and arranged his household accordingly. Mrs. Brant, however,—the Queen mother she might be styled in Europe—preferred the customs of her people, and soon after the death of her husband returned to the Mohawk Village on the Grand River, where she ever afterward resided.

The young Chief was born at the Mohawk Village on the 27th of September, 1794—being at the time of his father's decease thirteen years of age. He received a good English education at Ancaster and Niagara, under the tuition of a Mr. Richard Cockrel ; but through life improved his mind greatly, by the study of the best English authors, by associations with good society, and by travel. He was a close and discriminating observer of the phenomena of nature, upon which he reasoned in a philosophical spirit. Amiable and manly in his feelings and character, and becoming well acquainted with English literature, his manners were early developed as those of an accomplished gentleman.

When the war of 1812–'15, between the United States and England, broke out, the Mohawks, true to their ancient faith, espoused the cause of the latter, and the *Tekarihogea* took the field with his warriors. He was engaged in many of the actions on the Niagara frontier, in all of which his bearing was chivalrous and his conduct brave. His first effort was at the battle of Queenston—commenced so auspiciously for the American arms by the gallant and daring Van Rensselaer, and ended so disastrously by reason of the cowardice of the militia on the American side, who refused to cross the river and secure the victory which had been so bravely won.

There were incidents marking that battle, however, involving the conduct of the young Chief, and connected with the life of an American officer whose name from that day forth has been identified with the military glory of his country, which forbid that the transaction should be thus summarily despatched. Aside, moreover, from the part borne by John Brant in the battle, and the exciting incidents to be related, sufficient of themselves to form a chapter that might well be entitled "the romance of history," many facts connected with that singular engagement have to this day remained unwritten.

The command of the Niagara section of the American frontier, during the Autumn of 1812, had been committed by Governor Tompkins to Major General Stephen Van Rensselaer, the senior officer of the State Cavalry of New-York. Attached to his staff was Colonel Solomon Van Rensselaer, an officer who, as a subaltern in the regular service, had signalized himself by his undaunted bravery, and coolness and intrepidity in action, during the Indian wars, and particularly under the command of General Wayne at the Miamis. The situation of General Van Rensselaer had been exceedingly embarrassing during the whole period of his command, or nearly three months before the movement under review. His selection for that post by the Commander-in-chief of New-York, considering the adverse state of their political relations, was deemed an equivocal act on the part of the Governor. But, although opposed to the policy of the war, and in the possession of the first paternal estate in America, and in the enjoyment of every blessing which can sweeten life, General Van Rensselaer hesitated not to comply with the call of his country, and took the field immediately.* After reconnoitering the frontier from Ogdensburgh to Lake Erie, he determined to establish his head-quarters at Lewiston, on the Strait of Niagara. After the failure of the expedition of General Hull, who had been ingloriously captured with his army at Detroit, the next point of attack upon the enemy's country was obviously the Canadian peninsula at Niagara. But the season for active military operations had almost glided away under the tardy levy of regular troops, and the uncertain assemblages of the militia; and it was October before General Van Rensselaer found himself in force to warrant offensive operations. His solicitude, not only for the interests of the public service and the honor of his country, but for his own reputation, determined him to strike a blow at the enemy if possible,† in order to obtain a position for winter-quarters on the Canada shore. Added to which was the manifestation of a strong and impatient desire by the militia to be led against the enemy. This desire rose to such a height that resistance seemed scarcely possible, and patriotism was apparently passing the limits of subordination.‡ Indeed, the determination of the militia was expressed to the

* Memoirs of General Wilkinson.   † Ibid.
‡ Low's History of the War.

General through various channels, as an *alternative*, that they must have orders to *act* against the enemy or they would go home.* Nor was the General himself less desirous of action than his troops professed to be. He felt that the disgrace of the American arms at Detroit, at the opening of the campaign, could only be wiped away by a brilliant close of it; and that unless a signal blow should be struck, the public expectation would be disappointed; all the toil and expense of the campaign would be thrown away; and, worse than all, the whole would be tinged with dishonor.†

Impressed by considerations like these, and encouraged by the apparent desire of the militia to take the field, dispositions were made for an attack upon Queenston Heights, with a view of moving thence upon Fort George at Niagara, which it was proposed to carry by storm, and then take up the quarters of the army there for the winter—an excellent position for obtaining supplies, and making the necessary arrangements for opening the campaign early in the following Spring. ‡ General Brock, the British commander on the opposite shore of the river, was watching the motions of the Americans with unwearied vigilance; but a spy, who had been despatched across the river, having returned with the erroneous information that that officer had moved in the direction of Detroit with all his disposable force, arrangements were made by General Van Rensselaer for crossing the river and attacking Queenston Heights early on the morning of the 11th of October. The design, however, was frustrated, either by the ignorance, the cowardice, or the treachery of a boatman, who had been selected as the leading waterman for his skill and steadiness. The enterprise was to be led by Colonel Solomon Van Renssalaer.—"The corps " designated for the expedition, and principally composed of " militia, assembled punctually and in good order at the place of " rendezvous, and, with the exception of the weather, which was " wet and windy, every thing wore a propitious aspect. But " when, after long and patiently abiding the pelting of a north- " easterly storm, the embarkation was ordered and the boats call-

* General Van Rensselaer's official report.
† Letter of General Van Rensselaer to Governor Tompkins, Oct. 8, 1812.
‡ Ibid.

" ed for, none were found to be in readiness; and on inquiry it
" was discovered that the person having charge of them had
" not only withdrawn himself, but had carried with him all the
" oars necessary for the service. For this unexpected occur-
" rence there was no remedy but patience; the expedition was
" accordingly suspended, and the troops sent back to their can-
" tonments."*

The impatience of the militia continuing, and having received a reinforcement of three hundred and fifty regular troops
under Lieutenant-colonel Chrystie, the General determined to
renew the attempt before daylight on the morning of the 13th.
Colonel Van Rensselaer was to command the expedition as
before, and lead the attack with three hundred militia, to be followed by Lieutenant-colonel Chrystie with three hundred regulars. Lieutenant-colonels Chrystie and Fenwick had agreed
to waive rank, and serve under Colonel Van Rensselaer.
Lieutenant-colonel Fenwick, with Major Mullaney, was to follow Chrystie with three hundred and fifty regular troops and
some pieces of artillery, after whom the greater body of the
militia were to succeed in order. Such is an outline of the dispositions for the movement on the morning of the 13th of October. Meantime Lieutenant-colonel, (now Major-general Scott)
had arrived with his regiment of artillery at Schlosser, two
miles above the Falls, and twelve from Lewiston, on the day
before the engagement. Having heard from Colonel Stranahan,
of the Otsego militia, whose regiment, stationed at the Falls, was
on the move, that an expedition of some kind was contemplated
by General Van Rensselaer, Scott, then young, and ardent as
he is now, impatient of an early opportunity to meet an enemy,
mounted his horse and rode full speed to Lewiston. He forthwith presented himself to the Commanding General, from whom
he learned the character of the enterprise on foot, and of whom
he solicited the privilege of taking a part. The General replied that the details had all been arranged—that Colonel Solomon Van Rensselaer was to have the command, and that Lieutenant-colonels Fenwick and Chrystie had waived their rank,
and were to serve under that officer. But such was the urgency
of Scott, that the General gave him permission to accompany

* General Armstrong's Notices on the war of 1812.

the expedition as a volunteer, if he also would waive his rank. This proposition was declined ; but as Scott was anxious to bring his regiment down to Lewiston, it was ultimately stipulat ed that he might select a position upon the bank of the river, and use his artillery to such advantage as opportunity might afford.   Under this arrangement he hastened back to his regi ment at Schlosser, which, although wearied by its long journey, was nevertheless, by a forced march, over horrible roads, brought down to Lewiston all in good time in the evening.   Scott again importuned for permission to participate directly in the enter prise.   But in vain.   Had he been in the field, his rank in the line of the regular service would have given him the command of a Colonel of militia—in which only Van Rensselaer bore a commission ; and as the whole project had originated with the latter, the commanding General designed that he should reap the laurels in expectancy.

It would be foreign from the purpose of this narrative to dwell upon the variety of untoward and vexatious circumstan ces which delayed, and had nearly caused a total failure of, the enterprise.   Suffice it to say, that after those difficulties had been in part surmounted, the expedition departed upon its peril ous undertaking.   It has already been remarked that the enemy was keeping a vigilant watch over the motions of the Americans, and they had discovered indications of a move ment of some kind during the last few preceding days.   The narrowness of the river, without the agency of spies, enabled them to make these observations ; added to which the sound of the oars had been heard, so that, instead of being surprised, the enemy was measurably prepared for Van Rensselaer's reception. Indeed, a fire was opened before the boat of Colonel Van Rens selaer had reached the shore, and Lieutenant Rathbone was kill ed in the Colonel's boat.   Two companies of regular troops, however, and Captains Armstrong and Malcom, had previously landed without annoyance or discovery.*

Other boats successively followed, and the landing of two hundred and thirty-five men was effected, although the detach ments first arriving suffered severely from the fire of the enemy, especially in the loss of their officers.   The troops formed

* Armstrong's Notices of the War.

under a very warm fire, climbed the bank, Van Rensselaer himself leading the detachment, and routed the enemy at the point of the bayonet without firing a shot. In this operation Ensign Morris was killed, and Captains Armstrong, Malcom, and Wool were wounded, the latter slightly. Colonel Van Rensselaer himself was a severe sufferer, having received one ball in his hip, which passed out at his spine, two in his thigh, one of which lodged, two in his leg, and a sixth in his heel. Lieutenant-colonel Fenwick was also severely wounded, and Colonel Chrystie slightly. Indeed Captain Wool, himself wounded also, was now the senior officer fit for duty. The gallant leader, concealing his wounds under his great-coat as long as he could, immediately on the retreat of the enemy toward the town, ordered Captain Wool, the senior officer capable of duty, to ascend the mountain and carry the battery, giving him a direction for the movement by which he would avoid the fire of the enemy's artillery—placing Lieutenants Randolph and Gansevoort, who volunteered, at the head of the little column, and Major Lush, another volunteer, in the rear, with orders to put to death the first man who should fall back.* This enterprise was gallantly executed by Captain Wool, and the battery was carried " without much resistance."† Colonel Van Rensselaer, however, unable longer to sustain himself, fell to the ground soon after the party had filed off before him ; but he did not lose his consciousness, and the pains of his wounds were soon alleviated by the shouts of victory.

Meantime, the most intense anxiety was felt on the American shore to learn the result of the daring attempt; and before it was well light, the painful intelligence was received that the gallant leader had fallen, covered with wounds. And upon the heels of that unpleasant news, the report came that Colonel Fenwick had also fallen, dangerously wounded. Had Scott been in the field, Fenwick would have ranked him, being the oldest in commission. Chrystie was younger in rank than Scott ; but while the latter was again urging to be sent across, Chrystie

* Wilkinson's Memoirs.

† Report of Captain Wool. The officers engaged in storming the battery were Captains Wool and Ogilvie; Lieutenants Kearney, Huginen, Carr, and Sammons of the 13th regiment; Lieutenants Gansevoort and Randolph of the light artillery, and Major Lush of the militia.

himself appeared at General Van Rensselaer's marquée, having received a slight wound in the hand.　Scott was now entitled to the post he had been seeking, and was immediately gratified with directions to cross the river, and assume the command.

But while these arrangements were concerting on the American side, and before Lieutenant-colonel Scott had arrived at the scene of action, another important act in the changing drama of the day had been performed.　The landing of the Americans had been opposed by the light company of the 49th regiment of grenadiers, and the York volunteer militia, together with a small number of Indians.　The light troops had been dislodged by the Americans on ascending the heights, and an eighteen pounder battery taken.*　The fortress on the heights, carried by Captain Wool, was manned by a detachment of the grenadiers, the whole numbering, as was supposed, one hundred and sixty regulars.†　The heights having been cleared of the enemy, who retired upon the village of Queenston, the Americans were allowed to repose a short time upon their laurels.　But the respite was brief.　General Brock being at Niagara when the action commenced, was startled from his pillow by the roar of the artillery ; but so rapid were his movements, that he arrived at Queenston ere the grey of the morning had passed, accompanied by his Provincial aid-de-camp, Lieutenant-colonel McDonell.‡　Placing himself immediately at the head of four companies of his favorite 49th grenadiers and a body of militia, General Brock advanced for the purpose of turning the left of the Americans, and recovering the ground that had been lost.　A detachment of one hundred and fifty men, directed by Captain Wool to take possession of the heights above the battery, and hold General Brock in check, was compelled to retreat by superior numbers. An engagement ensued, in the course of which, after some fighting, the Americans were driven to the edge of the bank.　With great exertions, Captain Wool brought his men to a stand, and directed a charge immediately on the exhaustion of his ammunition.　This order was executed, though with some confusion. It was nevertheless, effectual, and the enemy in turn were driven to the verge of the heights, where Colonel McDonell, having his horse shot under him, fell, himself mortally wounded.§　In the

---

* Chrystie's account of the Canadian War.
† Wilkinson's Memoirs.　　‡ Chrystie.　　§ Captain Wool's official Report.

meantime General Brock, in attempting to rally his forces, received a musket ball in his breast, and died almost immediately. The last words he uttered as he fell from his horse, were, " Push on the brave York Volunteers."* The enemy thereupon dispersed in every direction ;† and Captain Wool, receiving at that time a small reinforcement of riflemen from the American side, set about forming a line on the heights, fronting the village, detaching flanking parties, and making such other dispositions as were first prompted by the exigencies of the occasion.

It was at this point of time, being yet early in the morning, that Lieutenant-colonel Scott arrived on the heights, where he found the troops, both regulars and volunteers, in considerable disorder. He immediately announced his name and rank, and assuming the command, with the assistance of his adjutant, an officer of great activity and intelligence, brought them into line. On counting his men, he found that of regular troops ·there were three hundred and fifty rank and file, all told, and two hundred and fifty-seven volunteers, under General Wadsworth and Colonel Stranahan, the former of whom at once waived his rank in favor of Scott. Just before Scott had arrived upon the ground, Captain Wool had ordered Lieutenants Gansevoort and Randolph, with a detachment of artillery, to drill out the eighteen pounder heretofore spoken of as having been taken from the enemy, at a point some distance below the crest of the heights, but which had been spiked before its capture. Hearing of the circumstance, and being told that the gun had been spiked only with a ramrod, Scott hurried away in person to direct the process of extracting this impediment to its use. He was not long absent, and on reascending the heights, great was his astonishment to find a cloud of Indians in the act of rushing upon his line, tomahawk in hand, while his troops were breaking, and evidently on the point of a general flight. The Indians bore down fiercely, and were, some of them, within ten paces of his men, when he gained his place just in season to prevent total disorder, and bring them to the right about, facing the enemy, upon whom they were turning their backs. All this was but the work of a moment. The Indians, finding this sudden change in the mode of their reception, recoiled ; and after a sharp en-

* Chrystler.   † Captain Wool.

gagement, were compelled to retreat. Their leader was a dauntless youth, of surprising activity; dressed, painted and plumed *en Indien*, cap-a-pied.

The Americans, it will be recollected by those familiar with the history of the war, retained possession of the heights, and of the little fortress they had taken, during several hours —undisturbed by the regular troops of the enemy, who was waiting for reinforcements from Fort George at Newark, six miles below. But they were incessantly harassed by the Indians, who hovered about them, occasionally advancing in considerable numbers, but who were invariably put to flight when seriously engaged by the Colonel's handful of an army. The stripling leader of the Indians was of graceful form and mould, and, as already remarked, of uncommon agility. He was often observed by Colonel Scott, and others, and was always accompanied by a dark, stalwart chief, evidently of great strength, who was subsequently known as Captain Jacobs. It was discovered that these two Indians in particular were repeatedly making a mark of Scott, who, like the first monarch of Israel, stood a full head above his soldiers, and who was rendered a yet more conspicuous object by a new and brilliant uniform, and a tall white plume in his hat. The conduct of these two Indians having been particularly observed by an officer, a message was instantly sent to Scott upon the subject, with his own overcoat, advising the Colonel to put it on. But the disguise was declined ; and the Indians, having taken refuge in a wood at some distance on the left, were driven thence by a spirited charge, gallantly led by Scott in person.

By these successive actions, however, the numbers of the Americans, both regulars and volunteers, had been sadly reduced, the wounded having been sent across the river to the American shore in the few boats not rendered useless by the enemy's fire in the morning. The British column, led by General Sheaffe, the successor of General Brock, was now discovered advancing in the distance from Niagara. Its approach, though slow and circumspect, was steady and unremitting ; and of its character and objects there could be no doubt.* The column with which General Sheaffe was thus advancing, consisted of three hundred and fifty men of the 41st regiment, se-

* General Armstrong's Notices.

veral companies of militia, and two hundred and fifty Indians.
Reinforcements, both of troops and Indians, arriving from Chippewa, the force of the enemy was augmented to eight hundred.*
Major-General Van Rensselaer, having crossed the river before
he made this discovery, hastened back to his own camp, to make
another appeal to the militia to cross over to the rescue of the
little band of their own countrymen, now in such imminent
peril. But in vain. Not a man could overcome his constitutional scruples about crossing the confines of his own country;
and for more than two hours the troops and volunteers upon
the heights were allowed to behold an advancing enemy, in
numbers sufficient to overwhelm them, while by looking over
their right shoulders they could see an army of American militia, abundantly sufficient to defeat the approaching column, and
maintain the victories of the morning.† The march of General
Sheaffe was protracted by an extensive detour to the west, beyond
the forest heretofore spoken of as having been a shelter to the
Indians. Scott and his officers, in consideration of their own
diminished numbers, marvelled greatly at this fatiguing measure
of precaution on the part of the enemy, but were afterward informed by the officers into whose hands they fell, that the enemy
had no idea that the diminutive force they saw upon the heights
constituted the whole of the army they were marching to encounter.

During the breathing-time thus enjoyed by the Americans, and
prolonged by the extreme caution of the enemy, a note from General Van Rensselaer was received by General Wadsworth, informing him of the facts heretofore stated respecting the cowardice of
the militia, and advising a retreat. The General stated that not
a company could be prevailed upon to cross the river; that he

* This is the estimate of the Canadian historian, Robert Chrystie. Colonel
Chrystie of the American forces, in his estimate, stated the force of Sheaffe at from
four to five hundred regulars, with four pieces of artillery, from five to six hundred
militia, and three hundred Indians.

† "Neither entreaty nor threats, neither arguments nor ridicule, availed any
thing. They had seen enough of war to satisfy them that it made no part of their
special calling; and at last, not disdaining to employ the mask invented by faction to cover cowardice or treason, fifteen hundred able-bodied men, well armed and
equipped, who a week before boasted largely of patriotism and prowess, were now
found openly pleading constitutional scruples in justification of disobedience to the
lawful authority of their chief."—*General Armstrong's Notices of the War.*

had himself seen the movements of the enemy, and knew that they were too powerful to be resisted by the handful of men upon the heights; and that he would endeavor to furnish boats and cover a retreat. Still, he left it optional with Wadsworth and his officers, to govern themselves according to circumstances under their own more immediate view. A consultation of the officers was immediately held; but nothing was decided upon. Meantime the enemy continued to approach, but with undiminished circumspection—"manœuvering from right to left, and "from left to right, and countermarching nearly the whole "length of the American line twice, as if determined to count "every man in the ranks, and to make himself familiar with "every foot of the position before he hazarded an attack."* This deliberation gave time for renewed councils on the part of the American officers. A retreat, however, was considered hopeless; whereupon Colonel Scott literally mounted a stump, and made a short but animated address to his soldiers:—"We can- "not conquer; we may fall; we must die," said Scott; "but if "we die like soldiers, we effect more by our example of gallantry "upon a conquered field, than we could ever have done for our "countrymen if surviving a successful one." A unanimous shout of approval answered the stirring appeal. Nor were the militia volunteers, who had continued faithful through the morning skirmishings, backward in seconding the determination. Indeed, though inexperienced, there were no braver men upon the field than Wadsworth and Stranahan.† The British advanced steadily in column, reserving their fire, as did the Americans, excepting the single piece of artillery in their possession, until they came within eighty paces. Several well-directed and effective fires succeeded—the Americans maintaining their ground firmly until actually pricked by the bayonets of the enemy. They then retreated toward the river, the side of the steep being at that day covered with shrubs, which enabled the soldiers to let themselves down from one to another, with sufficient deliberation to allow an occasional return of the fire of their pursuers. Presently, however, the Indians came springing down from shrub to shrub after them; which circumstance

---

* General Armstrong's Notices of the War.

† The late Colonel Farrand Stranahan, of Cooperstown. General Wadsworth and Colonel Stranahan have both since deceased.

somewhat accelerated the retreat of the Americans. On reaching the water's edge not a boat was at command ; and to avoid the galling fire of the pursuers, Scott drew his men farther up the river, to obtain shelter beneath the more precipitous, and, in fact, beetling cliffs.

Escape was now impossible, and to fight longer was not only useless but madness. After a brief consultation with Gibson and Totten, therefore, (the latter officer having returned to the field in the afternoon,) a capitulation was determined upon. A flag was accordingly sent, with a proposition. After waiting for some time without any tidings, another was sent, and afterward yet another—neither of which returned ; and it subsequently appeared that the bearers had been successively shot down by the Indians. Scott thereupon determined to go with the flag himself. But while preparing to execute his hazardous purpose, his attention was attracted by two of his men, who were deliberately stripping themselves to the skin. On inquiring their motive, they replied that they might as well drown as be hanged, as they were sure to be if taken, since they acknowledged themselves to be deserters from the ranks of the enemy. Saying which they plunged into the dark torrent flowing madly along in its mighty eddies and whirlpools. It was a fearful leap, but both succeeded in reaching the American shore in safety, and the Colonel afterward saw and conversed with them.

But to resume. Colonel Scott having determined to bear the fourth flag himself, Totten's cravat was taken from beneath his stock for that purpose. Totten and Gibson both resolved to accompany their commander, who, being the tallest, bore the handkerchief upon the point of his sword. Keeping close to the water's edge, and sheltering themselves as well as they could behind the rocks, the Indians continually firing in the meantime, they passed down until the bank afforded no farther protection, when they turned to the left to take the road. But just as they were gaining it, up rose the two Indians who had been aiming at Scott in the morning—the young and agile chief, and the more muscular Captain Jacobs—who both sprang upon them like tigers from their lairs. Scott remonstrated, and made known the character in which he was seeking the British commander, but to no purpose. The Indians grappled with them fiercely, and Jacobs succeeded in wrenching the sword from the

Colonel's hand. The blades of Towson and Chrystie instantly leaped from their scabbards, and the Indians were raising their hatchets when a British serjeant rushed forward, hoarsely exclaiming—"*Honor!*" "*Honor!*"—and having a guard with him, the combatants were separated, and Colonel Scott was conducted to the presence of General Sheaffe. to whom he proposed a surrender, and with whom terms of capitulation were speedily arranged—the General at once saying that they should be treated with all the honors of war. Orders were immediately given that the firing should cease; but these orders were not promptly obeyed, which caused a remonstrance from Colonel Scott, and finally a peremptory demand to be conducted back to his troops. This prolonged fire was from the Indians, whom General Sheaffe admitted he could not control, as they were exceedingly exasperated at the amount of their loss. Scott passed a rather severe rebuke upon an enemy who avowed allies of such a character; but officers being ordered among them in all directions, they were presently compelled to desist.

The prisoners surrendered by Scott numbered one hundred and thirty-nine regular troops, and one hundred and fifty-four volunteers, just—the Colonel accurately counting them o t himself.* They were all marched down to Newark, (now Niagara,) the same evening, where the Colonel and his two principal officers were quartered in a small tavern, having invitations the first evening to dine with General Sheaffe. While waiting for the arrival of an officer to conduct them to the General's quarters, another incident occurred, equally spirited, and even more start-

---

* When, shortly afterward, the general order of Sheaffe appeared, it was announced that two hundred of the Americans were drowned and nine hundred taken prisoners. Colonel Scott immediately called upon General Sheaffe, and remonstrated against such an exaggeration; since he had himself counted his own men, and knew that the number was less than three hundred, all told. Sheaffe replied that the numbers he had announced had been reported to him, and he felt strong confidence in the accuracy of the statement. In conclusion, he invited Scott to go to the barracks and see for himself. He did so; and to his deep mortification found that the statement of the general order was true! On an investigation of the discrepancy, it appeared that the number of prisoners had been swollen to that amount by several hundred cowardly rascals of the militia, who, upon landing on the Canadian shore, had availed themselves of the darkness and other facilities, to hide themselves away among the clefts of the rocks; where they had remained in concealment during the day, and were only dragged by the legs from their lurking, places by the British troops after the surrender. So much for militia.

ling than the scene with the two Indians by the road-side. Just
at twilight, a little girl entered the parlor, with a message
that somebody in the hall desired to see the " tall officer."
Colonel Scott thereupon stepped out of the parlor, unarmed, of
course, into the hall, which was dark and narrow, and withal
incommoded by a stairway; but what was his astonishment on
again meeting, face to face, his evil geniuses, the brawny Captain Jacobs and the light-limbed chief! The Colonel had shut
the door behind him as he left the parlor; but there was a
sentinel standing at the outer door, who had improperly allowed
the Indians to pass in. The dusky visitors stepped up to the
Colonel without ceremony, and the younger, who alone spoke
English, made a brief inquiry as to the number of balls which
had cut through his clothes, intimating astonishment that they
had both been firing at him almost the whole day, without
effect. But while the young Indian was thus speaking, or
rather beginning thus to speak—for such, subsequently, seemed
to be the import of what he meant to say—Jacobs, rudely seizing
the Colonel by the arm, attempted to whirl him round, exclaiming in broken English, " Me shoot so often, me sure to have hit
somewhere." " Hands off, you scoundrel," cried Scott, indignant at such freedom with his person, and adding a scornful expression reflecting upon the Indian's skill as a marksman, as he
flung him from him.

The Indians drew instantly both dirk and tomahawk, when,
with the rapidity of lightning, Scott, who had fortunately espied
a number of swords standing at the end of the passage, seized one
from its iron sheath, and placed himself in a posture of defence
against the menacing Indians. As they stood in this picturesque
attitude, Scott with his sword ready to strike, and the Indians with
their tomahawks and dirks in the air, frowning defiance upon
each other,—both parties awaiting the first blow,—Colonel Coffin, who had been sent with a guard to conduct Scott to the
General's quarters to dinner, sprang into the passage, and cried
" Hold !" Comprehending at a glance the dangerous position of
Scott, he interfered at once, by sharp remonstrance, and also
by weapon, in his defence. Jacobs, exasperated, turned upon
Colonel Coffin, and, uttering a menace, his companion also
unguardedly turned to observe the issue of the new combat.
The scene was of the most exciting and earnest character. The

Indians having thus turned upon Coffin, one of them exclaimed
—" I kill you !" Scott instantly raised his sabre, which was
heavy and substantial, so that a descending blow would have
fallen upon both the savages at once, and called out, " If you
strike, I will kill you both !" For a moment they stood
frowning ; the piercing eyes of the Indians gleaming with wild
and savage fury, while Scott and Coffin alike looked upon both
with angry defiance, all with upraised arms and glittering
steel. Recovering somewhat from the gust of passion into
which they had been thrown, the Indians then slowly dropped
their arms and retired. The officer who thus came to the rescue, was the aid of General Sheaffe, whose errand was to conduct the Colonel to dinner, and who, by this timely arrival,
probably saved his life. It can hardly be necessary to mention
who was the young chief that had sustained himself so actively
and bravely through the day, as the reader will already have
anticipated the name—JOHN BRANT—the successor of the great
Captain, his father, who, as has already been stated, though
not eighteen years of age, had that day, for the first time, led
his tribe upon the war-path. Beyond doubt it was no part
of the young Chief's design to inflict injury upon the captive
American commander. His whole character forbids the idea,
for he was as generous and benevolent in his feelings as he was
brave. Having been exhausting much ammunition upon the
Colonel during the day, this visit was one of curiosity, to ascertain how near they had come to the accomplishment of their object. Like Cassius, the Indian bears anger as the flint does fire,
though not always cold again so soon. It was the same with
Scott. Neither would allow of personal freedom—the Colonel
did not fully comprehend the object of their visit, and a sudden
rencontre, that had well nigh proved fatal, was the consequence.*

In the successive battles fought on that hardly-contested fron-

* General Sheaffe is an American by birth, and he took an early opportunity of
explaining to Colonel Scott how it happened that, most reluctantly, he was in arms
against the land of his birth. He stated that he was a lad at the commencement ot
the war of the American Revolution, living with his widowed mother at Boston.
While the British army was in the occupancy of that town, Earl Percy's quarters were
in the house of his mother. His Lordship manifested a strong degree of partiality for
him, and took him away with a view of providing for him. He gave him a military
education, and placed him in the army, purchasing commissions and promotion
for him as far as promotion can be acquired by purchase in the British service. His

tier during the years 1813 and 1814, young Brant, as the Indian leader, sustained himself with great credit, as well for his bravery as for his intelligence and activity.   In the course of the extraordinary campaign of 1813, commenced so brilliantly for the American arms at York, and followed up in the same spirit and with the same success at Fort George, (Niagara,) and yet attended with such surprising disasters as the capture by the enemy of Generals Chandler and Winder, and the surrender of Colonel Bœrstler at the Beaver Dams, young Brant had several opportunities of distinguishing himself.   He was in the affair of Fort George, under General Vincent, when that fortress was so gallantly carried by the American troops under the immediate command of Major-general Lewis.

After Vincent retired into the interior, with a view of taking up a position at Burlington Heights, and after the disaster of Winder and Chandler at Forty Mile Creek, Colonel Bœrstler was pushed forward with six hundred men of all arms—dragoons, artillery and infantry—to dislodge a strong picquet of the enemy posted in a stone house about two miles beyond a hilly pass called the Beaver Dams, seventeen miles from Fort George.*   Arriving at the Beaver Dams, Colonel Bœrstler was surprised by a large body of Indians under the conduct of young Brant and Captain William J. Kerr, numbering about four hundred and fifty warriors.   The battle was maintained for about three hours—the Indians, of course, fighting after their own fashion, in concealment—having apparently surrounded Colonel Bœrstler in the woods.   Indeed, the enemy must have conducted the battle with remarkable adroitness; for Colonel Bœrstler, galled upon all sides, dared neither to advance nor retreat, while the result of every observation was a conviction that he was surrounded by far superior numbers.   At length Lieutenant Fitzgibbons, of the 49th enemy's regiment, arriving on the ground with forty-six rank and file, sent a flag to Colonel Bœrst-

subsequent promotion to the rank of Major-general had been acquired by service. The breaking out of the war had found him stationed in Canada.   He lost no time in stating his reluctance to serve against his own countrymen, and solicited a transfer to some other country.   But his request had not been complied with at the time of the events now under review.   For his exploit in capturing Scott and his little band at Queenston Heights, he was created a Baronet.

  * General Armstrong.

ler, demanding a surrender. After some parleying—the British
lieutenant magnifying the number of their troops, and pretending to conduct the negotiation in the name of Major De Haren,*
not forgetting a few occasional suggestions touching the horrors
of an Indian massacre—Colonel Bœrstler, having neither reserve to sustain, nor demonstration to favor him,† surrendered
his detachment as prisoners of war.   This battle occurred on the
24th of June, and was a brilliant affair for young Brant, since
it was fought by the Indians alone, not a single cartridge being
expended by the regular troops of the enemy.‡

After this achievement, young Brant participated in almost
all the skirmishes that took place on the Niagara frontier while
the American army occupied Fort George and the village of
Niagara ; and in the summer of 1814 he was engaged in the
memorable battles of Chippewa, Lundy's Lane, and Fort Erie,
while that post was invested by the British forces.   In all these
engagements his conduct was such as to command the admiration not only of his own people, but of the British officers—
affording promise to all who marked his prowess, of becoming
a very distinguished warrior.

At the close of the war, having attained the age of manhood,
John Brant, and his youthful sister Elizabeth, the youngest of
his father's family, returned to the head of Lake Ontario, and
took up their residence in the " Brant House"—living in the
English style, and dispensing the ancient hospitalities of their
father.   Lieutenant Francis Hall, of the British service, who
travelled in the United States and Canada in 1816, visited the
Brant House, and saw the old lady Chieftainess at that place.

---

* Chrystie's History of the War in Canada.

† General Armstrong's " Notices."

‡ Letter to the author from Colonel William J. Kerr. This singular battle was
the subject of much controversy at the time, and of not a little ridicule.   The American accounts first published, stated that Bœrstler was attacked by five hundred
regular troops and one hundred Indians   Colonel Bœrstler's own account of the
affair dwells largely upon the great odds in numbers against him ; but although the
reader is left to infer that he fought long against regular troops as well as Indians, yet
the fact is nowhere expressly stated.   The Colonel maintained that it was an ill-
advised expedition, detached in consequence of false information comm nicated by
Major Cyrenius Chapin, commanding a detachment of volunteers.   The Major,
he averred, behaved like a consummate coward during the engagement.   In regard
to the battle itself, there is no doubt that the Colonel was out-generalled by Captain
Kerr and young Brant, and having been kept at bay for several hours, was at
length induced to surrender by stratagem.

He also speaks highly of the youthful Chief, John, as "a fine
" young man, of gentlemanlike appearance, who used the Eng-
" lish language agreeably and correctly, dressing in the English
" fashion, excepting only the moccasins of his Indian habit."—
Lieutenant Hall also visited the Mohawk village on the Grand
River, where Elizabeth happened at that time to be, and of
whom he gives an interesting account in his notice of the Brant
family, their situation, and the people as he found them. Speaking of Thayendanegea, this intelligent traveller remarks:—
" Brant, like Clovis, and many of the early Anglo-Saxon and
" Danish Christians, contrived to unite much religious zeal
" with the practices of natural ferocity. His grave is to be seen
" under the walls of his church. I have mentioned one of his
" sons: he has also a daughter living, who would not disgrace
" the circles of European fashion : her face and person are fine
" and graceful : she speaks English not only correctly, but ele-
" gantly; and has, both in her speech and manners, a softness
" approaching to oriental languor. She retains so much of her
" native dress as to identify her with her people, over whom she
" affects no superiority, but seems pleased to preserve all the ties
" and duties of relationship. She held the infant of one of her
" relations at the font, on the Sunday of my visit to the church.
" The usual church and baptismal service was performed by a
" Doctor Aaron, an Indian, and an assistant priest ; the congre-
" gation consisted of sixty or seventy persons, male and female.
" Many of the young men were dressed in the English fashion,
" but several of the old warriors came with their blankets fold-
" ed over them like the drapery of a statue ; and in this dress,
" with a step and mien of quiet energy, more forcibly reminded
" me of the ancient Romans than some other inhabitants of this
" continent who have laid claim to the resemblance. Some of
" them wore large silver crosses, medals, and trinkets on their
" arms and breasts ; and a few had bandeaus, ornamented with
" feathers. Dr. Aaron, a grey-headed Mohawk, had touched
" his cheeks and forehead with a few spots of vermilion, in
" honor of Sunday. He wore a surplice, and preached ; but his
" delivery was monotonous and unimpassioned. Indian elo-
" quence decays with the peculiar state of society to which it
" owed its energy."*

* Hall's Travels, pp. 135, 136.

Three years afterward, in 1819, James Buchanan, Esq., H.
B. M. consul for the port of New-York, made the tour of Upper
Canada, accompanied by two of his daughters. In the course
of his journey Mr. Buchanan visited the Brant House, of
which circumstance he subsequently published the following
agreeable account in his little volume of Indian sketches :—

"After stopping more than a week under the truly hospitable
roof of the Honorable Colonel Clarke, at the Falls of Niagara.
I determined to proceed by land round Lake Ontario, to York ;*
and Mrs. Clarke† offered to give my daughters a letter of introduction to a Miss Brant, advising us to arrange our time so as
to sleep and stop a day or two in the house of that lady, as she
was certain we should be much pleased with her and her
brother. Our friend did not intimate, still less did we suspect,
that the introduction was to an Indian prince and princess.
Had we been in the least aware of this, our previous arrangements would all have given way, as there was nothing I was more
anxious to obtain than an opportunity such as this was so well
calculated to afford, of seeing in what degree the Indian character would be modified by a conformity to the habits and comforts of civilized life.

"Proceeding on our journey, we stopped at an inn, romanti-
cally situated, where I determined to remain all night. Among
other things I inquired of the landlord if he knew the distance
to Miss Brant's house, and from him I learned that it was about
twenty miles farther. He added, that young Mr. Brant had
passed that way in the forenoon, and would, no doubt, be return-

---

* Now Toronto, or, more properly, Taranto, which is the Indian name.

† Mrs. Clarke was the daughter of the late Dr. Robert Kerr, of Niagara, and
grand-daughter of Sir William Johnson, by Molly Brant. She was of course by
blood one quarter Mohawk. Colonel Clarke's residence was upon the banks of the
Niagara, a short distance above the great cataract. His gardens and grounds were
extensive, highly cultivated, and laid out with the taste of a landscape gardener—
wash'd by the mighty stream thundering over the rapids past it on one side, and
bounded on the other of its sides by a deep, dark glen, of rocks, and trees, and wild
turbulent waters. Mrs. Clarke was a lady of noble appearance, of highly cultivated
mind and manners, and of sincere and unostentatious piety. Her husband died
two or three years since; and a letter to the author, from her brother, Colonel Kerr,
of Brant House, received while these pages were in preparation for the press, announced her decease, on the 2d of March, 1837. An agreeable visit at her seat, in
September preceding her decease, enlightened by her eloquence and vivacity, will
not soon be forgotten.—*Author*.

ing in the evening, and that if I wished it, he would be on the look-out for him. This I desired the landlord to do, as it would enable me to intimate our introduction to his sister, and intention of waiting on her the next morning.

"At dusk Mr. Brant returned, and being introduced into our room, we were unable to distinguish his complexion, and conversed with him, believing him to be a young Canadian gentleman. We did not, however, fail to observe a certain degree of hesitation and reserve in the manner of his speech. He certainly expressed a wish that we would do his sister and himself the favor of spending a few days with them, in order to refresh ourselves and our horses; but we thought his style more laconic than hospitable. Before candles were brought in, our new friend departed, leaving us still in error as to his nation.

"By four o'clock in the morning we resumed our journey. On arriving at the magnificent shores of Lake Ontario, the driver of our carriage pointed out, at the distance of five miles, the house of Miss Brant, which had a very noble and commanding aspect; and we anticipated much pleasure in our visit; as besides the enjoyment of so beautiful a spot, we should be enabled to form a competent idea of Canadian manners and style of living. Young Mr. Brant, it appeared, unaware that with our carriage we could have reached his house so soon, had not arrived before us; so that our approach was not announced, and we drove up to the door under the full persuasion that the family would be apprised of our coming. The outer door, leading to a spacious hall, was open. We entered, and remained a few minutes, when, seeing no person about, we proceeded into the parlor, which, like the hall, was for the moment unoccupied. We therefore had an opportunity of looking about us at our leisure. It was a room well furnished, with a carpet, pier and chimney glasses, mahogany tables, fashionable chairs, a guitar, a neat hanging book-case, in which, among other volumes, we perceived a Church of England Prayer Book, translated into the Mohawk tongue. Having sent our note of introduction in by the coachman, and still no person waiting on us, we began to suspect (more especially in the hungry state we were in,) that some delay or difficulty about breakfast stood in the way of the young lady's appearance. I can assure my readers that a keen morning's ride on the shores of an American lake, is an exer-

cise of all others calculated to make the appetite clamorous, if
not insolent.   We had already penetrated into the parlor, and
were beginning to meditate a farther exploration in search of
the pantry, when, to our unspeakable astonishment, in walked
a charming, noble-looking Indian girl, dressed partly in the native and partly in the English costume.   Her hair was confined
on the head in a silk net, but the lower tresses, escaping from
thence, flowed down on her shoulders.   Under a tunic or morning dress of black silk, was a petticoat of the same material and
color, which reached very little below the knee.   Her silk stock-
ings and kid shoes were, like the rest of her dress, black.   The
grace and dignity of her movement, the style of her dress and
manner, so new, so unexpected, filled us all with astonishment.
With great ease, yet by no means in that common-place mode
so generally prevalent on such occasions, she inquired how we
found the roads, accommodations, &c.   No flutter was at all
apparent on account of the delay in getting breakfast ; no fidget-
ting and fuss-making, no running in and out, no idle expressions of regret, such as 'O! dear me! had I known of your
coming, you would not have been kept in this way ;' but with
perfect ease she maintained conversation, until a squaw, wearing a man's hat, brought in a tray with preparations for breakfast.   A table cloth of fine white damask being laid, we were
regaled with tea, coffee, hot rolls, butter in water and ice coolers,
eggs, smoked beef, ham, and broiled chickens, &c. ; all served in
a truly neat and comfortable style.   The delay, we afterward
discovered, arose from the desire of our hostess to supply us
with hot rolls, which were actually baked while we were waiting.   I have been thus minute in my description of these comforts, as they were so little to be expected in the house of an
Indian.

   " After breakfast Miss Brant took my daughters out to walk,
and look at the picturesque scenery of the country.   She and
her brother had previously expressed a hope that we would stay
all day ; but though I wished of all things to do so, and had determined, in the event of their pressing their invitation, to accept
it, yet I declined the proposal at first, and thus forfeited a pleasure which we all of us longed in our hearts to enjoy ; for, as
I afterward learned, it is not the custom of any uncorrupted
Indian to repeat a request if once rejected.   They believe that

those to whom they offer any mark of friendship, and who give a reason for refusing it, do so in perfect sincerity, and that it would be rudeness to require them to alter their determination or break their word. And as the Indian never makes a show of civility but when prompted by a genuine feeling, so he thinks others are actuated by similar candor. I really feel ashamed when I consider how severe a rebuke this carries with it to us who boast of civilization, but who are so much carried away by the general insincerity of expression pervading all ranks, that few indeed are to be found who speak just what they wish or know. This duplicity is the effect of what is termed a high state of refinement. We are taught so to conduct our language, that others cannot discover our real views or intentions. The Indians are not only free from this deceitfulness, but surpass us in another instance of good-breeding and decorum, namely, of never interrupting those who converse with them until they have done speaking; and then they reply in the hope of not being themselves interrupted. This was perfectly exemplified by Miss Brant and her brother; and I hope the lesson my daughters were so forcibly taught by the natural politeness of their hostess, will never be forgotten by them, and that I also may profit by the example.

" After stopping a few hours with these interesting young Indians, and giving them an invitation to pay us a visit at New-York, which they expressed great desire to fulfil, and which I therefore confidently anticipated, we took our leave with real regret on all sides. As we passed through the hall, I expected to see some Indian instruments of war or the chase; but perceiving the walls were bare of these customary ornaments, I asked Mr. Brant where were the trophies that belonged to his family? He told me, and I record it with shame, that the numerous visiters that from time to time called on him, had expressed their desire so strongly for these trophies, that one by one he had given all away; and now he was exempt from these sacrifices by not having any thing of the kind left. He seemed, nevertheless, to cherish with fondness the memory of these relics of his forefathers. How ill did the *civilized* visiters requite the hospitality they experienced under the roof whose doors stand open to shelter and feed all who enter!

" As all about our young hostess is interesting, I will add

some farther particulars. Having inquired for her mother
she told me she remained generally with her other sons and
daughters, who were living in the Indian settlement on the
Grand River, that falls into Lake Erie : that her mother preferred being in the wigwams, and disapproved, in a certain
degree, of her and her brother John's conforming so much to
the habits and costumes of the English."

In the opening chapter of the present work, the Rev. Dr.
Stewart, formerly a missionary in the Mohawk Valley, and subsequently Archdeacon of the Episcopal church of Upper Canada,
was several times referred to as authority for a variety of particulars in the early life of the elder Brant. The sketches of
his life thus referred to, were in fact written by the present honorable and venerable Archdeacon Strachan, of Toronto, from
conversations with Dr. Stewart, and published in the Christian
Recorder, at Kingston, in 1819. There were portions of those
sketches which gave offence to the family of Thayendanegea,
and his son and successor entered upon the vindication of his
father's character with great spirit. Dr. Strachan had used an
unfortunate epithet in reference to the old Chief, and virtually
charged him with having been engaged in the bloody affair of
Wyoming ; accused him of having entertained designs hostile
to the interests of the crown ; of wavering loyalty ; and, before
his death, of intemperance. These and other matters, contained in the before-mentioned sketches, tending seriously to detract
from the respect previously entertained for the memory of the
father, were repelled with vigorous and virtuous indignation by
the son in the course of a correspondence with the Reverend
Archdeacon ; and were it not for the circumstance that the matter
was in the end satisfactorily adjusted, some extracts from this
correspondence might here be presented, by way of exhibiting
the tact and talent with which a Mohawk Chief could manage
a controversy in the field of letters. The offensive statements
in the sketches of the Christian Recorder were clearly shown
to have arisen from mistakes and misrepresentations ; and in the
course of the explanations that ensued, the conduct of the
Archdeacon " was most honorable." *

The difficulties between the Mohawks and the Provincial
Government, respecting the title to the lands of the former,

---

* Letter of William Johnson Kerr to the author.

which the elder Brant had so long labored, but in vain, to adjust, yet continuing unsettled, in the year 1821 John Brant, alias Ahyouwaèghs, was commissioned to proceed to England, as his father had been before him, to make one more appeal to the justice and magnanimity of the parent government. He urged his claim with ability, and enlisted in the cause of his people men of high rank and influence. Among these was the Duke of Northumberland, the son of the old Duke—the Lord Percy of the American Revolution, and the friend of his father, who had deceased in 1817. The Duke, like his father, had been adopted as a warrior of the Mohawks under the aboriginal cognomen of *Teyonhighkon;* and he now manifested as much zeal and friendship for the Mohawks, in the controversy which had carried John Brant to England, as the old Duke had done for Thayendanegea twenty years before. The young chief likewise found an active and efficient friend in Saxe Bannister, Esq., a gentleman bred both to the navy and the law, who had resided for a time in Upper Canada. Mr. Bannister espoused the cause of the Indians with laudable zeal, and wrote several papers for the consideration of the ministers in their behalf.* The result was, that before leaving England in 1822, the agent received a promise from the Secretary of the Colonies, Lord Bathurst, that his complaints should be redressed to his entire satisfaction. Instructions to that effect were actually transmitted to the Colonial Government, then administered by Sir Peregrine Maitland, and Ahyouwaèghs returned to his country and constituents with the well-earned character of a successful diplomatist.

But the just expectations of the Chief and his people were again thwarted by the provincial authorities. The refusal of the local government to carry into effect the instructions from the ministers of the crown, the pretexts which they advanced, and the subterfuges to which they resorted as excuses for their conduct, were communicated by the chief to his friend the Duke of Northumberland, by letter, in June, 1823. He also wrote simultaneously to Mr. Bannister upon the subject. A correspondence of some length ensued between the Chief and those gentlemen, and repeated efforts were made to compass a satis-

---

* Mr. Bannister afterward held an appointment in New South Wales, and subsequently still was Chief Justice of the colony of Sierra Leone, where he died.

factory and final arrangement of the vexed and long-pending controversy. But these efforts were as unsuccessful in the end as they had been in the beginning.

While in England upon this mission, the young Chief determined to vindicate the memory of his father from the aspersions that had been cast upon it there, as he had already done in his own country. Campbell's " *Gertrude of Wyoming* " had then been published several years. The subject, and general character of that delightful work, are too well and universally known to require an analysis in this place. With a poet's license, Mr. Campbell had not only described the valley as a terrestrial paradise, but represented its inhabitants as being little if any inferior, in their character, situation, and enjoyments, to the spirits of the blessed. Into a community thus innocent, gay, and happy, he had introduced the authors of the massacre of 1778, led on by " the monster Brant." This phrase gave great offence to the family of the old chief, as also did the whole passage in which it occurred. The offensive stanzas purport to form a portion of the speech of an Indian hero of the tale, an Oneida Chief, who is made to interrupt a domestic banquet, under most interesting circumstances, in the following strains, prophetic of danger near at hand :—

> " But this is not the time,"—he started up,
> And smote his heart with woe-denouncing hand—
> " This is no time to fill the joyous cup,
> " The mammoth comes,—the foe,—the monster Brant,—
> " With all his howling, desolating band ;—
> " These eyes have seen their blade, and burning pine
> " Awake at once, and silence half your land.
> " Red is the cup they drink—but not with wine :
> " Awake, and watch to-night ! or see no morning shine !
>
> " Scorning to wield the hatchet for his tribe,
> " 'Gainst Brant himself I went to battle forth :
> " Accursed Brant ! he left of all my tribe
> " Nor man, nor child, nor thing of living birth :
> " No ! not the dog that watch'd my household hearth
> " Escaped that night of blood, upon our plains !
> " All perish'd—I alone am left on earth !
> " To whom nor relative, nor blood remains,
> " No !—not a kindred drop that runs in human veins !"

This paraphrase of the celebrated speech of Logan—less poetical, by the way, than the original—was illustrated by notes, asserting positively that Brant was the Indian leader at Wyoming, and proving his cool-blooded ferocity by citing the anecdote from Weld's Travels, quoted, for denial, as a note on a preceding page. John Brant had previously prepared himself with documents to sustain a demand upon the poet for justice to the memory of his father; and in December, 1821, his friend Bannister waited upon Mr. Campbell, with an amicable message, opening the door for explanations. A correspondence ensued, only a portion of which has been preserved among the papers of John Brant; but in a note of the latter to the poet, dated the 28th of December, the young chief thanked him for the candid manner in which he had received his request conveyed by Mr. Bannister. The documents with which the Chief had furnished himself for the occasion, were thereupon enclosed to Mr. Campbell, and the result was a long explanatory letter from the poet, which has been very generally re-published. Candor, however, must admit that that letter does but very partial and evidently reluctant justice to the calumniated warrior. It is, moreover, less magnanimous, and characterised by more of special pleading, than might have been expected.*   In addition to this, it appears, by a communication from the young chief to Sir John Johnson, dated January 22, 1822, that Mr. Campbell had not only expressed his regret at the injustice done the character of his father, but had promised a correction in the next edition—then soon to be published. This correction, however, was not made, as it should have been, in the text, but in a note to the subsequent edition; and although, at the close of that note, Mr. Campbell says, for reasons given, that " the name of Brant remains in his poem only as a pure and declared character of fiction," yet it is not a fictitious historical character, and cannot be made such by an effort of the imagination. The original wrong, therefore, though mitigated, has not been fully redressed, for the simple reason that it is the poem that lives in the memory, while the note, even if read, makes little impression, and is soon forgotten.†

* See close of the Appendix.

† The note referred to, is as follows :—" I took the character of Brant in the poem " of Gertrude from the common histories of England, all of which represented him " as a bloody and bad man, (even among savages,) and chief agent in the horrible " desolation of Wyoming. Some years after this poem appeared, the son of Brant,

During his sojourn in London, the young chief seems to have paid considerable attention to the public institutions, particularly those of a humane and benevolent character. He was introduced by Mr. Butterworth to the British and Foreign School Society; and in his diary mentions an interesting visit to the Royal College of Physicians and Surgeons. Other objects of interest or curiosity, which attracted his attention, were noted in his diary, a small fragment of which only remains among his papers. The following entry is not very flattering to British beauty :—

" *Thursday Evening*, 16th *May*, 1822, I went to Mr. C. A Tulk's, M. P. party, to hear a little music. There were twenty-two ladies—one only pretty—Casweighter, said to be the best violin player in Europe, and Solly, celebrated for the guitar and piano. I met a gentleman well acquainted with my father—formerly of the Queen's Rangers."

But his attention to other matters did not lead him to forget fulness of the moral wants of his people. The war between the United States and Great Britain, the principal seat of which was in the vicinity of the Mohawks' territory, had had a most unhappy effect upon their social condition. Their farms had been neglected, their buildings had suffered from the same cause, as also had their church and schools. It is likewise probable, that after the decease of Thayendanegea, in the absence of a directing master mind, there had been but little advance in the work of public instruction before the war ; and it was the design of young Brant, on his return to Canada, to resuscitate and extend the schools among his nation. For this purpose he procured

---

" a most interesting and intelligent youth, came over to England; and I formed an
" acquaintance with him, on which I still look back with pleasure. He appealed to
" my sense of honor and justice, on his own part and on that of his sister, to retract
" the unfair assertion which, unconscious of its unfairness, I had cast on his father's
" memory. He then referred to documents which completely satisfied me that the
" common accounts of Brant's cruelties at Wyoming, which I had found in books
" of travels, and in Adolphus's and similar histories of England, were gross errors ;
" and that, in point of fact, Brant was not even present at that scene of desolation."
* * * * * "I ascertained, also, that he often strove to mitigate the cruelty of
" Indian warfare. The name of Brant, therefore, remains in my poem, a pure and
" declared character of fiction." This is something like knocking a man down, and then desiring that he would regard the blow as purely a phantasy of the imagination.

an appropriation, in 1822, from the New-England Corporation
for the civilization of Indians, which had been chartered as far
back as 1662.   After his return to Grand River, the young chief
entered zealously upon the work, as appears from an active correspondence maintained for several years with the officers of
that institution.   The following extracts, from a mass of his
letters, are given, not only as examples of his epistolary style,
but for the purpose of showing the extent and nature of the
exertions he was making, and the prospects of good which were
opening upon him:—

> JOHN BRANT, (AHYOUWAEGHS) TO JAMES GIBSON.
> " *Mohawk Village, Grand River, U. C.* }
>   " *19th June,* 1824. }

"   *   *   *   I have attended to the subject of your
letters with the greatest satisfaction, and I hope that the report
I am now about to make to you, will be equally satisfactory
to the humane and benevolent members of the New England
Corporation.   I set out with observing that the appointed
teacher conducts himself in every point of view corresponding
to our expectations.   The children are particularly taught
religious and moral duties ; the hours of prayer are rigidly
attended to ; and on the Sabbath the scholars attend divine
service.   Cleanliness is strictly enforced, and all laudable means
are resorted to in order to excite a liberal spirit of emulation.
Corporeal punishment is discountenanced, except in cases of
flagrant indifference.   Upon the whole, I have the pleasure of
announcing, through the medium of you, Sir, to the Corporation,
that the donation so liberally applied, will, in my opinion, be
attended with the most salutary effects.   It is an agreeable sight
to observe the rising generation of the aborigines employed in
acquiring knowledge, and in a spirit of true worship attending
divine service on the Sabbath.

    *   *   *   *   *   *   *   *   *   *

    " One of our tribes, the Oneidas,* are very anxious to have a
school established for them.   The chiefs have assured me that

---

* A section of the Oneida nation.   After the war of the Revolution, portions of
all the Six Nations emigrated to the new Mohawk territory, although the majority
of all the nations, except the Mohawks, remained within the United States—on
their ancient territory.

not less than thirty children would attend the school if established.

*   *   *   *   *   *   *   *   *

" Seven of the oldest children in our school read in the Mohawk Prayer-book, repeat the catechism, and answer responses in church.   The others use our primers, and spell very well in them to seven and eight syllables.   The number of scholars is twenty-one.   *   *   *   I am sensible of the generous aid that the Corporation have already afforded, and I am requested by the Chiefs of my tribe to return their sincere thanks to the members of the New England Corporation.

" I am, Sir,

" Your very obedient servant,

" J. BRANT,

" *Ahyouwaeghs*

" *James Gibson, Esq.*
" *Treasurer New England Corporation.*"

THE SAME TO THE SAME.

" *Mohawk Village, Grand River, U. C.*
19*th July*, 1826.

" DEAR SIR,

" After having visited the schools which are supported by the New England Corporation, where more than sixty children are taught to read and write in the Mohawk dialect and the English language, I beg to communicate to you the state of the church in our village.   It being the first built in the province, is now in a very dilapidated state, and we have not the funds to rebuild.   We have made an allotment of two hundred acres of land for the use of a resident clergyman, and fifty acres for the use of the school ; and we have appropriated six hundred dollars, or £150 province currency, toward defraying the expenses of building a parsonage; and although that sum is quite insufficient for the object, yet it is the utmost we can do, considering the circumstances and wants of our respective tribes.   We would be very thankful if we could obtain pecuniary aid sufficient to finish the parsonage and rebuild our church; and would rejoice to have a resident clergyman amongst us, who would not consider it too laborious frequently to travel to our several hamlets, to preach the Gospel of the meek and lowly

Jesus; to visit the sick; and always to evince, not only by preaching, but by example, his devotion to the church of Christ.

"I am, dear Sir,

"Your friend and servant,

"J. BRANT."

LETTER FROM THE SAME TO THE SAME.

"*Mohawk Village, Grand River, U. C.*
October 27, 1828.

"DEAR SIR,

"I have the pleasure to acknowledge your communication of the 17th August last, subjoining copies of the resolutions of the New England Corporation at a meeting held on the 8th of March, 1825. Permit me to repeat the grateful sentiments formerly expressed on the part of my tribe to the members of the Corporation for their liberal contributions, as also for the farther support they have now afforded to the most efficient and practical plans of promoting education and the diffusion of knowledge among the Mohawks.

"I have received a letter from the Rev. Mr. West, dated at New-York; but have not as yet arranged any plans with that gentleman relative to his mission; being satisfied, that after a personal conference and actual observation, we can in a much better way arrange such measures as may appear most beneficial.

"Mr. West mentions that he will visit me in the month of May next. I anticipate much satisfaction in meeting the reverend gentleman. It is undoubtedly the best mode of ascertaining our relative situations, circumstances, &c. &c. This I ardently desire for several reasons. It will enable the company to judge how far it may be useful to extend the means of education, and of the probable results; as also the difficulties in which, for very many years, a continuation of unfavorable circumstances has involved the Five Nations. To effect a complete change in manners and customs, that have been long established, will indeed be an arduous task. Let not the difficulties terrify us from the attempt. The more arduous, the more animating— inasmuch as if the attempt succeed, the reward will be great. Not that those who commence this work of humanity are to flatter themselves with the hope of seeing the complete effect of their labors ; time will be required ; and when the foundation is laid in the spirit of sincerity, no doubt can remain that, with the help of God, the edifice will be raised.

" With respect to that part of your letter which refers to the religious faith of a part of the Five Nations, I beg for a short time to defer a reply ; as it embraces a variety of important considerations, in connexion with the attempt to introduce religious instruction among them. The first great restraint, as to civilization, is removed ; I mean by their local situation, in possessing permanent, or rather fixed places of residence. The commencement must be among the youth, with mildness and assiduity. To render the task not only a good, but a lasting work, it will be necessary to obtain the consent of parents. Care should be taken to explain matters, that the object of instruction be understood as clearly as possib'e by the parents.

" In my next I shall draw on you for the amount appropriated for the building of the Mohawk and Oneida school-houses, as also for the schoolmaster at Davis's hamlet. This is a proper season for entering into contracts for building, as our sleighing season is nigh at hand, which affords great facility in the way of collecting materials. As you have not mentioned Lawrence Davids, I shall continue to draw for his salary as usual, out of the £200 appropriated by the Corporation in 1822.

" In my next I will tell you how the scholars get on. All my letters have been on business. I will in a few days write in a more friendly way, for I remember your kindness to me at Epsom.

" I beg my best respects to the Governor, Mr. Solly, and the other members of the Corporation, with whom I have the pleasure to be acquainted.

" I am, very truly, Dear Sir,

" Your obedient servant,

" J. BRANT.

" *Ahyouwaeghs.*

"*James Gibson, Esq.,*
  " *Treasurer New England Corporation, London.*"

These letters breathe the spirit of an enlarged and noble phi lanthropy, guided by true wisdom. The writer had formed a just estimate of the importance of the work in which he was

engaged, and the difficulties to be encountered ; and he had the
sagacity to perceive the only practicable method of accomplishing it—a knowledge of the only means that could be successfully adapted to the end.   The society of which he was the
judicious almoner appreciated his worth, and in the year 1829
presented him with a splendid silver cup, bearing the following
inscription :—

Presented by the New England Corporation,
Established in London by charter, A. D. 1662, for the civiliza-
tion of Indians,
To JOHN BRANT, Esq.,
Ahyouwaeghs,
One of the Chiefs of the Mohawk Nation,
In acknowledgement of his eminent services in promoting the
objects of the Corporation.   A. D. 1829.

In the year 1827, Ahyouwaeghs was appointed by the Earl
of Dalhousie, then Commander-in Chief of the British American provinces, to the rank of Captain, and also Superintendent
of the Six Nations.   It was early in the same year that the
Chief heard that a liberty had been taken with his name in the
American newspapers, which kindled in his bosom feelings of
the liveliest indignation.   Those familiar with that deep and
fearful conspiracy in the western part of New-York, in the Autumn of 1826, which resulted in the murder of William Morgan by a small body of over-zealous freemasons, will probably
remember that the name of John Brant appeared in a portion of
the correspondence connected with that melancholy story.   The
circumstances were these : It was well ascertained, that in the
origin and earlier stages of that conspiracy no personal injury
was designed against the unhappy victim of Masonic fanaticism.
The immediate object of the conspirators was to send Morgan
out of the country, under such circumstances, and to so great a
distance, as to ensure his continued absence.   But they had adjusted no definite plans for the execution of that purpose, or
distinct views upon the subject of his destiny.   Having abduct-
ed and illegally carried him away, those entrusted with his safe-
keeping found him upon their hands, and knew not what to do
with or whither to send him.   In this dilemma, one of their pro-

jects was to convey him to Quebec, and procure his enlistment on board of a British man of-war. Another suggestion, under the supposition that the Mohawk chief was a freemason himself, and would of course embark in any practicable scheme to prevent the disclosures of the secrets of freemasonry, which Morgan was in the act of publishing when seized, was, that Brant should take charge of the prisoner, and cause his transfer by the Indians to the North-western Fur Company. But every device for the banishment of the unhappy man failed, and he was buried at the solemn hour of midnight in the rocky caverns of the Niagara. The suggestion in regard to the transfer of the prisoner to Ahyouwaeghs, however, became public, and for a time it was supposed by those unacquainted with his character, that he might have been consulted in regard to that murderous transaction. The imputation was most unjust, and was repelled with a spirit becoming the man and his race, as will appear by the following letter :—

To the Editor of the York Observer.

' Wellington Square, Feb. 29, 1827.

"Sir,

"I have read a paragraph in the New-York Spectator of the 16th instant, wherein it is stated that the fraternity at Niagara had sent for me to receive and sacrifice the unhappy Morgan, of whom so much has been lately spoken.

"You will oblige me by contradicting this report, which is wholly false. Neither in that instance, nor any other, has such a barbarous proposal been made to me; nor do I believe the man exists who would dare to wound my feelings in such a heinous manner.

" I know nothing of the man, nor of any transaction relating to him ; and I am much surprised that my name has been called in question.

" I am, Sir, your's respectfully,

" J. Brant."

In the year 1832 John Brant was returned a member of the Provincial parliament for the county of Haldimand, comprehending a good portion of the territory originally granted to the Mohawks. The right of the Indians to this territory yet depended upon the original proclamation of Sir Frederick Haldimand, which, according to the decision of the courts of Upper Canada, conveyed no legal title to the fee of the land. The Indians had been in the practice of conveying away portions of their lands by long leases—for the term of nine hundred and ninety-nine years—and a large number of those persons by whose votes Brant was elected, had no other title to their real estate than leases of that description. As the election laws of Upper Canada very wisely require a freehold qualification for county electors, Mr. Brant's return was contested by the opposing candidate, Colonel Warren, and ultimately set aside, and the Colonel declared to be duly chosen.*

It was of but small moment to either candidate, however, which of the two should be allowed to wear the parliamentary honors. The desolating scourge of India—the cholera—was introduced upon the American continent in the Summer of that year, commencing its ravages at Quebec ; and among the thousands who fell before the plague, as it swept fearfully over the country of the great lakes, were JOHN BRANT—AHYOUWAEGHS —and his competitor.

He was a man of fine figure and countenance, and great dignity of deportment, though by no means haughty—having the unassuming manners of a well-bred gentleman. "The first " time I ever saw him, was at a court at Kingston, where he acted " as an interpreter on the trial of an Indian charged with mur- " der. Another Indian was a witness. One of the Indians was " a Mohawk and the other a Chippewa, of the Mississagua tribe. " It was necessary, therefore, that the questions should be inter- " preted to the witness in one language, and to the prisoner " in the other, which afforded me an opportunity to compare " the sounds of the one with the other ; and the harsh and " guttural language of the Mohawk† was, indeed, singularly con- " trasted with the copiousness and smoothness of the Chippewa. " But what impressed me most on the trial, was the noble ap- " pearance of Brant, and the dignity and composure with which " he discharged his duty."‡

* Letter to the author from the Hon. M. S. Bidwell, who sat in Parliament with the Mohawk Chief.

† Not "harsh and guttural," when spoken by the youngest daughter of Joseph Brant.

‡ Letter to the author from the Hon. M. S. Bidwell.

Ahyouwaeghs was a member of the Church of England, though not a communicant. A number of his friends and relations were with him when he died, all of whom believed his death was that of a happy and sincere Christian. In closing the present imperfect sketch of this remarkable man, who had but just attained the prime of manhood, and was cut off as it were in the dawn of a career bright with hope and brilliant with promise, the Christian philanthropist may pause a moment in the contemplation of at least one proud example of what letters and civilization may accomplish with the sons of the American forest.

Elizabeth, the youngest daughter of Joseph Brant, whose name has already been repeatedly mentioned in the foregoing pages, was married several years ago to WILLIAM JOHNSON KERR, Esq. son of the late Dr. Robert Kerr of Niagara, and a grandson of Sir William Johnson. Mrs. Kerr, as the reader must have inferred from what has been previously said respecting her, was educated with great care, as well in regard to her mental culture as her personal accomplishments. With her husband and little family she now occupies the old mansion of her father, at the head of Lake Ontario—a noble situation, as the author can certify from personal observation. Though fully conscious of the delicacy due to a lady living in unostentatious retirement, yet, as the daughter of Joseph Brant, the author trusts that, should this page meet her eye, the enthusiasm of her father's biographer may plead his apology for introducing her before the public—more especially as it shall be done in the language of one of the fair companions* of his journey :—

* * * " Let, then, my reader present to himself a lady of rather more than middling stature, of dignified, reserved, and gentle address, most pleasing in person, and attired in a costume sufficiently Indian to retain the flow and drapery, but donned with the ease, adaptation, and grace, so peculiarly the attributes of an elegant mind.

" Let my reader mark the keen, penetrating glance of that dark eye, as now it rests upon the stranger, whose too eager interest might be deemed obtrusiveness, or anon, its soft, tender, or melting expression, when it falls upon the portraits of her

* Miss Ann Elizabeth Wayland.

brother, is cast upon her father's miniature, or bides upon her children.

" Let him mark the haughty curl .of that lip as she speaks of those who depreciate her people, its sarcastic curve when she alludes to the *so-called* delineations of her father's character, or its fond smile as she looks upon her husband; let him have before him a being in whom mind rules every action, and predominates above all ; and let him attach this idea to one who glories in the fact, that the blood of the Mohawk courses in her veins ; and he will know the daughter of Joseph Brant. But no ; he must yet learn that this mind and these energies are devoted not alone to her immediate circle ; but have been exerted most faithfully for the improvement and well-being of her race. She has, within a few years, translated portions of the New Testament into her vernacular, and is devising various means for the elevation of the Indian character."

Colonel Kerr, her husband, is the eldest of three brothers, William Johnson, Walter, and Robert, all of whom bore commissions, and fought the Americans bravely on the Niagara frontier during the last war. They were likewise all wounded, and two of them taken prisoners, and brought to Greenbush and Pittsfield, whence they escaped, striking first upon Schoharie, and thence across the country from the Mohawk Valley, through the woods to the St. Lawrence—though, it is believed, not both at the same time. Walter was accompanied in his escape and flight by a fellow-prisoner named Gregg. In the course of their travels through the county of St. Lawrence, they fell in with a courier going from the American commander at Sackett's Harbor to General Wilkinson, then below, on his unsuccessful approach to Montreal. The fugitives had the address to pass themselves off for Yankees looking for lands, and obtained from the express such information as they desired. Gregg was disposed to rob him of his dispatches, but Walter Kerr would not consent. He subsequently died from the effects of his wound in London. Inheriting a share of Indian blood, from their grandmother, Molly Brant, the young Kerrs have been represented to the author by an American gentleman, who has known them well, "as being alike fearless in battle, and full of stratagem."

On the death of her favorite son, John, the venerable widow of Joseph Brant,* pursuant to the Mohawk law of succession heretofore explained, being herself of the royal line, conferred the title of TEKARIHOGEA upon the infant son of her daughter, Mrs. Kerr. During the minority, the government is exer cised by a regency of some kind; but how it is appointed, what are its powers, and at what age the minority terminates, are points unknown to the author. The infant chief is a fine-looking lad, three quarters Mohawk, with an eye piercing as the eagle's. But the people over whom he is the legitimate chief—the once mighty Six Nations—the Romans of the new world—whose conquests extended from Lake Champlain west to the falls cf the Ohio, and south to the Santee—WHERE ARE THEY? The proud race is doomed; and Echo will shortly answer, WHERE?

* This remarkable Indian princess died at Brantford, on the Grand River, on the 24th day of November, 1837—thirty years, to a day, from the death of her husband. Her age was 78 years.

NOTE TO THE FOURTH EDITION.

Since the 1st edition of this work was printed, the author has ascertained that his account of the battle of Queenston is not complete, nor entirely accurate, although pains were taken to consult the best authorities, and all known to be extant. The reader, therefore, is requested to examine that account again, commencing at page 505, with the following amendments and additions.

The American force that first crossed the river consisted of *three* companies, viz., those of Captains Wool, Malcom and Armstrong. They were not undiscovered by the British, but were seen and fired upon before they reached the bank. The enemy, however, fled as the Americans landed, and the three companies mounted the bank and formed in line fronting the heights, Captain Wool commanding, as the senior officer. A few moments afterward, Captain Wool was informed of Col. Van Rensselaer's landing, and ordered to prepare for storming the heights— and soon the command was brought him to march. The detachment did march to the base of the heights, where it was ordered by an aid from Col. Van Rensselaer to halt; and in a few minutes it was attacked by a party of British from Queenston, which, after a short but severe struggle, was repulsed. In this affair, Lieut. Wallace and Ensign Morris were killed, and Captains Wool, Malcom and Armstrong, and Lieut. Lent, wounded.

Shortly after this success, word was brought to Captain Wool that Col. Van Rensselaer was mortally wounded, and the detachment was ordered to return to the bank of the river. Captain Wool repaired to the Colonel, and volunteered to storm the battery on the heights—and this service was gallantly performed by the three companies of the 13th Infantry under his command, and a small detachment of artillery commanded by Lieuts. Gansevoort and Randolph. Through some cause, (probably the severe wounds of Col. Van Rensselaer,) full credit was not given to Captain Wool, in the official accounts, for his successful gallantry. From this point the narrative is correct, as it proceeds on page 507.

APPENDIX.

APPENDIX.

No. I.

[REFERENCE FROM PAGE 95.]

DESCRIPTION OF FORT PLAIN.

THE following is said to be a correct drawing of Fort Plain, sometimes erroneously called Fort Plank.*

The Fort was situated on the brow of the hill, about half a mile
north-west of the village, so as to command a full view of the valley,
and the rise of the ground, for several miles in any direction; and
hence it doubtless derived its name, because its beautiful location
commanded a "*plain*" view of the surrounding country. It was
erected by the government, as a fortress, and place of retreat and
safety for the inhabitants and families in case of incursions from
the Indians, who were then, and, indeed, more or less during the
whole Revolutionary war, infesting the settlements of this whole region. Its form was an octagon, having port-holes for heavy ordnance and muskets on every side. It contained three stories or
apartments. The first story was thirty feet in diameter; the se-

---

* Fort Plank, as it is written in the books, was situated two and a half miles from
Fort Plain. The true name was Fort Blank, from the name of the owner of the
farm on which it stood—Frederick Blank.

sond, forty feet ; the third, fifty feet; the last two stories projecting five feet, as represented by the drawing aforesaid. It was constructed throughout of hewn timber about fifteen inches square ; and, beside the port-holes aforesaid, the second and third stories had perpendicular port-holes through those parts that projected, so as to afford the regulars and militia, or settlers garrisoned in the fort, annoying facilities of defence for themselves, wives, and children, in case of close assault from the relentless savage. Whenever scouts came in with tidings that a hostile party was approaching, a cannon was fired from the fort as a signal to flee to it for safety.

In the early part of the war there was built, by the inhabitants probably, at or near the site of the one above described, a fortification, of materials and construction that ill comported with the use and purposes for which it was intended. This induced government to erect another, (Fort Plain,) under the superintendence of an experienced French engineer. As a piece of architecture, it was well wrought and neatly finished, and surpassed all the forts in that region. After the termination of the Revolutionary war, Fort Plain was used for some years as a deposit of military stores, under the direction of Captain B. Hudson. These stores were finally ordered by the United States Government to be removed to Albany The fort is demolished. Nothing remains of it except a circumvallation or trench, which, although nearly obliterated by the plough, still indicates to the curious traveller sufficient evidence of a fortification in days by-gone.—*Fort Plain Journal, Dec.* 26, 1837.

No. II.

[REFERENCE FROM PAGE 153.]

Copy of another paper in the same hand-writing, taken with the letter to General Haldimand from Dr. Smith.

" April 20, 1781.
" FORT STANWIX.

" THIS post is garrisoned by about two hundred and sixty men, under the command of Colonel Courtlandt. It was supplied with provision about the 14th of last month, and Brant was too early to hit their sleys; he was there on the 2d; took sixteen prisoners. A nine-inch mortar is ordered from Albany to this fort, to be supplied against the latter end of May. The nine months' men raised are to join Courtlandt's.

"25th May.—Fort Stanwix is entirely consumed by fire, except two small bastions; some say by accident, but it is generally thought the soldiers done it on purpose, as their allowance is short; provision stopped from going there, which was on its way.

John's Town.

" At this place there is a captain's guard.

"Mohawk River.

" There are no troops, or warlike preparations (as yet) making in this quarter; but it is reported, that as soon as the three years and nine months' men are raised, they will erect fortifications. From this place and its vicinage many families have moved this winter, and it is thought more will follow the example this spring.

" Schenectady.

"This town is strongly picketed all round; has six pieces of ordnance, six pounders, block-houses preparing. It is to be defended by the inhabitants; (except about a dozen) are for Government. There are a few of Courtlandt's regiment here; a large quantity of grain stored here for the use of the troops; large boats building to convey heavy metal and shot to Fort Stanwix.

" Albany.

" No troops at this post, except the Commandant, General Clinton, and his Brigade Major. Work of all kinds stopped for want of provisions and money. The sick in the hospitals, and their doctors, starving. 8th May—No troops yet in this place; a fine time to bring it to submission, and carry off a tribe of incendiaries.

" Washington's Camp.

"The strength of this camp does not exceed twenty-five thousand. Provisions of all kinds very scarce. Washington and the French have agents through the country, buying wheat and flour. He has sent to Albany for all the cannon, quick-match, &c., that was deposited there. Desertions daily from the different posts. The flower of the army gone to the southward with the Marquis De La Fayette.

" May 8th. They say Washington is collecting troops fast.

" Southern News.

" On the 15th of March, Lord Cornwallis attacked General Green at Guilford Court House, in North Carolina, and defeated him with the loss on Green's side of thirteen hundred men killed, wounded, and missing; his artillery, and two ammunition wagons taken, and Generals Starns and Hegu wounded.

" May 20th. Something very particular happened lately between here and New-York, much in the King's favor, but the particulars kept a secret.

" Eastern News.

" The inhabitants between Albany and Boston, and several precincts, drink the King's health publicly, and seem enchanted with the late proclamation from New-York. By a person ten days ago from Rhode Island, we have an account that the number of land forces belonging to the French does not amount to more than three hundred; that when he left it, he saw two of the French vessels from Chesapeake much damaged and towed in; that several boats full of wounded were brought and put into their hospitals, and that only three vessels out of the eight which left the island escaped, the remainder brought into York. Out eastward of Boston is acting on the Vermont principle.

" State of Vermont.

" The opinion of the people in general of this State is, that its inhabitants are artful and cunning, full of thrift and design. About fifteen days ago Colonel Allen and a Mr. Fay was in Albany. I made it my particular business to be twice in their company; at which time I endeavored to find out their business, and on inquiry I understood from Colonel Allen that he came down to wait on Govenor Clinton, to receive his answer to a petition which the people of Vermont had laid before the Assembly; that he had been twice at the Governor's lodging, and that the Governor had refused to see or speak to him. Allen then said he might be damned if ever he would court his favor again: since that time they have petitioned the Eastern States to be in their Confederacy, to no purpose. I heard Allen declare to one Harper that there was a North Pole and a South Pole; and should a thunder-gust come from the south, they would shut the door opposite to that point and open the door facing the north.

" 8th May. By this time it is expected they will be friendly to their King; various opinions about their flag.

" Saratoga.

" At this post there is a company belonging to Van Schaick's regiment, lately come from Fort Edward; which garrison they left for want of provision; and here they are determined not to stay for the same reason. A fort erecting here by General Schuyler. Two hundred and fifty men at this place.

" Fort Edward.

" Evacuated. Now is the time to strike a blow in these parts. A party toward Johnstown, by way of Division, and a considerable body down here, will effect your wish.

General Intelligence.

"Norman's Kill, Nisquitha, Hillbarrack, and New-Scotland, will immediately on the arrival of his Majesty's troops, join and give provision. Several townships east of Albany and south-east, are ready to do the like. Governor Trumbull's son was hanged in London for a spy : he had several letters from Dr. Franklin to some lords, which were found upon him.* No mention in the last Fishkill papers that Greene obliged his Lordship to retreat, as has been reported. The Cork fleet, of upward of one hundred sail, are safely arrived in York. No hostile intentions on foot against the Province of Canada.

"May 25. I just received a line from T. H. but before his arrival, I despatched a courier on the point of a sharp weapon, to which I refer you; and lest that should miscarry, I send you my journal, from which, and the extract sent forward, you may, if it arrives, form something interesting. For God's sake, send a flag for me. My life is miserable. I have fair promises, but delays are dangerous."

With the above was taken another paper in the same hand-writing, of which the following is a copy :

"Y. H. is disobedient, and neither regards or pays any respect to his parents : if he did, he would contribute to their disquiet, by coming down contrary to their approbation and repeated requests.

"The necessaries you require are gone forward last Tuesday by a person which the bearer will inform you of. I wish he was in your company, and you all safely returned, &c.

"My life is miserable. A flag—a flag, and that immediately, is the sincere wish of

"H. Senior."

* The reference here is to Colonel John Trumbull, the former Adjutant General of the northern department, who, so far from having been hanged at the time mentioned, is yet living, (Feb. 1838,) having served his country faithfully and successfully in a high civil capacity since the war of the Revolution, but, more to its glory still, by his contributions to the arts. It is true, that at the time referred to by the writer of these memoranda, Colonel Trumbull was in London. He had repaired thither to study the divine art which he has so long and successfully cultivated, under the instruction of his countryman, West, and with the tacit permission of the British ministers. Owing, however, to the intrigues of some of the American loyalists in London, who hated him bitterly, he was arrested in London during the Autumn of 1780, on a charge of treason, and committed to the common prison. He had a narrow escape, especially as great exasperation was kindled by the execution of André, and it was hoped that an offset might be made in the person of the son of a rebel Governor. West interceded with the King, and Trumbull was liberated. Colonel Trumbull's Memoirs, which are in course of preparation, will contain an interesting account of this affair, which was most disgraceful to those who compassed his arrest.—*Author.*

No. III.

[REFERENCE FROM PAGE 165.]

1.

A FIRM fortress is our God, a good defence and weapon :
He helps us free from all our troubles which have now befallen us.
The old evil enemy, he is now seriously going to work ;
Great power and much cunning are his cruel equipments,
There is none like him on the earth.

2.

With our own strength nothing can be done, we are very soon lost :
For us the right man is fighting, whom God himself has chosen.
Do you ask, who he is ? His name is Jesus Christ,
The Lord Jehovah, and there is no other God ;
He must hold the field.

3.

And if the world were full of devils, ready to devour us,
We are by no means much afraid, for finally we must overcome
The prince of this world, however badly he may behave,
He cannot injure us, and the reason is, because he is judge ;
A little word can lay him low.

4.

That word they shall suffer to remain, and not to be thanked for
   either :
He is with us in the field, with his Spirit and his gifts.
If they take from us body, property, honor, child and wife,
Let them all be taken away, they have yet no gain from it,
The kingdom of heaven must remain to us.

[The above is from a hymn book A. D. 1741. In one printed in 1826, and now
in use in Pennsylvania, the following is added :]

5.

Praise, honor and glory to the Highest God, the Father of all
   Mercy.
Who has given us out of love His Son, for the sake of our defects,
Together with the Holy Spirit.   He calls us to the Kingdom :
He takes away from us our sins, and shows us the way to heaven ;
May He joyfully aid us.   Amen.

No. IV.

[REFERENCE FROM PAGE 167.]

Colonel Gansevoort's Address to the late 3d New-York Regiment.
[Regimental Orders.]
"*Saratoga,* Dec. 30th, 1780.

"THE Colonel being by the new arrangement necessitated to quit the command of his regiment, and intending to leave this post on the morrow, returns his sincerest thanks to the officers and soldiers whom he has had the honor to command, for the alacrity, cheerfulness, and zeal, which it affords him peculiar satisfaction to declare they have so frequently evinced in the execution of those duties which their stations required them to discharge, and for their attention to his orders, which, as it ever merited, always had his warmest approbation.

"Though he confesses that it is with some degree of pain he reflects that the relation in which they stood is dissolved, he will endeavor to submit without repining to a circumstance which, though it may have a tendency to wound his feelings, his fellow-citizens who form the councils of the states have declared would be promotive of the public weal.

"In whatever situation of life he may be placed, he will always with pleasure cherish the remembrance of those deserving men who have with him been sharers of almost every hardship incident to a military life. As he will now probably return to that class of citizens whence his country's service at an early period of the war drew him, he cordially wishes the day may not be very remote when a happy peace will put them in the full enjoyment of those blessings for the attainment of which they have nobly endured every inconvenience and braved many dangers.

"P. GANSEVOORT."

An Address to Colonel Peter Gansevoort, by the Officers of his Regiment, on his retiring from service, in consequence of the new arrangement ordered by Congress.

"*Saratoga,* Dec. 31, 1780.

"SIR,

"Permit us, who are now with reluctance separated from your command, and deprived of the benefits which we frequently experienced therefrom, to declare our sentiments with a warmth of affection and gratitude, inspired by a consciousness of your unwearied attention to the welfare, honor, and prosperity of the Third New-York Regiment, while it was honored by your command.

" We should have been peculiarly happy in your continuance with us. From our long experience of your invariable attachment to the service of our country, your known and approved abilities, and that affable and gentlemanlike deportment by which (permit us to say) you have so endeared yourself to officers and soldiers, that we cannot but consider the separation as a great misfortune.

" Although your return to the class of citizens from whence our country's cause, at an early period, called you, it is not a matter of choice in you, nor by any means agreeable to us ; yet it cannot but be pleasing to know that you retire with the sincerest affection, and most cordial esteem and regards of the officers and men you have commanded.

" We are, with the utmost respect,

" Sir,

" Your most humble servants,

Jas. Rosekrans, Major,	B. Bogardus, Lieutenant,
Corn's. T. Gansen, Captain,	J. Bagley do.
J. Gregg, do.	Chrs. Hatton, do.
Leonard Bleeker, do.	W. Magee, do.
Geo. Sytez, do.	Prentice Bowen, do.
Henry Tiebout, do.	Saml. Lewis, do.
Hunloke Woodruff, Surgeon,	John Elliot, Surgeon's Mate,
J. Van Rensselaer, Paymaster,	Benj. Herring, Ensign,
Douw T. Fonday, Ensign,	Gerrit Lansing, do.

No. V.

[Reference from Page 236.]

At a meeting of the principal inhabitants of the Mohawk District, in Tryon County, Colonel Joseph Throop in the Chair,

Taking into consideration the peculiar circumstances of this country, relating to its situation, and the numbers that joined the enemy from among us, whose brutal barbarities in their frequent visits to their old neighbours, are shocking to humanity to relate :

They have murdered the peaceful husbandman and his lovely boys about him, unarmed and defenceless in the field. They have, with a malicious pleasure, butchered the aged and infirm ; they have wantonly sported with the lives of helpless women and children ; numbers they have scalped alive, shut them up in their houses, and burnt them to death. Several children, by the vigilance of their friends, have been snatched from flaming buildings ; and, though tomahawked and scalped, are still living among us ; they have made more than three hundred widows, and above two thousand orphans in this county ; they have killed thousands of cattle and horses that rotted in the field ; they have burnt more than two millions of bushels of grain, many hundreds of buildings, and vast stores of forage; and now these merciless fiends are creeping in among us again, to claim the privilege of fellow-citizens and demand a restitution of their forfeited estates ; but can they leave their infernal tempers behind them, and be safe or peaceable neighbors ? Or can the disconsolate widow and the bereaved mother reconcile her tender feelings to a free and cheerful neighborhood with those who so inhumanly made her such ? *Impossible !* It is contrary to nature, the first principle of which is self-preservation : it is contrary to the law of nations, especially that nation, which, for numberless reasons, we should be thought to pattern after. Since the accession of the House of Hanover to the British throne, five hundred and twenty peerages in Scotland have been sunk, the Peers executed or fled, and their estates confiscated to the crown, for adhering to their former administration after a new one was established by law. It is contrary to the eternal rule of reason and rectitude. If Britain employed them, let Britain pay them ! We will not.

Therefore, *Resolved unanimously,* that all those who have gone off to the enemy, or have been banished by any law of this state, or those who we shall find tarried as spies or tools of the enemy, and encouraged and harbored those who went away, shall not live in this district on any pretence whatever ; and as for those who have washed their faces from Indian paint, and their hands from the innocent blood of our dear ones, and have returned either openly or covertly, we hereby warn them to leave this district before the twentieth of June next, or they may expect to feel the just resentment of an injured and determined people.

We likewise unanimously desire our brethren in the other districts in this county to join with us, to instruct our representatives not to consent to the repealing any laws made for the safety of the state, against treason or confiscation of traitors' estates ; or to passing any new acts for the return or restitution of Tories.

By order of the Meeting,

May 9, 1783.   JOSIAH THROOP, Chairman.

At a meeting of the freeholders and inhabitants of Canajoharie District, in the County of Tryon, held at Fort Plain in the same district, on Saturday the 7th day of June, 1783, the following resolves were unanimously entered into. Lieutenant Colonel Samuel Clyde in the Chair:

Whereas, In the course of the late war, large numbers of the inhabitants of this county, lost to every sense of the duty they owed their country, have joined the enemies of this state, and have, in conjunction with the British troops, waged war on the people of this state; while others, more abandoned, have remained among us, and have harbored, aided, assisted, and victualled the said British troops and their adherents; and by their example and influence have encouraged many to desert the service of their country, and by insults and threats have discouraged the virtuous citizens, thereby inducing a number to abandon their estates and the defence of their country: *and whereas,* the County of Tryon hath, in an especial manner, been exposed to the continued inroads and incursions of the enemy, in which inroads and incursions the most cruel murders, robberies, and depredations have been committed that ever yet happened in this or any other country; neither sex nor age being spared, insomuch that the most aged people of each sex, and infants at their mothers' breasts, have inhumanly been butchered; our buildings (the edifices dedicated to the service of Almighty God not excepted) have been reduced to ashes; our property destroyed and carried away; our people carried through a far and distant wilderness, into captivity among savages (the dear and faithful allies of the merciful and humane British!) where very many still remain, and have by ill usage been forced to enter into their service.

And whereas, Through the blessings of God and the smiles of indulgent Providence, the war has happily terminated, and the freedom and independence of the United States firmly established:

And whereas, It is contrary to the interests of this county, as well as contrary to the dictates of reason, that those persons who have, through the course of an eight years' cruel war, been continually aiding and assisting the British to destroy the liberties and freedom of America, should now be permitted to return to, or remain in this county, and enjoy the blessings of those free governments established at the expense of our blood and treasure, and which they, by every unwarrantable means, have been constantly laboring to destroy,

Resolved, That we will not suffer or permit any person or persons whatever, who have during the course of the late war joined the enemy of this state, or such person or persons remaining with

us, and who have any ways aided, assisted, victualled, or harbored
the enemy, or such as have corresponded with them, to return to, or
remain in this district.

Resolved, That all other persons of disaffected or equivocal character, who have by their examples, insults, and threatenings, occasioned any desertions to the enemy, or have induced any of the virtuous citizens of this county to abandon their habitations, whereby
they were brought to poverty and distress. And all such as during
the late war have been deemed dangerous, shall not be permitted to
continue in this district, or to return to it.

Resolved, That all such persons now remaining in this district,
and comprehended in either of the above resolutions, shall depart
the same within one month after the publication of this.

Resolved, That no person or persons, of any denominations whatever, shall be suffered to come and reside in this district, unless
such person or persons shall bring with them sufficient vouchers of
their moral characters, and of their full, entire, and unequivocal
attachment to the freedom and independence of the United States.

Resolved, That we will, and hereby do associate, under all the ties
held sacred among men and Christians, to stand to, abide by, and
carry into full effect and execution, all and every the foregoing reso
lutions.

Resolved, That this district does hereby instruct the members in
Senate and Assembly of this state from this county, to the utmost
of their power to oppose the return of all such person or persons
who are comprehended within the sense and meaning of the above
resolutions.

Ordered, That the preceding votes and proceedings of this district be signed by the Chairman, and published in the New-York
Gazetteer.

SAMUEL CLYDE, *Chairman.*

No. VI.

[REFERENCE FROM PAGE 288.]

"AT a meeting of the President and Fellows of Harvard College,
June 5th, 1789—

"*Voted*, That the thanks of this Corporation be presented to Colonel Joseph Brant, Chief of the Mohawk Nation, for his polite
attention to this University, in his kind donation to its library of
the Book of Common Prayer of the Church of England, with the

Gospel of Mark, translated into the Mohawk language, and a Primer
in the same language

"Attest,   JOSEPH WILLARD, *President*."

No. VII.

[REFERENCE FROM PAGE 312.]

SAINCLAIRE'S DEFEAT.

'TWAS November the fourth, in year of ninety-one,
We had a sore engagement near to Fort Jefferson;
Sinclaire was our commander, which may remembered be,
For there we left nine hundred men in t' West'n Ter'tory.

At Bunker's Hill and Quebec, where many a hero fell,
Likewise at Long Island, (it is I the truth can tell,)
But such a dreadful carnage may I never see again
As hap'ned near St. Mary's upon the river plain.

Our army was attacked just as the day did dawn,
And soon were overpowered and driven from the lawn:
They killed Major *Ouldham*, *Levin*, and *Briggs* likewise,
And horrid yell of savages resounded thro' the skies.

Major *Butler* was wounded the very second fire;
His manly bosom swell'd with rage when forc'd to retire;
And as he lay in anguish, nor scarcely could he see,
Exclaimed, "Ye hounds of hell, O! revenged I will be."

We had not been long broken when General *Butler* found
Himself so badly wounded, was forced to quit the ground:
"My God!" says he, "what shall we do; we're wounded every man
Go, charge them, valiant heroes, and beat them if you can."

He leaned his back against a tree, and there resigned his breath,
And like a valiant soldier sunk in the arms of death;
When blessed angels did await, his spirit to convey;
And unto the celestial fields he quickly bent his way.

We charg'd again with courage firm, but soon again gave ground,
The war-whoop then re-doubled, as did the foes around;
They killed Major *Ferguson*, which caused his men to cry,
"Our only safety is in flight, or fighting here to die."

' Stand to your guns," says valiant *Ford*, " let's die upon them there,
Before we let the sav'ges know we ever habored fear."
Our cannon balls exhausted, and artillery-men all slain,
Obliged were our musket-men the en'my to sustain.

Yet three hours more we fought them, and then were forc'd to yield,
When three hundred bloody warriors lay stretched upon the field.
Says Colonel *Gibson* to his men, " My boys, be not dismayed,
I'm sure that true Virginians were never yet afraid.

" 'Ten thousand deaths I'd rather die, than they should gain the
     field :"
With that he got a fatal shot, which caused him to yield.
Says Major *Clark*, " My heroes, I can here no longer stand,
We'll strive to form in order, and retreat the best we can."

The word ' Retreat' being past around, there was a dismal cry
Then helter-skelter through the woods, like wolves and sheep they
     fly ;
This well-appointed army, who, but a day before,
Defied and braved all danger, had like a cloud pass'd o'er.

Alas ! the dying and wounded, how dreadful was the thought,
To the tomahawk and scalping-knife, in mis'ry are brought ;
Some had a thigh and some an arm broke on the field that day,
Who writhed in torments at the stake, to close the dire affray

To mention our brave officers is what I wish to do ;
No sons of Mars e'er fought more brave, or with more courage true.
To Captain *Bradford* I belonged, in his artillery ;
He fell that day amongst the slain, a valiant man was he.

No. VIII.

[REFERENCE FROM PAGE 314.]

Narrative of the Captivity and Sufferings of Massy Harbison, in the
Spring of 1792, who resided in the neighborhood of Pittsburgh, to-
gether with the Murder of her children, her own Escape, &c.

ON the return of my husband from General St. Clair's defeat, mentioned in a preceding chapter, and on his recovery from the wound he
received in the battle, he was made a spy, and ordered to the woods
on duty, about the 22d of March, 1792.   The appointment of spies

to watch the movements of the savages was so consonant with the desires and interests of the inhabitants, that the frontier now resumed the appearance of quiet and confidence. Those who had for nearly a year been huddled together in the block-house were scattered to their own habitations, and began the cultivation of their farms. The spies saw nothing to alarm them, or to induce them to apprehend danger, till the fatal morning of my captivity. They repeatedly came to our house, to receive refreshments and to lodge. On the 15th of May, my husband, with Captain Guthrie and other spies, came home about dark, and wanted supper; to procure which I requested one of the spies to accompany me to the spring and spring-house, and Mr. William Maxwell complied with my request. While he was at the spring and spring-house, we both distinctly heard a sound like the bleating of a lamb or fawn. This greatly alarmed us, and induced us to make a hasty retreat into the house. Whether this was an Indian decoy, or a warning of what I was to pass through, I am unable to determine. But from this time and circumstance, I became considerably alarmed, and entreated my husband to remove me to some more secure place from Indian cruelties. But Providence had designed that I should become a victim to their rage, and that mercy should be made manifest in my deliverance.

On the night of the 21st of May, two of the spies, Mr. John Davis and Mr. Sutton, came to lodge at our house, and on the morning of the 22d, at day-break, when the horn blew at the block-house, which was within sight of our house, and distant about two hundred yards, the two men got up and went out. I was also awake, and saw the door open, and thought, when I was taken prisoner, that the scouts had left it open. I intended to rise immediately; but having a child at the breast, and it being awakened, I lay with it at the breast to get it to sleep again, and accidently fell asleep myself.

The spies have since informed me that they returned to the house again, and found that I was sleeping; that they softly fastened the door, and went immediately to the block-house; and those who examined the house after the scene was over, say both doors had the appearance of being broken open.

The first thing I knew from falling asleep, was the Indians pulling me out of the bed by my feet. I then looked up, and saw the house full of Indians, every one having his gun in his left hand and tomahawk in his right. Beholding the dangerous situation in which I was, I immediately jumped to the floor on my feet, with the young child in my arms. I then took a petticoat to put on, having only the one in which I slept; but the Indians took it from me, and as many as I attempted to put on they succeeded in taking from me.

so that I had to go just as I had been in bed. While I was struggling with some of the savages for clothing, others of them went and
took the two children out of another bed, and immediately took the
two feather beds to the door and emptied them. The savages immediately began their work of plunder and devastation. What they
were unable to carry with them, they destroyed. While they were
at their work I made to the door, and succeeded in getting out, with
one child in my arms and another by my side; but the other little
boy was so much displeased by being so early disturbed in the morning, that he would not come to the door.

When I got out, I saw Mr. Wolf, one of the soldiers, going to the
spring for water, and beheld two or three of the savages attempting
to get between him and the block-house; but Mr. Wolf was unconscious of his danger, for the savages had not yet been discovered. I
then gave a terrific scream, by which means Mr. Wolf discovered
his danger, and started to run for the block-house: seven or eight
Indians fired at him, but the only injury he received was a bullet in
his arm, which broke it. He succeeded in making his escape to the
block-house. When I raised the alarm, one of the Indians came up
to me with his tomahawk, as though about to take my life; a second
came and placed his hand before my mouth, and told me to hush,
when a third came with a lifted tomahawk, and attempted to give
me a blow; but the first that came raised his tomahawk and averted
the blow, and claimed me as his squaw.

The Commissary, with his waiter, slept in the store-house near
the block-house; and upon hearing the report of the guns, came to
the door to see what was the matter, and beholding the danger he
was in made his escape to the block-house, but not without being
discovered by the Indians, several of whom fired at him, and one of
the bullets went through his handkerchief, which was tied about his
head, and took off some of his hair. The handkerchief, with several bullet holes in it, he afterward gave to me.

The waiter, on coming to the door, was met by the Indians, who
fired upon him, and he received two bullets through the body and
fell dead by the door. The savages then set up one of their tremendous and terrifying yells, and pushed forward, and attempted to scalp
the man they had killed; but they were prevented from executing
their diabolical purpose by the heavy fire which was kept up through
the port-holes from the block-house.

In this scene of horror and alarm I began to meditate an escape,
and for that purpose I attempted to direct the attention of the Indians from me, and to fix it on the block-house; and thought if I
could succeed in this, I would retreat to a subterranean rock with

which I was acquainted, which was in the run near where we were. For this purpose I began to converse with some of those who were near me respecting the strength of the block-house, the number of men in it, &c., and being informed that there were forty men there, and that they were excellent marksmen, they immediately came to the determination to retreat, and for this purpose they ran to those who were besieging the block-house, and brought them away. They then began to flog me with their wiping sticks, and to order me along. Thus what I intended as the means of my escape, was the means of accelerating my departure in the hands of the savages. But it was no doubt ordered by a kind Providence, for the preservation of the fort and the inhabitants in it; for when the savages gave up the attack and retreated, some of the men in the house had the last load of ammunition in their guns, and there was no possibility of procuring any more, for it was all fastened up in the store-house, which was inaccessible.

The Indians, when they had flogged me away along with them, took my oldest boy, a lad about five years of age, along with them, for he was still at the door by my side. My middle little boy, who was about three years of age, had by this time obtained a situation by the fire in the house, and was crying bitterly to me not to go, and making bitter complaints of the depredations of the savages.

But these monsters were not willing to let the child remain behind them: they took him by the hand to drag him along with them, but he was so very unwilling to go, and made such a noise by crying, that they took him up by the feet and dashed his brains out against the threshold of the door. They then scalped and stabbed him, and left him for dead. When I witnessed this inhuman butchery of my own child, I gave a most indescribable and terrific scream, and felt a dimness come over my eyes next to blindness, and my senses were nearly gone. The savages then gave me a blow across my head and face, and brought me to my sight and recollection again. During the whole of this agonizing scene I kept my infant in my arms.

As soon as their murder was effected, they marched me along to the top of the bank, about forty or sixty rods, and there they stopped and divided the plunder which they had taken from our house; and here I counted their number, and found them to be thirty-two, two of whom were white men painted as Indians.

Several of the Indians could speak English well. I knew several of them well, having seen them go up and down the Alleghany river. I knew two of them to be from the Seneca tribe of Indians, and two of them Munsees; for they had called at the shop to get their guns repaired, and I saw them there.

We went from this place about forty rods, and they then caught my uncle, John Currie's horses, and two of them, into whose custody I was put, started with me on the horses, toward the mouth of the Kiskiminetas, and the rest of them went off toward Puckety. When they came to the bank that descended toward the Alleghany, the bank was so very steep, and there appeared so much danger in descending it on horseback, that I threw myself off the horse in opposition to the will and command of the savages.

My horse descended without falling, but the one on which the Indian rode who had my little boy, in descending, fell, and rolled over repeatedly; and my little boy fell back over the horse, but was not materially injured. He was taken up by one of the Indians, and we got to the bank of the river, where they had secreted some bark canoes under the rocks, opposite to the island that lies between the Kiskiminetas and Buffalo. They attempted in vain to make the horses take the river. After trying some time to effect this, they left the horses behind them, and took us in one of the canoes to the point of the island, and there they left the canoe.

Here I beheld another hard scene, for as soon as we landed, my little boy, who was still mourning and lamenting about his little brother, and who complained that he was injured by the fall in descending the bank, *was murdered*.

One of the Indians ordered me along, probably that I should not see the horrid deed about to be perpetrated. The other then took his tomahawk from his side, and with this instrument of death *killed and scalped him*. When I beheld this second scene of inhuman butchery, I fell to the ground senseless, with my infant in my arms, it being under, and its little hands in the hair of my head. How long I remained in this state of insensibility, I know not.

The first thing I remember was my raising my head from the ground, and my feeling myself exceedingly overcome with sleep. I cast my eyes around, and saw the scalp of my dear little boy, fresh bleeding from his head, in the hand of one of the savages, and sunk down to the earth again upon my infant child. The first thing I remember after witnessing this spectacle of wo, was the severe blows I was receiving from the hands of the savages, though at that time I was unconscious of the injury I was sustaining. After a severe castigation, they assisted me in getting up, and supported me when up.

Here I cannot help contemplating the peculiar interposition of Divine Providence in my behalf. How easily might they have murdered me! What a wonder their cruelty did not lead them to effect it! But, instead of this, the scalp of my boy was hid from my view.

and, in order to bring me to my senses again, they took me back to the river and led me in knee deep; this had its intended effect. But "the tender mercies of the wicked are cruel."

We now proceeded on our journey by crossing the island, and coming to a shallow place where we could wade out, and so arrive to the Indian side of the country. Here they pushed me in the river before them, and had to conduct me through it. The water was up to my breast, but I suspended my child above the water, and, through the assistance of the savages, got safely out.

From thence we rapidly proceeded forward, and came to Big Buffalo; here the stream was very rapid, and the Indians had again to assist me. When we had crossed this creek, we made a straight course to the Connequenessing creek, the very place where Butler now stands; and from thence we travelled five or six miles to Little Buffalo, and crossed it at the very place where Mr. B. Sarver's mill now stands, and ascended the hill.

I now felt weary of my life, and had a full determination to make the savages kill me, thinking that death would be exceedingly well-come when compared with the fatigue, cruelties, and miseries I had the prospect of enduring. To have my purpose effected, I stood still, one of the savages being before me and the other walking on behind me, and I took from off my shoulder a large powder horn they made me carry, in addition to my child, who was one year and four days old. I threw the horn on the ground, closed my eyes, *and expected every moment to feel the deadly tomahawk.* But to my surprise the Indians took it up, cursed me bitterly, and put it on my shoulder again. I took it off the second time, and threw it on the ground, and again closed my eyes with the assurance that I should meet death; but, instead of this, the savages again took up the horn, and with an indignant, frightful countenance, came and placed it on again. I took it off the third time, and was determined to effect it; and therefore threw it as far as I was able from me, over the rocks. The savage immediately went after it, while the one who had claimed me as his squaw, and who had stood and witnessed the transaction, came up to me, and said, " well done, I did right, and was " a good squaw, and that the other was a lazy son of a b—h; he might " carry it himself." I cannot now sufficiently admire the indulgent care of a gracious God, that at this moment preserved me amidst so many temptations from the tomahawk and scalping knife.

The savages now changed their position, and the one who claimed me as his squaw went behind. This movement, I believe, was to prevent the other from doing me any injury; and we went on till we struck the Connequenessing at the Salt Lick, about two miles above

Butler, where was an Indian camp, where we arrived a little be-fore dark, having no refreshment during the day.

The camp was made of stakes driven in the ground sloping, and covered with chesnut bark, and appeared sufficiently long for fifty men. The camp appeared to have been occupied for some time; it was very much beaten, and large beaten paths went out from it in different directions.

That night they took me about three hundred yards from the camp, up a run, into a large dark bottom, where they cut the brush in a thicket, and placed a blanket on the ground, and permitted me to sit down with my child. They then pinioned my arms back, only with a little liberty, so that it was with difficulty that I managed my child. Here, in this dreary situation, without fire or refreshment, having an infant to take care of and my arms bound behind me, and hav-ing a savage on each side of me who had killed two of my dear children that day, I had to pass the first night of my captivity.

Ye mothers, who have never lost a child by an inhuman savage, or endured the almost indescribable misery here related, may never-theless think a little (though it be but little) what I endured; and hence, now you are enjoying sweet repose and the comforts of a peaceful and well-replenished habitation, sympathize with me a little, as one who was a pioneer in the work of cultivation and civilization.

But the trials and dangers of the day I had passed had so com-pletely exhausted nature, that, notwithstanding my unpleasant situa-tion, and *my determination to escape if possible*, I insensibly fell asleep, and repeatedly dreamed of my escape and safe arrival in Pittsburgh, and several things relating to the town, of which I knew nothing at the time, but found to be true when I arrived there. The first night passed away, and I found no means of escape, for the savages kept watch the whole of the night, without any sleep.

In the morning, one of them left us to watch the trail or path we had come, to see if any white people were pursuing us. During the absence of the Indian, who was the one that claimed me, the other, who remained with me, and who was the murderer of my last boy, took from his bosom his scalp, and prepared a hoop and stretched the scalp upon it. Those mothers who have not seen the like done by one of the scalps of their own children, (and few, if any, ever had so much misery to endure,) will be able to form but faint ideas of the feelings which then harrowed up my soul! I meditated revenge! While he was in the very act, I attempted to take his tomahawk, which hung by his side and rested on the ground, and had nearly succeeded, and was, as I thought, about to give the fatal blow; when, alas! I was detected.

The savage felt me at his tomahawk handle, turned round upon me, cursed me, and told me I was a *Yankee;* thus insinuating he understood my intention, and to prevent me from doing so again, faced me. My excuse to him for handling his tomahawk was, that my child wanted to play with the handle of it. Here again I wondered at my merciful preservation, for the looks of the savage were terrific in the extreme; and these, I apprehend, were only an index to his heart. But God was my preserver.

The savage who went upon the look-out in the morning came back about 12 o'clock, and had discovered no pursuers. Then the one who had been guarding me went out on the same errand. The savage who was now my guard began to examine me about the white people, the strength of the armies going against them, &c., and boasted largely of their achievements in the preceding fall, at the defeat of General St. Clair.

He then examined into the plunder which he had brought from our house the day before. He found my pocket-book and money in his plunder. There were ten dollars in silver, and a half a guinea in gold in the book. During this day they gave me a piece of dry venison, about the bulk of an egg, and a piece about the same size the day we were marching, for my support and that of my child; but owing to the blows I had received from them in my jaws, I was unable to eat a bit of it. I broke it up, and gave it to the child.

The savage on the look-out returned about dark. This evening, (Monday the 23d,) they moved me to another station in the same valley, and secured me as they did the preceding night. Thus I found myself the second night between two Indians, without fire or refreshment. During this night I was frequently asleep, notwithstanding my unpleasant situation, and as often dreamed of my arrival in Pittsburgh.

Early on the morning of the 24th, a flock of mocking birds and robins hoverd over us, as we lay in our uncomfortable bed, and sung, and said, at least to my imagination, that I was to get up and go off. As soon as day broke, one of the Indians went off again to watch the trail, as on the preceding day, and he who was left to take care of me, appeared to be sleeping. When I perceived this, I lay still and began to snore as though asleep, and he fell asleep.

Then I concluded it was time to escape. I found it impossible to injure him for my child at the breast, as I could not effect any thing without putting the child down, and then it would cry and give the alarm; so I contented myself with taking from a pillow-case of plunder, taken from our house, a short gown, handkerchief, and child's frock, and so made my escape ; the sun then being about half an hour high.

I took a direction from home, at first, being guided by the birds before mentioned, and in order to deceive the Indians, then took over the hill, and struck the Connequenessing creek about two miles from where I crossed it with the Indians, and went down the stream till about two o'clock in the afternoon, over rocks, precipices, thorns, briars, &c., with my bare feet and legs. I then discovered by the sun, and the running of the stream, that I was on the wrong course, and going from, instead of coming nearer home. I then changed my course, ascended a hill, and sat down till sunset, and the evening star made its appearance, when I discovered the way I should travel ; and having marked out the direction I intended to take the next morning, I collected some leaves, made up a bed and laid myself down and slept, though my feet being full of thorns, began to be very pain. ful, and I had nothing still to eat for myself or child.

The next morning, (Friday, 25th of May.) about the breaking of the day I was aroused from my slumbers by the flock of birds before mentioned, which still continued with me, and having them to guide me through the wilderness. As soon as it was sufficiently light for me to find my way, I started for the fourth day's trial of hunger and fatigue.

There was nothing very material occurred on this day while I was travelling, and I made the best of my way, according to my know-ledge, towards the Alleghany river. In the evening, about the going down of the sun, a moderate rain came on, and I began to prepare for my bed by collecting some leaves together, as I had done the night before ; but could not collect a sufficient quantity without setting my little boy on the ground ; but as soon as I put him out of my arms he began to cry. Fearful of the consequence of his noise in this situation, I took him in my arms, and put him to the breast im-mediately, and he became quiet. I then stood and listened, and *distinctly heard the footsteps of a man coming after me* in the same direction I had come ! The ground over which I had been travel-ling was good, and the mould was light ; I had therefore left my foot-marks, and thus exposed myself to a *second captivity !* Alarmed at my perilous situation, I looked around for a place of safety, and *providentially* discovered a large tree which had fallen, into the tops of which I crept, with my child in my arms, and there hid myself securely under the limbs. The darkness of the night greatly assist-ed me, and prevented me from detection.

The footsteps I heard were those of a savage. He heard the cry of the child, and came to the very spot where the child cried, and there he halted, put down his gun, and was at this time so near that I heard the wiping stick strike against his gun distinctly.

My getting in under the tree, and sheltering myself from the rain, and pressing my boy to my bosom, got him warm, and most providentially he fell asleep, and lay very still during the time of my danger at that time. All was still and quiet, the savage was listening if by possibility he might again hear the cry he had heard before. My own heart was the only thing I feared, and that beat so loud that I was apprehensive it would betray me. It is almost impossible to conceive or to believe the wonderful effect my situation produced upon my whole system.

After the savage had stood and listened with nearly the stillness of death for two hours, the sound of a bell, and a cry like that of a night-owl, signals which were given to him from his savage companions, induced him to answer, and after he had given a most horrid yell, which was calculated to harrow up my soul, he started, and went off to join them.

After the retreat of the savage to his companions, I concluded it unsafe to remain in my concealed situation till morning, lest they should conclude upon a second search, and being favored with the light of day, find me, and either tomahawk or scalp me, or otherwise bear me back to my captivity again, which was worse than death.

But by this time nature was nearly exhausted, and I found some difficulty in moving from my situation that night; yet, compelled by *necessity* and a love of self-preservation, I threw my coat about my child, and placed the end between my teeth, and with one arm and my teeth I carried the child, and with the other arm groped my way between the trees, and travelled on as I supposed a mile or two, and there sat down at the root of a tree till the morning. The night was cold and wet; and thus terminated the fourth day and night's difficulties, trials, hunger, and danger.

The fifth day, Saturday, 26th May, wet and exhausted, hungry and wretched, I started from my resting-place in the morning as soon as I could see my way, and on that morning struck the head waters of Pine Creek, which falls into the Alleghany about four miles above Pittsburgh; though I knew not then what waters they were, but crossed them; and on the opposite bank I found a path, and discovered in it two mockasin tracks, fresh indented, and the men who had made them were before me, and travelling on the same direction that I was travelling. This alarmed me; but as they were before me, and travelling in the same direction as I was, I concluded I could see them as soon as they could see me; and therefore I pressed on in that path for about three miles, when I came to the forks where another branch empties into the creek, and where was a hunter's camp, where the two men, whose tracks I had before discovered and followed, had been, and kindled a fire and breakfasted, and had left the fire burning.

I here became more alarmed, and came to a determination to leave the path. I then ascended a hill, and crossed a ridge toward Squaw run, and came upon a trail or path. Here I stopped and meditated what to do; and while I was thus musing, I saw three deers coming toward me in full speed; they turned to look at their pursuers; I looked too with all attention, and saw the flash of a gun, and then heard the report as soon as the gun was fired. I saw some dogs start after them, and began to look about for a shelter, and immediately made for a large log, and hid myself behind it; but most providentially I did not go clear to the log; had I done so, I might have lost my life by the bites of rattle-snakes; for as I put my hand to the ground to raise myself, that I might see what was become of the hunters and who they were, I saw a large heap of rattle-snakes, and the top one was very large, and coiled up very near my face, and quite ready to bite me. This compelled me to leave this situation, let the consequences be what they might.

In consequence of this occurrence, I again left my course, bearing to the left, and came upon the head waters of Squaw run, and kept down the run the remainder of that day.

During the day it rained, and I was in a very deplorable situation; so cold and shivering were my limbs, that frequently, in opposition to all my struggles, I gave an involuntary groan. I suffered intensely this day from hunger, though my jaws were so far recovered from the injury they sustained from the blows of the Indians, that wherever I could I procured grape vines, and chewed them for a little sustenance. In the evening I came within one mile of the Alleghany river, though I was ignorant of it at the time; and there, at the root of a tree, through a most tremendous night's rain, I took up my fifth night's lodgings; and in order to shelter my infant as much as possible, I placed him in my lap, and placed my head against the tree, and thus let the rain fall upon me.

On the sixth (that was Sabbath) morning from my captivity, I found myself unable, for a very considerable time, to raise myself from the ground; and when I had once more, by hard struggling, got myself upon my feet, and started upon the sixth day's encounter, *nature was so nearly exhausted, and my spirits were so completely depressed*, that my progress was amazingly slow and discouraging.

In this almost helpless condition, I had not gone far before I came to a path where there had been cattle travelling; I took the path, under the impression that it would lead me to the abode of some white people, and by travelling it about one mile, I came to an un-inhabited cabin; and though I was in a river bottom, yet I knew not where I was, nor yet on what river bank I had come. Here I was seized with the feelings of despair, and under those feelings I went to the threshold of the uninhabited cabin, and concluded that I would *enter and lie down and die;* as death would have been to me an *angel of mercy* in such a *situation,* and would have removed me from all my misery.

Such were my feelings at this distressing moment, and had it not been for the recollection of those sufferings which my *infant* would endure, who would survive for some time after I was dead, I should have carried my determination into execution. Here, too, I heard the sound of a cow-bell, which imparted *a gleam of hope to my de-sponding mind.* I followed the sound of the bell till I came opposite to the fort at the Six Mile Island.

When I came there, I saw three men on the opposite bank of the river. My feelings at the sight of these were better felt than described. I called to the men, but they seemed unwilling to risk the danger of coming after me, and requested to know who I was. I replied that I was one who had been taken prisoner by the In-dians on the Alleghany river on last Tuesday morning, and had made my escape from them. They requested me to walk up the bank of the river for a while, that they might see if the Indians were making a decoy of me or not; but I replied to them that my feet were so sore that I could not walk.

Then one of them, James Closier, got into a canoe to fetch me over, and the other two stood on the bank, with their rifles cocked, ready to fire on the Indians, provided they were using me as a decoy. When Mr. Closier came near to the shore, and saw my haggard and dejected situation, he exclaimed, " who, in the name of God, are you?" This man was one of my nearest neighbors before I was taken; yet in six days I was so much altered that he did not know me, either by my voice or my countenance.

When I landed on the inhabited side of the river, the people from the fort came running out to the boat to see me: they took the child from me, and now I felt safe from all danger, I found myself unable to move or to assist myself in any degree: whereupon the people took me and carried me out of the boat to the house of Mr. Curtus.

Here, when I felt I was secure from the ravages and cruelties of the barbarians, for the first time since my captivity my feelings re-turned with all their poignancy. When I was dragged from my bed and from my home, a prisoner with the savages; when the inhuman butchers dashed the brains of one of my dear children out on the door-sill, and afterward scalped him before my eyes; when they took and tomahawked, scalped, and stabbed another of them before me on the island; and when, with still more barbarous feelings, they afterward made a hoop, and stretched his scalp on it; nor yet, when I endured hunger, cold, and nearly nakedness, and at the same time my infant sucking my very blood to support it, I never wept. No! it was too, too much for nature. A tear then would have been too great a luxury. And it is more than probable, that tears at these seasons of distress would have been fatal in their consequences; for savages despise a tear. But now that my danger was removed, and I was delivered from the pangs of the barbarians, the tears flowed freely, and imparted a happiness beyond what I ever experienced before, or ever expect to experience in this world.

When I was taken into the house, having been so long from fire, and having endured so much from hunger for a long period, the heat of the fire, and the smell of the victuals, which the kindness of the people immediately induced them to provide for me, caused me to faint. Some of the people attempted to restore me and some of them put some clothes upon me. But the kindness of these friends would, in all probability, have killed me, had it not been for the providential arrival from down the river, of Major M'Culley, who then commanded the line along the river. When he came in and saw my situation, and the provisions they were making for me, he became greatly alarmed, and immediately ordered me out of the house, from the heat and smell; prohibited my taking any thing but the whey of buttermilk, and that in very small quantities, which he administered with his own hands. Through this judicious management of my almost lost situation, I was mercifully restored again to my senses, and very gradually to my health and strength.

Two of the females, Sarah Carter and Mary Ann Crozier, then began to take out the thorns from my feet and legs; and Mr. Felix Negley, who now lives at the mouth of Bull Creek, twenty miles above Pittsburgh, stood by and counted the thorns as the women took them out, and there were one hundred and fifty drawn out, though they were not all extracted at that time, for the next evening, at Pittsburgh, there were many more taken out. The flesh was mangled dreadfully, and the skin and flesh were hanging in pieces on my feet and legs. The wounds were not healed for a considerable time. Some of the thorns went through my feet and came out on the top. For two weeks I was unable to put my feet to the ground to walk

Besides which, the rain to which I was exposed by night, and the heat of the sun, to which my almost naked body was exposed by day, together with my carrying my child so long in my arms without any relief, and any shelter from the heat of the day or the storms of the night, caused nearly all the skin of my body to come off, so that my ody was raw nearly all over.

The news of my arrival at the station spread with great rapidity. The two spies took the intelligence that evening as far as Coe's station, and the next morning to Reed's station, to my husband.

As the intelligence spread, the town of Pittsburgh, and the country for twenty miles round, was all in a state of commotion. About sunset the same evening, my husband came to see me in Pittsburgh, and I was taken back to Coe's station on Tuesday morning. In the evening I gave the account of the murder of my boy on the island. The next morning (Wednesday) there was a scout went out, and found it by my direction, and buried it, after being murdered nine days.

Copy of a Letter from Mr. JOHN CORBLY, *a Baptist Minister, to his friend in Philadelphia, dated*

Muddy Creek, Penn, Sept. 1, 1792.

"DEAR SIR,

" The following are the particulars of the destruction of my unfortunate family by the savages:—On the 10th May last, being my appointment to preach at one of my meeting houses, about a mile from my dwelling-house, I set out with my loving wife and five children for public worship. Not suspecting any danger, I walked behind a few rods, with my Bible in my hand, meditating. As I was thus employed, on a sudden I was greatly alarmed by the shrieks of my dear family before me. I immediately ran to their relief with all possible speed, vainly hunting a club as I ran. When within a few yards of them, my poor wife observing me, cried out to me to make my escape. At this instant an Indian ran up to shoot me. I had to strip, and by so doing outran him. My wife had an infant in her arms, which the Indians killed and scalped. After which they struck my wife several times, but not bringing her to the ground, the Indian who attempted to shoot me approached her, and shot her through the body; after which they scalped her. My little son, about six years old, they dispatched by sinking their hatchets in his brains. My little daughter, four years old, they in like manner tomahawked and scalped. My eldest daughter attempted an escape by concealing herself in a hollow tree, about six rods from the fatal scene of action. Observing the Indians retiring, as she supposed, she deliberately crept from the place of her concealment, when one of the Indians, who yet remained on the ground, espying her, ran up to her, and with his tomahawk knocked down and scalped her. But, blessed be God, she yet survives, as does her little sister whom the savages in the like manner tomahawked and scalped. They are mangled to a shocking degree, but the doctors think there are some hopes of their recovery.

"When I supposed the Indians gone, I returned to see what had become of my unfortunate family, whom, alas! I found in the situation above described. No one, my dear friend, can form a true conception of my feelings at this moment. A view of a scene so shocking to humanity quite overcome me. I fainted, and was unconsciousl. orne off by a friend, who at that instant arrived to my relief.

"Thus, dear sir, have I given you a faithful, though a short narrative of the fatal catastrophe; amidst which my life is spared, but for what purpose the Great Jehovah best knows. Oh, may I spend it to the praise and glory of His grace, who worketh all things after the counsel of his own will. The government of the world and the church is in his hands. I conclude with wishing you every blessing, and subscribe myself your affectionate though afflicted friend, and unworthy brother in the gospel ministry,

"JOHN CORBLY"

No. IX.

[REFERENCE FROM PAGE 376.]

Miamis Rapids, May 7th, 1794.

Two Deputies from the Three Nations of the Glaize arrived here yesterday, with a speech from the Spaniards, brought by the Delawares residing near their posts, which was repeated in a council held this day, to the following nations now at this place, viz:—

Wyandots,	Mingoes,
Ottawas,	Munseys,
Chippawas,	Nanticokes.

GRAND-CHILDREN AND BRETHREN,

We are just arrived from the Spanish settlements upon the Mississippi, and are come to inform you what they have said to us in a late council. These are their words:

Children Delawares, *Six Strings White Wampum.*

☞ "Pointing to this country." When you first came from that country to ask my protection, and when you told me you had escaped from the heat of a great fire that was like to scorch you to death, I took you by the hand and under my protection, and told you to

look about for a piece of land to hunt on and plant for the support
of yourselves and families in this country, which the Great Spirit
had given for our mutual benefit and support. I told you at the same
time that I would watch over it, and when any thing threatened us
with danger, that I would immediately speak to you ; and that when
I did speak to you, that it would behove you to be strong and listen
to my words.   *Delivered six Strings White Wampum.*

The Spaniard then, addressing himself to all the nations who
were present, said,—

CHILDREN, These were my words to all the nations here present,
as well as to your grand-fathers, the Delawares. Now, Children, I
have called you together to communicate to you certain intelligence
of a large force assembling on the Shawanoe river to invade our
country. It has given me very great satisfaction to observe the
strong confederacy formed among you, and I have no doubt of your
ready assistance to repel this force.

CHILDREN, You see me now on my feet, and grasping the tomahawk to strike them.

CHILDREN, We will strike them together. I do not desire you to
go before me, in the front, but to follow me. These people have too
long disturbed our country, and have extinguished many of our
council-fires. They are but a trifling people compared to the white
people now combined against them, and determined to crush them
for their evil deeds. They must by this time be surrounded with enemies, as all the white nations are against them. Your French Father also speaks through me to you on this occasion, and tells
you that those of his subjects who have joined the Big-knives, are
only a few of his disobedient children who have joined the disobedient in this country ; but as we are strong and unanimous, we hope,
by the assistance of the Great Spirit, to put a stop to their mischie-
vous designs.   *Delivered a bunch Black Wampum.*

CHILDREN, Now I present you with a war-pipe, which has been
sent in all our names to the Musquakies, and all those nations who
live toward the setting of the sun, to get upon their feet and take
hold of our tomahawk ; and as soon as they smoked it they sent it
back, with a promise to get immediately on their feet to join us and
strike this enemy. Their particular answer to me was as follows :

"FATHER, We have long seen the designs of the Big-knives
"against our country, and also of some of our own color, particularly
"the Kaskaskies, who have always spoke with the same tongue as the
"Big-knives. They must not escape our revenge ; nor must you,
"Father, endeavor to prevent our extirpating them. Two other
"tribes of our color, the Piankishaws and the Cayaughkiaas, who have

"been strongly attached to our enemies the Big-knives, shall share "the same fate with the Kaskaskies."

CHILDREN, You hear what these distant nations have said to us, so that we have nothing farther to do but put our designs in immediate execution, and to forward this pipe to the three warlike nations who have so long been struggling for their country, and who now sit at the Glaize. Tell them to smoke this pipe, and to forward it to all the Lake Indians and their northern brethren; then nothing will be wanting to complete our general union from the rising to the setting of the sun, and all nations will be ready to add strength to the blow we are going to make. *Delivered a War-Pipe.*

CHILDREN, I now deliver you a Message from the Creeks, Cherokees, and Choctaws and Chickasaws, who desire you to be strong in uniting yourselves; and tell you it has given them pleasure to hear you have been so unanimous in listening to your Spanish Father; and they acquaint you that their hearts are joined to ours, and that there are eleven nations of the southern Indians now on their feet, with the hatchet in their hand, ready to strike our common enemy. *Black Strings of Wampum.*

The Deputies of the Three Nations of the Glaize, after speaking the above speeches from the Spaniards, addressed themselves to the several nations in council, in the following manner:

BROTHERS, You have now heard the speeches brought to our council at the Glaize a few days ago from the Spaniards, and as soon as they heard them and smoked the pipe, their hearts were glad, and they determined to step forward and put into execution the advice sent them. They desire you to forward the pipe, as has been recommended, to all our northern brethren, not doubting but as soon as you have smoked it, you will follow their example; and they will hourly expect you to join them, as it will not be many days before the nearness of our enemies will give us an opportunity of striking them. *Delivered the Pipe.*

BROTHERS, Our Grand-fathers, the Delawares, spoke first in our late council at the Glaize, on this piece of painted tobacco and this painted Black Wampum, and expressed their happiness at what they had heard from their Spanish Father and their brethren to the westward, and desired us to tell you to forward this tobacco and Wampum to the Wyandots, to be sent to all the Lake Indians, and inform them that in eight days they would be ready to go against the Virginians, who are now so near us, and that according to the number of Indians collected, they would either engage the army or attempt to cut off their supplies. The Delawares also desired us to say to the Wyandots, that, as they are our elder brethren, and took the lead in all our affairs last summer, it was thought strange that none of them were now there to put the resolution then formed into execution. It is true, some of them went last Fall when it was thought too late, and the assembling of the nations put off till spring; but the spring is now far advanced, and none of them have yet come.

Delivered the Tobacco and Wampum.

Egouchouay answered for all the nations present :—

BROTHERS, I am happy at the good news you have told us, and we will immediately go and collect all our people, and be with you as soon as possible.

(Signed)   A. McKEE, D. A. I. A

A true copy, THOMAS TALBOT.

No. X.

[REFERENCE FROM PAGE 406.]

THE CHIEFS TO SIR JOHN JOHNSON.

" Grand River, Feb. 6, 1802.

" OUR DEAR FRIEND,

" We take the opportunity of Moses Johnson's going to Canada, to trouble you with this the easiest method that tne distance of our situation from each other allows of, to communicate our sentiments to you. We wish to acquaint you, that last Fall, at our usual meeting at the beach, we made a speech to Captain Claus, which he has not yet fully answered. It was principally respecting the letter you wrote to Captain Brant, when you was at Niagara last summer, which we were sorry to find so severe; and as we are sensible that he has never attempted any thing to the detriment of the British interest, we were much surprised to find that his conduct seemed to give umbrage there. As to the uneasiness you mentioned prevailed at Grand River, we are entirely ignorant of any such thing among us who manage the affairs of the tribes living here; and as he is our appointed agent, he yet never acts without our approbation in whatever regards the public; consequently, if any of his transactions have given offence, we are all equally culpable. Therefore, if customs are so much changed with you, that the following the tracks of our predecessor gives umbrage, we hope, from our ancient friendship, you will inform us wherein it injures the interests of our brethren, for then our regard for their welfare will cause us to desist; and if there is a change in politics, don't let us remain ignorant of it; for ignorance might cause us unwittingly to give offence. As you know that not long ago a friendly correspondence and union with the different nations seemed to give pleasure to our brothers, we yet remain of the same sentiments, for we could not lightly drop what we took so much pains to begin; and we can yet hardly persuade ourselves that you have changed your sentiments; but if it is the case, we hope you will do us the favor fully to acquaint us, that we may not be liable to give uneasiness where we really mean none.

"I have the honor to be

"Your humble and most obed't servt.,

(Signed) "AARON HILL.

"In behalf of the Chiefs of the Mohawk, Oghkwaga, Onondaga, Cayuga, and Seneca Nations, living on the Grand River."

No. XI.

[REFERENCE FROM PAGE 411.]

GOVERNOR CLINTON TO CAPTAIN BRANT.

"*Greenwich, 1st December,* 1799.

"DEAR SIR,

"On my return from the country about a month ago, I was favored with your letter of the 4th of September. I am much gratified by the determination you express of furnishing Doctor Miller with the information he requested of you, and I hope, as the work for which it is wanted is progressing, you will find leisure to do it soon. I am confident he will make a fair and honorable use of it; and, as far as he shall be enabled, correct the erroneous representations of former authors respecting your nations.

"I am surprised to find that you have not received my answer to your letter of the 11th January last. It was inclosed and forwarded as requested, to Mr. Peter W. Yates of Albany. Had it reached you, I presume you will find, from the copy I now inclose, it would have been satisfactory; but as a particular detail of what passed between the Coghnawagoes and me, respecting their lands, may be more agreeable, I will now repeat it to you as far as my recollection will enable me :—

"In the Winter of 1792–1793, our Legislature being in session in

Albany, a committee from the seven nations or tribes of Lower Canada attended there, with whom I had several conferences. They complained that some of our people had settled on their lands near Lake Champlain and on the River St. Lawrence, and request-ed that Commissioners might be appointed to inquire into the matter, and treat with them on the subject. In my answer to their speeches I mentioned that it was difficult to define their rights and their boun-daries; that it was to be presumed that the Indian rights to a con-siderable part of the lands on the borders of the lake had been ex tinguished by the French Government before the conquest of Canada, as those lands, or the greater part of them, had been granted to indi-viduals by that government before that period. In their reply, they described their southern boundary as commencing at a creek or run of water between Forts Edward and George, which empties into South Bay, and from thence extending on a direct line to a large meadow or swamp, where the Canada Creek, which empties into the Mohawk opposite Fort Hendrick, the Black and Oswegatchie Rivers have their sources. Upon which I observed to them that this line would interfere with lands patented by the British Government previous to the Revolution, and particularly mentioned Totten and Crossfield's purchase and Jessup's patent; but I mentioned, at the same time, that I was neither authorised nor disposed to controvert their claims, which I would submit to the Legislature, who I could not doubt would pay due attention to them, and adopt proper mea-sures to effect a settlement with them upon fair and liberal terms. This I accordingly did; and some time after Commissioners were ap-pointed to treat with them in the presence of an agent of the United States, the result of which I find you are informed of.

" I believe you will readily agree that no inference could be drawn from any thing that passed on the above occasion to countenance the charge made against your nations. The mentioning and inter-ference of their boundaries. as above stated, with tracts patented under the British Colonial Government, could certainly have no allu-sion to the cessions made by the Six Nations, or either of them, to the state; especially as (if I recollect right) those cessions are of the territory of the respective nations by whom they were made without defining them by any particular boundaries, and subject only to the reservations described in the deed.

" I wish it was in my power to transmit you copies of their speeches and my answers at full length; but it is not, for the reasons men-tioned in my former letter. Should they, however, be deemed necessary by you, I will endeavor to procure and forward them. In the meantime you may rest assured that what I have above related is the substance of them.

"I am, with great regard and esteem,

"Your most obed't servant,

"GEO. CLINTON.

"*Col. Joseph Brant.*"

No. XII.

[REFERENCE FROM PAGE 416.]

CERTIFICATE OF GENERAL CHAPIN.

I CERTIFY I have been personally acquainted with Captain Joseph Brant for fourteen years past; that during this time have frequently been with him in treaties and councils held between the people of the United States and the Five Nations of Indians. That during the time aforesaid, my father, Israel Chapin, Esq. held the office of Indian affairs for the Five Nations of Indians, under the President of the United States; and during his agency, Captain Brant was several times in the States in transacting business of importance. At one time, in particular, he was invited to the seat of Government of the United States for the purpose of consulting upon means for restoring the Indians then hostile to the United States to a general peace; which visit occasioned some suspicions and censures against Captain Brant by certain characters residing in the province where he belonged. That, through the instigation of certain persons, jealousies have arisen, not only among some white people, but among his own also. That the jealousies of his own people are easily awakened; and solely upon this ground they have proceeded in the Indian forms to disown him as a Chief. That the Seneca Indians, with some others residing within the territory of the United States, who have had the disposal of a considerable part of the Five Nations' lands, and have sold, and do actually receive annuities from the people of the United States annually for the same, have been the principal actors in deposing him. That after the death of my father I succeeded him in the office, as aforesaid, and during my own agency had frequent meetings with Captain Brant in Indian councils, &c. And I do further certify, that during the whole of my acquaintance with Captain Brant, he has conducted himself with honor and integrity. That, so far from conducting himself in secrecy, or in any way inclining to alienate himself from the British government, or in doing

ing you at the King, your Great Father's council-fire at Niagara. I then addressed you on the business of your land transactions. I informed you then that General Hunter had taken your affairs into his most deliberate consideration, and what the result of those considerations were.

Since that time some people have come forward to pay for the township which was sold to Mr. Beasley and his associates; and the only thing which now remains upon the minds of your trustees, and which they cannot answer for, (unless you, in the most public manner, express your satisfaction,) is the statement made by Mr. Beasley of monies said to have been paid on your account to your agent, Captain Brant.

I will here explain to you the sums said to have been paid; and if you are satisfied, the necessary discharges will then be given, and your business, I hope, carried on in future more to your satisfaction, and also of the others concerned.

Brethren, The following sums are stated by Mr. Beasley to have been paid by him, and boards delivered by his order.

[Here follows the statement of the pecuniary transactions of Captain Brant, as the agent of the Mohawk Nation, which there is no occasion to transcribe in this place.]

If you wish to consult among yourselves before you give your answer, as I wish you to do, I shall wait until you are ready, as it is necessary that this business should come to a close; but do not let us hurry, take time and weigh the matter well; if you are satisfied that the statement of the account is just, I will lay before you a paper to sign, which shall be explained to you, that you may perfectly comprehend and understand it.

I must farther inform you, that I hope every man that attends for the purpose of executing the above papers may keep from liquor, as I am determined no name shall appear there, unless the whole council are perfectly sober.

Before we cover the fire to-day, I must inform you that the King's Council, with the approbation of General Hunter, have given themselves a great deal of pains in inquiring and seeing that justice should be done to the Six Nations in this business, for which I am confident you will acknowledge yourselves sensible.

I have further to mention to you, that the Governor in Council have thought it for the advantage, benefit, and interest of the Six Nations, that Sir John Johnson should be added as a Trustee for the Six Nations, but it is left for you to consider and say whether he is, or is not, to be added to those who are now acting for you.

No. XIV.

[REFERENCE FROM PAGE 418.]

PROCEEDINGS of a Council held at the Grand River, the 29th day of June, 1804, with the Six Nations, viz : Mohawks, Oneydas, Onondagas, Cayougas, Senecas, and Tuscaroras; and the following Nations,—Tutulies, Delawares, and Nanticokes.

Present,

Lieut. Col. Brock, 49th *Reg't. Commanding,*
William Claus, Esq., *Dept'y Sup't Gen. of Indian Affairs.*
James Gwins, Esq., *Agent of Indian Affairs.*
Lieut. Cary, 49th *Regiment.*
Lieut. Stretton, 49th *Regiment.*
William Dickson, Esq.
Richard Beasley, Esq.
Alexander Stewart, Esq.
Mr. W. I. Chew, *Store-keeper and Clerk Indian Dep*
Benj. Fairchild, } *Interpreters Indian Dep.*
J. B. Rousseau, }

The Deputy Superintendent General addressed the Chiefs as fol follows :—

BRETHREN, It gives me great satisfaction to meet you at this place, and in presence of so many of the King's officers and others this day, to renew our assurances of friendship, which I hope will continue uninterrupted as long as the waters run.

I dispel the darkness which hangs over you by reason of your many losses. I most heartily wish you may enjoy a serene and clear sky; so that you may be able to see your brethren from the sun-rising to the sun-setting.

BRETHREN, I must admonish and exhort you that you will at all times, but more especially at this juncture, pluck from your hearts and cast away all discords, jealousies, and misunderstandings which may subsist among you, or which any evil spirits may endeavor to raise in your breasts.

I therefore, with this Wampum, make this Council-room clean from every thing offensive, and hope that you will take care that no snake may creep in among us, or any thing that may obstruct our harmony. *Bunch of Wampum.*

BRETHREN, I have but a few words to speak, as the fewer that is said the easier you will understand and comprehend. Last year, about the time your corn was getting hard, I had the pleasure of see-any thing that might be prejudicial to the Indians ; on the other hand, he has frankly avowed that he would strenuously adhere to the Government and interest of the people to which he belonged ; that his honor and friendship for the Indian nations were so near his heart, that nothing should occasion him to do any thing incompatible with his duty ; and that his own time and trouble have been expended and greatly prolonged in doing every thing in his power to promote the interest of his nation and those allied to them. And Captain Brant having called on me to certify my opinion as aforesaid, I am free to declare to any who may be concerned, that from a long and intimate acquaintance I have good reason to make the remarks as aforesaid.

Israel Chapin,
Agent of Indian Affairs for the Five Nations.

Canandaigua, in the western part of the ⎰
   State of N. Y., Oct. 28th, 1805.   ⎱

No. XIII.

[Reference from Page 417.]

CERTIFICATE OF CAPTAIN LEONARD AND OTHERS.

We, the subscribers, certify, that in the month of April last there came to Fort Niagara about forty Seneca Indians, among whom were the Farmer's Brother, Red Jacket, Jack Berry, and other Chiefs. While at Niagara, detained by ice, we heard them say in public and private conversation, that they were going into Upper Canada for the express purpose of breaking Captain Brant, a Mohawk Chief. We also certify that the Seneca Chiefs above named reside within the United States.

Given under our hands at Fort Niagara, this 20th day of October, 1805.

W. Leonard, Capt. U. S. Artillery,
G. Armistead, Lieut. U. S. Artillery.
H. M. Allen, Lieut. U. S. Artillery,
Robert Lee, Col. of the Revenue.

I shall now retire, and when you have finished consulting, I shall be ready to attend you. [*Large Bunch of Wampum.*]

30*th June.*   Present the same as yesterday.

I am much pleased that you have so clearly comprehended what I said to you yesterday, and as you are unanimously agreed to admit of the account as just, the following is the paper which it will be necessary for your principal people to sign; but before I go further, I must tell you that your expressions of friendship for me draws from me the warmest sense of feeling. I shall ever endeavor to preserve your esteem and regard, and you may rest assured that my constant exertions shall be for your interest and happiness.

We, the Sachems and principal War Chiefs, Warriors, and prin- cipal women of the Six Nations, having taken into mature conside- ration the said account, and having examined the several items and entries therein, and the whole having been explained to us in the fullest manner, declare that we perfectly understand and compre- hend the same; do hereby unanimously approve thereof as just and true; and do fully admit and acknowledge that the several sums of money set down and charged in the said account as payments made by Mr. Beasley, to and for the use of the Six Nations, were really and truly made; and that the boards and materials charged in the same accounts were actually furnished by Mr. Beasley, also to and for the use of the Six Nations.

In testimony whereof, the aforesaid Sachems, principal War Chiefs, Warriors, and principal Women of the Six Nations, in behalf of the Body of the said Six Nations, have to these presents (done in tripulate) set our hands and affixed our seals at the Council House at the Mohawk Village on the Grand River, this 30th day of June, in the year of our Lord, 1804, and forty-fourth year of his Majesty's reign.

	his		his
Tekarihoken	⋈	Gonesseronton	⋈
	mark		mark
	his		his
Thaweyogearat	⋈	Shagogeaseronni	⋈
	mark		mark
	his		his
Oghnaongoghton	⋈	Ojageghte	⋈
	mark		mark
	his		her
Otoghseronge	⋈	Waorighonti	⋈
	mark		mark

Aonghwinjaga	his ⋈ mark	Tekaenyongh	his ⋈ mark
Otyoghwawagon	his ⋈ mark	Ogongksaneyont	his ⋈ mark
Aghstugwaresera	his ⋈ mark	Thaosonnenghton	his ⋈ mark
Tekahentakwa	her ⋈ mark	Teghsitaasgowa	his ⋈ mark
Oghsonwalagette	his ⋈ mark	Arenghoot	his ⋈ mark
Yoghstatheagh	her ⋈ mark	Nihaweanaagh	his ⋈ mark
Araghkwente	his ⋈ mark	Karrhageayate	his ⋈ mark
Oghgwarioghseta	his ⋈ mark	Kaweanontye	her ⋈ mark

We do certify that the within proceedings were held in our presence, and that the accounts and different items were explained to the Sachems, War Chiefs, and principal Women under the direction of the Deputy Superintendent General of Indian Affairs; that they seemed perfectly to understand and comprehend the same, and acknowledged that they did so, and were perfectly satisfied therewith. We do also certify that those whose names, marks, and seals are hereunto affixed, as well as the whole Council, were perfectly sober when they executed the within.

Council Room, Grand River, 30th June, 1804.

ISAAC BROCK, Col. 49th Regt.

Commissioners.

WILLIAM CAREY, Lieut. 49th Regt.

WILLIAM STRATTON, Lieut. 49th Regt.

After finishing, the usual ceremony of taking leave was gone through, and [A large bunch of Wampum delivered.]

No. XV.

[REFERENCE FROM PAGE 423.]

COUNCIL HELD AT NIAGARA.

[THIS speech was made by Capt. Brant at Niagara to Col. William Claus, Deputy Superintendent General of Indian affairs—after John Norton, alias Teyoninhokârâwen, had returned from England, who had been sent there by Capt. Brant.

W. J. KERR.]

BROTHER,—We have now come to this place, the Council-fire of our Great Father the King, to explain, in a public manner, the foundation of our claim to the lands we now possess, the attempts made in this country to curtail and invalidate our title to them, and latterly the means taken to obstruct the just decision of his Majesty's Right Honorable Privy Council on the subject.

BROTHER,—In the year 1775, when hostilities had commenced, the Mohawks, always faithful to the royal interest, brought off the Indian Department, in company with the Oghkuagas, from the Mohawk River to Canada. Upon our arrival there, this conduct was approved of by Sir Guy Carleton, who, in a public Council, desired us to take up the hatchet and defend our country, and that any losses we might sustain by the war, he promised should be replaced.

When the support given the Americans by the various European powers gave us reason to apprehend, that the war might take such an unfavorable conclusion as to deprive us of the happiness of return to our homes, and to the re-enjoyment of our forsaken lands, we applied to Sir Frederick Haldimand, then Governor and Commander-in-Chief, for a confirmation of General Carleton's promise; this he readily granted us, and we have it now in our possession.

When the line drawn at the peace, and the manner in which that was concluded, left us no hopes of regaining our former possessions, we applied to His Excellency Sir Frederick Haldimand for a grant in the Bay of Quinté.

On this becoming known to the Senecas and others at Buffalo Creek, they upbraided us with having treated them unfairly, after having been the most forward to engage in the royal cause, and having drawn them into the contest, now to abandon them in the present critical situation, to be exposed alone to such retaliation as revenge might urge the Americans to attempt.

We were struck with the justness of their argument, and in consequence relinquished the place we had first chosen, and applied for
the Grand River in lieu of it; as there being more conveniently
situated either to give assistance to our brethren, if assistance was
wanted, or to afford them a comfortable asylum should superior
numbers oblige them to retreat. His Excellency expressed his
satisfaction at our determination, and the terms of his grant will
confirm the accuracy of this assertion.

In a little time the Senecas were relieved from their apprehensions, they remained on their lands, and sold them gradually to the
Americans; for which they receive annually six thousand five hundred dollars, besides four thousand five hundred dollars which they
get in common with others of the Six Nations inhabiting within the
territories of the United States, from whom also several of their
Chiefs receive pensions; with these arrangements they have appeared
to remain contented on the reserves they have retained.

General Haldimand was on the eve of embarking for Europe
when he executed the grant. This we may suppose to have been the
reason why it was not registered at Quebec; and from this circumstance, shortly after the formation of the Canadian government, an
attempt was made to curtail our land.

After we came to a proper understanding on this head, from the
consideration that the animals were becoming scarce for the hunters,
we proposed leasing a part of our lands, not in our power to occupy,
to receive therefrom an annual income; the leasing was objected to
by the Executive, but they were sold with the sanction of the Canadian Government, and mortgaged for the payment of the interest;
the incumbrances, however, annexed to these arrangements, have
prevented us as yet deriving the benefit therefrom we had reason to
expect.

We have asked for a confirmation of the remaining lands, that
our posterity might enjoy in security the benefits of our industry,
and of their own; but this request has never yet met with an
answer.

What we asked for, seemed to be of such a nature as not to render it necessary to apply to higher authority than there was in this
country, (providing the inclination should be favorable to grant us
our requests,) was the reason we persevered in entreating for a satisfactory decision of the Executive for many years; notwithstanding
repeated retardments in our business, we were reluctant to trouble
his Majesty's Government in Britain with so trifling an affair.

However, at the time my nephew Teyoninhokârâwen desired to

go to Europe to serve in the war, we hoped, should an opportunity occur for him to make representation of our situation, it might expedite the conclusion of the business to our satisfaction. This he was well enabled to do from his knowledge of the subject, and authorized as being an adopted Chief: as such, I gave him letters of introduction to my friends there; and from the generosity and love of justice, which ever distinguishes his Majesty's Government, and is peculiarly prevalent in the British nation, it appears he was attended to, and in consequence of his representation, letters in our favor were wrote to the Government here.

BROTHER,—You then, as Agent for Indian Affairs, sent notice to the Grand River, as we have evident proof, through the medium of a Cayuga Chief named Tsinonwanhonte, who acquainted the other Chief of that tribe, Okoghsaniyonte, that Teyoninhokârâwen had been making use of their names to their detriment, and that I had got to my highest, and would soon fall; that the method they were to take to prevent evil arriving to them, was to come to Niagara, protest against and disavow all the proceedings of Teyaninhokârâwen, depose me from being chief, and disannul all that we had done from the time we formed the settlement.

The Chiefs of the Grand River would not listen to this, but many of the common people were thereby prevailed on to go to Buffalo Creek on the American side. There they held a Council with the Senecas and others of the Five Nations living within that territory, made new chiefs contrary to our established customs, came to Niagara, complied in every respect with your desires; so as to contradict the application of Teyoninhokârâwen on our behalf, and prevent him obtaining that confirmation to our grant which he hoped for from the justice of his Majesty's Government, and which apparently was on the point of being accomplished to our satisfaction.

BROTHER,—We protest against this your proceeding for these reasons, that you knew the Five Nations living within the American territories, and who composed the principal part of that council, were not the real proprietors of the Grand River, according to Sir Frederick Haldimand's Grant; neither did they deserve to be so from their subsequent conduct since we settled there; that several of these Chiefs were pensioners to the United States; that the names of many who were not Chiefs were sent to England, and that none of the principal men from the Grand River were there. Those who were made chiefs at Buffalo, we cannot allow of, as being contrary to all authority and custom, as well as their ignorance of public affairs rendering them absolutely unfit for such a situation.

The Farmer's Brother and Red Jacket, two of these Chiefs, pensioners to the United States, a few years ago at Hartford, in the Assembly of the Connecticut State, declared " that they were subjects to the United States, and would never cross the river, kissing the medal of General Washington in token of their steady attachment to the United States, vowing that they would ever remain united."

Is it such men as these you should represent as being the proprietors of the Grand River ? No ; they were granted to us as loyalists, that had fought and lost our lands in support of his Majesty's interests ; and the love we bear our Great Father the King, and the desire we have of living under his protection, is the reason we set so great a value on these lands, and persevere to obtain a confirmation of them. Neither is there any reason why you should prefer the title or claims of the opposite party of our own dialect, inhabiting at present the same village with us ; but who have joined those people in opposition, to promote anarchy among us. Before the war, they lived at Fort Hunter, and had sold the most of their lands before hostilities commenced ; what they lost, therefore, is more to be imputed to their imprudence than to their loyalty. This was not the case with us of Canajoharie or Oghkwaga. When we took up the hatchet, our lands remained almost entire and unbroken, like those of the tribes to the westward.

BROTHER,—We, the principal Chiefs of that part of the Five Nations inhabiting the Grand River, who obtained the grant from General Haldimand in consequence of our services and losses, now affirm that we approve in every respect of the representation of our affairs made by Teyoninhokârâwen in England ; and also of his request in our behalf ; but so much having been said on the subject for these many years past renders so necessary a discussion, that we entreat the Government to direct an inquiry to be made into the conduct of those concerned.

BROTHER,—Since we appointed Trustees by the direction of the Executive in this province, we have found the appointment very insufficient, both as to the speedy execution of our business, as also to the giving us the proper security for the property which may pass through their hands. The confidence we ever entertained of being protected in all our rights by our Great Father, caused us to remove to the place we now occupy within his dominions. We therefore petition that his Majesty's Government appoint such other medium for the transaction of our business as to their wisdom may appear proper, and which to us may be more satisfactory and secure.

BROTHER,—You know, that some years ago our Council-fire was

taken from Buffalo Creek and kindled at the Onondaga Village on the Grand River ; it is there that in a general Council we determined on what we now communicate at the Council fire-place of our Great Father, in consequence of our being made acquainted with the effect the Council held here last spring twelvemonth had in England.

We have delayed some time, in hopes to have had previously a fair discussion of the affair at our General Council, and to have convinced the people of Buffalo Creek of the mistake they had fallen into, in thinking that they had any right to hold councils at their village to interfere in our land affairs ; especially as our Council-fire, which had been extinguished by the Americans, was now rekindled under the protection of our Great Father, at the Grand River ; from whose benevolence we now hold that land, of which the Onondagas, the keepers of our Council-fire, are joint proprietors ; which is not the case at Buffalo Creek on the American side ; for which reason it certainly deserves the preference, as most likely of duration through the blessing of God and the support of our Great Father the King. From the time that our forefathers formed the confederacy, it has been with these that the General Council Fire-place has been kept, and there that every thing relating to the welfare of the whole has been deliberated on ; and, as such, it was regarded by all the neighboring nations.

BROTHER :—It is with pain and regret we have to observe that you received, as Trustee, thirty-eight thousand dollars of our money near two years ago, and that you have not since accounted to us for principal or interest, or given us any satisfactory account of the application of the same ; and we therefore are so convinced that you have forfeited our esteem and confidence, that we desire our Great Father will appoint some other person to superintend our affairs, and render us that justice, which, as strict adherents in loyalty and attachment to our Great Father, we have so long and faithfully deserved.

[Additional Memoranda, by Captain Brant.]

The Agent had deferred meeting us the three preceding days, giving for the reason, that he waited for a Mr. Selby from Detroit ; but the Chiefs gaining information that this gentleman's arrival was uncertain, insisted on meeting him that day between twelve and one o'clock, he came with the commanding officer. Col. Proctor said, as he had before said, he would not meet them in Council ; so he remained in resolution, and would not hear them, giving the same excuse for it ; but as this had never been the case before, nor the attendance of Mr. Selby required at any former council, the chiefs resolved to deliver their sentiments in the house built by his Majesty for that purpose, where they were assembled in the presence of several officers of the garrison, of Judge Thorpe, Mr. Weeks, Mr. Addison, Mr. Edwards, and several other gentlemen of the place.

Okoghsenniyonte, a Chief of the Cayugas, then rose, and expressed the general approbation of what was said, alleging it was the sentiment of the whole ; that the satisfaction they had felt on having the lands granted them according to the promise of his Majesty's representatives, was greatly weakened and disappointed by the disputes raised against their title, and the right to make the use of it they desire.

No. XVI.

[REFERENCE FROM PAGE 453.]

" *New-York, 1st Dec.* 1837.

" DEAR SIR,

" In the year 1797, I visited Col. Brant on his return from Philadelphia to his home on Grand River, seventy miles north of Niagara, in company with Doctor Dingly and Doctor Priestley, at *the Hotel kept by Mr. James Batten*, corner of John and Nassau streets. He appeared to be in good health and spirits, rather inclined to corpulency, of the middling stature, his dress that of a private citizen ; was very communicative. In the course of our interview he told us of his reception at the Court of St. James, spoke of our revolutionary war, and the active part he took, assisted by the English, which he now had reason to regret ; would never again take up the tomahawk against these United States ; gave us a pressing invitation to call and see him at his residence on Grand River ; stated that he had large possessions, and could make his friends very comfortable ; that he had many black slaves, which he had taken prisoners in the revolutionary war, who appeared to be happy, and entirely willing to live with him ; pleased with the Indian habits and customs, and never expressed a wish to return into civil society, where they were sure to be slaves to the white people, as they had been before the war. He seemed to be pleased with the attention he had received from the citizens of New-York. We took leave of him, and promised if either of us ever visited that part of Canada, we would call and see him

I think Doctor Priestley, in his tour of the United States, did call and see him.

"Respectfully, your ob't serv't,

"JEROMUS JOHNSON.

" *William L. Stone, Esq.*"

No. XVII.

[REFERENCE FROM PAGE 480.]

" *London, April 2d,* 1803.

"MY DEAR COL. JOSEPH BRANT,

"Years may have banished me out of the temple of your memory, but I have not yet forgot you, Sir William Johnson, his Lady and children. You will graciously receive this letter, which is to inform you that I esteem and reverence the virtues of Great Hendrick, yourself, and those of the Mohawk nation and their Allies; while I do not admire the policy, humanity, and justice of the English nation towards the Mohawks and their Allies, in aiding and assisting their enemies to rob them of their territory and country, and compelling them to seek shelter and lands amongst the Ottawawas and Mississagas, formerly their enemies, by the arts and intrigues of the French. The Christian rules are good and excellent; yet few Christians of the Roman and Protestant kind love or practise those rules. What is remarkable to me is, that Popes, Bishops, Nobles and Kings, who ought to be wise in doctrine and example, are the greatest strangers and enemies to Christianity.

"The reason of such conduct, no doubt, is pride; yet Solomon, in wisdom great, says, 'Pride was not made for man.' I conclude, therefore, that great men in state and church, having robbed Lucifer of his pride, they stole all his cruelty, and so became legislators; made laws to deprive the multitude of rational freedom, and plunder Gentiles without sin, because they are honest and good; and not Christians.

"The Pope, in 1492, gave, by his Bull to the King of Spain, all America, only because America was owned by the Gentiles, and because the Pope was, by his claim, successor of Christ, ' to whom God had given the heathen for his inheritance, and the western parts of the earth for his possession.' Had the Apostles and Christian Bishops, for the first six hundred years, understood Christ's words, 'I have other sheep which are not of this fold, them I will gather in,' the Pope would have not been content with his triple crown, which represents Asia, Africa, and Europe, but would have put on a quadruple crown to include America.

"It is evident that Christ commissioned his twelve Apostles to teach and baptize the people in Asia, Africa, and Europe, but not in America ; for Christ said to them, 'I have other sheep which are not of this fold, them I will gather in,' and not depend on the twelve Apostles to do that benevolent work.

"What right then could the Pope, in 1492, have over America, when his predecessor, St. Peter, and the other eleven Apostles, held no commission in America or over America. Hence, as the King ot Spain had no valid title to America from the Pope, what right has the King of England in and over America, who is an excommunicated heretic from the church of Rome. I conclude that the people of America belong to '*the fold of Christ*,' not to the fold of the twelve Apostles, because God gave America to Christ, Psalm 2, v. 8, the Pope, Kings, and Bishops in the old world, have not, and never had, any divine authority in America, over Christ's sheep, the Gentiles ; of course they are usurpers, robbers, and deceivers.

"I consider you, Sir, as the Chief of the Mohawks, and the other five nations of Indians, the legal and just owners of the country lying between the waters St. Lawrence, Ontario, Lake Erie, Lake Champlain, and Hudson's River to the forks of Susquehannah, which you have lost for fighting your Gentile brethren in behalf of English Christians ; and the good and honest Mississagas have in part lost their country, for fighting you, their Gentile brethren, in behalf of French Christians. Thus, I see you and the Mississagas have been crucified like Christ between two thieves, (i. e.) Jews and Romans. I have seen so much of Christian knavery and policy, that I am sick of Europe, which loves war and hates peace ; therefore I want and long to have a wigwam near Great Pontiack, King by divine right of the Mississaga Nation and Tribes near Detroit and Lake Michigan. Great Pontiack has adopted my grandson, Nikik, Samuel Peters Jarvis. Should you judge it proper to explain my obligations to Great Pontiack,* and thereby induce the Great Chief to patronize me also, I will go with Nikik to Michigan, and teach Nikik the rules and laws, how he shall defend in all shapes his brothers and sisters of the Mississaga Nation.

"I beg you to accept a portrait of Nikik my grandson, a captain and prince of the Mississagas, by creation of Great Pontiack ; as I suppose he is successor of the wise and great Pontiack, King and Lord of that country, A. D. 1760.

* It would seem from these references to Pontiac, that the eccentric writer of this letter was ignorant of his death years before.—*Author*.

"I know you and your generosity and benevolence, and therefore ask you to accept my gratitude, and to give me, (via.) Mr. Jarvis, such an answer as your goodness shall dictate to be due to, Sir,

"Your friend and servant,

"SAMUEL PETERS."

No. XVIII.

[REFERENCE FROM PAGE 487.]

THE following brief but very interesting account of a French Colony, located in the town of Pompey, in the year 1666, is taken from "A Memoir on the Antiquities of the western parts of the State of New-York," by De Witt Clinton.

After informing us that the statement is collected partially from the Sachems of the Six Nations, and partly from a manuscript journal of one of the French Jesuits, he proceeds to remark :—

"From the Jesuits' journal it appears, that in the year 1666, at the request of Karakontie, an Onondaga chieftain, a French Colony was directed to repair to his village, for the purpose of teaching the Indians arts and sciences, and to endeavor, if practicable, to civilize and christianise them.

"We learn from the Sachems, that at this time the Indians had a fort, a short distance above the village of Jamesville, on the banks of a small stream near ; a little above which, it seems, the chieftain, Karakontie, would have his new friends *sit down*. Accordingly they repaired thither and commenced their labors, which being greatly aided by the savages, a few months only were necessary to the building of a small village.

"This little colony remained for three years in a very peaceable and flourishing situation, during which time much addition was made to the establishment, and, among others, a small chapel, in which the Jesuit used to collect the barbarians, and perform the rites and ceremonies of his church.

"But the dire circumstance which was to bury this colony in oblivion, and keep their history in secret, was yet to come. About this time, (1669,) a party of Spaniards, consisting of twenty-three persons, arrived at the village, having for guides some of the Iroquois, who had been taken captive by the southern tribes. It appears evident that this party came up the Mississippi, as it has been ascertained that they passed Pittsburg, and on to Olean Point ; where, leaving their canoes, they travelled by land. They had been informed by some of the southern tribes that there was a lake at the north of them, whose bottom was covered with a substance shining and white,* and which they took, from the Indians' description, to be silver ; and it is supposed that the idea of enriching themselves upon this treasure, induced them to take this long and desperate journey ; for silver was the first thing inquired for on their arrival, and on being told that none was ever seen in or about the Onondaga lake, they became almost frantic, and seemed bent upon a quarrel with the French, and charged them with having bribed the Indians, and even those who had been their guides, that they would not tell where the mines might be found. Nor dare they, finding the French influence to prevail, venture out on a search, lest the Indians might destroy them. A compromise was however made, and both parties agreed that an equal number of each should be sent on an exploring expedition, which was accordingly done. But the effect of this upon the minds of the Indians was fatal. Upon seeing these strangers prowling the woods with various kinds of instruments, they immediately suspected some plan to be in operation to deprive them of their country.

"Nor was this jealousy by any means hushed by the Europeans. The Spaniards averred to the Indians that the only object of the French was to tyrannize over them ; and the French, on the other hand, that the Spaniards were plotting a scheme to rob them of their lands.

"The Indians by this time becoming equally jealous of both, determined, in private council, to rid themselves of so troublesome neighbors. For aid in this, they sent private instructions to the Oneidas and Cayugas, who only wanted a watchword to be found immediately on the ground. The matter was soon digested, and the time and manner of attack agreed upon. A little before day-break, on *All-Saints* day, 1669, the little colony, together with the Spaniards, were aroused from their slumbers by the roaring of fire-arms and the dismal war-whoop of the savages. Every house was immediately fired or broken open, and such as attempted to escape from the flames met a more untimely death in the *tomahawk*. Merciless multitudes overpowered the little band, and the Europeans were soon either lost in death or writhing in their blood ; and such was the furious prejudice of the savages, that not one escaped, or was left alive to *relate the sad disaster*. Thus perished the little colony, whose labors have excited so much wonder and curiosity.

* The salt crystallizes at the present time on the grass and upon the naked earth in the immediate vicinity of the springs, though the water of the lake is fresh.

"The French in Canada, on making inquiries respecting the fate of their friends, were informed by the Indians that they had gone towards the south, with a company of people who came from thence, and at the same time showing a *Spanish coat of arms* and other national trinkets, confirmed the Canadian French in the opinion that their unfortunate countrymen had indeed gone thither, and in all probability perished in the immense forests. This opinion was also measurably confirmed by a Frenchman who had long lived with the Senecas, and who visited the Onondagas at the time the Spaniards were at the village, but left before the disaster, and could only say that he had seen them there."

This history accounts, in the opinion of its learned author, for the appearance at this place of a small village, with evident remains of a blacksmith's shop, &c. to be seen at the first settlement of the country by the English. The account appears every way credible, and the explanation satisfactory. But in several other places in the country, the remains of blacksmiths' shops have been discovered, and in some instances the tools used by the trade. A blacksmith's vice was found, buried deep in the ground, on a farm in Onondaga Hollow, about three-fourths of a mile south of the turnpike. But the existence of a fort near this spot, every vestige of which is now nearly obliterated, readily accounts for the existence of these relics of civilization. In the cultivation of the lands lying upon the Onondaga Creek, innumerable implements of war and of husbandry have been found, scattered over a territory of four or five miles in length. Swords, gun-barrels, gun-locks, bayonets, balls, axes, hoes, and various other articles made of iron, have been found, and many of them are still preserved. I have now in my possession a sword that was dug up on the farm at present owned by Mr. Wyman, where have been found all the different kinds of articles mentioned above. On this farm, also, was found a stone of considerable dimensions, on which were rudely carved some European characters. But the stone has been lost, and the import of the characters is not remembered. It is proper also to remark here, that a stone, which has been preserved, and is now in the Albany museum, was found some years ago in the town of Pompey, containing inscriptions. The stone was of an oblong figure, being fourteen inches long by twelve broad, and is eight inches in thickness. It had in the centre of the surface the figure of a tree, with a serpent climbing it, and the following is a *fac simile* of the characters that were inscribed upon each side of the tree.

Leo X De   The tree, &c.   Ls
Vix 1520   † ∩

" We have here the true chronology of the pontificate of Leo X., and, without doubt, the year in which the inscriptions were made. This pontiff came to the papal chair in the year 1513 or 1514, and consequently the sixth year of his pontificate would be as stated above. The inscription may be thus translated :—' Leo X. by the grace of God ; sixth year of his pontificate—1520.' The stone was doubtless designed as a sepulchral monument, and the letters Ls were probably the initials of the name of the person whose grave it designated. The Cross informs us that the deceased was a Catholic, and the inverted U, was probably some other emblem, which the hand of time had in a great measure effaced. The supposition is not incredible that this stone was carved by a Spanish hand on or near the spot where it was found, and there deposited by him. Mexico was settled by the Spaniards in 1521. But previously to this period, Spanish adventurers frequently arrived upon the American coast. Florida was discovered by them in 1502. The French voyager Verrazano explored nearly the whole coast of the present United States in 1524, but a little subsequent to the date which forms the subject of our inquiry. And De Soto, who had been constituted Governor of Cuba and President of Florida, performed his celebrated expedition into the interior of America, having with him six hundred men, as early as 1538. He spent four years in the country, and as Florida then extended to an indefinite point in the north, embracing all that tract of country which has since been called Virginia, and as mention is made by his historian of ' extreme cold,' and of a place called *Saquechama*, it is reasonable to conjecture that they penetrated to the north as far as the *Susquehannah*.* But in the course of his travels, he fell in with a body of natives, who had with them a Spaniard by the name of John Ortez, of Seville. He had then been a captive for nearly ten years. It is not incredible, when all these facts are taken into consideration, that eight years anterior to the time of Ortez being taken prisoner, two or three, or half a dozen Spaniards, should have been taken by misfortune or the spirit of adventure to Pompey Hill, where one of them dying, the survivor or survivors prepared and placed this monument over his remains. It is also quite possible, that the visit of the Spanish adventurers, to which the narrative furnished by De Witt

* See Sandford's Aborigines, p. cxiv. note. Also, " Yates and Moulton's Hist." p. 11.

Clinton and recited above, relates, was at a period much earlier than that which he assigns for it.   De Soto himself was amused by similar stories told him by the savages of the existence of gold and silver in regions that were always beyond him.   In this way he was taken many hundred leagues into the bosom of a country filled only with savages, and never before trodden by the foot of an European.   But he returned vexed to find that he had been amused only with golden dreams.   The story of a lake at the north, whose bottom was lined with silver, was sufficient to fire the bosom of a Spaniard with an ungovernable spirit of daring in pursuit of that object ; and as the date of this enterprise was left to be established by tradition, that erring chronicler of events, it is altogether probable that a mistake in time, sufficient to explain the subject of our inquiry, was committed.   However this may be, there can be little doubt but Spaniards, carried there as captives or allured by the love of gold, were at Pompey Hill as early as 1520.—*Lectures of Rev. Mr. Adams, of Syracuse, (N. Y.)*

No. XIX.

[Reference from Page 487.]

Since the text of the present volume was written, the Antiquarian world has been gratified by a publication issued by the Society of Northern Antiquities of Copenhagen, which is creating a great sensation among men of letters.   It is entitled

" Antiquitates Americanæ, sive Scriptores Septentrionales rerum Ante-Columbianarum in America.   (Antiquities of America, or Northern writers of things in America before Columbus.)   Hafniæ, 1837, 4to. pp. 486."

The following summary notice of this most important work is copied from the New Haven Chronicle of the Church, of December 15, 1837 :—

This interesting and erudite volume is composed of ancient Icelandic histories relative to America, being mostly accounts of voyages of discovery to this country, made by the Northmen in the 10th, 11th, 12th, and 13th centuries, that is, anterior to the time of Columbus.   To these are added critical and explanatory notes, chronological and geneological tables, archælogical and geographical disquisitions, concerning the migration of the Northmen to this country, their first landing-places, and earliest settlements, with the vestiges of the same now remaining.   We give the following sum

mary of the conclusions drawn by the authors of this work in reference to the discovery and settlement of this country by the Norwegians.

In the spring of 986, Eric the Red emigrated from Iceland to
Greenland, and formed a settlement there. In 994, Biarne, the son
of Heriulf Bardson, one of the settlers who accompanied Eric, returned to Norway, and gave an account of discoveries he had made
to the south of Greenland. On his return to Greenland, Leif, the son
of Eric, bought Biarne's ship, and with a crew of thirty-five men, embarked on a voyage of discovery, A. D. 1000. After sailing some
time to the south-west, they fell in with a country covered with a
slaty rock, and destitute of good qualities ; and which, therefore, they
called *Helluland,* (Slate-land.) They then continued southerly, until they found a low, flat coast, with white sand cliffs, and immediately back, covered with wood, whence they called the country
Markland, (Woodland.) From here they sailed south and west,
until they arrived at a promontory which stretched to the east and
north, and sailing round it, turned to the west ; and sailing westward,
passed between an island and the mainland, and entering a bay
through which flowed a river, they concluded to winter there.

Having landed, they built houses to winter in, and called the place
Lefsbuthir, (Leifs-booths.)   Soon after this they discovered an
abundance of vines, whence they named the country *Vinland* or
Wineland.   Antiquarians have been much puzzled to know where
Vinland was located ; but the Antiquarian Society, to whose exertions
we owe the above work, after the most careful examination of all the
evidence on the subject, do not hesitate to place it at the head of Nar-
raganset Bay, in Rhode Island.   Every thing in the description of
the voyage and country agrees most exactly with this.   The promontory extending east and north, corresponds closely with that of
Barnstable and Cape Cod, and the islands they would encounter
immediately upon turning west, would be Nantucket and Martha's
Vineyard.

Two years after, 1002, Thorwold, the brother of Leif, visited Vinland, where he spent two years, and was finally murdered by the
natives. Before his death, he coasted around the promontory, and
called the north end, now Cape Cod, *Kjalarnes,* (Keel-Cape.) He
was killed and buried on a small promontory, reaching south from
the mainland, on the west side of the Bay, inclosed by the promontory of *Kjalarnes,* and which answers most accurately to the strip
of land on the east side of Plymouth Harbour, now called Gurnet's
Point. The Norwegians called it *Krassanes,* (Crossness or Cross-

land,) because the grave of Thorwold had a cross erected at both ends.

In 1007, three ships sailed from Greenland for Vinland, one under the command of Thorfinn Karlsefne, a Norwegian of royal descent, and Snorre Thorbrandson, of distinguished lineage; one other commanded by Biarne Grimalfson and Thorhall Gamlason; and the third by Thorward and Thorhall. The three ships had 160 men, and carried all sorts of domestic animals necessary for the comfort and convenience of a colony. An account of this voyage, and a history of the country, by Thorfinn Karlsefne, is still extant, and forms one of the documents in the *Antiquitates Americanæ*. They sailed from Greenland to *Helluland*, and passing *Markland*, arrived at *Kjalarnes*, whence sailing south by the shore of the promontory, which they found to consist of trackless beaches and long wastes of sand, they called it *Furthurstrandir*, (Wonder-Strand, *or* Beach;) whether on account of the extensive sandy shore, or from the mirage and optical illusion so common at Cape Cod, it is impossible to determine. Passing south, they sailed by the island discovered by Leif, which they called *Straumey*, (Stream-Isle,) probably Martha's Vineyard, and the straits between *Straumfjothr*, (Stream-Firth,) and arrived at Vinland, where they spent the winter. The Bay into which they sailed, they called *Hópsvatn*, and their residence received the name of *Hóp*, (*English* Hope, *Indian* Haup,) the identical *Mount Hope*, so much celebrated as the residence of King Philip. After various successes, Thorfinn returned to Greenland, and finally went to Iceland and settled.

From a comparison of all the remaining accounts of these voyages, the *geographical, nautical* and *astronomical facts* contained in them, with the natural history and geography of this country when first settled by the whites, there can be little doubt that *Vinland* has been correctly located by the learned Society. By similar evidence it also appears, that *Markland* was what is now called Nova Scotia; that *Litla Helluland* (Little Helluland) was Newfoundland; and that *Helluland it Mikla*, (Greater Helluland,) was the coast of Labrador. We ought also to have observed above, that *Straumfjothr* (Stream-Firth) probably included the whole of Buzzard's Bay.

Of the *climate* of Vinland, the Northmen say, it was, when they were there, so mild, that cattle would live out-doors during the year; that the snow fell but lightly, and that the grass continued to be green in some places nearly all winter. Among the *productions* of Vinland, were abundance of vines, a kind of wild wheat, (*maize,*) a beautiful wood which they called *mazer* (Birdseye-maple, *Acer Sac-*

charinum,) a great variety of forest animals, Eider Ducks in great
plenty ; and the rivers and bays they describe as filled with fish, among
which they reckon salmon, halibut, whales, &c. It is also said by
the same historians, that the sun rose at half past seven o'clock in
the shortest days, which is the exact time it rises at Mount Hope.

Subsequent to this time, explorations were made to the south of
Vinland along the eastern shore, and judging from the fragments of
voyages, it would seem that some penetrated as far south as Florida.
The whole country south of Chesapeake Bay is called by them
Hvitramannaland, (white-man's-land,) or *Ireland it Mikla,* (Ireland
the Great.) In 1121 Vinland was visited by Bishop Eric, and as
there is no account of his return, it seems probable that he spent
his days there.   Other explorations were made by the Norwegians
and Greenlanders to the north, who penetrated as far as Barrow's
Straits, which they called *Króksfjorthr,* (Kroks-Firth *or* Strait,) and
the land on the northern side, now known as the Cumberland Mountains, they denominated *Kroksfjartharheithi,* (Barren-highlands-of-
Kroks-Strait.) There are several other particulars we should be
glad to notice, but the length of this article will not allow.

Among other matters, curious and important, contained in this
valuable publication from Copenhagen, not noted by the New-Haven
Chronicle, are one or more readings of the celebrated hierogly-
phic inscription upon " Dighton Rock," in Fall River, Massachusetts, and of which no satisfactory explanation has previously been
given.   These Northern Antiquaries profess at length to have mas-
tered that inscription.   They pronounce the characters to be Ru-
nic, and read therein a confirmation of their theory, that a settlement was formed by the Northmen at Fall River as early as the
tenth century.   But this is not all.   Since the work of the Copenhagen Antiquaries has been published, another discovery has been
made in the immediate neighborhood of Dighton Rock, which is
equally curious and important as connected with this investigation.
The discovery referred to may be considered the most interesting
relic of antiquity ever discovered in North America, viz :—the remains of a human body, armed with a breast-plate, a species of mail,
and arrows of *brass ;* which remains we suppose to have belonged
either to one of the race who inhabited this country for a time *anterior* to the so-called Aborigines, and afterwards settled in Mexico
or Guatamala, or to one of the crew of some Phœnician vessel, that,
blown out of her course, thus discovered the western world long before the Christian era.

These remains were found in the town of Fall River, in Bristol county, Massachusetts, about eighteen months since.

In digging down a hill near the village, a large mass of earth slid off, leaving in the bank, and partially uncovered, a human skull, which on examination was found to belong to a body buried in a sitting posture ; the head being about one foot below what had been for many years the surface of the ground. The surrounding earth was carefully removed, and the body found to be enveloped in a covering of coarse bark of a dark color. Within this envelope were found the remains of another of coarse cloth, made of fine bark, and about the texture of a Manilla coffee bag. On the breast was a plate of brass, thirteen inches long, six broad at the upper end and five at the lower. This plate appears to have been cast, and is from one eighth to three thirty-seconds of an inch in thickness. It is so much corroded, that whether or not any thing was engraved upon it has not yet been ascertained. It is oval in form—the edges being irregular, apparently made so by corrosion.

Below the breast-plate, and entirely encircling the body, was a belt composed of brass tubes, each four and a half inches in length, and three sixteenths of an inch in diameter, arranged longitudinally and close together ; the length of a tube being the width of the belt. The tubes are of thin brass, cast upon hollow reeds, and were fastened together by pieces of sinew. This belt was so placed as to protect the lower parts of the body below the breast-plate. The arrows are of brass, thin, flat, and triangular in shape, with a round hole cut through near the base. The shaft was fastened to the head by inserting the latter in an opening at the end of the wood, and then tying it with a sinew through the round hole—a mode of constructing the weapon never practised by the Indians, not even with their arrows of thin shell. Parts of the shaft still remain on some of them. When first discovered the arrows were in a sort of quiver of bark, which fell in pieces when exposed to the air.

The skull is much decayed, but the teeth are sound, and apparently those of a young man. The pelvis is much decayed, and the smaller bones of the lower extremities are gone.

The integuments of the right knee, for four or five inches above and below, are in good preservation, apparently the size and shape of life, although quite black.

Considerable flesh is still preserved on the hands and arms, but none on the shoulders and elbows. On the back, under the belt, and for two inches above and below, the skin and flesh are in good preservation, and have the appearance of being tanned. The chest is much compressed, but the upper viscera are probably entire. The arms are bent up, not crossed; so that the hands turned inwards touch the shoulders. The stature is about five and a half feet. Much of the exterior envelope was decayed, and the inner one appeared to be preserved only where it had been in contact with the brass.

The following sketch will give our readers an idea of the posture of the figure and the position of the armor. When the remains were discovered, the arms were brought rather closer to the body than in the engraving. The arrows were near the right knee.

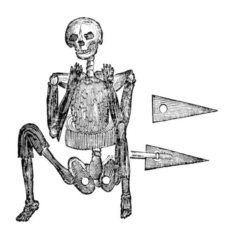

The preservation of this body may be the result of some embalming process; and this hypothesis is strengthened by the fact, that the skin has the appearance of having been tanned; or it may be the accidental result of the action of the salts of the brass during oxydation; and this latter hypothesis is supported by the fact, that the skin and flesh have been preserved only where they have been in contact with, or quite near, the brass; or we may account for the preservation of the whole by supposing the presence of *saltpetre* in the soil at the time of the deposit. In either way, the preservation of the remains is fully accounted for, and upon known chemical principles.

That the body was not one of the Indians, we think needs no argument. We have seen some of the drawings taken from the sculptures found at Palanqué, and in those the figures are represented with breast-plates, although smaller than the plate found at Fall

River. On the figures at Palenqué the bracelets and anklets appear to be of a manufacture precisely similar to the belt of tubes just described. These figures also have helmets precisely answering the description of the helmet of Homer's μεγας κορυθαίολος Εκτωρ.

No. XX.

[REFERENCE FROM PAGE 499.]

WE the subscribers, having been requested to give our opinion with regard to the religious and moral character of the late Capt. Joseph Brant, and the state of his mind as it appeared to us at its dissolution—hereby declare, that having lived a number of years a near neighbor of his, (our farms adjoining the place of his residence,) we were intimately acquainted with him ; in conversation he would often begin the subject, and dwell upon the duties that we owed one to another. He was a believer in the Christian religion, and was brought up in the doctrine of the Episcopal Church of England, of which he was a member when he died. During his illness we were often with him, and were present at his dissolution. During his sickness, (which was painful,) he was patient and resigned, and appeared always thankful to his friends for the attention paid to him. It is our opinion that during his sickness, and at the close of it, he was possessed of his rational faculties, and that he lived and died in the faith of the Christian religion.

AUGUSTUS BATES,
ASAHEL DAVIS.

Wellington Square, U. C. }
August 15th, 1837. }

No. XXI.

[REFERENCE FROM PAGE 526.]

Letter to the Mohawk Chief Ahyonwaeghs, commonly called John Brant, Esq. of the Grand River, Upper Canada.

London, January 20, 1822.

SIR,

Ten days ago I was not aware that such a person existed as the son of the Indian leader Brant,* who is mentioned in my poem "Gertrude of Wyoming." Last week, however, Mr. S. Bannister of Lincoln's Inn, called to inform me of your being in London, and of your having documents in your possession which he believed would change my opinion of your father's memory, and induce me to do it justice. Mr. Bannister distinctly assured me that no declaration of my sentiments on the subject was desired but such as should spontaneously flow from my own judgment of the papers that were to be submitted to me.

I could not be deaf to such an appeal. It was my duty to inspect the justification of a man whose memory I had reprobated, and I felt a satisfaction at the prospect of his character being redressed, which was not likely to have been felt by one who had wilfully wronged it. As far as any intention to wound the feelings of the living was concerned, I really knew not, when I wrote my poem, that the son and daughter of an Indian chief were ever likely to peruse it, or be affected by its contents. And I have observed most persons to whom I have mentioned the circumstance of your appeal to me, smile with the same surprise which I experienced on first receiving it. With regard to your father's character, I took it as I found it in popular history. Among the documents in his favor I own that you have shown me one which I regret that I never saw before, though I might have seen it, viz. the Duke of Rochefoucault's honorable mention of the chief in his travels.† Without meaning, however, in the least to invalidate that nobleman's respectable authority, I must say, that even if I had met with it, it would have still offered only a general and presumptive vindication of your father, and not such a specific one as I now recognize. On the other hand, judge how naturally I adopted accusations against him which had stood in the Annual Register of 1779, as far as I knew, uncontradicted for thirty years. A number of authors had repeated them with a confidence

* The name has been almost always inaccurately spelt Brandt in English books.

† The following testimony is borne to his fair name by Rochefoucault, whose ability and means of forming a correct judgment will not be denied. "Col. Brant is an Indian by birth. In the American war he fought under the English banner, and he has since been in England, *where he was most graciously received by the King,* and met with a kind reception from all classes of people. His manners are semi-European. He is attended by two negroes; has established himself in the English way; has a garden and a farm; dresses after the European fashion; and nevertheless possesses much influence over the Indians. He assists at present (1795) at the Miami Treaty, which the United States are concluding with the western Indians. He is also much respected by the Americans; and in general bears so excellent a name, that I regret I could not see and become acquainted with him."— *Rochefoucault's Travels in North America.*

which beguiled at last my suspicion, and I believe that of the public at large. Among those authors were Gordon, Ramsay, Marshall, Belsham, and Weld. The most of them, you may tell me, perhaps, wrote with zeal against the American war. Well, but Mr. John Adolphus was never suspected of any such zeal, and yet he has said in his History of England, &c. (vol. iii. p. 110) "that a force of sixteen hundred savages and Americans in disguise, headed by an Indian Col. Butler, and a half Indian of *extraordinary* ferocity named Brant, lulling the fears of the inhabitants (of Wyoming) by treachery, suddenly possessed themselves of two forts, and *massacred* the garrisons." He says farther, "that *all* were involved in unsparing slaughter, and that even the devices of torment were exhausted." He possessed, if I possessed them, the means of consulting better authorities; yet he has never to my knowledge made any atonement to your father's memory. When your Canadian friends, therefore, call me to trial for having defamed the warrior Brant, I beg that Mr. John Adolphus may be also included in the summons. And after his own defence and acquittal, I think he is bound, having been one of my historical misleaders, to stand up as my gratuitous counsel, and say, "Gentlemen, *you must acquit my client, for he has only fallen into an error, which even my judgment could not escape.*"

In short, I imbibed my conception of your father from accounts of him that were published when I was scarcely out of my cradle. And if there were any public, direct, and specific challenges to those accounts in England ten years ago, I am yet to learn where they existed.

I rose from perusing the papers you submitted to me certainly with an altered impression of his character. I find that the unfavorable accounts of him were erroneous, even on points not immediately connected with his reputation. It turns out, for instance, that he was a Mohawk Indian of unmixed parentage. This circumstance, however, ought not to be overlooked in estimating the merits of his attainments. He spoke and wrote our language with force and facility, and had enlarged views of the union and policy of the Indian tribes. A gentleman who had been in America, and from whom I sought information respecting him in consequence of your interesting message, told me that though he could not pretend to appreciate his character entirely, he had been struck by the *naïveté* and eloquence of his conversation. They had talked of music, and Brant said, "I like the harpsichord well, and the organ still better; but I like the drum and trumpet best of all, for they make my heart beat quick." This gentleman also described to me the enthusiasm with which he spoke of written records. Brant projected at that time to have written a History of the Six Nations. The genius of history should be rather partial to such a man.

I find that when he came to England, after the peace of 1783, the most distinguished individuals of all parties and professions treated him with the utmost kindness. Among these were the late Bishop of London, the late Duke of Northumberland, and Charles Fox. Lord Rawdon, now Marquis of Hastings, gave him his picture. This circumstance argues recommendations from America founded in personal friendship. In Canada the memorials of his moral character represent it as naturally ingenuous and generous. The evidence afforded, induces me to believe that he often strove to mitigate the cruelty of Indian warfare. Lastly, you affirm that he was not within many miles of the spot when the battle which decided the fate of Wyoming took place, and from your offer of reference to living witnesses, I cannot but admit the assertion. Had I learnt all this of your father when I was writing my poem, he should not have figured in it as the hero of mischief. I cannot, indeed, answer by anticipation what the writers who have either to retract or defend what they may have said about him, may have to allege ; I can only say that my own opinion about him is changed. I am now inclined exceedingly to doubt Mr. Weld's anecdote, and for this reason : Brant was not only trusted, consulted, and distinguished by several eminent British officers in America, but personally beloved by them. Now I could conceive men in power, for defensible reasons of state politics, to have officially trusted, and even publicly distinguished at courts or levees, an active and sagacious Indian chief, of whose private character they might nevertheless still entertain a very indifferent opinion. But I cannot imagine high-minded and high-bred British officers forming individual and fond friendships for a man of ferocious character. It comes within my express knowledge that the late General Sir Charles Stuart, fourth son of the Earl of Bute, the father of our present Ambassador at Paris, the officer who took Minorca and Calvi, and who commanded our army in Portugal, knew your father in America, often slept under the same tent with him, and had the warmest regard for him. It seems but charity to suppose the man who attracted the esteem of Lord Rawdon and General Stuart to have possessed amiable qualities, so that I believe you when you affirm that he was merciful as brave. And now I leave the world to judge whether the change of opinion, with which I am touched, arises from false delicacy and flexibility of mind, or from a sense of honor and justice.

Here, properly speaking, ends my reckoning with you about your father's memory; but as the Canadian newspapers have made some remarks on the subject of Wyoming, with which I cannot fully coincide, and as this letter will probably be read in Canada, I cannot conclude it without a few more words, in case my silence should seem to admit of propositions which are rather beyond the stretch of my creed. I will not, however, give any plain truths which I have to offer to the Canadian writers the slightest seasoning of bitterness, for they have alluded to me, on the whole, in a friendly and liberal tone. But when they regret my departure from historical truth, I join in their regret only in as far as I have unconsciously misunderstood the character of Brant, and the share of the Indians in the transaction, which I have now reason to suspect was much less than that of the white men. In other circumstances I took the liberty of a versifier to run away from fact into fancy, like a school-boy who never dreams that he is a truant when he rambles on a holiday from school. It seems, however, that I falsely represented Wyoming to have been a terrestial paradise. It was not so, say the Canadian papers, because it contained a great number of Tories ; and undoubtedly that cause goes far to account for the fact. Earthly paradises, however, are not earthly things, and Tempe and Arcadia may have had their drawbacks on happiness as well as Wyoming. I must nevertheless still believe that it was a flourishing colony, and that its destruction furnished a just warning to human beings against war and revenge. But the whole catastrophe is affirmed in a Canadian newspaper to have been nothing more than a fair battle. If this be the fact, let accredited signatures come forward to attest it, and vindicate the innocence and honorableness of the whole transaction, as your father's character has been vindicated. An error about him by no means proves the whole account of the business to be a fiction. Who would not wish its atrocity to be disproved ? But who can think it disproved by a single defender, who writes anonymously, and without definable weight or authority ?

In another part of the Canadian newspapers, my theme has been regretted as dishonorable to England. Then it was, at all events, no fable. But how far was the truth dishonorable to England ? American settlers, and not Englishmen, were chiefly the white men calling themselves Christians, who were engaged in this affair. I shall be reminded, perhaps, that they also called themselves Loyalists. But for Heaven's sake let not English loyalty be dragged down to palliate atrocities, or English delicacy be invoked to conceal them. I may be told that England permitted the war, and was therefore responsible for its occurrences. Not surely universally, nor directly. I should be unwilling to make even Lord North's administration answerable for all the actions of Butler's rangers; and I should be still more sorry to make all England amenable either for Lord North's administration, or for Butler's rangers. Was the American war an unanimous and heartfelt war of the people? Were the best patriots and the brightest luminaries of our Senate for, or against it? Chatham declared that if America fell she would fall like the strong man—that she would embrace the pillars of our constitution and perish beneath its ruins. Burke, Fox, and Barré kindled even the breasts of St. Stephen's chapel against it; and William Pitt pronounced it a war against the sacred cause of Liberty. If so, the loss of our colonies was a blessing, compared with the triumph of those principles that would have brought Washington home in chains. If Chatham and Pitt were our friends in denouncing the injustice of this war, then Washington was only nominally our foe in resisting it; and he was as much the enemy of the worst enemies of our constitution, as if he had fought against the return of the Stuarts on the banks of the Spey or the Thames. I say, therefore, with full and free charity to those who think differently, that the American war was disgraceful only to those who were its abettors, and that the honor of Englishmen is redeemed in proportion as they deprecate its principles and deplore its details. Had my theme even involved English character more than it does, I could still defend it. If my Canadian critic alleges that a poet may not blame the actions of his country, I meet his allegation, and deny it. No doubt a poet ought not for ever to harp and carp upon the faults of his country; but *he may be her moral censor, and he must not be her parasite.* If an English poet under Edward III. had only dared to leave one generous line of commiseration to the memory of Sir William Wallace, how much he would have raised our estimation of the moral character of the age! There is a present and a future in national character, as well as a past, and the character of the present age is best provided for by impartial and generous sentiments respecting the past. The twentieth century will not think the worse of the nineteenth for regretting the American war. I know the slender importance of my own works. I am contending, however, against a false principle of delicacy that would degrade poetry itself if it were adopted;—but it never will be adopted.

I therefore regret nothing in the historical allusions of my poem, except the mistake about your father. Nor, though I have spoken freely of American affairs, do I mean to deny that your native tribes may have had a just cause of quarrel with the American colonists. And I regard it as a mark of their gratitude that they adhered to the royal cause, because the governors, acting in the king's name, had been their most constant friends ; and the colonial subjects, possibly at times their treacherous invaders. I could say much of European injustice towards your tribes, but in spite of all that I could say, I must still deplore the event of Christians having adopted their mode of warfare, and, as circumstances then stood, of their having invoked their alliance. If the Indians thirsted for vengeance on the colonists, *that* should have been the very circumstance to deter us from blending their arms with ours. I trust you will understand this declaration to be made in the spirit of frankness, and not of mean and inhospitable arrogance. If I were to speak to you in that spirit, how easily and how truly could you tell me that the American Indians have departed faster from their old practices of warfare, than Christians have departed from their habits of religious persecution. If I were to preach to you about European humanity, you might ask me how long the ashes of the Inquisition have been cold, and whether the slave-trade be yet abolished ? You might demand, how many—no, how few generations have elapsed since our old women were burnt for imaginary commerce with the devil, and whether the houses be not yet standing from which our great-grandmothers may have looked on the hurdles passing to the place of execution, whilst they blessed themselves that they were not witches ! A horrible occurrence of this nature took place in Scotland during my own grandfather's life-time As to warlike customs, I should be exceedingly sorry if you were to press me even on those of my brave old ancestors, the Scottish Highlanders. I can, nevertheless, recollect the energy, faith, and hospitality of these ancestors, and at the same time I am not forgetful of the simple virtues of yours.*

---

* Considering the filial motives of the young chief's appeal to me, I am not afraid that any part of this letter, immediately relating to him, will be thought ostentatious or prolix. And if charitably judged, I hope that what I have said of myself and of my poem will not be felt as offensive egotism. The public has never been troubled with any defences of mine against any attacks on my poetry that were more literary : although I may have been as far as authors generally are from bowing to the justice of hostile criticism. To show that I have not been over-anxious about publicity, I must mention a misrepresentation respecting my poem on Wyoming which I have suffered to remain uncontradicted for ten years. Mr. Washington Irving, in a biographical sketch prefixed to it in an American edition, described me as having injured the composition of the poem by shewing it to friends who struck out its best passages. Now I read it to very few friends, and to none at whose suggestion I ever struck out a single line. Nor did I ever lean on the taste of others with that miserable distrust of my own judgment which the anecdote conveys. I knew that

I have been thus special in addressing you from a wish to vindicate my own consistency, as well as to do justice to you in your
present circumstances, which are peculiarly and publicly interesting.
The chief of an aboriginal tribe, now settled under the protection of
our sovereign in Canada, you are anxious to lead on your people in
a train of civilization that is already begun.   It is impossible that
the British community should not be touched with regard for an Indian stranger of respectable private character, posses ng such useful and honorable views.   Trusting that you will amply succeed in
them, and long live to promote improvement and happiness amidst
the residue of your ancient race,

I remain, your sincere well-wisher,

THOMAS CAMPBELL.

Mr. Irving was the last man in the world to make such a misrepresentation inten
tionally, and that I could easily contradict it; but from aversion to bring a petty
anecdote about myself before the world, I forbore to say any thing about it.   The
case was different when a Canadian writer hinted at the patriotism of my subject.
There he touched on my principles, and I have defended them, contending that on
the supposition of the story of Wyoming being true, it is a higher compliment to
British feeling to reveal than to palliate or hide it.

THE END